A New Jersey Anthology

A New Jersey Anthology

SECOND EDITION

Edited by

Maxine N. Lurie

RIVERGATE BOOKS

AN IMPRINT OF
RUTGERS UNIVERSITY PRESS
NEW BRUNSWICK, NEW JERSEY, AND LONDON

Publication of this volume has been made possible, in part, by a gift from Nicholas G. Rutgers IV and Nancy Hall Rutgers to support books about New Jersey.

Library of Congress Cataloging-in-Publication Data

A New Jersey anthology / edited by Maxine N. Lurie. — 2nd ed.
    p. cm.
  Includes bibliographical references and index.
  ISBN 978-0-8135-4744-2 (hardcover : alk. paper)
— ISBN 978-0-8135-4745-9 (pbk. : alk. paper)
  1. New Jersey--History.   I.   Lurie, Maxine N., 1940–
  F134.5.N4 2010
  974.9—dc22

                                                      2009025371

A British Cataloging-in-Publication record for this book is available from the British Library.

Visit our Web site: http://rutgerspress.rutgers.edu

Manufactured in the United States of America

To all three generations of my family,
for keeping me sane (most of the time):
Jon, David and Hikari, Debbie and Jason, Daniel and Katherine
Zachary, Chiyo, Magnolia, and Colby

Contents

Preface

The first edition of this book grew out of a perceived need for a book of readings on New Jersey history that could be used in courses on New Jersey or United States history taught at both the college and high school levels. At times it also happily appealed to the general reader, those curious to learn more about the state in which they lived. I remember when I started to put it together, I met Richard P. McCormick in Alexander Library at Rutgers University and he asked me "but how will you chose" what to include? His point was that much had been written about New Jersey, in both book and article format. While selection has not been easy, I used several guidelines both in the first, and in this the second, edition of the book. First, the selections deliberately cover the chronological scope of New Jersey history, to give readers a sense of how the state has developed and changed over time. Second, they try to illustrate the varieties of history. Thus, the selections include political, social, and legal history. Several are from biographies or analytical works. Third, an attempt was made to pick pieces that are interesting to read and that deal with important issues (what constitutes a fair trial, treatment of workers, or housing policy). I hope all will engage readers, leading them in the process to think about the questions with which historians wrestle, while also learning more about New Jersey.

Each selection is preceded by a headnote, which provides questions to be considered while reading. Because many of the selections in this edition come from books rather than from articles in scholarly journals, some of the headnotes provide additional background context from the larger work. All of them try to present issues and methods that have engaged historians, and they end with a list of suggested readings for those inclined to follow up either on the particular topic or the historical genre. In all, ten of the seventeen chapters are new. The changes were made to reflect scholarship done in the last fifteen years, adding new information or interpretations. Others have been added to increase the scope of topics covered—thus two chapters in this volume deal with war (the American Revolution and the Civil War) in two very different ways. They are included in response to the recognition that Americans have more often been at war than at peace, and that, even when not fought on New Jersey soil, wars have impacted the state's citizens. In addition, the introduction has been updated to bring the story closer to the present, while the footnotes have been expanded to incorporate recent scholarship.

When the first edition was published I thanked a number of people. This work still reflects their assistance: Jonathan Lurie; Susan Schrepher and Richard P. McCormick of Rutgers University; Kathryn Grover and Robert Burnet then at the New Jersey Historical Society. I have now accumulated additional debts for assistance with this second edition. These include Felicitas Ruetten, Elizabeth Schiller, Shayle Abelkop, and the staff of the Teaching, Learning, and Technology Center at Seton Hall University for their help with scanning and proofreading entries; the Provost and Office of Grants and Research Services for financial assistance for production costs; and Seton Hall University for the sabbatical that enabled me to finish this and another project. For help with images: Laura M. Poll at Monmouth Historical Association; Lauren Morrell, Office of the Curator, the Supreme Court of the United States; Bob Leach and John Beekman at Jersey City Public Library; Joanne Nestor at the New Jersey State Archives; David Kuzma, Erica Gorder, Bonita Craft Grant, and the staff at Special Collections and University Archives, Rutgers University; Michael Siegel at the Rutgers Cartography Lab; Jill Slaight, New-York Historical Society; James Osbourn. Newark Public Library. And, of course, the authors who consented to the inclusion of their work. Also Linda Epps at New Jersey Historical Society; Marlie Wasserman, Christina Brianik, and Marilyn Campbell at Rutgers University Press for their help in making this project work.

Maxine N. Lurie
April 2009

A NEW JERSEY ANTHOLOGY

Blueberry picker on the Lower Bank, Burlington County, about 1960. Despite its industrial image, New Jersey has been largely rural throughout much of its history; areas of the state remain devoted to the production of fruits and vegetables. Augustine Collection Photographs, Special Collections and University Archives, Rutgers University Libraries.

Introduction

Brief Overview of New Jersey History

Although a relatively small state, only 4.8 million acres in area, New Jersey has a long and complex history. Its past is full of paradoxes and contradictions that make it a challenge to study and understand. Primarily an agricultural state for most of its history, New Jersey was also one of the earliest to turn to manufacturing and chemical research. Today, while continuing to call itself the "Garden State," it has both the highest population density in the country and the largest number of hazardous waste sites. Although the state is seemingly paved from one end to another with cities that sprawl into adjacent suburbs, large areas remain devoted to horse farms, cornfields, orchards, nurseries, blueberry bushes, and cranberry bogs. For much of its past, New Jersey has been conservative in politics, policies, and attitudes, but it has also been in the forefront of reform efforts and judicial decisions. Although an old state—the so-called cockpit of the Revolution, with numerous historical markers to attest to that designation—it has largely failed to develop an identity of its own.

Early on, New Jersey was described as a "barrel tapped at both ends," caught between bigger, and better-known, New York and Pennsylvania.[1] It was a thoroughfare, "the corridor state," a place one traveled through by horse, train, and then car to get somewhere else. Even today the primary image for outsiders is of the New Jersey Turnpike lined with belching oil refineries. As such it has become the butt of national jokes and has been called, among other names, "the armpit of America."[2] The tendency for even New Jersey residents to identify with their neighbors has been symbolized by the lack, until rather recently, of a television station broadcasting from within the state's borders. Former governor Thomas Kean's "New Jersey and You, Perfect Together" ad campaign was aimed, at least in part, at creating a positive image and personality for an entity more than three hundred years old.

History itself explains New Jersey's identity crisis. At an early point it was divided into an "east" and "west" (later transformed into "north" and "south"). Political disagreements followed these divisions. Also, from the beginning diversity characterized its development. The state ranges geographically from an extensive seashore, fertile plains, and "barren" pinelands to muted mountains.[3] From the colonial period on its population included a variety of ethnic and religious groups.

1

One result of all this diversity has been much disagreement. Thomas Fleming suggests New Jersey's motto "might well be '[d]ivided we stand,'" for, he notes, "few states have equaled the multiplicity and duration of New Jersey's internal quarrels."[4]

New Jersey has long had a dubious reputation for its politics and its "justice." In 1944 the *Elizabeth Daily Journal* observed that "few states have been so cursed with political gangsters as New Jersey." Notorious figures include Lord Cornbury in the eighteenth century and "Boss" Frank Hague in the twentieth, both frequently cited as examples of corruption. Governor James McGreevey, whose brief tenure ended with a resignation in 2004, extended the saga into the twenty-first century.[5] There are numerous examples of election returns falsified by a variety of methods—ballot boxes being stuffed, polls remaining open for ten weeks in 1789, gerrymandered districts such as the "Horseshoe" created in Hudson County in 1871 and several odd shapes designed in 1992. To avoid detection, poll books have been burned, and even a judicial ruling obtained that ballot boxes could be opened but the contents not examined. New Jersey presented the first Congress with the first disputed federal election, not the state's last. In 1894 two senates tried to occupy the statehouse in Trenton simultaneously.[6]

All this political skulduggery, and more, is a consequence of both the numerous divisions within the state and a long record of closely contested politics. Although political parties have come and gone in New Jersey, the balance within the state, whether between Federalists and Jeffersonian-Republicans, Jacksonian-Democrats and Whigs, or modern-day Democrats and Republicans, has generally been close. Voters have frequently changed their party choice from one election to the next. Their independent attitudes often have meant that the governor and the majority of the legislature came from different parties.[7]

New Jersey has also had a long history of opposition to taxes, in part a function of the state's rural, conservative nature. In the colonial period, government was financed through paper money, with the interest earned by its loan serving in lieu of taxes.[8] During the nineteenth century the state obtained money first by granting a railroad monopoly and then by liberal incorporation laws—both in return for fees. Not until the 1970s, with status as a wealthy urban state long since reached, did New Jersey enact laws providing for sales and income taxes to support public services. As a result, the state long lagged behind much of the rest of the country in funding educational facilities and other services. Residents still feel the effects of this slow development. Because of the long dearth of higher educational opportunities, the state continues to send a disproportionately high number of students outside its borders to college and often loses their brainpower permanently as a consequence.

By the early twenty-first century, although New Jersey regularly ranked as the wealthiest (or alternatively the second wealthiest) state in the nation, it faced increased fiscal problems. Additional state services (from parks to pensions), previous tax cuts, and deficit spending contributed to higher taxes, while increasing fears of declining competitiveness. Involved in the service- and technology-oriented postindustrial economy, New Jersey has repeatedly been impacted by national financial downturns.

Where New Jersey has been in education, politics, economy, and culture makes its present more comprehensible. Residents can be proud of some, though not all, of their state's history, and they should not sell it short. Their little state is complex and interesting. In addition, it often indicates where the rest of the nation is headed.

◆ ◆ ◆ ◆ ◆ ◆

As elsewhere on the North American continent, Indians were the first inhabitants of New Jersey. Their population has been estimated at between eight and twelve thousand, most of them Lenni Lenapes (also called the Delawares), at the time of European contact. And, as elsewhere in early America, their numbers were decimated by the diseases brought by Europeans. The American Indian population of New Jersey, it is estimated, quickly dwindled to between twenty-four hundred and three thousand in 1700, to less than one thousand in 1763, and to fewer than two hundred by 1800. Those who did not succumb to illness were pushed out by land-hungry white settlers. They went first to West Jersey, then to Pennsylvania or New York, and, ultimately, to Oklahoma and Canada.[9] Although the first whites to make contact with this original American Indian population were probably French, Spanish, and English fishermen or traders, the earliest European settlers were Dutch and Swedes. In 1609 Henry Hudson explored both New Jersey's coast and the river that took his name. His efforts were followed up by the Dutch West Indies Company in 1621. The Dutch were primarily interested in establishing trading posts to obtain furs, and they concentrated their efforts more on the east side of the river. In addition, conflicts with American Indian inhabitants forced their eastward retreat to New Amsterdam in 1643 and 1655. As a result the Dutch were few in number and short on success: by 1660 their settlements in New Jersey consisted of isolated residents and the fortified hamlet of Bergen.

The Dutch were not the only newcomers to the region, nor were they alone in having difficulties with the native population. In 1638, when the New Sweden Company established an outpost on the Delaware, Governor Johan Printz (known as "Big Belly" because he weighed more than four hundred pounds) wrote that he would like "a couple of hundred Soldiers" on hand "until we broke the necks of all of them in the river."[10] The soldiers were not forthcoming, and the Swedes, after several confrontations with the Dutch, surrendered their claims to the region in 1655. At that time, an estimated four hundred Swedes and four thousand Dutch populated the entire Delaware valley (not just New Jersey).[11]

Commercial rivals of the English in Europe and elsewhere, the Dutch did not retain their hegemony in America for long. Their colony provided a further source of conflict because it physically divided the northern and southern portions of the empire the British were building. As a result, in 1664 Charles II granted his brother, the Duke of York, a widespread American colony incorporating parts of present-day New York, New Jersey, and Maine. The Duke sent Richard Nicolls off as governor and head of a military expedition designed to intimidate the Dutch. It did, and the English flag was raised over New Amsterdam without a shot being fired.[12]

Scarcely had Nicolls left England when the Duke turned over the "most improvable part" of his dominions to George Carteret and Lord John Berkeley, two English noblemen who had remained loyal to the Stuarts during their exile at the time of the English civil wars. In the meantime Nicolls had granted two tracts of land in what would be called "Nova Caesarea" or "New Jersey." The first, Elizabeth-Town, went to a group of Puritans from Connecticut; the second, Monmouth, went to a mixture of Quakers and Baptists from New England. In 1666 other Puritans purchased land from the Indians and established Newark. Because the new proprietors refused to recognize these titles, they proved a long-term source of contention in the colony.[13]

The proprietary period in New Jersey lasted from 1664 to 1702, a brief but confusing time. Rapid division and sale of proprietary shares created an ever-changing group of proprietors. Berkeley sold half the province to a group of Quakers headed by John Fenwick and Edward Byllynge in 1674. Carteret's portion went to another group of Quakers, including a number of Scottish investors, in 1682. As a result there were actually two New Jerseys, West and East, each with its own governor and legislature. First Berkeley and Carteret, and then the later proprietors of the two sections, provided "Concessions" and "Constitutions" that incorporated such important concepts as representative government (including consent to taxation), religious toleration, and trial by jury.[14] Despite these political concessions, designed to attract settlers to the province, relations between residents and proprietors were not always smooth. There was a "Revolution" in East Jersey in 1672, disorder in West Jersey in 1681, and a number of disturbances in both provinces in the late 1690s. As a consequence of their troubles in governing, and also because of challenges to their authority from England, the proprietors surrendered their political claims to the province (but not their title to the land) in 1702.

When New Jersey became a royal province in 1703 it contained about ten thousand residents, an ethnic mix of Indians, Dutch, Swedes, English, and Scots and a religious mix of Puritans, Quakers, Baptists, Presbyterians, and Anglicans, among others. The legacy of division into an east and west continued to have political ramifications even though there was once again a single "New Jersey." The diversity that would characterize the state into the present was already obvious and significant.

The royal period in New Jersey history divides into two portions, 1703–1738 and 1738–1776. Initially, the colony shared its governor with New York and elected a separate legislature. The result was a series of governors who paid little attention to New Jersey, and that small amount usually boded no good—for most of them were more concerned with lining their own pockets than with the welfare of the colony. The first, Lord Cornbury, has been described as a greedy transvestite, a "detestable maggot." He is alleged to have accepted first a bribe from the eastern proprietors and then the contents of a "blind tax" collected by their opponents. The "Ring" that surrounded him engaged in a large-scale land grab.[15] A successor, William Burnet, accepted one thousand pounds for "incidentals" from the assembly and promptly signed a bill it desired. William Cosby appeared in the colony only once in four years and fought with its leading politicians. Only Robert Hunter stands out for his honesty, skill, and attempt to clean up politics. Bribery, disputed elections, and raucous disagreements thus early became part of New Jersey politics.[16]

In 1738 Lewis Morris was appointed the first separate royal governor of New Jersey. Although a native son, he proved no more responsive to New Jersey residents than his predecessors. The assembly wanted paper money; he wanted a higher salary. Neither would make concessions, and the colony's government was thus locked in a stalemate. Financial disagreements also plagued two of his successors. Both Jonathan Belcher and Francis Bernard tried to obtain support for England's efforts in the Great War for Empire, only to have the assembly refuse, claiming "poverty." The aid that was given, after the French and Indians appeared to threaten the western frontier of the colony, came through deficit financing (paper money). At the end of the French and Indian Wars, New Jersey had the largest per capita debt of any colony.[17] Throughout this period New Jersey politicians divided into numerous factions that jockeyed for power both among themselves and with the royal governors around the issues of paper money, taxation, and ending the rioting (particularly between 1735 and 1755) caused by controversies over land titles. The result, as in other colonies, was to increase the power of the colonial assembly.[18]

Also significant in this period was the religious revival known in the American colonies as the Great Awakening. George Whitefield, the English minister who conducted revival meetings up and down the Atlantic coast, stopped and spoke in New Jersey several times. Similar efforts were led by such native sons as Gilbert Tennent among the Presbyterians and Theodore Frelinghuysen among members of the Dutch Reformed Church.[19] In addition to conversions, the Awakening led to the splitting of churches by warring factions and to the creation of educational institutions such as the College of New Jersey (Princeton) in 1746 and Queens College (Rutgers) in 1766.[20]

In the 1760s New Jersey, diverse in religion and population, had a primarily rural economy. The total population was approximately one hundred thousand; the largest "city," Elizabethtown, probably had fewer than one thousand residents. Although there were both rich and poor people, it was basically a middle-class society; Governor Belcher described it as the "best country I have seen for middling fortunes, and for people who have to live by the sweat of their brows." It was also a provincial community primarily concerned with local affairs. England was far away. Provincialism slowly lessened over the years until this small colony suddenly found itself caught in the center of the whirlwind known as the American Revolution.

In 1763, William Franklin, a young lawyer and the illegitimate son of Benjamin Franklin, was appointed governor of New Jersey. He was destined to be the last royal official to hold this position.[21] With the Great War for Empire ended, England moved to bring under control both its additional territory and the large debt it had acquired in the course of that conflict. Two measures passed by Parliament particularly affected New Jersey. The Currency Act restricted paper money issues used to finance the colonial government and its war debt. The Stamp Act imposed a direct tax on legal documents and other items.

Despite its rural, conservative atmosphere, New Jersey did not entirely escape the furor raised by the Stamp Act throughout the American colonies. Lawyers resolved to do no business requiring the stamps; William Coxe, the local stamp agent, could not rent a house for fear it would be destroyed. The assembly claimed that "all Taxes laid upon us without our Consent" were "a fundamental infringement of the Rights and privileges Secured to us as English Subjects and by Charter." New Jersey protested the stamp tax, but without urban crowds there were no riots comparable to those in Massachusetts, and without firebrands like Patrick Henry there were no radical statements such as those coming from Virginia.

An economic boycott of English goods helped induce Parliament to repeal the Stamp Act. But the principles behind American objections were not recognized in England, and the law was replaced in 1767 by the Townshend Acts, which imposed taxes on lead, paper, paint, and tea. In protest, Americans resorted to nonimportation agreements. Along with other legislatures, New Jersey's petitioned the king. Again Parliament backed off. The acts were repealed, except for a symbolic tax on tea, which became an issue after the passage of the Tea Act in 1773.

To ensure that the tax on tea would not be paid, Bostonians threw the leaves into the harbor. New Jersey radicals staged their own "tea party" by burning a shipment at Greenwich, while college students in Princeton vowed not to drink the brew. England responded with the Intolerable Acts, closing Boston Harbor and altering Massachusetts's governmental structure. Designed to divide the colonies, the policies had the opposite effect. Americans sent aid to Boston and also began to arm. While New Jerseyans participated in these colonial protests, the colony was never in the vanguard of patriot activity. Small, provincial, conservative, lacking a newspaper of its own, it was more concerned with the robbery of the provincial treasury in 1768 and the ensuing controversy than with developments in the larger world around it.[22]

New Jersey thus moved slowly, hesitantly, toward revolution. After July 1774, two governments coexisted in the colony with a new Provincial Congress gradually siphoning authority from the old royal legislature. During this process Franklin not only held on to his position longer than any other royal governor but also used his influence to try to keep New Jersey in the empire. He almost succeeded. At one point in 1775 New Jersey's delegates from the Continental Congress returned to plead with the assembly not to break ranks; later, three representatives from other colonies were sent to ensure that New Jersey remained true to the "common cause."

In June 1776, fourteen months after fighting had begun at Lexington and Concord, the Provincial Congress finally ordered Franklin arrested and deported to Connecticut. New, more radical delegates were sent from New Jersey to the Continental Congress. Richard Stockton, Abraham Clark, John Witherspoon, John Hart, and Francis Hopkinson arrived in time to sign the Declaration of Independence. But New Jersey still hedged its bets. It wrote a constitution referring to itself as a "colony" and stating that the document would be "null and void" if a reconciliation with the king should occur.

The constitution of 1776, written in haste as British forces landed on nearby Staten Island, reflected the times in other ways as well. It provided that a legislature, elected annually, would choose a governor. This official was further weakened by the lack of veto and appointment powers. Although including property qualifications to vote and hold office, the constitution granted the right to vote to "all inhabitants . . . of full age"—a provision that enabled some women and blacks to vote until 1807.[23] In spite of defects that soon became clear, the brief document served until 1844.

The first state governor elected under its terms was William Livingston, a wealthy New York Whig lawyer who had recently moved to New Jersey to enjoy a peaceful country existence. Instead he spent the wartime years with a price on his head, constantly moving to avoid capture by the British. New Jersey had become a corridor through which the armies of both sides marched while local loyalist and patriot forces confronted one another in what frequently amounted to a nasty civil war.[24] In addition to numerous skirmishes, several major battles of the war were fought within the state—Trenton in 1776, Princeton in 1777, and Monmouth in 1778. The Continental army spent three winters in New Jersey, two in Morristown (the winter of 1779–1780, when it snowed twenty-eight times, was reputed to be the worst of the century) and one in Middlebrook (now Bound Brook).

Caught between contending forces, disagreeing with neighbors and relatives, New Jerseyans chose different sides. A relatively high number of its citizens remained loyal to the crown, some serving with the British forces. William Franklin, after being "exchanged" and released from his Connecticut prison, headed the detested Board of Associated Loyalists in New York City. Southern and western New Jersey contained many Quaker pacifists who tried to remain neutral. Some residents shifted sides depending on whether American or British soldiers were standing on their doorstep. The Baroness von Riedesel, wife of the highest-ranking Hessian officer to serve the British in America, described three visits to the Van Horne home in Middlebrook. On the first the family announced their loyalty to the king; during the second, when American officers were present, they stayed up late singing, "God save great Washington! God damn the King"; on the third visit, they asked her to assure the king of their support. Other New Jerseyans were consistently and fiercely tied to the patriot cause, some paying for this with imprisonment, loss of property, and their lives. It was a difficult time for all—until the British sailed out of New York harbor in 1783.[25]

The war ended in New Jersey, at least officially. The peace treaty was received while Congress met in Princeton, and George Washington wrote his farewell address to the troops at Rocky Hill. The consequences of the war were few but dramatic in New Jersey—independence, greater local control, public and private buildings in ruins, the removal of loyalists to England or Canada, and lowered property qualifications for voters. Because the state was still primarily rural and conservative, other changes came about more slowly.[26] Though glad that the "late unpleasant times" were over, New Jersey entered the Confederation period of the 1780s with economic problems of its own and fearful of the pitfalls it thought the national government faced under the Articles of Confederation. In 1778, before ratifying the Articles, the legislature questioned how the new government would handle western lands, as well as its ability to tax or to control state tariffs on trade. Increasingly concerned with these problems, in 1786 the state refused the national requisition for money. Similar sentiments led to the appointment of delegates to the Annapolis Convention later that year with instructions to work for change in the Articles, and then to the quick selection of representatives to the Philadelphia Convention.[27]

New Jersey played a significant role in the writing of the United States Constitution. Its delegation, through the efforts of William Paterson, proposed a "small state" plan, basing representation on states as equal units rather than on each state's population. The contingent stubbornly adhered to this proposal until a compromise was devised and was incorporated into the design of the U.S. Senate.[28] When the document was completed it was sent on to the states for ratification, a process that was protracted and difficult in many places, but not in New Jersey. Because provisions of the new Constitution corrected the defects of the Articles to which New Jersey residents had previously objected, there was little debate over its contents. A convention ratified quickly and unanimously, making the state the third "pillar" in the new nation. To celebrate, the delegates retired to a local Trenton tavern, ate dinner, and drank thirteen toasts in honor of the occasion—the last to the United States and "liberty."

The unanimity of 1787 gave way to the disagreements of 1789 as diverse, closely contested politics returned to the state. In the first election, a wild, bitter affair, the divisions were primarily sectional and personal.[29] As the 1790s continued, issues came to resemble those debated throughout the country. Reflecting national concerns (particularly economic policies and foreign affairs), New Jersey residents divided into Federalists and Jeffersonian-Republicans.

Particularly divisive were the Jay Treaty of 1795, a copy of which was burned in Flemington because it was seen as favoring England, and the Alien and Sedition Acts of 1798, criticized for the restrictions they imposed on freedom of speech and the press. Under the terms of the latter a Newark man, Luther Baldwin, was tried and convicted of sedition because he said he wished that a cannon salute to visiting President John Adams had hit his posterior. Republican newspapers noted the fine of $150 for this "heinous" crime and concluded that "joking could be dangerous even in a free country."[30]

Until 1800 the Federalists dominated New Jersey politics. Afterward, except for a Federalist resurgence during the War of 1812, the Republicans controlled most political offices, although, as usual, New Jersey elections were close. Both sides created state political conventions, legislative caucuses, and party newspapers to build and keep support, all of which increased popular participation and stimulated greater public discussion of issues.[31]

The Jeffersonian-Republicans increased the size of the nation with the Louisiana Purchase and embroiled it in controversies with both England and France. In 1812 the United States again went to war with England over, among other issues, maritime rights. New Jersey, with a relatively small foreign trade and numerous Quakers, briefly returned the antiwar Federalists to power. The legislature condemned the war as "inexpedient, ill-timed" and "dangerous," while the militia refused to serve outside the state's boundaries (as did the forces of many other states). Yet when the war ended with Andrew Jackson's spectacular victory at the Battle of New Orleans, many state residents felt a sense of pride in their nation (even though the larger conflict was actually a draw).[32]

A surge of nationalism and a decline of political opposition followed the war in the United States. The "Era of Good Feelings" was characterized by one-party politics as the Federalist Party, because of its opposition to the war, declined precipitously. However, even in this period political disagreements in New Jersey did not entirely disappear; they just revolved again around older, local issues. Clearer divisions reappeared in the state and nation with the election of 1824 and the Jacksonian period it inaugurated.

In the meantime, significant developments in transportation and industrialization took place in New Jersey. As the state linking New York and Pennsylvania, as well as North and South, New Jersey was particularly involved in what has been called the "transportation revolution," the rapid development of roads, steamboats, clipper ships, railroads, and canals after 1800.[33] From 1801 to 1829 the legislature chartered fifty-one companies to build and operate "turnpikes," privately constructed roads that charged tolls. New Jersey investors built and operated steamboats in competition with New York inventors who claimed a monopoly. Thomas Gibbons constructed and Cornelius Vanderbilt operated the *Bellona,* whose flag proclaiming "New Jersey must be free" defied authority from across the Hudson. In 1824 the United States Supreme Court ruled in *Gibbons v. Ogden* that only the federal government could regulate commerce; no state could grant a monopoly over interstate traffic. Colonel John Stevens built the first steam locomotive in the country and in an 1825 demonstration ran it around a circular track in Hoboken at the speed of six miles per hour. He was later involved in the establishment of a railroad line that connected Philadelphia and New York. The canal mania that swept the country led to the construction of the Morris Canal in the northern portion of the state and the Delaware and Raritan Canal in the central part.[34] The consequences of these developments were profound. Canal barges transported coal from Pennsylvania mines and helped fuel industrialization. Railroads crisscrossed the state carrying tourists to the Shore. Politics was also transformed. In 1830 the legislature chartered the Joint Companies (the Delaware and Raritan Canal and the Camden and Amboy Railroad). In return for a minimum payment of $30,000 a year to the state (sufficient then to cover most of the budget), the railroad received a monopoly of the route between New York and Pennsylvania.

The company also exercised a predominant influence in state and local politics; New Jersey was sometimes called the "state of Camden and Amboy." Despite critics who charged that the costs were high, the service poor, and the road unsafe, the monopoly continued until 1873. Two years earlier the lines had been leased to the Pennsylvania Railroad for 999 years, which meant that no longer could the company claim special privileges as a purely state institution. The Penn system used the tracks, operated the canal, and competed with other lines now also running through the state.

Along with changes in transportation came early industrialization. In 1791 the state chartered the Society for Useful Manufactures, which purchased the site of the Passaic River's Great Falls, the second largest waterfall in the eastern United States, as a source of waterpower. The company established Paterson as a center for manufacturing and, although an initial failure, by the mid-nineteenth century its mills were producing cotton and silk textiles, as well as various machines (including locomotives). South Jersey manufactured iron and glass, Trenton companies made ceramics and other products; in the north, Newark became a center for leather goods and beer, Plainfield for hats, New Brunswick for rubber and wallpaper. Cities grew, the labor force changed, by 1840 the state was no longer totally rural, and by 1860 it was an important center for manufacturing.[35]

In New Jersey and elsewhere, animated politics returned with the election of 1824 and the subsequent creation of the "second-party system." The election began as a four-way race between John Quincy Adams, Andrew Jackson, Henry Clay, and William Crawford. It ended with the House of Representatives electing Adams as president; Henry

Clay was appointed his secretary of state. Adams had charges of "corrupt bargain" ringing in his ears while Jackson immediately began campaigning for 1828. Two parties based on economic and political disagreements as well as personalities and patronage eventually emerged from the political battles that followed: the Jacksonian-Democrats and the Whigs. Although complicated by the state's own diversity, the divisions within New Jersey reflected those in the nation as a whole but diverged on the question of banks and corporations. State elections were, as usual, close—so close that in 1838, in what was dubbed the Broad Seal War, Whig delegates certified as victors by the governor (using the state seal) were challenged by Democratic opponents. A Democratic Congress refused to seat the Whigs, ensuring their control of the House of Representatives. Once again, as in 1789, a New Jersey political brawl had spilled over to Washington.[36]

In addition to a revival of partisan politics, the Jacksonian era brought an increased interest in political and social reform. Some of the political developments typical of the period in other states had already occurred in New Jersey, including the broadening of suffrage and the use of political conventions. Others, particularly constitutional change, came later to the state. Not until 1844, long after most of its neighbors, was the Revolutionary Constitution of 1776 replaced. Governor Daniel Haines viewed it as simply "incompatible with the present age." The legislature had spent an inordinate amount of time on special acts (most frequently to grant divorces) and on political appointments. The state lacked independent courts and had a weak governor who was not popularly elected. The Constitutional Convention revamped the original document, but compared to what other states chose to do the resultant reforms were modest. Under the new constitution, New Jersey elected governors every three years, but they could not serve consecutive terms and possessed a veto that could easily be overridden. State senators were elected for three-year terms, assemblymen for one. The constitution established a separate chancellor for courts of equity and a court of appeals, banned legislative divorces, made provisions for amendments, and included a bill of rights. Like its predecessor, it was a document that, despite its defects, survived for a long time. Not until 1947 did New Jersey replace it.[37]

The Jacksonian period also spawned myriad social reforms. Fueled by economic changes, population growth, evangelical religion, and the development of humanitarianism, reformers, particularly in the North and Old Northwest, turned to remodeling society and its institutions. They were particularly interested in debtors, drunkards, prisoners, and the "insane" and promoted model communities, education, and abolition. But New Jersey's endemic conservatism inhibited reform, and its predominantly rural character made social problems less visible than they were in more rapidly urbanizing states.

Still, reform in New Jersey in this period reflected the concerns of American society at large, and it increasingly involved the remodeling or creation of institutions. New Jersey renovated its prisons to provide a system of individual cells, then thought to be more conducive to rehabilitation. But one historian concluded that the resultant system of solitary confinement unfortunately created "more madmen than repentants."[38] "Madmen" themselves were the object of concern as Dorothea Dix and others lobbied the state legislature to create a mental asylum, eventually built in 1848.[39] Reformers hoped the new jail would prevent recidivism of convicts, while the asylum would cure the sick.

Other reformers worked to keep debtors out of state institutions altogether. An 1830 report on imprisonment for debt stated, "We know of nothing worse in the whole length and breadth of the land than in New Jersey." Legal revisions in 1844 made it no longer possible to imprison someone for owing as little as five dollars; no longer would half the jail population of the state consist of debtors unable to earn money to repay what they owed because of their incarceration.[40]

While other reformers attempted to improve schools; some created Utopian communities, models that would avoid the problems brought by industrialization, commercialism, and competition. In New Jersey they established the North American Phalanx in Red Bank in 1843. It lasted twelve years and spawned the shorter-lived Raritan Bay Union near Perth Amboy in 1853. Both communities attempted to build alternative methods of social organization and a more cooperative life. The Red Bank group combined farming and industry, private and communal life, so that all could work according to their "strengths and tastes." Disagreements over religion, the value of various trades, and the quality of intellectual life, however, weakened the organization. A fire compounded its problems, and the group disbanded in 1855.[41] These efforts paralleled such contemporaneous attempts elsewhere as the Shaker communities, Brook Farm in Massachusetts, and Robert Owens's New Harmony in Indiana. These experiments intrigued later reformers, including those who would attempt such projects from the 1870s to the 1960s.[42]

On a practical level, though, neither Utopian communities nor improved schools lasted beyond this period. By 1830 there were pauper schools for the poor and academies for the rich, but free public education was nonexistent in New Jersey. As other northern states created public schools, New Jersey failed to act. The state's first superintendent of education, appointed in 1848, wrote that a "merciful man . . . would not winter his horse" in existing district schoolhouses.[43] In 1855 the first normal school, or teachers college (which became Trenton State College and is now the College of New Jersey), was established, but not until 1871 did state laws begin to provide truly "free" elementary schools.[44] In the early twenty-first century the state and its courts still argue over how these institutions should be funded.

The fact that New Jersey moved slowly in some areas is shown dramatically in the length of time it took to abolish slavery in the state and the way this act was ultimately accomplished. Slaves in colonial New Jersey worked on farms, in the iron industry, and in private households. They were more prevalent in the eastern section than in the Quaker-dominated western region. Although the American Revolution increased abolitionist sentiment by adding a political commitment to natural rights to the currents of Quaker theology, the state did not pass a law for abolition until 1804. It was the last northern state to do so, and even then it was made "gradual" so that slavery was not totally abolished in the state until the Thirteenth Amendment was adopted in 1865.

Other northern states, such as New York and Pennsylvania, also provided for gradual emancipation, but the last slaves were freed in those states earlier than they were in New Jersey. Even so, freedom came more quickly than William Griffith, president of the New Jersey Antislavery Society in 1804, anticipated: he had predicted that it might take "a century" before slavery was "eradicated from our country." New Jersey's conservatism accounts for much of the delay the state's enslaved African Americans encountered. Slaves were property, and state politicians were unwilling to confiscate it in one fell swoop; instead, they freed the children of slaves born after 1804 as they came of age (twenty-five for males, twenty-one for females) on the grounds that they would then have repaid their masters, through their labor, for their initial investment. The freedmen, frequently described as "degraded" and "rejected," remained at the bottom of the economic and social heap, but their new status was still preferable. One former slave declared that he "wouldn't be a slave ag'in, not if you'd give me the best farm in the Jarsies."[45] New Jersey's conservative position on this issue is also apparent in its handling of fugitive slaves. While other northern states moved to block the application of federal fugitive slave laws within their boundaries by adopting personal liberty laws, New Jersey passed its own law to assist southerners in recovering their property. But an 1836 law required jury trials to prove that slaves were truly fugitives before they were returned to their southern owners.

Although a northern state, New Jersey has been called a "border state" because of its attitudes during the Civil War. Actually, the state supported the war effort and even raised more troops when first asked than it was required to do. However, the Democratic Party remained strong, and a considerable amount of sympathy existed for the South. The "Opposition Party" was slow to take the name "Republican" and, though it objected to the extension of slavery in the West, it was not inclined to attack the institution in the South. New Jersey was the only free state not to give all its electoral votes to Lincoln in 1860 and to vote for General George McClellan (then living in West Orange) in 1864. State Democrats divided: some thought the South should be free to secede, a few even that New Jersey should join the Confederacy, but most supported Lincoln's efforts to keep the Union together. When they dominated the legislature in 1863 the more radical Democrats pushed for the passage of "peace resolutions" and chose "Copperhead" Colonel James W. Wall to finish an uncompleted term as United States senator. Newspaper editors in the state also divided. Some opposed the war and the draft, the Democratic *Newark Journal* going so far as to ask those who desired "to be butchered" in Mr. Lincoln's war to "step forward at once." These complex divisions, including the continuance in power of the Democratic Party, also occurred in neighboring New York and Pennsylvania, while opposition to the draft led to rioting in New York City. But New Jersey met most of its commitments. In the end an estimated 88,305 New Jerseyans served the Union during the war, and 6,300 of these men died.

In many ways New Jersey's ambivalence on the Civil War characterized the state through much of its history and reflected the state's endemic hesitancy to act. Its diverse population and its continued tendency to generate close and changing election results (now a consequence of divisions between Democrats and Republicans) also kept conflict alive in the state. When the Republicans won in 1865, Charles E. Elmer praised God that New Jersey residents had finally "returned from all manner of wickedness and declared themselves Loyal and true to the Union." But he spoke too soon: political controversy reemerged shortly afterward in the state's bifurcated response to Reconstruction.[46]

Reconstruction was a seesaw process for the nation as a whole. The president contended with Congress for power, and the victorious North argued with the defeated South over the position of the states within the Union and of African Americans within American society. New Jersey's positions on these questions were complicated. First Democrats, then Republicans, then Democrats, then Republicans controlled the state legislature, the governor's office, or both. Between 1865 and 1870 the state both rejected and accepted the Thirteenth, Fourteenth, and Fifteenth Amendments. In addition to close elections that resulted in power shifting between parties, the state's actions reflected a residual support for states' rights and for the South, and a degree of long-standing racism that characterized most of the North and was not distinctive to New Jersey.[47]

Even as the country coped with the Civil War, Reconstruction, and their aftermath, it moved on to other issues. In national politics Democrats and Republicans took positions on the tariff, civil service reforms, and prohibition, but New Jersey politicians did not always follow their party's platform. Not all New Jersey Democrats supported free trade; not all Republicans favored local option laws forbidding liquor sales. Contests were close as politicians tailored their appeals to various interests, and late nineteenth-century voters turned out in large numbers. Politics provided entertainment, recreation, and jobs. Generally, Democrats were more successful in electing governors until the mid-1890s; then Republicans had the edge. The depression of 1893, dislike of William Jennings Bryan and his "free silver" platform, and the taint of corruption took their toll on the Democrats. Not until Woodrow Wilson ran for governor in 1910 would they return to power. By then, election law reforms, modern advertising techniques, declining party loyalty, the development of motion pictures, and the rise of professional sports had combined to reduce the percentage of voters who went to the polls.[48]

The last third of the nineteenth century was marked by rapid and interconnected growth in industrialization, immigration, and urbanization. Alongside these developments emerged sometimes stark contrasts between rich and poor, management and labor, and morality and popular recreation. The contradictions and problems of the age generally were mirrored in New Jersey. And by 1900 the state had become even more diverse and complex.

By the 1870s New Jersey had attracted new industries such as oil refineries, rubber production, and large-scale services such as insurance companies. Modern research laboratories whose inventions were designed, tested, and marketed by supporting companies appeared. Thomas Edison's facilities, first at Menlo Park and then at West Orange, were precursors to the seven hundred research laboratories of a century later; today New Jersey is still prominent in the nation in research and development spending, some of it now through its universities. By the 1890s numerous chemical and pharmaceutical firms (along with polluted waterways) were also established.[49]

The "robber barons" of this age also devised new methods of organizing and conducting business. In addition to the light bulb, the phonograph, the motion picture, and new uses for oil products and steel, they invented the trust. In the 1890s, as New Jersey discovered the value of such combinations as a new source of state revenue, it became the home of the trusts. Liberal laws encouraged national companies to incorporate in the state—for a fee. A single building in Jersey City contained "offices" for more than 1,200 corporations; the 7 largest companies in the country and 150 of the top 298 were chartered in the state in 1904. Not everyone found this state enterprise admirable. Lincoln Steffens, the noted Progressive reformer, called New Jersey the "Traitor State." The influence that the trusts exercised in state politics fed a growing interest in reform.[50]

The trusts, insurance companies, and, later, public utility corporations were not the only politically weighty entities in New Jersey. Railroad companies had been significant since before the Civil War, and afterward they proliferated; track mileage nationwide expanded tremendously. Within the "corridor state," routes leading toward New York City achieved ever-greater significance. Tax exemptions for railroad property and methods of evaluating that property became an issue in state and local politics (particularly in Jersey City) from at least the 1880s to the 1940s.[51] In addition, rapidly growing cities awarded franchises for "traction companies" (trolley car lines) and for water, gas, and electric services. The opportunities for "honest graft" (and dishonest) multiplied.[52] In the 1890s speculators built racetracks, some legal, others not, and gambling became a significant interest as well. William E. Sackett, writing of the period, stated that it was "almost unheard of" for anyone opposed to the railroads to be elected in New Jersey, but the other "interests" exerted considerable influence as well.[53]

While some New Jerseyans became rich—indeed, very rich—at the same time others toiled long and hard for little pay. Brewers in Newark worked fourteen to eighteen hours a day, six days a week, and another six to eight hours on Sundays; they earned between twenty and twenty-five dollars a month.[54] In 1886 they struck for shorter hours and better wages. Paterson, which became the scene of a nationally publicized strike in 1913, contained numerous textile mills where women and children worked as many as thirteen hours a day in unhealthy and sometimes dangerous conditions. At the same time silk manufacturer Catholina Lambert built a home, literally a castle, on the mountain overlooking the city and stocked it with paintings by such European masters as Rembrandt.[55] Other wealthy industrialists flocked to Morristown where they built "cottages" (resembling those of Newport, Rhode Island, erected in the same period) containing thirty rooms or more.[56] This took place at the same time that such cities as Newark literally packed residents like sardines into flimsy tenement houses lacking adequate ventilation and sanitation.[57] With such contrasts in lifestyle it is not surprising that Paterson alone experienced 137 strikes between 1881 and 1900. The period from 1870 to 1900 was one of frequent, and sometimes bitter and violent, incidents of labor unrest in New Jersey, as in many other parts of the country.

The workers who labored in the Paterson mills, as had those who helped all of America industrialize, came from many different lands. In the early nineteenth century immigrants had arrived in large numbers from Ireland and Germany; the Irish built canals, while the Germans operated breweries. In the late nineteenth century immigrants came from Poland, Italy, Russia, and other southern and eastern European countries. They worked in the fields in South Jersey as well as in factories in the northern part of the state. Most flocked to the cities, where work was most plentiful. The size of this immigration and a sense of its impact can be gleaned from statistics in the 1910 census. Twenty-seven percent of the state's population was foreign-born, slightly lower than in New York but higher than in Pennsylvania. In Paterson, the foreign-born made up 36 percent of the population; in Passaic, they were 52 percent. The foreign-born constituted 16 percent of the population in the United States as a whole at the time. New Jersey was unusually diverse before the Civil War, but by the early twentieth century its heterogeneity had entered another dimension. To some it had become "a virtual tower of Babel, a confusion of tongues and creeds." Distinctive ethnic neighborhoods arose, but the great variety of backgrounds, languages, and religions that resulted from this influx made the organization of labor unions complex and difficult. In addition, the large numbers of Catholics, particularly in such places as Jersey City, at times led to political backlash on the part of older Protestant residents.[58]

Although New Jersey's diversity was not new, the rate of expansion of its population, its degree of urbanization, and change in the nature of its agriculture were novel developments of the turn of the century. In the twenty-five years after 1890 the population almost doubled, reaching nearly three million by 1915. Farm acreage peaked in 1879. Afterward, the state became more urban than rural, and what its farmers grew changed. In the colonial period they had concentrated on beef, cattle, and wheat. Increasingly, dairy and chicken farming become more significant, as did vegetables both for the market and the new canning industry. The Joseph Campbell Company began processing produce in 1869; the company and tomatoes long remained important in South Jersey. Cranberries and blueberries were raised in bogs and the Pine Barrens. Later, nurseries produced trees, shrubs, roses, and bedding plants when suburbs began to grow, especially after 1950.[59]

The late nineteenth century was also the time when popular forms of recreation and entertainment now taken for granted first developed. Football, baseball, horse racing, golf, tennis, and bicycling became increasingly available and affordable to spectators and participants of different classes.[60] Large numbers of tourists began to vacation at New Jersey lake and seashore resorts, made accessible in large part by railroads. Sloops and stagecoaches brought visitors to Cape May from Philadelphia after the War of 1812, but Long Branch did not become *the* vacation spot until 1869, when President Grant discovered its delights—and could arrive in a private railroad car. The rich and famous flocked there until the Democrat Grover Cleveland was elected in 1884; then the fickle wealthy took off for the newest faddish place. In the 1880s Lakewood had nearly one hundred hotels that helped entertain the well-to-do. The largest and best-known resort of the period was Atlantic City, but it tended to attract a crowd of middle- and working-class people who came for day-long excursions on railroad coaches. They walked on the boardwalk, waded in the water, rode the Ferris wheel, ate saltwater taffy, and did the things visitors still do, except patronize legal casinos (which were unavailable before 1976).[61]

By the late nineteenth century even resorts, particularly Atlantic City, confronted problems as the contradictions between Victorian values and practices became increasingly apparent. The gap between morality and reality symbolized larger problems in American society. Offended by political corruption, the stark differences between rich and poor, the growth of trusts, and the restrictions on economic opportunity this growth implied, reformers of the Progressive era sought changes. Motivated by faith in democracy, efficiency, progress, and the possibility of social justice, they proposed a whole series of reforms in government, education, the workplace, and neighborhoods. New Jersey, still conservative and slow to react, gradually joined in the collective din for change until, for a brief time while Woodrow Wilson was governor, the state actually stood in the forefront of the Progressive movement.

In New Jersey, as in some other states, Progressivism started on the local level as a reform movement within the Republican Party called the "New Idea." Gradually, the Democratic Party also issued calls for reform. Mark Fagan and George L. Record in Jersey City pushed for better schools, more public parks, honest and efficient government, and (particularly important in Jersey City) equal taxation for railroads.[62] They and others also sought restrictions on corporations, an end to "perpetual franchises," institution of the direct primary, and other limits on the powers of political bosses. Women joined various civic clubs and pushed for such reforms as conservation of the Palisades, pure-food and -drug legislation, school improvements, the establishment of a women's college (Douglass College, as part of Rutgers University), and the right to vote. Some of them also helped organize settlement houses in urban areas designed to provide education and services particularly for immigrants. Efforts at reform moved on to the state level during the governorships of Franklin Murphy and John Franklin Fort, although their successes were limited; it was left to Woodrow Wilson to implement major changes.[63] For a brief time, New Jersey had a forceful governor able to muster enough legislative support for reform measures.

Wilson himself seemed an unlikely candidate for the role of Progressive reformer. Born in Virginia and the son of a Presbyterian minister, he had become a professor of political science and then president of Princeton University in 1902. His efforts to bring changes to that Ivy League institution ran into difficulties over the question of eating clubs (still a controversial issue) and the location of the graduate school. Seen as a conservative who could be controlled, he was the choice of the Democratic Party's political bosses for governor in 1910, but at the outset of the campaign Wilson broke with the bosses, especially James Smith Jr. of Newark, and appealed to reformers in both parties for support. As governor he proceeded to push actively for a series of laws embodying Progressive ideals. In short order the legislature enacted election reforms providing for direct primaries, banned corrupt practices by regulating campaign contributions, created a public utilities commission empowered to regulate the industry, and established workmen's compensation. Later additions were the "Seven Sister" acts designed to end New Jersey's role as a haven for corporations (repealed, however, in 1920 because they reduced state revenues). In 1912, when Republicans regained control of the state legislature, Wilson went on to campaign for and to win the presidency.[64]

As president, Wilson carried Progressivism to the national level. While he was in office the world went to war and, despite Wilson's urgings to remain neutral in "thought and deed," the United States was drawn into the conflict. The large number of Germans in New Jersey meant that there was sympathy for the Axis cause at first, but the state went on to support the Allies and the war effort as a whole.

As elsewhere in the country, patriotism was sometimes carried to an extreme. Reflecting the national xenophobia, residents of western Morris County changed the name of their community from German Valley to Long Valley, while Hamburg, Dresden, and Bismark streets in Newark became Wilson, London, and Pershing. The state commissioner of education assured the public that all teachers were loyal. But if they were not, they were expected to "at once resign and get out of the schools."[65]

During the war, New Jersey served as a center for wartime industrial production, as a major shipping point, and as a training ground for troops. The state manufactured munitions, chemicals, ships, and airplanes. Sixteen military complexes were established for training and assembling troops, the largest of them Camp Merritt in the north and Camp Dix in the south. Thirteen hundred buildings were constructed at Merritt, only to be abandoned after the war. Hoboken became a major point for the embarkation of soldiers; 40 percent of those who went to Europe passed through its port.[66] Some of these wartime enterprises had a lasting impact on the state as they increased its industrial base.

As the war came to an end, the United States adopted Prohibition. The temperance movement, including an advocacy of total abstinence, had waxed and waned over the nineteenth century, but it attracted greater support during World War I when advocates argued that drinking was "foreign" (Germans drank beer) and an unproductive use of grain crops. Passage of the Eighteenth Amendment in 1917 divided Americans, and New Jersey residents, along ethnic, religious, and urban-rural lines. It was also not easily enforced, particularly in a state with such a long coastline. In 1929 James M. Doran, national administrator for the program, stated, "We regard New Jersey as one of the hardest spots to handle in the entire country." By 1933 the nation had given up trying to "handle" liquor by forbidding it, and Prohibition was repealed.[67]

Prohibition came to an end as the country struggled with the worst depression in its history. The stock market crash in 1929 was the symbolic beginning of a disastrous financial decline caused by imbalances in the world, as well as the American, economy. New Jersey, with its large industrial base, was particularly vulnerable. By 1932 the unemployment rate in the state was 30 percent. The national average was 25 percent, but in some industrial cities fully half of the laboring population was unemployed.

As local and state governments ran out of funds, they turned to the federal government, which, after the election of Franklin D. Roosevelt in 1932, responded with the numerous initiatives of the New Deal.[68] Designed to provide relief for those in need, to reform the economy so as to prevent a recurrence of depression, and to experiment with alternatives for the future, the New Deal was meant to "prime the pump," to put people to work so that they could earn money, spend it, and in the process revive the economy. A variety of "alphabet soup" agencies ran construction projects, operated theaters, and took surveys. New Jersey obtained new post offices, hospitals, stadiums (in Jersey City and at Rutgers), and schools. Conservationists created a national park at Jockey Hollow near Morristown, site of the Continental Army's encampment during the American Revolution, and artists decorated the then-new terminal at Newark Airport. Jersey City particularly benefited from this largesse as the Democratic Party funneled projects for the state through Frank Hague in return for the votes his political machine turned out for Roosevelt. The enormous medical center built there was a monument to this collaboration.[69]

Another project in New Jersey was designed both to create work and serve as a model community. The New Deal created greenbelt cities across the nation to combine employment, the amenities of urban living, and the restful qualities of a rural landscape. Several were built outside Washington, D.C., Cincinnati, Ohio, and Milwaukee, Wisconsin; one, originally called Jersey Homesteads, was placed in South Jersey. The community initially attracted Jewish residents and socialists from New York City, mostly garment workers, who wished to live in a rural cooperative environment. Plans called for a self-contained community with a factory, a farm, and homes. Houses were little cinderblock affairs built quickly (though not inexpensively as intended). The manufacturing enterprise has long since been abandoned, but the town of Roosevelt, as it is now called, survives, along with some of its original residents.[70] By 1938, although prosperity had not entirely returned to the nation or state, the New Deal began to run out of steam. Conservative Democrats and reviving Republicans blocked new programs and even rolled back some existing ones. More important were problems caused by the rise of Germany and Japan. With the outbreak of war in Europe in 1939, foreign affairs took more and more of the nation's attention. After Pearl Harbor the United States went to war without the divisions and doubts that had accompanied its entry into World War I.[71]

New Jersey's role in World War II was very similar to the one it played in World War I. The state served primarily as a manufacturing center and a site for training troops. Factories turned out ships, airplanes, munitions, medical supplies, processed foods, and other goods in ever-increasing amounts.[72] Fort Dix, the Kilmer facility, and other installations in the state trained troops and prepared them for embarkation. Atlantic City hotels were used as hospitals. The naval station at Lakehurst sent blimps, and the Civil Air Patrol at Pomona sent airplanes, to look for German submarines off the Jersey coast. Before the war was over, more than two million men and women had been processed through New Jersey for service overseas. When the veterans returned they swamped Rutgers and other colleges to take advantage of the liberal educational provisions of the GI Bill of Rights.

The war years also saw a struggle in New Jersey over revisions of the state constitution. Elected on the Democratic ticket in 1940 as a prospective counterweight to Frank Hague and his "machine," Governor Charles Edison, a son of the inventor, called for change in the document, then nearly one hundred years old.[73] It was difficult to amend, placed severe and antiquated limits on the power to borrow money, and had put in place a decentralized executive department whose ability to cope with modern problems was limited. In addition, the court system had become the "most complicated . . . in any English speaking state." Revising the constitution became a partisan political issue. Hague opposed it, rural county officials feared losing equal representation in the state senate, and the war proved a distraction. Both Edison and his successor in office, Walter Evans Edge, failed in their attempts to obtain a new document. Hague's opposition was decisive. He feared any changes that would increase the power of New Jersey's governors—undoubtedly at his expense.

But in 1947, as the nation moved on to the problems of postwar adjustment and the emerging "cold war," New Jersey acquired a new governor, Republican Alfred E. Driscoll. Determined to enact constitutional changes, he created bipartisan support for revisions and deliberately included representatives from as many of the diverse groups in New Jersey as possible. A special convention met for the summer in the Rutgers University Gymnasium and collectively wrote a document designed to modernize the government and satisfy previous critics, including Frank Hague.

The Constitution of 1947 unified the executive branch and simplified the court system. It provided for a strong governor to be elected to a four-year term. Governors could succeed themselves once and had significant veto powers. Provisions for collective bargaining, a bill of rights, and a first-in-the-nation antidiscrimination clause also became part of the revised constitution. The document was further altered in 1966 to meet the U.S. Supreme Court's standard of "one man one vote"; representation in the state senate became proportional to population rather than being set at three senators per county.[74] These constitutional changes were truly significant. Long regarded as politically backward, New Jersey became an example that other states studied. It emerged with an increasingly active governor and a model court system. Local and county governments (and their politicians) became less important; old-fashioned boss control, such as Hague had exercised, increasingly became a thing of the past. Attention began to focus more on Trenton, and gradually New Jersey became a modern state—able to shape a role for itself, and perhaps, finally, even an identity of its own.[75]

In the postwar period, the rapid expansion of suburbs, the related decline of cities, the increase in state services supplied to residents, changes in the economy, and a new wave of immigration all contributed to altering the state. New Jersey became more diverse, particularly in terms of population, than ever before. But it also became more homogenous as divisions between north and south and between rural and urban areas became less pronounced as suburbs and new industries filled the spaces between them.

"Suburbs" were not new to America, or to New Jersey, in the 1950s. But the number, size, and the speed with which they grew were novel. The rapid growth was a consequence of the postwar population boom, extensive highway construction, cheaper methods of mass producing "tract" houses, and federal mortgage programs. The New Jersey Turnpike was completed in 1953 and the Garden State Parkway a year later. Both opened regions of the state for settlement as they made it feasible for people to commute.[76] The later construction of such interstate routes as 78, 80, and 287 spread development further. By 1960 New Jersey was the most densely populated state in the nation; by 1980, 70 percent of its people lived in the suburbs. There was a political impact as well: Republicans and Democrats spread more evenly throughout the state, and the number of registered independents increased.

As the suburbs grew, many of the cities declined. At first the exodus was led by those who wanted a house surrounded by a green lawn.[77] After the riots of the 1960s, in which twenty-three people died and damage to property exceeded $10 million, residents who feared remaining in Newark, Camden, Plainfield, and other cities plagued by violence and crime left in a stampede. Cities lost population; Camden declined from 124,000 in 1950 to 85,000 in 1988. The cities also lost revenues at a time when funds became more essential to support services to the largely poor population left behind.[78] Not until the mid-1980s did urban renewal begin to reverse the situation. The Gateway project in Newark, an aquarium in Camden, and a reconstructed downtown in New Brunswick were designed to revive those cities. But changes have been slow, frequently controversial, and sometimes displaced poorer residents and older businesses.

A response to the increasing inequalities between wealthy suburbs and poor cities came in the New Jersey Supreme Court's *Mt. Laurel* decision, which prohibited suburbs from using zoning laws to exclude prospective poor or African American residents. After several modifications and legislative action, the state created a Council on Affordable Housing to work out plans by which suburbs could either build low-income housing or contribute to its construction in cities.[79] Nearly forty years later the efforts are ongoing and still controversial.

Since World War II, New Jersey industry has also changed. Much of it moved to the suburbs, and manufacturing, particularly "heavy" industries, moved to the American South and then overseas. Electronics companies, pharmaceutical firms, communications headquarters, and various research facilities became a larger part of the economic mix.

Enormous office complexes, such as those on the Route 1 corridor, sprouted up as service industries grew more important. And, though it still displays the sign "Trenton makes, the world takes," the state capital is now primarily a government center, housing state and federal office buildings and courthouses.[80]

New Jersey's population not only grew but changed after World War II. The 1950s saw a large influx of Hungarians, the 1960s Cubans and South Americans, the 1970s Vietnamese, the 1980s and afterward Asians, Africans, and Middle Eastern Muslims.[81] Entirely new ethnic differences and neighborhoods are visible. As the population, road mileage, and suburbs grew, so did the services provided by the state. Programs supported by Governor Richard J. Hughes in the 1960s reflected the Great Society initiatives of the Johnson administration. Additional parks, cultural and educational facilities, and an expanded Newark Airport appeared. Rutgers grew from a small institution into a major state university, state teachers colleges became institutions with a wider mission, and new county colleges were built, some of them from scratch.[82]

In 1945 New Jersey still had no statewide tax. To finance the new services provided in the years that followed, the government ultimately turned to sales and income taxes. New Jersey had never willingly taxed much and did not begin to do so without a political struggle even as late as the 1960s. Only after 1976, when the state supreme court closed the schools because financing them solely through property taxes was held to be inherently unequal, did the legislature pass an income tax. A series of court cases, starting with *Abbott v. Burke* in 1985, attempted to make school districts closer in funding and the quality of education they offered, but in 2009 the goal had not yet been met.[83] At that point the state was viewed as having the highest cumulative taxes in the nation.

In addition to school funding, New Jersey in the 1990s and into the first decade of the next century was faced with a number of other problems. Ironically, some were a consequence of its positive adjustment to economic change and continued population growth, others to the impact of international terrorism and global warming. New Jersey's participation in the postindustrial economy, with its emphasis on technology and financial and other service industries, left it vulnerable to repeated downturns in the national economy, including the dot-com bust in the early 1990s, fallout from the September 11, 2001, attack on the World Trade Center, and the international banking crisis of 2008. Unfortunately, many who lived in New Jersey but worked in Manhattan lost their lives as a consequence of terrorism, while others perished in the wars in Iraq and Afghanistan.[84]

New Jersey's continued population growth during this period produced sprawl as development pushed further out from urban areas, butting up against the limits of its small size. The result was an increased interest in land preservation and the creation of three major areas with limits on development (the Pinelands, formerly known as the Pine Barrens; Meadowlands; and the Highlands). Congestion also meant greater concern with pollution, toxic waste sites, and garbage disposal. At the same time, climate change increased incidents of flooding, as it provoked interest in solar energy and wind power. Increasingly the state and its people have been caught up in not just national but also international changes.

At the beginning of the twenty-first century, New Jersey was a very different place than it was even in 1945. Yet in some ways it has shown remarkable constancy over more than three hundred years. Its population is still diverse, the range of ethnic and religious groups wider than ever before. The contests between its political parties remain close, and though sectional differences are muted, they still exist.[85] New Jersey continues to develop a sense of identity, but finds it difficult to select symbols to prove it. Former Governor Kean's 1982 slogan, "New Jersey and You, Perfect Together," conveyed a positive message, but an effort to replace it in 2006 came up empty.[86] Perhaps this failure encapsulates the complex, contradictory, paradoxical, and interesting aspects of New Jersey history since the seventeenth century.

Notes

1. This description of New Jersey is usually attributed to Benjamin Franklin but may have originated with James Madison.

2. Poking fun at New Jersey is not a new practice. It has apparently been done from the beginning. An example, clearly not the earliest, is the comment of about 1871 by Senator James W. Nye of Nevada, who declared that no one was "too degraded" for citizenship: "We have New Jersey, and all things considered, it has proven a success." Quoted in Eric Foner, *Reconstruction: America's Unfinished Revolution, 1863–1877* (New York, 1988), 497. For views of and from the turnpike, see Angus Gillespie and Michael Rockland, *Looking for America on the New Jersey Turnpike* (New Brunswick, N.J., 1989).

3. Charles A. Stanfield, *A Geography of New Jersey: the City in the Garden* (New Brunswick, N.J., 1998); Frank Kelland and Marylin Kelland, *New Jersey: Garden or Suburb* (Dubuque, Iowa, 1978); Peter O. Wacker, *Land and People: A Cultural Geography of Preindustrial New Jersey; Origins and Settlement Patterns* (New Brunswick, N.J., 1976); Paul G. E. Clemens and Peter O. Wacker, *Land Use in Early New Jersey: A Historical Geography* (Newark, N.J., 1995).

4. Thomas Fleming, *New Jersey: A History* (New York, 1977; reprint, 1984), 3–4.

5. "Inside the Scandals: James E. McGreevey's Grab for love and power, his misguided allegiances, and his plan for redemption," *New Jersey Monthly*, November 2004, 68–75, 94.

6. William Nelson, "Early Legislative Turmoils in New Jersey," *American Magazine of History* (1905): 221–231; Richard P. McCormick, "New Jersey's First Congressional Election, 1789: A Case Study in Political Skulduggery," *William and Mary Quarterly* ser. 3, 6 (1949): 237–250; Richard P. McCormick, *The History of Voting in New Jersey* (New Brunswick, N.J., 1953); William E. Sackett, *Modern Battles of Trenton*, vol. 1 (Trenton, N.J., 1895); John D. Venable, *Out of the Shadow: The Story of Charles Edison* (East Orange, N.J., 1978) 167–168; John Reynolds, "'The Silent Dollar': Vote Buying in New Jersey," *New Jersey History* (hereafter cited as *NJH*) 98 (1980): 191–211; and Dayton David McKean, *The Boss: The Hague Machine in Action* (Boston, 1940).

7. Richard P. McCormick, "An Historical Overview," in *Politics in New Jersey*, ed. Alan Rosenthal and John Blydenburgh (New Brunswick, N.J., 1975), 1–30; Stanley N. Worton, *Reshaping New Jersey: A History of Its Government and Politics* (Trenton, N.J., 1997).

8. Donald L. Kemmerer, "A History of Paper Money in Colonial New Jersey, 1668–1775," *Proceedings of the New Jersey Historical Society* (hereafter cited as *Proc. NJHS*) 74 (1956): 107–144; Donald L. Kemmerer, "The Colonial Loan Office System in New Jersey," *Journal of Political Economy* 47 (1931): 867–874; Frederick R. Black, "Provincial Taxation in Colonial New Jersey, 1704–1735," *NJH* 95 (1977): 21–47; and John W. Cadman Jr., *The Corporation in New Jersey: Business and Politics, 1791–1875* (Cambridge, Mass., 1949), 425–428, 440–441.

9. Herbert C. Kraft, *The Lenape: Archeology, History, and Ethnography* (Newark, N.J., 1986); Herbert C. Kraft, *The Lenape-Delaware Indian Heritage: 10,000 B.C.–A.D. 2000* (Elizabeth, N.J., 2001); Clinton A. Weslager, *The Delaware Indians: A History* (New Brunswick, N.J., 1972); Clinton A. Weslager, *The Delaware Indian Westward Migration: With the Texts of Two Manuscripts (1821–1822) Responding to General Lewis Cass's Inquiries About Lenape Culture and Language* (Wallingford, Pa.,1978); Gregory Dowd, *The Indians of New Jersey* (Trenton, N.J., 1992); Amy C. Schott, *Peoples of the River Valleys: The Odyssey of the Delaware Indians* (Philadelphia, 2007).

10. Kraft, *The Lenape*, 201.

11. Clinton A. Weslager, *Dutch Explorers, Traders, and Settlers in the Delaware Valley, 1609–1664* (Philadelphia, 1961); Clinton A. Weslager, *The English on the Delaware: 1610–1682* (New Brunswick, N.J., 1967); Adrian C. Leiby, *The Early Dutch and Swedish Settlers of New Jersey* (Princeton, N.J., 1964); and Firth Haring Fabend, *A Dutch Family in the Middle Colonies, 1660–1800* (New Brunswick, N.J., 1991); Carol E. Hoffecker, Richard Waldron, Lorraine E. Williams, and Barbara E. Benson, eds., *New Sweden in America* (Newark, Del., 1995); Frank J. Esposito, "The Lenape and the Swede: Indian and White Relations in the Delaware River Region, 1638–55," *NJH* 112 (1994): 1–14; David F. Winkler, "Revisiting the Attack on Pavonia," *NJH* 116 (1998): 3–15.

12. Richard P. McCormick, *New Jersey from Colony to State, 1609–1789* (Newark, N.J., 1981); John Pomfret, *Colonial New Jersey: A History* (New York, 1973); Wesley Frank Craven, *New Jersey and the English Colonization of North America* (Princeton, N.J., 1964).

13. John Pomfret, *The New Jersey Proprietors and their Lands* (Princeton, N.J., 1964); John Pomfret, *The Province of West New Jersey, 1609–1702: A History of the Origins of an American Colony* (Princeton, N.J., 1956); John Pomfret, *The Province of East New Jersey, 1609–1702: The Rebellious Proprietary* (Princeton, N.J., 1962).

14. Julian Boyd, *Fundamental Laws and Constitutions of New Jersey* (Princeton, N.J., 1964).

15. His bad reputation has been challenged by Patricia U. Bonomi in *The Lord Cornbury Scandal: The Politics of Reputation in British America* (Chapel Hill, N.C., 1998).

16. Marc Mappen, "The First Bribe," in *Jerseyana: The Underside of New Jersey History* (New Brunswick, N.J., 1992), 17–21; Mary Lou Lustig, *Robert Hunter 1666–1734: New York's Augustan Statesman* (Syracuse, N.Y., 1983).

17. Eugene R. Sheridan, *Lewis Morris, 1671–1746: A Study in Early American Politics* (Syracuse, N.Y., 1981); Michael C. Batinsky, *Jonathan Belcher: Colonial Governor* (Lexington, Ky., 1996); Colin Nicolson, *The "Infamous Governor" Francis Bernard and the Origins of the American Revolution* (Boston, 2001).

18. Thomas L. Purvis, *Proprietors, Patronage, and Paper Money* (New Brunswick, N.J., 1987); Michael Batinsky, *New Jersey Assembly, 1738–1775* (Lanham, Md., 1987); Brendon McConville, *These Daring Disturbers of the Public Peace: The Struggle for Property and Power in Early New Jersey* (Ithaca, N.Y., 1999).

19. Milton J. Coalter, Jr., *Gilbert Tennent, Son of Thunder* (Westport, Conn., 1986); James Tanis, *Dutch Calvinist Pietism in the Middle Colonies: A Study in the Life and Theology of Theodorus Jacobus Frelinghuysen* (The Hague, 1967), 78–86; Randall Balmer, *A Perfect Babel of Confusion: Dutch Religion and English Culture in the Middle Colonies* (New York, 1989).

20. George P. Schmidt, *Princeton and Rutgers: the Two Colonial Colleges of New Jersey* (Princeton, N.J., 1964).

21. Larry R. Gerlach, *William Franklin: New Jersey's Last Royal Governor* (Trenton, N.J., 1975); Willard S. Randall, *A Little Revenge: Benjamin Franklin and His Son* (Boston, 1984); and Sheila Skemp, *William Franklin: Son of a Patriot, Servant of a King* (New York, 1990).

22. Larry R. Gerlach, *Prologue to Independence: New Jersey in the Coming of the American Revolution* (New Brunswick, N.J., 1976); Larry R. Gerlach, "Politics and Prerogatives: The Aftermath of the Robbery of the East Jersey Treasury in 1768," *NJH* 90 (1972): 133–168; Larry R. Gerlach, ed., *New Jersey in the American Revolution, 1763–1783: A Documentary History* (Trenton, N.J., 1975).

23. Charles R. Erdman, *The New Jersey Constitution of 1776* (Princeton, N.J., 1929); Maxine N. Lurie, "Envisioning a Republic: New Jersey's 1776 Constitution and Oath of Office," *NJH* 119 (2001): 3–21; Edward Raymond Turner, "Women's Suffrage in New Jersey," *Smith College Studies in History* 1 (1916): 165–187; Marion Thompson Wright, "Negro Suffrage in New Jersey, 1776–1875," *Journal of Negro History* 33 (1948): 171–175; Irwin N. Gertzog, "Female Suffrage in New Jersey, 1790–1807," *Women and Politics* 10 (1990): 47–58.

24. Alfred Bill, *New Jersey and the Revolutionary War* (Princeton, N.J., 1964); Leonard Lundin, *Cockpit of the Revolution: The War of Independence in New Jersey* (Princeton, N.J., 1940); Adrian C. Leiby, *Revolutionary War in the Hackensack Valley: The Jersey Dutch and the Neutral Ground* (New Brunswick, N.J., 1980); David Hackett Fischer, *Washington's Crossing* (New York, 2004); Barbara Mitnick, ed., *New Jersey in the American Revolution* (New Brunswick, N.J., 2005).

25. Precise estimates of numbers of loyalists are difficult to make and depend on definitions (active or not, for example, or including neutrals or not). See A. V. D. Honeyman, "Concerning the New Jersey Loyalists in the Revolution," *Proc. NJHS* 51 (1933): 117–133; Ruth M. Keesey, "Loyalism in Bergen County, New Jersey," *William and Mary Quarterly* ser.

3, 18 (1961): 558–576; Paul H. Smith, "New Jersey Loyalists and the British 'Provincial' Corps in the War for Independence," *NJH* 87 (1969): 67–78; C. C. Vermeule, "The Active Loyalists of New Jersey," *Proc. NJHS* 52 (1934): 87–95; and Susan Burgess Shenstone, *So Obstinately Loyal: James Moody, 1744–1809* (Montreal, 2000).

26. Gregory Evans Dowd, "Declarations of Dependence: War and Inequality in Revolutionary New Jersey, 1776–1815," *NJH* 103 (1985): 47–67.

27. Richard P. McCormick, "The Unanimous State," *Journal of Rutgers University Libraries* 23 (1958): 4–8; Richard P. McCormick, *Experiment in Independence: New Jersey in the Critical Period, 1781–1789* (New Brunswick, N.J., 1950); Mary R. Murrin, *To Save This State from Ruin: New Jersey and the Creation of the United States Constitution, 1776–1789* (Trenton, N.J., 1987).

28. Maxine N. Lurie, "The New Jersey Intellectuals and the United States Constitution," *Journal of Rutgers University Libraries* 49 (1987) 65–87; John E. O'Connor, *William Paterson: Lawyer and Statesman, 1745–1806* (New Brunswick, N.J., 1979).

29. McCormick, "New Jersey's First Congressional Election," 237–250.

30. James M. Smith, "Sedition, Suppression, and Speech: A Comic Footnote on the Enforcement of the Sedition Law of 1798," *Quarterly Journal of Speech* 40 (1954): 284–287; James M. Smith, *Freedom's Fetters: The Alien and Sedition Laws and American Civil Liberties* (Ithaca, N.Y., 1956), 270–274; Douglas Bradburn, "A Clamor in the Public Mind: Opposition to the Alien and Sedition Acts," *William and Mary Quarterly*, ser. 3, 65 (2008): 565–600).

31. Rudolph J. Pasler and Margaret C. Pasler, "Federalist Tenacity in Burlington County, 1810–1824," *NJH* 87 (1969): 197–210; Rudolph J. Pasler and Margaret C. Pasler, *The New Jersey Federalists* (Rutherford, N.J., 1975); Carl E. Prince, "Patronage and a Party Machine: New Jersey Democratic-Republican Activists, 1801–1816," *William and Mary Quarterly*, ser. 3, 21 (1964): 571–578; Carl Prince, *New Jersey's Jeffersonian Republicans: The Genesis of an Early Party Machine, 1789–1817* (Chapel Hill, N.C., 1967); Walter R. Fee, *The Transition from Aristocracy to Democracy in New Jersey, 1789–1829* (Somerville, N.J., 1933).

32. Peter D. Levine, "The New Jersey Federalist Party Convention of 1814," *Journal of Rutgers University Libraries* 33 (1969): 1–8; Harvey Strum, "New Jersey Politics and the War of 1812," *NJH* 105 (1987) 37–69; Harvey Strum, "New Jersey and the Embargo, 1807–1809," *NJH* 116 (1998): 16–47.

33. George Rogers Taylor, *The Transportation Revolution, 1815–1860* (New York, 1962).

34. Wheaton J. Lane, *From Indian Trail to Iron Horse: Travel and Transportation in New Jersey, 1620–1860* (Princeton, N.J., 1959); Archibald D. Turnbull, *John Stevens: An American Record* (New York, 1928); Maurice Baxter, *The Steamboat Monopoly: Gibbons v. Ogden, 1824* (New York, 1972); George Dangerfield, "The Steamboat Case," in *Quarrels That Have Shaped the Constitution*, ed. John A. Garraty (New York, 1987), 57–69; Barbara N. Kalata, *A Hundred Years, a Hundred Miles: New Jersey's Morris Canal* (Morristown, N.J., 1983); Crawford Clark Madeira, *The Delaware and Raritan Canal: A History* (East Orange, N.J., 1941).

35. Joel Schwartz, *The Development of New Jersey Society* (Trenton, N.J., 1997), 23–59; Joseph Gowaskie, *Workers in New Jersey History* (Trenton, N.J., 1996); Susan Hirsch, *Roots of the American Working Class: The Industrial Crafts in Newark, 1800–1860* (Philadelphia, 1978); Levi R. Trumbull, *A History of Industrial Paterson* (Paterson, N.J., 1882); Kim Voss,

The Making of American Exceptionalism: The Knights of Labor and Class Formation in the Nineteenth Century (Ithaca, N.Y., 1993); Paul E. Johnson, Sam Patch, The Famous Jumper (New York, 2003).

36. Richard P. McCormick, "Party Formation in the Jacksonian Era," Proc. NJHS 83 (1965): 161–173; Richard P. McCormick, The Second American Party System: Party Formation in the Jacksonian Era (Chapel Hill, N.C., 1966), 124–134; Herbert Ershkowitz, The Origins of the Whig and Democratic Parties: New Jersey Politics, 1820–1837 (Washington, D.C., 1982); Peter D. Levine, "The Rise of Mass Parties and the Problem of Organization: New Jersey, 1829–1844," NJH 91 (1973): 91–107; Peter D. Levine, "The Behavior of State Legislative Parties in the Jacksonian Era: New Jersey, 1829–1844," Journal of American History 62 (1975): 591–607; Peter D. Levine, The Behavior of State Legislative Parties in the Jacksonian Era: New Jersey, 1829–1844 (Rutherford, N.J., 1977); Michael J. Birkner and Herbert Ershkowitz, "'Men and Measures': The Creation of the Second Party System in New Jersey," NJH 107 (1989): 41–59.

37. Peter D. Levine, "The Constitution of 1844: Constitutional Reform and Legislative Behavior in Nineteenth Century New Jersey," in Development of the New Jersey Legislature from Colonial Times to the Present, ed. William C. Wright (Trenton, N.J., 1976); John E. Bebout, The Making of the New Jersey Constitution: Introduction to the Proceedings of the New Jersey State Constitutional Convention of 1844 (Trenton, N.J., 1945).

38. Quoted in Fleming, New Jersey, 114. See also James Leiby, Charity and Correction in New Jersey (New Brunswick, N.J., 1967), chapter 2.

39. Frederick M. Herrmann, "The Political Origins of the New Jersey State Insane Asylum, 1837–1860," in Jacksonian New Jersey, ed. Paul A. Stellhorn (Trenton, N.J., 1979), 84–101; Leiby, Charity and Correction, chapter 3; David Gallaher, Voice for the Mad: The Life of Dorothea Dix (New York, 1995); Thomas Brown, Dorothea Dix: New England Reformer (Cambridge, Mass., 1998).

40. Michael A. Lutzker, "Abolition of Imprisonment for Debt in New Jersey," Proc. NJHS 84 (1966): 1–29.

41. Herman Belz, "The North American Phalanx: Experiment in Socialism," Proc. NJHS 81 (1963): 215–247; George Kirchmann, "Why Did They Stay? Communal Life at the North American Phalanx," in Planned and Utopian Experiments: Four New Jersey Towns, ed. Paul A. Stellhorn (Trenton, N.J., 1980), 10–27; Jayme A. Sokolow, "Culture and Utopia: The Raritan Bay Union," NJH 94 (1976): 89–100; George Kirchmann, "Unsettled Utopias: The North American Phalanx and the Raritan Bay Union," NJH 97 (1979): 25–36; Maud H. Greene, "Raritan Bay Union, Eagleswood, New Jersey," Proc. NJHS 68 (1950): 1–20; Marie Marmo Mullaney, "Feminism, Utopianism, and Domesticity: The Career of Rebecca Buffum Spring, 1811–1911," 104 NJH (1986): 1–22.

42. See Perdita Buchan, Utopian New Jersey: Travels in the Nearest Eden (New Brunswick, N.J., 2007), for a discussion of some of the later communities in the state.

43. Fleming, New Jersey, 114.

44. Joel Schwartz, "The Education Machine: The Struggle for Public School Systems in New Jersey Before the Civil War," in Jacksonian America, ed. Paul A. Stellhorn (Trenton, N.J., 1979), 102–119; Nelson R. Burr, Education in New Jersey, 1630–1871 (Princeton, N.J., 1942).

45. Simeon R Moss, "The Persistence of Slavery and Involuntary Servitude in a Free State (1685–1866)," *Journal of Negro History* 35 (1950): 289–314; Giles R. Wright, *Afro-Americans in New Jersey: A Short History* (Trenton, N.J., 1989); Larry A. Greene, "A History of Afro-Americans in New Jersey," *Journal of the Rutgers University Libraries* 56 (1994): 4–71; Arthur Zilversmit, "Liberty and Property: New Jersey and the Abolition of Slavery," *NJH* 88 (1970): 215–226; Arthur Zilversmit, *The First Emancipation: The Abolition of Slavery in the North* (Chicago, 1967); Graham Russell Hodges, *Root and Branch: African Americans in New York and East Jersey, 1613–1863* (Chapel Hill, N.C., 1999); Graham Russell Hodges, *Slavery and Freedom in the Rural North* (Madison, Wis., 1997).

46. Alan A. Siegel, *For the Glory of the Union: Myth, Reality, and the Media in Civil War New Jersey* (Rutherford, N.J., 1984); Charles M. Knapp, *New Jersey Politics during the Period of Civil War* (New York, 1924); William C. Wright, "New Jersey's Military Role in the Civil War Reconsidered," *NJH* 92 (1974): 197–210; Maurice Tandler, "The Political Front in Civil War New Jersey," *Proc. NJHS* 83 (1965): 223–233; Mark Lender, *One State in Arms: A Short Military History of New Jersey* (Trenton, N.J., 1991), 48–66; William Gillette, *Jersey Blue: Civil War Politics in New Jersey 1854–1865* (New Brunswick, N.J., 1995); William J. Jackson, *New Jerseyans in the Civil War: For Union and Liberty* (New Brunswick, N.J., 2000); Alan S. Siegel, *Beneath the Starry Flag: New Jersey's Civil War Experience* (New Brunswick, N.J., 2001).

47. Foner, *Reconstruction*; Larry A. Greene, "The Emancipation Proclamation in New Jersey and the Paranoid Style," *NJH* 91 (1973): 108–124; Jonathan Lurie, "Mr. Justice Bradley: A Reassessment," *Seton Hall Law Review* 16 (1986): 342–378; Leslie H. Fishel Jr., "Northern Prejudice and Negro Suffrage, 1865–1870," *Journal of Negro History* 39 (1954): 8–26.

48. John F. Reynolds, *Testing Democracy: Electoral Behavior and Progressive Reform in New Jersey, 1880–1920* (Chapel Hill, N.C., 1988); Sackett, *Modern Battles of Trenton*; Richard A. Hogarty, *Leon Abbett's New Jersey: The Emergence of the Modern Governor* (Philadelphia, 2001).

49. Arthur C. Tressler and John R. Pierce, *The Research State: A History of Science in New Jersey* (Princeton, N.J., 1964); Paul Israel and Robert D. Friedel, *Edison's Electric Light: Biography of an Invention* (New Brunswick, N.J., 1986); Martin V. Melosi, *Thomas A. Edison* (New York, 1990); Schwartz, *Development of New Jersey Society*, 37–59; Paul Israel, *Edison: A Life of Invention* (New York, 1998).

50. Charles W. McCurdy, "The Knight and Sugar Decision of 1895 and the Modernization of American Corporation Law, 1869–1903," *Business History Review* 53 (1979): 304–342; Christopher Grandy, "New Jersey Corporate Chartermongering, 1875–1929," *Journal of Economic History* 49 (1989): 677–692.

51. Hermann K. Platt, "Jersey City and the United Railroad Companies, 1868: A Case of Municipal Weakness," *NJH* 91 (1973): 249–265; Hermann K. Platt, "Railroad Rights and Tideland Policy: A Tug of War in Nineteenth-Century New Jersey," *NJH* 108 (1990): 35–57; Richard J. Connors, *A Cycle of Power: The Career of Jersey City Mayor Frank Hague* (Metuchen, N.J., 1971); Venable, *Out of the Shadow*; Eugene M. Tobin, "In Pursuit of Equal Taxation: Jersey City's Struggle Against Corporate Arrogance and Tax Dodging by the Railroad Trust," *American Journal of Economics and Sociology* 34 (1975): 213–224; Harley L. Lutz, *The Taxation of Railroads in New Jersey* (Princeton, N.J., 1940).

52. On "honest" and "dishonest" graft, see William L. Riordon, ed., *Plunkitt of Tammany Hall: A Series of Very Plain Talks on Very Practical Politics, Delivered by Ex-senator George Washington Plunkitt, the Tammany Philosopher, From His Rostrum—the New York County Court House Bootblack Stand* (New York, 1963), 3–6.

53. Sackett, *Modern Battles of Trenton*; Reynolds, *Testing Democracy*.

54. John T. Cunningham, *New Jersey: America's Main Road* (New York, 1966), 224.

55. Philip B. Scranton, ed., *Silk City: Studies on the Paterson Silk Industry, 1860–1940* (Newark, N.J., 1985); James D. Osborne, "Italian Immigrants and the Working Class in Paterson: The Strike of 1913 in Ethnic Perspective," in *New Jersey's Ethnic Heritage*, ed. Paul A. Stellhorn (Trenton, N.J., 1978), 10–34; Delight W. Dodyk, "Women's Work in the Paterson Silk Mills: A Study in Women's Industrial Experience in the Early Twentieth Century," in *Women in New Jersey History*, ed. Mary R. Murrin (Trenton, N.J., 1985), 11–28; Anne Huber Tripp, *The I.W.W. and the Paterson Silk Strike of 1913* (Urbana, Ill., 1987); Nancy Fogelson, "They Paved the Street with Silk: New Jersey Silk Workers, 1913–1924," *NJH* 97 (1979): 133–48; Robert H. Zeiger, "Robin Hood in the Silk City: The I.W.W. and the Paterson Silk Strike of 1913," *Proc. NJHS* 84 (1966): 182–95; Steve Golin, "Bimson's Mistake; Or, How the Paterson Police Helped to Spread the 1913 Strike," *NJH* 100 (1982): 57–86; Steve Golin, "The Paterson Pageant: Success or Failure?" *Socialist Review* 69 (1983): 45–78; Steve Golin, *The Fragile Bridge: Paterson Silk Strike, 1913* (Philadelphia, 1988); Martin Green, *New York, 1913: The Armory Show and the Paterson Silk Strike Pageant* (New York, 1988).

56. Marjorie Kaschewski, *The Quiet Millionaires: The Morris County That Was* (Morristown, N.J., 1970); John W. Rae and John W. Rae Jr., *Morristown's Forgotten Past—"The Gilded Age": The Story of a New Jersey Town, Once a Society Center for the Nation's Wealthy* (Morristown, N.J., 1980).

57. Stuart Galishoff, *Newark: The Nation's Unhealthiest City, 1832–1895* (New Brunswick, N.J., 1988).

58. Rudolph Vecoli, *The People of New Jersey* (Princeton, N.J., 1965); the quote appears on 210. Douglas V. Shaw, *The Making of an Immigrant City: Ethnic and Cultural Conflict in Jersey City, New Jersey, 1850–1877* (New York, 1976); Douglas V. Shaw, *Immigration and Ethnicity in New Jersey History* (Trenton, N.J., 1994) For an example of religion and related conflict see Samuel T. McSeveney, "Religious Conflict, Party Politics, and Public Policy in New Jersey, 1874–75," *NJH* 110 (1992):18–44. .

59. Hubert G. Schmidt, *Agriculture in New Jersey: A Three-Hundred-Year History* (New Brunswick, N.J., 1973). Paul G. E. Clemens, *The Uses of Abundance: A History of New Jersey's Economy* (Trenton, N.J., 1992), summarizes changes in agriculture and industry over time.

60. John T. Cunningham, "Games People Played: Sports in New Jersey History," *NJH* 103 (1985): 1–31; Foster Rhea Dulles, *America Learns to Play* (New York, 1940); Donald J. Mrozek, *Sport and American Mentality, 1880–1910* (Knoxville, Tenn., 1983).

61. John Brinckmann, *The Tuckerton Railroad: A Chronicle of Transport to the New Jersey Shore* (privately printed, 1973); Harold F. Wilson, *The Story of the Jersey Shore: A Social and Economic History of the Counties of Atlantic, Cape May, Monmouth and Ocean*, vols. 1 and 2 (New York, 1953); Charles E. Funnell, *By the Beautiful Sea: The Rise and High Times of That Great American*

Resort, Atlantic City (New Brunswick, N.J., 1983); Jeffrey M. Dorwart, *Cape May County, New Jersey: The Making of an American Resort Community* (New Brunswick, N.J., 1992).

62. Eugene M. Tobin, "'Engines of Salvation' or 'Smoking Black Devils': Jersey City Reformers and the Railroads, 1902–1908," in *The Age of Urban Reform: New Perspectives on the Progressive Era*, ed. Michael H. Ebner and Eugene M. Tobin (London, 1977), 142–155; Eugene M. Tobin, "The Progressive as Politician: Jersey City, 1896–1907," *NJH* 91 (1973): 5–23.

63. Ransom E. Noble, *New Jersey Progressivism before Wilson* (Princeton, N.J., 1946); Michael H. Ebner, "Redefining the Success Ethic for Urban Reform Mayors: Fred R. Low of Passaic, 1908–1909," in Ebner and Tobin, *Age of Urban Reform*, 86–101; Joseph Lincoln Steffens, *Upbuilders* (New York, 1909), 3–93; John D. Buenker, "Urban, New-Stock Liberalism and Progressive Reform in New Jersey," *NJH* 87 (1969): 79–104; Eugene M. Tobin, "The Progressive as Humanitarian: Jersey City's Search for Social Justice, 1890–1917," *NJH* 93 (1975) 77–98; Eugene M. Tobin, "The Commission Plan in Jersey City, 1911–1917: The Ambiguity of Municipal Reform in the Progressive Era," in *Cities in the Garden State: Essays in the Urban and Suburban History of New Jersey*, ed. Joel Schwartz and Daniel Prosser (Dubuque, Iowa, 1977), 71–84; Ella Handen, "In Liberty's Shadow: Cornelia Bradford and Whittier House," *NJH* 100 (1982): 49–69; Ella Handen, "Social Service Stations: New Jersey Settlement Houses Founded in the Progressive Era," *NJH* 108 (1990): 1–29; Martin Paulsson, *The Social Anxieties of Progressive Reform: Atlantic City, 1854–1920* (New York, 1994); Bernard A. Olsen, *A Billy Yank Governor: The Life and Times of New Jersey's Franklin Murphy* (West Kennebunk, Me., 2000).

64. Arthur F. Link, *Wilson: The Road to the White House* (Princeton, N.J., 1947); David W. Hirst, *Woodrow Wilson, Reform Governor: A Documentary Narrative* (Princeton, N.J., 1965); Henry A. Turner, "Woodrow Wilson and the New Jersey Legislature," *Proc. NJHS* 74 (1956): 21–49; James D. Startt, *Woodrow Wilson and the Press: Prelude to the Presidency* (New York, 2004).

65. Continuation of an emphasis on 100 percent Americanism and intolerance for differences was reflected in the 1920s in the rise of the Ku Klux Klan. See Howard B. Furer, "The Perth Amboy Riots of 1923," *NJH* 87 (1969): 211–232; Mappen, "The Klan," in *Jerseyana*, 166–170; David M. Chalmers, *Hooded Americanism: The First Century of the Ku Klux Klan, 1865–1965* (New York, 1965), especially chapter 35, "Methodists and Madness in the Garden State," 243–253.

66. Lender, *One State in Arms*, 75–82; Howard B. Furer, "Heaven, Hell, or Hoboken: The Effects of World War I on a New Jersey City," *NJH* 92 (1974): 147–169; Chad Millman, *The Detonators: The Secret Plot to Destroy America and the Epic Hunt for Justice* (New York, 2006).

67. Quoted in Cunningham, *New Jersey*, 288. J. C. Furnas, *The Life and Times of the Late Demon Rum* (New York, 1965); Norman H. Clark, *Deliver Us from Evil: An Interpretation of American Prohibition* (New York, 1976); Mappen, "Keeping New Jersey Sober," in *Jerseyana*, 176–179.

68. Richard A. Noble, "Paterson's Response to the Great Depression," *NJH* 96 (1978): 87–98; Clemens, *Uses of Abundance*, 79–85.

69. Connors, *Cycle of Power*; McKean, *The Boss*; George C. Rapport, *The Statesman and the*

Boss: A Study of American Political Leadership Exemplified by Woodrow Wilson and Frank Hague (New York, 1961); Lyle W. Dorsett, "Frank Hague, Franklin Roosevelt and the Politics of the New Deal," *NJH* 94 (1976): 23–35; Mark S. Foster, "Frank Hague of Jersey City: 'The Boss' as Reformer," *NJH* 86 (1968): 106–117; Richard J. Connors, "Politics and Economics in Frank Hague's Jersey City," in *New Jersey since 1860: New Findings and Interpretations*, ed. William C. Wright (Trenton, N.J., 1972), 76–91; Hildreth York, "The New Deal Art Projects in New Jersey," *NJH* 98 (1980): 133–171.

70. Edwin Rosskam, *Roosevelt, New Jersey: Big Dreams in a Small Town and What Time Did to Them* (New York, 1972); Paul K. Conklin, *Tomorrow a New World: The New Deal Community Program* (Ithaca, N.Y., 1959); Joseph L. Arnold, *The New Deal in the Suburbs: A History of the Greenbelt Town Program, 1935–1954* (Columbus, Ohio, 1971); Buchan, *Utopian New Jersey*, 173–201.

71. Unlike World War I, German Americans did not sympathize with the homeland. See Mappen, "Swastikas in Sussex County," *Jerseyana*, 205–209; Martha Glaser, "The German-American Bund in New Jersey," *NJH* 92 (1974): 33–49.

72. The Kearney shipyards employed six thousand people in 1939, compared to forty thousand in 1942. For general background see Allan M. Winkler, *Home Front U.SA.: America during World War II* (Arlington Heights, Ill., 1986); David Kennedy, *Freedom from Fear: The American People in Depression and War, 1929–1945* (New York, 1999); and, on New Jersey, Lender, *One State in Arms*, 82–96.

73. Dorsett, "Frank Hague"; Venable, *Out of the Shadow*, 164–215.

74. Richard J. Connors, *The Process of Constitutional Revision in New Jersey: 1940–1947* (New York, 1970); Venable, *Out of the Shadow*, chapter 12; Alan Shank, *New Jersey Reapportionment Politics* (Rutherford, N.J., 1969); Vorhees E. Dunn Jr., "The Road to the 1947 New Jersey Constitution: Arthur T. Vanderbilt's Influence on Court Reform, 1930–47," *NJH* 104 (1986): 23–41; Maxine N. Lurie, "The Twisted Path to Greater Equality: Women and the 1947 Constitution," *NJH* 117 (1999): 39–58.

75. Gerald M. Pomper, ed., *The Political State of New Jersey* (New Brunswick, N.J., 1986); Alan G. Tarr and Mary C. A. Porter, *State Supreme Courts in State and Nation* (Westport, Conn., 1988); Robert A. Carter, "Meese, Brennan and Jersey Judicial Activism," *New Jersey Lawyer* 120 (August 1987): 27–30.

76. John E. Bebout and Ronald J. Grele, *Where Cities Meet: The Urbanization of New Jersey* (Princeton, N.J., 1964), 52–77; Linda Keller Brown and Patricia Vasilenko, "Time, Space, and Suburbanities: The Social-Spatial Structure of Essex, Union, and Morris Counties in the Twentieth Century," in *Cities of the Garden State*, 85–108; Herbert J. Gans, *The Levittowners: Ways of Life and Politics in a New Suburban Community* (New York, 1967); Lizabeth Cohen, *Consumer Republic: The Politics of Mass Consumption in Postwar America* (New York, 2003); Howard Gillette Jr., *Camden after the Fall: Decline and Renewal in a Post-Industrial City* (Philadelphia, 2005); Bryant Simon, *Boardwalk of Dreams: Atlantic City and the Fate of Urban America* (New York, 2004); Kevin Mumford, *Newark: A History of Race, Rights, and Riots in America* (New York, 2007); Ann Marie T. Cammarola, *Pavements in the Garden: The Suburbanization of Southern New Jersey Adjacent to the City of Philadelphia, 1769 to the Present* (Madison, N.J., 2001).

77. Philip Roth, *Goodbye Columbus* (New York, 1959). Although fiction, this novel offers a good description of the movement from Newark to the suburbs.

78. Barbara B. Jackson and Kenneth J. Jackson, "The Black Experience in Newark: The Growth of the Ghetto, 1870–1970," in *New Jersey since 1860*, 36–59; Judith F. Kovisars, "Trenton Up Against It: The Prescription for Urban Renewal in the 1950s and 1960s," in *Cities of the Garden State*, 161–75; John T. Cumber, *A Social History of Economic Decline: Business, Politics, and Work in Trenton* (New Brunswick, N.J., 1989).

79. Jerome G. Rose and Robert E. Rothman, eds., *After Mt. Laurel: The New Suburban Zoning* (New Brunswick, N.J., 1977); David L. Kirp, John P. Dwyer, and Larry A. Rosenthal, *Our Town: Race, Housing, and the Soul of Suburbia* (New Brunswick, N.J., 1995); Charles M. Haar, *Suburbs Under Siege: Race, Space, and Audacious Judges* (Princeton, N.J., 1996).

80. Schwartz, *Development New Jersey Society*, 60–72.

81. Henry Bischoff, "Caribbean Peoples in New Jersey: An Overview," *NJH* 113 (1995): 1–30; S. Miltra Kalita, *Suburban Sahibs: Three Immigrant Families and Their Passage from India to America* (New Brunswick, N.J., 2003).

82. Donald R. Raichle, "Richard J. Hughes, Frederick M. Raubinger, and the Struggle for New Jersey Public Higher Education," *NJH* 114 (1996): 19–47.

83. Deborah Jaffe, *Other People's Children: The Battle for Justice and Equality in New Jersey's Schools* (New Brunswick, N.J., 2007).

84. Alvin S. Felzenberg, *Governor Tom Kean: From the New Jersey Statehouse to the 9–11 Commission* (New Brunswick, N.J., 2006), 405–442; Gail Sheehy, *Middletown, America: One Town's Passage from Trauma to Hope* (New York, 2003); Kristen Breitweiser, *Wake-Up Call, The Political Education of a 9/11 Widow* (New York, 2006).

85. Pomper, *The Political State of New Jersey*; Jeffrey M. Stonecash and Mary P. McGuire, *The Emergence of State Government: Parties and New Jersey Politics, 1950–2000* (Madison, N.J., 2003); Barbara G. Salmore and Stephen A. Salmore, *New Jersey Politics and Government: The Suburbs Come of Age*, 3rd ed. (New Brunswick, N.J., 2008); Felzenberg, *Governor Tom Kean*; Sandy McClure, *Christie Whitman: A Political Biography for the People* (Amherst, N.Y., 1996); Art Weissman, *Christine Todd Whitman: The Politics of Character* (New York, 1996).

86. "New Jersey Looking for a New State Slogan," *USA Today*, May 8, 2006.

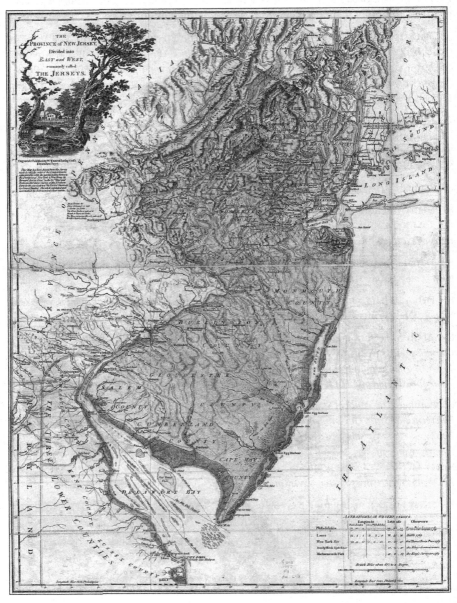

Although the colony was formally divided into East Jersey and West Jersey for only twenty-eight years, until 1702, the proprietors of each province retained title to the land and granted dividends in each into the nineteenth century. The two north-south lines on this 1778 map, engraved and published in London by William Faden, reflect earlier disputes over the boundary between the two Jerseys. Geography and Map Division, Library of Congress.

1

Historians who study American colonial history have necessarily been concerned with establishing the sources of American institutions. Out of this interest has come a long-standing debate over whether the baggage settlers brought to the New World—political and social ideas as well as clothes, tools, and designs for houses—was more formative than the ways in which their new surroundings forced them to create institutions. In the nineteenth century, historians from George Bancroft to the first professional, university-trained Ph.D.'s of the 1870s and 1880s traced the origins of American political institutions to the Anglo-Saxons of England and their German Teutonic heritage. Later Frederick Jackson Turner countered these arguments by emphasizing instead the singular impact of the New World environment, particularly the "frontier," on American ideas, institutions, and attitudes.

This argument long continued to concern colonial historians. David Grayson Allen's *In English Ways* (1982) argued that the experiences English settlers brought with them to Massachusetts were most important for understanding the communities they created. According to Allen, these experiences, particularly political and agricultural practices, varied greatly among groups emigrating from different English regions and help explain some of the conflicts between settlers and settlements in that colony. England in the seventeenth century was changing rapidly, moving in stages from older communal farming arrangements to "modern" individualistic practices. Massachusetts settlers left England at a time of political conflict and civil war, of disagreement over ideas and institutions.

Although the historical debate about the relative influences of culture and environment has mainly been argued from the examples of New England and Virginia, it has clear implications for the study of New Jersey history. What kinds of political institutions did the English (or, for that matter, their predecessors, the Dutch and Swedes) establish in New Jersey? New Jersey was a proprietary colony; titles to its government and land were granted by the king to individual "lords," not to a corporation as had been the case in Massachusetts and Virginia. The proprietors determined the form of government and method of land distribution.

What were the sources of the proprietors' ideology? What problems did they face in putting it into effect? The following chapter deals in part with the difficulties proprietors confronted in maintaining and exercising what they saw as their rightful political powers. Challenges to their political authority came from both English officials and residents of the colony, but why? Did conditions in New Jersey foster some of this opposition? Did these conditions make the very idea of proprietors somehow inappropriate or obsolete?

A related issue occupying colonial, and other, historians is the idea of American "exceptionalism." The notion of this nation's singularity was central to Turner's frontier thesis. Louis Hartz in *The Liberal Tradition in America* (1955) argued that America was different from Europe because it had never gone through the feudal stage of development. As a result the country had a truncated political spectrum; the range from conservative to liberal was much shorter than in other countries. Americans, he concluded, are and have always been "liberals." If, as the following article suggests, colonial proprietors (New Jersey's included) represent a continuation of feudalism, then is it true that Americans escaped so completely this aspect of world history? Does New Jersey show us that the truth is somewhat more complicated than the Hartz thesis has alleged?

Hartz defined liberalism in reference to a Europe that had experienced a feudal past and socialist present, a conservative nobility opposed to change and a radical proletariat in favor of it. Americans instead were "born free"; they were liberals in the Lockean sense whose political divisions (compared to Europe's) were telescoped into a middle ground. Some American historians, seeing greater divergence than Hartz, have used the words "conservative," "liberal," and "radical" to describe political differences, interpretations of the Constitution, willingness to use government power, and support for change. But the definitions of these terms and how they have been used have changed over time. What "conservative" meant to Alexander Hamilton in 1790 is not the same as what it meant to Rush Limbaugh in 2009. How would you define these terms?

Even those who, accepting Hartz's thesis, see America as a liberal society have sometimes disagreed on what being liberal means in the context of republican ideology. They have postulated a divergence between "classical" and "liberal" republicanism: classical republicanism looked to the past, emphasized the community or the family, and was satisfied with a subsistence economy; liberal republicanism looked to the future, stressed the individual, and rewarded competitive and acquisitive actions. Part of the historical debate centers on when Americans became individualistic capitalists driven by the desire for commercial success. Some historians suggest that the move from an interest in communal self-sufficiency to an individualist interest in commercial markets took place between 1790 and 1820; others position it between 1830 and 1850 during a "market revolution." How do these ideas apply to groups such as the Board of Proprietors of East Jersey, who over two centuries evolved into a modern corporation?

The exceptional nature of the United States is claimed (or, more recently, denied) on the basis of comparative historical analysis. By examining several countries, or a number of American colonies, similarities and differences become apparent that help build a clear understanding of the singularity of a place. When New Jersey is examined from a comparative perspective, it appears in some ways unique. What experiences peculiar to the colony made New Jersey unique in this period? At the same time, New Jersey was part of the British Empire and then the new United States. As such it shared ideas, institutions, and ethnic and religious groups with its neighbors. It also shared such experiences as royal control and the American Revolution. What events and issues specifically did New Jerseyans share with other settlers of the New World?

Suggested Readings

Allen, David Grayson. *In English Ways: The Movement of Societies and the Transferal of English Local Law and Custom to Massachusetts Bay in the Seventeenth Century*. Chapel Hill: University of North Carolina Press, 1981.

Bender, Thomas, ed. *Rethinking American History in a Global Age*. Berkeley: University of California Press, 2002.

Craven, Wesley Frank. *New Jersey and the English Colonization of North America*. Princeton, N.J.: Van Nostrand, 1964.

Cunningham, John T. *The East of Jersey: A History of the General Board of Proprietors of the Eastern Division of New Jersey*. Newark: New Jersey Historical Society, 1992.

Hartz, Louis. *The Liberal Tradition in America: An Interpretation of American Political Thought since the Revolution*. New York: Harcourt Brace, 1955.

McCormick, Richard P. *New Jersey from Colony to State, 1609–1789*. 1964. Reprint, Newark: New Jersey Historical Society, 1981.

McConville, Brendan. *Those Daring Disturbers of the Peace: The Struggle for and Power in Early New Jersey*. Ithaca, N.Y.: Cornell University Press, 1999.

Pomfret, John. *Colonial New Jersey: A History*. New York: Scribner, 1973.

———. *The Province of East New Jersey, 1609–1702: The Rebellious Proprietary*. Princeton, N.J.: Princeton University Press, 1962

———. *The Province of West New Jersey, 1609–1702: A History of the Origins of an American Colony*. Princeton, N.J.: Princeton University Press, 1956.

Purvis, Thomas L. *Proprietors, Patronage, and Paper Money*. New Brunswick, N.J.: Rutgers University Press, 1986.

Turner, Frederick Jackson. "The Significance of the Frontier in American History" (1893). In *Frontier and Section: Selected Essays*. Englewood Cliffs, N.J.: Prentice Hall, 1961, 37–62.

Weeks, Daniel J. *Not for Filthy Lucre's Sake: Richard Saltar and the Anti-proprietary Movement in East New Jersey, 1665–1707*. Bethlehem, Pa.: Lehigh University Press, 2001.

* * * * * *

New Jersey: The Unique Proprietary

Maxine N. Lurie

New Jersey, it has been suggested, has received little attention from historians because it was an "average" colony lacking in "distinctive characteristics."[1] Pausing only long enough to classify New Jersey as a "middle colony," many historians have then gone on to study its more interesting neighbors. But New Jersey has had an unusual and important political and legal history. In the colonial period it underwent a metamorphosis from a feudal institution to a corporation, a transformation unique in North America and one that prefigured modern business structures. Further distinctions also differentiate New Jersey from the other proprietary colonies it superficially resembled and show that it began and evolved in unique ways.[2]

The original English grant for the colony in 1664 came from the Duke of York, not the king. The question of whether the duke had the same power to confer political control as he had to convey a land title to the early proprietors marked politics in New Jersey from its inception. The ultimate resolution of the question split control of the land from title to the government. Before the resolution, the difficulties the proprietors encountered in exercising governmental authority in the period to 1702 were compounded by a series of splits among the proprietors themselves. Although New Jersey was one of several multiple proprietorships, shares in it were fractionalized to an extraordinary degree, a fragmentation exacerbated by the way land was granted as dividends to these fractional holders. In addition, New Jersey was the only proprietary colony broken into two—East and West Jersey—with ownership of each half vested in different groups. The boards of proprietors created in the seventeenth century have survived to the present, but they changed from groups of feudal lords to the precursors of modern corporate boards.

Pennsylvania Magazine of History and Biography 111 (1987): 76–97. Reprinted by permission of the Historical Society of Pennsylvania.

❖ ❖ ❖ ❖ ❖ ❖

New Jersey was initially part of the grant given to James, Duke of York, by his brother Charles II on March 12, 1664.[3] Later that year, the duke conveyed part of his territory to Sir George Carteret and Lord John Berkeley, two friends and supporters from the interregnum. Berkeley sold his half in 1674 to John Fenwick and Edward Byllynge, two Quakers whose involved affairs and subsequent disagreements complicated the colony's early history.[4] In 1676, Byllynge, the Quaker trustees handling the dispute between Fenwick and Byllynge, and Carteret signed a Quintpartite Agreement dividing the colony into East and West Jersey. George Carteret died in 1680; two years later, his widow sold what had by then become East Jersey to a consortium of twelve members, a group which soon doubled its membership. The twenty-four East Jersey proprietors were predominantly Quaker, and approximately half were Scots. In 1687 Byllynge's heirs sold his West Jersey shares to Dr. Daniel Coxe, an avid English speculator, and in 1691 Coxe sold most of his shares to the West Jersey Society, an investment company.

All of New Jersey's proprietors—from Berkeley and Carteret to the West Jersey Society—assumed that they had purchased the right to the government as well as the land of their colony.[5] But the original grant, a reconveyance from the Duke of York, did not specifically mention powers of government. The proprietors' assumptions about their right to rule were early challenged by jealous colonial officials in New York. The Province of New York had lost some of its best lands and customs revenues to the newly established Jersey colony; New York officials worked aggressively in an attempt to squash an independent government in New Jersey.[6] The power issue was not completely resolved until the Jersey proprietors surrendered their charter on April 15, 1702.

Further confusing matters was the Dutch recapture of New York and New Jersey, lasting from July 1673 until November 1674. When the Treaty of Westminster returned the land to Charles II, the king issued a confirmatory grant to the Duke of York. The duke, in turn, issued to Carteret for East Jersey a brief release, which only mentioned the right to the soil; no release for West Jersey was issued to Byllynge and Fenwick. It was not until 1680 that the duke confirmed the sale of West Jersey to the Quakers.[7] The Dutch reconquest and subsequent English regrants served to confuse further the situation because, once again, the new documents did not spell out the proprietors' rights in governing New Jersey.

Still other problems emerged. Clashes between New York and

New Jersey authorities, along with pressure on the Duke of York by his friend William Penn, led the duke in 1680 to submit the legal questions around the Jersey colony to Sir William Jones, an eminent English lawyer, for his opinion. Jones found that New York officials did not have the authority to collect customs duties in New Jersey, inferring from this that New Jersey proprietors had the right to govern their colony. The Jones Decision clarified, for the moment at least, New Jersey's right to an independent government, but it did not resolve who could exercise this right in West Jersey.[8]

Acting upon the Jones Decision, the duke—perhaps inadvertently— identified only Edward Byllynge by name in confirming the political rights of the West Jersey proprietors. Byllynge asserted sole right to the government. Resident proprietors disputed this claim but lost the argument before Quaker arbitrators in England in 1684. In 1687 Byllynge's heirs sold the right to the government to Dr. Daniel Coxe, who later sold it to the West Jersey Society. Thus, in West Jersey title to the land and title to the government were clearly separated. This did nothing to clarify political relationships among colonists, New York officials, or the English government. The disagreements and frequent transfers of political rights in West Jersey did not help the proprietors of either section who later tried to validate their claims to the government of the Jerseys in the 1690s.

Confusion expanded when the proprietors of both East and West Jersey agreed, under pressure, to surrender their governments to James II so that the province could be included in the Dominion of New England. With the Glorious Revolution, proprietary government returned to both East and West Jersey in 1692, but the political dissension remained.

After 1696 English officials deliberately contributed to a confused state of affairs by forcing the proprietors to surrender their governments to the Crown. They did this by refusing to grant approbation to proprietor-selected governors (Jeremiah Basse, then Andrew Hamilton), approbation required under the Navigation Act of 1696. This led the colonists to challenge the legitimacy of those governors, a challenge that undermined the proprietors' authority and contributed to disorder and confusion in both Jerseys from 1698 to 1702. The Board of Trade evidently believed that approving the governors would recognize the proprietors' right to govern. This action was part of a campaign against all proprietary colonies in a concerted effort to tighten control over the empire as a whole. New Jersey, as the weakest colony, gave way first. Although some of the same questions were raised about Penn's right to govern Delaware (as part of Pennsylvania), he and his heirs ultimately withstood the challenges. In the end, the significant distinction is not that New Jersey relinquished power that Pennsylvania did not, but that threats to the New Jersey proprietors' right to govern surfaced first, lasted longest, and were most profound.

Much of the political disorder and confusion characterizing New Jersey under the proprietors was a direct consequence of the proprietors' questionable right to govern. Other proprietary colonies also experienced frequent political disputes and disorder. In spite of New Jersey's label as the "rebellious" colony,[9] several of the proprietary colonies were in constant uproar. Maryland was in almost perpetual turmoil during the seventeenth century. In 1681 Lord Culpeper, governor of Virginia, wrote that his neighboring colony was "in torment" and "in very great danger of falling to pieces."[10] Writing about Virginia, Edmund Morgan referred to "lazy Englishmen."[11] They might also have been characterized as unruly and difficult to govern. There were rebellions in both North and South Carolina. New Yorkers refused to pay taxes and duties in the 1680s unless they had an assembly, while Penn's settlers gave him many difficult times. William Penn thought his settlers quarrelsome, wicked, "disingenuous," and "unsatiable."[12] These general complaints about the "nature" of English colonists were most pronounced in the proprietary colonies.[13]

In New Jersey, conflicts erupted in the 1670s over quitrents, and in the 1690s, in both East and West Jersey, over quitrents and the qualifications and approvals for the office of governor. Disputes over rents and land titles along the borders with New York (as well as between the two sections of New Jersey itself) punctuated the 1740s and 1750s. Aggravating the disagreements among proprietors and settlers were questions as to who really held the right to govern and boundary disputes that jeopardized land titles.

Other colonies witnessed political battles, unrest, and rebellions, but only New Jersey had two of its colonial governors literally dragged from their beds and carted off to prison in another colony (New York) for having had the audacity to govern. Imprisonment was the fate of both Philip Carteret of East Jersey in 1675 and John Fenwick of West Jersey in 1677 and 1678. Carteret indignantly wrote that Sir Edmund Andros of New York had

> sent a Party of Soldiers to fetch me away Dead or alive, so that in the Dead Time of Night broke open my Doors and most barbarously and inhumanly and violently hailed me out of my Bed, that I have not Words enough sufficiently to express the Cruelty of it; and Indeed I am so disabled by the Bruises and Hurts I then received, that I fear I shall hardly be a perfect Man again.[14]

John Fenwick founded the town of Salem and asserted his right, as a West Jersey proprietor, to govern the new settlement. And as a result, he complained,

> my house was beset, my door broken down, and my person seized on in the night time by armed men sent to execute a paper ordered from the Governor of New York, to whom I was sent prisoner in the depth of winter by sea—his order being to bring me in dead or alive—where he tried me, himself being judge, keeping me imprisoned for the space of two years and about three months.[15]

Only in New Jersey, too, can one find the governor of one colony seizing a ship, half of which was owned by the governor of another colony. Thus, Lord Richard Bellomont of New York seized the *Hester*, half of which Jeremiah Basse of East Jersey owned, in a dispute over the collection of customs duties. The dispute ultimately involved the question of the right to New Jersey's governments. It ended with the surrender when the proprietors agreed to give up their "pretended" rights to govern.[16]

New Jersey's cloudy political situation claimed another casualty. The Jersey proprietors—like those in Maryland, New York, Pennsylvania, and Carolina—planned that much of their population would be concentrated in cities, designating some of them centers for government and trade. The West Jersey proprietors hoped to make Burlington such a "chief city"; the East Jersey proprietors in 1682 declared their intention to build a "principal town" at Perth Amboy, "which by reason of situation must in all probability be the most considerable for merchandise, trade and fishing, in those parts."[17] With the exception of Philadelphia, these planned proprietary "cities" remained little more than villages throughout the colonial period.

This was especially the case in New Jersey, where even in 1797 there was "no town of very considerable trade, size, or importance."[18] Officials of the colony of New York—who sought to prevent the development of ports in neighboring New Jersey before 1700—were partially responsible for this state of affairs; so too was the tendency of the more fully developed cities of New York and Philadelphia to drain trade and commerce from the colony. But other reasons, unique to New Jersey, led to the failure of urban development. Colonial cities were ports, centers designated to receive imports and collect customs; New Jersey's ports fell victim to the proprietors' questionable rights to govern and to collect customs. By the time New Jersey became a royal province her cities could not compete successfully with firmly established ports to the north and south.

❖ ❖ ❖ ❖ ❖ ❖

New Jersey proprietors were not unique in wanting to profit from their lands. But their extraordinarily long land tenure was unusual, and it had far-reaching consequences for the colony and state. The Jersey proprietors obtained their grants or purchased their shares because they expected profit from land sales or rentals, from produce or rent from proprietary farms, and, on occasion, from trading or manufacturing enterprises. Although specific figures are relatively scarce, it seems clear that in New Jersey as elsewhere colonization proved to be an expensive outlay offering few immediate returns. Only shares kept until the second or third generation realized significant returns. As in Maryland and Pennsylvania, these long-range profits generally derived from increased land values as the colony grew and matured.

Early land sales and rentals did not produce much money for a number of reasons. "Sales" prices and rents were difficult to collect; proprietary agents often kept inaccurate records; and money itself was scarce.[19] In addition, the legal mechanisms for enforcing land contracts were inadequate. In some cases, the assemblies declined to create such procedures; in others, local juries refused to issue judgments. Zealous proprietors—like those in East Jersey—faced a hostile populace whose animosity increased with rent collection efforts. William Penn in 1707 advised James Logan, his agent, to "cherish or threaten tenants as they give occasion for either," but neither cherishing nor threatening availed much in Pennsylvania, New Jersey, or other proprietary colonies.[20]

Settlers also avoided land payments by squatting or by deliberately neglecting to take out proprietary titles and pay rents. In East Jersey towns, some settlers claimed that titles from Indians (Newark) or titles obtained prior to the arrival of proprietary agents (Elizabethtown) were sufficient and that, under these titles, payments to the proprietors were not required. Boundary disputes served as another excuse for nonpayment; residents argued that these disputes "rendered them unsafe in paying their Quit rents."[21] New Jersey was not alone in these difficulties. Townspeople on Long Island insisted that Indian titles predating the Duke of York's patent exempted them from his rents, while settlers in Pennsylvania and Maryland used boundary disputes to justify withholding payments.[22]

Nor was the problem of trying to obtain returns from land sales and rents restricted to the early years of settlement. Controversy over rents contributed to disorder in New Jersey in the 1740s and 1750s. Continued difficulties in collecting rents led the East Jersey proprietors to liquidate their holdings after the American Revolution.[23] James Parker, the most active member of the East Jersey Board of Proprietors in this period, complained that constant vigilance was necessary to obtain returns.[24] Again the New Jersey experience was not unusual; at the time of the Revolution arrears in Pennsylvania were enormous.[25]

In fact in East Jersey and elsewhere the proprietors' right to any rents was questioned. Thus Lewis Morris argued at one point that the proprietors'"quit rents are an unjust tax upon us and our heirs forever," while Maryland Protestants at the time of the Davyes-Pate uprising in 1676 maintained that they had transported themselves "into this Country, purchased the land from the Indians with loss of Estate and many hundred mens lives (yea thousands)" and had defended themselves, "whereby our land and possessions are become our Owne."[26]

The proprietors tried to increase their profits by other means. In Maryland, Carolina, Pennsylvania, and New Jersey they established farms and manors to be run by themselves or their agents. Thus, six Scottish proprietors of East Jersey took joint title to some of their dividend lands, pooled resources, sent tenants to the colony, and waited for returns. But returns never materialized.[27] At other times proprietors sought profits by establishing trading posts to supply settlers with necessities. Maryland, Carolina, and Pennsylvania proprietors, as well as the Scottish proprietors of East Jersey, Dr. Daniel Coxe, and the West Jersey Society also, tried, unsuccessfully, to profit from fishing, fur trading, and manufacturing.

In the early years, expenses clearly outran returns. Expenses included fees for charters, land purchases from the Indians, and the transportation of settlers and supplies. Thus, George Carteret spent money to send approximately thirty colonists with Philip Carteret, the first governor; members of the West Jersey Society transported three men and a "few" families; some of the Scottish proprietors in East Jersey pooled their money to send ships and about 250 settlers to the colony.[28] They were evidently not reimbursed for their efforts, and they lost money. Much the same situation occurred in Pennsylvania, Maryland, and Carolina. This is why proprietors preferred that settlers come at their own expense whenever possible, and why they used headrights to entice them. They also tried to have large investors bring settlers with them at no cost to the proprietor. For example, in New Jersey Berkeley and Carteret granted to Major Nathaniel Kingsland and Captain William Sandford a tract of 15,300 acres in 1671, on condition they settle ten families "besides their own" within seven years.[29]

There were also expenditures for the costs of government and for defense. The proprietors tried to get the colonists to pay for these items, but with varying success. Even when the proprietors succeeded, it usually took them many years and a struggle with the colonial legislatures before the colonists accepted responsibility for these expenses.

New Jersey, just prior to the division, and West Jersey, in 1693, passed taxes to meet some government expenses. But when they surrendered the province to the king in 1702, the East Jersey proprietors maintained that they had always underwritten the government. This is confirmed by the earlier statement by the assembly that "the planters and Inhabitants of this Province have been at Equal Charges with the proprietors in England, in that they have made all Highwayes, bridges, Landings and prisons, etc." and would pay nothing more because "they were not willing to maintain a government against themselves."[30]

Yet an additional financial burden diminished the return on funds invested in New Jersey. Fractionalized ownership led to regular trading in proprietary shares; each transfer of title required that previous proprietors be bought out, leading to additional expenses and a drain on profits. Though difficult to document, these expenses must be taken into account before the profits of an individual proprietor can be calculated. Of the other proprietaries, only in Carolina did such transfers occur; nowhere did the transfers happen with the frequency and cost of New Jersey. Berkeley sold West Jersey to Fenwick and Byllynge for £1,000. Byllynge then sold ninety shares at £350 each. The widow of George Carteret sold East Jersey for £3,400. And the West Jersey Society bought twenty shares of West Jersey, two shares of East Jersey, and other New Jersey property from Dr. Daniel Coxe for £4,800.[31] The Society sold 1,600 shares of stock at a par value of £10 each. This process continued into the eighteenth century.

◆ ◆ ◆ ◆ ◆ ◆

It should not come as a surprise that the Jersey proprietors profited little, if at all, in the early years of their grants. The only returns to Berkeley and Carteret were the sales prices they received when they sold their respective halves. Subsequent proprietors of both East and West Jersey did not make money before 1702. The East Jersey proprietors had expected that they would realize over £500 sterling annually from rents alone. In 1696, however, total income from rents was nearer £200, enough to cover the governor's salary, but leaving nothing for the proprietors.[32] The West Jersey Society generally sold rather than rented land. By 1702, the Society had disposed of £6,000 worth of land, but the money (if any was indeed collected) was never returned to investors in England. Nor were there many remittances after 1702. Lewis Morris, who long served as agent for the Society, was dismissed in the 1730s for having failed to send funds to the proprietors.[33]

Over the long term, the Jersey proprietaries became profitable investments. Individual proprietors who held on into the eighteenth century, and even those who invested then, profited from the sale of proprietary shares, from the sale of lands obtained as dividends, and perhaps even from rents. The same held true for the last proprietors of Maryland and Pennsylvania, who realized revenues from rents and land sales up to the Revolution and received some compensation for losses afterward. Some in East Jersey thought the Revolution a close call and feared the same fate as Baltimore and the Penns.[34] But the New Jersey proprietors survived even the Revolution. Land dividends continued to be granted, both in East and West Jersey, into the nineteenth century. In addition, after 1800 the East Jersey Board declared the first cash dividend for proprietors and distributed money derived from the sale of United States government securities. In some ways, then, New Jersey had the most successful proprietors of all. Their very perseverance brought them into the era of the early American corporation.

❖ ❖ ❖ ❖ ❖ ❖

The fragmentation of ownership in East and West Jersey—a pattern which did not appear elsewhere—also moved the proprietary toward a corporate form. Although multiple ownership was in some ways a consequence of the long continuation of the proprietorship, it was a process that began early and from the outset had the momentum for continued fractionalization. Carolina was another multiple proprietorship, but one in which the number of shares never increased. In fact, the *Fundamental Constitutions of Carolina* was based on the fact that shares were not divisible; the frame of government assumed that there would always be eight "lords," with each responsible for a distinct area of government. Over the sixty-six years of the proprietorship, only forty individuals served in those roles; even though at the time of the surrender of the charter in 1729 only two of the original families remained.[35] At times some of the Carolina titles were in the hands of minors. Two shares were involved in litigation. The surrender itself took ten years, because ownership of one quarter of the province was unclear. But there always were eight shares.[36]

The East Jersey's *Fundamental Constitutions* was based, by contrast, on the expectation of increased fractionalization of holdings. The constitution provided for limits on the impact that this pattern of ownership would have on the government of the colony. To keep one proprietor from dominating the others, the constitution prohibited anyone from holding more than a one twenty-fourth interest. Likewise, to prevent proprietors from "squandering" their interest in the government, holders of less than a one ninety-sixth interest lost their political role.[37] These provisions controlling access to government recognized that an unlimited number of individuals could own shares in the land. As that possibility approached realization in the eighteenth century, the East Jersey proprietors restricted membership on its board of directors to those owning at least a quarter share (one ninety-sixth) in the proprietary. But there were no limits on how often a share could be subdivided; holders of even the smallest fraction were still entitled to land dividends. The same fractionalization of proprietary shares occurred in West Jersey, though title—first under Edward Byllynge, then under Dr. Daniel Coxe and the West Jersey Society—to the government there was kept intact. West Jersey differed, then, from East Jersey in denying fractional holders a say in government matters. But both East and West Jersey granted land dividends to holders of even the smallest fraction of a proprietary share.

The number of shareholders in East and West Jersey increased rapidly. East Jersey went from 12 to 24 to 85 shareholders in the 1680s alone, and the size of individual holdings dropped quickly to a twenty-fourth and then a forty-eighth share. By the eighteenth century, even a ten-thousandth share was recorded.[38] West Jersey went from 2 share-holders in 1674 to 120 by 1683, and from one hundred full shares to holdings of one sixty-fourth of one of those shares.[39] Splitting hold-ings further was the West Jersey Society, created in 1691. This holding company owned two shares of East Jersey, twenty shares of West Jersey, and parcels of land in New Jersey and Pennsylvania; speculators traded in the shares of the society.[40]

The fractionalization that contributed to the evolution of the New Jersey proprietorship had other consequences as well. Almost all of the original proprietors in each colony were economically or politically prominent and influential men. Many were involved in one way or another in more than one colonial enterprise. But as time passed and proprietary titles devolved upon others, the status of the proprietors as a group declined, and with it their ability to protect their colonies. This pattern of development was true everywhere, but it was exacerbated in New Jersey.

Berkeley and Carteret, the original proprietors of New Jersey, were royalist supporters of the Crown during the exile years of the civil war period, and they held significant government posts in the Restoration government.[41] Their Jersey holdings later went to men who lacked equivalent status and influence. Neither John Fenwick nor Edward Byllynge in West Jersey were politically prominent and influential, while the men who purchased the one hundred shares from them in later years were even less "weighty." In East Jersey the twelve propri-etors included several Scottish lords (who later took the wrong side in the Glorious Revolution), but the group was mainly comprised of Quaker polemicists, tailors, and merchants. With the exception of William Penn, these men lacked influence at court. As the twelve proprietors became twenty-four, and then more, their individual status and influence further declined. At the time of the charter's surrender, only Penn stood out as significant.[42] This problem of diminished standing persisted into the eighteenth century, diluting the power and influence of the Jersey proprietors.

After 1674, New Jersey—begun as one colony—was in fact two, divided into an east and west, with each section owned by different proprietors. Carolina had been split north and south, because distance between the two early centers of settlement made one government impracticable. But both Carolinas belonged to a single group of proprietors. Similarly, Delaware and Pennsylvania were administered separately for political and religious reasons, although both were the property of the Penns. In New Jersey, the impact of this unusual division was felt long after the surrender of the charter reunited the two halves into a single royal colony. In fact, the political and economic consequences continued into and beyond the eighteenth century. As a result of the separation of New Jersey into eastern and western divisions, there were two capitals, two treasurers, a sectionally balanced council, and an extraordinary political factionalization of the colony.

The West Jersey proprietors appointed Burlington as their capital; East Jersey proprietors selected Perth Amboy. The surrender agreement alternated governmental meetings between the two towns. From 1702 to 1776, alternate meeting places was customary practice, set aside only when royal governors argued that ill health or the press of business required the legislature to meet elsewhere.[43] When William Franklin, the last royal governor of New Jersey, pushed for the building of a formal governor's house, his request mentioned the need for two such residences.[44]

The situation changed with the Revolution. Both Governor William Livingston and the legislature were forced to move about the state in an effort to avoid capture by the British. The government continued to wander after the war. Meeting thirty-five times from 1776 to 1791, the legislature sat in Burlington, Perth Amboy, Princeton, and Trenton. The state considered each when attempting to locate a single, permanent capital.[45] In 1790 Tench Coxe wrote William Paterson that New Jersey should "soon . . . fix [its] Government in one place" in order to promote manufacturing and stability. Coxe argued for a site accessible to oceangoing ships, suggesting "Brunswick & its Vicinity" as the most suitable.[46] His selection was ignored; the next year the legislature choose Trenton, and for the first time since the 1670s New Jersey had one capital.

Even after reunification, the historic division of the colony multiplied the number of factions in New Jersey. In the period from 1703 to 1729, Governors Cornbury, Hunter, and Burnet contended with competing East Jersey factions led by Scottish proprietors, English proprietors, and Nicolls patentees as well as such West Jersey factions as the West Jersey Society, Quakers (who were often also resident West Jersey proprietors), and Anglicans (including the West Jersey proprietor Colonel Daniel Coxe). The political divisions continued into the 1780s and constituted the fundamental cleavage of the Confederation period. The Revolutionary War had heightened sectional antagonisms. East Jersey was more frequently affected by fighting, and West Jersey Quakers refused to help militarily or economically. Disagreements over the use of paper currency after 1783 also followed sectional lines. But the bitter fight between East and West Jersey proprietors over the boundary line between their sections—an issue kept constantly before the legislature from 1782 to 1786—most clearly continued and aggravated "the traditional internal split within the state."[47] The political impact continued into the next century, long surviving the formal division into East and West Jersey, which lasted only from 1674 to 1702.

❖ ❖ ❖ ❖ ❖ ❖

Perhaps the most enduring legacies of the proprietary period were the boards of proprietors established to handle business in both East and West Jersey. These associations have survived to the present.[*] Both have evolved into modern corporations. In the process, the New Jersey proprietorship transformed itself from a feudal lordship to a capitalist company.

Of the five grants, proprietary in origin, for mainland colonies, two—Carolina and New Jersey—were "multiple" proprietorships. That is, the original grants for these colonies went to more than one individual. These multiple proprietorships exhibited some similarities. Proprietors in both colonies contributed money to the ventures and became, in effect, shareholders. Those who did not contribute monetarily were later held ineligible for returns. The Carolina proprietors agreed in 1663 to require periodic contributions of £25 each. At the end of three years, six of them had laid out £100 each; two never met their obligations.[48] Each proprietor in East Jersey was asked to put £300 into a common fund to meet the purchase price and initial expenses. Other

---

*Editor's note: The East Jersey Board ceased to exist in 1998, after this article was written.

assessments followed. And the 1725 agreement which reorganized the East Jersey Board of Proprietors required contributions toward common expenses. The West Jersey Society expected shareholders to pay up to £10 per share for expenses; in the first twenty-seven months assessments totaled £5 5s per share. Over the years, the Society collected £8,108 of the £9,200 to which it was entitled.[49]

The proprietors of East Jersey created a board to manage their affairs in 1685; West Jersey created a council to do the same in 1688. Both entities were formed in the colony; the entities themselves remained in America. In this regard, both differed from the board of directors for Carolina, and, for that matter, the West Jersey Society, which were located in England. The Jersey proprietors also differed from their Carolina counterparts in that they did not give up their lands with the surrender of their charters. The Jersey proprietaries persevered, surviving even the American Revolution.[50] As a result, the proprietors of New Jersey went from being feudal lords to being corporate stockholders, a status recognized in the late nineteenth century when the East Jersey Board of Proprietors convinced a state legislative committee that the board was a corporation, even though it lacked a formal corporate charter. The board argued successfully that its organization and operation predated the state.[51]

The survival of the New Jersey proprietors as a modern corporation is especially noteworthy because the beginnings of this transformation can be seen as early as the 1670s and 1680s. A similar process started in Carolina, but there the proprietorship did not survive to make the final transformation. According to John Pomfret, the "Carolina proprietorship, the prototype of New Jersey's, was . . . a feudal fief rather than a trading company, and it embodied the ideas of a landed nobleman rather than those of a London merchant."[52] In their actual operations, multiple proprietorships early on combined feudal fief and company. As feudal arrangements broke down, the New Jersey proprietorship ultimately became simply a company.

◆ ◆ ◆ ◆ ◆ ◆

There is a connection between the nature of the New Jersey proprietorship and the political problems experienced by her proprietors. New Jersey started out with two feudal lords who sold their proprietorships to groups rather than individuals. These groups were not "lords" in the traditional sense of the term; nor were they partners; nor, at least originally, corporations. A lord could have political power, but it was not as clear that a quasi-corporation (not yet a recognizable corporate body) could possess such authority. Thus the changing nature of the New

Jersey proprietorship complicated the question of political control, which was confused from the outset by the Duke of York's grant to Berkeley and Carteret. In this sense the dispute over political control in New Jersey is really symptomatic of a more fundamental change, which was nothing less than the transformation from a feudalistic entity to a modern one.

Notes

An earlier version of this paper was presented before the Seminar for New Jersey Historians sponsored by the New Jersey Historical Commission and the Department of History, Princeton University. I would like to thank the New Jersey Historical Commission for a research grant, Rutgers University Libraries for research leave, Richard P. McCormick and John Murrin for pointing out things I had not considered, and Jonathan Lurie for reading drafts.

1. Richard P. McCormick, *New Jersey from Colony to State* (Newark, 1981), x. In contrast, John Pomfret, in *Colonial New Jersey: A History* (New York, 1973), xvi, points to New Jersey as "unique," citing as justification its divided proprietorship, the proprietors' ownership of the soil only, and the complex land system.

2. For a comparative discussion of the proprietary colonies, see Maxine Neustadt Lurie, "Proprietary Purposes in the Anglo American Colonies: Problems in the Transplantation of English Patterns of Social Organization" (Ph.D. diss., University of Wisconsin, 1968).

3. This grant included territory that sprawled from Maine to New Jersey and incorporated Long Island, Martha's Vineyard, and Nantucket Island.

4. Byllynge was in bankruptcy and later claimed Fenwick's involvement was as a trustee to protect Byllynge, the real owner. William Penn arbitrated the dispute, and Quaker trustees were appointed to handle Byllynge's affairs. They divided the proprietorship into one hundred shares, awarding ninety to Byllynge and ten to Fenwick.

5. The Quakers said they had been "induced" to buy Berkeley's half by the "powers of government" included in the conveyance "because to all prudent men the government of any place is more inviting than the soil for what is good land without good laws." They wanted the government to "assure people of an easy and free and safe government" without which settlers would not come "for it would be madness to leave a free and good and improved country, to plant in a wilderness." Letter from the West Jersey Trustees to the Duke of York's Commissioners, 1680, quoted in John Clement, "William Penn and His Interest in West New Jersey," *Pennsylvania Magazine of History and Biography* 5 (1881): 324; Samuel Smith, *History of New Jersey* (Burlington, N.J., 1765), 117–118.

6. See the discussion of the problems of John Fenwick and Philip Carteret.

7. In 1683 he confirmed the sale from Carteret to the twenty-four proprietors.

8. This was not a definitive resolution of the question, because English officials later maintained that the duke could not convey his political rights to another party.

9. John Pomfret, *The Province of East New Jersey, 1609–1702: The Rebellious Proprietary* (Princeton, N.J., 1962).

10. Quoted in Michael G. Hall, Lawrence H. Leder, and Michael G. Kammen, eds., *The*

Glorious Revolution in America: Documents on the Colonial Crisis of 1689 (Chapel Hill, N.C., 1964), 143.

11. Edmund Morgan, *American Slavery, American Freedom: The Ordeal of Colonial Virginia* (New York, 1975), chapter 3.

12. Penn to James Harrison, November 20, 1686, Papers of David Lloyd and Others Relating to Pennsylvania (materials from the Pennsylvania Historical Society microfilmed and presented to the Wisconsin Historical Society by Roy Lokken); Penn to [?], April 8, 1704, ibid.; Penn to Logan, May 18, 1708, *Penn-Logan Correspondence, Memoirs of the Historical Society of Pennsylvania* (Philadelphia, 1872), 10, 271 (hereafter cited as *Penn-Logan Correspondence.)*

13. Richard Dunn, *Sugar and Slaves: The Rise of the Planter Class in the English West Indies, 1624–1713* (New York, 1972), makes this clear by illustrating the difficult time both proprietary and royal governors experienced in the West Indies colonies. Even within England it was difficult for authorities to exercise their power in certain rural areas. See Robert W. Malcolmson, "'A set of ungovernable people': The Kingswood Colliers in the Eighteenth Century," in, *An Ungovernable People, The English and Their Law in the Seventeenth and Eighteenth Centuries*, ed. John Brewer and John Styles (New Brunswick, N.J., 1980), 85–86. This may indicate that disorder and rebelliousness were endemic to the peripheral areas of the state and empire. That it was more characteristic in the proprietary colonies is shown by the fact that of eighteen "rebellions" in America between 1645 and 1760, thirteen occurred in the proprietaries, five in royal colonies, and none in the charter colonies. For a list of the eighteen, see Richard M. Brown, "Violence and the American Revolution," in *Essays on the American Revolution*, ed. Stephen Kurtz and James H. Hutson (New York, 1973), 85–86; the calculations are mine. A 1701 pamphlet noted that "in some of the Proprieties, the Hands of the Government are so feeble, that they can not protect themselves against the Insolencies of the Common People, which makes them very subject to Anarchy and Confusion." Louis B. Wright, ed., *An Essay Upon the Government of the English Plantations on the Continent of America* (repr., San Marino, Calif., 1945), 37.

14. In William A. Whitehead, ed., *Documents Relative to the Colonial History of State of New Jersey* (Newark, 1880), 1:316 (hereafter cited as Whitehead, *Documents Relative to New Jersey*). See also Edwin Hatfield, *History of Elizabeth, New Jersey* (New York, 1868), 189–195. Andros acted to prevent establishment of New Jersey's right to an independent government. He demanded that Carteret cease operating a separate government, and then he had Carteret tried in New York for resisting this order. The jury verdict found Carteret not guilty, but the court ordered him to desist anyway.

15. In John Pomfret, *The Province of West New Jersey, 1609–1702: A History of the Origins of an American Colony* (Princeton, N.J.: Princeton University Press, 1956), 84. Fenwick was tried in New York in 1677 but because his deeds to West Jersey were held in England by John Eldridge and Edmund Warner (to whom he had mortgaged his property), he could offer no proof of his position. He was fined by the court and required to give security for good behavior. He was arrested again in 1678 and held in New York. In 1683 William Penn bought out Fenwick's interests and claims; shortly afterward West Jersey political rights were recognized as inhering in Edward Byllynge.

16. The dispute started in 1693 over the right of the New Jersey proprietors to create ports free from New York jurisdiction and customs collections. After 1696, East and West Jersey proprietors petitioned the Board of Trade to recognize New Jersey's rights to free ports. In 1697 the board agreed there were no regulations against New Jersey ports. But later the same year Attorney General Sir Thomas Trevor and Solicitor General Sir John Hawles ruled

that because the power to designate ports was not given to the Duke of York, he could not have transferred this power to the New Jersey proprietors. The proprietors proposed a test case; the Board of Trade then moved to tie the right to ports to the right to the government. The proprietors feared they might lose such a test, refused the arrangement, and turned to devising an acceptable surrender agreement. In a final ironic development, the Hester Case, which served as the test the proprietors had decided to avoid, ended in Basse's favor. The chief justice stated he was not convinced New York had jurisdiction over New Jersey. But it was too late; the proprietors had already conceded.

17. *Brief account of the province of East-Jersey, in America, published by the present proprietors, for the information of all such persons who are or may be inclined to settle themselves, families and servants in that country* (Edinburgh, 1682), in Smith, *History of New Jersey*, 542.

18. Robert Proud, *History of Pennsylvania* (Philadelphia, 1797), 1:166. In 1740, Lewis Morris wrote to the Duke of Newcastle that Perth Amboy and Burlington "are both Inconsiderable places and like to remain so, neither of them fit for the seat of government, nor so convenient scituated for that purpose as some others." William A Whitehead, ed., *The Papers of Lewis Morris, Governor of the Province of New Jersey, from 1738 to 1746* (New York, 1852), 121.

19. In the early years, proprietors often "sold" land and reserved a quitrent; in this case, the annual rents were lower than those on land which was simply rented.

20. Penn to Logan, 1707, *Penn-Logan Correspondence*, 10:229.

21. Remonstrance of Assembly to Governor Gookin, May 7, 1709, *Minutes of the Provincial Council of Pennsylvania, Colonial Records of Pennsylvania* (Philadelphia, 1852), 2:455.

22. J. R. Brodhead, *History of the State of New York 1609–1691* (New York, 1871), 2:71, 109; Alexander Flick, *History of the State of New York* (New York, 1933), 2:85–86; J. M. Neil, "Long Island, 1640–1691: The Defeat of Town Autonomy" (master's thesis, University of Wisconsin, 1963), 62–64, 70, 86; Jerome Reich, *Leisler's Rebellion: A Study of Democracy in New York 1664–1720* (Chicago, 1953), 13–14, 23.

For problems with rents in Pennsylvania and Maryland, see *Penn-Logan Correspondence*, 9:102, 262, 365–366; 10:25, 50, 123, 303; *Papers Relating to the Provincial Affairs of Pennsylvania, Pennsylvania Archives*, series 2 (1878), 7:65; Beverley W. Bond, *The Quit-rent System in the American Colonies* (New Haven, Conn., 1919), 161–162.

23. Gary Horowitz, "New Jersey Land Riots 1745–1755" (Ph.D. diss., Ohio State University, 1966); Thomas L. Purvis, "Origins and Patterns of Agrarian Unrest in New Jersey, 1735 to 1754," *William and Mary Quarterly* 39 (1982): 600–627; Introduction, *The Minutes of the Board of Proprietors of the Eastern Division of New Jersey from 1764–1794*, ed. Maxine N. Lurie and Joanne R. Walroth (Newark, 1985), 4:xxi–xlii.

24. Parker wrote, "Where ever I turn my Eyes as a Landlord or as a Proprietor of Lands in Common or unlocated the greatest Destruction presents itself and such a licentious Behaviour in the people in general that Really people who have not their Interests immediately under their Eyes have only but a very gloomy prospect." Letter to John Stevens, January 11, 1786, Stevens Family Papers, MG 409, #272, New Jersey Historical Society, Newark.

25. In 1779 this was estimated at £118,569 4s. 6 1/2d.; Bond, *Quit-rent,* 161n.

26. "Letter of Lewis Morris to the people of Elizabethtown, July 13, 1698," *New Jersey Historical Society Proceedings* 14 (1877): 185; "Huy and Cry," (1676) in *Proceedings of the Council of Maryland* 5 (1887): 140. See also: *New York Post Boy,* June 9, 1746, Letter to Mr.

Parker; the author attacked the proprietors' right to land, on the grounds that "No Man is naturally intitled to a greater Proportion of the Earth, than another," and stated that he who took vacant land and "bestowed his Labour on it" should have "the Fruits of his Industry." In William Nelson, ed., *Newspaper Extracts 1740–1750*, vol. 2, *New Jersey Archives* 12 (Paterson, N.J., 1895), 308–309.

27. Ned Landsman, "The Scottish Proprietors and the Planning of East New Jersey," in *Friends and Neighbors: Group Life in America's First Plural Society*, ed. Michael Zuckerman (Philadelphia, 1982); Ned Landsman, *Scotland and Its First American Colony, 1683–1765* (Princeton, N.J., 1985), part 2.

28. Wesley Frank Craven, *New Jersey and the English Colonization of North America* (Princeton, N.J., 1964), 48; Frederick Black, "The Last Lords Proprietors of West Jersey: The West Jersey Society, 1692–1702" (Ph.D. diss., Rutgers University, 1964), 262–265; "Account of Shipment to East Jersey in August, 1683, by Some of the Proprietors," Whitehead, *Documents Relative to New Jersey* 1:464–469; John Pomfret, "The Proprietors of the Province of East New Jersey, 1682–1702," *Pennsylvania Magazine of History and Biography* 77 (1953): 261; John Pomfret, *The Province of East Jersey*, 197–198.

29. "Some Early New Jersey Patentees paying Quitrents," *New Jersey Historical Society Proceedings* 48 (1930): 233.

30. October 29, 1686, *Journal of the Governor and Council of East Jersey* (1890), *New Jersey Archives* 13:169.

31. John Pomfret, *The New Jersey Proprietors and Their Lands* (Princeton, N.J. 1964), 25–26, 36–39, 73–74; Anthony Q. Keasbey, "Purchase of East New Jersey," *New Jersey Historical Society Proceedings* 17 (1882): 24; William T. McClure, "The West Jersey Society, 1692–1736," *New Jersey Historical Society Proceedings* 74 (1956): 3–4.

32. Pomfret, *The Province of East Jersey*, 298–299; Pomfret, *The New Jersey Proprietors and Their Lands*, 51, 55–56. Andrew Hamilton wrote William Dockwra in 1688 about £950 raised by a group of East Jersey proprietors for investment in the colony. Hamilton observed that the money was "sunk and gone"; a note appended to the letter about twenty years later added that there was "nothing left for so much money but the bare land." Whitehead, *Documents Relative to New Jersey* (Newark, 1881), 2:27–34.

33. Black, "Last Lords Proprietors," 56, 269; McClure, "The West Jersey Society, 1692–1736," 8; John Strassburger, "'Our Unhappy Purchase': The West Jersey Society, Lewis Morris and Jersey Lands, 1703–36," *New Jersey History* 98 (1980): 97–115.

34. Memo on Reasons why Books should be Returned, n.d., William Alexander Papers, New-York Historical Society, Box 43 (hereafter Alexander Papers). At this point the proprietors feared the New Jersey legislature "in their present levelling mood [would] follow the example of Pennsylvania in taking possession of the whole." It is difficult to document the profits precisely, but occasional figures are suggestive. James Alexander, prominent East Jersey proprietor in the first half of the eighteenth century, died in 1756. His papers contain several lists of property obviously enumerated to facilitate division among his heirs. One group of lands, the Sussex lands, appears on a list showing that portion on which mortgages were held, as well as what was left to be sold. The whole is valued at £5439.9.5 proclamation money or £5892.15.2 New York money. "An Account of What Remains Due of the Sussex Lands for Rights Sold," n.d., Alexander Papers, Box 1a.

35. William S. Powell, *The Proprietors of Carolina* (Raleigh, N.C., 1963), 10; Kemp P. Battle, "The Lords Proprietors of Carolina," *North Carolina Booklet* 4 (1904): 5–37; Herbert R.

Paschal, "Proprietary North Carolina: A Study in Colonial Government" (Ph.D. diss., University of North Carolina, 1964), 98–114.

36. The two original families that remained were Colleton and Carteret, and Carteret kept his portion of the lands. Also the two shares which were disputed were claimed or held for more than one individual, but they were not divided the way New Jersey shares were.

37. This rule was violated by Arendt Sonmans, who held more than one full share. The quotation is from *A Brief Account of the Province of East New Jersey in America: Published by the Scots Proprietors Having Interest There* (Edinburgh, 1683), 13; see also "Fundamental Constitutions of East Jersey," in *Fundamental Laws and Constitutions of New Jersey*, ed. Julian Boyd (Princeton, N.J., 1964).

38. Pomfret, *The Province of East Jersey*, appendix: "Transfers and Fractioning 1683–1702," 397–399. Many references to fractional holders appear in the four volumes of the *Minutes of the Board of Proprietors of the Eastern Division of New Jersey*, ed. George Miller, vols. 1–3; Lurie and Walroth, *The Minutes of the Board of Proprietors*, vol. 4.

39. Pomfret, *The Province of West Jersey*, 124, 285–289, gives one example of a conveyance that read "1/32 of 3/90 of 90/100."

40. The West Jersey Society remained in existence in England until 1923. McCormick, *From Colony to State*, 48.

41. John Berkeley had served during the civil war in the Royal Army and then as secretary, treasurer, and financial manager for the Duke of York. He was rewarded for his services in 1658 by being made Baron Berkeley of Stratton on Cornwall. After the Restoration he served as a member of the Privy Council and as a commissioner of the Admiralty. In 1670 he was appointed a lord lieutenant of Ireland, and from 1675 to his death in 1678 he served as ambassador extraordinary to France.

As early as 1626 George Carteret had been appointed governor of the Isle of Jersey and in 1640 Treasurer of the Navy. During the civil wars he provided shelter in his province for Edward Hyde, Lord Clarendon, a favorite of Charles II, and also for the Duke of York. There is some evidence that in 1650 Charles tried to recompense him with the grant of an island near Virginia. After 1660, he served as a member of the Privy Council, Vice Chamberlain of the Household, Treasurer of the Navy, and Lord of the Admiralty.

Berkeley and Carteret were distinguished by the services they had rendered the Duke of York and the king, as well as by the fact that they both served with James in the navy. These associations help explain their roles in the proprietorship of Carolina as well as that of New Jersey.

42. There is a list of proprietors, their holdings, and their occupations in Pomfret, *The Province of West Jersey*, Appendix: "The Proprietors of the One Hundred Shares of West New Jersey," 285–289; Pomfret, *The Province of East Jersey*, Appendix: "Transfers and Fractioning 1683–1702," 397–399; John Pomfret, "The Proprietors of the Province of West New Jersey, 1674–1702," *Pennsylvania Magazine of History and Biography* 75 (1951): 117–146; Pomfret, "The Proprietors of the Province of East New Jersey," 251–293.

43. The legislature met in Trenton in 1745 at the request of Governor Lewis Morris who noted that he had been ill and "reduced almost to a Skeleton." In 1752 Governor Belcher called the legislature to Elizabethtown as an "Extraordinary Necessity" because his physicians advised against a longer "Journey at this time of the year." Whitehead, *Documents Relative to New Jersey* (Newark, 1882), 6:257; Frederick W. Ricord, ed., *Documents Relative to New Jersey, Journal of the Governor and Council* (Trenton, 1891), 4:393, 398.

44. Correspondence between Franklin and the Lords of Trade, in *Documents Relative to New Jersey*, ed. Frederick W. Ricord and William Nelson (Newark, 1885), 9:385–386, 396, 404.

45. Mary Alice Quigley and David E. Collier, *A Capitol Place: The Story of Trenton* (Woodland Hills, Calif., 1984), 35. Twenty-two of the thirty-five times the legislature met in Trenton.

46. Tench Coxe to William Paterson, January 11, 1790, William Paterson Papers, Rutgers University Libraries, oversized. I thank Kenneth Bowling for pointing out this letter.

47. Richard P. McCormick, *Experiment in Independence: New Jersey in the Critical Period 1781–1789* (New Brunswick, N.J., 1950), 100, 135–57. McCormick quotes Noah Webster that "the jealousies between East and West Jersey . . . [are] almost az great az between the northern and suthern states" on the seat of government and any other matter.

48. First meeting of the Proprietors, May 25, 1663, in *The Shaftesbury Papers and other Records Relating to Carolina, Collections of The South Carolina Historical Society*, ed. Langdon Cheves (Charleston, S.C., 1897), 5:5; Account 1663, C05/286 Carolina Entry Book, May 1663–October 1697, 221ff (LC microfilm ACLS British MSS Project PRO Reel #1); *Carolina Lords Proprietors' Accounts of Disbursements and Receipts, 1663–1666, listing Fees in Passing ye Charter and Duplicate of Carolina* (Charleston, S.C., 1963). Neither Sir William Berkeley nor Clarendon ever paid in any money.

49. *A Brief Account of the Province of East New Jersey in America* (1683), 12; Instructions to Governor Laurie, July 20, 1683, in *The Grants, Concessions and Original Constitutions of the Province of New Jersey*, ed. Aaron Leaming and Jacob Spicer (Philadelphia, 1881), 171–173; Agreement of the Proprietors about the land, 1684, ibid., 186–187; Instructions to the Governor and Commission Land, July 3, 1685, ibid., 211; Account of the Several Rates or Assessments laid upon the Proprietors of East Jersey, September 23, 1690, Whitehead, *Documents Relative to New Jersey* 2:37–40; Agreement of the Members of the West Jersey Society for the managing and improving of their lands, March 4, 1692, ibid., 2:73–80; Accounts of the Disbursements by the Proprietors of East Jersey upon the Publick Affairs of the Province, ibid., 2:202–205; George Miller, ed., *The Minutes of the Board of Proprietors of the Eastern Division of New Jersey* Perth Amboy, 1949), 1:49–50; Black, "Last Lords Proprietors," 1–2, 75–82, 102–111, 182.

50. Memo on Reasons why Books should be Returned, n.d., Alexander Papers, Box 43.

51. *Report of the Joint Committee to Investigate the Acts and Proceedings of the Board of Proprietors of East Jersey, Touching the Rights and Interests of the State, And of the Citizens Thereof* (Trenton, 1882), 39–40.

52. Pomfret, *Colonial New Jersey*, 22.

This is the portrait that for a number of years was described as being of Lord Cornbury, the first royal governor of New Jersey. Patricia Bonomi questions both the allegation that Cornbury wore women's clothing and that the image represents him. In response to her research the New-York Historical Society changed its description of the painting to read "Unidentified Woman [Formerly Edward Hyde, Lord (Viscount) Cornbury] by unidentified artist, early Eighteenth Century; oil on canvas, 49 ¼ x 38 ⅞ inches; accession # 1952.80." Collection of the New-York Historical Society.

2

Lord Cornbury (1661–1723) was appointed governor of New York and New Jersey in 1702. As a successful soldier, member of Parliament, and cousin of Queen Anne, he was welcomed in both colonies with great fanfare, and with the hope that he would bring calm to troubled regions. In 1710 he returned to England, leaving turmoil, especially in New Jersey. Historians have long ranked him as the worst governor New Jersey ever had; in 1965 Arthur Pierce described him as "A Governor in Skirts," "Striding along the ramparts of Fort Anne in New York . . . in feminine attire," with his hand always out "itching" for money. Descriptions of his cross-dressing appeared in several contemporary letters sent to England, while accusations that he accepted bribes and misappropriated money appeared in the Remonstrance of the New Jersey assembly.

In 1998 Patricia Bonomi published *The Lord Cornbury Scandal*, arguing that he was an able man condemned by a "culture pervaded by gossip, satire, slander, and sexual innuendo." The real problem was that he arrived at a time when the empire was trying to both consolidate its control and strengthen the Church of England. He was the first royal governor of New Jersey, appointed after the proprietors of East and West Jersey surrendered their political claims to the Crown and at a point when the governments of what had been two colonies were merged into one. In furthering the aims of empire and church he ran afoul of colonial politicians and religious dissenters, who blackened his name in order to have him recalled to England. What they really opposed was his policies. Bonomi concludes that Cornbury was not guilty of the charges. The conflicting tales illustrate how historical interpretations change, and sometimes are very different. The reader, whether a historian, student, or interested citizen, needs to evaluate the arguments and evidence before deciding which interpretation makes more sense.

In the section of the book reproduced here Bonomi examines specifically the portrait used since the 1950s to illustrate books and articles discussing Cornbury, showing "him" in woman's clothing. She questions the attribution. What reasons does she give, and is she convincing? Does

Bonomi prove her negative argument (the painting is not Cornbury), or just raise questions? The selection and the book as a whole also raise a series of questions about the nature and practice of politics in colonial New Jersey (as well as other colonies and England itself), gender roles, the use of evidence, the power of myths in history, and the possible truth about Lord Cornbury's career as a colonial governor.

British and American historians who have looked at politics in England and its colonies in the late seventeenth and eighteenth century have tried to describe when and how political parties developed, and whether or not they approximate modern parties. Not surprisingly, there is disagreement about when things happened, and even what to call what appeared to be happening. As England reeled from civil war to Restoration to the Glorious Revolution and then the Hanoverian succession, political divisions were numerous and sometimes complex. They have been characterized as Cavalier vs. Puritan, court vs. country, Tory vs. Whig, factions vs. parties, or a mix of more than one set of entities. Colonial politics reflected and were impacted by what happened in England, along with local divisions. New Jersey politics were particularly complicated. New Jersey was divided into East and West until 1702, and there were numerous factions in each section: two sets of proprietors further divided by internal disputes (East Jersey had resident Scottish and English proprietors, who disagreed on land policies, as well as conflicts with those remaining in London); religious differences (there were Anglicans, Quakers, Dutch Reform, Presbyterians, and others); and different views, for example, about preparedness during wartime, further complicated by ethnic differences. Some historians have seen the divisions, both before and after 1702, as simply proprietary vs. anti-proprietary parties, others as a shifting set of factions throughout the period. Descriptions and analysis offered by historians vary, but however the local political scene is described there is no question that Cornbury stepped into a minefield.

Even as political divisions worked themselves out in England, the American colonies, and New Jersey in particular, the "press" developed, and became a tool for political discussion and attacks. Newspapers became common, along with pamphlets and flyers. Opponents turned to the use of satire, innuendo, and character attack. At a time when gender roles were becoming more defined and religious dissenters more disapproving of perceived sexual transgressions, scandal, real or fabricated, could become a tool used against political opponents. Surely everyone can think of recent modern examples, including specifically New Jersey ones, where this has taken place. Does this though make colonial political "parties" equivalent to modern ones? If not, what does?

In presenting her arguments that previous historians have been mistaken about Cornbury, Bonomi challenges their use of evidence. Four letters written by three of Cornbury's foes in New York and New Jersey are the major source of stories about him; complaints from colonial politicians opposed to new policies that he brought with him are the basis for charges of corruption. The portrait, most likely painted after his death, and labeled more than a century later, has been taken as proof of his activities on the "ramparts" of New York's fort. Historians, though, are not working in a court of law where proof must be beyond a reasonable doubt. In fact, they often have limited evidence available and can only offer tentative conclusions. How much evidence is needed, and how likely is it to be found, to prove him "guilty as charged"?

The Cornbury legend is one that state historians have long told, with a chuckle, looked at as a good story. Do we now have to worry whether it is real or a myth? And if it is but a myth, do historians, who are after all committed to finding the truth about the past, have to discard it? Did Cornbury wear women's clothes and accept bribes, or was he a modernizing reformer trying to help create a better imperial system? Why were charges of cross-dressing raised about him, but no other colonial governor? Is there perhaps something behind the story, or was he just the victim of vicious political practices in a time of change?

Suggested Readings

Bucholz, Robert. *The Augustan Court of Queen Anne and the Decline of Court Culture.* Stanford, Calif.: Stanford University Press, 1993.

Harris, Tim. *Politics Under the Later Stuarts: Party Conflict in a Divided Society, 1660–1715.* London: Longman, 1993.

Jones, J. R. *Country and Court: England, 1658–1714.* Cambridge, Mass.: Harvard University Press, 1978.

Lustig, Mary Lou. *Robert Hunter 1666–1734, New York's Augustan Statesman.* Syracuse, N.Y.: Syracuse University Press, 1983.

Newcomb, Benjamin. *Political Partisanship in the American Middle Colonies, 1700–1776.* Baton Rouge: Louisiana State University Press, 1995.

Olson, Alison Gilbert. *Anglo-American Politics, 1660–1775: The Relationship Between Parties in England and Colonial America.* Oxford: Clarendon Press, 1973.

Pierce, Arthur. "A Governor in Skirts." *New Jersey Historical Society Proceedings* 83 (1965): 1–9.

Purvis, Thomas L. *Proprietors, Patronage, and Paper Money: Legislative Politics in New Jersey, 1703–1776*. New Brunswick, N.J.: Rutgers University Press, 1986.

Sheridan, Eugene. *Lewis Morris 1671–1746: A Study in Early American Politics*. Syracuse, N.Y.: Syracuse University Press, 1981.

Tully, Alan. *Forming American Politics: Ideals, Interests, and Institutions in Colonial New York and Pennsylvania*. Baltimore, Md.: Johns Hopkins University Press, 1994.

Weeks, David. *Not for Filthy Lucre's Sake: Richard Saltar and the Antiproprietary Movement in East New Jersey, 1665–1707*. Bethlehem, Pa.: Lehigh University Press, 2001.

◆ ◆ ◆ ◆ ◆ ◆

Lord Cornbury Redressed:
The Governor and the Problem Portrait

Patricia U. Bonomi

One of the most curious artifacts of the eighteenth-century British Empire is a painting, hanging in the New-York Historical Society, that is said to be a portrait of Edward Hyde, Viscount Cornbury, in women's clothes. At least that is what viewers have been told—that Cornbury is indeed the subject—ever since his lordship's name became associated with the painting in the late eighteenth century. At first glance the portrait seems to offer prima facie evidence for the long-accepted view that Cornbury was a cross-dresser. But is the person in the portrait Lord Cornbury? Or might the painting simply constitute a particularly exuberant, if compelling, legacy of the rumors spread by Cornbury's political foes in the early eighteenth century? These questions suggest some intriguing possibilities concerning the portrait's history, which might be considered as a prelude to exploring the larger political culture of Cornbury's time.

Early History of The Portrait

Lord Cornbury died in 1723. Throughout the sixty-two years of his life and for three-quarters of a century thereafter, not a word seems to have been recorded in the colonies or England about a painting of him in women's clothes. His name was first associated with the portrait in England in 1796, the occasion being a visit by Horace Walpole and George James "Gilly" Williams, one of Walpole's Strawberry Hill circle of literary gentlemen, to the country estate of a friend, Sylvester Douglas, Lord Glenbervie. The three men were recalling stories about Katherine Hyde, Duchess of Queensberry, a famous eighteenth-century beauty. This reminded Walpole, son of Robert Walpole and thus heir to

From Patricia U. Bonomi, *The Lord Cornbury Scandal: The Politics of Reputation in British America* (Chapel Hill: University of North Carolina Press, 1998), 13–26. Reprinted by permission of the University of North Carolina Press.

old Whig tales, of a story about her cousin Lord Cornbury, "the mad Earl (as he [Walpole] called him)," which Glenbervie recorded in his diary as follows: "He was a clever man. His great insanity was dressing himself as a woman. Lord Orford [Walpole] says that when Governor in America he opened the Assembly dressed in that fashion. When some of those about him remonstrated, his reply was, 'You are very stupid not to see the propriety of it. In this place and particularly on this occasion I represent a woman (Queen Anne) and ought in all respects to represent her as faithfully as I can.'" At this point Williams volunteered that his father "told him that he has done business with him [Cornbury] in woman's clothes. He used to sit at the open window so dressed, to the great amusement of the neighbours. He employed always the most fashionable milliner, shoemaker, staymaker, etc. Mr. Williams has seen a picture of him at Sir Herbert Packington's in Worcestershire, in a gown, stays, tucker, long ruffles, cap, etc."[1]

A saucy story indeed, and one that points to a transvestite Cornbury not only in the colonies but also in England. The portrait mentioned by Williams is undoubtedly the one on view today at the New-York Historical Society; the description of the clothing matches, and it was from the Pakington family that the painting, purchased at auction by the society in 1952, descended. Yet the closest we can come to a source specifically attaching Cornbury's name to this painting is a thread spun by three merry gentlemen on a bibulous evening seven decades after Cornbury's death.

All three were well-known gossips. William Hazlitt called Walpole the "very prince of gossips," whose "mind, as well as his house, was piled up with Dresden china." Glenbervie, for his part, is said by the editor of his diaries to have "loved gossip" and to have recorded it with such abandon that his stories should be viewed with "a reservation of judgment." Williams is described as "one of the gayest and wittiest of his set in London society," qualities borne out by his droll, gossipy correspondence with George Selwyn.[2]

Williams could have been no more than seventeen when his father, a law reporter and member of Gray's Inn, told him the cross-dressing story some sixty years earlier. Gray's Inn is adjacent to Holborn, a street in London where transvestites publicly exhibited themselves in the early decades of the eighteenth century; a number of them, in full regalia, were hauled from Holborn through the streets to the workhouse in 1714 and perhaps again in the 1720s to the Old Bailey. That Lord Cornbury—a peer of the realm and first cousin to Queen Anne—could have been among their number or had displayed himself in women's clothes at open windows, and the fact gone unrecorded in any public or private document until three-quarters of a century after his death, is extremely unlikely.[3] It is more likely that Williams, or perhaps Glenbervie, conflated Williams's sixty-year-old transvestite story with Walpole's even older one about Cornbury in the colonies.

Williams could possibly have been told during his visit to Pakington's Worcestershire seat that the figure in the portrait was Cornbury. A letter from the son of Lord Sandys of Worcestershire, dated September 16, 1796, reported to the art cataloguer Sir William Musgrave on three paintings owned by Pakington, including one described as "The Second E. of Clarendon in Women's cloaths." Cornbury was in fact the third Earl of Clarendon, having acceded to the title in 1709. Though we cannot know for certain whether Sandys, Williams, or some third party first linked Cornbury to the portrait, what information we do have points to a date circa 1796.[4]

Why was the attribution made at that time? Again, we must guess. But it does happen that the date coincides with a period in which English society had become inordinately absorbed with the issue of cross-dressing. This was owing to the presence in their midst of the famous Chevalier d'Eon de Beaumont (1728–1810) of ambiguous gender. The chevalier's story is somewhat elusive. Toward the end of the Seven Years' War, d'Eon—after performing valorous service for France as a captain of the elite Corps of Dragoons—had been dispatched to England to help negotiate a peace treaty, after which he remained in London, supposedly to spy for Louis XV. By the mid-1770s London was aflutter with rumors that d'Eon was in fact a biological woman, news to this effect, including stories of cross-dressing, having issued from the Continent. Soon a debate was raging in the English press over whether d'Eon was man, woman, or hermaphrodite, and thousands of pounds were wagered on the question.[5]

The chevalier, after losing his patrons in France, took up permanent residence in England in 1783. Never able to shake off the transvestite gossip, and increasingly destitute, he staged public fencing matches, allegedly dressed on occasion in women's clothes. Between 1794 and 1796, such exhibitions, according to the newspapers, drew large crowds at Bath, Brighton, Southampton, Oxford, Birmingham, and Worcester— the last being but a short distance from the Pakington estate.[6]

The English fascination with cross-dressing in the late eighteenth century may well have given new life to the old story about Cornbury, contributing to his association with the Pakington portrait in a way we may never fully trace.

Cornbury's name was attached to the portrait more or less officially in 1867, when the painting was publicly displayed in an exhibition of national portraits at London's South Kensington Museum. By that time, and probably for that occasion, a label had been affixed to the frame identifying the sitter as Cornbury. Still there today, the label bears, not a curator's authoritative description, but a quotation from British historian Agnes Strickland's *Lives of the Queens of England*, published in 1847: "Among other apish tricks, Lord Cornbury [the "half-witted son" of "Henry, Earl of Clarendon"] is said to have held his state levees at New York, and received the principal Colonists dressed up in complete female court costume, because, truly, he represented the person of a female Sovereign, his cousin—german queen Anne."[7] Strickland offered only one specific source, a letter written to Hanover in 1714 by the German diplomat Baron von Bothmer relaying the rumor that when in "the Indies" Cornbury "thought that it was necessary for him, in order to represent her Majesty, to dress himself as a woman." The exhibition catalogue noted that the portrait was on loan from Sir J. S. Pakington and added, on cue from Strickland, that Cornbury "is said to have dressed himself in woman's clothes in order to represent her Majesty Q. Anne at New York."[8]

On July 18, 1867, the *New-York Daily Tribune* carried a special correspondent's report on the exhibition, including a brief discussion of the portrait. The correspondent noted that Cornbury was depicted "in female low-necked evening dress, it being his idea of loyalty to his Queen to dress like her!" He went on to quote the same picturesque passage from Strickland that appeared on the label. The *Tribune* story constitutes the first mention of the portrait in any known American source, printed or manuscript. Once the story appeared, the way was open for a luxuriant expansion of the Cornbury legend in the United States.[9]

Speculations: Expert and Otherwise

One reason Americans knew nothing about the portrait before 1867 is that it was very likely painted not in the colonies, as has sometimes been assumed, but in England. Most American specialists I consulted on this point agree that in the early eighteenth century no artist sufficiently skilled to produce a painting of this sort—even one modeled on a figure in an English mezzotint engraving, as was common in colonial portraiture—was working in North America.[10] A survey of portraits by such provincial artists as Gerret Duyckinck, Evert Duyckinck III, Nehemiah Partridge, John Watson, and Peter Vanderlyn—all painting in New York or New Jersey during or shortly after Cornbury's tenure as governor—seems to support that opinion. Their naive rendering of their sitters' features and their inexperience in dealing with light make it probable that the portraitist, though not an artist of the first rank, was working in England.[11] It seems a fair guess, too, that if a colonial had been taking a satirical poke at the governor—or, to put the most extreme case, if Cornbury had actually posed for the artist—word of the portrait would have got around.

Robin Gibson of the National Portrait Gallery in London, the leading expert on the Hyde family paintings known as the Clarendon Collection, commented on the New-York Historical Society portrait: "I feel certain that the so-called portrait of Lord Cornbury is a perfectly straightforward British provincial portrait of a rather plain woman c. 1710." Gibson thinks it unlikely that the portrait was painted in the colonies: "Although I do not think it would be possible to positively identify either the artist or the sitter of the portrait in question, it seems to me the sort of portrait which might have been painted of a well-to-do woman living well outside London society, perhaps in the north of England. It is not necessarily of a member of the aristocracy." But might the portrait be an English caricature of Cornbury, as some have suggested? Gibson thinks not. "Caricature portrait paintings (certainly in Britain at this date) are unknown, to me and extremely rare at any time. Any caricature would have taken the form of an engraving or drawing."[12] This seems to rule out the possibility of a prank specifically aimed at Cornbury: a caricature, intended for circulation, would not have been done in oils. Further, if the portrait were of English origin, it could not have been produced during Cornbury's tenure as governor in North America—unless the subject happened to be someone else.

Might Cornbury have sat for the portrait after returning to England in 1710? This seems unlikely, given the absence during his lifetime of the notice such a portrait would have occasioned. For all their love of scandal in the eighteenth century, English gossips and political diarists seem never to have identified Cornbury as a transvestite or imputed to him any other kind of androgynous peculiarity. Of the eighteenth-century connoisseurs who examined the famous Clarendon Collection, not one remarked that it included unusual portraits, much less one of Cornbury in women's clothes. George Vertue, tireless visitor to country seats and preeminent commentator on eighteenth-century painting, described the pictures at Cornbury Hall, Oxfordshire, which he saw in 1729, as "that Noble Collection of portraits."[13]

If there existed other authenticated likenesses of Cornbury, standards of comparison against which the portrait likeness could be measured, some of the mystery might be dispelled. A few candidates have turned up. One is an early nineteenth-century sketch made from an ivory carving—apparently a kind of cameo—that is said to represent the third Earl of Clarendon (Cornbury). But the sketch artist, Silvester Harding, did not say why he believed the ivory, now lost, depicted the third earl. The figure is attired in armor with a lace cravat at the throat and a swag of cloth over the right shoulder, a costume in which gentlemen were often portrayed from the 1680s to the 1720s.[14]

Supposing for the moment that Harding was right, how do the features in his sketch compare with those in the New-York Historical Society painting? The heavy eyes and full mouth are not incompatible with those of the New York portrait, though the pendulous lower lip is absent. The rather weak chin of the sketch does not match the long chin of the painting. Nor does the low forehead in the sketch resemble the unusually high one in the portrait. The noses are not at all alike, turning up in Harding's drawing and down in the portrait.[15]

Another ostensible likeness of Cornbury is an engraving that illustrates a history of New Jersey published in 1902. When copied to illustrate subsequent writings about Cornbury, the engraving was retouched and darkened, making it appear increasingly sensuous. Actually, the person in the engraving is not Cornbury at all. The author of the New Jersey history, Francis Bazley Lee, seems to have been rather a rascal. To illustrate his florid account of Cornbury's governorship, Lee used a portrait from James Grant Wilson's *Memorial History of City of New York* (1892) where the subject is clearly identified as the Duke of Marlborough. Lee removed Marlborough's name from beneath the picture, replaced it with Cornbury's signature from a different page in Wilson's history, added a sketch of the family estate, Cornbury Hall, from yet another page, and passed off the composite as authentic Cornburiana.[16] Such knavery in our own century raises fresh fancies about the scruples of more interested parties in previous centuries.

Another supposed likeness of Cornbury, one never published or discussed in previous writings about him, turned up in Geneva, Switzerland. This portrait, a miniature painted on vellum, is in the collection of the Geneva Museum of Art and History. The only identifying mark on the portrait itself is an inscription on the reverse side, "J. L. Durant fecit anno 1681." On the right side of the oval case in which the picture rests is a second inscription, in a different hand and of unknown date. It identifies the sitter as "Milord Edouard Hide, Comte de Cornbury" and notes that the portrait was deposited in Geneva's Bibliothèque Publique by order of the city council. At some point the miniature apparently fell into private hands. It was included in a gift to the city in 1846 and transferred permanently to the museum in 1870.[17]

As it happens, Geneva is not an entirely unexpected place to find traces of Cornbury. The young viscount lived in the city from early 1680 until May 1682 while a student at l'Académie de Calvin, an institution known in the seventeenth century for educating young European gentlemen of rank. Moreover, he received a singular honor in 1680 when at eighteen he was chosen for a leading role in the city's premier civic festival, l'Exercice de l'Arc—a day given over to military drills, shooting contests, and lavish banquets featuring multiple toasts. In ancient times, the best marksman among the citizens of the town had customarily been acclaimed "king" of the Arquebuse Drill, or troop of musketeers, and it may have been for his skill in musketry that Cornbury received the extraordinary honor of being chosen king in 1680 and perhaps again in 1681. It is quite possible that the Genevan artist Jean-Louis Durant (1654–1718) painted a miniature of Cornbury to mark the occasion.[18]

The figure in the portrait is draped in blue cloth with orange fringe, the same colors used by the drill in 1680 when Cornbury was made king, and the unusual blue bow suggests some kind of costume or "club tie." The sitter appears to be about the right age (in 1681 Cornbury was nineteen); the luminous blue eyes and fair skin might be expected in a young man whose grandfather, the Earl of Clarendon, was still quite blond in his forties and whose mother was once described as having "a complexion of dazzling fairness."[19] Further, the person represented in the miniature could be seen to bear some resemblance to Harding's sketch, most notably in the full mouth, fleshy chin, and round face. (At the least, the miniature and the cameo sketch look more like each other than either looks like the figure in the New-York Historical Society portrait.) Still, one cannot be certain that the miniature depicts the young viscount, because the artist did not identify his sitter and nothing is known about the circumstances in which Cornbury's name was subsequently assigned to the portrait. The most we can say, in view of the considerable evidence for Cornbury's connection to the miniature, is that we may now have a notion of what one artist thought he looked like as a young man. In any event, neither the Harding sketch nor the miniature is likely to put an end to speculation about the New-York Historical Society portrait, given the necessarily subjective quality of any effort to compare them.

One of the most challenging questions concerning the society's painting is why a portrait of Cornbury, if such it was, should turn up at the Worcestershire estate of the Pakington family. There was no blood tie or even close marital connection between the Hyde and Pakington families, nor did they, so far as can be determined, ever own property in the same counties. That the portrait might have been passed to, or become mixed with, the Pakington collection thus seems improbable. The Pakington family papers include many items from the eighteenth century. One is a 1786 "Inventory of Household Furniture Belonging To the Honorable Sir Herbert Pakington Baronet, at His House At Westwood Near Worcester." A number of portraits of unidentified women (possibly including the later titled "Cornbury" portrait) were among the items inventoried a mere ten years before Cornbury's name was associated with the famous painting, yet none was described as "curious," the common designation for anything out of the ordinary.[20]

One English historian has suggested that Pakington might have bought the painting for the amusement of his guests. Perhaps so. Yet it may also be that Lady Theresa Lewis, a Hyde descendant who in the mid-nineteenth century also tried without success to trace the portrait's provenance, spoke more wisely that she knew when she observed that as portraits moved from estate to estate and family to family the names of their sitters were often forgotten, sometimes to "live again with fresh names in the hands of the fresh owners."[21]

At my request, the New-York Historical Society agreed in 1990 to undertake a full scientific investigation of the painting. Examination showed that the picture carries no signature or other markings that would help to date it or to identify the artist.[22] The canvas is linen of a type used during the seventeenth and eighteenth centuries in both England and North America; the frame dates from the nineteenth century. Radiography revealed no underdrawing, no tampering with an original figure, and no clues to the portrait's provenance. Pigment analysis, it was thought, held out the best hope, for had the sitter's dress been painted with Prussian blue, the portrait could have been dated to post-1730–1735, after Cornbury's death. Analysis of cross-sections of pigment by a specialist at the Los Angeles County Museum showed, however, that the paint was smalt and indigo of types used in both the colonies and England well before and long after Cornbury's time.[23]

❖ ❖ ❖ ❖ ❖ ❖

So: contemporary evidence for Cornbury's cross-dressing is elusive; no scientific findings or evidence of the portrait's provenance point to Cornbury; the information on the label attached to the frame is spurious by modern standards; the picture was probably painted in England. It would appear that one of the most influential pieces of evidence for the charge that Cornbury was a transvestite must be declared factitious.

It is significant, moreover, that Cornbury's name became associated with the portrait at a time when cross-dressing, owing to the Chevalier d'Eon, was much in the news. At the close of the American Revolution, George Washington himself was accused in an English newspaper of being "of the female sex" and was grouped with other military cross-dressers—Joan of Arc, Hannah Snell, and the Chevalier d'Eon. It was perhaps fortunate for the Americans, the journalist concluded, that

General Washington's "Circumstance was not known at a more early Period of the Contest."[24] Within two months of the appearance of this story, Washington was caricatured in a British magazine dressed in women's clothes.

Thus were Cornbury and Washington both mocked as cross-dressers in a century notable for political satire and gossip, whose practitioners wantonly employed sexual innuendo.[25] That Cornbury was in such good company suggests the fresh possibilities in a scrutiny of the man and the political climate of his time.

Notes

1. Francis Bickley, ed., *The Diaries of Sylvester Douglas (Lord Glenbervie)*, 2 vols. (London, 1928), 1:76–77 (October 9, 1796).

2. For Walpole quotation, see Peter Sabor, "Horace Walpole as a Historian," *Eighteenth-Century Life* 11 (1987): 5. Sabor concludes that Walpole's primary interpretive aim as a historian "was to be original, tendentious, and, above all, interesting" (8). Bickley, *Diaries of Douglas*, 1:vii; *Dictionary of National Biography* (hereafter *DNB*), 61:400–401; John Heneage Jesse, *Memoirs of the Court of England: George Selwyn and His Contemporaries*, vol. 1 (Boston, 1843), esp. 121–159.

3. Williams's father, William Peere Williams, died in 1736, when his son was either sixteen or seventeen years of age *(DNB*, 61: 469–470). Gerald Howson, *Thief-Taker General: The Rise and Fall of Jonathan Wild* (London, 1970), 62–63; Randolph Trumbach, "London's Sodomites: Homosexual Behavior and Western Culture in the Eighteenth Century," *Journal of Social History* 11 (1977–1978): 1–33.

Cornbury's London residence at the time was Somerset House, a former royal palace, whose windows were at a safe remove from the public gaze. Raymond Needham and Alexander Webster, *Somerset House, Past and Present* (London, 1905).

4. Whether Sandys's letter was written before or after Williams's visit to Worcestershire is unknown. The letter is included in Musgrave's manuscript catalogue, "Painted Portraits in Many of the Public Buildings and Capital Mansions of England," Add. Mss. 639 I, fol. 239, British Library.

An inventory of furnishings, including paintings, at the Pakington estate in 1786 makes no reference to a Clarendon painting; see Hampton Collection, accession no. 4739, parcel I (viii), fol. 1 (microfilm), Worcestershire Records Office, Worcester, England.

5. The most thoroughly researched biography is Gary Kates, *Monsieur d'Eon Is a Woman: A Tale of Political Intrigue and Sexual Masquerade* (New York, 1995); see also Kates, "D'Eon Returns to France: Gender and Power in 1777," in *Body Guards: The Cultural Politics of Gender Ambiguity*, ed. Julia Epstein and Kristina Straub (New York, 1991), 189. Consult with some caution Cynthia Cox, *The Enigma of the Age: The Strange Story of the Chevalier d'Eon* (London, 1966); and Marjorie Garber, *Vested Interests: Cross-Dressing and Cultural Anxiety* (New York, 1992), 259–266. The chevalier's published memoirs are in significant part spurious; see Antonia White, trans., and Robert Baldick, introduction, *Memoirs of*

Chevalier d'Eon (London, 1970), xiv; and J. Buchan Telfer, *The Strange Career of the Chevalier D'Eon de Beaumont* . . . (London, 1885).

6. Lynne Friedli, "'Passing Women'—A Study of Gender Boundaries in the Eighteenth Century," in *Sexual Underworlds of the Enlightenment*, ed. G. S. Rousseau and Roy Porter (Chapel Hill, N.C., 1988), 245; Cox, *Enigma of the Age*, 84, 126–127, 190–159. For these duels the chevalier is said to have been garbed either as a woman or in the uniform of a dragoon (Cox, *Enigma of the Age*, 126–127). The British Library possesses putative journals and letterbooks of d'Eon in which he is alternately addressed as "Chevalier" or "Mademoiselle"; see Add. Mss. 29993, 29994.

7. The description, though slightly altered for the label, is attributed to Agnes Strickland (*Lives of the Queens of England*, 12 vols. [London, 1847], 12:132). The New-York Historical Society added its own descriptive label in 1995 indicating that the identity of the sitter has been challenged; it reads: "Unidentified artist, early 18th century. *Edward Hyde (Viscount Cornbury)* (1661–1723). Oil on canvas. Purchase 1952.80. The name of Eduard Hyde, Viscount Cornbury, royal governor of New York Colony (1702–1708), was first associated with this portrait at the end of the 18th century. Recent research done on the painting has called the identity of the sitter into question."

8. Baron von Rothmer to Jean de Robethon, The Hague, June 16, 17 14, Stowe Mss. 227, vols. 1 17–1 19, British Library. The rumor, spread to Whig circles in England (with which Rothmer was allied) in correspondence from three colonials, may have taken on new life after 1775 when Rothmer's letter was translated from French to English. See James Macpherson, comp., *Original Papers; Containing the Secret History of Great Britain, from the Restoration to the Accession of the House of Hannover*, 2 vols. (London, 1775), 2:626.

The catalogue description reads in full: "Edward Hyde, Lord Cornbury, after ward 3d Earl of Clarendon (–1723). Painter [ ]. Sir J. S. Pakington, Rt. M.P. Only s, of Henry, 2d E.; Master of the Horse to P. George of Denmark; Gov. of New York in the reign of Anne; marr. Catherine, dau. of Henry, Lord O'Rrien, eld. son of Henry E. of Thomond; is said to have dressed himself in woman's clothes in order to represent her Majesty Q. Anne at New York; d. 31 March, 1723. Half-length, standing; in female dress, with low body and jewels. Canvas, 49 X 39 in." *Catalogue of the Second Special Exhibition of National Portraits, Commencing with the Reign of William and Mary and Ending with the Year MDCCC, on Loan to the South Kensington Museum., May 1, 1867* (London, 1867), 40. Though the figure is more or less seated, the painting described is unquestionably the one that hangs today in the New-York Historical Society.

9. See, e.g., "A Governor in Petticoats," *Historical Magazine* (Morrisania, N.Y.), 2d ser., 11 (1867): 169, J. Romeyn Brodhead, "Lord Cornbury," *Historical Magazine* 111 (January 1868): 71–72; James W Gerard, "The Dongan Charter of the City of New York," *Magazine of American History*, XVI (July 1886), 41; and James Grant Wilson, *The Memorial History of the City of New York: From Its First Settlement to the Year 1892*, 4 vols. (New York, 1892–1893), II, 88.

10. The late Mary Black, former curator of painting at the New-York Historical Society, wrote: "I do not think the painting is of the period of Cornbury's presence in the province. . . . I doubt that it was painted in America." Moreover, in her survey of artists' account books and diaries in the society archives, she encountered no mention of the painting (Black to author, May 17, 1989). Ruth Piwonka, New York museum and history

consultant, notes, "The portrait does not resemble the style of any painters known to be working in America circa 1705" (Piwonka to author, May 18, 1986).

Ellen G. Miles of the National Portrait Gallery, Washington, D.C., does not rule out a colonial artist, pointing to New York's Gerardus Duyckinck (1695–1746) as a painter worthy of consideration, though Gerardus, only fifteen when Cornbury returned to England in 1710, would have had to paint him at a later date. Miles further notes that the New-York Historical Society painting is in the style of early eighteenth-century portraiture; she believes it is, not a caricature, but a serious painting (Miles to author, February 15, 1989, and August 1993). For more on Gerardus Duyckinck, see Richard H. Saunders and Ellen G. Miles, *American Colonial Portraits, 1700–1776* (Washington, D.C., 1987), 144–147.

11. For these and other eighteenth-century painters, see Waldron Phoenix Belknap Jr., *American Colonial Painting: Materials for a History* (Cambridge, Mass., 1959); Ian M. G. Quimby, ed., *American Painting to 1776: A Reappraisal* (Charlottesville, Va., 1971); Mary Black, "Contributions toward a History of Early Eighteenth-Century New York Portraiture: Identification of the Aetatis Suae and Wendell Limners," *American Art Journal*, 12, no. 4 (Autumn 1980): 4–31; John Hill Morgan, *John Watson, Painter, Merchant, and Capitalist of New Jersey, 1685–1768* (Worcester, Mass., 1941; orig. publ. as American Antiquarian Society *Proceedings*, 50, pt. 1 [1940]: 225–317); and Saunders and Miles, *American Colonial Portraits*. For more on the use of mezzotints, see Belknap, *American Colonial Painting*; Charles Coleman Sellers, "Mezzotint Prototypes of Colonial Portraiture . . . ," *Art Quarterly* 20 (1957): 407–468; and Frederick A. Sweet, "Mezzotint Sources of American Colonial Portraits," *Art Quarterly* 14 (1951): 148–157.

12. Robin Gibson to author, July 30, 1990. See Gibson's *Catalogue of Portraits in the Collection of the Earl of Clarendon* (Wallop, Hampshire, 1977).

13. Nor is there any mention in Vertue's voluminous writings on early eighteenth- century English painting of an unusual portrait of Lord Cornbury. The original Vertue notebooks are in the British Library; for Cornbury Hall entries, see Add. Mss. 23070, fol. 66, British Library. A detailed inventory of the Clarendon Collection, made in 1751 when Cornbury Hall was sold by the Hyde family, appears in Vernon J. Watney, *Cornbury and the Forest of Wychwood* (London, 1910), appendix 18; and in Lady Theresa Lewis, *Lives of the Friends and Contemporaries of Lord Chancellor Clarendon: Illustrative of Portraits in His Gallery*, 3 vols. (London, 1852), 3:239–435.

Among viewers of the collection was Horace Walpole. In 1751 the paintings were divided between two lines of Hyde descendants. Walpole saw one half of the collection in 1761 and the other half in 1786 while visiting the owners' estates. He gives a fairly detailed description of the paintings but remarks no oddities; see Paget Toynbee, ed., "Horace Walpole's Journals of Visits to Country Seats etc.," *Walpole Society* 16 (1927–1928): 38; W. S. Lewis, A. Dayle Wallace, and Edwine M. Martz, eds., *Horace Walpole's Correspondence* (New Haven, Conn., 1965), 33:541.

14. The drawing was one of many included in an illustrated edition of the first Earl of Clarendon's *History of the Rebellion and Civil Wars in England* (1702–1704), 31 vols. (Oxford, 1837), 4:102, a celebrated eyewitness account. David Piper, comp., *Catalogue of Seventeenth-Century Portraits in the National Portrait Gallery, 1625–1714* (Cambridge, 1963), 89 and plates; M. H. Spielmann, *British Portrait Painting to the Opening of the Nineteenth Century*, 2 vols. (London, 1910), vol. 1.

15. For Hyde family members, see Gibson, *Catalogue of Portraits*, plates 27–30. But see also Timothy H. Breen, "The Meaning of 'Likeness': American Portrait Painting in an Eighteenth-Century Consumer Society," *Word and Image*, 6 (1990): 325–350.

To continue the "likeness" game—a particularly conjectural sport when dealing with formal eighteenth-century portraiture—a glance at extant paintings of Cornbury's immediate family members suggests a certain refinement of feature and bearing as well as a fairness of complexion and hair, characteristics significantly absent in the New-York Historical Society portrait. On such grounds as these one might be more inclined to connect the painting to the Pakington family, judging from the rather coarse features of Sir John Pakington (1672–1727) as depicted in a portrait that hangs today in the Worcester Guildhall.

16. Compare the initial illustration in Francis Bazley Lee, *New Jersey as a Colony and as a State*, 4 vols. (New York, 1902), facing 1:390, with that in Duane Lockard, *The New Jersey Governor: A Study in Political Power* (Princeton, N.J., 1964), 25. The retouched print was then used to illustrate a story about Lord Cornbury in the *New York Times*, June 3, 1990. For the original illustrations, see James Grant Wilson, *Memorial History of the City of New York* (New York, 1892–1893), 11, 59, 71, 55. Lee's account of Cornbury's governorship is in Francis Bazley Lee, *New Jersey as Colony and State* (New York, 1902), vol. 1, chapters. 11–12. This representational sequence illustrates two of this book's themes: the untrustworthiness of pictorial evidence and the subjectivity of history.

17. Inventory item no. G 60, Miniatures Series, Musée d'Art et d'Histoire, Geneva; Fabienne X. Sturm, conservator, Musée de l'Horlogerie et de l'Emaillerie, Section du Musée d'Art et d'Histoire, to author, July 7, 1992. I am much indebted to Sturm, to archivists at the State Archives of Geneva, and to Livio Fornara at the Bibliothèque d'Art et d'Archéologie for assistance in researching Cornbury's sojourn in that city.

The handwritten inscription on the back of the miniature, it might be noted, is in the style of the later seventeenth and early eighteenth centuries.

18. Charles Rorgeaud, *Histoire de l'Université de Genève, I, L'académie de Calvin, 1559–1796* (Geneva, 1900), 441. According to a local history, in 1680, "le comte de Cornbury tenta sa chance, il fit deux coups meilleurs que son prédécesseur, 'et le dernier proche la broche'"; Eugene Louis Dumont, *Exercices de l'arquebuze et de la navagation* (Geneva, 1979), 114, n. 3. For the history of the festival and Cornbury's investiture as king in 1680, see Ernest Naef, "Les exercices militaire à Genève," *Genava: Bulletin du Musée d'Art et d'Histoire de Genève* 11 (1933): 110–120; for 1681, see n.s., 14 (1966): 59 and n. 10.

Durant, a native of Geneva, was known primarily as an ornamental engraver and painter in enamel; see Leo R. Schidlof, *La miniature en Europe* . . . (Graz, 1964), 1:236.

19. For the description of Cornbury's mother, see Anthony Hamilton, *Memoirs of the Comte de Gramont* (London, 1930), 112.

20. Hampton Collection, accession no. 4739, parcel 1 (viii), fol. 1 (microfilm).

The closest link between the two families is that Sir John Pakington's first wife's mother was Margaret Hyde, daughter of the Right Reverend Alexander Hyde, Bishop of Salisbury (1665–1667), who was a first cousin of Cornbury's grandfather, the first Earl of Clarendon. See John Pakington to Mr. Wotton, October 22, 1726, Add. Ms. 2412 l, II, fol. 14, British Library; E. A. R. Barnard, "The Pakingtons of Westwood," *Worcestershire Archeological Society, Transactions*, N.S., 13 (1937): 28–47; and *DNB*, 15:91–95. It is possible that

Cornbury and Sir John (1671–1727) knew each other, because both were Tories and served together in the House of Commons in the late seventeenth century. Yet there is no evidence of correspondence between them or any other indication in family or official papers that they were in any way close.

21. Richard Davenport-Hines to *Times Literary Supplement*, May 18–24, 1990; Lewis, *Lives of Friends and Contemporaries of Clarendon*, 1:33–34. Lady Theresa could find no link between the Pakington and Hyde families and no account of how the portrait became part of the Pakington collection.

22. The chiaroscuro, or shadowing, of the sitter's face (which the casual observer might mistake as evidence of a latent beard and mustache) was characteristic, however, of painting at the turn of the eighteenth century.

23. This information is based on a number of consultations with Holly Hotchner and Richard Kowall of the New-York Historical Society Conservation Laboratory and Kowall to author, January 4, 1990. I gratefully acknowledge their assistance.

24. Though the London editor called the story "improbable," he ran it on the front page beside other foreign news. Washington's secret was supposedly revealed in a deathbed confession by his wife; that Martha Washington did not die until 1802 seems not to have deterred the scandalmongers. See the *Daily Advertiser* (London), January 25, 1783. The *Advertiser* gave as its original source the *Pennsylvania Gazette* of November 1782; a scan of the newspaper for those and other likely dates turns up no such story.

25. Peter Wagner, *Eros Revived: Erotica of the Enlightenment in England and America* (London, 1988); George deF. Lord et al., eds., *Poems on Affairs of State: Augustan Satirical Verse, 1660–1714*, 7 vols. (New Haven, Conn., 1963–1975); David Foxon, *Libertine Literature in England, 1660–1745* (New Hyde Park, N.Y., 1965); W. A. Speck, "Political Propaganda in Augustan England," Royal Historical Society, *Transactions*, 5th ser., 22 (1972): 17–32.

The Battle of Monmouth occurred at the end of June 1778, when British troops, who had abandoned Philadelphia and were moving to New York City, clashed with the patriot forces that had
been following them. This was one of the largest battles of the Revolution. It has often been seen
by historians as a draw, but Washington claimed victory as his forces had held their own and
fought the British to a standstill. Emanuel Leutze (1816–1868), Washington at the Battle of
Monmouth. Oil on canvas, dated 1857. Monmouth County Historical Association, Freehold,
New Jersey; gift of the descendants of David Leavitt, 1937.

3

Of all the wars in which New Jersey's residents have been involved, the American Revolution had the greatest direct impact on its territory. The state, sometimes labeled as the "crucible," "crossroads," and "cockpit" of the Revolution, was in the middle of the fighting for seven out of the eight long years of this war. In many places the Revolutionary War was also a bitter civil war pitting neighbors, former friends, and relatives against one another. In the following chapter Mark Lender evaluates the state's role in the war and notes that several hundred small battles, and a number of major ones, including Trenton, Princeton, and Monmouth, took place in New Jersey. Yet when the story of the Revolution is told, attention most often has been placed first on the fighting further north, especially in Massachusetts in 1775 and early 1776 at the outset of the war, and then after 1779 on the southern campaigns. In 1940 Leonard Lundin complained that New Jersey had been given "scant attention" in accounts of the war. It has fared a little better recently, with a focus on Washington's crossing of the Delaware in book and film, and with the official federal designation of a large swath of territory as part of a new "Crossroads of the American Revolution" district. Even so, how can the relative lack of past attention be explained?

When attention is given to New Jersey's role in the Revolution, there have been different interpretations, as there are of the war in general. One issue is explaining just why the state was at the center of so much fighting. What role did New Jersey's geographic location play in the fact that it was caught up in the war? What would have happened had the British army been able to take all of the state, and keep control of it? Where in the state did most of the fighting occur? Next, what was there about the state's economy that drew in both the British and the rebels? What did they want in or from New Jersey?

When historians do turn to New Jersey in this war, they most often describe the beginning, for good reason, as a disaster. The usual account is of New Jersey's failure to mount resistance to the British invasion in the autumn of 1776, the incompetence and sometimes nonexistence of the militia. Washington is described as quickly retreating across the state in disarray, his army nearly disbanded, while large numbers of intimidated residents took oaths of loyalty to Britain. In addition, many residents were loyalists, or, including a large number of Quakers, just wanted to remain neutral. The state has been described as demoralized and "completely cowed." This stage of the war was followed by the Battle of Trenton, part of the "ten critical days," a pivotal point in the Revolution. Was the state really totally demoralized, and had all resistance actually disappeared before December 26, 1776? Just when, according to Lender, did the tide begin to shift?

After the battles at Trenton and then Princeton in early January 1777, an exhausted Continental army took refuge in Morristown. It would return later in the war, eventually spending a total of three winters in or near that small town. How does Lender explain this? What was there about Morristown that led the army to spend so much time there? What made its location so important? Was it only geography, or were there other reasons for its selection?

Another question has to do with changes that took place in the state as the war continued. In the end, New Jersey was invaded several times, most significantly in 1776 and 1778, but also later, in 1780. The first time the British aimed to take and hold the state, the second to cross it unhindered on their way from Philadelphia to New York City, and the last to capture Washington, his army, and supplies in the Watchung Mountains. They failed at each attempt, but Lender does see changes in how the state responded. What was different, and why? What changed in New Jersey over time?

Some estimates put the number of loyalists in New Jersey as one-third, or perhaps more, of the population. Residents from all walks of life, including William Franklin, the last royal governor, turned out and fought to keep the colony British. Their activities helped make New Jersey a dangerous place to live throughout the Revolution. The loyalists spied on the patriots, raided their homes, kidnapped leaders, and served in special military units. Despite all this, they were, ultimately, not effective. What limited the role that the loyalists played in New Jersey?

The chapter also raises larger issues about the American Revolution, arguing in fact that examining New Jersey helps explain the war as a whole. What kind of war was the American Revolution? How was it fought? In large or small battles? By a few people or, over the course of time, many individuals? Was it won by the Continental army, or did the often disparaged militia play an important role? As both armies passed through New Jersey or fought around its edges, they took cattle, grain, wagons, and other supplies. This was a pattern repeated in the southern theater of the war. Why were the British and Hessian depredations especially resented, more than those of hungry rebels? Why in the end did the British lose and the patriots win in New Jersey and then in the larger war?

Americans like to think of themselves as a peaceful society, but historians have pointed out, especially in recent times, that they have more often than not been at war. Every generation has seen soldiers go off to fight somewhere. But only during the Revolution was New Jersey's soil hotly contested. If you had lived in New Jersey during this period, what might you have faced? Where in the world today could one find a similar experience?

Suggested Readings

Bill, Alfred Hoyt. *New Jersey and the Revolutionary War.* Princeton, N.J.: Van Nostrand, 1964.

Dwyer, William. *The Day is Ours!* New York: Viking, 1983.

Ferling, John. *Almost a Miracle: The American Victory in the War of Independence.* New York: Oxford University Press, 2007.

Fischer, David Hackett. *Washington's Crossing.* New York: Oxford University Press, 2004.

Kwasny, Mark V. *Washington's Partisan War, 1775–1783.* Kent, Ohio: Kent State University Press, 1996.

Leftkowitz, Arthur. *The Long Retreat.* New Brunswick, N.J.: Rutgers University Press, 1998.

Leiby, Adrian C. *The Revolutionary War in the Hackensack Valley: The Jersey Dutch and the Neutral Ground, 1775–1783.* New Brunswick, N.J.: Rutgers University Press, 1962.

Lundin, Leonard. *Cockpit of the Revolution: The War for Independence in New Jersey.* Princeton, N.J.: Princeton University Press, 1940.

McCulloch, David. *1776.* New York: Simon and Schuster, 2005.

Middlekauff, Robert. *The Glorious Cause: The American Revolution 1763–1789.* 1982. Rev. ed. New York: Oxford University Press, 2005.

Ward, Harry M. *General William Maxwell and the New Jersey Continentals.* Westport, Conn.: Greenwood Press, 1997.

The "Cockpit" Reconsidered: Revolutionary New Jersey as a Military Theater

Mark Edward Lender

In war, as in real estate, location can be everything; during the War for Independence, location virtually decreed that New Jersey would be one of the chief military theaters. Situated between the de facto rebel capital in Philadelphia and the chief British garrison in New York City, the state was the contested middle ground. Armies maneuvering in either direction had to plan operations in the province. Generations of historians have referred to New Jersey as the "Cockpit of the Revolution," and from a purely quantitative perspective, the term is apt.[1] More fighting took place in New Jersey than in any other state: between October 16, 1775, with the seizure and destruction of the British transport *Rebecca & Francis* on Brigantine Beach, and a final incident on April 3, 1783, with a fugitive loyalist near Tuckerton, the state and its rivers and coastal waters were the scene of at least some 296 battles, skirmishes, and naval engagements—and one authoritative compilation has counted over 600.[2] Revolutionary New Jersey was a dangerous place.

If the fighting was frequent, it was also varied and complex. There were major battles between Continental and British regulars; there were smaller-scale actions involving mixed Continental and militia forces; and there were patrolling skirmishes where both sides got off no more than a few shots. Some fights involved only irregular forces operating under local authority or completely on their own initiative, occasionally with little interest in the wider war. Maritime privateers used New Jersey's rivers and coasts to wage war as a matter of free enterprise. In some instances, one side or the other tried to force a decisive action—to inflict a campaign-winning or even war-winning defeat; other

From *New Jersey in the American Revolution,* edited by Barbara Mitnick (New Brunswick: Rutgers University Press, 2005), 45–60. Reprinted by permission of the author.

actions aimed only at harassing enemy outposts or foraging operations, disrupting communications, or simply terrorizing neighborhoods. Bitter local actions reflected the civil war "within the war" between Whigs and loyalists. New Jersey was host to war in virtually all of its guises.

Location helped determine not only the frequency of combat but also the activities of the armies when not actually on campaign, for war also included recruiting, planning, training, civil and political relations, supply and intelligence operations, communications, and all the rest of the minutia of maintaining armed forces in the field. It was simply waiting for the enemy to make a move. Washington spent about half of the War for Independence in the state, devoting most of his time and attention to these noncombat tasks. In addition, New Jersey commanded the lines of communication between New York and Philadelphia, and its roads and rivers were important to each side. Rebels and redcoats both tried to exploit the state's physical geography: the British tried to force major actions on the plains of central New Jersey, terrain suited to traditional European tactics, while Washington used the defensive landscapes of northern New Jersey to establish relatively secure base and headquarters areas.

The frequency and duration of military operations meant that military concerns intruded prominently into daily affairs. For almost eight years, war, or the prospect of war, was a fact of life, and residents learned to live with it and interacted routinely with the military. Local farms fed both armies, often involuntarily, and pillaging troops from both sides did enormous property damage. Civilians also supplied combatants with intelligence, helped with recruiting, and, among patriots, rotated in and out of the militia. Thus distinctions between soldiers and civilians often blurred, and civilians would be very much a part of the war effort.

Indeed, the military experience of New Jersey became a microcosm of the wider war. The conflict assumed such scope and complexity that it touched on virtually every military question raised in other theaters. Granted, New Jersey's location made it a battleground, but how did such factors as terrain, supply, and communications shape actual operations? How, for example, did the British cope with the tactical problems inherent in operations in the interior of the state? How did patriots counter British superiority in numbers, naval support, maté-riel, and experience? To what extent did civilians play a role in active operations? And how, of course, did these matters help explain the ultimate victory of patriot arms? A focus on New Jersey offers a broader understanding of the conflict, and this essay argues that to understand events in the "Cockpit of the Revolution" is to understand the military history of the Revolution generally.

Early Operations: Retreat and Revival

The war came to New Jersey through the happenstance of geography: it engulfed the state because of New Jersey's proximity to operations in and around New York City.[3] There were several early incidents in New Jersey, mostly militia brushes with British vessels or crews coming ashore to forage, all minor affairs. The real force of the war struck only in the summer of 1776. In August, the British landed on nearby Staten Island, and, beginning in September, General William Howe, the British commander in chief, launched assaults that successively drove Washington from New York City and its environs—and then across New Jersey. On December 8, the remnants of Washington's army crossed the Delaware River into the relative safety of Pennsylvania.

The rebel cause appeared on the verge of collapse. Washington was battered, and most local militia had scattered. Thousands of New Jersey residents had declared allegiance to the king, and some had taken up arms against the patriots. Even the state legislature had dispersed. In fact, the seeming lack of nerve and disaffection of patriots bothered Washington even more than General Howe. "I think our affairs," Washington wrote his brother,

> are in a very bad situation; not so much the apprehension of Genl. Howe's army, as from the defection of New York, Jerseys and Pennsylvania. In short, the conduct of the Jerseys has been most infamous. Instead of turning out to defend their country and affording aid to our Army, they are making their submissions as fast as they can. If they the Jerseys had given us any support, we might have made a stand at Hackensack and after that at Brunswick, but the few Militia that were in arms, disbanded themselves . . . and left the poor remains of our Army to make the best we could do of it.[4]

New Jersey, with its stores of produce, strategic location, and ambivalent revolutionaries, seemed secure for the crown.[5]

Yet the British had not finished off Washington's battered corps. Howe believed—with some reason—that the rebel army would largely disintegrate by spring. In his view, it was better to allow winter to run its destructive course with the rebels; he could clean up any pathetic remnants later. Thus, on December 13 the British general ordered his command into winter quarters. Detachments would hold key towns across central New Jersey—including New Brunswick, Princeton, Trenton, and Burlington—thereby maintaining security and communication. Howe admitted that these commands were too far apart to support one another; but he considered trouble very unlikely, and if there was any, he expected the garrisons to hold out until the arrival of reinforcements.[6] His decision constituted one of the greatest blunders of the war.

Howe had badly misread the situation. As the initial trauma of invasion faded, New Jersey patriots began to rebound. By mid-December, militia had engaged the British in some two dozen actions. Small enemy units venturing into the countryside did so at their peril, and even large bodies could run into trouble. On December 17, for example, at Hobarts Gap, militia stopped 800 redcoats short of Morristown.[7] (Royal success at the gap would have been disastrous for the Americans; at the very least, it would have denied the safe haven of the village [Morristown] to Washington's men after Trenton and Princeton. Patriot naval harassment prevented the British from establishing winter headquarters at Burlington, and when they moved inland to Bordentown, militia patrols kept them on alert. By late December, things were so bad around Trenton that the garrison commander, Colonel Johann Rall, needed an escort of 100 men with artillery support to get a dispatch through to Princeton. Comfortable in New York, Howe missed the import of this, but many of his field commanders in New Jersey were getting nervous.[8] The state was not pacified, the interior was dangerous, and the New Jersey militia, so scorned by Washington only a week before, had revived.

Patriot political authorities also recovered from the initial shock of invasion. Most New Jersey officials were able to maintain civil order, work with militia units in dealing with Tory activity, and retain contact with senior patriot military leaders. Patriot command and control remained functional, and resistance in New Jersey was increasingly well organized.[9] Popular support for continued resistance grew as well, spurred in part by reactions to the Royal Army. Troop conduct was egregious and alienated even many residents originally well-disposed toward the crown. Soldiers pillaged freely; farms and homes were looted, public buildings were damaged or destroyed, and there were incidents of personal violence and rape. Tabulated damage claims reached the modern equivalent of millions of dollars.[10] By late 1776, Howe had lost whatever chance he had to win New Jersey's hearts and minds.

The British commander also underestimated Washington. During the retreat, Washington had lost heavily to desertion, expired enlistments, and matériel shortages, but his army remained operational. Reinforcement and logistics efforts faltered but never collapsed. Even before crossing into Pennsylvania, the rebel general had been looking for a chance to strike back; once across the Delaware, he focused on plans for a counterattack.[11] Frantic efforts to rally reinforcements succeeded. Washington was no match for the British main body, but he scraped together enough of a force to target the isolated British detachment at Trenton. He planned the operation for Christmas night.

The plan almost misfired. Washington had wanted an attack in three columns, but weather and river conditions prevented this, and only the commander in chief's column of some 2,500 men got across the Delaware in force. He and his own column attacked by themselves and, aided by the fortunes of war, achieved complete tactical surprise. The Battle of Trenton was more a raid than a major engagement. The serious fighting lasted only forty-five minutes, but Hessian defeat was complete: Rall was mortally wounded, over 100 were killed or wounded, and another 918 fell prisoners. Washington lost only 3 wounded and 2 frozen to death during the initial advance.[12] Knowing the British would have to react, Washington quickly withdrew to Pennsylvania—but he had struck a startling blow.

He also had regained Howe's attention. Trenton was more an embarrassment than a major defeat, but Howe understood its impact on patriot morale—which was euphoric—and that it reflected a deteriorating military situation. Circumstances demanded a decisive response, and on January 2, three days after Washington had again occupied Trenton along Assunpink Creek, Howe dispatched Lord Cornwallis toward the village with some 6,000 men. Washington was in trouble; a British rush across the Assunpink Bridge could have pushed him into the Delaware River. But confronted with a rebel delaying action, Cornwallis reached Trenton only at dusk. When a halfhearted attempt at the bridge failed, he decided against a night action. He would "bag the fox" in the morning.[13] Thus for the second time in the campaign, a British general elected not to make a final thrust against a vulnerable rebel army.

The mistake was fully the equal of Howe's earlier decision to end the campaign. Daybreak found the Americans gone. In a classic *ruse de guerre*, Washington had left a few militia to keep campfires burning and make the noise of an army and then slipped away along an unguarded road. Early on January 3, just outside Princeton, his forces collided with some 700 redcoats and, after an initial check, overwhelmed them in a brief but violent action. Once again, Washington quickly left the field—and wisely, inasmuch as a furious Cornwallis had countermarched and was closing rapidly.[14] The patriot general also decided not to attempt a descent on New Brunswick and seize a lightly guarded British pay chest. His men were tired, and he headed out of harm's way; by January 7, his army was safely at Morristown. The so-called ten crucial days were over and, with them, perhaps Britain's best chance to win the war on the battlefield.

The Lessons of '76

The main British army, of course, remained undefeated—but it hardly mattered. The reverses at Trenton and Princeton left British commanders off balance, and unsure of Washington's next move, Howe gave up most of New Jersey. For the rest of the winter, the Royal Army held only a strip of territory between Perth Amboy and New Brunswick.

With Howe's withdrawal, patriot authorities quickly reasserted political control. The significance of this for the rest of the war was stark: the British army would command only the territory on which it stood. As the British moved on, the rebels, almost always hovering on their flanks, moved in and reestablished themselves. The courts, law enforcement, local markets, public records—including the land titles so vital to an agricultural economy—all remained in patriot hands. Without control of these critical social and political assets, the British stood little chance of rekindling any broad New Jersey allegiance to George III. They never did root out the rebel civil structure in New Jersey, a defeat as telling as any they suffered on the battlefield.

This failure sealed the loyalists' fate. With the British retreat, hundreds, and eventually thousands, of Tories who had come out for the king during the early days of the invasion were left to look to themselves. They stood no chance. The resurgence of patriot military and civil authority included a settling of accounts with the loyalists, who were crushed as a political force. In early 1777, for example, at Morristown, the Council of Safety condemned thirty-five loyalists taken in arms. Two Tory officers were duly hanged, at which point the committee put an offer to the remaining men: join their officers on the gallows or enlist in the Continental army. They enlisted.[15] In June of the same year, the state legislature passed the first of a series of acts allowing the condemnation and sales of Tory estates. The seizures struck at the economic base of loyalism, and hundreds of families lost everything, forcing many to seek protection behind British lines in New York.[16] Measures like these had the desired effect: they broke the back of loyalism as an effective threat to the Revolution. There was no pretense at allowing what might be termed "fair play" (or civil liberties, for that matter) for the Tories. This was a civil war, and loyalists were the internal enemy. Just as Whig families fled to avoid the British onslaught in late 1776, early 1777 found Tories trying to escape their patriot neighbors. It was a grim reversal of fortunes and demonstrated to loyalists everywhere that they were safe nowhere beyond the immediate presence of British troops.[17]

There was no effective counterrevolution in New Jersey. The loyalists fought on but never established an effective regional base to support a revival of royal political authority. Tories waged a persistent guerilla war, and some 2,450 served as regulars for the king, but they could not dislodge the Whig grip on the political apparatus of the state.[18] In the spring of 1777, the long-term importance of all of this may not have been fully apparent, but it was clear enough that New Jersey loyalists were as embittered and demoralized as their patriot neighbors were reanimated.

A New War: The Morristown Encampment and Its Consequences

As patriots and the British pondered the impact of the 1776 campaign, Washington took up quarters in the Arnold Tavern at Morristown. His choice of destinations was limited after Trenton and Princeton, and he settled on the town because it was relatively secure. The terrain favored the defensive. The town was on high ground, protected south and east by the Great Swamp and the Watchung Mountains. As an added precaution, troops built a hilltop redoubt close to the center of town. As there never was an attack, the post became known as Fort Nonsense, but it made good sense in early 1777.[19]

As a base area, Morristown was almost ideally located. Before the war, it was a hamlet of only 250 people, but the population was friendly, and a rebel political structure was firmly in place, a boon to army administration as it dealt with civilian authorities and state militia. Local farms were productive, a key factor in sustaining growing numbers of troops and animals. The town's location also facilitated communications. Morristown was situated to control new inland transport routes that ran from New England through New York State and northern New Jersey and hence to points south. It was also ideal for intelligence gathering. Units posted in the Watchung Mountains kept an eye on the British in the New Brunswick area, and those on the Hudson Palisades watched the enemy garrison in New York—and these outposts reported regularly to Morristown. In addition, the village screened approaches to New Jersey's nascent iron and gunpowder industries, resources increasingly helpful to patriot munitions supply.[20] Such a base was vital for a successful insurgency, and Morristown remained in service until 1782, earning informal status as military capital of the Revolution.

Washington made good use of his time at Morristown. Between January and April, he created a new Continental army able to fight a protracted war. The one-year enlistments of 1775 were gone, replaced by troops enrolled for three years or "for the war." All recruits received cash bounties of $20, and the "for-the-war" men were promised 100 acres of land.[21] In an agricultural world, 100 acres offered an entrée to yeoman status, a real inducement to the young or poor with little previous stake in society. The result was an army of rank and file largely from the lower socioeconomic strata, with a middle-class or wealthy officer corps.[22] The arrangement afforded Washington the promise of stable regiments, and over time he intended to train "a respectable army" capable of meeting the redcoats on equal terms.

Again, location helped. Suited to the defensive, Morristown also provided a staging point for offensive operations, and Washington was looking for small fights. Between January and April, patriots fought some eighty actions, mostly across from New York and around the strip of British-occupied territory between New Brunswick and Perth Amboy.[23] A primary goal was to keep the British out of the countryside and away from New Jersey's ample stores of food and forage. No one would refer to New Jersey as the "Garden State" until the nineteenth century, but the state was renowned for its agriculture, and Howe had intended to feed his army from local farms. But foraging parties frequently met opposition, and the British had no choice but to cover foragers with armed escorts, which drained resources and nerves.

Two examples illustrate the point. On February 8, no less than Lord Cornwallis marched from New Brunswick at the head of over 2,000 redcoats and Hessians. His target was the store of food and forage at Quibbletown (now in Piscataway Township). But a patriot attack killed and wounded over 60 men at the cost of 6 rebels dead and another 20 wounded. This was a high price for hay. Two weeks later, 1,500 troops on a foraging operation at Spanktown (modern Rahway) were attacked by 1,000 rebels who not only disrupted the foraging but punished the column all the way back to Perth Amboy. It was Napoleon who later famously noted that armies "traveled on their stomachs," but Washington was equally aware of the fact, and he made the British fight just to eat.[24] Without a battle-tested army, Washington had found a winning formula: "By keeping four or five hundred men well advanced," he wrote another officer, "we not only oblige them to forage with parties of 1,500 and 2,000 to cover, but every now and then, we give them a Smart Brush."[25] Hessian Captain Johann Ewald, who served in many of the foraging actions, thought much the same thing. The British army, he noted in his diary, "would have been gradually destroyed through this foraging."[26]

In the end, patriots won the "forage war."[27] Washington simply made the New Jersey countryside too dangerous, and for the British, the loss of the state as a granary was a major disaster, ultimately forcing British commissaries to import the bulk of their foodstuffs from Ireland, a hugely expensive and time-consuming operation. Transatlantic supply operations compelled one of the largest maritime efforts in British history, and the supply ships required naval escorts to ward off swarms of American privateers. Consequently, the Royal Navy, one of the real advantages the British enjoyed over the rebels, had to divert considerable strength from other operations.[28] Thus the cumulative effect of small battles such as Spanktown and Quibbletown—and scores of others—had far-reaching implications.

The forage war also served another important purpose. The practice of sending small units into harm's way provided invaluable field experience; troops learned the practical skills of soldiering even as Washington reorganized the army. By late spring, when he was ready to consider more ambitious operations, a significant proportion of the men had seen at least some action. When the general moved south in April and May, his army was not entirely green.

1777: Middlebrook and After

Success at Morristown allowed Washington to confront the British more directly in the spring. Again, he enjoyed the advantage of location, shifting his base of operations to the Watchung Mountains at Middlebrook. Washington was on excellent defensive terrain and virtually dared Howe to come after him.[29] Perhaps recalling the horror of Bunker Hill, the royal commander never did.

Instead, Howe tried to lure Washington down—but the patriot chief refused to be lured. Once more, location told against the British. Howe's plans for 1777 called for a strike on Philadelphia, and the shortest route was across New Jersey. But such a march would force him to cross the Delaware, perhaps in the face of Washington's army. He could not risk this. Thus in mid-June, in a final effort to bring the rebels to battle, he feigned an evacuation of New Jersey, hoping Washington would come down from the hills. Washington reacted cautiously, noting that whatever the British were doing, they had retained their artillery.

Thus when Howe turned to fight on June 26, he met only advanced American detachments. The day saw a series of sharp engagements between Oak Tree, Scotch Plains, and Westfield. But when Washington declined a general action and pulled back to the Watchungs, Howe quit the state.[30]

Major consequences followed. Refusing to march across New Jersey, Howe went to Pennsylvania by sea. Landing at the head of Chesapeake Bay in late August, he took until mid-September to break through Washington's troops (who had plenty of time to march from New Jersey) and into Philadelphia.[31] Yet holding the city depended on the ability to feed and supply the army, and after his experience in New Jersey, Howe understood the problems inherent in local foraging. Thus the British needed control of the Delaware River, allowing navy transports to supply the city. Until river navigation was secure, Philadelphia was not.[32]

This meant more fighting, as two rebel forts commanded the river. Fort Mifflin sat on Mud Island, just off the Pennsylvania mainland; across from Fort Mifflin was Fort Mercer, in Red Bank, New Jersey.* On October 19, British artillery opened on Fort Mifflin, and on October 22 some 2,000 Hessians assaulted Fort Mercer. It was a slaughter: firing from concealed positions, the Continentals killed or wounded 400.[33] Fort Mercer held out until November, abandoned only after the evacuation of Fort Mifflin made the New Jersey post untenable. The British had won the Delaware and seemingly the campaign. But it was a costly victory: the fighting had consumed over a quarter of Howe's effective strength.[34]

The delays in taking Philadelphia helped doom another British army. Even as Howe was dealing with Forts Mifflin and Mercer, the troops of General John Burgoyne were coming to grief at Saratoga, New York. Howe's orders from London never specifically required him to assist Burgoyne, but his operations in Pennsylvania concluded at so late a date as to preclude a supporting deployment. Burgoyne was lost, and soon afterward the French recognized American independence and declared war on Britain. What had begun as a colonial rebellion had become an international war—a godsend to the Americans.

Thus the period from January to June 1777 marked an extraordinary passage in arms. Washington rebuilt the Continental army as a credible force and worked effectively with militia and civilian authorities to maintain control of the countryside. He used locations at

---

*Editor's note: There are two Red Banks in New Jersey: this one on the lower Delaware River and another in Monmouth County.

Morristown and Middlebrook to offset superior British numbers and experience, and without risking a major battle, he compelled the British to commit vast and unanticipated resources to feed themselves and their animals. He made it too dangerous for the British to leave their garrisons in anything but major force, and he kept them off balance tactically as well as strategically. Finally, he cost the British invaluable time during the spring, a delay with disastrous consequences for the royal cause. True, he lost Philadelphia, a blow to rebel pride—but in the end it hardly mattered. Later in the war, notably in the Yorktown campaign, Washington certainly equaled his performance in the first half of 1777—but he never surpassed it.

The Monmouth Campaign and American Military Maturity

The French declaration of war altered the military equation. Confronted with a widening war, the British realized that they could not fight everywhere. Bitterly, they elected to forgo pursuit of a military decision in the North, redeploy troops to protect vital Caribbean colonies, and invade the southern states. The crown hoped that southern Tories would rally in numbers sufficient to restore royal authority. The new strategy meant abandoning Philadelphia. But the Royal Navy lacked the transports to evacuate the entire army and terrified loyalists, who were well aware of what had happened to New Jersey Tories the previous year. Thus, on June 18, 1778, the new British commander in chief, General Henry Clinton, began to march 12,000 troops and camp followers overland to New York—directly across New Jersey.[35]

The march brought on the longest single day of fighting of the entire war. Clinton reached Freehold, in Monmouth County, only on June 26; poor roads, hot and rainy weather, and patriot harassment had slowed his movement, and the redcoat army needed a rest. Washington, breaking camp directly from his winter quarters at Valley Forge, had followed the British into New Jersey. Clinton had resumed his trek early on June 28, when the Continental vanguard, under Charles Lee, struck his rear. A strong counterattacked pressed Lee, but Washington brought up the main army by midday, and the lines stabilized after bitter fighting. The afternoon was spent in a spectacular cannonade and localized American attacks, all in brutal heat. The battle was a tactical draw, although Clinton had the worst of it. That night, Clinton broke off and eventually got his army safely back to New York.

The Battle of Monmouth was an important benchmark in the war, a measure of rebel progress in arms. Changes effected the previous winter at Valley Forge had vastly improved the Continental army. French arms and equipment reached the army in quantity, and training improved under the tutelage of General Frederick von Steuben. Recruiting operations began to replenish depleted ranks, and some states, including New Jersey, even sent draftees to the Continental regiments. The artillery arm reorganized, and quarter-master operations, placed in the capable hands of General Nathaniel Greene, got supplies moving to camp. When it became clear that a New Jersey campaign was a possibility, Greene stockpiled supplies along probable lines of March. The army that broke camp in June 1778 was a rejuvenated force.

Monmouth was the first test of the new Continentals, and they did well against the best regiments in the British army. There were still serious problems. Field communications and resupply were not on a par with the British, there were too few mounted troops, and Washington's staff still lacked experience in conducting large-scale operations.[36] But on the whole, the Continentals were a force to reckon with at Monmouth, and even the British conceded as much. The battle marked the "coming of age" of the Continental army—a maturing of the force Washington had begun to build at Morristown in early 1777.

Monmouth also reflected the civilian commitment to the war. In 1776, the effects of the first British invasion were devastating: much of the militia dispersed, residents fled in alarm, many loyalists came out to declare for the king, and state government scattered. The story was different in 1778. Militia rallied and operated effectively with the Continentals, few Tories came out, and state government followed events carefully. Most civilians were hostile to the invaders. They hid valuables and drove livestock into the woods and swamps, passed information on British movements to militia and Continental troops, and assisted enemy deserters. Some picked up weapons and joined the fight. By 1778, the British faced a civilian population willing to support rebel troops while denying vital intelligence, supplies, and moral support to the crown. Even with an enemy army in their midst, state patriots remained firmly in political and civil control. In military terms, the Monmouth campaign was an important passage of arms, but in addition, it was a telling measure of the extent to which New Jersey was lost to the empire.

The Long War: Skirmishes, Raids, and Exhaustion to 1783

In the aftermath of Monmouth, the focus of active operations shifted to the South, although this did not diminish the significance of New Jersey's military role. After a mild winter at Middlebrook in 1778–1779, the army endured the appalling 1779–1780 winter—the coldest ever recorded—at Morristown. This experience shook the army profoundly.

Snows were four to six feet deep; pay was five months late; firewood, food, and forage were scant. Deteriorating rebel finances exacerbated problems—the army had no money to purchase local produce—and some troops pillaged just to survive. By January 1780, Washington had to impress supplies and take stern measures to protect civilian property from desperate soldiers. By spring, troop protests verged on mutiny.[37] Open revolt flared the following winter. On New Year's Day 1781, the Pennsylvania line mutinied at Morristown, and the troops marched for Philadelphia to demand satisfaction from Congress. Emissaries met them at Trenton, however, and most men returned to duty with promises of better conditions and, in some cases, discharges. Shortly thereafter, Washington put down rebellious New Jersey Continentals at Pompton, shooting two ringleaders.[38] It was as close as the army had come to dissolving since the darkest days of 1776.

Yet these episodes, however bitter, served to underscore the value of New Jersey's secure location. Even in the bleak winter of 1780, there was plenty of food in the state, and when Washington impressed it, he was able to work through established civil authorities. This expedited the process and limited the political damage inherent in a blunt military seizure of private property.[39] Nor were the British able to take advantage of the mutinies. In 1780 and 1781, Morristown's protected location kept them from learning the full scope of patriot difficulties until it was too late to act. In late August and early September of 1781, the British also missed the import of a rapid and skillfully disguised march across the state. Continental and French troops moved south from positions around New York and Rhode Island to arrive in Virginia in October—to trap Cornwallis at Yorktown.[40] Washington and French general the Comte de Rochambeau made good use of New Jersey's interior communications routes. Even when not a battlefield, New Jersey remained vital ground.

Until the end, however, the war of skirmishes and raids continued in New Jersey. After Monmouth—that is, after the end of major combat—the state saw 266 small-scale incidents.[41] Some were well-planned raids against specific targets—blockhouses, prominent individuals, forage operations, and the like—while others were the result of rival groups stumbling across one another. Casualties were usually minimal. In January 1779, for example, the *New Jersey Gazette* reported the death of three "Pine-Banditti" at the hands of Monmouth County militia; in May 1781, militia and Tories skirmished in Shrewsbury with no known casualties.[42] In aggregate, however, hundreds were killed, wounded, or captured—hardly "small" losses in a state with fewer than 130,000 residents.

Some of these operations were larger. In 1779, 400 Continentals stormed the British outpost on Paulus Hook (modern Jersey City), taking 158 prisoners and killing or wounding another 50. The following year, 400 Hessians struck rebel positions at Hoppertown in Bergen County, killing or capturing some 49 men.[43] But these were raids, never intended to capture and hold territory or settle a decisive point. As such, they were of a piece with rest of the local hit-and-run actions. The northern war had devolved into a grinding series of small-unit and guerrilla operations; such wars usually ended through attrition and exhaustion rather than a knockout blow, and neither side was capable of throwing such a punch.

The only exception to the "desultory war," as Washington termed it, came in 1780. In June, British commanders in New York learned of the Continental near-mutiny at Morristown. Unsure of what was really happening, they launched a reconnaissance in force into New Jersey. On June 7, about 5,000 British and Hessians drove inland toward Springfield. Continental and militia resistance stopped them at Connecticut Farms (now Union), which the British burned before pulling back to Elizabethtown. On June 23, General Clinton, just returned from the invasion of the Carolinas, reinforced the troops and sent them in again. With luck, they could force Hobarts Gap, as they had failed to do in 1776, and get to Morristown. Tough opposition stopped them at Springfield, which they also burned before pulling out for good—harassed virtually every step of the way by infuriated local militia.[44] It was the last major British incursion into the state.

The Battle of Springfield was instructive. By 1780, property damage, a shattered economy, and the near-constant threat of enemy raids had left New Jersey residents profoundly war-weary. Yet this did the British little good. The burning of Connecticut Farms and Springfield reflected their understanding that civilian New Jersey was against them and that raids, no matter how severe, would not dislodge patriot authority. They also knew that these same civilians were the source of the militia that sniped at their flanks. Enough militia came out to cooperate with the Continental regulars to make a penetration of the state interior prohibitively expensive. The British could still handle the patriot regulars, but they could not wage war successfully against a war-wise populace.

The naval war also lost none of its intensity. Between late June 1778 and 1783, there were 108 engagements on New Jersey's rivers or off its immediate coasts.[45] Many of these actions were privateer assaults on British shipping bound in and out of nearby New York, and predations were a galling and expensive drain on the British merchant fleet. In 1777 alone, privateer operations drove up marine insurance rates 20 percent, and captured goods became important to the patriot war effort and to the civilian economy. British attempts to strike at the privateers also motivated several shore engagements, including a large attack in 1778 on General Casimir Pulaski's cavalry at Osborne (or Minnock) Island.[46] To the end of the war, however, New Jersey's privateers were a thorn in the British side.

The partisan warfare, ashore or afloat, was intertwined with New Jersey's civil war. Unable to reestablish themselves in their home state, refugee Tories raided actively from New York. Many of their operations came under the aegis of the Board of Associated Loyalists, headed by New Jersey's deposed royal governor, William Franklin. They fought like what they were: men with nothing left to lose. Black troops, often escaped New Jersey slaves, were active participants, sometimes in ventures against the neighborhoods of former masters.[47] The civil aspect of the war was the most likely to target specific civilians, and it engendered some of the deepest bitterness of the era.

"The Banks of the Delaware": Retrospection on a War

In the end, failure to hold and pacify New Jersey, or any substantial part of it, weighed heavily against the British war effort. With the British unable to maintain a significant presence in the state, their hopes of a rebel political collapse never materialized. Indeed, the patriot civil structure proved resilient even during the darkest periods of the war, and Whig political authority only consolidated as the war lengthened. This proved of critical importance to the military effort. Firmly in place, local Whig committees and courts dealt with suspected Tories and offered a constant source of vigilance against counterrevolution. Loyalists had no chance to reassert the authority of the crown in New Jersey. Civilian officials also worked with Continental military authorities in matters of civil-military relations, including Continental recruiting and commissary operations. The assistance rendered in impressing supplies for the army in 1780 was a case in point. None of this worked perfectly everywhere or all of the time—but civil authority, even when embattled, kept the state in the war.[48]

Significantly, the political infrastructure lay in back of the militia— the armed embodiment of the civil structure. Militia participation was never complete or equitable: perhaps 30 percent of the state's eligible manpower was lost to loyalism or Quaker pacifism, and militia laws allowed the well-to-do to hire substitutes to serve for them.[49] There also were shirkers who did their best to avoid their tours of duty, and there were frequent complaints about dilatory militia responses in times of crises. Thus Governor William Livingston complained that military burdens fell disproportionately on the shoulders of the "willing."[50] But war is seldom fair, and enough men did serve to make the militia effective. Never intended to fight major battles—that was obvious in November 1776—the militia learned to handle local tasks admirably. It bore the brunt of the "desultory war" of skirmishes and raids, security patrolling and intelligence gathering, and intimidation of loyalists. Militiamen eventually learned to work well with the patriot regulars, and they did good service at Monmouth, Springfield, and smaller operations with the Continentals. To a considerable degree, then, New Jersey became a society in arms and, with Washington's regular army, a full military partner in holding the state for the Revolution. It was this partnership that won the war.

Skillful patriot use of New Jersey's location and terrain contributed as well. Protected positions at Morristown and Middlebrook provided the secure bases necessary to support organizational as well as operational missions. Washington used them to counter British numbers and assume the posture of a "force in being"—perhaps not strong enough to challenge the redcoats directly but too strong to ignore. Certainly Howe considered Washington too strong to attack on good defensive ground or to leave in his rear; he could never entice Washington into the open for a decisive battle in New Jersey, even as the rebel general used terrain and position to support persistent and damaging "brushes" with the enemy without risking a major defeat. Location helped level the playing field, which advantaged only the rebels.

The same was true of New Jersey's strategic interior. In patriot hands, the interior was an invaluable sanctuary, of which Morristown was the paramount example. This region also offered relatively secure communications, including the best links between the northern and southern colonies, which was amply demonstrated in the march of Washington and Rochambeau to Yorktown. In addition, it protected many of New Jersey's contested farms, which contributed far more to patriot than to British commissaries—again, a fact with serious and adverse consequences for the crown.

No British commander found the key to operations in the New Jersey interior. This was the lesson of scores of small battles and of some larger ones such as Hobarts Gap and Springfield. British forces could pass through the state—Clinton proved that in 1778—but not without moving in major force, not without a fight, and not with any intention of lingering. This lesson was confirmed repeatedly elsewhere during the rest of the war. Small enemy forces were always at risk, and far from bases of supply, reinforcement, or naval support, even sizeable British formations would come to grief on battlefields across the colonies. In varying degrees, Bennington, King's Mountain, and, in perhaps the best examples, Saratoga and Yorktown were the New Jersey experience writ large. The American interior was dangerous and the British never learned to tame it.

The last Continental troops filed out of the Morristown encampment on August 29, 1782 (fittingly, they were from the New Jersey Brigade).[51] It was the last of many marches through the state, so many that New Jersey has earned informal recognition as the "Crossroads of the American Revolution." In their various marches, the British never subdued New Jersey, but they always understood its military importance. No one was clearer on this than Lord Cornwallis. At a social moment after his surrender at Yorktown, he was gracious and candid enough to offer a toast to Washington: "And when the illustrious part your Excellency has borne in this long and laborious contest becomes matter of history, fame will gather your brightest laurels rather from the banks of the Delaware than from those of the Chesapeake."[52]

Notes

1. For example, Leonard Lundin, *Cockpit of the Revolution: The War for Independence in New Jersey* (Princeton, N.J.: Princeton University Press, 1940).

2. Calculating the precise number of the battles and skirmishes is probably impossible: not all records of the war have survived, and not all actions were recorded. The count of over 600 (actually 607) engagements or incidents is found in David C. Munn, comp., *Battles and Skirmishes of the American Revolution in New Jersey* (Trenton, N.J.: Department of Environmental Protection, Bureau of Geology and Topography, 1976). Munn counted every military incident and based his tally on detailed archival and local historical sources. The lower figure is from Howard Peckham, *The Toll of Independence* (Chicago: University Press, 1974) 125, 141. This is a valuable source and accurate for the engagements reported, but it looks at the national scene and is based on a much narrower examination of New Jersey sources. In yet another count, the National Park Service database of Revolutionary War actions also lists 296 actions in New Jersey (National Park Service, *Crossroads of the American Revolution in New Jersey: Special Resource Study* [Philadelphia: U.S. Department of the Interior, National Park Service, Philadelphia Support Office, 2002], 5). There is no disagreement, however, on the fact that New Jersey was the site of more engagements than any other state. Munn's *Baffles and Skirmishes* is the most comprehensive and reliable source, however, and is cited most often in this essay.

3. For overviews of military operations in New Jersey, see Alfred Hoyt Bill, *New Jersey and the Revolutionary War* (Princeton, N.J.: D. Van Nostrand, 1964); and Lewis F. Owen, *The Revolutionary Struggle in New Jersey, 1776–1783* (Trenton: New Jersey Historical Commission, 1975).

4. Washington to John Augustine Washington, December 18, 1776, John C. Fitzpatrick, ed., *The Writings of George Washington* (Washington, D.C.: U.S. Government Printing Office, 1931–1944), 6:397–398.

5. Howe was pleased with the campaign; see Ira D. Gruber, *The Howe Brothers and the American Revolution* (New York: Athenaeum, 1972), 148–149; and Troyer Steele Anderson, *The Command of the Howe Brothers during the American Revolution* (New York: Oxford University Press, 1936), 204–209.

6. Howe is quoted at length on this point in Anderson, *The Command of The Howe Brothers*, 206.

7. Mark Edward Lender, "Small Battles Won: New Jersey and the Patriot Military Revival," *New Jersey Heritage* 1 (2002): 33–34.

8. Ibid., 34–35.

9. While he marshaled his forces in Pennsylvania, for example, Washington was able to communicate with civil, militia, and Continental officers in the state. See Washington's detailed letter of December 12, 1776, to New Jersey militia general Philemon Dickinson, then near Trenton (Fitzpatrick, *The Writings of George Washington*, 6:358). Washington sent equally explicit instructions to Continental general William Maxwell at Morristown on December 21, 1776 (ibid., 6:414–416). On December 20, 1776, he also informed the president of Congress that he wanted Maxwell "to harass and annoy the Enemy in their Quarters and cut off their Convoys" (ibid., 6:407).

10. Patriot rank and file did their share of plundering as well but not on a scale approaching British activity. Inventories of damages were tallied under a law of December 1781 (Acts of the . . . General Assembly of the State of New Jersey) and are now in the New Jersey State Archives as "Damages by the British Army, 1776–1782" and "Damages by the American Army, 1776–1782."

11. In his letter to his brother of December 18, 1776, Washington noted that he had wanted to stand at Hackensack or at New Brunswick (Fitzpatrick, *The Writings of George Washington*, 6:398). On December 7, even as his army had begun to cross the Delaware into Pennsylvania, Washington led a column back toward Princeton, pulling back only when intelligence informed him that the British were advancing in strength (ibid., 6:335–336).

12. Washington related his account of the Trenton action in a letter to General Alexander McDougall on December 28,1776: "I crossed over to Jersey on the Evening of the 25th about nine Miles above Trenton with upwards of 2000 Men and attacked three Regiments of Hessians, consisting of 1500 Men about 8 o'clock next Morning. Our Men pushed on with such rapidity, that they soon captured four pieces of Cannon out of Six, Surrounded the Enemy, and obliged 30 Officers and 886 privates to lay down their Arms without firing a Shot. Our loss was only two Officers and two or three privates wounded" (ibid., 6:448). The standard history of the battle is William S. Stryker, *The Battles of Trenton and Princeton* (1898; repr., Trenton, N.J.: Old Barracks Association, 2001). For a briefer account that emphasizes the element of chance in the outcome at Trenton, see Mark Edward Lender, "Reversals of Fortune: The Trenton and Princeton Campaign of 1776–1777," *New Jersey Heritage* 1 (2002): 17–29; Trenton casualties are noted on 25.

13. However prosaic and however fixed in legend, there is little evidence that Cornwallis actually used the term. What is certain is his belief that Washington would still be across Assunpink Creek on the morning of January 3. See Don Higginbotham, *The War of American Independence: Military Attitudes, Policies, and Practice, 1763–1789* (New York: Macmillan, 1971), 169; and Stryker, *The Battles of Trenton and Princeton*, 268–269.

14. Washington's account of the Assunpink and Princeton operations is in Washington to the President of Congress, January 5, 1777, Fitzpatrick, *The Writings of George Washington*, 6:467–470.

15. Andrew M. Sherman, *Historic Morristown, New Jersey: The Story of Its First Century* (Morristown, N.J.: Howard Publishing, 1905), 248–249. Records of the actual trial, and a similar Council of Safety proceeding at Morristown, are in *New Jersey v. James Hiss* to *New Jersey w. John Parks*, Morris County Court of Oyer and Terminer, Minutes, Boxed MSS, New Jersey State Library [now in New Jersey State Archives]; Military Record of Captain Moses Estey [copy of original], New Jersey Department of Defense MSS, New Jersey State Archives. According to available records, these "Tory Continentals" served with records no less distinguished than those of soldiers enlisted under more "patriotic" circumstances. Troop service records are in Revolutionary Veterans File, New Jersey Department of Defense MSS, and New Jersey State Archives.

16. Dennis P. Ryan, *New Jersey's Loyalists*, vol. 20 of *New Jersey's Revolutionary Experience* (Trenton: New Jersey Historical Commission, 1975), 18–19.

17. On the fate of the Tories, see ibid., 23–26. In February 1776, the same lesson was learned in bloody fashion at Moore's Creek Bridge in North Carolina, an engagement that broke early loyalist activity in the South as decisively as the New Jersey experience did in the North. See Christopher Ward, *The War of the Revolution*, 2 vols. (New York: Macmillan, 1952), 1:663–664.

18. This is not to say that loyalists did not maintain a foothold in New Jersey. They garrisoned Sandy Hook for most of the war, and there was a Tory post on Paulus Hook in modern Jersey City. Unlike the patriot base at Morristown, however, these lodgments never served as secure areas covering civil administration or as depots or encampments for major military formations intended to take and hold territory. The Tory regulars served under Cortlandt Skinner, the last royal attorney general of New Jersey, turned British brigadier. They were tough troops, and they campaigned in theaters from the Middle colonies to the South. After the war, most survivors found new homes in Canada. Their defeat stemmed from no lack of courage. There were the six regiments of Skinner's Greens, so called because of their green uniforms. The Continental army seldom boasted more than three New Jersey regiments. The record of Skinner's regiments is traced in Paul H. Smith, "New Jersey Loyalists and the British 'Provincial' Corps in the War of Independence," *New Jersey History* 87 (1969): 69–78; and William S. Stryker, *The New Jersey Volunteers in the Revolutionary War* (Trenton, N.J.: Naar, Day and Naar, 1887).

19. A good overview of Morristown as a headquarters and encampment, including its advantageous location, is in Bruce W. Stewart, *Morristown: A Crucible of the American Revolution*, vol. 3 of *New Jersey's Revolutionary Experience* (Trenton: New Jersey Historical Commission, 1975).

20. On iron production, see David L. Salay, "Production of War Material in New Jersey During the Revolutionary War," in *New Jersey in the American Revolution III: Papers Presented at the Seventh New Jersey History Symposium, 1975*, ed. William C. Wright (Trenton: New Jersey Historical Commission, 1976), 13–16. At the time of Washington's arrival, Morristown also had the only powder mill in New Jersey (Fred Bartenstein and Isabel Bartenstein, *A Report on New Jersey's Revolutionary Powder Mill* [Morristown, N.J.: Morris County Historical Society, 1975]).

21. Worthington C. Ford et al., eds., *Journals of the Continental Congress, 1774–1789*, 34 vols. (Washington, D.C.: Library of Congress, 1904–1937), 5:762–763.

22. James Kirby Martin and Mark Edward Lender, *A Respectable Army: Be Military Origins of the Republic, 1763–1789* (Arlington Heights, Ill.: Harlan Davidson, 1982), 90–92.

23. David C. Munn, comp., *Battles and Skirmishes of the American Revolution in New Jersey* (Trenton: Department of Environmental Protection, Bureau of Geology and Topography, State of New Jersey, ca. 1976), 127–128.

24. Operations to prevent British foraging also served to preserve New Jersey food and forage supplies for patriot forces. In fact, the Americans at Morristown and other points had enough food during 1777.

25. Fitzpatrick, *The Writings of George Washington*, 7:96–97.

26. Johann Ewald, *Diary of the American War: A Hessian Journal*, trans. and ed. Joseph P. Tustin (New Haven, Conn.: Yale University Press, 1979), 55.

27. Credit for the term goes to Jared C. Lobdell, "Six Generals Gather Forage: The Engagement at Quibbletown, 1777," *New Jersey History* 102 (1984): 35.

28. David Syrett, *Shipping and the American War, 1775–83: A Study of British Transport Organization* (London: University of London, Athlone Press, 1970).

29. Martin and Lender, *A Respectable Army*, 80–81.

30. Accounts of why Howe chose not to march across New Jersey vary; see Gruber, *The Howe Brothers*, 198; and Anderson, *The Command of the Howe Brothers*, 238. For Howe's account, see William Howe, *The Narrative of Lieut. Gen. Sir William Howe in a Committee of the House of Commons . . .*, 2nd ed. (London: printed by H. Baldwin, 1779).

31. For the Philadelphia campaign, see Martin and Lender, *A Respectable Army*, 80–83. Washington used the New Jersey transportation network to reach Philadelphia long before Howe.

32. Washington saw the holding of the river forts as critical. "Gen'l Howe's Situation in Philadelphia will not be the most agreeable; for if his supplies can be stopped by water, it may easily be done by land." He dared to "hope that the acquisition of Philadelphia may instead of his good fortune; prove his [Howe's] ruin" (Fitzpatrick, *The Writings of George Washington*, 9:422–423).

33. For a graphic description of the fight, see Frank H. Stewart, *History of the Battle of Red Bank* (Woodbury, N.J.: Board of Chosen Freeholders of Gloucester County, 1927).

34. The definitive account of the defense of the river forts is John W. Jackson, *The*

Pennsylvania Navy, 1775–1781: The Defense of the Delaware (New Brunswick, N.J.: Rutgers University Press, 1971); for a shorter version, see Mark Edward Lender, *The River War: The Fight for the Delaware, 1777* (Trenton: New Jersey Historical Commission, 1979).

35. Although dated, the standard account of the Monmouth campaign remains William S. Stryker, *The Battle of Monmouth*, ed. William Starr Myers (Princeton, N.J.: Princeton University Press, 1927).

36. As a result of poor staff work, for example, a major patriot contingent under General Daniel Morgan, in position on the exposed enemy right and within sound of the guns on June 28, never got into the fight. Redcoat officers were still better at handling large commands in complex operations.

37. Martin and Lender, *A Respectable Army*, 161.

38. The full story of the Pennsylvania and New Jersey mutinies is in Carl Van Doren, *Mutiny in January* (New York: Viking, 1943).

39. "Instructions to Officers to Collect Provisions," January 8, 1780, Fitzpatrick, *The Writings of George Washington*,17:360–362; Washington to the Magistrates of New Jersey, January 8,1780, ibid., 17:62- 65.

40. On the precise march routes, see National Park Service, *Crossroads of the American Revolution*, 26.

41. This total is tabulated from the chronological list of engagements in Munn, *Battles and Skirmishes*, 132–141.

42. *New Jersey Gazette*, February 3, 1779, *New Jersey Archives*, 2nd ser., 5:264–265.

43. Munn, *Battles and Skirmishes*, 81; Peckham, *The Toll of Independence*, 55, 69; detail on the skirmishing around Hoppertown is in Adrian C. Leiby, *The Revolutionary War in the Hackensack Valley: The Jersey Dutch and the Neutral Ground* (New Brunswick, N.J.: Rutgers University Press, 1980), 246–251.

44. Thomas Fleming, *The Forgotten Victory: The Battle for New Jersey, 1780* (New York: Reader's Digest Press, 1973). Ewald, the Hessian jaeger captain, thought that the militia was especially effective at Springfield; see his *Diary*, 244–246.

45. Tabulated from the chronological list of engagements or incidents in Munn, *Battles and Skirmishes of the American Revolution*, 132–141. Not all of these encounters involved shooting, but the seizure of an enemy vessel driven ashore by weather or run aground was still of military importance.

46. Franklin W. Kemp, *A Nest of Rebel Pirates* (Batsto, N.J., Batsto Citizens Committee, 1966), 9, 47–50; *Political Magazine and Parliamentary, Naval, Military, and Literary Journal*, January 1761, 60, quoted in ibid., 103.

47. On loyalist African American combatants, see Frances D. Pingeon, *Blacks in the Revolutionary Era*, vol. 14 of New Jersey's Revolutionary Experience series (Trenton: New Jersey Historical Commission, 1975), 21–23; for a specific example of a raid involving black loyalists, see Clement Alexander Price, *Freedom Not Far Distant: A Documentary History of Afro-Americans in New Jersey* (Newark: New Jersey Historical Society, 1980), 69.

48. This is the general conclusion of Bernstein, "New Jersey in the American Revolution."

49. Mark Edward Lender, "The Conscripted Line: The Draft in Revolutionary New Jersey," *New Jersey History* 103 (1985): 25.

50. *Votes and Proceedings of the General Assembly of the State New Jersey*, August–October 1777, 159–160.

51. B. Stewart, *Morristown*, 23.

52. Quoted in National Park Service, *Crossroads of the American Revolution*, 25.

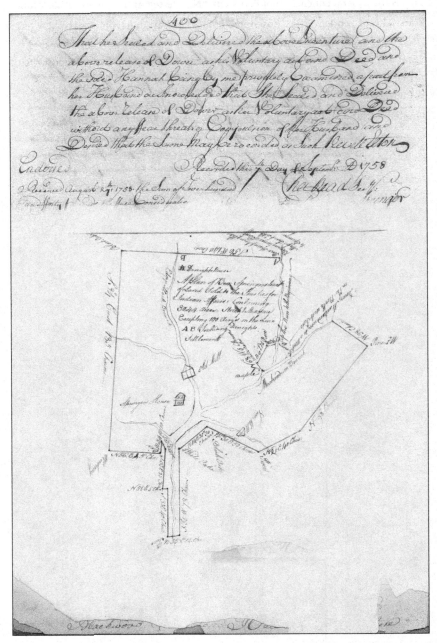

During the French and Indian War, New Jersey created a reservation for the Delaware who remained in the colony. By 1800 few were still there; they then arranged to move to New York to join with the Stockbridge Indians. Original Survey of the Brotherton Indian Reservation, Burlington County, New Jersey, ca. 1758. New Jersey State Archives, Department of State.

4

Ever since the American Revolution, historians have disagreed on its causes and consequences. In the twentieth century this disagreement became a split over emphasizing consensus or conflict, economic interests or ideology. The disputes continue even as each generation has focused on different aspects of what happened. In *The History of Political Parties in the Province of New York, 1760–1776* (1909), Carl Becker postulated that two simultaneous revolutions occurred in America, the first against England, and the second based on economic interests, over who should rule at home—conservatives or radicals, wealthy property owners and merchants, or poorer farmers and craftsmen. Becker's ideas were later applied to an examination of the war's effects by J. Franklin Jameson in *The American Revolution Considered as a Social Movement* (1926). Jameson argued that the Revolution brought greater democracy and significant changes in four areas—the "status" of people, land ownership, commerce, and thought. In his view the Revolutionary conflict produced considerable change.

For those historians who instead have seen continuity as the more important thread in American history, the Revolution was one stitch in an ongoing seam. Change occurred gradually in colonial America. Considerable "democracy" as well as basic political premises existed both before and after the Revolution. The conflict was primarily with England, and American aims were "conservative," not radical, because the colonists' main objective was to protect their existing "rights as Englishmen."

The disagreement over how much and what kind of change the Revolution brought was heightened from the 1960s on by the increasing interest of scholars in studying history from the bottom up. American history had long been the story of upper-class white males, while the society itself was heterogeneous from the start. Social historians were concerned with the actions of "inarticulate" people, those who left no written record, had been ignored while those of "great men," the wealthy upper classes who left a trail of manuscript letters, pamphlets, newspaper articles, and other documents, were excessively studied. The imbalance thus distorted the account of what had actually happened in the past.

To determine whether the American Revolution conserved what already existed or brought radical changes, social historians have urged the necessity of examining the lives of everyday people (poor farmers, laborers, mariners), as well as those usually excluded from the political arena (African Americans, women, and American Indians). Adding these groups to the mix changed the perspective. Despite the claim in the Declaration of Independence that all individuals were "created equal," this was not how these groups were treated at the time. The question has then becomes what in their lives changed (and what did not), when, and how rapidly. The chapter that follows looks at the experience of the Delaware, often called Lenape, Indians of New Jersey, and the ways in which they were impacted by the Revolution. This provides another lens through which to examine the consequences of the Revolution, and adds another issue to the discussion. A later chapter will look at blacks; include women, and for all three groups the question becomes who in the end benefited from the Revolution, and who did not?

Americans tend to think of the Revolution, despite all the devastation of the war, as having positive results; after all, it created their nation. But recent scholars looking at the impact of the Revolution on Indian groups have seen it as a disaster. Collin Calloway in *The Revolution in Indian Country* (1995) argued that the war was a "no-win situation." It became a civil war within some native communities as they divided over whether to remain neutral (often not possible) or join with the British or Americans. On the frontier it became a "total war" as (usually) patriot forces burned corn and destroyed villages. In the end, those who fought with the British, the larger number of Indians, shared in the defeat and lost their lands, while those who sided with the patriots "found that republican blessings were reserved for white Americans." After the war settlers moved west in larger numbers, while treaties took Indian lands, forcing one group after another farther west, impacting other tribes.

By the time of the Revolution there were few Indians left in New Jersey. In 1740 they are estimated to have been less than one percent of the population. Most of those who remained through the Revolution had left by 1800, or blended into the general population. When did New Jersey's Indians leave and why? Was it before, during, or after the Revolution? During the Revolution, Lorraine Williams notes, the Delaware in New Jersey and elsewhere were "caught in the middle." In what sense? And in the end does she see what happened to Indians in and from New Jersey as a total disaster?

Historians have given a number of explanations for the fate of Native

Americans. First is that the ideology of the Revolution, the emphasis on republicanism, was at the root of their treatment. It placed great importance on an individual's independence but placed blacks (most of whom were slaves), women (who were usually legally dependent on fathers and then husbands), and Indians (seen as "savages") in a dependent category. A second explanation is that the long history of warfare in the colonial period, especially along the frontier, resulted in fear and distrust. This was exacerbated in the Revolution by British use of native fighters. Third was the insatiable European-American desire for land, and their prejudiced view that Indians did not really use it. Which of these explanations help understand what happened to the Delaware? What examples can you find where these explanations fit how they were treated in New Jersey, or, for those who moved, in the Ohio country?

Remember Jameson, who, though not discussing Indians, did point to changes in the "status" of people, and in land ownership, brought by the Revolution. How did Indians fare in these categories? Were they better or worse off after the Revolution? Was there anything they could have done differently as they faced what Herbert Kraft called "dark and troublesome times"? Was there anything that white citizens could have done differently? And, finally, while there were few Indians left in New Jersey by 1800, where did they all go, and where are they today?

Suggested Readings

Calloway, Collin G. *The American Revolution in Indian Country: Crisis and Diversity in Native American Communities*. New York: Cambridge University Press, 1995.

Dodyk, Delight W. "'Troublesome Times A-Coming': The American Revolution and New Jersey Women." In *New Jersey in the American Revolution*, edited by Barbara Mitnick. New Brunswick, N.J.: Rutgers University Press, 2005.

Dowd, Gregory. "Declaration of Independence: War and Inequality in Revolutionary New Jersey, 1776–1815." *New Jersey History* 103 (1985): 47–67.

———. *The Indians of New Jersey*. Trenton: New Jersey Historical Commission, 1992.

Gerlach, Larry R. *Prologue to Independence: New Jersey in the Coming of the American Revolution*. New Brunswick, N.J.: Rutgers University Press, 1976.

Gertzog, Irwin. "Female Suffrage in New Jersey, 1790–1807." *Women and Politics* 10 (1990): 47–68.

Jameson, J. Franklin. *The American Revolution Considered as a Social Movement*. Princeton, N.J: Princeton University, 1926.

Kerber, Linda K. *Women of the Republic: Intellect and Ideology in the American Revolution*. Chapel Hill: University of North Carolina Press, 1980.

Kraft, Herbert C. *The Lenape-Delaware Indian Heritage: 10,000 B.C.–A. D. 2000*. Elizabeth, N.J.: Lenape Books, 2001.

Norton, Mary Beth. *Liberty's Daughters: The Revolutionary Experience of American Women, 1750–1800*. Boston: Little Brown, 1980.

Schutt, Amy C. *Peoples of the River Valleys: The Odyssey of the Delaware Indians*. Philadelphia: University of Pennsylvania Press, 2007.

Tolles, Frederick B. "The American Revolution as a Social Movement Reconsidered." *American Historical Review* 60 (1954): 1–12.

Weslager, Clinton Alfred. *The Delaware Indians: A History*. New Brunswick, N.J: Rutgers University Press, 1972.

Wood, Gordon. *The Radicalism of the American Revolution*. New York: Knopf, 1992.

♦ ♦ ♦ ♦ ♦ ♦

Caught in the Middle:
New Jersey's Indians
and the American Revolution

Lorraine E. Williams

On May 12, 1779, General George Washington received a delegation of Delaware Indians at his headquarters at Middlebrook, New
Jersey.[1] "Delaware" was the name the English had given to the native
peoples sixteenth- and seventeenth-century explorers found occupying
the area that is today all of New Jersey, northern Delaware, eastern
Pennsylvania, southeastern New York, and southwestern Connecticut.
The native peoples called themselves "Lenape," but by the 1740s they
had come to refer to themselves as "Delawares" when they dealt with
the English.

The delegation was escorted by George Morgan, a resident of the
farm "Prospect" in Princeton, New Jersey, adjoining the land of the
College of New Jersey (today Princeton University). Morgan was also
the agent for Indian Affairs for the central states. In his care on the visit
were three Delaware boys—eight-year-old George Morgan White Eyes,
the son of Chief White Eyes, Morgan's good friend; sixteen-year-old
John Killbuck, the son of Chief Killbuck; and eighteen-year-old Thomas
Killbuck, Chief Killbuck's half brother. The boys were to be schooled in
Princeton under Morgan's supervision. Young White Eyes would go on
to graduate from the college in 1789.[2]

Washington greeted the Delawares with a military parade and
made a speech emphasizing the importance of the recent treaty alliance between the two parties to the future of each. The Delawares had
become the first American Indian nation to conclude a treaty with the
new United States in September 1778.[3] They had pledged that they
would

From *New Jersey in the American Revolution*, edited by Barbara Mitnick (New
Brunswick, N.J: Rutgers University Press, 2005), 101–112. Reprinted by permission of the author.

give a free passage through their country to the troops aforesaid [the American forces], and the same to conduct by the nearest and best ways to the posts, forts or towns of the enemies of the United States, affording to said troops such supplies of corn, meat, horses, or whatever may be in their power for the accommodations of such troops . . . [and] engage to join the troops . . . with such a number of their best and most expert warriors . . . and act in concert with them.[4]

In exchange for the Delawares' support of the Americans' effort against the British, the United States had promised to provide a fort for the Indians' safety against retaliation from the British or their Indian allies and to provide the trade goods—metal tools, guns, and cloth—upon which the Indians had become dependent.

This first treaty of the young rebellious nation followed the format of older treaties made by the British with North American Indians for more than a hundred years. It was also the format the United States would follow in other treaties it would make with Indian allies. But this treaty of 1778 concluded with a clause that had never before appeared in a North American treaty and would never appear again: "[S]hould it for the future be found conducive for the mutual interest of both parties to invite any other tribes who have been friends to the interest of the United States, to join the present confederation, and to form a state whereof the Delaware nation shall be the head, and have a representation in Congress."[5] Chief White Eyes is credited with the idea that the nation's fourteenth state should be an Indian state. He signed the treaty along with Chiefs Killbuck and Captain Pipe. Perhaps the urgent desire to make this first treaty with the Indians made the United States offer a status of equality to the Delawares that it would never offer again.

The Delawares who visited Washington at Middlebrook were not, however, from New Jersey. These Delawares had come to the state from villages in the Ohio country (the colonial name for the drainages of the Allegheny and Ohio rivers). They were offering to guide the American forces along the western frontier between the American stronghold at Fort Pitt (present-day Pittsburgh) and Fort Detroit, the British stronghold to the north in Canada. Washington was welcoming the Delawares back to their old homeland for only a brief visit. Then they were to journey to Philadelphia, where Congress was in session. These Delawares' home in 1779 was no longer in New Jersey or any of their ancestral lands on the East Coast. It was out on the western frontier. There they had been caught solidly in the middle of the American Revolution between the British and the Americans. Both combatants at first argued that all Indians should remain neutral; later, each demanded military aid from them. The Delawares had to choose a side. They picked the United States and hoped they had made the right choice.

At the beginning of the American Revolution there were Delawares still living in New Jersey. They had English names, and if they owned land, it was by English law as members of the colonial population. Perhaps as many as 200 Delawares occupied a colonial reservation, Brotherton, in Burlington County. There is no record of George Washington or the Congress meeting with these New Jersey Delawares. They were not a numerous and separate society to be courted as potential allies. When New Jersey declared itself a state in 1776, the Delawares within its borders became citizens of a state in rebellion and at war, and the reservation population at Brotherton became wards of the state (formerly, they had been wards of the colonial government). These Delawares were caught between the combatants' armies, which were to crisscross New Jersey repeatedly. Indeed, the constant warfare in the state earned New Jersey the name "Cockpit of the Revolution."

By 1776, the Delawares were dispersed widely across North America, below Canada and east of the Mississippi River. They lived in radically different circumstances in and out of New Jersey. How had this come to be? How well did these two populations—the Delawares on the Ohio and those in New Jersey—survive while being caught in the middle of the American Revolution?

A Complex Colonial History for New Jersey's Indians

The Europeans who first explored and then attempted to establish colonies in what is today New Jersey encountered the Lenape living in small, unfortified settlements, moving seasonally to hunt, fish, collect shellfish and wild plant foods, and grow corn, beans, and squash. During the seventeenth century, the Dutch, Swedes, and English competed for colonial sovereignty over the area and also competed with one another for the Indians' furs and wampum or sewant (strings or belts of small shell beads for which Indians were eager to trade). The furs brought high prices in European markets, and the wampum was much prized by Indians farther from the coast, particularly the Iroquoian groups such as the Five (later the Six) Nations of New York and the Susquehannocks of Pennsylvania. Until the English won total control of what became New Jersey and New York in 1664 by the conquest of the Dutch colony of New Netherland (which had conquered New Sweden in 1655), colonists were few in number. Aside from the Dutch-Indian warfare around New Amsterdam (New York City after 1664) in the 1640s, relations between the Indians and the various European colonists in New Jersey were largely peaceful. The small numbers of colonists did not keep the Indians from using their territory in traditional ways, and the Europeans were welcomed as a source of the metal tools, guns, and cloth the Indians avidly sought in exchange for wampum, furs, and sometimes corn and deer meat.

This peaceful situation did not long outlive the English conquest of 1664. Not only did more and more settlers arrive from Great Britain, but New Jersey also attracted settlers from New England. By the 1720s, the numbers of colonists were interfering with the Indians' access to resources. With the fur-bearing mammals trapped out, the Indians had only their lands to exchange for the tools and cloth they desired—and needed. The Indians were learning the hard lesson that the English idea of land ownership denied them access to continuing to hunt, fish, or cut down trees even on large expanses the colonists owned but did not yet occupy. Since the colonists most coveted the best farmland, the Indians were quickly dispossessed of any but marginal agricultural land.

At this point, some Delawares decided they could no longer live with the Europeans and took advantage of an invitation from the Miami Indians to move west to the Ohio country, recently depopulated by the fur wars of the Iroquois. The Miamis welcomed the Delawares, as did the Iroquois, who claimed the Ohio territory by conquest but had sent few of their own people to settle there.[6] There was plenty of room for the Delawares to farm, hunt, and fish and even to revive the fur trade as a way to secure European goods. In the Ohio country, the British and the French competed for the influence among the Indian bands and for access to their furs. This competition provided the Indians with many material and political advantages.

In the 1730s and 17490s, Delawares who became disaffected with New Jersey life continued to migrate to the Ohio country. By the late 1740s, there were at least three Delaware villages on the Allegheny River near Fort Pitt. These villages were surrounded by those of other refugee Indians from the eastern colonies, including Shawnees, Senecas, and Mohawks.[7] Sometimes different Indian peoples shared towns. In 1748, Conrad Weiser, a colonel emissary, found that Shingass Old Town (named for the Delaware chief who lived there) was occupied by both Delawares and Mohawks.[8]

Indians who remained in New Jersey from the 1720s through the 1750s tried to adapt to a life enclosed within a Euro-American population. No longer able to follow traditional subsistence patterns, these Delawares become wage laborers to supplement the meager farming and hunting still available to them. They worked at such jobs as harvesting crops, building houses, and coastal whaling.

They also learned to make the European-style wood-splint baskets that the colonists needed for domestic and agricultural use. Delaware Valley Indians became extremely successful basket makers and are credited with starting an adaptation to colonial life that spread to other Indian groups from the Carolinas to southeastern Canada. Teedyescunk (also commonly spelled "Teedyuscung"), the leading Indian signer of the 1758 agreement to relinquish to the colony of New Jersey all Indian land claims south of the Raritan River, had supported himself for decades before as a basket and broom maker.

By 1758, Teedyescunk and many other Delawares had moved either to Easton, Pennsylvania, or to the Susquehanna River valley farther west, seeking pockets of land not yet overrun by colonists. With the onset of the Seven Years' War in 1756 (popularly called the French and Indian War in British America), the Delawares in the Susquehanna Valley and the Ohio country supported the French. They had old scores to settle with the English colonists and hoped to gain a better supply of trade goods from the French. Governor Francis Bernard initiated negotiations to extinguish Indian land claims in New Jersey as part of an effort to end the Delawares' raids from Pennsylvania into the northwestern part of New Jersey.[9]

Many New Jerseyans who lived nowhere near the frontier feared attacks by the Indians still living among them within the colony. In an effort to calm the public, the colonial government required resident Indians to register with a magistrate, take a loyalty oath, and wear a red ribbon to show they were friends rather than foes.

When this did not produce calm, in 1758 Governor Bernard created the Brotherton reservation in Burlington County. It was to be a haven for all Indians south of the Raritan River who cared to move there. Near the present town of Indian Mills, the reservation's location offered several advantages. A house and at least one sawmill were already on the property. The land adjoined the pinelands, where the Indians could continue to hunt and forage free of the colonists who disdained the pinewoods as "the barrens."

Governor Bernard described the new reservation in 1759 with evident satisfaction.

> It is a tract of Land Very suitable for this purpose, having soil good enough, a large hunting country and a passage by water to the Sea for fishing . . . & has a saw mill upon it which serves to provide them with timber for their own use & to raise a little money for

other purposes. [W]e laid out the plan of a town to which I gave
the Name of Brotherton & saw an house erected being one of ten
that were ready prepared.[10]

The location of Brotherton had another advantage—it was in an
area heavily populated by English Quakers, who had long promoted
an attitude of friendship and solicitude toward the Indians. The development of the nearby Atsion Iron Works after 1766 also offered the
Indians employment and a company store from which to buy provisions.[11]

At Brotherton, Presbyterian missionary John Brainerd could
continue the ministry to the Delawares his brother, David, had begun
in the 1740s. A log meetinghouse was built, and Brotherton became
both a reservation and a mission community when John Brainerd was
appointed guardian of the Indians there in 1762.[12]

Not all Indians still living in New Jersey moved to Brotherton,
which seems never to have had a population of more than 300. The
1758 treaty made specific reference to Indians continuing their fee
simple rights to lands they already held as individuals. In the 1760s,
John Brainerd ministered to Indians living in areas near Brotherton and
referred to Indians still living in Monmouth County.[13]

By the 1760s, the Indians in New Jersey had adopted English
names. They had been missionized by different Christian denominations. The Quakers and the Presbyterians had been most active. The
latter were supported by the Presbyterian Society for Propagating
Christian Knowledge, based in Scotland. The Scottish society collected
and sent funds for the Indians' benefit, which were dispensed by the
College of New Jersey at Princeton. With this support, John Brainerd
was able to establish a school at Brotherton, at least one graduate of
which attended the college at Princeton. The funds were important
to the quality of life at Brotherton because the colonial government
expected the reservation to be self-supporting after its initial investment in construction and moving costs.

The disaffected New Jersey Indians who crossed the Delaware and
filtered westward were drawn to the Moravian Brethren at Bethlehem,
Pennsylvania. The Moravians baptized numbers of Delawares and settled
some of their converts in nearby mission towns. The mission towns
proved to be unpopular with both the local colonists in Pennsylvania
and with non-Christianized Indians. After the French and Indian War,
the disaffected Delawares still living in eastern Pennsylvania (along
the west bank of the Delaware and in the Susquehanna River valley)
moved west to join the Delaware settlements in the Ohio country, and
the Moravians moved with them. Missionaries John Heckewelder and

David Zeisberger ministered to the Indians in the Ohio settlements and began new "praying towns" there. An English trader named Cresap visited one of them in 1775 and described it this way: "Christianized under the Moravian Sect, it is a pretty town consisting of about sixty houses, and is built of logs and covered with Clapboards. It is regularly laid out in three spacious streets which meet in the centre, where there is a large meeting house built of logs sixty foot square covered with Shingles, Glass in the windows and a Bell."[14]

After the French and Indian War, the Delawares moved their villages away from Fort Pitt into the valley of the Muskingum River (a tributary of the Ohio). By 1775, therefore, there were two distinct populations of Delaware Indians. One still lived in New Jersey, extremely anglicized and adapted to life within the colony. The other lived in the Ohio territory. The latter maintained in their villages on the Muskingum freedom from colonial oversight but had become dependent upon commerce with the colonists for tools and clothing. In fact, during Cresap's 1775 trading visit, a veteran trader told him that to be accepted by the Indians he met, he should wear a calico shirt as they did, not the buckskins the Indians associated with the land-hungry colonial frontiersmen.[15]

In both New Jersey and the Ohio country there were professedly Christian communities of Delawares—Moravian towns in the Ohio country and the Presbyterian Brotherton reservation in New Jersey. The American Revolution would bring drastic changes to the Delawares in both locations.

On the Frontier

In 1775, the Ohio country Delawares were divided about how to deal with the Americans. Chiefs White Eyes and Killbuck believed it was possible to coexist with the settlers, even as the colonists expanded their settlements westward. White Eyes, in particular, supported the influence of the Moravian missionaries among the Delawares. Captain Pipe believed any accommodation to the settlers moving into the Ohio country would only cost the Delawares land and autonomy. At the beginning of the Revolutionary War, these leaders vied for control of their people as they tried to decide which side to support.

Although both the British and the Americans at first urged the Indians on the western frontier to remain neutral, the Indians were immediately affected by the disruption of trade the hostilities caused. The Americans had difficulty supplying trade goods while mobilizing resources for the war effort to the east. But the British could continue supplying "their" Indians through Canada. It was not long, as the

Indians had expected, before entreaties for neutrality became entreaties to join one side or the other. George Washington was particularly concerned that an eruption of warfare by the frontier Indians against the western settlers should force him to draw off forces he needed to use against the British in the middle states, specifically in New Jersey. He had gained firsthand experience of the frontier Delawares when, as a young colonel of the Virginia militia, he had been sent during the French and Indian War to their territory in an unsuccessful attempt to attach them to the English cause.[16] In the 1770s, the Moravian missionaries pressured the Delawares strongly to join the American cause. Like most dissenting Protestants, the Moravians thought their future religious freedom lay with the Americans.

At the same time, the Delawares were subjected to pressures from the Iroquois, nominal overlords of the Ohio country, who continued their long-standing support of the British. The Delaware leaders wanted to choose the right side. They had backed the losing French in the previous war; this time, they wanted to back the winner. But it was difficult to foretell who that would be.

After much debate, the Delawares agreed to support the Americans and concluded the treaty of 1778. Unfortunately, by the time their delegation visited Washington at Middlebrook in 1779, the relationship was already under stress. Chief White Eyes, the leading supporter of the treaty, had been killed earlier that year by some Americans he was guiding in conformity with treaty provisions.[17] The Americans feared Indian reaction to his murder. They reported falsely that the chief died of smallpox. They brought his son and Killbuck's son and half brother from the frontier, nominally for their protection but perhaps also to serve as hostages should the Delawares break the treaty.

As the Delaware delegation traveled toward New Jersey in 1779, Colonel Daniel Brodhead, the commander at Fort Pitt, wrote to Washington about a plot to kill the visiting Indians and thereby plunge the frontier into an Indian war. Washington did not receive the message until after the Indians had left Middlebrook. He sent George Morgan a warning to take particular care during the Indians' visit to Philadelphia and added that he had ordered Brodhead to meet them with a military escort on their return to ensure safe passage back to their villages.[18]

Once back in the Ohio country and lacking White Eyes's strong support for the Americans, the Delawares found that they also lacked the fort Congress had promised them to protect their villages and the trade goods they needed to survive. It was not long before Captain Pipe took his group to join the British at Detroit. The Delawares who continued to back the Americans were helpless in the face of attacks by other Indians who were supplied by the British.

In 1782, the last blow to the Delaware-American alliance was the murder by Pennsylvania militia of ninety-six Delaware men, women, and children at the Moravian mission settlement of Gnadenhutten.[19] Killbuck was forced to retreat for protection to the Americans at Fort Pitt as a wave of anti-American feeling swept through the Delaware settlements on the frontier. The enmity engendered outlasted the end of the Revolution. The western Delawares continued to war with the United States until they were finally defeated in 1794. The disheartened Moravians moved their converts to Canada, where their descendants remain today. The remaining frontier Delawares again moved westward, away from the incoming settlers, and eventually they settled in Oklahoma, where there are today two reservations populated by Delawares who well remember their roots in New Jersey.

There turned out to be no winning side for any of the Indians on the western frontier. By the Treaty of Paris, which concluded the Revolutionary War in 1783, the British ceded to the United States all frontier lands westward to the Mississippi River, including the lands of their own Indian allies. In consolation, the British offered their Indian allies the option to move to reservations in Canada.

In New Jersey

From its creation in 1776, the state of New Jersey seems to have ignored the Indians still living within its boundaries. Unlike decades earlier, there seems to have been no fear that these Indians would connect with the Delawares on the frontier. We know that some Indians in the state served in the American military forces during the Revolutionary War. They were following a long-standing tradition of volunteering for military service that John Brainerd reported.[20] The Indians at Brotherton participated in the war effort through their work at the nearby Atsion Iron Works. Atsion was active throughout the Revolution and supplied the Continental army and navy with shot and other military products.[21] The Indians must have been particularly dependent on the ironworks and its company store, as there is no record of the state supporting the reservation during the war. With the severing of ties between Great Britain and New Jersey, funds were also no longer available to the Indians from the Scottish Society for Propagating Christian Knowledge.

In 1777, worried about his family's safety and lacking financial support for his ministry to the Indians, John Brainerd moved to Deerfield in Cumberland County, where he died in 1781. No missionary to the Indians was appointed to succeed him. The Indians at Brotherton and in the surrounding area lost not only pastoral care but a spokesman of consequence to protect their rights. Southern New Jersey Quakers had also spoken for the Indians' rights, but the Quakers lost status in the eyes of other New Jerseyans because of their pacifism. The Indians, even on the reservation, were very much left to their own devices in war-torn New Jersey.

The records provide no evidence of New Jersey Indians' struggles during the Revolution, but we do know that the population at Brotherton declined. In 1801, the state bought the reservation lands from the remaining Indians. The fewer than a hundred Indians still resident there wished to join the Stockbridge Indians in New York State. After this move, Bartholomew Calvin, the Brotherton Indian who had attended the College of New Jersey, petitioned the New Jersey government for an award of $2,000 in return for the Indians' relinquishing their hunting and fishing rights south of the Raritan River. The state legislature granted the funds and assisted the Indians in meeting their expenses in relocating to Wisconsin, where their descendents can be found today.[22]

During the Revolutionary War and the years afterward, most of New Jersey's Indians who remained in the state blended ever more into the general population. There was no category of "Indian" in the state census of 1790. Indians who remained were henceforth citizens of the state and the nation, a status that reservation Indians of the West would not gain until 1924. New Jersey's resident Indians survived the Revolutionary War and its aftermath, and a few communities, such as Monmouth County's Sand Hill Delawares, were able to maintain a clear group identity into the 1950s. Many residents in New Jersey today still proudly claim Indian ancestors among the Delawares who remained in the state in the seventeenth and eighteenth centuries.

Notes

1. George Washington, "Speech to the Delaware Chiefs," John C. Fitzpatrick, ed., *The Writings of George Washington from the Original Manuscript Sources, 1745–1799* (Washington, D.C.: U.S. Government Printing Office, 1931–1944)), 15:53–56.

2. "George Morgan White Eyes," in Ruth L. Woodward and Wesley Frank Craven, *Princetonians, 1784–1790* (Princeton, N.J.: Princeton University Press, 1991), 442–452.

3. Washington, "Speech to the Delaware Chiefs," 53; "Treaty with the Delawares, 1778," in *Indian Affairs, Laws and Treaties*, ed. Charles J. Kappler, 2:3–5 (Washington D.C.: United Stated Government Printing Office, 1904).

4. "Treaty with the Delawares," 2:3.

5. Ibid., 2:5.

6. Charles E. Hunter, "History of the Ohio Valley," in *Handbook of North American Indians: Northeast*, ed. Bruce G. Trigger, 15: 590 (Washington, D.C.: Smithsonian Institution, 1974).

7. Conrad Weiser, "The Journal of Conrad Weiser, Esqr., Indian Interpreter, to the Ohio," in *Early Western Travels, 1748–1846*, ed. Reuben Gold Thwaites, 21–43 (Cleveland: Arthur H. Clark, 1904).

8. Ibid., 26.

9. Anthony F. C. Wallace, *King of the Delawares: Teedyuscung, 1700–1763* (Philadelphia: University of Pennsylvania Press, 1949), 18.

10. *New Jersey Archives*, 1st ser., 9:174–175.

11. Arthur D. Pierce, *Iron in the Pines: the Story of New Jersey's Ghost Towns and Bog Iron* (New Brunswick, N.J.: Rutgers University Press, 1957), 31.

12. *New Jersey Archives*, 1st ser., 9:355–358.

13. Rev. Thomas Brainerd, *The Life of John Brainerd, Missionary to the Indians of New Jersey* (Philadelphia, 1865), 385, quoting John Brainerd.

14. Samuel Thornely, ed., *The Journal of Nicholas Creswell, 1774–1779* (New York: Dial Press, 1924), 106.

15. Ibid., 103.

16. George Washington to Governor George Clinton, May 29, 1778, Fitzpatrick, *The Writings of George Washington*, 11:473; Washington to the Board of War, August 3, 1778, ibid., 12:265–266; George Washington, "Journal," June 21, 1754, ibid., 1:88.

17. "George Morgan White Eyes," 443.

18. George Washington to Colonel George Morgan, May 21, 1779, Fitzpatrick, *The Writings of George Washington*, 15:113.

19. R. Pierce Beaver, "Protestant Churches and the Indians," in *Handbook of North American Indians*, William C. Sturtevant, gen. ed., vol. 4, *History of Indian-White Relations*, ed. Wilcomb E. Washburn (Washington, D.C.: Smithsonian Institution, 1988), 433.

20. Mark E. Lender, "The Enlisted Line: The Continental Soldiers of New Jersey" (Ph.D. diss., Rutgers University, 1975). Daughters of the American Revolution, *African American and American Indian Patriots of the American Revolutionary War* (Washington, D.C.: National Society of the DAR, 2001), 127–128. Brainerd, *The Life of John Brainerd*, 316, quoting John Brainerd in 1759.

21. Pierce, *Iron in the Pines*, 34.

22. Edward McM. Larrabee, "Recurrent Themes and Sequences in North American Indian-European Culture Contact," *Transactions of the American Philosophical Society*, n.s., 66, part 7 (Philadelphia: American Philosophical Society, 1976): 17.

A fervent republican and a signer of the Declaration of Independence, Abraham Clark (1726–1794) felt the Constitution should be ratified despite his concern about the rights of such small states as New Jersey and the kind of national government the document created. Portrait Collection, Special Collections and University Archives, Rutgers University Libraries.

5

Historical debate over the Confederation period of the 1780s and the adoption of the United States Constitution continues the disagreement about whether the American Revolution was evolutionary or revolutionary. Here, too, historians tend to see either conflict or consensus and continuity to reflect the actions Americans took to establish fundamental laws for their new nation.

The debate centers around two issues. The first deals with the nature and severity of the problems experienced by the national and state governments under the Articles of Confederation. Was this truly, as the late-nineteenth-century historian John Fiske described it, a critical period in American history? Or were the problems exaggerated by conservatives then, and by historians since? The second and related question is whether the Constitution was really necessary.

These issues were first clearly presented in Charles Beard's *An Economic Interpretation of the Constitution of the United States* (1913). Written at the height of the Progressive period, it reflected the concerns of that era with class and economic conflict. Beard thus argued, in a deliberately provocative manner, that the spirit of the Revolution was embodied in the Declaration of Independence and the Articles of Confederation. The Constitution represented a successful counterrevolution by conservatives who shared an interest in preserving particular forms of property (money, securities, manufacturing, trade, and shipping). Furthermore, because few could, or did, vote for the Constitution, America's sacred document was the result of an undemocratic conspiracy; the revered Founding Fathers were actually pursing their own self-interest. Merrill Jensen supported Beard's argument in *The Articles of Confederation* (1940) and *The New Nation* (1950) by maintaining that, with some alterations, the Articles would have sufficed for the new nation. Recently a neo-Progressive argument has been presented by Woody Holton in *Unruly Americans and the Origins of the Constitution* (2007) and others.

The consensus view of this period is quite different. Such historians as Edmund Morgan, in *The Birth of the Republic, 1763–89* (1956), maintained that the logic of both events and developing political theory led directly from the Declaration of Independence to the Articles of Confederation and then on to the Constitution. The later document was the fulfillment, not the denial, of the spirit of the Revolution. The faults of the Articles and disorders of the 1780s were indeed real. The Founding Fathers were public-spirited men, concerned with finding solutions to political and economic problems and not with lining their own pockets.

Some historians were specifically critical of Beard. Robert E. Brown and Katherine B. Brown, in *Virginia, 1705–1786: Democracy or Aristocracy?* (1964) and other works, saw the widespread political participation of the colonial period continuing after the Revolution. Forrest McDonald, in *We the People* (1958), presented a complex picture of various economic groups, with different interests in each state, relating in various ways to the Constitution and its provisions. He concluded that states that functioned independently of the national government and had done well under the weak Articles opposed the Constitution, while others, which were dependent or had experienced problems during the Confederation period, favored it. In a later work, *Novus Ordo Seclorum* (1985), McDonald turned to the philosophical ideas behind the Constitution, to the connection between ideology and action. For him the Constitution represented the culmination of the Revolution. It was the creative work of practical men who, from the ideas of their times as well as their own experiences, produced a new form of government to solve the problems of their country.

New Jersey presents some interesting problems in the context of this historiographical debate. As the following article shows, conflict and disagreement was pronounced in New Jersey during the 1780s over the payment of Revolutionary war debts and the use of paper money. How and why did residents of the state divide over these issues? Was their disagreement based on class or economic interests, or were other factors involved, such as sectionalism?

New Jersey residents disliked the Articles of Confederation from the outset, long before proposals arose at the Constitutional Convention to replace them with a totally new document. And despite the disagreements over economic issues New Jersey voted for the Constitution quickly and unanimously; on this matter there was clear agreement. How can the apparent shift from conflict to consensus within the state be explained? How did the problems of the 1780s enhance discontent? Were New Jersey's founding fathers, such as William Paterson and William Livingston, protecting their own private interests in supporting the Constitution, or were they protecting the public interest of their constituents? Is the Constitution the fulfillment or overthrow of the Revolution? If the Constitution undid the Declaration, why did John Witherspoon, the firebrand Whig president of the College of New Jersey, sign the Declaration, serve in Congress under the Articles, and support the Constitution in the state ratifying convention?

New Jersey was after all a small state that lacked the historical independence of North Carolina or Rhode Island. Do Forrest McDonald's categories (independent or dependent) help in understanding New Jersey's response to the Constitution? What other reasons were there for the state's support of the Constitution?

Suggested Readings

Beard, Charles. *An Economic Interpretation of the Constitution of the United States.* 1913. Reprint, New York: Macmillan, 1941.

Beeman, Richard, Stephen Botein, and Edward C. Carter II, eds. *Beyond Confederation: Origins of the Constitution and American National Identity.* Chapel Hill: University of North Carolina Press, 1987.

Bogin, Ruth. *Abraham Clark and the Quest for Equality in Revolutionary Era, 1774–1794.* Rutherford, N.J.: Fairleigh Dickinson University Press, 1982.

Brown, Robert E. *Charles Beard and the Constitution: A Critical Analysis of "An Economic Interpretation of the Constitution."* Princeton, N.J.: Princeton University Press, 1956.

Holton, Woody. *Unruly Americans and the Origins of the Constitution.* New York: Hill and Wang, 2007.

Jensen, Merrill. *The Articles of Confederation: An Interpretation of the Social-Constitutional History of the American Revolution, 1774–1781.* Madison: University of Wisconsin Press, 1940.

———. *The New Nation: A History of the United States, 1781–1789.* New York: Knopf, 1950.

Lurie, Maxine N. "Colonel John Stevens, the Overlooked Federalist from New Jersey." *New Jersey History* 111 (Fall/Winter, 1993): 58–106.

———. "The New Jersey Intellectuals and the United States Constitution." *Journal of Rutgers University Libraries* 69 (1987): 65–87.

McCormick, Richard P. *Experiment in Independence: New Jersey in the Critical Period, 1781–1789.* New Brunswick, N.J.: Rutgers University Press, 1950.

———. "The Unanimous State." *Journal of Rutgers University Libraries* 23 (1958): 4–8.

McDonald, Forrest. *Novus Ordo Seclorum: The Intellectual Origins of the Constitution.* Lawrence: University Press of Kansas, 1985.

Murrin, Mary R. *To Save This State from Ruin: New Jersey and the Creation of the United States Constitution, 1776–1789*. Trenton: New Jersey Historical Commission, 1987.

O'Connor, John E. *William Paterson: Lawyer and Statesman, 1745–1806*. New Brunswick, N.J.: Rutgers University Press, 1979.

New Jersey
and the Two Constitutions

Mary R. Murrin

The English settled New Jersey in the mid-1660s, shortly after wresting the area from its original colonizers and their main commercial rivals, the Dutch. After the restoration of Charles II in 1660, his brother James, Duke of York, mounted a successful expedition against New Netherland. In 1664 James conveyed what is now New Jersey to two supporters of the royal court, John Lord Berkeley and Sir George Carteret. They had full title to the soil; they assumed they had governmental powers as well. The duke's chosen governor, Richard Nicolls, unaware of the duke's grant to Berkeley and Carteret, parceled out considerable acreage to various settlers.

Despite the uncertainty as to their legal right to rule, Berkeley and Carteret immediately drew up a frame of government for the new colony. Their "Concessions and Agreements" of 1665 offered liberal political and religious rights to prospective settlers. Yet initial harmony quickly yielded to conflict largely over the payment of quit rents and the competing land claims caused by the duke's grants of power to both a governor and the two proprietors. A brief Dutch reconquest in 1673–74 was largely uneventful, but the retrocession to England brought with it significant change.

In 1674 Berkeley sold his share to Edward Byllynge and John Fenwick, and in 1676 Carteret agreed to a partition of the province into East and West Jersey. For the next quarter century West Jersey developed under Quaker influence, while Carteret's East Jersey became more heterogeneous, attracting not only English Quakers but also Dutch immigrants from New York, Puritans from New England, Anglicans from

In *The Constitution and the States: The Role of the Original Thirteen in the Framing and Adoption of the Federal Constitution*, edited by Patrick T. Conley and John P. Kaminski (Madison, Wis.: Madison House Publishers, 1988), 55–75. Reprinted by permission of Madison House Publishers, Inc., part of Rowman and Littlefield Publishers, Inc.

England, and both Presbyterians and Quakers from Scotland. The West Jersey proprietors issued a liberal frame of government, the West Jersey Concessions, in 1677. Like their East Jersey counterpart, the Concessions were designed to attract settlers. Both guaranteed the basic rights of Englishmen, freedom of conscience, access to land, and participation in government. Both established general assemblies with elected lower houses. However, the West Jersey Concessions spelled out the powers of the assembly in greater detail and specified individual liberties, such as trial by jury, protection from arbitrary arrest, the secret ballot and a liberal code of laws. The East Jersey assemblies adopted a stringent criminal code modeled on the Duke's Laws of 1665.

During the period of division, both Jerseys were beset by complicated questions of land ownership and by repeated challenges from New York to their independent status. In 1702 the proprietors, unable to rule effectively, surrendered all governing rights to the Crown. East and West Jersey became a single royal colony. Edward Hyde, Lord Cornbury, a cousin of Queen Anne, was New Jersey's first royal governor. Until 1738 the governor of New York also served, under separate commission, as governor of New Jersey, but beginning with Lewis Morris, New Jersey was permitted its own royal governor.

The proprietors retained their property interests, and New Jersey continued to be plagued with land disputes well after the Revolution. A Board of Proprietors of East Jersey (established in 1684 and headquartered in Perth Amboy) and a similar organization for West Jersey (established in 1688 and headquartered in Burlington) have continued in existence to the present day.*

Problems under the Articles of Confederation

At the close of the Revolutionary War, New Jersey faced many of the same difficulties besetting other states. However, internal differences complicated the state's response to problems of debtor-creditor relations, currency, and the Continental debt. Distinctive patterns of ethnicity, land use, trade, and religion established during the proprietary period, when New Jersey was two colonies, were still evident. But although the two regions, East and West Jersey, were at loggerheads on possible solutions to these postwar problems, a decade of experience trying to resolve them made the state as a whole receptive to the Constitution. New Jerseyans believed the Articles of Confederation to be seriously flawed and were united on two major issues troubling the new nation—the disposition of western lands and Congress's need for a secure income.

---

*Editor's note: The East Jersey Board dissolved in 1998.

The New Jersey legislature made its position on the Confederation quite clear in 1778. On June 16 it sent a remonstrance to the Continental Congress listing a number of objections to the proposed Articles of Confederation and urging their revision. The memorial New Jersey submitted devoted much space to issues of revenue, trade regulation, and western lands—topics of great importance during the next decade.

The legislature called for fixed state boundaries within five years, argued that Congress should have sole authority to regulate trade and impose customs duties, and observed that Congress should have authority over western lands so that all states might benefit rather than a few. On this last point the legislature observed plaintively, "Shall such States as are shut out by Situation from availing themselves of the least Advantage from this Quarter, be left to sink under an enormous Debt, whilst others are enabled, in a short Period, to replace all their Expenditures from the hard Earnings of the whole Confederacy?"

Congress listened, but it rejected the proposed revisions. In July, New Jersey delegate Nathaniel Scudder wrote to John Hart, the speaker of the New Jersey Assembly, urging the legislature to direct its delegates to ratify the Articles despite any disadvantages to the state. He pointed out that small states could be at a severe disadvantage if Congress began amending the Articles. Warning of the "fatal Consequences" should the Articles not be ratified and America be discovered to be "a Rope of Sand," Scudder asserted that "every State must expect to be subjected to considerable local Disadvantages in a general Confederation." In November, still convinced the Articles needed substantial revision, the legislature relented. New Jersey was the eleventh state to ratify, followed by Delaware and Maryland, two other small states that objected to the absence of any provision for the western lands.

New Jersey's objections were understandable. The Articles, which largely continued the constitutional relationship established under the Continental Congress, gave the Confederation Congress no power to tax, impose customs duties, or regulate trade (except by treaty). Under the Articles, and indeed after 1779, Congress no longer paid its bills simply by printing paper money. All governmental expenses, such as those required by the prosecution of the war and the servicing of the Continental debt, depended upon a system of requisition. Congress met its expenses by assessing each state a quota of the total amount. New Jersey had no source of income to satisfy these requisitions except by imposing direct taxes on its citizens. A small state with fixed boundaries, New Jersey had no western lands, no real port, and negligible foreign trade. Her merchants shipped through the ports of Philadelphia and New York City, and both New York and Pennsylvania exacted heavy import duties. As one historian has observed, New Jersey was like "a barrel tapped at both ends."

The Social Structure

New Jersey was an agricultural state: somewhere between 70 and 80 percent of the population of 150,000 owed its living in some way to the land. No town boasted more than 1,500 inhabitants. But despite the state's overall rural character, East and West Jersey exhibited important differences.

Dutch, English, Scots-Irish, Irish, and Germans made up the bulk of East Jersey's white population. Most of the state's black population of 10,000 (the majority of whom were slaves) lived in the northern part of the state, especially Bergen and Somerset counties. Economically, East Jersey was in New York City's orbit. It was a region of small family farms which produced little for sale. A few small manufactories and ironworks and a number of artisans and shopkeepers completed the economic picture. Four of the state's largest towns—Newark, Elizabeth Town, Perth Amboy, and New Brunswick—were in East Jersey. English Calvinist and Dutch Reformed were the predominant religions; the Episcopal Church attracted fewer members.

West Jersey's population was more homogeneous, primarily English, with a few Germans, Finns, and Swedes. Politically it was dominated by Quakers who had not been enthusiastic supporters of either the war or measures to pay for the war. Economically the region looked to Philadelphia. Farms were larger, more prosperous than East Jersey's and produced some crops for sale. West Jersey escaped much of the devastation of the war, and few Continental creditors lived there.

Postwar Problems

The state, especially the northern part, was a major theater of battle between 1776 and 1780. One historian has called it "the cockpit of the Revolution." The clashing armies and the guerrilla warfare between patriots and the large loyalist population damaged and destroyed farms, houses, and towns. Farmers received payment for only a portion of the goods taken or destroyed. In 1779–80, when currency problems were at their height, federal officers left certificates or promises to pay. At war's end New Jersey was not only devastated; her citizens, particularly those in East Jersey, held a sizable portion of the notes and certificates which constituted the Continental debt.

The economic depression of the mid-1780s had a profound effect on relations between New Jersey's creditors and debtors. People who

had speculated in land and goods on the easy credit of the infla-
tionary wartime economy found themselves in debt as the economy
contracted. The depression affected the entire American economy.
British closure of the West Indies to American shipping cut off a major
trade outlet. American merchants, who had restocked their wares on
credit as the war ended, found few customers for their goods. A series of
crop failures brought severe hardship to New Jersey's farmers, already in
difficulty from wartime devastation, debt, and high taxes. The number
of lawsuits for recovery of debt mushroomed.

East Jersey legislators tended to support any measures, such as
paper-money bills, that helped the many debtors among their constituents and to vote against measures which required the spending of
money. West Jersey legislators, often wealthier than their East Jersey
counterparts and representing fewer debtors, opposed measures favoring
debtors, including paper-money bills. A postwar dispute over the location of the dividing line between East and West Jersey significantly
weakened the creditor influence within the legislature. The two boards
of proprietors had surrendered political power when the Jerseys became
a single royal colony in 1702, but they retained title to considerable
amounts of land. The dispute over an improperly located dividing line
occupied the attention of both groups of proprietors for several years as
they argued the case before the legislature. Loath to offend potentially
friendly legislators, the East Jersey proprietors mounted no opposition
to pro-debtor legislation. They won their case, but the two groups of
proprietors, which might otherwise have combined to form a united
pro-creditor front, exerted little or no influence on politics.

Paper Money

The Assembly passed a number of pro-debtor measures in the early
1780s, including bills forcing creditors to accept paper money rather
than specie, delaying court proceedings, releasing jailed debtors from
confinement, and preventing the forced sale of debtor estates at reduced
value. Creditors found the latter measure particularly reprehensible and
believed that debtor-relief bills violated the sanctity of contracts and
damaged public and private credit.

The 1785 session was marked by a fierce debate over a paper-money
or loan office bill. The proposed loan office would issue paper money
and lend it, at interest, to borrowers with sufficient landed security.
Borrowers would repay the money in regular installments. As the loans
were repaid, the principal would be withdrawn from circulation and
destroyed. The interest payments would go to the state treasury for
government expenses. The loan office had proved a convenient fiscal

expedient in the past, especially in the middle colonies, and New Jersey's colonial experience with the device had been reasonably successful. The loan office debate provoked sharp exchanges from three of New Jersey's most influential political figures—Abraham Clark, William Livingston, and William Paterson.

Abraham Clark (1726–1794) was a figure of signal importance in New Jersey during the 1770s and 1780s. A signer of the Declaration of Independence, he either sat in the New Jersey Assembly or represented New Jersey in Congress for most of the period from 1776 to 1794. A man of fervent republican sympathies, he was the acknowledged champion of New Jersey's many indebted farmers, a position he eloquently presented in a series of anonymous newspaper essays and in a pamphlet entitled *The True Policy of New-Jersey, Defined*. Clark loathed privilege, distrusted lawyers, and had few kind words for merchants. At home he was a major advocate of paper money and other debtor-relief measures. In the wider arena he feared the economic power of New York and Pennsylvania over New Jersey and favored some expansion of congressional power, including a grant to the national legislature of authority over western lands. He represented New Jersey in the Annapolis Convention in September 1786, but he refused to accept appointment to the federal convention.

William Livingston (1723–1790) was governor of New Jersey from 1776 to his death in 1790. He served as one of New Jersey's delegates to both the First and Second Continental congresses before his selection as governor. Livingston was an accomplished polemicist, and his "Primitive Whig" essays made a forceful case for the hard-money, pro-creditor position. He served as one of New Jersey's delegates to the Constitutional Convention, but age and ill-health limited his contribution.

William Paterson (1745–1806) was a strong nationalist and, like Livingston, a vigorous Whig and staunch defender of property rights. A lawyer, Paterson was involved in two of the most divisive issues in New Jersey politics during the 1780s—the dividing-line controversy and debtor-creditor disputes. Paterson served in New Jersey's first and second provincial congresses, as New Jersey's attorney general, as one of New Jersey's delegates to the Constitutional Convention, and later as governor and then associate justice of the United States Supreme Court.

Advocates of the loan office bill argued that it would provide a necessary circulating medium for specie-poor New Jersey. Money did not circulate widely in the state's weak economy. In consequence, citizens found it difficult to pay either their debts or their taxes. Clark scornfully described the loan office opponents as "artful, designing men" and pictured creditors as "money-men . . . wishing for greater power to grind the faces of the needy."

Opponents of the loan office bill argued that paper money was a direct attack on the sanctity of contracts because it inevitably depreciated. If debtors were allowed to pay creditors in depreciated currency, creditors would be cheated of the amounts rightfully owed them. According to their arguments, money was not scarce; debtors were simply lazy individuals attempting to evade the payment of lawful debts. Livingston described debtors as "idle spendthrifts" and looked forward to the day "when laws [would] be made in favor of creditors instead of debtors; and when no cozening, trickish fraudulent scoundrel [should] be able to plead legal protection for his cozenage, tricks, frauds and rascality." Paterson argued for a decrease in the amount of money available because such a measure would "introduce a Spirit of Industry & Frugality . . . [and] compel people to work for the Bread they eat, and not go about seeking whom they may devour."

The legislature finally passed the paper-money bill in May 1786. The measure may have done little to relieve the situation of those in the most dire straits, but the legislature's attention to the agrarian discontent may have spared New Jersey from the kind of trouble Massachusetts experienced with Shays' Rebellion.

The weight of private debt made the problem of public debt more urgent. With no revenue from ports or western lands, New Jersey could meet congressional requisitions only by taxing its hard-pressed citizens, many of whom were the same Continental creditors Congress was raising money to pay. Not surprisingly, New Jersey was a strong advocate of alternative means to finance the central government.

During the war Congress and the states created several varieties of financial paper—certificates issued to pay for military supplies, notes given soldiers and militiamen in payment for services, and legal-tender paper money. Wartime inflation reduced its value nearly as fast as it was printed. Most of this financial paper was issued by Congress and constituted the Continental debt. New Jersey's citizens held about one-eleventh of this debt, a large amount for such a small state. This high percentage was attributable to the state's situation as a major theater of war.

Congress made several attempts to deal with its currency and debt problems. In 1780 it called in the old currency at a proportion of 1 to 40 and asked the states to issue new paper money. New Jersey arranged to redeem the old currency, but the new issue depreciated rapidly despite the state's vigorous efforts to maintain its value.

Many New Jerseyans had little faith in the new currency and declined to accept it. The controversy over its value developed largely along sectional lines. West Jersey legislators, whose region had little to lose because it had little of the old currency, favored redemption of the new issue at current rather than face value. East Jerseyans favored redemption at the higher face value. This would benefit the region's creditors and satisfy its fiscal conservatives, who viewed redemption at current depreciated value as a faithless repudiation of honestly incurred debt. Sectional divisions within the legislature prevented any resolution of the issue until after the October 1784 elections, when the political makeup of the Council (the upper house) changed. The Council and Assembly finally agreed on redemption at the depreciated value.

Western Lands

New Jersey's problems with the Confederation extended well beyond the currency issue. Many states were disturbed by the absence of any provision in the Articles for the disposition of trans-Appalachian lands claimed by some of the states under their colonial charters. New Jersey and other landless states, wanting to limit the western claims of states like Virginia, argued that the former Crown lands belonged in common to the Union. New Jersey's position was prompted both by its precarious economic situation and by the presence in the legislature of men who had invested in speculative land companies.

The land companies' claims to western lands were based on Indian deeds they had purchased. However, Virginia and other states, citing their original charters, claimed the same territory. In 1780 the New Jersey Assembly appointed a committee to investigate its citizens' western land claims. The Indiana Company, which counted many prominent citizens of New Jersey among its investors, was represented on the committee. Not surprisingly, the committee's report concluded that the lands belonged to the states in common. In December 1780 the Assembly sent Congress a memorial based on this report.

In January 1781 Virginia offered to cede the northern part of its western claim if all prior Indian claims were voided and Virginia's rights to the remaining territory were confirmed. New Jersey, among other states, objected strenuously. In October 1781 the New Jersey Assembly instructed its delegates to the Confederation Congress to oppose the cession and demand a resolution of the Indiana Company claim. Congress rejected Virginia's proposal in November, and the issue remained unresolved until March 1784, when Congress finally accepted the partial cession in a compromise which incorporated an understanding that the Indian grants would not be upheld.

Dissatisfied with the proposed compromise, New Jersey attempted to bring the land dispute before the Confederation as a suit between the states of Virginia and New Jersey. When this failed, New Jersey voted against the Virginia land cession. As late as March 1786, long after the land question had been resolved, New Jersey's legislature continued to instruct the state's delegates to oppose any western lands bill if the legislation might benefit one state exclusively.

New Jersey considered the western lands to be important, both as a source of revenue for the central government and as a prime area where the state's many impoverished farmers might seek a new start. However, the opening of the West to settlement depended upon the free navigation of the Mississippi River, and New Jersey's position on this issue differed from that of other northern states.

Britain had conceded the right to free navigation of the Mississippi River in the Treaty of Paris of 1783, but Spain actually controlled the region. To protect their territory, the Spanish closed the river to American shipping in 1784. Further, they demanded the renunciation of any American claim to free navigation of the Mississippi as the price of a commercial treaty.

Most of the northern states were quite willing to give up free navigation for a commercial treaty with Spain. A treaty would provide commercial opportunities for eastern cities hard-pressed by the postwar economic depression and give the new nation some commercial standing. Continued closure of the Mississippi River would prevent expansion into the West, an area all regions expected the South to dominate, and thus keep southern power in check.

The South promoted the opening of the West not only because expansion would increase its own influence but because the South feared the West might opt for independence if it were not brought into the Confederation quickly.

John Jay of New York, the American secretary for foreign affairs, concluded that to insist on free navigation was futile, and he requested a change in his instructions. In August 1786 Congress agreed to Jay's proposed revision. Initially, two of New Jersey's three delegates supported revision. Virginia, convinced New Jersey might be persuaded that the opening of the West coincided with her best interests, directed James Madison to buttonhole Abraham Clark at the Annapolis Convention. Madison convinced Clark, who in turn helped persuade the New Jersey legislature to instruct the state's congressional delegates to restore the original demand for free navigation of the Mississippi.

A Spanish commercial treaty attractive to northern states blessed with ports and shipping industries was of little interest to a state with neither. The value of the western lands depended on opening the area for settlement. Once Congress controlled the western lands, New Jersey favored any course increasing their value.

New Jersey's Fiscal Problems with Congress

Congress's efforts to put its financial house in order did not end with the currency plan of 1780. In February 1781, before ratification of the Articles was complete, Congress asked the states to amend the document and give it the authority to levy a 5 percent tariff on certain imports—a move New Jersey favored heartily. Twelve states approved the 1781 impost, but passage required the assent of all thirteen. Rhode Island's negative vote killed the plan.

In September 1782, Congress made an emergency requisition on the states to pay the interest on the national debt. New Jersey's legislature took no action, an oversight which irritated the state's many Continental creditors. Stung by the public response, the legislature passed the required legislation in June 1783. In December the legislature moved to protect these creditors and bypass the requisition system it considered inequitable. It directed the state treasurer to pay the money directly to the federal public creditors resident in New Jersey rather than forward it to the Confederation treasury.

Meanwhile, Congress was again at work on a scheme to secure a regular source of income. In April 1783 it asked the states for the authority to levy a 5 percent tariff on certain goods for a period of twenty-five years. The proceeds would be used for public debt payments. In addition, it requested a supplemental revenue, also for twenty-five years, and the cession of all Crown lands still held by the states.

The New Jersey legislature had little reason to believe all thirteen states would agree to this impost when they had not approved the previous one. Nevertheless the legislature approved the duty and the land cession, but it delayed action on the supplemental revenue. In December 1783 the legislature authorized the necessary tax. It made it payable in paper money and ordered the printing of an amount equal to New Jersey's quota of the supplemental revenue. But as it did with the emergency requisition, it ordered the state treasurer to pay New Jersey creditors of the United States directly rather than forwarding any monies to the Confederation treasury. In December 1784 the legislature reaffirmed its decision and ordered the state treasurer to make no further payments on congressional requisitions until the states approved the impost.

As expected, all thirteen states did not ratify the financial plan. The significance of New Jersey's refusal to meet the requisition escaped notice because Congress made no new call for funds until September 1785, when it issued a requisition couched in language that enraged New Jersey's legislators. Congress announced it would not be responsible for interest payment made by any state to its own Continental creditors after January 1786. Further, it refused to issue interest certificates to public creditors of any state which failed to comply with the requisition.

The legislature fumed. New Jersey had expected to be reimbursed at some future point for the payments made to Continental creditors. In a December 9 letter to the state's congressional delegation, New Jersey assemblyman Abraham Clark noted that New Jersey had incurred considerable expense by shouldering the financial burdens of Congress and was now about to be penalized for doing so. He also observed that New Jersey's citizens had lent money to Congress as private citizens. No action of the legislature of the state where they resided should interfere with repayment. Supplying New Jersey's share of the requisition required oppressive taxes, said Clark; moreover, the state's hard-pressed citizens also paid tariffs to both New York and Pennsylvania, contributing handsomely to *their* state treasuries. Clark described the requisition as a scheme to subvert the impost, the only practicable means of raising a revenue. The requisition system of Congress was "a burden too unequal and grievous for this State to submit to." In February the legislature resolved to take no action on the requisition until the impost was passed. And until the impost was passed, the state's congressional delegation was to vote against any expense to New Jersey unless the measure benefited the state or the Union in general.

Congress was shocked by New Jersey's defiant posture and quickly dispatched Charles Pinckney of South Carolina, Nathaniel Gorham of Massachusetts, and William Grayson of Virginia to placate the legislators and plead with them to reconsider. Pinckney painted a gloomy picture of the dissolution of the Confederation should the New Jersey legislature remain recalcitrant, and he touched on the grim consequences of such a breakup for small states like New Jersey. He suggested that a proper remedy to the perceived difficulties with the Confederation might be a state call for a general convention to amend the Articles. The legislators discussed the matter for three days and agreed to rescind the vote, but they continued to insist that the requisition system was unreasonable.

New Jersey's change of heart was more cosmetic than real. The state took no steps to comply with the requisition. Indeed, few states made any attempt to supply the requisitioned funds. By June 1786 Congress was nearly out of money.

New Jersey's fiscal rebellion lent considerable weight to calls for some reform of the Articles. Congress had coped as best it could with the unwieldy requisition system. New Jersey's refusal to comply with that system, which it perceived as grossly unfair, made the fragility of the Union apparent.

New Jersey Delegates in the Constitutional Convention

Virginia's invitation to a September 1786 convention at Annapolis to discuss congressional power over trade followed closely upon New Jersey's refusal to honor the requisition. New Jersey sent three delegates—Abraham Clark, William Churchill Houston, and James Schureman—and equipped them with liberal instructions. The trio was authorized to examine the trade of the United States and the several states, to consider a uniform system of trade regulations, and to deal with other matters as well.

It was an interesting delegation. Clark advocated some expansion in the authority of Congress and was particularly concerned about the economic domination of New Jersey by New York and Pennsylvania. Houston (1746–1788) was a prominent lawyer whose specialties were tax and financial questions. Schureman (1756–1824) was a prominent New Brunswick merchant who had served in both the New Jersey Assembly and the Confederation Congress. He was a staunch nationalist and a determined opponent of all paper-money measures.

Delegations from New Jersey, Virginia, New York, Delaware, and Pennsylvania attended the convention. No delegation arrived with the same instructions. Delegates from New Hampshire, Rhode Island, Massachusetts, and North Carolina did not arrive in time; the other states ignored the call. Under these circumstances the convention could reach no conclusions. However, the delegates returned to their states with a report proposing that another convention be held in Philadelphia in May 1787 and noting that "the Idea of extending the powers of their Deputies, to other objects than those of Commerce which has been adopted by the State of New Jersey . . . will deserve to be incorporated into that of a future Convention." Congress approved the recommendation in February 1787.

New Jersey, Pennsylvania, Virginia, Delaware, and North Carolina named delegates to the Constitutional Convention before Congress even endorsed the idea. With the exception of Rhode Island, which ignored the convention entirely, the remaining states chose delegates between February and June, in part spurred by the specter of armed resistance raised by Shays' Rebellion in Massachusetts.

New Jersey finally settled on William Livingston, Jonathan Dayton, William Paterson, David Brearly, and William Churchill Houston as delegates. Houston did not attend, possibly because of illness.* David Brearly (1745–1790) was a prominent lawyer who had helped draft

---

*Editor's note: "Brearly" is at times spelled "Brearley." Houston did attend, although very briefly.

the New Jersey constitution in 1776. He was the chief justice of the New Jersey Supreme Court from 1779 to 1789 and a judge of the U.S. District Court from 1789 to his death. He was a strong opponent of paper money and became a Federalist.

Jonathan Dayton (1760–1826) was the youngest man at the convention. He was a captain during the Revolutionary War but early established a reputation for imprudence. A member of a wealthy family, he owned large amounts of public securities and was an enthusiastic land speculator. At the convention he was a vigorous exponent of the rights of small states. Though considered Clark's protégé, Dayton became a Federalist.

Paterson proved to be the most important member of the delegation, though all five men went on to hold important state or federal office under the new Constitution.

The delegates to the Philadelphia Convention faced no easy task. First, they had to reach agreement on how radically to reform the Articles. Further, they had to achieve consensus on the amount of authority to be given the central government and how the states might be protected both from each other and from the central government.

Governor Edmund Randolph, head of the Virginia delegation, presented a series of resolutions on May 29. This Virginia Plan, drafted by Madison, called for a bicameral Congress with proportional representation. The lower house would be elected by the people, the upper house by the lower from a slate of nominees proposed by the state legislatures. Congress would choose the executive and could veto all state laws contravening the federal constitution. At least one supreme court and a system of inferior courts would make up the judicial branch. A council of revision consisting of the executive and several members of the judiciary would have a veto over the legislature.

The small states, including New Jersey, objected because the Virginia Plan would place them at a disadvantage. The larger states would control both houses and the executive. On June 15, Paterson presented a plan based on a reform of the Articles rather than an entirely new frame of government. This proposal would retain the Confederation's principle of equal representation for each state. In addition, Congress would receive limited power to tax and to regulate interstate and foreign commerce. The states would be freed from the requisition method of finance. Congress would control the disposition of western lands and could negotiate freely with foreign powers. The Paterson scheme also contained a provision making federal law and treaties "the supreme law of the respective states." This suggestion became the basis for the "supreme law of the land" clause in Article VI of the final document.

New Jersey's delegation was actually responsible for two proposals in support of equal representation. Brearly suggested that all existing state boundaries be redrawn, providing for thirteen precisely equal states. The convention made approving noises about the desirability of equitable boundaries, but it took no action.

The convention debated Paterson's scheme (also called the New Jersey or Small State Plan) for three days before rejecting it and deciding to use the Virginia Plan as the basis for debate. The small states continued to oppose proportional representation because it embodied some of their worst fears about the domination of small by large states. In July the convention broke the stalemate when it accepted a compromise calling for a two-house legislature, one house with representation based on population and the other with each state receiving equal representation.

Once New Jersey was assured of some form of equal representation, its delegation found the new Constitution quite a suitable frame of government, since it provided useful solutions for many of the problems New Jersey had first cited in 1778 when responding initially to the Articles.

The provisions allotting the federal government the power to regulate commerce (foreign and interstate), issue currency, and govern western lands, and the language upholding the sanctity of contracts, addressed the concerns of both East and West Jerseyans.

Stripping the states of the power to exact their own tariffs removed an economic burden from New Jersey and dissipated considerable hostility toward New York and Pennsylvania. The opening of the West would not only provide the new government a source of income but also secure new opportunities for New Jersey's many impoverished farmers.

Throughout the Confederation period the state had suffered from depreciated currency and debt problems. New Jersey held a substantial portion of the Continental debt and had shouldered the heavy burden of interest payments to the state's Continental creditors, a burden the legislature believed should be the concern of the central government. There was little reason for any area of New Jersey to object to a new government which proposed to assume this debt. And New Jerseyans, appalled at the multiple and depreciating currencies and periodic repudiations of the Confederation years, were pleased with the prospect of a more stable financial system.

The form of government the convention produced owed more to Virginia's contribution than New Jersey's. Paterson's scheme rearranged the elements of the Confederation; Randolph's restructured the government. Still, New Jersey's contribution to the constitutional process was significant. The legislature's exasperation with the Confederation's mode of finance finally led to the flat refusal to comply with the requisition. This stand certainly encouraged the pursuit of more sweeping change among those states which sent delegations to Annapolis. New Jersey's broad instructions to its delegates were cited as a model, and the New Jersey Plan provided a useful corrective to the Virginia Plan.

The Constitution Ratified

The Philadelphia Convention's handiwork became public knowledge quickly. The full text of the Constitution appeared in the *Trenton Mercury* and in a New Brunswick broadside on September 25. In the first three weeks of October the legislature received several petitions from citizens of Salem, Gloucester, Middlesex, and Burlington counties calling for a ratifying convention. All expressed approval of the new frame of government; the most fervent was one from Salem, which read in part, "Nothing but the most immediate adoption of it can save the United States in general, and this state in particular, from absolute ruin."

Congress authorized the states to call ratifying conventions in late September. A month later, on October 29, the New Jersey legislature unanimously passed resolutions calling for a state convention. The elections were without incident, and on December 11 the delegates convened in Trenton at the Blazing Star Tavern. Information about the convention's deliberations is scanty. According to the account published in the *Trenton Mercury*, the delegates spent December 11–13 selecting officers, discussing rules, reading the legislature's authorizing resolution, and examining the Constitution. On December 14, 15, and 16 the Constitution was analyzed section by section. On December 18 the Constitution was again read, debated, and unanimously approved. A ceremonial procession to the courthouse for a public reading followed ratification. The celebration was punctuated by fifteen rounds of musket fire, thirteen for the new nation and one each for Delaware and Pennsylvania, which had ratified before New Jersey. The delegates then repaired to a nearby tavern, seeking a more convivial atmosphere for the expression of their satisfaction with the completed task. The newspaper account makes it plain that the joy of the occasion was fixed in every heart and expressed with liquid abandon. The convention adjourned on December 19, but not before passing a final resolution promoting a location in New Jersey for the nation's capital. Months later the New Jersey legislature offered a large site not far from Trenton, but to no avail.

New Jersey's hopes of luring the new federal capital (authorized by Article I, Section 8, of the Constitution) to a site on the Delaware may have added to the state's enthusiasm for the new Constitution.

Congress had actually met in Princeton in 1783 after the delegates departed Philadelphia in some haste, fleeing an angry contingent of Continental soldiers demanding back pay.

New Jersey's attempt to capture the federal capital ran afoul of both sectional rivalries and the struggle between those favoring a strong national government and those who did not. Congress, in turn, voted first for a site on the falls of the Delaware, then for two sites (one on the Delaware, one on the Potomac), then again for the site on the Delaware. Victory seemed within New Jersey's grasp, but lack of money made state construction of the buildings impossible. Though the South eventually prevailed, a New Jersey site was still a possibility while the state was engaged in the ratification process.

New Jersey had every reason to view the Constitution favorably, and there is no evidence of any substantial opposition to it within the state. None of the commentaries from beyond the state's borders indicated any doubt that New Jersey would ratify and do so quickly. Indeed, most of the debate in the new nation over the Constitution took place after New Jersey ratified. Abraham Clark, who could have registered significant opposition when the document was laid before Congress, remained quiet during ratification. Virginia's Richard Henry Lee proposed that Congress append a series of amendments detailing basic rights before forwarding the document to the states for ratification. His proposal, which included the provision for a second convention, might well have consigned the Constitution to defeat. Clark did not support Lee, and ten months later he explained his position in a letter to Thomas Sinnickson, a prominent Salem, New Jersey, merchant. Clark conceded he had not liked the Constitution because he believed it erected a consolidated rather than a federal government, and one which was unnecessarily oppressive. However, he had believed the document should be forwarded to the states as written, without approval or disapproval by the Confederation Congress, and he had hoped that the states would amend it as necessary.

The brief period of unanimity in New Jersey was not to last. Sectional divisions within the state had long been an important feature of political life. The two regions were different economically, socially, religiously, and ethnically. New Jerseyans were deeply divided over problems facing the state in the 1780s—debtor-creditor issues and the controversy over the loan office. The two regions agreed on little else but the deficiencies of the Confederation. The Constitution appealed to both sides. But the hostilities which had been expressed so forcefully in the loan office controversy and during the legislature's efforts to deal with the intense debtor-creditor situation reappeared during the first federal election. New Jersey's moment of concord then gave way to the accustomed pattern of sectional antagonisms, but these abated once more as the state achieved the distinction on November 20, 1789, of becoming the first to ratify the congressionally proposed Bill of Rights.

Essay on Sources

The major study of New Jersey during the Confederation period and the state's position on the Constitution is Richard P. McCormick, *Experiment in Independence: New Jersey in the Critical Period, 1781–1789* (New Brunswick, N.J., 1950). The New Jersey chapter in the present volume [*The Constitution and the States* (1988)] as well as a longer study, Mary R. Murrin, *To Save This State Prom Ruin: New Jersey and the Creation of the United States Constitution, 1776–1789* (Trenton, N.J., 1987), is based on McCormick's work.

For information on population, ethnic, religious, and land-use patterns, see Peter O. Wacker, *Land and People: a Cultural Geography of Preindustrial New Jersey; Origins and Settlement Patterns* (New Brunswick, N.J., 1975), especially chapters 3–5. On politics and social structure, see Jackson Turner Main, *Political Parties before the Constitution* (Chapel Hill, N.C., 1973), chapters 1, 6, 12, and 13, and, by the same author, *Social Structure of Revolutionary America* (Princeton, N.J., 1965), chapters 1, 3, and 6. Information on wartime devastation can be found in Howard Peckham, ed., *Toll of Independence: Engagements and Battle Casualties of the American Revolution, 1763–1783: A Documentary History* (Trenton, N.J., 1975), which is a fertile source for quotations on wartime damage. On matters economic, see E. James Ferguson, *The Power of the Purse: A History of American Public Finance, 1776–1790* (Chapel Hill, N.C., 1961), chapters 1–4, and John J. McCusker and Russell R. Menard, *The Economy of British America, 1607–1789* (Chapel Hill, N.C., 1985), especially chapter 9. On state and sectional rivalries, see Joseph L. Davis, *Sectionalism in American Politics, 1774–1787* (Madison, Wis., 1977), and Peter Onuf, *Origins of the Federal Republic: Jurisdictional Controversies in the United States, 1775–1789* (Philadelphia, 1983), chapters 1, 2, 4, and 7.

For biographical information on the major figures, see Paul S. Stellhorn and Michael Birkner, eds., *The Governors of New Jersey, 1664–1974: Biographical Essays* (Trenton, N.J., 1982), pp. 77–81, for Livingston; John E. O'Connor, *William Paterson, Lawyer and Statesman, 1745–1806* (New Brunswick, N.J., 1979), and James McLachlan, *Princetonians, 1748–1768: A Biographical Dictionary* (Princeton, N.J., 1975), pp. 437–440, for Paterson; Ruth Bogin, *Abraham Clark and the Quest for Equality in the Revolutionary Era, 1774–1794* (Rutherford, N.J., 1982); Richard A. Harrison, *Princetonians, 1776–1783: A Biographical Dictionary* (Princeton, N.J., 1981), pp. 31–42, for material on Dayton; and the McLachlan volume of *Princetonians*, pp. 643–647, for Houston.

Important sources of documentary material include Edmund C. Burnett, ed., *Letters of Members of the Continental Congress* (Washington, D.C., 1934; reprinted 1963), vols. 7 and 8; Merrill Jensen, John P. Kaminski, and Gaspare J. Saladino, eds., *The Documentary History of the Ratification of the Constitution* (Madison, Wis., 1976–), vols. 1, 3, and 13; the "Primitive Whig" essays from the *New Jersey Gazette*, courtesy of the William Livingston Papers project at New York University; and the pamphlet now identified as the work of Abraham Clark, *The True Policy of New Jersey, Defined* (Elizabeth-Town, N.J., 1786), in the Special Collections Department at Alexander Library, Rutgers University.

A former Federalist, Garret D. Wall (1783–1850) was selected governor of New Jersey by a Jacksonian Republican legislative caucus in 1829. Though he declined to serve, his election marked the revival of partisan politics in the state. In 1834 he was elected to the U.S. Senate, where he strongly supported the economic policies of both Jackson and Van Buren. Portrait Collection, Special Collections and University Archives, Rutgers University Libraries.

6

The men who wrote the Constitution of the United States in 1787 shared the assumption that political parties were bad because they could not help but be divisive. They declared as a consequence that parties should not and would not develop, and the structure of government they devised was based on this assertion. James Madison in *The Federalist Papers* foresaw the development of conflicting "interest" groups that would represent the different needs of American citizens. But he did not envision the political parties that quickly appeared in the 1790s, nor the two-party system that has characterized United States politics throughout most of its history.

As a result, Americans have tinkered with their political system to make it work under conditions for which it was not originally designed. Historians in turn have tried to explain when and why parties appeared and how they developed and operated. Historians have also examined which voters have been attracted to which parties and why there were usually two parties (not more, as in Italy, or fewer, as in the former Soviet Union). The first American party system arose between 1791 and 1795 on the foundation of real political, economic, and ideological differences among Americans. The resultant Federalist and Jeffersonian-Republican parties fought over policies and offices until after the War of 1812, when the Federalist Party declined because of its opposition to the war and a surge in nationalist feeling at its end. The election of 1824 was marked by a revival of political contests and followed by the re-emergence of a two-party system that Richard P. McCormick referred to as "the second party system" (1966).

Historians have tried to address numerous questions about this system. The first question is when parties actually emerged. The initial contest (on the national level, the presidential election of 1828) was between John Quincy Adams, representing the National Republicans, and Andrew Jackson of the Jacksonian Democrats. A division emerged between Whigs and Democrats, but when? Or, more precisely, when did this split emerge on the national level and in different states, specifically New Jersey? Did the second-party system develop because of national issues, state interests, or a combination of both?

The second question concerns ideology. Historians have suggested that philosophical differences stimulated the creation of political parties. Whigs favored an active government, one that assisted in the development of commerce and manufacturing. Democrats preferred a limited government and a laissez-faire economy. The first represented the elite and wealthy, the second small farmers and workers. But American political parties have seldom been diametrically opposed in their viewpoints; they more often comprise coalitions of different interest groups. Thus, for example, it is necessary to ask if all Whigs in New Jersey were wealthy, and if all of them agreed on policy matters. If not, other factors must have influenced the development of parties.

An alternative explanation revolves around personalities. John Quincy Adams and Andrew Jackson were very different. As John William Ward notes in *Andrew Jackson: Symbol for an Age* (1953), Adams represented the East and was more intellectual; Jackson, by contrast, was seen as the western man of action. Each appealed to some voters and politicians and alienated others. But do voters support parties based on subjective likes and dislikes alone? Is this a sufficient explanation for the emergence of parties?

Whether ideology or personality accounts better for the creation of political parties, historians have noted the tendency of parties to be self-perpetuating. They become "electoral machines," winning offices for candidates by gathering votes and rewarding supporters with patronage appointments once in power. Recipients of jobs and other prizes support the party in the next election by voting and otherwise using their influence. In *The Behavior of State Legislative Parties in the Jacksonian Era: New Jersey, 1829–1844* (1977), Peter Levine argues that such structural factors help explain what held together a diverse coalition.

Other historians have claimed that cultural differences have had greater influence in sustaining the party system. Herbert Ershkowitz, in *The Origin of the Whig and Democratic Parties: New Jersey Politics 1820–1837* (1982), argues that the "Whigs drew their support from evangelical Protestants, the Democrats had a constituency which included the Irish, German, and nonevangelical Protestants." Political scientists today might observe that Mormons are Republicans. But is there a uniform or strong correlation between ethnic, religious, and social background and party affiliation? If so, why does a particular religious or ethnic group support one party over another?

A related issue concerns the connection between the "first" and "second" party systems. Progressive historians claimed that in the debate over the Constitution, Federalists became members first of the Federalist and then the Whig parties. Anti-Federalists became Jeffersonian-Republicans and then Democrats. Thus they posited a continuity in American politics based on class and ideological differences. Revisionists (the name given historians who challenge traditional interpretations of the past) have seen discontinuity in membership. Some Federalists, such as Joseph Bloomfield in New Jersey, became Jeffersonian-Republicans. Others switched affiliation from the Jeffersonian-Republicans to the Whigs. Did issues, personalities, ideology, or cultural differences guide these changes? Finally, it is possible that the second-party system started for one set of reasons, then continued for another? What is certain is that the intrusion of new arguments (free soil and abolition) proved divisive in the 1850s, leading to the rise of a third-party system.

Suggested Readings

Birkner, Michael J., and Herbert Ershkowitz. "'Men and Measures': The Creation of the Second Party System in New Jersey." *New Jersey History* 107 (1989): 41–59.

Chambers, William Nisbet, and Walter Dean Burnham, eds. *The American Party System: Stages of Development.* New York: Oxford University Press, 1967.

Ershkowitz, Herbert. *The Origin of the Whig and Democratic Parties: New Jersey Politics, 1820–1837.* Washington, D.C.: University Press of America, 1982.

Levine, Peter D. *The Behavior of State Legislative Parties in the Jacksonian Era: New Jersey, 1829–1844.* Rutherford, N.J., 1977.

———. "State Legislative Parties in the Jacksonian Era: New Jersey, 1829–1844." *Journal of American History* 62 (1975): 591–607.

McCormick, Richard P. *The Second American Party System: Party Formation in the Jacksonian Era.* Chapel Hill: University of North Carolina Press, 1966.

Nadworny, Milton. "New Jersey Workingmen and the Jacksonians." *Proceedings of the New Jersey Historical Society* 67 (1949): 185–198.

Pessen, Edward. *Jacksonian America: Society, Personality, and Politics.* 1969. Rev. ed. Homewood, Ill.: Dorsey Press, 1978.

Renda, Lex. "The Dysfunctional Party: The Collapse of the New Jersey Whigs, 1849–1853." *New Jersey History* 116 (1998): 3–57.

Sellers, Charles G. *The Market Revolution: Jacksonian America, 1815–1846.* New York: Oxford University Press, 1991.

Wilentz, Sean. *The Rise of American Democracy: Jefferson to Lincoln.* New York: Norton, 2005.

◆ ◆ ◆ ◆ ◆ ◆

Party Formation in New Jersey in the Jackson Era

Richard P. McCormick

American political historians have long been intrigued with the Age of Jackson and especially with the political ferment occasioned by Jackson's entrance upon the national political scene. Although it has always been apparent that the Jacksonian era was marked, among other features, by the formation of a new two-party system, the circumstances that gave rise to the parties have remained shrouded in obscurity. Our difficulties may be attributed largely to the fact that we have looked to events in the national capital to provide an understanding of the course of politics, whereas the crucial arena for observing party formation was in the individual states. It is therefore of some interest to examine political developments in New Jersey in that exciting period.

In the decade following the Treaty of Ghent, political interest and activity in New Jersey were on the decline. Traditional political distinctions between Federalists and Democratic-Republicans were somehow nurtured and kept alive, but on a statewide basis the party of Jefferson had such a preponderance of numbers that the Federalists ceased to enter any contest above the county level. They could not expect to win state offices, for all officials—including the governor—were chosen by the joint meeting of the legislature. Neither could they hope to elect one of their party to Congress, for congressmen in New Jersey were elected on a general ticket. Nevertheless, the Federalists remained at least the equal of their opponents in five of the state's thirteen counties, and they were a threat in three or four others.[1]

The Democratic-Republican Party by 1824 was a mature organization that had enjoyed almost uninterrupted control of the state since 1801. It gave the appearance of being a well-constructed, smoothly functioning machine, its main parts being the township

Proceedings of the New Jersey Historical Society 83 (1965): 161–173. Reprinted by permission of the author and the New Jersey Historical Society.

committees, county conventions, and state convention. The last body—made up of delegates from each county—met biennially to nominate a congressional slate and quadrennially to name presidential electors. Because of the decentralized nature of New Jersey politics, control of the party was not vested in a small clique, but was instead dispersed among the county chieftains. This condition, together with the fact that the party had not for many years been challenged on the state level and was therefore not well unified by the spur of competition, was to explain in part the breaking up of the party in the mid-1820s.[2]

The character of the election machinery in New Jersey was also to be of significance in the impending upheaval, for it was well adapted to mass participation in politics. Elections were held on the second Tuesday and Wednesday in October, except in presidential years, when electors and congressmen were chosen in November. All elections were by ballot, which could be either written or printed. In practice they were almost always printed, thereby facilitating straight party voting. The township was the voting unit and contained either one or two polling places. There was a legal requirement that adult males must be taxpayers in order to vote, but even if there had been a serious disposition to enforce this qualification, the techniques for doing so were inadequate. Consequently there was virtually universal white manhood suffrage.[3] During the years of apathy that followed the decline of Federalism, however, only a minority of voters went to the polls. Indeed, the most striking change that was to mark the Jackson era was the extraordinary increase in the size of the electorate.

Although there had been occasional rumblings of interest in the presidential question earlier in the year, it was not until late in 1823 that New Jersey began to rouse itself from its political lethargy.[4] From the first there was a marked lack of unanimity among political leaders in their choice of presidential candidates; Calhoun, Crawford, and Adams all had substantial support within the ranks of the Democratic-Republicans.[5] Jackson's star was the last to rise, and there was little in the way of an organized campaign in his behalf until June 1824, when a public meeting in Salem issued a call for the friends of the General to gather in Trenton in September.[6]

The Jackson state meeting, attended by delegates from only seven of the thirteen counties, named an eight-man electoral ticket, at least three members of which were Federalists.[7] The movement was now well launched, and it is pertinent to ask who launched it. The evidence points fairly conclusively to the ubiquitous and notorious Colonel Samuel Swartwout of New York City. This former participant in the

Burr Conspiracy, who was also a close friend of Andrew Jackson, was actually the chairman of the Jackson state convention, even though his connection with New Jersey was a tenuous one.[8] He was probably linked to the Salem meeting through Aaron Ogden Dayton, the nephew of another of his conspiratorial associates, Jonathan Dayton, for Aaron Ogden Dayton—a former Federalist—was secretary of both the Salem meeting and the state meeting.[9]

When the official Democratic-Republican state convention met on October 19, the Jacksonians entered into a combination with the Crawfordites and forced the adoption of an electoral ticket made up of five Jackson and three Crawford men. The supporters of Adams thereupon withdrew and named their own set of electors.[10] Not content with the five-eighths of a loaf that the convention had awarded them, the ardent friends of Jackson assembled again a week later, on October 25, and formed an all-out Jackson ticket.[11]

Eight days later the election opened, and for two days the people of New Jersey experienced the unfamiliar excitement of participating in a genuine presidential contest. Only once before—in 1808—had they been presented with the opportunity of voting for opposing slates of electors, and on that occasion over 33,000 ballots had been cast.[12] Now—in 1824—only 18,400 men voted. This figure approximated one-third of the potential electorate. By a narrow margin of 1,000 votes, Jackson triumphed over Adams and carried nine of the thirteen counties.[13]

Under the circumstances, Jackson's victory must be regarded more as a successful and surprising political coup than as the result of a popular crusade. With the regular organization of the Democratic-Republican Party badly divided, the Jackson forces seized the initiative, created their own organization, and carried on a skillful campaign. It is impossible to discern any clear-cut bases for the cleavage between Jacksonians and Adamsites. Considerations of personal political expediency rather than concern with fundamental principles determined the allegiance of political leaders.[14]

No small share of the credit for Jackson's victory must be given to the leadership provided by former Federalists. Long denied an opportunity to rise to positions of state and national prominence, they eagerly climbed aboard the Jackson bandwagon, which was driven by Samuel Swartwout, and many of them were subsequently to become prominent Jacksonian officeholders.[15]

Such excitement as had been engendered by the presidential contest quickly subsided. The state elections in 1825 went off quietly, voters returned to their traditional party allegiances, and there seemed to be no general awareness that a new political era was at hand. In

1826, however, when the biennial state convention of the Democratic-Republican Party met, the "presidential question" was once more a divisive factor, and the session broke up in disorder, never to meet again. Each faction then met separately and nominated its own Congressional ticket.[16] One newspaper editor gave a succinct explanation of what lay behind the conflict: "Why simply that one man shall go *out* of, and another *into* office."[17]

In the October elections, the contest was between the Jackson Party and the Adams—or Administration—Party. The Adamsites scored an easy victory, carrying the state by 5,000 votes out of a total of 25,000.[18] Again, this election was not a decisive test, for the Jacksonians had decided to wait until 1828 to make an all-out campaign. Their organization was rudimentary, in contrast to that of the Adamsites, which was largely the organization of the old Democratic-Republican Party, revived and strengthened by administration support and patronage.[19]

Soon after the state elections in 1827, which aroused little interest and resulted in a slight gain by the Jacksonians, the political pot began to bubble vigorously.[20] The Jacksonians led off with a state convention held on the anniversary of the Battle of New Orleans. With evident enthusiasm, they named their electoral ticket and appointed a central state committee headed by Garret D. Wall.[21] The Adamsites held their convention on Washington's Birthday with a host of new faces—many of them former Federalists—conspicuous among the leaders of the session.[22] Quite obviously, the period of proscription had ended, and the Federalists were now participating fully in both the Jacksonian and Adamsite camps.

As the critical fall elections approached, campaigning by both parties reached an unprecedented peak of intensity. Early in October the state election was held, and it gave the Adamsites a victory by the slight margin of a thousand votes.[23] Some two weeks later—on October 23—the "Jackson Republican Convention," as it was now called, assembled again in Trenton. With every evidence of harmony, a congressional ticket evenly divided between former Federalists and former Democratic-Republicans was nominated.[24]

On November 4th and 5th the voters of the state responded to the pressures exerted on them by the two well-organized and vigorous party machines by turning out more than 45,000 strong. Weeks later, when the official returns were finally published, they learned that Adams had triumphed by a majority of nearly 2,000 votes and had carried all but four counties.[25] The real triumph, however, lay with the political managers of both parties who, without appeals to issues or to economic interest, had succeeded in bringing to the polls almost three times as many men as had cast ballots in 1824.

Seventy-two percent of the adult white males voted in 1828 as compared with 31 percent four years earlier. Vigilance committees, poll committees, township committees, county conventions, party organs, pamphlets, broadsides and personal appeals had all combined to arouse the voters and make them feel the urgency of the contest. No discernible issues, either state or national, were involved, other than those that centered on personalities. But the common man—the man who had rarely been stimulated to vote in national elections—now went to the polls, and he cast his vote as enthusiastically against as for the glamorous figure of Andrew Jackson.[26]

With the removal of their personal figure head from the presidential office, the Adamsites were dispirited and ineffective in 1829, and the Jacksonians swept the state for the first time since 1824.[27] Garret D. Wall, former Federalist, and foremost leader of the Jackson Party, was elected to the governorship, but he declined and accepted instead the appointment of United States district attorney. Thereupon his future son-in-law, Peter D. Vroom, also a former Federalist, was chosen governor.[28]

Conscious of the growing strength of their party organization at the local level, but aware of the fact that they had not been able to win a statewide election since their surprise triumph in 1824, the Jacksonians decided to change the rules of the game to suit their own ends in 1830. In control of the legislature, they enacted a law postponing the congressional election in 1830 until late December, thus separating the state from the national election.[29] They had reason to fear the strength of their opponents, now organized under the National Republican banner behind a new hero, Henry Clay. Their strategy was probably sound, for although they retained control of the legislature, they lost the congressional contest by a margin of nearly 1,100 votes out of a total of about 29,000.[30] The defeat of the Jacksonians was in part attributable to internal dissension, which manifested itself in the state convention and resulted in the choice of a congressional ticket that displeased many in the party.[31] Although the party regained control of the legislature in 1831, its margin was slight, and it was evident that the election of 1832 was going to be fiercely contested by two well-matched foes.[32]

It was at this period—in the early 1830s—that a significant new influence made its appearance in New Jersey politics. During the years 1830–1832 the legislature chartered the Delaware and Raritan Canal Company and the Camden and Amboy Railroad Company, which, merged together as the Joint Companies, were granted a monopoly of the canal and railroad traffic across the state between New York and Philadelphia. For many years to come, this extremely valuable monopoly privilege was to be the target of attack by hostile transportation interests and was to be a major issue in state politics. Because the monopoly had been created by a Jacksonian legislature, and because many of the Jackson leaders were closely identified with the Joint Companies, the destinies of the party and the monopoly were intertwined. Correspondingly, those interests opposed to the monopoly were generally to be found in the National Republican—or Whig—Party. The rival transportation groups were especially active in the years 1832 to 1837, and during this period party politics were to be in many ways a projection of transportation politics.[33]

The influence of the transportation factor was evident as the parties prepared for the election of 1832. The five-member Jackson central committee, appointed in mid-March, included three directors of the Joint Companies and the editor of the leading pro-monopoly newspaper.[34] When the National Republicans held a Young Men's Convention in April, the presiding officer was the president of the Joint Companies' leading antagonist, the New Jersey Railroad and Transportation Company, and the secretary was a director of the same railroad.[35]

In addition to the transportation issue, the campaign also revolved around the bank question, which both parties agitated vigorously for popular effect. Elaborate organizations were perfected, with "Young Men" committees for the first time supplementing the work of the regular party machinery. Shortly before the October state elections, the county conventions met as usual to nominate candidates for the legislature and to elect delegates to the state conventions.[36] Forty thousand men turned out to vote for members of the legislature, an unprecedented total for a state election, and the National Republicans won this first test of strength by a small majority.[37]

A month later, however, when the national election took place, the tables were turned and the Jacksonians eked out a victory by the narrow margin of 463 votes out of the record total of over 47,000.[38] Seventy percent of the adult white males voted. This indecisive triumph was the signal for the exultant editor of the chief party organ to proclaim:

> Hereafter we know no other name but *Democracy*—and the support of the administration is the *only* test of Democracy. The name of Jackson was but the signal—the watchword at which we rallied to the old Democratic landmarks—let us now maintain our stand upon the *old party principles,* and the *old party name.*[39]

In 1833—as in 1829—the Jacksonians overwhelmed their opponents, who could arouse little popular enthusiasm now that the magic name of Clay no longer served as their symbol of unity.[40] The Democrats showed nearly the same strength they had in 1832, but the National Republican vote declined sharply, especially in South Jersey, where it fell off as much as 50 percent in certain counties. Religious issues, growing out of the Hicksite-Orthodox split among the Quakers, contributed to the defeat of the National Republicans, as did the deterioration of their party organization.[41]

Looking forward to the 1834 election, the anti-Jacksonians seized upon the removal of the deposits from the Bank of the United States as the issue upon which they hoped to rally support. When New Jersey's two senators refused to heed the instructions of the Democratic legislature on this question, they became—with the Bank—centers of party controversy. Reports of the endless debates in Congress kept the issue alive, although the local Democratic leadership was inclined to view the whole matter as remote, artificial, and even somewhat annoying. "If you were to stop talking," wrote Governor Vroom to Democratic Congressman James Parker, "people would not know that anything was the matter."[42]

But the "Bankites" continued to fulminate against Jackson, and their activities came to a head early in April when delegates from all parts of the state met in Trenton, ostensibly to memorialize Congress on the subject of the deposits. In reality, however, the meeting organized what very soon became known as the Whig Party.[43] It was the state committee appointed by this Bank meeting that later issued the call for a Whig State Convention to meet in August.[44]

The Democrats, despite some minor defections over the Bank controversy, remained substantially the same party in leadership and organization that they had been since 1828.[45] They held a state meeting in May for the purpose of drafting a set of resolutions approving the policies of the administration, at the same time appointing party committees. In September, 670 delegates gathered in Trenton for the regular Democratic State Convention and with machine-like precision went through the formalities of renominating the old congressional ticket.[46]

With both parties once again highly organized for what was universally regarded as a major contest, the total vote rose to a new high of 53,862—indicating that 78 percent of the adult white males had gone to the polls. The Democrats elected their congressmen by a majority of 1,000 votes and also retained control of the legislature.[47] Political observers agreed that the deciding factor in producing the Democratic victory was the vote cast by the Hicksite Quakers against the Whig ticket.[48]

With the election of 1834, a decade of transition in the history of political parties in New Jersey came to an end. For the next two decades, the Democrats and the Whigs, both well organized and usually evenly matched, were to contest for supremacy. Although the principles that distinguished one from the other were far from clear, each was able to command the firm allegiance of multitudes of voters.

The Jackson-Democratic Party, as it emerged and developed during the decade under consideration, was a new political organization; it could not be considered as a lineal descendant of the Democratic-Republican Party. It owed its origins largely to Federalist leadership, and former Federalists continued to be its most conspicuous helmsmen after it had become the dominant party in the state. They were attracted to the Jacksonian cause because it offered them an opportunity to win political preferment, and they were able to gain high positions in the party at an early date because the Democratic-Republican stalwarts chose to regard Adams as the legitimate successor to the presidency. The party was not organized around a set of principles, nor did it adopt any body of doctrine during the decade. Made up of disparate elements, it found its unifying symbol in Jackson and its unifying drive in the desire to win office.

The decade witnessed a new type of competition between parties that were becoming increasingly institutionalized. Men of abilities were willing to devote considerable attention to party affairs because politics offered a respectable, exciting, and lucrative career. They mastered and applied techniques of mass organization, recently made possible by improvements in transportation, communication, and publication as well as by an electoral process that encouraged mass participation. Using these techniques with skill and energy, they competed intensely for votes. So well did they practice their profession that they succeeded in bringing to the polls nearly three-fourths of the adult white males in the state.

It would not be possible to find in this decade any evidence that the party situation reflected basic economic or social cleavages in the population. Certainly the Jacksonians were not participating in a class revolt or engaging in a radical crusade. Their most evident distinguishing characteristic subsequent to 1830 was their close identification with the monopoly of the Joint Companies. Before that date they were known chiefly for their allegiance to Jackson and for their partiality toward former Federalists. Their greatest accomplishment was so to arouse popular interest as to give new depth and meaning to the term "American Democracy."

Notes

1. The period is ably surveyed in Walter R. Fee, *The Transition from Aristocracy to Democracy in New Jersey, 1789–1829* (Somerville, N.J., 1933). As late as 1823, nineteen of the fifty-six legislators bore the Federalist label. *(New Brunswick) Fredonian*, October 23, 1823. Federalists survived in large part because the county was the major political unit. Moreover, as partisan tensions declined, the legislators agreed that members from each county should enjoy "Senatorial courtesy" in matters of local appointments; Federalist politicians then could win elections to the legislature in several counties and share in the spoils of office. L. Q. C. Elmer, *The Constitution and Government of the Province and State of New Jersey* . . . (Newark, 1872), 211.

2. Even on the county level, the lack of competition from the Federalists encouraged intra-party contests and the frequent launching of "Union" tickets made up of Democratic-Republicans and Federalists. *(New Brunswick) Fredonian*, October 22, 1818; *(Elizabeth) New Jersey Journal*, October 16, 1822, September 30, 1823; *Bridgeton Observer*, October 18, 1823.

3. *New Jersey Laws*, Acts of November 16, 1807, and June 1, 1820. Under this taxpayer qualification as many as three-fourths of the adult males actually cast ballots.

4. Gov. I. H. Williamson to Sen. Mahlon Dickerson, December 16, 1823, Mahlon Dickerson Papers, New Jersey Historical Society (hereafter NJHS).

5. *New Jersey Journal*, November 18, 1823; *(New Brunswick) Fredonian*, February 12, 19, 1824; Charles F. Adams, *Memoirs of John Quincy Adams,*12 vols. (Philadelphia, 1874–1877), 6:173–174, 253–254, 282–283, 479–480.

6. *Bridgeton Observer*, June 26, 1824. This Salem meeting was generally regarded at the time as marking the real start of the Jackson movement in New Jersey. "Amicus Republicae," *(New Brunswick) Fredonian*, September 8, 1824.

7. *(New Brunswick) Times*, September 22, 1824. The Federalists were James Parker, Joseph W. Scott, and John Beatty Jr.

8. Swartwout owned land with his brother in Bergen County. For the colonel's background and his relations with Jackson, see Henry F. Du Puy, "Some Letters of Andrew Jackson," *Proceedings of the American Antiquarian Society*, n.s., 30 (1921): 70–88. In mid-April, Swartwout had played a leading role in promoting Jackson's interests in New York City. *(New Brunswick) Fredonian*, April 15, 1824.

9. [Charles Robson], *The Biographical Encyclopaedia of New Jersey* (Philadelphia, 1877), 374–376.

10. *(New Brunswick)Times*, October 27, 1824, *(New Brunswick) Fredonian*, October 27, 1824.

11. *Bridgeton Observer*, October 30, 1824. This final ticket contained six of the eight names proposed by the September meeting; five of the eight named by the state convention.

12. Minutes of the Privy Council, II, November 12, 1808. New Jersey State Library. Down to 1804, and again in 1812, the electors were not properly chosen. In 1816 and 1820 there had been no contest.

13. *(New Brunswick) Times*, November 10, 1824; *(New Brunswick) Fredonian*, November 17, 1824.

14. *(New Brunswick) Fredonian*, November 10, 1824; Elmer, *Constitution*, 189, 220, 224–225.

15. Among the prominent Federalists who took the lead in supporting Jackson were Garret D. Wall, Peter D. Vroom, James Parker, Henry S. Green, Aaron Ogden Dayton, Joseph W. Scott and William Chetwood. James Parker to G. D. Wall, November 10, 1824, James Parker Papers, Rutgers University Library (hereafter RUL).

16. *(Newark) Sentinel of Freedom*, September 26, 1826; *(Trenton) Emporium*, September 30, 1826; *(Bridgeton) West Jersey Observer*, October 7, 1826; [S. J. Bayard], A *Sketch of the Life of Com. Robert F. Stockton* (New York, 1856), 60–62.

17. *(New Brunswick) Fredonian*, October 4, 1826. See also *West Jersey Observer*, October 7, 1826; *(Newark) Sentinel of Freedom*, September 26, 1826.

18. *(Newark) Sentinel of Freedom*, October 17, 1826; *(New Brunswick) Fredonian*, November 1, 8, 1826. The Adams Party won the legislature, 41–16, and carried all but three counties—Sussex, Warren, and Hunterdon.

19. *(Trenton) Emporium*, October 21, 1826; *(New Brunswick) Fredonian*, October 25, December 13, 1826; *(Newark) Sentinel of Freedom*, November 14, 1826; Bayard, *Stockton*, 63; Adams, *Memoirs*, 6:313–614.

20. *(Newark) Sentinel of Freedom*, October 23, 1827. Even as late as 1827, the old party labels still retained meaning in some counties. S. G. Opdycke to G. D. Wall, August 28, 1827, G. D. Wall Papers, RUL; *(New Brunswick) Fredonian*, September–October 1827.

21. *(Newark) Sentinel of Freedom*, January 15, 1828; *West Jersey Observer*, January 12, 1828. The electors were all former Democratic-Republicans, but the Federalists were assured that their claims would be recognized when the Congressional ticket was named. J. D. Westcott Jr. to G. D. Wall, January 18, 1828, G. D. Wall Papers, RUL.

22. *(Mt. Holly) New Jersey Mirror*, February 27, 1828. Two former Federalists, Theodore Frelinghuysen and Aaron Leaming, were placed on the electoral ticket, and others such as Joseph C. Hornblower, L. H. Stockton, C. C. Stratton, William Pearson and William B. Ewing were active delegates. *West Jersey Observer*, March 15, 1828.

23. *West Jersey Observer*, October 13, 1828. The new legislature was to have 34 Adamsites and 23 Jacksonians.

24. *West Jersey Observer*, November 1, 1828; *(Newark) Sentinel of Freedom*, October 23, 1828. The three Federalists were Vroom, Parker and Fowler. The "Administration State Convention," meeting on October 17, had named a congressional slate that contained only one known Federalist—T. H. Hughes of Cape May. *New Jersey Mirror*, October 29, 1828.

25. *(Newark) Sentinel of Freedom*, November 25, 1828; *West Jersey Observer*, December 6, 1828.

26. Elmer, *Constitution*, 226.

27. *(Newark) Sentinel of Freedom*, October 20, 1829. They carried nine counties and secured a 39–18 majority in the legislature.

28. Elmer, *Constitution*, 428–429.

29. *New Jersey Laws*, March 2, 1830. Normally the state and national elections would have been held together on the second Tuesday and Wednesday in October.

30. *New Jersey Mirror*, August 25, October 20, 1830; January 13, 1831.

31. *(Newark) Sentinel of Freedom*, November 16, December 7, December 21, 1830.

32. *New Jersey Mirror*, October 27, 1831.

33. Wheaton J. Lane, *From Indian Trail to Iron Horse* (Princeton, N.J., 1939), passim; Robert T. Thompson, "Transportation Combines and Pressure Politics," *Proceedings of the New Jersey Historical Society* 57 (1939): 1–15, 71–86.

34. *New Jersey Journal*, March 20, 1832.

35. *New Jersey Journal*, March 27, April 17, 1832. The directors of the New Jersey Railroad and Transportation Company were almost all National Republicans.

36. In Essex County the county conventions were not held until October 5 and 6, only ten days before the election. *New Jersey Journal*, September–October 1832.

37. Although they secured a two-to-one majority in the legislature, their statewide popular majority was under 2,000. *New Jersey Journal*, October 16, 1832; *(Trenton) Emporium*, October 30, 1832.

38. *(Trenton) Emporium*, November 24, 1832. The Anti-Masonic vote was 480, enough to have significantly affected the outcome. Jackson carried Sussex, Warren, Hunterdon, Monmouth, Bergen, and Somerset. South Jersey, Essex, Middlesex, and Morris went for Clay.

39. *(Trenton) Emporium*, November 10, 1832. Four years earlier, the same editor, Stacy G. Potts, had suggested to Garret D. Wall that the time had come for "the friends of Jackson to hoist the Republican flag." Evidently this proposal was regarded as being premature, for the Jackson label remained in use until 1832. Potts to Wall, November 8, 1828, G. D. Wall Papers.

40. *New Jersey Journal*, October 22, November 5, 1833; *(Trenton) Emporium*, October 12, 1833. The Democratic majority was nearly 7,000, and they won every county except Essex and Cape May.

41. The Hicksites voted Democratic, largely because of their animosity toward Theodore Frelinghuysen, who had been opposed to them in their lawsuit with the Orthodox.

42. Vroom to Parker, January 14, 1834, James Parker Papers. Two months later Vroom observed impatiently to Parker, "Neither of us can as yet see the end of the noise and clamor which the parasites of the Bank are endeavoring to excite and prolong." Vroom to Parker, March 15, 1834, ibid.

43. *New Jersey Journal*, April 8, 1834; Vroom to Parker, April. 4, 1834, James Parker Papers. The name "Whig" came into use in New Jersey late in April.

44. *New Jersey Journal*, July 15, 1834. The leading figures in the newly christened party were for the most part men who had heretofore not occupied conspicuous positions in politics. Many were young men; a few were seceding Jacksonians; others had earlier been

identified with the hierarchy of the old Democratic-Republican Party. Senators Samuel L. Southard and Theodore Frelinghuysen were the chief ornaments of the party.

45. Joseph W. Scott, Gen. Abraham Godwin, William Chetwood, and James Cook were some of the moderately prominent figures who deserted to the Whigs. See also Vroom to Parker, May 20, 30, 1834, James Parker Papers.

46. *New Jersey Journal,* May 27, Sept. 16, 1834.

47. *New Jersey Journal,* Oct. 21, Nov. 4, 1834. The Democrats carried Bergen, Morris, Sussex, Warren, Hunterdon, Somerset, Monmouth, and Gloucester.

48. *New Jersey Journal,* October 21, 1834; Vroom to Parker, May 30, 1830, James Parker Papers.

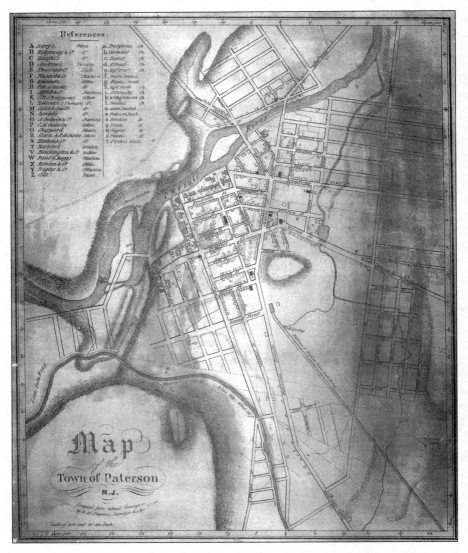

This 1833 map of Paterson shows the course of the Passaic River and the sluices built to carry water from the Great Falls to the mills. It includes a list of the mills that were in existence in 1833; most produced textiles. The map shows the falls (at the sharp bend in the river), and bridge above them, leading to the disputed pleasure gardens. Collections and University Archives, Rutgers University Libraries.

7

The period from about 1820 to 1850 is usually called the Jacksonian Era, or the Age of the Common Man. Historians have pointed to it as a time of great change; a market revolution, a transportation revolution, multiple reform movements, and the revivalism of the Second Great Awakening. The rise of Paterson, and the subtexts of the tale of Sam Patch and the creation of Forest Garden, all parts of the story Paul E. Johnson tells in the following selection, can help us understand aspects of New Jersey's history in this time period, and look at major issues of concern to historians.

Paterson was the brainchild of Alexander Hamilton and others who in 1792 created the Society for the Encouragement of Useful Manufactures (SUM), hoping to use water power from the Great Falls of the Passaic River to build the first planned industrial city in the country. The promoters assumed that manufacturing would build a stronger, more competitive nation. The project limped through ups and downs in the 1790s and War of 1812, then began to expand in the 1820s. By 1830 the town had seventeen cotton mills, producing 5,000,000 yards of cloth, and employing some 5,000 workers. Nationally, the time period saw an increase in production from 4,000,000 yards of cloth in 1817 to 323,000,000 by 1840. Most cotton cloth was produced in New England, but Paterson shared in developments even as it became better known for the production of locomotives and silk fabric. As the city industrialized, labor unrest increased; from 1824 to 1836 there were six strikes. In the 1830s workers pushed for a ten-hour day, and by the 1880s the demands were for eight hours. Strikes were frequent in Paterson, especially in the late nineteenth century, and in 1913 the much larger city that Paterson had become was the location of a famous walkout as silk workers left the mills en masse.

Sam Patch was descended from a New England Puritan family of declining fortunes. Originally farmers, with each generation they made do with smaller and smaller pieces of land as population increased and farms were divided. His father turned to shoemaking, and the family to employment in the new textile mills. Sam himself started working in the mills in Pawtucket, Rhode Island, at age seven, and by the mid-1820s he was a skilled boss mule spinner in Paterson. There, as the following selection shows, he challenged the local elites by attracting attention during their special events, and did so by dramatically leaping off a cliff and into the Great Falls. After he left Paterson, Patch went on to become an early American celebrity—he gave up mill work to become an entertainer. He jumped from heights at Hoboken, Niagara, and Rochester. Sadly, in the end a combination of alcoholism and daring proved fatal.

Sam Patch's life and adventures and the changing world in which he lived raise many issues, especially for labor historians. These scholars originally focused narrowly on trade unions, collective bargaining, and major strikes. By the 1960s and 1970s, reflecting democratization of the historical profession and the radicalism of the times, the perspective of the "new labor" historians had broadened to include numerous aspects of workers' lives. Particularly influential were E. P. Thompson's *The Making of the English Working Class* (1963) and the work of Herbert G. Gutman on American workers and the culture of their communities. An interest in women and minorities has been added. Recently, the view has grown even wider, to include slave and indentured as well as free labor, management, and global comparisons. Labor historians who have looked at the early nineteenth century are particularly interested in the shift from artisans and craftsmen to unskilled workers as mass production, factories, and machines were introduced. In the process, older master-journeymen teaching apprentices their craft in home workshops were replaced by large, impersonal businesses. Examining the new arrangements, historians look for divisions between workers and their bosses and try to pinpoint when class consciousness arose. They note conflict over the conditions of work (wages, hours, and the rules of work), and the extent and impact of child labor. In examining Sam Patch and his experiences, Johnson looks at many of these issues, and more.

What were the issues in Paterson in the 1820s that led workers to walk out in 1828? Why did the mill owners' change of the lunch hour provoke them? How was class consciousness exhibited in Paterson? How does the change in the way residents celebrated the Fourth of July help us understand increased economic divisions in the supposedly democratic Age of the Common Man? Historians have noted that early industrialization and the market and transportation revolutions raised the standard of living for many, as it made more goods available at lower prices. But capitalism also brought increased competition and the exploitation of workers who faced lower wages and poor working conditions. What were the working conditions in early Paterson in terms of wages and hours? Why were children used in the mills, and how were they treated? How, in his role as a boss mule spinner, did Patch treat them?

Forest Garden, Timothy B. Crane's project on the north bank of the falls where he hoped to build a refined recreational center, produced much opposition. Crane saw his efforts as improving on nature, providing facilities that would enable the pubic, or at least some members of it, to enjoy their leisure time. Why did Sam Patch and his fellow workers have a problem with the development of this area? Was it the cost of going there or were other issues involved as well?

Related to the fight over means of recreation in this period and later are the impact of religious revivalism and concerns about the use of alcohol. Early industrialization meant that greater quantities of alcohol were available, and at less cost, than before, helping the Jacksonian period become the time of the highest per capita consumption in American history. At the same time, factory work was regimented, and machinery increasingly dangerous; owners wanted sober workers operating their complex tools. Add religious objections to the consumption of alcohol, and the development of a temperance movement is not surprising. Alcohol proved a disaster first for Greenleaf Patch, Sam's father, and then for Patch himself. He used drink to bolster his courage before his death-defying leaps, only to meet a sad end in the falls of the Genesee at Rochester. What does his life tell us not just about the perils of drink and the costs of fame, but also about economic mobility in the Jacksonian era and the price of industrialization?

Suggested Readings

Brody, David. "The Old Labor History and the New: In Search of the American Working Class." *Labor History* 20 (1979): 111–126.

Dawley, Alan. *Class and Community: The Industrial Revolution in Lynn.* Cambridge, Mass.: Harvard Studies in Urban History, 1976.

Fink, Leon. "What Is To Be Done in Labor History." *Labor History* 43 (2002): 419–424.

Gish, Clay. "The Children's Strikes: Socialization and Class Formation in Paterson, 1824–1836." *New Jersey History* 110 (1992): 21–38.

Gowaskie, Joseph. *Workers in New Jersey History.* Trenton: New Jersey Historical Commission, 1996.

Gutman, Herbert G. *Work, Culture, and Society in Industrializing America: Essays in American Working Class and Social History.* New York: Knopf, 1976.

Hirsch, Susan. *Roots of the American Working Class: The Industrialization of Crafts in Newark, 1800–1860.* Philadelphia: University of Pennsylvania Press, 1978.

Laurie, Bruce. *Artisans Into Workers: Labor in Nineteenth-Century America.* New York: Hill and Wang, 1989.

Prude, Jonathan. *The Coming of the Industrial Order: Town and Factory Life in Rural Massachusetts, 1810–1860.* Cambridge: Cambridge University Press, 1983.

Schultz, Ronald. *The Republic of Labor: Philadelphia Artisans and the Politics of Class, 1720–1830.* New York: Oxford University Press, 1993.

Sellers, Charles Grier. *The Market Revolution: Jacksonian America, 1815–1846.* New York: Oxford University Press, 1991.

Troy, Leo. *Organized Labor in New Jersey.* Princeton, N.J.: D. Van Nostrand, 1965.

Trumbull, Levi.R. *A History of Industrial Paterson.* Paterson, N.J.: Carleton M. Herrick, 1882.

Wilentz, Sean. *Chants Democratic: New York City and the Rise of the American Working Class, 1788–1850.* New York: Oxford University Press, 1984.

Paterson

Paul E. Johnson

In his mid-twenties Sam Patch left Pawtucket and reappeared in Paterson, New Jersey—twelve miles west of New York City. We cannot know why he made the move, but Paterson was a good place for him: it was a bigger factory town than Pawtucket, and it sat beside a more famous waterfall.

Educated travelers knew Paterson as the site of Passaic Falls, one of the scenic wonders of North America. The young architect Benjamin Latrobe spent part of his honeymoon there in 1800, and suggested it as a good place for an American academy of landscape art. Passaic Falls, said Latrobe, "combine everything in themselves and in the magic circle of which they are the Center, of which Nature forms her sublimest Landscapes, excepting the ocean." Other cultivated visitors agreed that Passaic Falls provided a rare combination of the beautiful, the sublime, and the picturesque. The Passaic River widened and slowed above Paterson, then made an abrupt turn just at the brink and dropped seventy feet (second only to Niagara in the eastern United States) into a deep shaded pool. The falls, the dark and craggy rocks, the dangerous sheer cliffs on both banks, and the ancient forest that brooded over the scene were perfect expressions of natural power and primordial gloom. The view at the falls was "grand and beautiful," "sublime-almost terrific," "frightful," "a terrible prospect," "a scene of singular grandeur and beauty." Those who wanted to escape from these sublimities into the more reassuring picturesque could turn their backs to the falls and precipice and peer through the trees onto shaped land: a broad plain of farms and country roads in the eighteenth century and, after 1815, the sprawl of Paterson along the lower Passaic River.[1]

Paterson itself possessed a well-known history. It had been founded as the "National Manufacturing City" in 1792, with the active support of Secretary of the Treasury Alexander Hamilton, and with money from a joint-stock company called the Society for the Encouragement of Useful Manufactures (SUM). Pierre Charles L'Enfant, the French architect who had laid out the federal city of Washington, designed an ambitious and costly dam and millrace for the SUM. The project took two years to complete, and the first Paterson factory opened in 1794. The enterprise was premature: capital, skills, and markets for domestic manufactures were limited, and the Paterson factory closed its doors in 1796. The company leased a few mill sites in the early years of the nineteenth century, and a few more during the War of 1812. Then the commercialization of inland farming after 1815 created an exploding domestic demand for textiles and other American-made goods. Factories, mills, and forges sprang up along L'Enfant's old Paterson raceways, sending a flood of finished goods to the nearby entrepôt of New York, and from there to markets all over the United States. By 1827 Hamilton's ghost town was a manufacturing city of six thousand, described by a New Jersey newspaper (one that no longer apologized for such things) as "this flourishing Manchester of America."[2]

Sam Patch was among the thousands of workers who moved into Paterson in the 1820s. He found work as a mule spinner and, in September 1827, he performed a leap at Passaic Falls that got him into the newspapers for the first time. The jump was a challenge to the ambitions and pretensions of a Paterson entrepreneur. It was also, like all of Sam's performances, a grand and eccentric gesture thrown into contemporary conversations about nature and economic development, class and masculinity, and the proper uses of waterfalls.

A builder and sawmill owner named Timothy B. Crane had bought the forested north bank of Passaic Falls in August 1827. In September he turned it into a commercial pleasure garden, announcing that he would reshape the forest in the name of material and moral progress: "Although Nature has done more for this spot of earth, than perhaps any other of its size, to render it beautiful and interesting to the visitor, it is nevertheless susceptible of very great embellishments, from the hand of ART," and with that he improved the grounds with gravel walkways, imported bushes and trees, and a combined ice cream parlor and saloon. Crane called his establishment the Forest Garden. During the next few summers crowds went there for ice cream and conversation, and there were periodic circuses, Indian war dances, and displays of fireworks as well.[3]

The Forest Garden was an outdoor restaurant with facilities for putting on shows—a copy of Niblo's and the other summer gardens of New York City. But Crane and his supporters advertised it as something more: an artful refinement of raw nature that transformed a forbidding wilderness into an opportunity for aesthetic contemplation. The *Paterson Intelligencer* praised the Forest Garden as a retreat where "the refinements of taste and art [are] combined with the varied and romantic beauties of nature," and later congratulated Crane on his gardens and fireworks: "This rude spot, where the lonely visitor once heard nought but the wild roar of the noble Passaic . . . is now become the brilliant scene of science, added to the sublimity of nature." A satisfied customer agreed: "[Crane] has so far domesticated the wilderness of nature, and blended with it the improvements of art, that the Passaic Falls is no longer a place for the melancholy retirement of the horror-stricken wanderer, who seeks solitude as the only food for his bewildered imagination, but is now become the delightful scene of social gaity [sic] and interesting contemplation." The editor gave this advice to tired clerks and workingmen: cross the river and "greet the smiles of your friends amid the enchanting groves of the Forest Garden," "bid dull cares begone," "lounge at your pleasure under the illuminated Cedars of Lebanon," and, on the way home, "take a peep at the awful chasm below-listen for a moment to the tremendous roar of the troubled Passaic, [and] contrast the scene with your own quietude of mind." Social gaiety, sublimity, scenes of science, quietude of mind—all of it across the river from the factories and tenements of Paterson, New Jersey.[4]

Before receiving customers, Timothy Crane had to bridge the falls chasm that separated the Forest Garden from Paterson, and of all the improvements that he made, Crane was proudest of his bridge. He designed the thing himself. It was made of wood and covered, and its substructure was sided to form an arch. The sides were open, with latticed railings, affording a full view of the falls and chasm. Crane called it Clinton Bridge, after Governor De Witt Clinton of New York. Few of his fellow citizens could have missed the reason why, for in the 1820s Clinton was a hero to developers everywhere. He had promoted and then presided over the construction of the Erie Canal. Completed in 1825, the canal was a stupendous triumph of engineering that was opening the whole Great Lakes frontier to settlement and commerce. The Erie Canal stood as a magnificent icon of the triumph of American civilization over wilderness, and a lot of people were naming taverns, ferryboats, hotels, steam locomotives, and babies after De Witt Clinton.[5] . . .

◆ ◆ ◆ ◆ ◆ ◆

Through the late summer of 1827 Timothy Crane's workmen cleared land, planted bushes and trees, and assembled Clinton Bridge beside the falls. They finished at the end of September, and Crane announced that he would supervise his men as they pulled his bridge across the chasm and set it into place. He advertised his exhibition for the afternoon of Saturday, September 30. The factories would be closed. The whole town could come out and watch Clinton Bridge conquer Passaic Falls. It would be a big day for progress, and a bigger day for Timothy Crane.

Across the river in Paterson, twenty-eight-year-old Sam Patch watched Crane's improvements taking shape. Sam's life was not going well. For a time, he had operated a small Paterson candlewick mill in partnership with a man named Martin Branigan, but the partnership dissolved in 1826. Like Sam's purported enterprise with Kennedy near Pawtucket, the agreement seems to have ended in acrimony: Branigan pointedly announced that "All persons are forbid giving any further credit to the above firm, without the consent of [Branigan.]" Branigan—like Kennedy—stayed in business, and Sam Patch went off looking for employment elsewhere. In 1827 he was working as a mule spinner in Paterson's Hamilton Mills. He was also a solitary drinker who repeatedly boxed the ears of children who worked under him. (The boy who recounts these stories also tells us that Patch suffered bouts of delirium tremens, suggesting that he had been drinking heavily for a very long time.)[6]

Sam Patch, in short, was an angry and not particularly admirable victim of the huge social process that was creating places like Pawtucket and Paterson and granting money and respect to people like Timothy Crane. As he watched Crane boss his gardeners and bridge builders, an unhappy constellation of class anger and rum-soaked resentment took shape in the mind of Sam Patch. Sam let it be known that he would spoil Crane's day.

That Saturday all of Paterson turned out to watch Timothy Crane pull his bridge over the chasm. Constables patrolled the crowd looking for Sam Patch. They had locked him into a basement for safekeeping, but someone had let him out.[7]

Tim Crane swaggered through the afternoon, tugging at his whiskers and shouting instructions to his men, always with an eye on the crowd. The bridge rested on log rollers on the northern bank. Cables stretched across the chasm, and ropes and tackles waited to edge the bridge over the precipice and along the cables and to set it into place on the substructure. At last the workmen took their stations and pulled at the ropes, and Clinton Bridge edged slowly across Crane's fairy-tale landscape, moved by sweating men and by what the *Paterson Intelligencer* called "the exercise of a good deal of ingenuity and mechanical skill" on the part of Timothy Crane. As the bridge reached the cliff and began riding out over the cables, things went wrong: one of the log rollers slipped and dropped end over end into the pool below the falls, and the bridge lurched dangerously. Crane's men regained control and set it safely into place. Tim Crane looked up for applause, but the cheering was broken by shouts from the south bank. For there was Sam Patch, standing erect on a rock at the edge of the cliff. Sam spoke to the people near him. Then he stepped off.

It was a straight seventy-foot drop to the water below, and Sam took it in fine Pawtucket style. At the end he brought up his knees, then snapped them straight, drew his arms to his sides, and went into the water like an arrow. Tim Crane and his kidnapped audience stared into the chasm, certain that Sam was dead. But in a few seconds Sam shot to the surface. The crowd cheered wildly as Sam sported in the water, paddled over to Crane's log roller, took the trail rope between his teeth, and towed it slowly and triumphantly to shore.

Before he jumped, Sam Patch told the people on his side of the chasm that "Crane had done a great thing, and he meant to do another."[8]

At its simplest, Sam's leap at Clinton Bridge was an act of vandalism: Timothy Crane was an enterprising, successful man, and Sam Patch was a sullen failure who risked his life to ruin Crane's celebration. We might label the jump an act of drunken resentment and leave it at that. So it may have been. But the crowd applauded Sam Patch's leap, and the leap survived in the folklore of Paterson as an admirable performance. Something, it seems, had prepared the people of Paterson to enjoy Sam's assault on the festivities of Timothy Crane.[9]

A look into the past and future of Passaic Falls reveals the reason why: the Forest Garden was built on land that had once been a public playground, and Crane's improvements and the ways he managed them and talked about them aroused the sustained fury of his neighbors. Sam's leap, it turns out, was no isolated event. It was the opening shot in a twelve-year war over the north bank of Passaic Falls—a war that ultimately drove Timothy Crane into bankruptcy and away from the falls.

Crane and his supporters insisted that the north bank had been a useless, forbidding wilderness before he built the Forest Garden, but the working people of Paterson knew better. For them, the north bank was a valued retreat from the city and a place to play. A family named Godwin ran a tavern there about half a mile above the falls. An

English gentlewoman who visited in May 1827 pronounced it "quite a cockney place and crowded with Saturday and Sunday visitors." From Godwin's tavern, pathways led through the forest toward the falls. The land along these paths was privately owned, but no proprietor had ever changed the landscape or excluded the public. The woods were dense, and the rock base was crossed by deep cracks which most people assumed were the work of ancient earthquakes. One of the ravines led all the way down to the river below the falls. Pleasure seekers drank at Godwin's tavern (tea and lemonade as well as alcohol), hiked through the woods, threw stones into the chasm and dropped them into the crevasses, carved their names on trees and rocks, fished at the base of the falls (there were legends of two-hundred-pound sturgeon), or found quiet places to sit and enjoy the summer air. The bravest boys dove and swam in the pools above the falls, and Sam Patch leaped from the cliffs into the river at least once before his famous jump in September 1827. The working people of Paterson valued the falls ground: it was a wild and beautiful spot that belonged to everyone and no one, unimproved private property that was open to free public use. A boy who grew up in Paterson recalled that "the Falls have always been looked upon with pride by the citizens, and they expected it would always remain so. Some folks . . . even demanded that free access should be had by all."[10]

Crane took the north bank out of public hands and turned it into the Forest Garden, "a place of rational amusement." Crane's later advertisements invited "the poet and the painter" and the "man of leisure;" he hoped that refined out-of-towners would patronize his gardens, and he was particularly proud of a visit from the bishop of New York. He went out of his way to offer "the man of *labor and industry* a relaxation from the toils of his occupation." But he insisted that customers behave themselves, and he reserved the right to exclude those who did not. Welcome guests included "decent people," "ladies and gentlemen," "good society," those who were "respectable and orderly," and those who maintained "good order and decorum." He wanted customers who stayed on the walkways and out of the bushes, who conversed politely and never got drunk, and who contemplated trees without wanting to climb them.[11]

Timothy Crane's transformation of the old pleasure ground, along with his talk about art, nature, and De Witt Clinton, would have caused trouble in any event. But he compounded his crimes by charging a toll at Clinton Bridge. The toll was only two pennies, but Crane insisted on it. An occasional genteel guest objected to Crane's bad manners at the tollbooth, and even Crane's friends thought his zealous toll taking was "ungentlemanly." In 1831 Crane bought space in a newspaper to justify the toll. He pleaded that he had risked everything he owned in his north-bank improvements, and could survive only if he turned a profit. Closely tied to this argument was the next one: the toll was his one means of keeping the place decent and safe. Crane knew what happened when just anyone crossed Clinton Bridge: "1st. If the bridge were thrown open, the Garden would be occupied with a set of lazy, idle, rascally, drunken vagabonds. 2d. This would drive away all decent people. 3d. We should thereby lose all our income; and 4th. Our little ornaments and improvements would be defaced, ruined, and in fact, destroyed."[12]

Crane spoke from experience, for the Forest Garden had come under attack from the beginning. First, of course, was the opening-day leap of Sam Patch. Then, in his first season, Crane had to install spring guns to discourage "Night Poachers" who defaced his tollgate and entered the grounds to steal liquor. During business hours, drunken, foul-mouthed men insulted respectable customers and threw firecrackers at ladies' feet. Others cut down Crane's trees, broke his imported bushes, smashed his glassware, stole his lanterns, and hurled his tables and benches over the falls. Rowdiness and vandalism escalated into assaults on Crane and his family and employees. Crane's boys were kicked and beaten when they worked the tollgate; some attackers threatened to throw them into the river. The boys found trouble whenever they ran errands into town, and Crane himself could not walk safely in Paterson. At night, musket balls and doses of buckshot slammed into the walls and through the windows of buildings on the old pleasure ground. One of the worst of these attacks occurred on Christmas Night in 1828—a night when the lower orders traditionally settled scores with upper-class enemies.[13]

Throughout these assaults, Timothy Crane knew who his tormentors were. Some were well-dressed sports who might have passed as gentlemen. Others were men, Crane said, "from whom we might expect better things," who condoned the violence. But most were workingmen, and Crane singled out the English weavers and spinners as the worst: "They come into my gardens, and cut down my young trees, and mutilate my seats and tables and bridge, and get drunk and curse and swear, and use indecent language," and scare off respectable women and men.[14]

The attack on the Forest Garden was an early round in the contest over recreational space in industrializing America, a contest that regularly pitted the noise and physicality of working-class recreations against the privatized, contemplative leisure pursuits of the middle class. In Paterson the contest took on a particularly personal and violent edge, for many of Crane's attackers were people who had been his friends. Timothy Crane had been in Paterson since 1812, and as an architect, builder, speculator, and sawmill owner, he had watched his fortune grow with the town. His work, his public services, and his membership in the Episcopal Church brought him into cooperation with Paterson's leading families. His joviality and love of talk won him entry into other circles as well: between 1815 and 1823 he was an elected chief of Paterson's volunteer fire companies, and he was widely known as a storyteller, a genial braggart, and a friend to traveling acrobats and circus riders. A boy from the mills recalled that people had liked Timothy Crane. A lot of them called him Uncle Tim.[15]

Crane seems to have retained the goodwill of the community until he bought the land next to the falls. His decision to turn it into a romantic retreat for ladies and gentlemen transformed his relations with Paterson. Crane's old associations—the fire companies, the sawmill and the construction sites, the storytelling groups—had been with a democracy of males that excluded women. The Forest Garden, on the other hand, catered to respectable women and their male escorts, and it pointedly excluded the working-class men who had made up much of Crane's old social world.

The reasons for Crane's decision must remain a mystery. But we should note that the purchase of the north bank was the second big event of 1827 for Crane. In February he had married Maria Ryerson, daughter of one of the old families of New York City. He was a fifty-four-year-old widower; she was twenty-four and, by the time he bought his land in August, pregnant with their first child. Crane's marriage to this polished young woman, coupled with his withdrawal from the old male democracy and his new interest in exclusivity and romantic sentimentalism, suggests that he had determined to change his way of life. Timothy Crane was no longer one of the boys. He had become an inventor of American bourgeois culture.[16]

Viewed from the factories and poor streets of Paterson, Crane's Forest Garden was a vast provocation. It violated customary-use rights to the falls ground, and that alone would have started a fight. But Crane's personal transformation made it worse. Timothy Crane was breaking with the informal, democratic society of other men and redefining respectability and right behavior. The Forest Garden translated Paterson's familiar hierarchy of wealth into a new, undemocratic, and utterly unacceptable formula for the distribution of respect. That is when Paterson changed its mind about Timothy Crane. The people of Paterson may have admired Clinton Bridge. It was a straightforward conquest of nature and a fine feat of engineering. But at the end of the bridge there were tree stumps, gravel walkways, and orderly bushes and shrubs where their pleasure ground had been, and Uncle Tim was talking in strange new ways.

Crane's bridge raising in 1827 was a truly ambivalent celebration. Sam Patch resolved the ambivalence with a little speech about the democracy of worth and a spectacular reassertion of the freedom and physicality of the old north bank. Patch's leap was the first in a continuous series of assaults upon Timothy Crane. The Forest Garden never made money, and Crane's creditors began to seize the land within a year. He stayed on as manager, dodging rocks and demanding tolls all the way, until 1839. Then he abandoned his vandalized and neglected gardens and retired to a log cabin in a forested corner of the north bank, where he died in 1845. It was the end to a long and ugly war with the neighbors, a war that began the day Sam Patch sneaked past the constables and joined the crowd that had come to see Timothy Crane conquer Passaic Falls.[17]

Months after the episode at Clinton Bridge, when he had begun to jump professionally, Sam Patch offered an explanation of his leaps. Crane and other friends of progress had been spreading rumors. Some said the jump at Clinton Bridge had been the act of a madman. Others insisted that Patch was merely drunk, and Timothy Crane himself concocted the best story of all: Sam Patch had leaped for love. Patch was enamored of a young woman, you see, and she had turned him down. He had leaped not to humiliate Timothy Crane but to kill himself. Patch countered with his own explanation. "It is no melancholy event," he insisted. "I am perfectly sober and in possession of my proper faculties, and [leaping waterfalls] is nothing more than an art which I have knowledge of and courage to perform"—"an art," he went on, "which I have practiced from my youth."[18]

Art. It was an important word in the vocabularies of Sam Patch and Timothy Crane, but it had different meanings for the two. Crane used "art" as a crucial component in what might be called the language of progress, a language that described and legitimized what he was doing at Passaic Falls. Patch's use of the word derived from plebeian-democratic sensibilities that called Timothy Crane and his works into serious question. We might look at the episode at Clinton Bridge as a confrontation between the art of Sam Patch and the art of Timothy Crane.[19] . . .

◆ ◆ ◆ ◆ ◆ ◆

On July 4, 1828, Sam Patch leaped again at Passaic Falls. Later on the same day, Timothy Crane presented a display of fireworks at the Forest Garden. Crane's fireworks and Patch's leap were the first commercial entertainments ever advertised for Independence Day at Paterson: they were at it again.

Independence Day celebrations had been initiated by the political parties (the Jeffersonian Republicans in particular) of the early republic, and citizens had expressed Federalist and Jeffersonian versions of what America was about in speeches and parades. With the disappearance of the Federalists after 1815, the celebrations became nonpartisan and local, and something went out of them. Whole neighborhoods still turned out for the parades and nighttime fireworks, but most treated the Fourth as a festive day off from work, complete with theatrical performances, hunting parties, circuses, boat races, and complaints about drinking and gambling among the lower orders. The upper classes began to stay at home, or to spend the day in church, or to take exclusive pleasure trips.[20]

In Paterson, Independence Day celebrations in the late 1820s were a part of what was happening in the mills, on the streets, and on the north bank of Passaic Falls: the republic of useful arts was confronting Progress and the new inequalities of a mill city. The *Paterson Intelligencer*, which began publication in 1826, reported its first July Fourth celebration that summer. Representatives of the mechanics' and spinners' associations joined with "citizens" in a general committee of the day, which planned the festivities. The day began with a ringing of church bells, the playing of patriotic airs by the town band, and the firing of a cannon. But the centerpiece was the parade, led by a uniformed company of militia. The town band came second, followed by "Ladies" (almost certainly the wives and daughters of leading men) and female schoolteachers with their pupils, then men hoisting the cap of liberty and the American flag, then the town's civic leaders and clergy. Following the dignitaries came thirteen elderly citizens carrying the flags of the original thirteen states, accompanied by ten boys bearing banners of the newer states. Militia officers in uniform were followed by the associations of spinners, weavers, and other mechanics, marching trade by trade, carrying flags emblazoned with patriotic emblems and pictures of the tools and processes of their trades. The flags and the trade-by-trade marching order, along with the mechanics' participation in the planning of the day, sustained the tradition that the individual arts, in their making of shoes and houses and cotton cloth, fashioned the nation itself. (A citizen commented that the spinners were particularly striking in their white uniforms with green badges, and their blue banner with a spread eagle and depictions of the spinning process.) Male teachers and their pupils walked behind the mechanics and were followed by a final and inclusive contingent of "Citizens generally"— any white men, apparently, who wanted to march. A second company of militia brought up the rear.[21]

The parade began at ten o'clock in the morning and carried its pomp and noise through the streets. It ended at Brick Presbyterian Church, where the inclusiveness of the morning parade gave way to selective celebration. The town's leading men and women left the ranks and entered the church, where, according to one of them, "exercises suitable to the occasion were performed with a becoming sense of the sacred character of the place, and the honor due to the day." The minister offered a prayer, a lawyer read the Declaration of Independence, and the Orator of the Day (another lawyer) spoke with (according to the first lawyer) "masterly eloquence, which, combined with the beauty of thought, the aptness of allusion, and the force of classic illustration scattered throughout the composition, rendered this Oration a mental feast not soon to be forgotten, by those who partook of it." After songs by the choir, the lawyers, factory owners, and their ladies filed out of the church and rejoined the democratic parade that had waited outside.

The procession marched to Munn's Passaic Hotel. The militiamen fired their muskets into the air and disbanded. The crowd dispersed into festivities that the newspaper ignored, the ladies went off to an entertainment of their own, and the leading men of Paterson gathered in the hotel dining room. (The newspaper reported that the dinner was open to "all who choose," but the cost was a dollar a plate—a day's labor for most Patersonians.) There were food and speeches, and toward the end the innkeeper brought in a pie. He opened the pie and a white pigeon flew out bearing a very bad poem entitled "The Herald of America's Prosperity." ("O'er fields and plains by Nature blest / On lightsome wing I came," and on and on.) Thirteen toasts were proposed, commemorative of the thirteen original states: to the Nation, the People, the Heroes of the Revolution, the Republicans of Greece and South America, the New Jersey School Fund. The thirteenth toast, as was customary, went up to "Our Fair Country Women."

In the evening the banqueters rejoined the rest of Paterson for a grand flight of rockets, staged and paid for by the general committee of the day. Later, citizens could read that the Fourth had gone off with "harmony and good order," and with "unanimity manifested by all classes." It was a fine Fourth of July of the 1820s—a parade and fireworks staged and enjoyed by the whole town, and a sermon, readings, high-minded music, and banquet for the town's leaders. The festivities demonstrated republican hierarchy and celebrated the dignity and usefulness of white men—dignity that derived from daily work.

The festivities were similar in 1827: an inclusive, trade-based parade, a church service, an elite banquet, and a civic display of fireworks. The banquet ended with the usual toasts, but this year some of the toasts folded the language of the republic into the language of progress. There was a salute to American "Mechanical Genius" as manifested by the practical inventors Benjamin Franklin and Robert Fulton, and another to the American System of sheltering infant industries under protective tariffs—accompanied by the playing of "Yankee Doodle." Volunteer toasts saluted the rise of American manufactures and of Paterson in particular, while from outside came the sounds of another wedding of patriotism and progress: the engineer who was building the Morris Canal through Paterson (the canal linked the Pennsylvania coalfields with New York) set off thirteen explosions—"not only a loud but a profitable expression of patriotic feeling," according to a bemused Canadian visitor. The town leaders acted out their bipartisanship with dueling toasts to the Democrat Andrew Jackson and the National Republican Henry Clay, and there was a circumspect toast to "the Constitution" by Timothy Crane. But there were also toasts to Paterson's artisans and mechanics, phrased in the language of mutual usefulness and mutual respect: "In their industry and ingenuity the manufacturer has found . . . the best protection"; "may they be at all times united and free, and always maintain their integrity"; "the strong pillars upon which our prosperity rests. May they long maintain that respectable rank in society which they at present so deservedly occupy." Perhaps representatives of the workingmen's associations had again taken part in the planning and thus in the dinner (the planning session went unrecorded that year), or perhaps some among Paterson's elite in 1827 (at least at a civic and festive occasion, and toward the end of a lot of drinking) continued to fuse progress and the republic with respect for labor.[22]

The Fourth of July went differently in 1828. First, Patersonians learned that there would be no public fireworks. Instead, Timothy Crane promised a grand pyrotechnic display at the Forest Garden, on the far side of his tollbooth, to be witnessed only by subscribed ticket holders. Citizens then read that "a large and respectable meeting of Young Men" had planned the civic celebration and selected its officers and other dignitaries. The "Young Men" (a common code for ambitious and well-connected young men) neglected to invite women—either "Ladies" or female teachers—or "Citizens generally" to join the parade, though they did include the mechanics and spinners. The marching workers were duly noted, but only in the language of progress. (The newspaper account noted the banner carried by millwrights, "on which is exhibited in beautiful perspective the various implements and the mode of their application, by which this useful class of mechanics enables the manufacturer to render the natural elements so immanently subservient to the comfort and prosperity of this town.") The banquet was not attended by mechanics, nor were toasts given to their usefulness and patriotism. The usual salutes to the republic and founding fathers went up, but this time they were linked principally to entrepreneurial progress: to "Roads and Canals—important links in the chain which binds our union" (accompanied by "Meeting of the Waters," a tune composed for the opening of the Erie Canal); to "Domestic Manufactures—The Only Hope for National Independence" ("Heigh ho! The Cotton Spinners"); to "Literature, Science, and the Arts—The aliment of Freedom" ("Ode on Science").[23]

The day ended with Crane's fireworks, presented for an exclusive audience at the Forest Garden, "where the refinements of taste and art combined with the varied and romantic beauties of nature, to afford pleasure and satisfaction to the numerous company present."[24]

Celebrations in this new and exclusive "spirit of rational freedom," so different from the civic inclusiveness of earlier years, would continue into the 1830s. But July 4, 1828, did include one performance that the Young Men had not planned. At four-thirty in the afternoon, as advertised, Sam Patch leaped from the south side of Clinton Bridge. The plain people of Paterson, absent as usual from the ceremonies at the church and hotel, had been excluded from the planning, denied the civic fireworks show, denigrated in the parade, and ignored by the toastmasters. They marched in battalions to the falls to see Sam Patch. A New Yorker gasped that "the giddy precipices around the chasm were covered with a promiscuous multitude of both sexes whose curiosity had brought them together to see this singular feat of temerity." The local paper estimated the crowd at between three thousand and five thousand persons. (Paterson had six thousand residents.) They lined the cliffs, rank upon rank. At the appointed time Sam Patch stepped to the edge and stared down at the river. He took off his coat, vest, and shoes; perhaps he was wearing the spinner's uniform in which he had marched that morning. Some in the crowd pushed forward for a better view, nearly crowding those in front off the precipice. As the crowd regathered, Sam turned and delivered a short speech that few could hear and none recorded. Then he faced the precipice and leaped into the chasm. The *Intelligencer* granted that it was a "hazardous feat," "handsomely executed." Sam rose to the surface of the water as the crowd's anxious silence broke into wonder and a roar of applause.[25]

Though most of Paterson witnessed Sam's leap on the Fourth of July, it is doubtful that the town's merchants and manufacturers were among them, for Sam had scheduled his leap at an hour at which they almost certainly were still at the banquet, offering toasts to progress, patriotism, and each other. A news story about this leap was the first to report the phrase that became Sam's motto: "Some things can be done as well as others."[26]

Twelve days later Sam Patch announced that he would perform his "astonishing leap" once more, on Monday, July 28. On the same day as Sam's announcement—Wednesday, July 16—twenty-two Paterson manufacturers made an announcement of their own:

Notice. The subscribers hereby give notice to their *workers* and others, that after Saturday, the 19th July, 1828, they will stop their Mills and Factories, at half past seven o'clock, in the morning, for breakfast, and at one o'clock P.M. for dinner.

This arrangement we consider will divide the day in a more equal manner than heretofore, and prove of advantage to the workers.

The announcement changed the dinner hour from noon to one o'clock, and it met with resistance. A friendly newspaper stated that the owners "had the good of the children in view," though the same editor had earlier averred that they changed the lunch hour "for their own convenience." It really made no difference: the manufacturers' decree was certain to start a fight.[27]

In the mills, Sam Patch and the skilled Englishmen who were his peers read the proclamation and thought about it. It was only a small change in the routine of the working day, but a little reflection revealed what the bosses were trying to do. Signers of the decree owned all but two of the town's cotton mills and many of the foundries and factories. The new rule changed the lunch hour for nearly half of Paterson's manufacturing wage earners, and for many more than half of the job-holding children. In a mill town where most families depended on more than one breadwinner, and where workers went home for lunch, few wage-earning households would be unaffected. Put simply, twenty-two wealthy men had taken it upon themselves to complicate the domestic schedules of hundreds of Paterson families. Worse, they announced the new hour after a closed meeting and in language (they "hereby give notice") that assumed their right to dictate the conditions of work. The owners must have known that the adult male spinners and weavers would resist this attack on their authority over themselves and the children who worked under them, particularly when it came in the form of an arbitrary assertion of power by a closed-door combination of employers.[28]

The manufacturers posted their decree on Wednesday: the customary noon lunch hour would be in effect for the rest of the week, but when the mills reopened on Monday, lunchtime would be one o'clock.

Sam Patch was a boss mule spinner at the Hamilton Mills, and he must have been in the thick of the discussions that took place during the week. Many of the other boss spinners were veterans of the labor violence and repressed reform movements of industrial Lancashire. Described in newspapers as "Manchester *mobites*" subject to "the moral diseases of Europe" (the first of which, of course, was a propensity for rioting and labor radicalism), they were the terror of Timothy Crane and men like him. But in Sam Patch's world, they were the staunchest and most admirable of men. Sam was himself a twenty-one-year veteran of the mills, and three years earlier had witnessed and perhaps taken part in the Pawtucket walkout—the first textile strike in American history. While the spinners and weavers planned what they would do, Sam thought up a contribution of his own: he spread the word that on Saturday afternoon—after the factories had closed, and in the first hours of calm before what everyone knew would be a storm—he would again leap at Passaic Falls.[29]

The mills and factories closed at noon on Saturday. Workers left their machines and workbenches knowing that peace was at an end. There would be a day and a half of eerie quiet, and on Monday there would be trouble. The people of Paterson began that day and a half with a walk to Passaic Falls. They streamed out of their workplaces and out of the houses and grogshops in the lower neighborhoods, jostling and talking. Latecomers hurried past the last empty factory and around the embankment, and there stood the crowd waiting for Sam Patch. A New Yorker estimated the crowd at six to ten thousand: the whole town. At the appointed time, Sam strode out of the audience and stepped onto his rock. A part of the crowd stood at his back, with the deserted town behind them. Clinton Bridge and the falls were at his right and the basin was at his feet, and everywhere Sam turned he met the eyes of workmates and neighbors. He straightened, gathered himself, and stepped off and dropped with perfect grace into the gulf. Some person or persons had wanted to ensure that this grand gesture would be made: Sam collected fifteen dollars for the leap.[30]

(Again, we cannot know what Sam wore for this leap. But it is likely that he jumped, as he did in future leaps, in the white shirt and pants that were the parade uniform of the Paterson Association of Spinners. This uniform carried meanings—probably for Patch, certainly for the Englishmen who worked with him and witnessed his leap—that reached back to Manchester. After the defeat of Napoleon in 1815, workers in the textile towns of Lancashire, led again by the weavers and spinners, revived their demands for republican rights— in the faces of Britain's victorious aristocrats. The workers organized a great rally at St. Peter's Field, near Manchester, in 1819 to hear a speech advocating parliamentary reform. Soldiers who had been instructed to arrest the speaker charged into the crowd, killing several and injuring hundreds of others. Before the Massacre at Peterloo began, the cap of liberty [the symbol of international republicanism] was delivered to the podium by a group of women dressed in white with green trim. After the Massacre, Manchester spinners adopted white hats with green ribbons as a defiant and angry remembrance of the day. Hundreds of these men later migrated to the United States, and many of them found their way to Paterson over the next few years. The English spinners and their American compatriots marched in Paterson's July Fourth parades wearing suits of white cotton adorned with prominent green badges. The jumping attire of Sam Patch—the white uniform with the green badge removed—might have meant more to Sam's audience than the newspapers evidently understood.)[31]

On Monday the mill hands came to work on time and worked at their machines through the morning. When the clock struck noon they stopped. The spinners and weavers and the boys and girls who worked under them marched downstairs and out of doors. It was twelve o'clock. Time for lunch.

There are differing accounts of what happened next. An early report stated that the workers had gone out on strike on Monday afternoon and had become "very riotous and disorderly, and such as to keep the inhabitants of the place in continual apprehension." The same report announced (erroneously) that the militia was on its way from Newark. Another account had young strikers, encouraged by the incorrigible weavers and spinners, mobbing their opponents and threatening to throw them into the "ugly basin into which Mr. Patch jumps occasionally." The *Paterson Intelligencer* downplayed the violence, but admitted that the walkout "was indeed conducted with some noise and show of outrage." The known facts are these: the workers rioted on Monday afternoon, two hundred men and many more children and women were out on strike, and only two mills remained in operation—the two that had not tried to change the dinner hour.[32]

On Tuesday the weavers and mule spinners, joined by skilled journeymen from the smaller shops, held a meeting and issued two demands. First, they resolved to stay out on strike until the noon lunch hour was reinstated. Second, evidently enraged and emboldened by events, they demanded that the citywide workday be cut from eleven to ten hours. They would greet employers who agreed to the twelve o'clock lunch hour and the ten-hour day as "friends to their fellow citizens and to mankind in general." The others would not be friends at all. The mechanics would not work for them, and they would use "all legal means" to keep others from entering their degrading and dishonorable employment. The mechanics ended their meeting and went home. Later that night, someone set fire to one of the struck mills. Another sneaked into the weaving room of the Phoenix Mills—one of the two that remained in operation—and cut the warps with a knife.[33]

The owners stood adamant, and the strike continued through July. Not until early August did the papers announce that "the children have yielded their position and most of the mechanics returned quietly to work, to take their dinner at one o'clock. . . . The children are now perfectly docile and appear sorry for their misconduct." With the mills running and the power of the owners to set schedules at least temporarily acknowledged, the victorious manufacturers became kindhearted: by fiat (and not by the authority of riotous workingmen) they restored the lunch hour to twelve o'clock. Their newfound benevolence, however, did not extend to the weavers and spinners who had led the strike. During the angry days of late July, the owners had sworn that they would never rehire the chief troublemakers, though they were, as an anti-strike editor conceded, "among the best workmen." They carried out their threat: a New Yorker who visited Paterson reported, "The ringleaders of the mechanics, among whom are some of the Manchester *Mobites*, have been discharged."[34]

On August 6 Sam Patch jumped from a ship's mast into the Hudson River at Hoboken, cheered on by a crowd of New Yorkers who had gathered on a hotel lawn. Sam had not made his advertised leap at Passaic Falls on July 28. The leap on the Saturday before the strike was his last appearance in the records of Paterson. An editor claimed to have "learned that Mr. Patch has resolved to leap no more from the place he has chosen heretofor [sic]. Sam felt rather 'ugly' about it the last time."[35]

Notes

1. Quotations, in order: Edward C. Carter II, John C. Van Home, and Charles E. Brownell, eds., *Latrobe's View of America, 1795–1820: Selections from the Watercolors and Sketches* (New Haven, Conn., 1985), 167–68; *Manufacturer's and Farmer's Journal* (Providence, R.I.,), 27 September 1824; Eliza Southgate Bowne, A *Girl's Life Eighty Years Ago: Selections from the Letters of Eliza Southgate Bowne* (1887; Williamstown, Mass, 1980), 180; C. D. Arfwedson, Esq., *The United States and Canada in 1832, 1833, ad 1834* (London, 1834), 1:235; P. Stansbury, A *Pedestrian Tour of Two Thousand Three Hundred Miles, in North America . . . Performed in the Autumn of 1821* (New York, 1822), 16; *New-York Spectator*, 7 September 1827. On the view of Paterson from the falls ground, see Arfwedson, *The United States and Canada*, 1:136; J. Milbert, *Picturesque Itinerary of the Hudson River and Peripheral Parts of North America* (1828; Ridgewood, N.J., 1968), 260; Captain Frederick Marryat, *Diary in America*, ed. Jules Zanger (Bloomington, Ind., 1960), 80. See also Leo A. Bressler, "Passaic Falls: Eighteenth Century Natural Wonder," *Proceedings of the New Jersey Historical Society* 74 (April 1956): 99–106.

2. The only modern history of early Paterson is Howard Harris, "The Transformation of Ideology in the Early Industrial Revolution: Paterson, New Jersey, 1820–1840" (Ph.D. diss., City University of New York, 1985), esp. 137. On Hamilton's role, see John R. Nelson Jr., *Liberty and Property: Political Economy and Policymaking in the New Nation, 1789–1812* (Baltimore, 1987), 37–51. Newspaper quoted: *Sentinel of Freedom* (Newark, N.J.), 26 June 1827.

3. *Paterson Intelligencer,* 12 December 1827 (quotation); 28 July 1830 (war dances); 12 August 1829, 8 August 1832 (circus); 18 June 1828, 30 September 1829, 11 August 1830, 9 July 1828, 15 September 1830, 29 June 1831, 10 August 1831, 27 June 1832, 1 August 1832, 26 June 1833, 24 July 1833, 5 August 1835, 18 May 1836, 31 May 1836, 28 June 1837,6 June 1838 (fireworks).

4. *Paterson Intelligencer*, 30 June 1830, 30 September 1829, 21 July 1830, 9 July 1828.

5. *Paterson Intelligencer*, 10 October 1827; E. M. Graf, "Passaic Falls Bridges," *Bulletin of the Passaic County Historical Society* 3 (October 1944): 14; Frank L. Byrne, *Prophet of Prohibition: Neal Dow and His Crusade* (Madison, Wis., 1961), 7, 10, 18.

6. On Patch and child workers, Charles Pitman Longwell, *A Little Story of Old Paterson, as Told by an Old Man* (n.p., 1901), 37; on Sam's candlewick mill, *Paterson Intelligencer,* 19 July 1826. Branigan stays in business: Rev. Samuel Fisher's census of Paterson for 1827, copied in a letter to the author from James G. Ward, 16 January 1984.

7. The lockup story told in Longwell, *A Little Story*, 37–38, and Longwell, *Historic Totowa Falls* (Paterson, n.d.), 37. It is corroborated in the *Journal of Commerce* (New York), reprinted in the *New-York Evening Post*, 7 July 1828.

8. *New-York Evening Post*, 1 October 1827; *Paterson Intelligencer*, 10 October 1827. Longwell, *A Little Story*, 37–41, and *Historic Totowa Falls*, 36–39, reminiscing at a distance of seventy years, differs in some details from the contemporary story in the *New-York Evening Post*. In Longwell's version the bridge sways dangerously after the fall of the log roller, and this near-disaster provides the backdrop for Sam's leap. Longwell has Patch's pre-jump speech as "Now old Tim Crane thinks he has done something great; but I can beat him." Given the many decades that intervened between the two accounts, they are remarkably similar. When they differ, I follow the account in the *Post*.

9. Local memories of Sam's leap: Longwell, *A Little Story*, 37–41; Longwell, *Historic Totowa Fall*, 36–39; William Carlos Williams, *Paterson* (New York, 1963), 15–17. The *Intelligencer* published a cryptic account of the leap that received this response from the writer "No Quiz": "What a pity it is, that too much modesty should ever repress the brilliant coruscations of wit and genius. 0 that Quiz had done justice to the launch of Timothy Crane's bridge o'er the deep and yawning chasm at Passaic Falls, and the adventurous leap of Sam Patch, Esq. from the giddy height which overlooks the afore-said gulf! But, alas, we must now despair of ever having these memorable events, 'at which the little boys and girls did gape and stare,' given to us and embodied in the true quizzical style." He went on to what appears to be a defense of Timothy Crane against unspecified rumors: "Quiz is informed that Wormwood's ear has never been lent to such 'oft repeated tales,' but that the facts have come from other sources, and are incontro-vertible. Quiz is of course at liberty to laugh when he pleases; but with all due deference, would it not be well to select a subject at which he could laugh with a better grace?— this is so confoundedly like a forced laugh, that it sounds as if 'he mocked himself.' But there is another circumstance, which I suppose will also be laughed at by the whole attacked corps, who seem to have concentrated and marshalled all their forces, bringing up all the resources, 'little Trim' and all, which have been so sagaciously kept back, for the fatal moment when a last and desperate effort is to be made to prostrate a single individual, who, notwithstanding many sneers, does not appear to be beneath their notice: and it is this-that the individual did serve in the armies of these U. States, during the whole of the late war, with credit to himself and advantage to his country— and a part of the time under the immediate command of the lamented and gallant Pike, with whom, as I can prove from circumstances, he must have been a favorite and confi-dential officer. He shall stand, Mr. Editor, like a redoubt of granite, uninjured, amidst all this slanderous fire." *(Paterson Intelligencer*, 10 October 1827.) Another tantalizing and unresearchable note—possibly referring to Sam Patch—was printed in the *Intelligencer* on 10 January 1827: "The lines of 'S.P.' evince a very creditable feeling, but are not suffi-ciently finished for publication."

10. Longwell, *Historic Totowa Falls*, 40 (quote). Adlard Welby, *A Visit to North America and the English Settlements in Illinois, with a Winter Residence in Philadelphia* (London, 1821), 23–24; Stansbury, *A Pedestrian Tour*, 15–16; [Margaret Hunter Hall], *The Aristocratic Journey: Being the Outspoken Letters of Mrs. Basil Hall, Written during a Fourteen Months' Sojourn in America, 1827–1828*, ed. Una Pope-Hennessy (New York, 1931), 30; Marryat, *Diary in America*, 80–81; Norman F. Brydon, *The Passaic River* (New Brunswick, N.J., 1974), 109. Sam's early jump: *New-York Evening Post*, 7 July 1828. Sam advertised his second and third publicized jumps as his third and fourth.

11. *Paterson Intelligencer*, 11 May 1831, 7 July 1831, 14 July 1830, 12 August 1829; Rev. Isaac Fidler, *Observations on Professions, Literature, Manners, and Emigration in the United States and Canada, Made during a Residence There in 1832* (New York, 1833), 98.

12. Fidler, *Observations*, 96–97; *Paterson Intelligencer*, 20 June 1838, 27 June 1838, 11 May 1831 (Crane's explanation).

13. *Paterson Intelligencer*, 19 March 1828, 31 December 1828, 11 May 1831. On Christmas Night: Stephen Nissenbaum, *The Battle over Christmas* (New York, 1996); Susan G. Davis, "'Making Night Hideous': Christmas Revelry and Public Order in Nineteenth-Century Philadelphia," *American Quarterly* 34 (Summer 1982): 185–199.

14. Fidler, *Observations*, 97 (quote); *Paterson Intelligencer*, 11 May 1831.

15. On Timothy Crane: Longwell, *Historic Totowa Falls*, 38; Fidler, *Observations*, 96–97; Ellery Bicknell Crane, *Genealogy of the Crane Family. Volume I. Descendants of Henry Crane, of Whethersfield and Guilford, Conn., with Sketch of the Family in England* (Worcester, Mass, 1895), 1:102; William Nelson, ed., *The Van Houten Manuscripts: A Century of Historical Documents* (Paterson, 1894), 69–70; D. Stanton Hammond, comp., "Rev. Samuel Fisher's Census: Paterson, N.J., 1824–1832," *Bulletin of the Passaic County Historical Society* 4 (August 1958): 104; William Nelson and Charles A. Shriner, *History of Paterson and Its Environs* (New York, 1920), 2:406.

16. Albert Winslow Ryerson, *The Ryerson Genealogy: Genealogy of the Knickerbocker Families of Ryerson, Ryerse, Ryerss; also Adriance and Martense Families; all Descendants of Martin and Adriaen Reyersz (Ryerzen) of Amsterdam, Holland* (Chicago, 1916), 128; Crane, *Genealogy of the Crane Family*, 1:102.

17. Paterson bank seizes the property: *Paterson Intelligencer*, 26 March 1828 and 9 April 1828. Further legal troubles with the land: *Paterson Intelligencer*, 16 June 1830, 18 November 1835, 15 June 1836, 20 July 1836. The north bank remained contested territory for many years. In the 1850s a silk manufacturer bought the grounds and closed them off with the intention of building a house for himself. He reconsidered and turned the property into a privately owned "public" park, with the advertised intention of improving Patersonians. He too was harassed and vandalized until he quit the grounds. See Longwell, *Historic Totowa Falls*, 40, and Levi R. Trumbull, *A History of Industrial Paterson* (Paterson, 1882), 332–333. The land is now a public park, operated by the City of Paterson.

18. Fidler, *Observations*, 99–100, told the jumped-for-love story just after a conversation with Timothy Crane. Patch told his own story in the *Paterson Intelligencer*, 16 July and 2 July 1828.

19. Raymond Williams, *Culture and Society, 1750–1950* (New York, 1958), and *Keywords: A Vocabulary of Culture and Society* (New York, 1976). Williams's principal concern is with the dissociation of "art" from occupational skills (Sam Patch's definition) and its attachment to anti-occupations practiced by special people who operate apart from and above the workaday world, a redefinition that was not accomplished in the United States until at least the 1850s. A third use of the word (Timothy Crane's) stemmed from the old vocabulary used by Sam Patch, but reshaped in ways that gave "art" new entrepreneurial and developmental meanings. Crane's "art" is fully illustrated in the

historical and critical studies cited in note 25 [editor's note: this note in the original book has been deleted here]. Those studies and the works in labor history cited in note 20 [editor's note: this note in the original book has been deleted here] establish the centrality of Patch's and Crane's definitions of art in working-class and middle-class perceptions of economic development during the crucial years 1825–1850.

20. On celebrations of the Fourth of July, see Len Travers, *Celebrating the Fourth: Independence Day and the Rites of Nationalism in the Early Republic* (Amherst, Mass., 1997); David Waldstreicher, *In the Midst of Perpetual Fetes: The Making of American Nationalism, 1776–1820* (Chapel Hill, N.C., 1997); Simon P. Newman, *Parades and the Politics of the Street: Festive Culture in the Early American Republic* (Philadelphia, 1997), 83–119; Scott C. Martin, *Killing Time Leisure and Culture in Southwestern Pennsylvania, 1800–1850* (Pittsburgh, 1995), 71–101. More general studies of American festivities that have shaped the following paragraphs include Mary P. Ryan, *Civic Wars: Democracy and Public Life in the American City during the Nineteenth Century* (Berkeley, Calif., 1989); Ryan, "The American Parade: Representation of the Nineteenth-Century Social Order," in *The New Cultural History*, ed. Lynn Hunt (Berkeley, Calif., 1989), 131–153; Susan G. Davis, *Parades and Power: Street Theatre in Nineteenth-Century Philadelphia* (Philadelphia, 1986); Sean Wilentz, "Artisan Republican Festivals and the Rise of Class Conflict in New York City, 1788–1837," in *Working Class America: Labor, Community, and American Society*, ed. Michael H. Frisch and Daniel J. Walkowitz (Urbana, Ill., 1983), 37–77; Laura Rigal, "'Raising the Roof': Authors, Spectators, and Artisans in the Grand Federal Procession of 1788," *Theatre Journal* 48 (October 1996): 253–278.

21. Information in this and the following three paragraphs is from the *Paterson Intelligencer*, 21 June 1826, 6 July 1826, 12 July 1826.

22. *Paterson Intelligencer*, 11 July 1827 Canal explosions at Paterson: *Montreal Gazette*, 19 July 1827. On the emerging connections between technological progress and the Fourth of July in the 1820s, see David E. Nye, *American Technological Sublime* (Cambridge, Mass., 1994), 41–43.

23. *Paterson Intelligencer*, 4 June 1828, 18 June 1828, 25 June 1828, 2 July 1828, 9 July 1828.

24. Quotation from *Paterson Intelligencer*, 9 July 1828 and 8 July 1829. In subsequent years the mechanics' associations were not listed among the planners, and none of the official toasts mentioned them. There were now toasts to an abstracted "People." In 1830 the fire companies, apparently controlled by Jacksonian Democrats, held their own banquet. There were twelve cheers for "The People," and toasts not only to De Witt Clinton but to Thomas Paine, and to the Jacksonian Democrats' libertarian position on church and state. In 1831 the official banquet included the visiting Directors of the Paterson and Hudson Railroad, which had ritually begun construction on that day. In another hotel the Mechanics Institute (which, if it was like those in other towns, was an elite organization that provided rational education for ambitious and well-behaved mechanics) held a banquet of its own. Its vice president toasted "The Mechanics of Paterson—May their reputation for intelligence and patriotism be equal to their reputation for mechanical excellence; they will then assume that rank in Society to which their industry so justly entitled them" a rank that they had occupied unchallenged in

previous years. At the end of the day, the elite could choose between Crane's fireworks and a fancy-dress ball.

There was a related transformation in the official celebration of women. Women marched in the parades of 1826 and 1827—the schoolteachers with their children, the others apparently marching as a group, dressed as they pleased. Women were not mentioned in 1828, and the parade was rained out in 1829. They reappeared in the parade of 1830 as "Ladies, dressed in white"—an abstract, feminized purity. The thirteenth official toast was always made to women, transformed from "Our Fair Country Women" in 1826 to "The American Fair" in the following three years (followed in 1827 and 1828 by the playing of "Come Haste to the Wedding") to "Woman" in 1830. Judging by what the elite chose to celebrate, one would have to say that Paterson was transformed in the late 1820s from a town of useful mechanics and pretty women to a pantheon of Industry, Progress, and Woman. See the *Paterson Intelligencer*, late June through mid-July, 1826–31.

25. *Paterson Intelligencer*, 9 July 1828. The longer piece appeared in the *New York Journal of Commerce*, and was reprinted in the *New-York Evening Post*, 7 July 1828, and other papers.

26. Sam's motto: *New-York Evening Post*, 7 July 1828. Though the exact time for the official dinner was unannounced, its seems very safe to assume that the exclusive festivities were still in progress when Sam leaped at 4:30 p.m. The parade formed at 11 a.m. on that day, and marched through all the principal streets. Services at the church included a prayer, the reading of the Declaration of Independence, numerous songs by the choir, and the performance by the Orator of the Day, a speech that generally occupied more than an hour. There was then the parade to St. John's Hall, more festivities, a formal banquet, the thirteen regular toasts (each followed by a band performance), and even more volunteer toasts. In subsequent years the parade began at 10 a.m., with the banquet scheduled for 3 p.m. For times, see *Paterson Intelligencer*, 9 July 1828 (Sam's leap, parade starting time); 1 July 1829 and 4 July 1830 (parade and banquet starting times).

27. *Paterson Intelligencer*, 16 July 1828; *New-York Commercial Advertiser*, 31 July 1828.

28. This is the conclusion of Howard Harris, "The Transformation of Ideology in the Early Industrial Revolution," 296–308, and of Clay Gish, "The Children's Strikes: Socialization and Class Formation in Paterson, 1824–1836," *New Jersey History* 110 (Fall/Winter 1992): 21–38.

29. Quotes: *New-York Commercial Advertiser*, 6 August 1828; *New-York Evening Post*, 26 July 1828. On the Pawtucket strike, see Gary Kulik, "Pawtuckat Village and the Strike of 1824: The Origins of Class Conflict in Rhode Island," *Radical History Review* 17 (Spring 1978): 6–35.

30. *New-York Commercial Advertiser*, 24 July 1828; *New York Statesman*, 21 July 1828. *New York Enquirer*, 4 August 1828 (crowd estimate). Money: *New-Jersey Journal* (Elizabeth Town), 22 July 1828.

31. James Epstein, "Understanding the Cap of Liberty: Symbolic Practice and Social Conflict in Early Nineteenth-Century England," *Past and Present* 122 (February 1989): 101,110–111.

32. *New-York Evening Post*, 26 July 1828 (quote); *New-York Commercial Advertiser*, 26 July 1828, 31 July 1828 (quote); *Paterson Intelligencer*, 6 August 1828.

33. *New-York Spectator*, 1 August 1828; *New-York Enquirer for the County*, 29 July 1828; *New-York Commercial Advertiser*, 31 July 1828; *New-York Evening Post*, 30 July 1828; *Paterson Intelligencer*, 30 July 1828.

34. *New-York Commercial Advertiser*, 6 August 1828, 8 August 1828.

35. *New-York Commercial Advertiser*, 31 July 1828.

at two o'clock in the afternoon of said day, and then and there proceed to make an allotment between the said three townships of such poor persons as shall then be chargeable upon the townships of Roxbury and Pequanack; and that the township of Jefferson shall take and receive of the said townships of Roxbury and Pequanack, all such poor persons as may be reasonable for them to take, in proportion to the taxable property contained within their respective limits, and that the said township of Jefferson shall be entitled to receive from the said townships of Roxbury and Pequanack **Monies** their equal proportion of all monies which **raised for** hath been raised in said townships for the **the poor to** support of the poor, and remains unexpended **be divided.** at the time of such division; *Provided,* That if either of the committees chosen as aforesaid, **Proviso.** shall neglect to meet as aforesaid, it shall and may be lawful for such committee as shall meet, to proceed to such distribution of the poor, and such other business as is by this act prescribed and intended to be done.

AN ACT for the gradual abolition of slavery.

Passed February 15, 1804.

Sec. 1. BE IT ENACTED *by the coun-* **Everychild** *cil and general assembly of this state, and it is* **born of a** *hereby enacted by the authority of the same,* **slave after** That every child born of a slave within this **of July** state, after the fourth day of July next, shall be **next to be** free; but shall remain the servant of the owner **to remain** of his or her mother, and the executors, ad- **servants** ministrators or assigns of such owner, in the **males 25,** same manner as if such child had been bound **& females** **21 years of** **age.**

After considerable debate, New Jersey passed the Abolition Act of 1804, a gradual manumission law. Because of the way it was worded, slavery continued to exist in the state until the passage of the Thirteenth Amendment in 1865. Laws of New Jersey (1830 edition), Special Collections and University Archives, Rutgers University Libraries.

8

It is often assumed that slavery was the South's "peculiar institution," but actually until the American Revolution slaves were present in all of the thirteen colonies that would become the United States. Even after the Revolution, slavery continued in some areas of the North. In the end, New Jersey was the last northern state to pass an abolition law, and because that law provided for gradual emancipation there were still eighteen slaves left in 1865. They were freed by the Thirteenth Amendment.

From the late nineteenth century to the mid-twentieth century the dominant historical view of slavery in the United States was that it had not been so bad. An example of this is a 1924 statement by D. H. Gardner in the *Proceedings of the New Jersey Historical Society* that New Jersey slaves in the colonial period were "in the main, quite happy and contented." By the 1950s and 1960s, historians, reading such sources as advertisements for runaway slaves and narratives written by back abolitionists, presented a much darker picture, one of slaves with scars from beatings, forcibly separated from their families, and determined to escape. They also emphasized that slavery destroyed the African heritage and family structure. By the 1970s, new arguments appeared noting that in many places family life was re-created and African culture continued dispute the hardships of enslavement. Recent history has added an Atlantic or even global perspective to discussions of slavery.

The selection by Giles Wright on slavery and the American Revolution in New Jersey reflects the studies of the past half century, incorporating new information and interpretations. The story he tells is a mixed one, documenting the difficulties of slavery while noting the perseverance and accomplishments of slaves, as well as cultural continuities from Africa. While he concentrates on the impact of the Revolution, his piece can be used to examine a whole range of issues about slavery in the North. These include how the lives of northern slaves were different from those in the South; what, if any, changes the Revolution brought; why abolition took so long in New Jersey; and how blacks were treated once they obtained their freedom.

New Jersey is described as a "slave-owning society" rather than a "slave society" because, while it had the second highest proportion of slaves in the North (after New York), the numbers did not approach that of the South or Caribbean. In 1680 there were 200 slaves in the Jerseys, in 1770 there were 8,200, or possibly about 7 percent of the population compared to over 50 percent in places like South Carolina. Nor was slave labor essential to the economy as it was in areas producing tobacco, cotton, or sugar. Rather, New Jersey's farms were smaller, its crops more diversified, and its winters longer. That said, slave labor was used on farms, in iron manufacturing, and for domestic work in homes. By the time of the Revolution, Quakers no longer viewed slavery as acceptable, with the consequence that most slaves were held in East Jersey, while the number of free blacks increased in West Jersey, where many Quakers had settled. With these distinctions in mind, how does New Jersey slavery compare to that of other places, including the South? How did New Jersey laws treat slaves? In what ways was this different from how whites were treated? Were slaves whipped, hung, burned at the stake? Did they ever run away, try to revolt, or resist in other ways? Did the African heritage of slaves survive in New Jersey? What kinds of evidence can be used to answer these questions?

Chapter 4 of this volume, "Caught in the Middle: New Jersey's Indians and the American Revolution," deals with what happened to the Delaware Indians during and after the American Revolution, and similar questions can be asked for blacks, both free and slave. First, which side did they take, loyalist or patriot? Second, what was the consequence, were they better or worse off? The answer can depend on whether one sees the glass half empty or half full. Larry Greene, writing about blacks in New Jersey, concludes, "Most New Jersey slaves experienced little change in their status after the Revolution." Wright, on the other hand, sees the Revolution as a "watershed" moment. He emphasizes the active agency of those who used the chaos of the American Revolution to free themselves, the spread of ideas about equality, and the increase in manumissions. As the number of freed blacks rose, it became increasingly difficult to sustain the institution; successfully running away became easier, and a tipping point was reached. Yet the Revolution did not end slavery in New Jersey. Does Wright convince you that something significant happened? Would slavery have ended without the American Revolution? Wright uses 1810 as the final year to assess changes; what if he had used 1783 instead?

Abolition came late to New Jersey (at least for a northern state), with a gradual emancipation law passed in 1804. Under the terms of the law the children of slaves were to be freed when they came of age, essentially when they reached the point where their work had paid their owners for their cost. Why were many residents of the state reluctant to approve abolition, and how can historians explain the method used to accomplish it? Does it mean that owners were compensated for the loss of their property? Did they move toward abolition because they accepted the ideology of the Revolution, including the statement of the Declaration of Independence that "all men are created equal," or did they free their slaves because they owned so few of them that the economic consequences were insignificant? Which was more important, ideas or the "pocketbook"? Where do you think Wright stands on this issue?

Finally, what happened to African Americans in New Jersey after slavery? Greene has noted that abolition did not mean equal treatment, not "the acquisition of voting rights, the end of racial stereotypes, or the acceptance of the black presence in the state." What kinds of jobs could and did blacks have in New Jersey? What civil rights were they granted? Could they serve on juries, vote, or hold office? How long did it take, just when did changes occur, and has true equality been reached today?

Suggested Readings

Berlin, Ira, and Ronald Hoffman eds. *Slavery and Freedom in the Age of the American Revolution.* Charlottesville: United States Capitol Historical Society/University Press of Virginia, 1983.

Greene, Larry A. "A History of Afro-Americans in New Jersey." *Journal of the Rutgers University Libraries* 56 (1994): 4–71.

Hodges, Graham Russell. *Root and Branch: African Americans in New York and East Jersey 1613–1863.* Chapel Hill: University of North Carolina Press, 1999.

———. *Slavery and Freedom in the Rural North: African Americans in Monmouth County New Jersey, 1665–1865.* Madison, Wis.: Madison House, 1997.

McManus, Edgar J. *Black Bondage in the North.* Syracuse, N.Y.: Syracuse University Press, 1973.

Moss, Simeon F. "The Persistence of Slavery and Involuntary Servitude in a Free State (1685–1866)." *The Journal of Negro History* 35 (1950): 289–310.

Pingeon, Frances D. *Blacks in the Revolutionary Era.* Trenton: New Jersey Historical Commission, 1975.

Price, Clement A. *Freedom Not Far Distant: A Documentary History of Afro-Americans in New Jersey.* Newark: New Jersey Historical Society, 1980.

Quarles, Benjamin. *The Negro in the American Revolution.* Chapel Hill: University North Carolina Press, 1961.

Wolinetz, Gary K. "New Jersey Slavery and the Law." *Rutgers Law Review* 50 (1998): 2227–2258.

Wright, Giles R. *Afro-Americans in New Jersey: A Short History.* Trenton: New Jersey Historical Commission, 1989.

Zilversmit, Arthur. "Liberty and Property: New Jersey and the Abolition of Slavery." *New Jersey History* 88 (1970): 215–226.

◆ ◆ ◆ ◆ ◆ ◆

Moving Toward Breaking the Chains:
Black New Jerseyans
and the American Revolution

Giles R. Wright

In 1855, William Cooper Nell, abolitionist, lecturer, journalist, and a pioneering black historian, wrote *The Colored Patriots of the American Revolution*, perhaps the first full-length study to narrate the historical experience of black Americans.[1] This work also provided a nexus between persons of African descent and the American Revolutionary War.

In examining the intersection of the American Revolution and blacks in New Jersey, this present chapter is part of a rather extensive historiography; it continues in the tradition of Nell and other black historians, including William Wells Brown in the 1860s, George Washington Williams and Joseph T. Wilson in the 1880s, Benjamin Brawley in the 1920s, Luther P. Jackson in the 1940s, and Benjamin Quarles in the 1960s.[2] In doing so, it suggests that the War of Independence can be viewed as instructive in at least two significant ways; both go beyond a chronicling of blacks as participants in the war, the focus of the aforementioned studies.

First, the Revolutionary War marked a watershed—a juncture in history by which time several key developments had occurred in New Jersey black life: a large increase in the slave population since its introduction to New Jersey; the emergence of the slave family; the existence of a small free black population; and the cultural metamorphosis of Africans into African Americans. Second, the American Revolution can be considered in terms of its impact on black New Jerseyans. The nature of the war's meaning for this segment of the population in New Jersey is of course part of the conflict's effect on the lives of all northern blacks.

From *New Jersey in the American Revolution*, edited by Barbara Mitnick (New Brunswick, N.J.: Rutgers University Press, 2005), 113–137. Reprinted by permission of the author.

Given that it was the North, led by Vermont in 1777, that ushered in the "First Emancipation" (the initial full-scale effort to eliminate slavery in America), the central question remains whether the Revolution, through its cascading torrents of historical change, was the major reason for this occurrence—the disappearance of chattel bondage in the North. One school of thought has suggested that it was; its historians have argued that it was the Revolution's ideology of freedom, equality, and moral rectitude that dealt a crippling blow to the North's system of bondage. In 1961, for example, Leon Litwack noted:

> The liquidation of slavery in the North should not be considered simply on the grounds of profits and losses, climate and geography. Abolition sentiment generally ignored these factors and chose instead to emphasize one particular theme: that the same principles used to justify the American Revolution, particularly John Locke's natural rights philosophy, also condemned and doomed Negro slavery. Such an institution could not be reconciled with colonial efforts to resist English tyranny; indeed its existence embarrassed the American cause.[3]

Echoing these sentiments in 1967, Arthur Zilversmit ended his chapter on abolition during the American Revolution by writing:

> The years of the Revolutionary War had brought great gains for northern Negroes. . . . Undoubtedly the Revolutionary elan was a moving force behind the policy of abolition . . . In the preamble to their abolition acts, both Pennsylvania and Rhode Island appealed to the ideology of the American Revolution to justify their actions.[4]

In 1973, another historian, Edgar J. McManus, took a similar position:

> The greatest thrust for Negro freedom came during the Revolutionary era. Public opinion veered sharply against slavery almost in direct proportion to the deterioration of relations with England. White militants demanding political freedom for themselves found it difficult to justify chattel bondage for Americans of darker pigmentation. . . . Everywhere the natural rights doctrine espoused by the patriot party forced change in attitudes about the Negro and his place in American life.[5]

Other historians have questioned whether the spirit of liberty and equality generated by the American Revolution convinced appreciable numbers of northerners that bondage war morally wrong, contending that the northerners' effort to abandon slavery was rooted in economic factors. For example, some have argued that slavery disappeared in the North because the region's economy was not dependent on slave labor and that the relatively small number of slaves in that part of the country, where free white workers basically prevailed, made northern employers far less resistant to abolitionist efforts than southern slave-holders.[6] In explaining the institution's demise in New Jersey around the time of the Revolution in terms of fundamental economic determinants and considerations, Frances Pingeon has noted:

> During at least half of the eighteenth century the desperate need for labor of all kinds obscured the problem inherent in Northern slavery. With the approach of the Revolution, these tensions began to develop. It is my contention that conflicts arose more from economic need and social problems created by slavery in New Jersey than from Revolutionary ideology. The message of New Jersey Quakers and enlightened liberals of the Revolutionary epoch evoked a response in New Jersey because the strain of the slavery system in this particular society outweighed its advantages. The Revolution gave a moral strength to questions that were already being asked.[7]

Pingeon concluded that by the time of the Revolution, slavery in New Jersey had become uneconomical and was a dying institution. "The long New Jersey winters, which forced idleness on many Blacks employed in farming; the increased competition with white labor; and the ingrained prejudice against Blacks, a legacy of the colonial era, raised questions about the profitability of slavery," she observed.[8] Pingeon further indicated that the response of New Jersey slaveholders to this lack of economic benefit varied. Now viewing bondage as a matter of short-term speculation rather than a more permanent investment as in the South, some hired out their bond persons and collected their wages. Others sold their slaves in the nation's booming southern markets. Still others relocated to the South with their slaves.[9]

It appears that the Revolution itself succeeded in undermining slavery in New Jersey and served as a liberating instrument for New Jersey blacks. Perhaps it was the lofty egalitarian and libertarian rhetoric of the Revolution that helped weaken New Jersey bondage. At the same time, another factor of equal significance was at play: the chaos and turbulence spawned by the Revolution. The Revolution's severe dislocations invested black New Jerseyans with an unprecedented opportunity to realize their yearnings for freedom, and thus caught up in the vortex of the Revolution, they used their increased bargaining power to their own advantage. The Revolution thereby had a profound impact on black New Jerseyans, affecting their well-being and reshaping their lives in an unprecedented manner. The forces unleashed during the Revolutionary War in fact produced cataclysmic changes in the lives of black New Jerseyans that were still reverberating by 1810, a year that some have identified as the end of the Revolutionary War era.[10] Indeed, by marking 1810 as the end of an era that began in 1776, a period of considerable social upheaval, two key pieces of evidence of slavery's decline in New Jersey are accommodated: An Act for the Gradual Abolition of Slavery that was passed in 1804 and the unprecedented size of the free black New Jersey population in 1810.

Before the Revolution: 1630s–1776

Although by the time of the American Revolution New Jersey had not become what historian Philip D. Morgan has defined as a "slave society," one in which slavery is the determinative institution, it had become a "slave owning society."[11] It had come to possess an economy that featured a considerable reliance on enslaved labor, making the forced labor of blacks an important thread in New Jersey's social fabric. Indicative of this development was the immense growth in the slave population over the nearly 150 years slavery had been on New Jersey soil. Identified as numbering 200 in 1680, seemingly the earliest year for which New Jersey slaves were counted, by 1770 the total had reached 8,220, a roughly forty-fold increase.[12] This enabled New Jersey, on the eve of the American Revolution, to rank second only to New York among northern colonies in terms of actual numbers of blacks and their percentage of the total population. In addition, this expansion of New Jersey's blacks mirrored their overall growth in the American colonies. By the onset of the Revolution, the number of blacks in America had reached at an all-time high: approximately 500,000, roughly 20 percent of the total American population. It was the highest percentage of blacks ever to be found in this country.[13]

The growth of the New Jersey black population before the onset of the Revolution was understandable given the increase in demand for slave labor and the availability of Africans. This growth coincided with the rapid expansion of the transatlantic slave trade during the eighteenth century, a period that witnessed the arrival of 60 percent of all slaves brought into the New World. The trade's volume peaked in the 1780s when nearly 80,000 slaves per annum crossed the Atlantic from Africa. Initially coming into New Jersey from the West Indies (e.g., Barbados) and the southern mainland colonies (e.g., Virginia,

Georgia, the Carolinas) as incidental residue of the overall transportation of Africans across the Atlantic, by 1750 slaves were brought into New Jersey directly from the African continent, increasingly to be used to replace white indentured servants in the labor force. Between 1761 and 1765, regular advertisements of public auctions held in Coopers Ferry (present-day Camden) of slaves from West Africa appeared in Philadelphia newspapers, indicating the substantial influx of bondpersons into New Jersey during that period. The Seven Years' War (French and Indian War), which took place between 1756 and 1763, accentuated the demand for African slaves, since the participation of white males in the war limited their availability for indentured servitude. Moreover, expanded opportunities for economic advancement for workers in Europe also affected the demand for African slave labor in New Jersey.[14]

The increased dependency on slaves in New Jersey was particularly noticeable in its northern region, where the Dutch, who were the first to bring bondpersons into New Jersey and among the world's main traffickers in slaves during the seventeenth century, settled in large numbers. Northern New Jersey was thus, along with northern New England and the New York City area, part of the region in the North that featured the highest concentration of slaves. For example, by the mid-eighteenth century, enslaved men outnumbered propertyless single white men 262 to 194 in Monmouth County. Neighboring Middlesex County had 281 enslaved men and 81 free wage workers, white and black. The numbers for Bergen County for the same categories were 306 to 8. Conversely, slaves in the southern part of New Jersey were relatively few in number on the eve of the American Revolution—only about 5 percent of the total population in 1772.[15] They were part of an economy that was less diversified than that found in northern New Jersey, and they lived in a region that traditionally featured a greater availability of white workers.

With the rising need for Africans in New Jersey during the years leading up to the Revolution came an increase in their value, a point that runs counter to the notion of slavery's unprofitability. Prices seemingly reached a nadir around the mid-1730s, when the average cost of a male slave was about £20.[16] An examination of New Jersey estate inventories for the 1750–1760 decade, however, reveals an average price of roughly £47 for thirty-two males. After the Revolution, however, prices were substantially higher. Seventy-two men included in New Jersey estate inventories between 1794 and 1801 had an average value of roughly £76; twenty-seven of them were worth at least £100. Thus the average price had increased more than 50 percent beyond the 1750–1760 level.[17]

The growth of the New Jersey slave population by the time of the Revolution was also influenced by the ability of enslaved people to reproduce themselves. This process of natural increase among slaves in America was a key way in which American bondage could be distinguished from slave systems in other parts of the New World. Commenting on this prevailing pattern, as it was revealed in British slave colonies in the Caribbean, Morgan has written:

> In 1780 the number of blacks in British America was less than half of the total number of African emigrants received in the previous century and a half, whereas the white population exceeded its emigrant group almost three times over. The key to the black disaster lay in their experiences in the Caribbean, where about one in four Africans died within the first three years of residence and where sugar production proved a veritable destroyer of life. In this region as a whole, African slaves and their descendants never produced enough children to offset the staggering number of adult deaths.[18]

The increase in New Jersey's slave population was not without worry on the part of white New Jerseyans. Their preference was for laborers like themselves, considered more assimilable than Africans, who were perceived as uncivilized, primitive, savage, vicious, dangerous, and capable of the greatly dreaded acts of rebellion. Given the fact that whippings, brandings, and mutilations were common punishments even for free persons in colonial New Jersey, it is not surprising that harsh, severe, even barbaric punishment was regarded as essential to addressing the danger that subversive slaves posed. For example, the 1704 slave code provided that a slave guilty of stealing an item worth five shillings receive forty lashes on his or her bare back and be branded with the letter "T" on the left cheek near the nose.[19] Under this code, burning served as a punishment for slaves committing arson or murder and castration for "any carnal knowledge of a white woman." The 1713 slave code that replaced that of 1704, while removing castration and any allusion to burning, continued to prescribe severe penalties against slaves, allowing for immediate execution for such crimes as arson, rape, or murder.[20] Even minor infractions brought severe punishment. Examples include a 1751 law that subjected slaves to twenty lashes by the constable for meeting in groups of more than five or for being out of doors after 9:00 p.m. without their owner's permission. A 1760 law imposed a punishment of thirty lashes upon a slave for setting an illegal trap.[21]

The concern about acts of servile insurrection, one of several common forms of both overt and covert slave dissent (e.g., running away, theft, arson, sabotage, murder of slave owners, and feigning illness), was well-founded, for such acts are well documented in pre-Revolutionary New Jersey. In 1734, for example, two slave conspiracies were unearthed, perhaps New Jersey's first significant examples. Occurring miles apart, they nevertheless were remarkably similar. The first was discovered near Somerville, where it was alleged that hundreds of slaves plotted to gain their freedom by a massacre of whites. A belief by the slaves that their bondage was contrary to the orders of King George seemingly helped fuel their subversion. According to the plot, as soon as the weather became mild enough to permit them to survive in the woods, at some midnight agreed upon, all of the slaves were to rise and slay their owners. Buildings were to be set afire and the draft horses killed. Finally, having secured the best saddle horses, the conspirators intended to flee to the Indians and join them in support of the French. However, the impudent remarks of a drunken slave aroused suspicion of the plot and led to the arrest of several hundred bondmen, two of whom were hanged and many others flogged.[22]

In the second example, also in 1734, a group of slaves in Burlington County somehow became convinced that England had outlawed slavery and therefore they were being held in bondage illegally. Thus enraged against their owners, a large number formed a plot to gain their freedom by armed rebellion. A Philadelphia newspaper reported that it had been decreed by the leaders of the uprising that every male and female slave in every family was to rise at midnight and cut the throats of their masters and sons. They were not to meddle with the women, whom they intended to plunder and ravish the following day. As in the Somerville example, when the massacre was over, the rebels intended to seek refuge among the French and Indians. The plot failed after it was uncovered following an investigation prompted by a remark one of the plotters made while arguing with a white. He asserted that he was as good as any of the slave owners and they would soon know it. Although most of the county's slaves were suspected of complicity, only thirty of the ringleaders were brought to trial. One slave was hanged, several had their ears cut off, and the rest were severely flogged.[23]

A subsequent slave plot surfaced in 1741 in Hackensack, where three bondmen were burned alive after being convicted of setting fire to seven local barns. In 1772, in Perth Amboy, another slave plot was discovered when a slaveholder, alarmed by reports of a conspiracy, urged that all blacks, including seven of his own, be sent to Africa at their owners' expense.[24] Obsessive fear of a slave rebellion led the committee of correspondence in Shrewsbury and Freehold in 1775 to order that "all arms in the hands of or at the command of negroes, slave or free, shall be taken and secured by the militia officers of the several districts." This action was taken in response to "numerous and riotous meetings of negroes at unlicensed houses," which the committee perceived as threatening and fraught with dangerous implications.[25]

While the need for black labor overrode concerns about slave insurrections, it is likely that the growth in the population of black New Jerseyans by the time of the American Revolution would have been greater if not for the high mortality rates and decline in fertility that accompanied the arrival of slaves directly from Africa during the middle of the eighteenth century. These slaves lacked immunity to common diseases such as measles, whooping cough, and smallpox. Fertility also fell, it has been argued, because as slave owners replaced indentured servants, they preferred the replacements, like those they replaced, be single men without families.[26]

The slave family, the enslaved population's most important instrument for its survival, had also surfaced in New Jersey by the time of the American Revolution; a familial life—the African family—which had initially been destroyed through enslavement, had been rebuilt. The manner in which colonial slaves in New Jersey and elsewhere came to acquire a sense of being connected by blood—a feeling of affinity based on an awareness of common descent—is still not that well understood. However, it probably did involve the existence in New Jersey of several generations of native-born blacks, a more favorable balance of the sexes (still, males outnumbered females throughout the colonial period, reflecting the emphasis placed on importing black males for the labor force), and the defining among New Jersey slaves of new, non-African marital roles and familial structures (e.g., the extended family) that addressed the most obvious problem of physical separation.

The importance of early New Jersey slave families cannot be minimized, for they performed at least two vital functions. Slave families aided the process of natural reproduction, which, as previously noted, contributed to the size of the population of black New Jerseyans by the time of the American Revolution. Black families also served as socializing agents, helping younger generations acquire adaptive mechanisms that would facilitate their survival in the face of the stresses and strains of bondage.

Further, the early black family was connected to a common form of slave resistance. Bondpersons in New Jersey, as elsewhere in colonial America, frequently absconded from their owners in order to be reunited with family members. Extant runaway slave notices thus often provide some clues about the early formation of New Jersey slave families. The following few lines from a 1772 example revealing a man's interest in seeking out either his mother or wife offer insight into the level of familial consciousness among black New Jerseyans on the eve of the American Revolution.

> RUN-AWAY from the Subscriber, on Sunday Evening the 27th Day of December last, a Negro Man named Jack, about 33 Years old, a short spare Fellow. . . . He was purchased from Hendrick Emons, of Rockey-Hill in New Jersey, about 9 years ago, and it is supposed he is either gone that Way, where he has a Mother, or else to Anthony Ten Eyck's at Albany, where he has a Wife.[27]

Of course, not all New Jersey black families were enslaved and subject to being torn apart; the oldest consisted of free persons. Such families on the eve of the American Revolution were part of a small group of free blacks in New Jersey that numbered roughly 400 in all—about 5 percent of the total black population.[28]

Free blacks could be found in New Jersey as early as the 1680s. Some of the earliest had migrated from Manhattan to Bergen County, where they became owners of original Tappan land grants. They were Afro-Dutch, bearing such surnames as Van Donck, De Vries, and Manuel.[29] The pathway to joining free blacks was somewhat blocked in the aftermath of the rebellion of 1712 in neighboring New York, in which a group of slaves killed nine whites and wounded five or six more.[30] Alarmed over the prospects of similar insurrection on New Jersey soil, the legislature passed a law in 1713 that provided for greater strictures on the enslaved population; it required that a manumission (a formal act of freedom from slavery) be accompanied by a security or bond of £200 and a guarantee of £20 a year for the upkeep of any freed slave.[31] This financially prohibitive arrangement for most New Jersey slave owners would prove to be the greatest impediment to manumission efforts in pre-Revolutionary New Jersey. By 1776, most of those who comprised the small number of free blacks in New Jersey were either the descendants of seventeenth-century free blacks or manumittees who fell into one of two categories: those who through age or circumstance had become liabilities to their owners or those who were the descendants of mixed racial unions—mulattoes.

Perhaps the most notable native-born mulatto New Jerseyan who had been manumitted by the time of the American Revolution was Cyrus Bustill, an individual whose life actually intersected with the conflict. A native of Burlington, Bustill was born in 1732, the son of his owner, Samuel Bustill—an English-born Quaker and prominent lawyer—and his female slave, Parthenia. At his death in 1742, Samuel

Bustill left a will that gave Cyrus to his wife, Grace, who later sold him to a local baker—a Quaker—with the understanding that Cyrus undertake an apprenticeship that would enable him to purchase his freedom. By 1774, Cyrus had secured his freedom, opened a bakery in Burlington, and married. During the American Revolution, he worked at his trade in Burlington and, in all probability, baked bread for Washington's troops during the 1777–1778 winter ordeal at Valley Forge. While there is an oral tradition in the Bustill family that he even received a silver coin from Washington for such service, there is actual documentary evidence, also possessed by Bustill's descendants, that in fact he was given official commendation for his baking services for the Continental Army. After the war, he moved his family to Philadelphia, where he became one of the city's early black leaders; he was a founding member of the historic Free African Society in 1787 and later opened a school for black youth in his home. Bustill also would gain recognition as the great-great-grandfather of Paul Robeson, the celebrated twentieth-century singer, actor, and civil rights activist, arguably New Jersey's most illustrious native.[32]

The life of Bustill suggests the pioneering role that free blacks, given their greater personal autonomy, understandably played in the early life of black communities in America. In pre-Revolution New Jersey, however, they were victimized because of their color in ways similar to those in bondage. Although it failed enactment, a bill that came before the 1773–1774 session of the legislature illuminates the subordinate status sought for free blacks; it required manumitted slaves to pay taxes and fulfill all other duties of citizens, but it denied them the right to vote, serve as a witness except against each other, and marry whites. In addition, free blacks who ran into debt or who were sentenced to prison could be bound out as indentured servants.[33]

Free blacks were also in the forefront of the cultural transformation black New Jerseyans had experienced by the time of the American Revolution—from African to African American. On the eve of the Revolution, the great majority of New Jersey blacks were no longer complete aliens in a strange land. As uprooted Africans, they had indeed become hybrids or hyphenated Americans—new products of a two- pronged process of acculteration.[34]

Scholars are still debating the extent to which Africans maintained and transmitted their culture in the New World. One acknowledged process involved the melding of different traditional African customs into a pan-African culture and the retention of some aspects of this heritage—what have been termed Africanisms or African survivals. Affecting the preservation of African cultural traditions (the rekindling of African ways of thinking and behaving) was, of course, the arrival in

New Jersey of slaves directly from Africa. Their importation enhanced the possible infusion of New Jersey's native black population with first-hand knowledge of the continent and its cultural heritage.

One of the ways in which New Jersey slaves revealed a pan-African associational life was through African burial grounds. Suggesting a sense of unity and social cohesion, as well as solidarity and common purpose, these burial sites were probably the first public places where black New Jerseyans congregated. While the actual locations of such eighteenth-century places have yet to be unearthed in New Jersey, they have been discovered elsewhere; a neighboring example is the African Burial Ground in New York City. We can surmise, therefore, that they existed in New Jersey as well and could provide further evidence of the continuation of such African burial practices as the placing of favorite objects of the deceased on top of the grave. In fact, the Gethsemane Cemetery in Little Ferry, a burial place established in 1860 for Hackensack's African Americans, has yielded broken white pottery and clay pipes, also suggestive of death rituals derived from African peoples—in particular, the Bakongo of present-day Congo.[35]

Slave owners, aware of African cultural continuities present among their slaves, sometimes used them to their advantage. One example, drawing on supernatural beliefs associated with the practice of trial by ordeal in some African societies, was a 1767 case in which a slave was suspected of murdering a white man, but no evidence could be found against him. As a last resort, the suspected slave was ordered to touch the face of his victim; when blood then ran out of the dead man's nose, the slave was induced to confess, convicted of murder, and duly burned alive. New Jersey historian David Steven Cohen has pointed out that this incident also revealed the "bloody corpse" motif found throughout the Western world, perhaps an example of cultural syncretism.[36]

Through their cultural borrowing and reinterpretation, the acculturative process experienced by New Jersey Africans also involved the adoption of the beliefs and behavior patterns of their land of enslavement—the absorption of the culture of the larger society. African slaves revised their languages, for example, learning to speak such European languages as English, Dutch, and German. Their fluency naturally varied considerably; runaway notices often referred to fugitives who spoke "low Dutch," "Negro Dutch," or "bad English," as well as to those who exhibited a bilingual proficiency ("speaks good Dutch and English") and to those who could "read and write, and 'tis supposed will forge a pass."[37]

Clothing was another area that reflected the acculturative process. Again, advertisements for escaped slaves are instructive. In some instances, they document slaves having a taste for fine clothing, perhaps in imitation of wealthy slave owners. A 1773 notice that referred to three runaways from Hopewell, for example, showed that they wore or carried with them items that belied their lowly status. "A suit of black clothes, a brown silk camblet coat, three linen shirts, good shoes and stockings" described the first; "a yellowish brown close bodied coat, a vest, the foreparts calf-skin, with the hair on, new buckskin breeches, a new felt hat, good shoes and stockings" identified the second; and the last was in possession of "a green sagathy coat, a light coloured cut velvet vest, two striped Holland jackets, a brown coat, red great coat, a pair of leather breeches, three shirts, the one ruffled, a pair of tow trousers, a new castor hat, good shoes and stockings."[38]

Another example of the degree of Americanization present among black New Jerseyans before the Revolution is one captured on occasion in runaway slave notices. Witness a 1772 notice that identified a thirty-year-old runaway from "Boontown" (Boonton) as being "much addicted to strong drink."[39] Virtually all African societies from which slaves were taken had very strong strictures against intoxication for everyone except the elderly—those who, as a reward of old age, had earned the right to use intoxicants to excess. It would thus be virtually unthinkable in traditional African society for those as young as thirty to consume large quantities of intoxicating beverages.

Religion serves as an area where black New Jerseyans exhibited both African cultural continuities and the internalizing of Euro-American culture, drawing on the African past as well as the American present. By the time of the Revolution, many black New Jerseyans had been affected by the desire of white colonists to bring Africans to a belief in Christ and had become Quakers, Anglicans, Lutherans, Presbyterians, Moravians, or members of the Dutch Reformed Church. Through the example of William Boen, a conversion to Quakerism can be seen as informing nonviolent protest against slavery. Born into bondage in Mount Holly in 1735 and manumitted at age twenty-eight, Boen's antislavery convictions led him to refuse to use or wear any article manufactured or transported by enslaved labor.[40] By attaining a position of influence among early Lutherans, Arie Van Guinee also personified the religious acculturation that occurred among some early black New Jerseyans. In 1714, several years after moving to the Raritan Valley from New York City, where he was a member of a Lutheran congregation, he held the very first local Lutheran service in his home. Van Guinee later assisted in the baptisms of his niece and nephew and became a man of considerable means, purchasing sizeable plots of land over the years.[41]

In contrast to Boen and Van Guinee were those black New Jerseyans whose conversion to Christianity still allowed for the expression of their African religious heritage—the fusion of Christian and African religious beliefs and rituals. Often their conversion could be attributed to the Great Awakening that began in 1740, an evangelistic movement anchored in the notion of equality before God that featured camp meetings and revivals and an emphasis on immediate conversion rather than spiritual growth through study and discipline. It attracted New Jersey blacks, along with those in other colonies, because the emotional fervor and convulsive behavior it sanctioned permitted several African cultural survivals. One of those was the drumlike rhythmic hand clapping that accompanied their responsive singing; another was "spirit possession," the supreme religious experience so fundamental to traditional African religious beliefs and practices in which a deity momentarily takes over the mind and body of a devotee, allowing for a trance or altered state of consciousness. Behaving like a possessed person has persisted to the present day in some African American churches. Terms for the conduct include "shouting," "getting happy," and "getting the Holy Ghost."[42]

Naming practices among black New Jerseyans also offered proof of the coexistence of a long memory of Africa and newly acquired American ways. Such West African names as Sambo (of Hausa origin), Kuff (a derivative of the Akan "Kofi"), and Sukey (probably the Wolof female name "Suki") could be found among New Jersey slaves before the Revolution, as well as such African-sounding names as Bonturah, Cudjo, Mingo, Quameny, Quamino, Quaco, Quashee, and Jemima.[43] In answering to European names by the eve of the Revolution, however, black New Jerseyans also signaled a change in their identity. A perusal of pre-Revolution runaway slave notices, wills, and inventory lists reveals a common use of names clearly non-African, such as Tim, Peter, Jack, Joe, Sybil, Betty, Elizabeth, Sylvia, and Sarah. Among these names are some that suggested a kind of comic jest that played off the slaves' lowly status; for example, fanciful names like Free, Hero, and Prince were used, as were classical names such as Plato, Caesar, Phoebe, Cato, Pompei, Medea, and Chloe. That slave owners never carried these names themselves indeed suggests the degree to which they often sought to mock, ridicule, and demean their human property.

The use of aliases—multiple names—by runaway slaves, as a way of avoiding detection and capture, indicates still another manner in which the naming process revealed a degree of Americanization among New Jersey bondpersons. A 1771 notice, for example, indicated that Jem, a slave of Isaac Wilkins of Newark, "calls himself by several names of James, Gaul, Mingo, Mink, and Jim." A 1764 notice, stating that Jacob, of Freehold, New Jersey, "has several times changed his name, calling himself James Stuart, and James Pratt, &ct . . . he passes himself as an Indian," reveals a fugitive not only using several names but one artful enough in adapting to his environment to change his ethnic identity as well.[44]

Finally, New Jersey slaves in their daily work revealed skills associated with occupations in Africa, as well as those learned through their experiences in bondage. In the first category would be the work that New Jersey slaves did as farm laborers, cultivating grains for domestic use and export to the West Indies and raising hogs, cattle, and horses on small farms or small slave holdings. Women who toiled as house servants or were engaged in cooking, laundering, and spinning also fell into this category, as did male slaves serving as seafarers and dockworkers who drew upon work habits found among African groups situated close to bodies of water. Other occupations found among black New Jerseyans that were akin to African work traditions included blacksmithing, weaving, and one often mentioned in fugitive slave notices: fiddling, a talent related to that of professional musicians found among the West African coast who played stringed instruments such as the kora of the Mandingo people.[45]

Mining, at which blacks from Angola and the Congo were especially skilled, also engaged the services of New Jersey slaves. In fact, one of the largest mines in colonial America, employing over 200 slaves, was the Schuyler mine in lower Bergen County. It was discovered by an elderly black, whose reward was a "fancy dressing gown like his master and some pipe tobacco." In the mines, blacks worked with skilled and journeymen whites and indentured servants, as well as in skilled positions at forges and blast furnaces.[46]

By the onset of the Revolution, black New Jerseyans had become chimney sweeps, bakers, masons, farriers, coopers, wheelwrights, shoemakers, carpenters, and barbers—all radical departures from African work traditions. In one notable case, Peter Hill became one of the nation's earliest black clockmakers. Born a slave in 1767 in Burlington, Hill was able to serve an apprenticeship while in bondage to the clockmaker Joseph Hollingshed Jr. After gaining his freedom in 1795, Hill established his own workshop and purchased land in Burlington; he later moved his shop to Mount Holly. Hill's work revealed a cultural transformation that involved the traditional African perception of time, a critical function of the African cosmology or worldview that for some New Jersey slaves had been discarded by the time of the Revolution. In turn, they embraced a new concept of time, which became both linear as well as an abstraction measurable in such finite units as hours, minutes, and seconds. Essentially, they moved away from a sense of time derived from the repetitive rhythms of nature and the regularities of social life.[47]

The Revolution and After: 1776–1810

Considering the breakdown of traditional measures for the social control of bondpersons that accompanied the often near-anarchic conditions of the American Revolution, it is not surprising that two slave conspiracies were plotted in New Jersey during the Revolution. One occurred in Somerset County in 1776 and involved a group of slaves who armed themselves and attempted to unite against their owners. Three years later, in Elizabethtown, slaves, allegedly incited by the Tories, conspired to rise and murder their owners.[48] The liberation of the insurrectionists that would have resulted from the success of their insurgency helps to underscore the central place of the word "freedom" in any assessment of the Revolution's enormous impact on black New Jerseyans. In short, there occurred during the Revolutionary War era, the years between 1776 and 1810, impressive gains in the struggle to break the chains binding New Jersey's enslaved population. By 1810, slave imports had ceased; the number of free blacks had increased dramatically; and the slave population had been lowered appreciably.

The American Revolution radically altered black New Jerseyans' lives by greatly widening opportunities for slaves to escape the yoke of bondage. The most common escape route to liberty was through simply running away. Although it is difficult to quantify such slave flight during the Revolution, it is clear that the numbers of such men and women "exceeded those in any previous era."[49] They were certainly among the thousands of bondpersons in America who, as active agents in their own liberation, used the war's turmoil and tumult to flee from their owners. In the process, they helped shrink the number of American slaves by roughly 100,000 by the war's end, "the largest black escape in the history of North American slavery."[50] Second- and third-generation New Jersey–born slaves who had gained familiarity with the neighboring countryside therefore were especially prone to take flight, often passing themselves off as free blacks. As can be seen in the following slave notice, which appeared in the *Pennsylvania Packet*, January 4, 1780, even among slaves only briefly in New Jersey there was an inclination to use the war as a cover for flight:

> Was taken up, and is now confined to Trenton gaol, by the subscriber, living in New-Germantown, Hunterdon County, State of New Jersey, a young Negro Man, who says his name is Peter; he is nearly six feet high, of slender make, speaks and understands very little English, and appears to have been but a short time in America, had scarce any clothing. The owner is desired to apply, pay charges and take him away.[51]

Runaways were among the New Jersey slaves who gained their freedom through military service. As one scholar has noted, "Fugitives often fled to the opposing armies to seek freedom in return for military service. A New Jersey master reported in 1778 that his runaway had 'gone to join the enemy,' and another advertised that his Negro would probably 'endeavor to get . . . to the American camp, as he is fond of soldiery.'"[52]

The British were the first to encourage slave defections by offering freedom to fugitives who took refuge with their military forces. On November 7, 1775, John Murray, Lord Dunmore, the last royal governor of Virginia, declared martial law and promised freedom to any slave who was willing and able to take up arms in His Majesty's service. Other British commanders followed Dunmore's lead and recruited slaves; ultimately, approximately 1,300 blacks served with the British.[53] When the British left America at the end of the war, they carried an estimated 20,000 free blacks to Great Britain, the West Indies, and Canada (Nova Scotia); some of these eventually relocated to Sierra Leone. This number includes black New Jerseyans who were among the 3,000 who evacuated with the British from New York City in 1783, further reducing New Jersey's slave population.[54]

The most celebrated black who saw service with the British was a native New Jerseyan: Cornelius Titus, who later became known as Colonel Tye. A runaway slave from Monmouth County, he distinguished himself at the 1778 Battle of Monmouth, then went on to become the scourge of American patriots. Tye looted and raided farms, carrying off silver, clothing, and badly needed cattle for British troops in Staten Island and New York City. For these accomplishments, he and his men were paid handsomely, sometimes receiving five gold guineas. In September 1780, while attempting his greatest feat—the capture of Captain Josiah Huddy, who was famed for his leadership in raids against British positions in Staten Island and Sandy Hook, Tye was shot in the wrist. It was originally thought to be a minor wound, but within days lockjaw set in and, lacking proper medical treatment, Tye died. Pertinent to any assessment of Tye's importance to the British is the observation by Graham Hodges that "Tye's title is noteworthy." Hodges has noted that while the British army did not formally commission black officers, it often granted blacks officers' titles out of respect.[55]

Dunmore's proclamation helped move patriot commanders and decision makers to rethink their policy of excluding blacks, both slave and free, from the war—a policy that seemed to ignore the fact that blacks occasionally had served in colonial militias and had participated in the Revolution's first battles. Coupled with the fact that as the struggle for independence lengthened and the number of soldiers grew critically short, the proclamation prompted colonists to overcome their fears that a slave revolt or mass defections would result from the arming of slaves. By the end of the war, out of a total force of 300,000, roughly 5,000 blacks, had served the patriot cause.[56]

While we have no estimate of the number of black New Jerseyans who fought on the side of the patriots, we know that most of those who did came from southern New Jersey.[57] This area had the larger free black population and the greater physical presence of Quakers, who, as America's first organized abolitionists and despite their pacifism during the Revolution, were probably more willing to promise freedom to their slaves for wartime duty. Oliver Cromwell was among those black South Jerseyans who served with the patriots. Born free in 1752 in Columbus, Burlington County, Cromwell's distinction lies in part in his having lived to be 100 years old and his ability, at that age, to provide oral testimony regarding his participation in the war. Among the reminiscences recounted by Cromwell, who enlisted in a company attached to the Second New Jersey Regiment, was his having accompanied George Washington when he crossed the Delaware in 1776 and his participation in the battles of Princeton, Brandywine, Monmouth, and Yorktown. Adding luster to Cromwell's Revolutionary War service was Washington's signing on June 5, 1783, of Cromwell's honorable discharge as a private and Cromwell's receipt of a yearly federal pension of $96.[58]

With the change in the military policy of excluding blacks, New Jerseyans were among the American slave owners who now offered freedom to their slaves for war service, sometimes promising freedom if they served in their place. Benjamin Coe of Newark, owner of a slave named Cudjo, was among these. For serving as a member of the Continental army as a substitute for Coe, Cudjo not only received his freedom but nearly an acre of ground on High Street in Newark.[59] At the other end of the spectrum was the tragic case of Samuel Sutphen of Readington, Somerset County; it involved reneging on a promise of freedom for military service.

Born in 1747 into bondage in Somerset County, by the onset of the American Revolution Sutphen had become the principal farmhand on his owner's plantation. With the outbreak of hostilities, his owner, Barnardus LaGrange, sided with the loyalists and ultimately fled to British-occupied New York. His property was confiscated, and the ownership of Sutphen passed through two individuals before he was bought by Casper Berger, a tavern owner and member of the New Jersey militia. Berger promised to free Sutphen at the end of the war if he would serve in his stead. Sutphen accepted Berger's commitment and participated in numerous military engagements, but Berger failed to keep his promise. At the war's conclusion, Sutphen then experienced a succession of two owners. The widow of the second owner permitted him to earn money with which to purchase his freedom. Sutphen's story of injustice finally ended around 1805 with that purchase; he had endured a life of bondage until his mid-fifties.[60]

New Jersey also provided several examples of slaves whose participation in the war led to their freedom through action by the legislature. At the heart of their unusual cases was the question: What was to be the disposition of slaves who were part of the confiscated estates of loyalists?

The first of three slaves to be freed by legislative decree in New Jersey as a reward for American military service was Peter Williams, who belonged to a Tory from Woodbridge. Taken behind British lines by his owner, he escaped in 1780 and then served first with the state militia and later the Continental army until the end of hostilities. His manumission occurred in 1784 and established a precedent for the well-documented case of Prime, who belonged to a Princeton loyalist, Absalom Bainbridge, and whose case ended in November 1786 when the legislature passed an act manumitting him. Three years later a slave named Cato received his freedom in the same manner. Like Peter Williams, he belonged to a Woodbridge loyalist and served in both the state and Continental armies.[61]

The impact of the American Revolution also extended to the number of manumissions in New Jersey; there were considerably more after the Revolution.[62] Among those granting manumission to their slaves was William Livingston, New Jersey's first governor, who set his slaves free during the war, stating that bondage for "Americans who have almost idolized liberty" was "peculiarly odious and disgraceful."[63] Another New Jersey slaveholder who seemingly took to heart the Revolution's egalitarian and libertarian principles was Moses Bloomfield. Father of Joseph Bloomfield, the state's governor (1801–1802 and 1803–1812), Moses Bloomfield freed his slaves in a public ceremony on July 4, 1783, that celebrated the end of the war. Mounting a platform in Woodbridge, he stated: "As a nation, we are free and independent—all men are created equal, and why should these, my fellow citizens—my equals, be held in bondage? From this day forth they are emancipated and I here declare them free and absolved from all servitude to me and my posterity."[64]

The Revolution even emboldened slaves to seek freedom through the courts by attacking defects in title deeds and in some cases by challenging the very legality of bondage itself. The February 2, 9, and 16, 1780, editions of the *New Jersey Gazette*, for example, ran notices of one

New Jersey bondman suing for his liberty in which he warned prospective buyers that he expected "freedom, justice and protection . . . by the laws of the state."[65]

Aside from reducing the number of those in bondage in New Jersey, the American Revolution gave impetus to New Jersey's burgeoning abolitionist movement. In providing the perfect context for those opposed to slavery to voice their opposition, it helped foster an antislavery sentiment that led to the further weakening of New Jersey bondage. While earlier a denunciation of slavery had been couched largely in terms of its immorality, an antislavery position could now be based on slavery's existence running counter to the very pronouncements of liberty and equality used to justify rebellion against Great Britain. An excellent example of this is seen in the writing of David Cooper, a New Jersey Quaker who in 1785 joined with other Quakers to present a bill to the legislature seeking to abolish both slavery and the slave trade.[66] His attack on slavery, written in 1783 and titled *A Serious Address to the Rulers of America, On the Inconsistency of Their Conduct Respecting Slavery*, noted the incompatibility of slave ownership and the ideals of the Revolution. Urging his compatriots not to appear hypocritical to subsequent generations, Cooper eloquently penned the following:

> Ye rulers of America beware: Let it appear to future ages, from the records of this day, that you are not only professed to be advocates for freedom, but really were inspired by the love of mankind, and wish to secure the invaluable blessing to all; that, as you disdained to submit to the unlimited control of others, you equally abhorred the crying crime of holding your fellow men, as much entitled to freedom as yourselves.[67]

Although New Jersey generally lagged behind its northern neighbors in terms of antislavery efforts, such efforts were very much in evidence well before the American Revolution, enabling Cooper to draw on well-established antecedents. As early as 1696, the Quakers of West Jersey and southern Pennsylvania voted in their yearly meeting to recommend to their coreligionists that they cease the further importation of slaves.[68] Considerably later, the Quaker John Woolman, a native of Rancocas, Burlington County, became one of America's foremost early advocates of abolition. Believing that slaves should be freed by the personal action of their owners rather than by political measures, he traveled extensively throughout the colonies, from New England to the Carolinas, on horseback and by foot championing the cause of emancipation. His *Considerations on Keeping*

Negroes, first printed in 1754, is considered a benchmark among anti-slavery statements written in America.

Woolman's humanitarian message no doubt contributed to the 1769 tariff on the importation of slaves into New Jersey, which can be interpreted as an attempt to limit the expansion of slavery in the colony. It most certainly facilitated the action taken in 1776 by Pennsylvania and West Jersey Quakers who, in their respective yearly meetings, agreed to excommunicate those coreligionists who refused to divest themselves of bondpersons. It also probably influenced the numerous petitions that the colonial assembly received from Quaker counties in 1773 and 1774 that asked for duties that would end the importation of slaves into the colony, as well as for a law to ease the requirements for manumitting slaves. In 1775, a strong petition asking for an act "to set free all of the slaves now in the Colony" was presented to the assembly by fifty-two Quakers from Chesterfield in Burlington County.[69] These petitions are significant in that they mark a movement by Quakers to go beyond seeking to persuade those of their own faith of the immorality of bondage and to alter public policy instead; they sought to have their antislavery views sanctioned by law.

In 1786, in the aftermath of the American Revolution, Governor William Livingston gave impetus to the approach of employing legislation in the antislavery struggle by securing the passage of An Act to Prevent the Importation of Slaves into the State of New Jersey, and to Authorize the Manumission of Them Under Certain Restrictions, and to Prevent the Abuse of Slaves. As its title suggests, this landmark law banned slave imports by levying a fine of £50 for each slave imported from Africa after 1776 and £20 for each slave imported before 1776; encouraged manumission by allowing a slave owner to free a slave between twenty-one and thirty-five years of age and of sound mind and body without posting a bond of £200; and allowed owners to be indicted for the inhumane treatment of slaves.[70] Continuing this trend two years later, the state enacted legislation that forbade the removal of slaves from New Jersey without their consent; provided that slaves convicted of a criminal offense receive the same punishment as white lawbreakers; required slave owners to teach slave children to read; and permitted the state to seize and sell slave ships.[71]

A decade later, in 1798, New Jersey passed the Act Respecting Slaves, a more detailed slave code that repealed virtually all preexisting slave legislation. While a gradual abolition clause was removed from this bill, under its provisions slaves were now allowed to own real estate; the terminal age at which slaves could be manumitted was raised to forty from thirty-five; manumitted blacks could reside in any county; and the penalties for abusing slaves or failing to educate them were raised.[72]

It is likely that the more progressive attitude toward the treatment of slaves found in the aforementioned laws of 1786, 1788, and 1798 can be attributed to the Revolution, revealing another way in which the war helped to improve the plight of New Jersey bondpersons. Although the Revolution did not convince a majority of New Jersey inhabitants of the need for the outright support of manumission, the Revolution's emphasis on natural rights seemingly made these inhabitants more favorably disposed to ameliorating the conditions of bondage. Efforts to make New Jersey bondage less onerous seem to undercut the argument that New Jersey slavery declined because of its unprofitability; there appears to be little evidence that those inclined to rid themselves of slaves for economic reasons were in the forefront of any efforts to improve the well-being of New Jersey bondpersons.

The Revolution also seemingly produced a judicial climate in New Jersey more favorable to bondpersons, as the courts gave increasingly liberal interpretations to the laws governing manumission. In 1795, the state supreme court ruled that a mere promise of manumission, although unsubstantiated by legal consideration, created a valid claim to freedom. "It is far better to adopt this rule," the court declared, "than to suffer promises thus made . . . to be violated or retracted at pleasure."[73]

Another important step in the antislavery struggle in New Jersey was taken in 1793, when, at the instigation of the Pennsylvania Abolition Society, the state's first abolition society was formed. Representatives of the Pennsylvania society traveled to Burlington on January 26, 1793, and supervised the birth of the New Jersey Society for Promoting the Abolition of Slavery.[74] Focusing initially on "defending the rights of free blacks and winning some important cases for slaves wrongfully kept from freedom," it did not press for immediate and unconditional manumission, supporting instead the pattern of gradual emancipation already established in Pennsylvania in 1780 and to be established in New York in 1799.[75]

The year 1800 witnessed the kind of paradox that has often characterized the black historical experience in general and that in New Jersey in particular. On the one hand, in that year black bondage reached its peak in New Jersey; the state had a total of 12,422 slaves. Of this number, the overwhelming majority—11,915—were found in the northern counties, reflecting a similar regional imbalance that had characterized New Jersey slavery from its earliest days. On the other hand, the free black population, which stood at 2,762 in 1790, had increased to 4,402 ten years later, its highest to date. The southern counties, as they had in 1790 when they had 1,466 free blacks, accounted for most of these free blacks—2,374, almost 85 percent of the total black population of the southern counties.[76] These counties were part of the Delaware Valley, encompassing southeastern Pennsylvania and southern New Jersey, an area that has been termed the "Cradle of Emancipation," where black people were first emancipated in the United States on a massive scale. The dominant presence in this area of Quakers, the nation's first organized abolitionists, again helps to explain why the area led in the emergence of a free black population.

By 1804, the stage had been set for the final development in erasing the moral blot of bondage in post-Revolutionary New Jersey: the passage of New Jersey's first abolition law, An Act for the Gradual Abolition of Slavery. Success in the neighboring states helped New Jersey abolitionists to achieve this milestone. The Gradual Manumission Act passed in New York in 1799, like the Pennsylvania act of 1780, indeed exerted pressure on New Jersey. Could New Jersey remain a bastion of slavery, immune from the liberty offered in neighboring states? If it attempted to do so, would New Jersey slaves flee to join free black communities in the neighboring states?

In addition to the gradual abolition laws of Pennsylvania and New York, the position on manumission taken by the state's abolition society helped New Jersey's emancipation process to be a gradual one. In fact, realizing fully that the idea of total and immediate emancipation stood little chance of success, in February 1804 the society presented an impassioned plea for gradual abolition. While pointing out that slavery was indefensible "in a land of freedom, and by a people distinguished for reason and humanity," the plea stated that to emancipate those who were enslaved at present would violate the property rights of slaveholders. This argument, the plea continued, should not apply to the proposed emancipation of unborn blacks, "that to enslave Children to the latest posterity for the cost of the parent . . . is a satisfaction vastly disproportionate."[77]

Crucial to the nearly unanimous acceptance of the 1804 abolition law was the scheme to compensate owners for the ultimate loss of the children of their slaves, a plan first enacted in New York. Under the provisions of this act, all children born of slaves after July 4, 1804, were to be emancipated after serving apprenticeships to their mother's owner, females after twenty-one years of age and males after twenty-five.[78] In this concession to slave owners, which amounted to "the nearest approach to financial compensation to expropriated slaveholders in any northern emancipation law," the law provided that slave children over the age of one could be abandoned to the poorhouse, where they would be bound out to individuals who would receive compensation from the state for their maintenance.[79] Since the children were often bound to their former owners, the law benefited the latter because they now had an "apprentice" paid for by the state. The maintenance fees led to considerable abuse and fraud. Amid efforts to repeal the entire bill because it allegedly deprived individuals unconstitutionally of their property without their consent, the fees were discontinued by the legislature in 1811, the abandonment clause having been repealed in 1805.[80] Evidence that these children became a tremendous financial burden to the state is reflected in the fact that, in one year, the support of the bound children amounted to over 40 percent of the state budget. In terminating the payments, it was observed that in some instances, the state had paid the guardian, usually the former slave owner, more than the lifetime price of the slave.[81]

Passage of the 1804 abolition law made New Jersey the final state to join the effort to eradicate slavery in the North. What has been termed the "First Emancipation," the illegality of slavery in the North, was now a reality. Six years later, roughly a generation removed from the firing of the last shot at Yorktown (the Revolution's final battle), 75 percent of blacks in the North were free. Massachusetts, New Hampshire, and Vermont had no slaves; Pennsylvania and Rhode Island had black populations that were 97 percent free, Connecticut's 95 percent free, and New York's 63 percent free.[82] With 42 percent of its black population free, New Jersey ranked last in this regard, a fact not surprising given that its gradual abolition act had only been in existence since 1804. Sixteen years later, in 1820, the state's free black population was 62 percent, a percentage that compares somewhat favorably with the 63 percent reached in New York in 1810, some eleven years after its gradual abolition act went into effect.[83]

The free black population in New Jersey in 1810 stood at an all-time high: 7,843.[84] Of this number, the majority, for the first time, were found in the state's northern counties. Here free blacks numbered 4,316, compared to 3,527 in the southern counties, although in the latter they constituted 91 percent of the total black population as opposed to roughly 29 percent in the former—a drastic difference.[85] Still, New Jersey slavery, confined principally to the northern counties, especially Bergen, Somerset, Monmouth, and Middlesex, had started down the road to extinction; the growth of the free black population had become irreversible.

Although having escaped the bonds of involuntary servitude, by 1810 free New Jersey blacks were still the objects of hostility and discriminatory legislation from Revolutionary War–era white New Jerseyans; they faced hardship, persecution, and physical insecurity. In fact, the prolongation of slavery in New Jersey after the Revolution encouraged the notion that free blacks were actually slaves without masters; it helped to reinforce the willingness of the larger society to impose many social injustices and disabilities upon free black persons. They were denied the right to sit on juries or testify in court, subjected to curfews, restricted in their travels, confined to certain occupations, and not allowed to stand in the militia. While the 1798 slave code, for example, required that free blacks, both from other states as well as New Jersey, traveling outside their home county carry with them certificates of freedom signed by two justices of peace, perhaps the most egregious social disability they suffered was the loss of the franchise.[86] This occurred in 1807 when both single white women and blacks lost the right to vote that was given under the 1776 constitution to all persons worth £50. This would become the grievance that black New Jerseyans would campaign against most vigorously during the antebellum period. Yet despite the indignities and degradations experienced by free New Jersey blacks and regardless of hardship, persecution, and physical insecurity, their life was far preferable to bondage.

The significance of a relatively large free black population in New Jersey in 1810 as a consequence of the American Revolution cannot be exaggerated. Such freedom found expression in a more fully developed black associational life in New Jersey. Around 1800, for example, the black community's most precious and enduring social institution—the black church—began to emerge, committed from the outset to meeting both the spiritual and temporal needs of its members. Owing to their early appearance, black New Jersey churches are among the oldest to be found in the North. The Mount Pisgah African Methodist Episcopal (AME) Church in Salem is regarded as the earliest of these congregations; it was present at the first and organizing conference of the AME Church in Philadelphia in 1816. The formation of black churches—in particular, AME congregations—was facilitated by the presence of Richard Allen in southern New Jersey in the early 1780s. Founder of the AME Church and its first bishop, Allen had served as a wagon driver during the Revolution and at the end of the war traveled as an itinerant preacher in this area, as well as in southeastern Pennsylvania and Delaware.[87]

With the enlargement of the number of free blacks in the wake of the Revolution came another development worthy of mention: the darkening of the free black New Jersey population. This shift away from a population disproportionately mulatto increased the chances of success of darker-hued runaways. The greater chance of success in turn encouraged others to flee. The following statement by Ira Berlin regarding this process indeed applies to New Jersey: "The larger, darker-skinned free Negro population camouflaged fugitives, increased their chances of success, and encouraged still other blacks to make their way from slavery to freedom. The increase in runaways begun during the tumult of the Revolution continued into the postwar years."[88]

The American Revolution, more than any other single event, sounded the death knell for New Jersey slavery. While New Jersey slaves may have been hard-pressed to debate the ideological underpinnings of the war, they quickly fathomed how the war would be made to serve their interests and concerns, and they responded accordingly. To those who were escape-minded, it served as an unprecedented blessing. For others, it was the opportunity to parlay military service into freedom, an opportunity that was seized upon and applied to both of the opposing combatants. The war also aided the work of those who were opposed to slavery, their efforts to abolish black forced labor gaining momentum in the war's aftermath. The theory of natural rights and the slogans of liberty and independence that were promulgated to denounce the tyranny and despotism of the British now became the perfect justification for any number of anti-slavery activities, ranging from manumissions, to laws that sought to ease the treatment of the enslaved, to the creation of an abolitionist society. In short, as one study suggests in a reference that includes New Jersey, "the war itself proved the greatest solvent to the master-slave relation."[89]

The positive effects of the American Revolution on the lives of black New Jerseyans would also foreshadow the gains African Americans would derive from the nation's subsequent major wars—creating the ironic situation of blacks benefiting from armed conflicts that gave rise to considerable misery and suffering. Indeed, the Civil War led to the freeing of all of America's bondpersons, creating the "Second Emancipation," while World Wars I and II brought about the foremost development in twentieth-century African American life: the Great Migration, the unprecedented movement of black people out of the South in search of the Promised Land. Since New Jersey was the destination of many who trekked northward as part of the Great Migration seeking to escape the inequities, injustices, and cruelties of Jim Crowism in the South—considered by some to be a newer form of bondage—the story of the two world wars prompting black settlement in New Jersey can be viewed as connected to that of the American Revolution and black New Jerseyans. Both stories involve African Americans using war-related developments to improve their circumstances, to break the chains of bondage in seeking their right to life, liberty, and the pursuit of happiness—an ideal first given prominence by the American Revolution roughly 225 years ago.

Notes

1. William Cooper Nell, *The Colored Patriots of the American Revolution* (Boston: R. F. Wallcut, 1855).

2. See William Wells Brown, *The Negro in the American Revolution: His Heroism and Fidelity* (Boston: Lee Shepard, 1867); George Washington Williams, *A History of the Negro Race in America from 1619 to 1880. Negroes as Slaves, as Soldiers, and as Citizens; Together with a Preliminary Consideration of the Unity of the Human Family, an Historical Sketch of Africa, and an Account of the Negro Governments of Sierra Leone and Liberia* (New York: Putnam and Sons, 1883); Joseph T. Wilson, *The Black Phalanx: A History of the Negro Soldiers of the United States in the Wars of 1775–1812, 1861–65* (Hartford, Conn.: American Publishing, 1887); Benjamin Brawley, *A Social History of the American Negro: Being a History of the Negro Problem in the US., Including a History and Study of the Republic of Liberia* (New York: Macmillan, 1921); Luther Porter Jackson, *Virginia Negro Soldiers and Seamen in the Revolutionary War* (Norfolk, Va.: Guide Quality Press, 1944); and Benjamin Quarles, *The Negro in the American Revolution* (Chapel Hill: University of North Carolina Press, 1961). For a discussion of the writings of these historians and other historians of African descent, see Earl E. Thorpe, *The Central Theme of Black History* (Westport, Conn.: Greenwood Press, 1969); and Earl E. Thorpe, *Black Historians: A Critique* (New York: William Morrow, 1971). These studies examined the role of blacks in the war itself. Subsequent scholarship, of which this essay is a part, has examined the broad effects of Revolutionary War sentiment on slavery itself and, even more recently, the nature of northern black life during the era of the war. For a review of some of the recent historical literature—seven books—that deals with the effects of the American Revolution on black life and suggests that the war's effect on manumission in the North was basically "halting and conservative," see Douglas R. Egerton, "Black Independence Struggles and the Tale of Two Revolutions: A Review Essay," *Journal of Southern History* 54, no. 1 (February 1998).

3. Leon F. Litwack, *North of Slavery: The Negro in the Free States, 1790–1860* (Chicago: University of Chicago Press, 1961), 6–7. Regarding Vermont, it was the only state to adopt an antislavery clause in its constitution, which it did in 1777. A breakaway territory claimed by New Hampshire and New York, it was not one of the original thirteen colonies, being admitted to the Union in 1791. Pennsylvania was actually the first state to pass an abolition law, this occurring in 1780.

4. Arthur Zilversmit, *The First Emancipation: The Abolition of Slavery in the North* (Chicago: University of Chicago Press, 1967), 137–138.

5. Edgar J. McManus, *Black Bondage in the North* (Syracuse, N.Y.: Syracuse University Press, 1973), 150–151.

6. For example, see Gary B. Nash and Jean R. Soderlund, *Freedom by Degrees: Emancipation in Pennsylvania and Its Aftermath* (New York: Oxford University Press, 1991). They argue that slavery declined in Philadelphia around the time of the Revolution because of the tendency of slaveholders of a certain class (e.g., master artisans, ship captains, shopkeepers, and taverners—those having one or two slaves) to rid themselves of slaves. Given a fluctuating economy, in the place of slaves they hired wage laborers who could be employed and discharged at will. More affluent slave owners, in contrast, were inclined to retain their slaves in order to underscore their high social status.

7. Frances D. Pingeon, "Slavery in New Jersey on the Eve of Revolution," in *New Jersey on the American Revolution: Political and Social Conflict*, rev. ed., ed. William C. Wright, 50 (1970; repr., Trenton: New Jersey Historical Commission, 1974).

8. Ibid., 57.

9. Ibid., 58.

10. The years between 1770 and 1810 are identified as the "Revolutionary era" in Peter Colchin, *American Slavery: 1619–1877* (New York: Hill and Wang, 1993), 63; and Ira Berlin, "'The Revolution in Black Life," in *The American Revolution: Explorations in the History of American Radicalism*, ed. Alfred F. Young, 351 (De Kalb: Northern Illinois University Press, 1976).

11. For a full discussion of this distinction and its implications for slave life, see Philip D. Morgan, "British Encounters with Africans and African-Americans, circa 1600–1780," in *Strangers within the Realm: Cultural Margins of the First British Empire*, ed. Bernard Bailyn and Philip D. Morgan, 163–219 (Chapel Hill: University of North Carolina Press, 1991).

12. Ira Berlin, *Many Thousands Gone: The First Two Centuries of Slavery in North America* (Cambridge, Mass.: Harvard University Press, 1998), 369, table I.

13. Benjamin Quarles, "The Revolutionary War as a Black Declaration of Independence," in *Slavery and Freedom in the Age of the American Revolution*, ed. Ira Berlin and Ronald Hoffman, 285 (Charlottesville: United States Capitol Historical Society/University Press of Virginia, 1983).

14. Herbert S. Klein, *The Atlantic Slave Trade* (Cambridge: Cambridge University Press, 1999), 45; Pingeon, *Blacks in the Revolutionary Era*, vol.14 of *New Jersey's Revolutionary Experience* (Trenton: New Jersey Historical Commission, 1975), 14; Berlin, *Many Thousands Gone*, 179.

15. Berlin, *Many Thousands Gone*, 46,180,181; Pingeon, "Slavery in New Jersey," 49.

16. The price of £20 for a male slave is provided for Philadelphia by Nash and Soderlund in *Freedom by Degrees*. Given Philadelphia's proximity to New Jersey, it is assumed that a similar price existed in New Jersey for the same period.

17. Zilversmit, *The First Emancipation*, 42.

18. Morgan, "British Encounters with Africans," 161.

19. Gary K. Wolinetz, "New Jersey Slavery and the Law," *Rutgers Law Review* 50, no. 4 (Summer 1998): 2233.

20. Pingeon, "Slavery in New Jersey," 52.

21. Wolinetz, "New Jersey Slavery," 2236.

22. Henry Scofield Cooley, *A Study of Slavery in New Jersey* (Baltimore: Johns Hopkins University Press, 1896), 42.

23. McManus, *Black Bondage*, 132.

24. Pingeon, *Blacks in the Revolutionary Era*, 19; Herbert Aptheker, *American Negro Slave Revolts* (New York: International, 1943), 201–202.

25. Pingeon, *Blacks in the Revolutionary Era*, 19.

26. Berlin, *Many Thousands Gone*, 184.

27. Quoted in Clement Alexander Price, *Freedom Not Far Distant: A Documentary History of Afro-Americans in New Jersey* (Newark: New Jersey Historical Society, 1980), 44.

28. Since early census takers failed to differentiate between slaves and free blacks in New Jersey, the figure of 5 percent is a rough estimate based on the 3 percent figure given by Hodges for pre-Revolution Monmouth County in his *Slavery and Freedom in the Rural North: African Americans in Monmouth County, New Jersey, 1665–1865* (Madison, Wis.: Madison House, 1997), 64. It is likely that manumissions among Quakers by 1776 would have raised the percentage higher for the entire colony, hence the figure of 400 free blacks, roughly 5 percent of the 8,200 blacks listed for New Jersey for 1770. Donald R. Wright, *African Americans in the Colonial Era: From African Origins through the American Revolution*, 2nd ed. (Wheeling, Ill.: Harlan Davidson, 2000), 165, also notes that "before 1770 free blacks made up only about 5 percent of the colonial African-American population." Finally, in 1755 in Maryland, one of the few colonies for which a census of the free black population was taken prior to the Revolution, free blacks constituted 4 percent of the total black population. This would also seem to make an estimate of 5 percent for New Jersey reasonable. The figure for Maryland comes from Berlin, "'The Revolution in Black Life,'" 352.

29. For a discussion of these families, see David Steven Cohen, *The Ramapo Mountain People* (New Brunswick, N.J.: Rutgers University Press, 1988), 25–42.

30. Zilversmit, *The First Emancipation*, 14.

31. Cooley, *A Study of Slavery*, 45.

32. For a discussion of the life of Cyrus Bustill; see appendix A, "The Proud Bustills," 145–157, in Lloyd L. Brown, *The Young Paul Robeson: "On My Journey Now"* (Boulder, Colo.: Westview Press, 1997).

33. Zilversmit, *The First Emancipation*, 91–92.

34. The historian Ira Berlin has written considerably on the transformation of Africans into African Americans. See, for example, his "Time, Space, and the Evolution of Afro-American Society on British Mainland North America, "*American Historical Review* 85 (1980): 44–78.

35. Graham Russell Hodges, *Root and Branch: African Americans in New York and East Jersey, 1613–1863* (Chapel Hill: University of North Carolina Press, 1999), 258.

36. For discussion of this incident, see David Steven Cohen, *The Folklore and Folklore of New Jersey* (New Brunswick, N.J.: Rutgers University Press, 1991), 41–49.

37. Quoted in Price, *Freedom Not Far Distant*, 43.

38. Quoted in ibid., 44–45 The historians Shane White and Graham White have contended that the dress and hairstyles of some colonial and antebellum slaves not only perpetuated African cultural traditions but also served as a cultural defense against a dehumanizing system. See Shane White and Graham White, "Slave Hair and African American Culture in the Eighteenth and Nineteenth Centuries, "*Journal of Southern History* 61, no. I (February 1995): 45–76; and White and White, "Slave Clothing and African-American Culture in the Eighteenth and Nineteenth Centuries," *Past and Present* no. 148 (August 1995): 149–186.

39. Quoted in Price, *Freedom Not Far Distant*, 43.

40. Pingeon, *Blacks in the Revolutionary Era*, 9.

41. Hodges, *Root and Branch*, 86.

42. Discussions of spirit possession range from a focus on Africans, to African Americans, to New World African diaspora peoples in such countries as Haiti, Cuba, and Brazil. Examples include John S. Mbiti, *African Religions and Philosophy* (London: Heinemann, 1970); Robert Farris Thompson, *Flash of the Spirit: African and Afro-American Art and Philosophy* (New York: Random House, 1983); Robert L. Hall, "African Religious Retentions in Florida," in *Africanisms in American Culture*, ed. Joseph E. Holloway (Bloomington: Indiana University Press, 1990); and Maya Deren, *Divine Horsemen: Voodoo Gods of Haiti* (New York: Chelsea House, 1970). Among those who have written extensively on the phenomenon of spirit possession is the social anthropologist Sheila S. Walker. Her writings on this subject include *Ceremonial Spirit Possession in Africa and Afro-America: Forms, Meanings, and Functional Significance for Individuals and Social Groups* (Leiden, Netherlands: E. J. Brill, 1972), and "African Gods in America: The Black Religious Continuum," *Black Scholar* 11, no. 8 (November/December 1980): 25–36.

43. The African origins of certain names and words found among black Americans can be found in Lorenzo D. Turner, *Africanisms in the Gullah Dialect* (Ann Arbor: University of Michigan Press, 1947). David Mitros, ed., *Slave Records of Morris County, New Jersey: 1736–1841*, 2nd ed. (Morristown, N.J.: Morris County Heritage Commission, 2002), also proved useful in compiling the list of African and African-sounding names.

44. Hodges, *Root and Branch*, 118.

45. Ibid., 115. 'The following quotation from Pingeon's *Blacks in the Revolutionary Era*, 16, is also revealing: "Numerous advertisements for runaway slaves described them as possessing fiddles or other musical instruments which, according to their masters, they played with great skill."

46. Hodges, *Root and Branch*, 108–109.

47. An excellent source on how time has been perceived among peoples in Africa and the African diaspora of the New World is Joseph K. Adjaye, ed., *Time in the Black Experience* (Westport, Conn.: Greenwood Press, 1994).

48. Pingeon, "Slavery in New Jersey," 55.

49. Hodges, *Root and Branch*, 159.

50. Ibid.

51. Quoted in Price, *Freedom Not Far Distant*, 46.

52. McManus, *Black Bondage*, 154.

53. The figure of 1,300 black British arms-bearers has been culled from chapters 2, 7, 8, and 9 in Quarles, *The Negro in the American Revolution*. A figure of 1,000 black bearers of arms for the British appears in Mary Francis Berry and John W. Blassingame, *Long Memory: The Black Experience in America* (New York: Oxford University Press, 1982), 297; and James Oliver Horton and Lois E. Horton, *In Hope of Liberty: Culture, Community, and Protest among Northern Free Blacks, 1700–1860* (New York: Oxford University Press, 1997), 62.

54. Hodges, *Root and Branch*, 159.

55. Hodges, *Slavery and Freedom*, 97; see 96–104 for a full discussion of Tye's military exploits.

56. The figure of 5,000 for the number of blacks who bore arms on behalf of the patriot cause is a commonly accepted one. For example, see Quarles, *The Negro in the American Revolution*, ix. See also the standard text, John Hope Franklin and Alfred A. Moss Jr., *From Slavery to Freedom: A History African American*, 7th ed. (New York: McGraw Hill, 1994), 76.

57. Pingeon, *Blacks in the Revolutionary Era*, 21.

58. An entry on Oliver Cromwell appears in Rayford W. Logan and Michael R. Winston, eds., *Dictionary of American Negro Biography* (New York: W. W. Norton, 1982), 142. The oral history interview of Cromwell published in 1852 in the *Burlington (New Jersey) Gazette* appears in Sidney Kaplan, *The Black Presence in the Era of the American Revolution 1770–1800* (Greenwich, Conn.: New York Graphic Society, 1973), 47.

59. Simeon F. Moss, "The Persistence of Slavery and Involuntary Servitude in a Free State (1685- 1866)," *Journal of Negro History* 35 (1950): 301–302.

60. Hodges, *Root and Branch*, 141–142. The foremost authorities on Samuel Sutphen are William Schleicher and Susan Winter, whose forthcoming book on Sutphen is reflected in their essay "Patriot and Slave: The Samuel Sutphen Story," *New Jersey Heritage* 1, no. 1 (Winter 2002): 30–43.

61. Peter Williams and Cato are mentioned in Moss, "Persistence of Slavery," 301. For a discussion of the case of Prime, including his petition, see Giles R. Wright, "Prime: Another Resident of Brainbridge House," *Princeton History* no. 10 (1993): 60–66.

62. Berlin, *Many Thousands Gone*, 235.

63. Moss, "Persistence of Slavery," 299; Cooley, *A Study of Slavery*, 23.

64. Hodges, *Root and Branch*, 167–168.

65. McManus, *Black Bondage*, 153.

66. Hodges, *Slavery and Freedom*, 115.

67. Cooper's address is printed in its entirety in Gary B. Nash, *Race and Revolution* (Madison, Wis.: Madison House, 1990), 117–131.

68. Moss, "Persistence of Slavery," 292.

69. Cooley, *A Study of Slavery*, 22–23.

70. Wolinetz, "New Jersey Slavery," 2240–2241.

71. Ibid., 2241.

72. Zilversmit, *The First Emancipation*, 188–189.

73. McManus, *Black Bondage*, 173.

74. There is some discrepancy as to when New Jersey's first statewide abolition society was organized. The date of 1793 is given in Zilversmit, *The First Emancipation*, 173, and Pingeon, *Blacks in the Revolutionary Era*, 23, while the year 1786 is provided in Cooley, *A Study of Slavery*, 23, and Hodges, *Root and Branch*, 115.

75. Hodges, *Root and Branch*, 167.

76. See Giles R. Wright, *Afro-Americans in New Jersey: A Short History* (Trenton: New Jersey Historical Commission, 1988), 81–82, appendix 3.

77. Zilversmit, *The First Emancipation*, 192.

78. Ibid.

79. Robin Blackburn, *The Overthrow of Colonial Slavery 1776–1848* (London: Verso, 1988), 274.

80. Zilversmit, *The First Emancipation*, 198. Zilversmit notes that while the abandonment clause (section 3 of the 1804 abolition law) was repealed in 1805, the state continued down to 1811 to support some abandoned children because their maintenance had been contracted for prior to the repeal of the abandonment clause.

81. Ibid., 199; Pingeon, *Blacks in the Revolutionary Era*, 26–27.

82. Berlin, *Many Thousands Gone*, 372, table 2.

83. The figure for New Jersey is taken from in Wright, *Afro-Americans in New Jersey*, 80, appendix 2.

84. See ibid.; see also Berlin, *Many Thousands Gone*, 372, table 2.

85. See Wright, *Afro-Americans in New Jersey*, 82, appendix 3.

86. Wolinetz, "New Jersey Slavery," 2242–2243.

87. For a biographical sketch of Richard Allen, see Logan and Winston, *Dictionary of American Negro Biography*, 12–13.

88. Berlin, "The Revolution in Black Life," 359.

89. Ira Berlin, *Generations of Captivity: A History of African-American Slaves* (Cambridge, Mass.: Belknap Press of Harvard University Press, 2003), 102.

Thirteenth New Jersey Volunteers Monument, Gettysburg, Pennsylvania. The Battle of Gettysburg was a turning point in the Civil War. Bringing his Confederate forces up through the Shenandoah Valley, General Lee brought the war to the North. His defeat was the beginning of the end for the South. The bitterly fought battle is memorialized with monuments to the soldiers who had fought there, scattered through what is now a national historic park. New Jersey State Archives, Department of State.

9

During the American Revolution, military conflict was a frequent occurrence in New Jersey, but no Civil War battle took place on state soil. New Jersey did, however, become a political battleground as Republicans and Democrats, war supporters and those for peace at any price, took differing positions. The stand taken by the state has been a source of controversy ever since, as historians have tried to evaluate its role. At issue is whether the state was a northern state, border state, or southern sympathizer, as well as whether or not it met its manpower requirements from the Union. Although the precise number of soldiers who fought (and died) continues to be disputed, it is clear that men from the state served the Union throughout the war, participating in most major battles in the South and the West, as well as at Gettysburg in nearby Pennsylvania. A few, often with family ties to the South, served in the Confederate army. All who participated did so in what historians have seen as a war noted for its massive destruction of human life, setting a precedent in new weapons used and large numbers killed for the wars of the twentieth century; there were more than 620,000 casualties in the Civil War.

Starting in the early twentieth century, some historians, particularly Charles M. Knapp, have portrayed New Jersey as a southern-sympathizing "border state," resembling Maryland or Tennessee. In 1994 William Gillette challenged this view, arguing instead that New Jersey was a typical "mid-Atlantic" state, similar to its neighbors, New York and Pennsylvania. Evidence cited by the first group is that New Jersey had been slow to adopt abolition and still had some slaves in 1860. It voted against Lincoln in both 1860 and 1864, while Democrats maintained their control over the state government through most of the war. It also had vocal Copperhead politicians and newspaper editors, and important economic ties to the South. In 1861 and again in 1863 many New Jerseyans supported peace efforts, with some willing to take the South and slavery back into the Union. The second view counters that the state had a long history of close elections, noting that Lincoln and Douglas split New Jersey's electoral vote in 1860, while Lincoln's opponent in 1864, George McClellen, was from the state. Absentee balloting was not permitted, disenfranchising soldiers, most of whom would have voted for Lincoln. Finally, despite the number of "Peace" Democrats, and a small number of Copperheads, the "War" Democrats dominated. Joel Parker, the Democratic governor during most of the war, and his staff worked hard to help the Union effort, providing troops and supplies.

As a student, how do you decide which view of New Jersey is more accurate? Some perspective on the contradictions found in New Jersey can be gained by looking at the Shenandoah Valley. Edward L. Ayers, *In the Presence of Mine Enemies*, notes the complicated divisions in both the northern and southern sections of the valley, and also how opinions in each changed over time. There were few abolitionists in the Pennsylvania section, and a number of pro-unionists in the Virginia section. Many Americans, in both North and South, had reservations about the Civil War. For students of New Jersey and the Civil War, several possible conclusions follow. First, history is complicated, and second, it is not always easy to reconcile conflicting interpretations. But historians should try. To evaluate conflicting interpretations you need to look closely at the validity of arguments, importance of sources (cited in footnotes and bibliography), and the overall weight of the evidence. Then reach a judicious conclusion.

It is sometimes difficult not only to comprehend the big picture but also to get accurate facts. During the war itself, federal and state governments disagreed on whether New Jersey filled it quota of required troops as well as if and when it needed to resort to a draft. Right after the war John Y. Foster asserted that the state had more than met its obligations. Poet Walt Whitman, who spent the last twenty years of his life in Camden, stated that New Jersey had "quite a warlike record." More recently, historians have asserted that it failed to meet its quotas and lagged behind other states. As the war dragged on, New Jersey not only resorted to a draft but also paid higher and higher bounties to substitutes. While recruiting, it used "barrel scraping" that produced many unfit to serve due to health or age. What has made it difficult to get an accurate count that would enable us to judge New Jersey's role and compare it to other states was that men from New Jersey enlisted in military units from other states, and men from elsewhere enlisted in New Jersey units. Some signed up for nine months, others for three years. Some reenlisted and were then counted again. Those called up in the draft legally could, instead of serving, pay a fine or hire a substitute. Estimates for those who served vary from between 90,000 and 76,800;

for black soldiers estimates are between 1,185 and 3,092. These ranges make problematic a definitive conclusion about how much support there was for the war. Do you think modern counts of how many serve in the military are more or less accurate?

Why did men join the army or navy during the Civil War? At the outset of the war more were actually ready to sign than could be accepted, motivated by patriotism, or as Samuel Toombs said "love of country and hatred of the heresy of Succession." Few soldiers from New Jersey were abolitionists, although there were some; only later were they willing to support emancipation, and not all did. As in other wars, some went off to fight alongside friends, neighbors, and relatives. Others joined for the money—the pay during economic hard times, then the bounties. Letters, diaries, and memoirs can provide insight into their motives, but not all soldiers left a paper trail, and some were illiterate. Keep in mind, too, that historians question their sources. Do you think soldiers always accurately noted their motives?

In the selection that follows, Gottfried lets us join Union soldiers from New Jersey as they marched from place to place, and then fought, while participating in the Battle of Gettysburg. As you read, think about the horror and confusion of battle, the seemingly random chance involved in whether an individual lived, died, or suffered horrendous wounds. The everyday life of a soldier could be quite difficult, but small things provided satisfaction. Battles were not the only thing to fear: at a time when even the best medical practice could make matters worse, more men died from disease than from wounds. Gottfried shows the soldiers marching through heat and rain, sometimes without adequate food or shelter. Life for them was uncertain and exhausting.

New Jersey soldiers, those who survived and those who did not, left their tracks, and unfortunately their graves, on numerous Civil War battlefields. They are memorialized with statutes in New Jersey towns and by monuments at places like Gettysburg. The most important legacy to this particular war, however, was the ending of slavery in the United States. On this issue, and changes in race relations, New Jersey is remembered for its contradictory actions, rather than its bravery. As control of the legislature alternated between Democrats and Republicans, the state first rejected and then ratified each of the Reconstruction amendments: the Thirteenth ending slavery, the Fourteenth extending citizenship, and the Fifteenth providing the right to vote regardless of race. It took another hundred-plus years, though, before the latter two were given real meaning in the state and elsewhere.

Suggested Readings

Ayers, Edward L. *In the Presence of Mine Enemies: War in the Heart of America, 1859–1863*. New York: W. W. Norton, 2003.

Gillette, William. *Jersey Blue: Civil War Politics in New Jersey 1854–1865*. New Brunswick, N.J.: Rutgers University Press, 1995.

Jackson, William J. *New Jerseyans in the Civil War: For Union and Liberty*. New Brunswick, N.J.: Rutgers University Press, 2000.

Knapp, Charles M. *New Jersey Politics During the Period of the Civil War and Reconstruction*. Geneva, N.Y.: W. F. Humphrey, 1924.

McPherson, James M. *Battle Cry of Freedom: The Civil War*. New York: Ballantine Books, 1989.

Olsen, Bernard A., ed., *Upon the Tented Field: An Historical Account of the Civil War, as Told By the Men Who Fought and Gave Their Lives*. Red Bank, N.J.: Historic Projects, 1993.

Sears, Stephen W. *Gettysburg*. Boston: Houghton Mifflin, 2003.

Shaara, Michael. *The Killer Angels*. New York: Ballantine Books, 1974.

Siegal, Alan A. *Beneath The Starry Flag: New Jersey's Civil War Experience*. New Brunswick, N.J.: Rutgers University Press, 2001.

Toombs, Samuel. *New Jersey Troops in the Gettysburg Campaign: from June 5 to July 31, 1863*. Orange, N.J.: Evening Mail, 1888.

Tandler, Maurice. "The Political Front in Civil War New Jersey." *Proceedings of the New Jersey Historical Society* 83 (1965): 223–233.

Wright, William C. "New Jersey's Military Role in the Civil War Reconsidered." *New Jersey History* 92 (1974): 197–210.

Gettysburg

Bradley M. Gottfried

Facing the enemy in battle was the last thing anyone wanted, but General Lee had other ideas. If the Jerseymen had looked closely during the first week in June they would have seen clouds of dust swirling across the river to the southwest. They did not know it, but Lee was stealthily pulling his troops from their positions near Fredericksburg and marching them toward Culpeper Court House. From there, the Confederate army would enter the Shenandoah Valley, shielded from view by the Blue Ridge Mountains. Hooker knew the enemy camps were abandoned and he could see the dust clouds, but he was still befuddled from his infamous defeat at Chancellorsville.

Hooker sent his cavalry thundering toward Culpeper Court House on June 9 to learn Lee's location. The subsequent cavalry fight at Brandy Station was the largest ever on American soil. While the Federal horsemen experienced initial success, they were unable to break through the Confederate line to see that Lee had massed all but one infantry corps in the region. Prior to the battle, General Sedgwick was directed to move his corps to the river on June 6, crossing if necessary, to see what was going on. Hooker also gave him permission to seize civilians for questioning. Hooker was getting desperate.[1]

Sedgwick moved his entire corps toward the river and threw General Howe's Second Division across. Only General A. P. Hill's thinly stretched corps faced the mighty Federal army. Howe's men initially pushed Hill's men back and captured several prisoners in the process, but the Confederate defense stiffened as reinforcements arrived. Sedgwick reported to Hooker at 10:30 that night that three batteries were in his front and he could not "move 200 yards without bringing on a general fight." Although his orders were permissive, Sedgwick was cautious and wrote Hooker, "before bringing over the

From: Bradley M. Gottfried, *Kearny's Own: The History of the First New Jersey Brigade in the Civil War* (New Brunswick, N.J.: Rutgers University Press, 2005), 123–136. Reprinted by permission of the author.

rest of my corps, I await orders. I am satisfied that it is not safe to mass the troops on this side."

On June 4, the New Jersey Brigade had been put on the alert about two hours before daylight to be ready to break camp and move. The tents were to remain standing when they left at sunrise. The column formed and moved out of camp at the appointed time, but the march soon stopped, and the men waited all day for orders to proceed. These orders never arrived, nor did they arrive the following day. They finally received orders to proceed at 9:00 a.m. on June 6 and marched to within twenty rods of the riverbank at Franklin's Crossing. They spent the night here in a pouring rain. The men were not reassured when stretchers bearing the dead and wounded from Howe's expedition passed them that night.[2]

This was a tough time for the Twenty-third New Jersey Volunteers [editor's note: hereafter NJV]. With the expiration of their enlistments almost at hand, the regiment's men were unwilling to be ordered against Lee's army. Grumbling gave way to open anger, and they stacked their arms in protest. It was a mutiny—the worst ordeal for an officer. Colonel Grubb assembled his officers in his tent and discussed the options. He told them in no uncertain terms that he expected firmness and support. The conversation over, Grubb ordered "assembly" sounded and marched the men to the parade ground, where they formed a hollow square. The colonel spoke to his men about the reputation they had gained on several battlefields, how it was his duty to maintain this reputation, and asked them how they could meet their mothers, wives, sweethearts, "when the hooting rabble should tell them they had twice been beaten by the enemy and the third time were afraid to meet them?" The approach touched a nerve, for the men began yelling, "We will go" and "We are not afraid." The regiment joined its comrades in preparing to cross the river.

When they rose at 3:30 a.m. on June 7, the Jerseymen could see that it would be a beautiful day. Many attended Sabbath services at 9:00 a.m. A second service was just about to begin at sunset when bugles sounded. It was time for the First Division to cross the river to relieve the Second Division. The men worried that there was still enough light for the enemy's artillery to wreck havoc on their exposed lines, but to their relief no shots were fired. The brigade again occupied the Deep Run region, rotating details for picket duty. That night the First, Third, and Twenty-third NJV were on the picket line. The remaining units did not like having their backs to the river and Lee's army in front of them, so they spent considerable time during the night digging rifle pits.[3]

Although an artillery barrage and attack was anticipated on June 8, none came. Paul Kuhl wrote that "nothing happened to disturb us, except an occasional visitor in [the] shape of a minnie ball coming in close proximity to our ranks." Wondering what this meant, the Jerseyans built fires to prepare their morning coffee, but enemy snipers hiding in nearby houses made them dash for their rifle pits. The Federal artillery on the heights opened fire, smashing houses and sending the enemy snipers scampering to safety. After breakfast, the men deepened their rifle pits and added lunettes of sharpened sticks to discourage an enemy attack. Edmund Halsey noted that the results were "quite like forts." According to Oscar Westlake of the Third NJV, "I don't think they will attack us—we have thrown up some intrenchments [sic] and our Corps would be able to hold a large force of them if they should come down [on] us." Sporadic sniper fire continued disturbing the men.

June 8 was an exciting day for the men of the Twenty-third NJV. With its term of enlistment set to expire on June 13, the regiment was told to prepare for the trip home. The three hundred Yahoos bid their comrades a fond farewell and then recrossed the river. As might be expected, those men left behind were jealous of the nine-month regiment's good fortune. Charles Harrison noted that "[we] would have been grateful could we have gone with them." Paul Kuhl grudgingly wrote, the regiment "marched past us on their way home . . . they looked very happy, I suppose at the idea of being at home so soon again. They have done their duty well for a nine months Regts. And I am willing to give them all the honor they deserve."[4]

The remaining soldiers of the now weakened brigade, perhaps twelve hundred strong, were not upset when told they were being relieved by Newton's Third Division on June 9. After recrossing the river, many stripped, bathed, and washed their filthy clothes. Confederate batteries opened fire that night, but most of the shells passed harmlessly overhead. The men rested in camp until June 13, when ordered back to the river to help remove pontoon bridges after Newton's men had recrossed. All knew that something was up. The job took all night and some of the next morning to complete. Fearing that the enemy would appear on the opposite bank and open fire, the Jersey boys worked as quickly as they were able. Their task was made more difficult by a drunken colonel of the engineers who gave conflicting orders and generally hindered their activities. Their task finished, the men marched to the Lacy House on Stafford Heights, where they had breakfast and rested for the rest of the day. Accidentally left behind were two stretcher bearers, asleep in their tents, who later awoke to the "Good morning" of a Confederate officer as they were hustled off to the rear.

By June 13, General Hooker realized that he could no longer wait to move his army north to protect Washington. The army's new concentration point was along the Orange and Alexandria Railroad, and it would take the better part of the next week for the force to arrive. The VI Corps' route was through Dumfries, Greenwood, and Wolf Run Shoals.[5]

Daylight on June 14 found Wright's Division on the march, reaching Potomac Creek at about 1:00 p.m., where the men bivouacked. Many soldiers attended prayer service that evening before retiring to their tents for a well-deserved peaceful sleep. It would not come this night, for the bugles sounded at 9:00 p.m. and the men quickly broke camp. Hospital stores were fired as they left, causing one soldier to write, "I think the destruction of property there was needless, as it could have been easily shipped, had not the hospital functionaries fled in panic." The all-night march was made even more difficult because it was on an old corduroy road with loose logs. "We went stumbling and tripping among them with some hazard to limb and life," Alanson Haines reported. Regiments became intermingled as the men's fatigue heightened. The column finally halted for an hour's rest at Stafford Court House at about 3:30 a.m. on June 15. Some men just dropped where they were and slept in the two-inch-deep dust on the road surface. Then it was up again, and the terrible march continued. Temperatures soared as the sun climbed in the sky. So many men fell from the ranks that by the end of the march regiments were the size of companies. Benjamin Hough bitterly wrote, "they came verry [sic] near marched us to death." Sergeant Phineas Skellenger of the same regiment recalled that the "curces [sic] that was [sic] heaped on our Commanding Gen was awfull [sic]." Wright's aides were everywhere, yelling at the men to close ranks and maintain their killing pace. It was easier for them, as they were on horseback. Edmund Halsey began his diary entry on June 15 with, "*Hot,*" and later wrote, "The heat was *intense.* The fine dust being like a cloud in the air and was inhaled at every breath." According to Haines, "the men fell out in squads; some fainted, some were sunstruck." So many men had fallen by the side of the road that General Wright finally halted his command about two miles from Dumfries, permitting many men to rejoin the column. Continuing on, the division reached Dumfries, where it halted for the night in a meadow. June 15 was a day that the men would never forget. They did not know that Hooker, realizing he had dawdled too long in front of

Fredericksburg, now had to make up for lost time if he wanted to defend Washington.

The brigade was on the road again at daylight of June 16, this time without breakfast, and the grumbling intensified with each passing mile. After reaching Wolf Run Shoals on the Occoquan River at about noon, the Jerseymen were permitted to rest, bathe, and eat until 5:00 p.m. Then drums sounded the long roll and they wearily approached their stacked arms. A stack belonging to the Fifteenth NJV fell over, causing a rifle to discharge. The bullet clipped William Kelsey in the neck, possibly nicking his carotid artery. Quick thinking by the regiment's surgeon halted the bleeding and Kelsey survived, but his soldiering days were over.[6]

The late-afternoon march to Fairfax Station was a fairly short one, and the brigade went into camp and remained there the next day. Back on the road on June 18, the column finally reached its destination—on the other side of Fairfax Court House along the Aldie Pike. The brigade would remain here until June 26.

Noting that Confederate cavalry had entered Chambersburg, Oscar Westlake of the Third NJV believed that this was an isolated situation. "My opinion is that Lee wants to get Hooker with his army up into Maryland and then try to take Washington." Events would soon prove Westlake wrong. As the brigade broke camp and marched toward the Potomac River, the Jerseyans marveled at the copious amounts of supplies left behind by the Federal troops marching in front of them. Although efforts were made to destroy the discards, plenty of useful things were there for the taking. According to Haines, "hundreds of thousands of dollars worth of property had been destroy by the flames, or thrown away, to be gathered by the enemy, should they follow."

The enemy did not follow, as they were already far to the north. In fact, all but three of Lee's divisions were in Pennsylvania by June 26, and the others crossed the state line the following day. Learning of the enemy's advance into Pennsylvania, Hooker ordered his troops into Maryland on June 25. The now reconstituted VI Corps broke camp at 3:00 a.m. on June 26 and marched fifteen miles. Passing through Dranesville, the brigade camped one mile beyond it on the Washington and Leesburg Pike. Reveille sounded at 2:00 a.m. on June 27, but the Jerseyans did not begin their trek until between 9:00 a.m. and 10:00 a.m. on the wagon-clogged roads. The brigade finally reached the banks of the Potomac River near Edwards Ferry and waited for the wagon trains to cross. To the band's tune of "My Maryland," the New Jersey Brigade finally crossed back into the Union on the pontoon bridge at 5:00 a.m., and some men sang "Home Again." With Lee in Pennsylvania, the men had much to worry about, yet they remained upbeat. The corps camped for the night about a mile from the river at Poolesville.[7]

Almost completely recuperated from his latest bout with illness, General Torbert returned to the brigade, sending Colonel Penrose back to the Fifteenth NJV. This permitted Lieutenant Colonel Campbell to be assigned the Third NJV, which was without field officers. Because Colonel Buck was wounded, Lieutenant Colonel Charles Wiebecke commanded the Second NJV. The corps marched through Poolesville and Barnsville, then proceeded along the base of Sugar Loaf Mountain and halted about a mile from Hyattstown, Maryland, on June 28. It was a tiring eighteen-mile march. General Hooker was relieved of command in the early morning hours and replaced with Major General George Meade of the V Corps. Up before daylight on June 29, the men were on the road a short time later. They wondered when they would stop for breakfast, but they never did. The corps marched approximately twenty-four miles that day, through New Market and Riegelsville, before going into camp at New Windsor. Thoroughly exhausted from their long marches, the men threw themselves to the ground. The Jerseymen were not upset when the wagons and the rest of the corps passed them on the morning of June 30 while they continued resting. The reprieve ended at noon, when the brigade set off once more, marching through Westminster and Manchester, reaching the latter at about 10:00 p.m.

No one complained when told they would remain in camp on July 1 and rest their weary bodies. Farmers descended upon the corps in waves to sell their wares, and townspeople came to check out the camps. This all changed as darkness fell. Each regimental commander formed his men and, after conducting an inspection, ordered them into a square. Walking into the center of it, each officer recalled the unit's past bravely and discipline. They also read orders from General Meade about not straggling and other expectations of their new commander. The men knew that something must be up, and then heard that they would soon be back on the road, marching instead of sleeping. The column finally began its long march after 10:00 p.m. Although the enlisted men did not know it, the two armies had collided at Gettysburg, and the VI Corps was badly needed. The first two-mile march was in the wrong direction, so the corps had to backtrack, wasting four miles and valuable time.[8]

The march now continued through the night and into the next day. The officers knew how badly their troops were needed at Gettysburg, so they halted infrequently, and when they did, it was for about ten minutes or so—just enough time for the men to relieve themselves. The men constantly heard the phrase "Close ranks and don't straggle" from their officers. Singing and exchanging jokes helped pass the time and take their minds off the misery. The ordeal became more unbearable as the day wore on, however, and the temperatures increased, as did the dust. One officer in Bartlett's Brigade recalled that the "heat was deadly, dust filled our throats; but still the march was kept up . . . no time to rest, no time to eat, no time for any thing but suffering." While the men were clearly suffering, the officer noted the determination in their eyes—a look he had never seen before. The bands and drummers occasionally played to keep the men from falling asleep on their feet.

Civilians lined the road, making the hardships somewhat easier to bear. One Jerseyman wrote home that they "waved flags and in many ways testified their devotion to the cause." Many yelled out, "We thank you for coming." The civilians distributed bread and other delicacies until their supply gave out. Cherry trees lining the road were more generous, and the men gladly stripped them of their fruit. The townspeople of Littlestown, just south of Gettysburg, hoisted buckets of cool water onto horse blocks, and the men gratefully dipped their cups into them as they marched past. The column finally halted at about 1:00 p.m. on July 2. Some men made coffee, but most simply dropped where they were and immediately fell asleep. The march continued an hour later, and the column finally reached the battlefield between 3:30 and 4:00 p.m. The VI Corps had made an epic march of thirty-five miles in sixteen hours.[9]

Resting along the east bank of Rock Creek, the Jerseymen made coffee and threw off their clothes. Many bathed their blistered feet in the cool creek waters. This refreshed them, and one noted that their "patriotic spirit still prevailed." Heavy gunfire soon erupted to the southeast, causing some to jump to their feet. A dusty aide galloped up to the brigade and asked directions to General Sedgwick's headquarters. The men knew what this meant and immediately began collecting their belongings. The march was now at the double-quick toward Little Round Top at the southern part of the field, where two divisions in General Longstreet's First Corps were battering the Federal III and V Corps. "As we went through the woods and over the fields, shells were bursting in the air and minie balls singing close to our heads," Reverend Haines related. Passing a cavalcade of wounded and just plain scared Federal troops, the brigade halted a bit north of Little Round Top, close to the George Weikert house on Cemetery Ridge, where it formed a reserve. The First NJV formed at the foot of a small hill, the Fifteenth NJV formed behind it, and the Second and Third NJV continued the line to the right. The brigade's services were not needed, as the V Corps and part of the Third Division of the VI Corps were finally able to beat back the determined Confederate onslaught.

The men lay on their arms that night, but sleep did not come easily. Thousands of dying and wounded men filled the fields in front of them, and their dreadful cries rent the air all night. Some men ventured out with canteens to help quench the thirst of the wounded. The brigade moved southwest toward the northern part of Little Round Top on the morning of July 3. Because his three brigades were dispersed over the battlefield, General Wright turned the First New Jersey Brigade over to General Newton. Sniper fire was a problem, but few were hit, as the men hid behind the numerous rocks and boulders. General Torbert established his headquarters about forty feet behind the main line. Eating lunch, Torbert became annoyed when he realized that his men were throwing pebbles at him. He quickly strode toward his line and bellowed for his men to quit bothering him. This brought a general laugh from the men, and one yelled out, "Them's rebel bullets, General."[10]

The First NJV again formed the first line, with the Third NJV behind it. The Fifteenth NJV was deployed at right angles to the rest of the brigade, and the Second NJV was on the picket line. The men laid out their cartridges on the ground in front of them and waited. Some of the men picked up additional muskets. The quiet concerned the men. This ended with the massive cannonade that preceded the Pickett-Pettigrew-Trimble charge. A Jerseyman recalled that "most of the missiles passed over our heads harmlessly, bursting in the rear, or going too low, struck in the hill below us." Fewer than five men were wounded, as the troops ground their bodies into the dirt. When the cannon fire ended, the Jersey boys watched the awesome charge and awaited orders to move to the right to take on Pickett's Division. A soldier wrote, "with strange emotion we watched their coming; it was not fear, it was not surprise, but every man was silent, and grasped his weapon more closely." Charles Harrison called it "one of the grandest sights of the war . . . the Round Shot whistles through the air and the sharp crack of the Rifle is heard on all sides. The enemy charge our front but are cut down by hundreds and obliged to fall back in great confusion." The New Jerseyans were not needed to repel the charge, as the Federal troops to the right handled the reduced masses of

Confederates. The Third NJV replaced the Second NJV on the picket line later in the afternoon.

The Fourth NJV was missing from the brigade, as it was still on guard duty. Six of its companies were on the battlefield with the artillery reserve near Little Round Top, and the remaining companies were with the wagon train at Westminster. The regiment would not rejoin the brigade until November.[11]

The men slept better that night knowing that Lee's massive charge had failed and that it was unlikely he would try his hand against this sector again. The brigade's losses during the battle were minimal—ten wounded (Second NJV: six; Third NJV: one; Fifteenth NJV: three). Knowing the importance of this battle and learning of the heroic actions of the Second New Jersey Brigade, many men were disappointed in their minor role. Lieutenant Ellis Hamilton wrote home that his brigade "was not engaged at all being, by a singular freak by Gen. Sedgwiek, on the reserve."

Taking his Fifteenth NJV out on picket duty on July 4, Colonel Penrose ordered his men to stack their Enfield-type muskets and pick up Springfields that lay about the field in abundance. The latter rifles were considered superior, but some of the men grumbled that their Enfields "could shoot farther, and with more certainty of aim." Being on a battlefield after a fight was a new experience for the men. Dayton Flint wrote home, "it was a scene I hope never to witness again, and a sad 4th of July it was to us." The men spent considerable time burying the dead. Lucien Voorhees of the same regiment wrote home, "the pen cannot perform its duties in describing the horrible, ghastly scenes there visible." Sergeant Phineas Skellenger noted that "battelfiedl [sic] was the awfullest sight I ever saw—some of the dead lay 3 or 4 days before they was [sic] buried." The bodies turned black and became bloated under the hot July sun, polluting the air and sickening the men. Lieutenant Ellis Hamilton also reported on the numerous "pools of blood lying all around the ground." Heavy rains settling into the area that afternoon helped dissipate the smell and clean the landscape somewhat.[12]

The brigade was roused at 2:00 a.m. on July 5 with news that Lee's army was in full retreat. There was less enthusiasm about the rest of news—the VI Corps would lead the effort to bag them before they could reach Virginia. The brigade began the march at 11:00 a.m. at the van[guard] of the corps. Cautiously advancing in line of battle, with a heavy line of skirmishers in front of them, the Jerseyans approached the now-vacated enemy positions in the Wheatfield, picking up an enemy straggler here and there. They came upon Lee's rearguard about two miles from Fairfield. The brigade's skirmish line was initially thrown back on the line of battle, but when the entire line swept forward, it drove "the enemy from the woods and across the field beyond," recalled Reverend Haines. The Confederates were driven two miles before Sedgwick halted the advance. The Third NJV, which was the principal aggressor, had one man killed and two wounded, and a Rebel bullet tore off one of General Torbert's buttons. The enemy lost two killed and six captured.

The usual rotation occurred on July 6, so the First New Jersey Brigade was now in the rear of the corps. Finding the enemy in heavy numbers, the Second Division deployed while the First Division rested behind it. The march continued at 6:00 p.m., and the brigade marched all night to make up for lost time, arriving at Emmitsburg, Maryland, at daylight. After a short rest for breakfast, the pursuit of Lee's army continued at 6:00 a.m. on July 7. Marching along the foot of South Mountain, the column used a road described as "muddy, rocky, narrow." It was an interminable march that continued all day and into the night. The night was pitch dark and rain fell in torrents, drenching the men and forcing them to inch forward. They began wondering if their officers were confused and lost, but finally received orders at 10:00 p.m. to halt for the rest of the night. "It was a hard march[.] I never thought men could stand so much[.] Our rations run out the day before," reported Benjamin Hough. Without shelter tents, the men sought nonexistent cover and lay down in the mud as the rains continued. A lack of supper and coffee added to their misery. "The men considered the past two days as *rough* as any in the service, all things considered," noted Edmund Halsey in his diary. July 8 was somewhat easier, as the brigade did not break camp until late morning, and then marched only eight miles over the mountains to Middletown. The rain continued, and with each step the roads worsened. The Jerseyans rested in camp until 4:00 p.m. on July 9, when they made another eight-mile march, this time to Boonsborough. The column marched only three miles on July 10, then deployed in line of battle, as the enemy was near. The corps remained here the next day. Many took the opportunity to bathe in Antietam Creek. The corps marched about six miles on July 12, to within two miles of Hagerstown, Maryland. Torbert deployed his brigade in line of battle and aggressively advanced his skirmish line. When within 175 yards of the enemy, Torbert ordered a charge. The enemy pickets occupied rifle pits on a hill but quickly scrambled out of them and beat a hasty retreat. "You had oughte [*sic*] a have seen the rebs run," wrote Hough. Ellis Hamilton noted that the fight was a short one—twenty minutes, after which the "Rebs took to their heels." Three officers and four enlisted men were wounded at this action near Funkstown.[13]

The corps remained here on July 13, as the two picket lines constantly fired at each other. A unofficial truce was called that evening, and the opposing soldiers chatted and exchanged goods. A soldier in the Fifteenth NJV explained it as "such is war-one minute trying to take life and the next, perhaps, shaking hands." The officers discouraged these activities and, when observed, quickly put an end to them.

The brigade was on the road again on July 14, this time to Williamsport, about six miles away. Lee's army was here with its back to the Potomac River, as its pontoon bridge was destroyed and recent rains had raised the levels. The Confederates quickly built fortifications and awaited the enemy's attack. Meade took his time in bringing up his army. Oscar Westlake wrote home, "I think we will have a fight with them yet before they all get across the Potomac." However, Lee quickly crossed his men to safety prior to the attack. The VI Corps marched back to Boonsborough on July 15, taking all day to make the sixteen-mile march. The intense heat caused many to drop by the side of the road, but most caught up later that night. There was no rest for the weary, as the corps marched twenty miles the next day to Berlin via Middletown and Petersville. The heat was intense during these marches. Chaplain Haines wrote, "it seemed as if it was the intention of our general officers to kill us by hard marching." In reality, there was no need for these forced marches. Upon reaching Berlin, the corps was given a well-deserved three-day rest. The Jersey Brigade crossed the Potomac River on July 19 and marched eight miles to Wheatland, finally concluding the Gettysburg Campaign. Although the Jerseymen had played but a small role, they knew it was an important reserve one. According to General Torbert's report, the brigade had one killed and seventeen wounded during the campaign. While in Wheatland, General Torbert filed a brigade strength report that included 106 officers and 1,557 enlisted men, for a total of 1,663 (First NJV—356; Second NJV—448; Third NJV—367; Fifteenth NJV—492; Total—1,663). The report did not include the Fourth NJV, which was still on detached service.[14]

Most of the men were content that the army had decisively defeated Lee, but it was not until later that they learned that Meade had squandered a wonderful opportunity. Josiah Brown of the Second NJV wrote after the war that Lee's army was "permitted to recross to the 'sacred soil' thus resigning an opportunity of crushing the rebellion and closing the war. . . . True our force was exhausted and weakened and ill fitted to re-engage the enemy, yet were not we the victors and they the flying foe? They had no way of retreat. . . . But the bird had soon flown and we were booked for two more years of exhausting sacrifice and struggle."

◆ ◆ ◆ ◆ ◆ ◆

While the begrimed men of the First New Jersey Brigade waited to face Lee's army again, the Twenty-third NJV was still not home. Paul Kuhl had written to his sister on June 18, 1863, that the enemy's invasion of Pennsylvania was the time for the "nine months men to prove that they are not cowards. I say if they do not respond to the call to repel the invaders, they will prove themselves cowards." The Twenty-third NJV proved to be anything but. After reaching Beverly, New Jersey, the regiment was not immediately mustered out, as it took time to prepare the discharge papers and to rectify the sutlers' accounts. The men pitched their tents and waited. Colonel Grubb permitted about half the men to go on leave at a time while waiting there.[15]

The delay tested Grubb's patience. Finally journeying to Trenton on June 17, he implored the governor to hasten the discharge process. Although his men's discipline remained perfect, he was concerned that a nearby military hospital could cause the spread of disease. While there, a telegram arrived for Governor Parker with the news that the Rebels were in Pennsylvania. "Will your men go?" Grubb was asked, and he immediately responded, "Of course they will." Riding back to Beverly with Grubb, the governor gave an impassioned speech to the men of the Twenty-third NJV. Praising them for their service, he recognized that the Federal and state governments had no further claim on their time, but told them that the capital of Pennsylvania was in imminent danger. Parker ended his remarks by saying, "Now every man who will go to Harrisburg to-night, step three paces to the front." Every man stepped forward.

Grabbing their knapsacks and muskets, the men hopped aboard the trains bound for Philadelphia, arriving there about dusk that evening. They were greeted by cheering Philadelphians who feared that Lee's army was about to capture the city. The column marched to another train station to board trains bound for Harrisburg. None were there, so Grubb quartered his 369 men in the police station. The colonel was able to secure a train of open coal cars the following day, June 18, and the regiment finally arrived in Harrisburg at 1:00

p.m. that afternoon, The troops were surprised by the cool reception they received from the local citizens whose city was in danger. Meeting General Darius Couch, commander of this military district, Grubb was told to take his men to the Cumberland Valley Railroad Bridge over the Susquehanna River. Couch was concerned that the enemy would attempt to cross here, so he had the Twenty-third NJV dig rifle pits along the river. The regiment manned the pits for three days; then Couch again appeared and told Grubb that the enemy was falling back and the Army of the Potomac was advancing, so the Twenty-third could return to New Jersey to be mustered out. One veteran wrote that he, "without regret, quitted the inhospitable capital." The regiment reached Beverly and was mustered out of service on June 27. Although merely a nine-month regiment, it had distinguished itself on the battlefields of Fredericksburg and Chancellorsville. Many of the men later joined the Thirty-seventh and Fortieth NJV.[16]

Back on the front lines, the men of the First New Jersey Brigade reflected on the most recent campaign. Losses were minimal, but the long marches and other physical exertions had taken their toll. Sergeant Paul Kuhl wrote home, "such privations as we have undergone for the past month I did not think it in the power of man to stand. I never saw anything to compare with it, and hope I never will again, for it takes a person of iron constitution to stand it. I can very plainly feel the effects on myself, but a few weeks rest will bring me all right again."[17]

Notes

1. Bradley M. Gottfried, *Roads to Gettysburg* (Shippensburg, Pa.: White Mane, 2002), 6–19; *The War of the Rebellion: A Compilation of the Official Records of the Union and Confederate Armies* (Washington, D.C.: U.S. Government Printing Office, 1880–1901) [hereafter *OR*], ser. 1, vol. 27, pt. 3: pp. 12–13.

2. *OR*, ser. 1, vol. 27, pt. 3, pp. 12–13; Alanson A. Haines, *History of the Fifteenth Regiment New Jersey Volunteers* (New York: Jenkins & Thomas, 1883), 68–69; Camille Baquet, *History of Kearny's First New Jersey Brigade, 1861–1865* (Trenton, N.J.: MacCrellish & Quigley, 1910), 89.

3. John Y. Foster, *New Jersey and the Rebellion* (Newark: M.R. Dennis, 1868), 511–512; Haines, *Fifteenth,* 69; *Hunterdon Republican,* June 19, 1863; Edmund Halsey Diary, June 8, 1863, U.S. Army Military History Institute, Carlisle, Pa.

4. Haines, *Fifteenth,* 69–70; Halsey diary, June 9, 1863; E. L. Dobbins, "Fragments from the History of a Quaker Regiment," *War Talks by Morristown Veterans* (Morristown, N.J.:

Vogt Brothers, 1887), 34. Oscar Westlake to mother, June 12, 1863; Charles Alexander Harrison Diary, June 18, 1863, U.S. Army Military History Institute, Carlisle, Pa.; Paul Kuhl to brother, May 18, June 9, 1863, Paul Kuhl Papers, John Kuhl Collection (private); Paul Kuhl to sister, June 10, 1863, Paul Kuhl Papers.

5. Halsey diary, June 12, 1863; Benjamin Hough, *Letters from Home*, ed. Edna Raymond (Westtown, N.Y.: Town of Minisink Archives, 1988), 36; Phineas Skellenger to brother, June 21, 1863, Phineas Skellenger Papers, John Kuhl Collection (private); Haines, *Fifteenth*, 70–71; Joseph Bilby, *Three Rousing Cheers* (Hightstown, N.J.: Longstreet House, 1993), 80–81; Baquet, *Kearny's*, 90; Gottfried, *Roads*, 41–42, 53.

6. Halsey diary, June 14, 15, 1863; Hough, *Letters*, 3; Haines, *Fifteenth*, 72–73; *Hunterdon Republican*, June 26, 1863; Quincy Grimes to father, June 18, 1863, Quincy Grimes Papers, John Kuhl Collection (private).

This was the last complete letter that Grimes would write. An uncontrollable case of diarrhea that began in mid-July caused his death on September 8, 1863. Edmund Halsey called him a "quiet well behaved soldier-obedient to orders and much esteemed by all his comrades" (Halsey to sister, September 8, 1863, Halsey Letters, Rockaway Borough Library, Rockaway, N.J.).

7. Haines, *Fifteenth*, 73, 75; Oscar Westlake to mother, June 21, 1863, Oscar Westlake Papers, John Kuhl Collection (private); Gottfried, *Roads*, 143, 151; Halsey diary, June 27, 1863; Hough, *Letters*, 41.

8. Haines, *Fifteenth*, 76, 79, 91; Halsey diary, June 29, 30, 1863; Baquet, *Kearny's*, 91; Bradley M. Gottfried, *Brigades of Gettysburg* (New York: DaCapo Press 2002), 285–286; *Hunterdon Republican*, July 8, 1863; OR, ser. 1, vol. 27, pt. 1, p. 162.

9. Gottfried, *Brigades*, 286; F. W. Morse, *Personal Experiences in the War of the Rebellion* (Albany, N.Y.: Munsell Printer, 1866), 33–34; Halsey diary, July 2, 1863; OR, ser. 1, vol. 27, pt. 1, p. 658; *Hunterdon Republican*, July 10, July 17, 1863; Haines, *Fifteenth*, 79–80, 98.

10. *Hunterdon Republican*, July 17, 1863; Halsey diary, July 2, 1863; Haines, *Fifteenth*, 85, 87; OR, ser. 1, vol. 27, pt. 1, pp. 665, 668; Baquet, *Kearny's*, 91–93.

11. Halsey diary, July 3, 1863; Baquet, *Kearny's*, 91–92, 98, 208, 397–398; OR, ser. 1, vol., 27, pt. 1, p. 669; Haines, *Fifteenth*, 92; Harrison diary, July 3, 1863.

12. Haines, *Fifteenth*, 94–95; Ellis Hamilton to father, July 17, 1863, Hamilton Papers, Special Collections, Alexander Library, Rutgers University, New Brunswick, N.J.; Baquet, *Kearny's*, 97; Dayton Flint to sisters, *Washington Star*, February 22, 1911; Phineas Skellenger to brother, July 10, 1863; *Hunterdon Republican*, July 24, 1863; Ellis Hamilton to mother, July 9, 1863, .

13. OR, ser. 1, vol. 27, pt. 1, pp. 669–670; Halsey diary, July 5, 6, 8, 1863; Haines, *Fifteenth*, 98, 99–100; Hough, *Letters*, 44, 45; *Hunterdon Republican*, July 31, 1863; Ellis Hamilton to father, July 17, 1863.

14. Haines, *Fifteenth*, 100–101, 102; OR, ser. 1, vol. 27, pt. 1, pp. 658–670; Oscar Westlake to mother, July 11, 1863; *Hunterdon Republican*, July 31, 1863.

15. Josiah Brown, "Record of My Experiences during the Civil War From October 1, 1862 to July 1865," typed transcript, New Jersey Historical Society, Newark, 14; Paul Kuhl to sister, June 18, 1863; Baquet, *Kearny's*, 278.

16. Baquet, *Kearny's*, 279, 235, 280–281; Foster, *Rebellion*, 512–513.

17. Paul Kuhl to sister, July 11, 1863.

"Grand Promenade Atlantic City," 1905. *There is a long history of vacationers sending postcards of the places they visited to friends and relatives. In this case the site was Atlantic City and its boardwalk. The picture illustrates how visitors in an earlier period put on their best dresses, men with hats and women with umbrellas meant to ward off the sun. Some, rather than strolling, rode along in style on the rolling chairs. Postcard collection, Special Collections and University Archives, Rutgers University Libraries.*

10

As historians have studied different aspects of the past, their main interest has shifted since the 1960s from politics to economics, from laws to society, and, later, to culture. Political historians have focused on ideas and institutions, the formation of political parties, and voting requirements and patterns. Economic historians have considered industrialization, monetary policies and institutions, and the changing ways people have earned a living. Legal historians have analyzed constitutions and laws, judges' lives, and methods of handling crime. More recently, social historians have sought to re-create the lives of everyday people, to examine class and class differences. The following selection, from a social history of one resort town, deals with forms of entertainment and attitudes toward both class and recreation during the Victorian era in the United States.

In 1852, Absecon Island had only marshes and sand dunes to offer visitors. Less than thirty years later, Atlantic City had achieved national status. Who was attracted to this new resort? According to the publicity releases of its boosters it drew the rich and well-born from all over the East. In fact, the city's pull was far more limited in terms of both class and distance. Charles Funnell has raised questions about the relationship between class and entertainment. Did rich and poor enjoy the same forms of recreation and go to the same vacation places? Do they today? Are golf, tennis, and skiing, for example, sports for all classes? Who goes to minor league baseball games and such places as Canyon Ranch spas? What role does financial status, class, taste, and age play in how Americans choose to use their leisure time? Why has Funnell characterized Atlantic City as both "crude" and "magnificent"?

Atlantic City's entertainment created problems for many Victorian Americans because it made apparent some of the conflicts and contradictions in their society. Vacations were meant to be enjoyable, but pleasure and morality sometimes clashed. Most laborers worked six days a week, but on the seventh day, meant to be a day of rest, Sunday "blue laws" closed stores and prohibited the sale of liquor—and thus defined the limits of acceptable relaxation. Sunday was also the only day most tourists could make trips to the Shore, but the fact that the town's facilities stayed open so that visitors would make the most of their limited leisure time violated both laws and sensibilities. If amusements closed, visitors stayed away, and the resort's businesses made no profit.

Atlantic City was also advertised as a family resort at the same time that publications heralded the opportunities for singles to meet there. However, some of the forms of entertainment that drew single people, including saloons, gambling, and prostitution, offended families. Yet even those Victorians who established laws regulating entertainment did not always agree on or enforce "correct" standards. Does New Jersey still have "blue laws"? Where does law and society draw the line between pleasure and morality today?

Another interesting aspect of entertainment in the Victorian era is the impact of technological advance. Just as railroads opened areas of the country for settlement in the 1800s, made the transportation of goods easier and cheaper, and fueled industrialization by creating the need for large-scale production of iron and steel, they made Atlantic City possible. The resort was on a direct line from Philadelphia. Railroads enabled large crowds to travel inexpensively to Atlantic City, not for the summer or week as vacationers had done earlier, but for the day. Most Atlantic City tourists still spend only a day there.

Technology also provided new machines to entertain visitors once they came. The Ferris wheel, merry-go-round, and roller coaster were mechanical wonders that drew crowds as strongly as the ocean and the boardwalk did. Today, technological developments continue to provide both updated versions of older machines and new forms of entertainment. What kinds of rides are available at Great Adventure and Disney World, and how do they compare with those at Atlantic City a century ago?

Atlantic City drew workers as well as tourists. Many of those who labored to keep the city running were African American. How were these workers regarded and treated? Did segregation exist in Atlantic City, and, if so, what form did it take? Here, too, Victorians compromised moral and ethical standards with the desire for profits. How does the treatment of African Americans in the city compare with their treatment in other places during this time?

Atlantic City in the Victorian era was not unique; although it was larger and more famous, it resembled other Shore towns in many fundamental ways. Its story reveals much about general attitudes toward class, recreation, and race in the North.

Suggested Readings

Cunningham, John T. *The Jersey Shore*. New Brunswick, N.J.: Rutgers University Press, 1958.

Dulles, Foster Rhea. *America Learns to Play*. New York: D. Appleton-Century, 1940.

Foster, Herbert J. "Institutional Development in the Black Community of Atlantic City, New Jersey: 1850–1930." In *The Black Experience in Southern New Jersey*, edited by David C. Munn, 32–48. Camden, N.J.: Camden County Historical Society, 1985.

Johnson, Nelson. *Boardwalk Empire: The Birth, High Times, and Corruption of Atlantic City* . Medford, N.J.: Plexus, 2002.

Messenger, Troy. *Holy Leisure: Recreation and Religion in God's Square Mile*. Philadelphia: Temple University Press, 1999.

Mrozek, Donald J. *Sport and American Mentality, 1880–1910*. Knoxville.: University of Tennessee Press, 1983.

Paulsson, Martin. *Social Anxieties of Progressive Reform: Atlantic City: 1854–1920*. New York: New York University Press, 1994.

Simon, Bryant. *Boardwalk of Dreams: Atlantic City and the Fate of Urban America*. New York: Oxford University Press, 2004.

Uminowicz, Glenn. "Recreation in a Christian America: Ocean Grove and Asbury Park, New Jersey, 1869–1914." In *Hard at Play: Leisure in America, 1840–1940*, edited by Kathryn Grover, 8–38. Amherst: University of Massachusetts Press, 1992.

Wilson, Harold F. *The Story of the Jersey Shore: A Social and Economic History of the Counties of Atlantic, Cape May, Monmouth and Ocean*. 3 vols. New York: Lewis Historical Publishing, 1953.

———. "Victorian Vacations at the Jersey Shore." *Proceedings of the New Jersey Historical Society* 77 (1959): 267–271.

♦ ♦ ♦ ♦ ♦ ♦

Newport of the Nouveaux Bourgeois

Charles E. Funnell

Many different kinds of people patronized Atlantic City in the turn-of-the-century period, but the ambiance of the resort was lower middle class. From this class came the greatest number of visitors and the largest part of the city's revenue, and accordingly the atmosphere of Atlantic City was a product of lower-middle-class preferences and aspirations. Many people today believe, and some at the time asserted, that the city was then an upper-class resort. Articles appearing recently in popular magazines have offered a casual sketch of the gentility and elegance of the Victorian resort, its swell tone and distinguished patronage . . . , but here we . . . consider why it is basically erroneous. Bedizened, gauche, extravagant, conniving, ingenuous—Atlantic City from the start depended on the lower middle class for its success, and was the charming preposterous artifact of its customers' tastes.

Before beginning, it is necessary to consider the class structure applied here. The most useful divisions for the town's history are upper class, upper middle class, lower middle class, lower class, blacks, and bums. The upper class is divided into "society," defined strictly as individuals listed in the *Social Register* for Philadelphia, and the nouveaux riches, those enjoying wealth but not yet accepted by the traditional upper class. The upper middle class consists mainly of professional people, substantial businessmen, executives, and the like. Also, and importantly, newspaper editors. To the lower middle class belong lesser white-collar workers of all varieties, including the many different kinds of clerks staffing the commerce and retail trade of Philadelphia. Many of these are women, employed in growing numbers as salesgirls. The lower class consists of factory workers, male and female, and other laborers engaged in heavy, tedious, and generally unremunera-

From *By the Beautiful Sea: The Rise and High Times of That Great American Resort, Atlantic City*, by Charles E. Funnell, pp. 24–49. Copyright © 1975 by Charles E. Funnell. Used by permission of Alfred A. Knopf, a division of Random House, Inc.

tive work. Blacks include residents of Atlantic City and visitors from Philadelphia, and are properly considered apart from all classes of whites, in a period which witnessed the acme of racial sentiment in American society. Economically trivial but socially interesting, bums are the *Lumpenproletariat* of unemployed drifters and down-and-outs.

Many observers of Atlantic City believed, or liked to believe, that it was an expression of high society. A Pennsylvania Railroad pamphlet of 1889 spoke of the "representatives of the best society" which frequented the resort.[1] In 1897 a member of the Atlantic City Hotel Men's Association, expansively describing the future of the town in the twentieth century to a Philadelphia businessmen's group, predicted that a bicycle path recently built between the city and its resort would be improved to a broad highway for the wealthy: "A modern Appian way, upon which the rich and pleasure-loving people, blessed with fine horses, can drive down from Philadelphia in their carriages."[2] John F. Hall, editor of the *Daily Union*, boasted that "there is hardly a family of any prominence residing within a thousand miles of this favored region that has not at one time or another occupied, as host or guest, one of the beautiful homes which form the crowning glory of the town."[3] The resort's Easter Parade, one of the annual highlights, drew great crowds to promenade the Boardwalk. *Harper's Weekly* said of it in 1908: "Practically all of the Easter guests here are people of wealth and fashion. . . . Seventy-five per cent of their names figure in the social registers of their home cities."[4]

Such claims, of course, are immediately suspect. If they are to be believed, Atlantic City was hot on the trail of Newport for the patronage of the Four Hundred. Was the resort in fact laying hold of the fashionable clientele of the Quaker City?

An examination of the "hotel personals" which the *Daily Union* regularly printed in the 1890s is illuminating. While not captioned "social column," these lists clearly were the cream of the visiting crop in the newspaper's eyes. They were compiled from the registers of the principal (and most expensive) hotels that lined the Boardwalk, a selection device which simplified the editor's task, since these great structures embodied the town's most forceful claim to elegance and sophistication. An examination of twenty-six weekly lists—chiefly in 1890, 1893, and 1894, when they were prominently and extensively featured in the newspaper—yields 467 names of distinguished visitors.[5] These were all from Philadelphia (if a visitor came from a different city, the *Daily Union* noted that fact). A comparison of these names with the appropriate *Social Registers* yields 10 definite listings and 5 possible listings. Lest it be thought that the resort press was too yokel an affair to recognize society when they saw it, similar data from the *Philadelphia Inquirer* may be added.[6] Of 327 distinguished visitors to Atlantic City (1892, 1894, 1901),[7] 14 are found in the *Social Register*.[8] In addition, of 142 arrivals on a single day at a dozen hotels (including the prestigious Traymore, Windsor, and Chalfonte), 4 are listed.[9]

But perhaps Philadelphia society, while not thronging the hotels, maintained a sizable cottage community at the seaside. The Social Register Association published a summer edition in 1900 which gave 763 addresses of individuals or families, listed in the winter register at Philadelphia residences, who had summer homes elsewhere.[10] Only 31 of them gave a summer address for Atlantic City, and 7 of these are not private homes but hotels. Though this edition of the register gave the same information for society members from Baltimore, Washington, New York, Chicago, and Boston, only one individual from these cities had a summer residence at the resort. Taking the summer addresses of the first 200 Philadelphians in the register, we find fully half of them choosing the fashionable Philadelphia suburbs (such as Chestnut Hill and the Main Line), with most of the rest scattered among various northeastern resorts and foreign countries. Seven preferred Atlantic City. In sum, if high society was not utterly absent at the City by the Sea, there was something less than a surfeit of tweed on the Boardwalk.

Who were these "distinguished visitors" then? The brief descriptions attached to some of the names in the *Daily Union* give an idea.[11] They are offered as given, with no attempt to harmonize the syntax: "Pennsylvanic Cycle Co.," "the well known brick manufacturer," "a prominent official in the passenger department of the Pennsylvania Railroad," "candidate for District Attorney of Philadelphia," "a prominent businessman," "a prominent merchant," "a well known carpet manufacturer," "a prominent Philadelphia Civil Engineer," "a prominent member of the Quaker City bar," "manager . . . of the Philadelphia Press," "a well known Philadelphia letter carrier," "publisher and printer," "one of Philadelphia's most prominent physicians," "a well known Philadelphia shoe manufacturer," "a well known Philadelphia fruit dealer," "a prominent iron merchant," "Select Councilman of the Tenth Ward," "President of the Penn Mutual Life Insurance Co.," "President of the Fire Association of Philadelphia," "real estate agent," "publisher of The First Ward News," "of Common Council's," "the well known Philadelphia politician," "a prominent Philadelphia lumber merchant," "well known wholesale grocer of Philadelphia," "the 8th street shoe merchant," "Recorder of Deeds of Philadelphia." Also, twenty-one physicians.

These were the elite of business, manufacturing, government, publishing, and the professions. They were not high society. How a "well known Philadelphia letter carrier" made the list is anyone's guess; the inclusion seems ironic, but it was probably meant seriously. In six instances, ladies at the great hotels are specifically described as high society: "a pretty society lady of Germantown," "a popular acquisition to the large number of society representatives stopping at the Waverly," "a leader of society of Philadelphia," "a handsome blonde and prominent in Philadelphia social circles," and others.[12] Yet none of these ladies is listed in the *Social Register*. It cannot be said that a blueblood never trod the strand, but society stayed away from the town with marked assiduity. Most of the rich who did come were the men who gave the Gilded Age its name, the nouveaux riches who were forging industrial America and growing fat on the proceeds. With them came the upper middle class, who could afford some of the same luxuries in more modest degree. The pseudo-snobbery of resort literature was partly aimed at both groups. If they couldn't be invited to Newport, they could buy their way into Atlantic City, but they would have to share the city with the classes they were escaping from. One article put it in just these terms:

> The ultra-swell and almost no one else go to Lenox, Bar Harbor, Newport. Swell and near-swell and folks "just comfortable" go to places like Asbury Park. Into Atlantic City every day in the season are dumped ultra-, almost-, and near-swell, folks comfortable and uncomfortable, and absolutely every other kind by the thousands; for that's Atlantic City.[13]

There are numerous indications that those not having a vested interest in the promotion of the resort regarded it as lowbrow in atmosphere. The year 1894 was a black one for the national economy, but the *Philadelphia Inquirer* claimed that the resort had acquired new visitors from "influential society" and the "wealthy classes, ranging from the tens to the hundreds of thousands valuation." The author of the article, while seemingly sympathetic to the resort's interests, gave it a backhanded slap: "Some of these people came because they were tired of other resorts and wanted novelty, which they certainly get here, and others visited here because they could not afford to go to the more ultra and consequently much more expensive resorts."[14] In 1909 a visiting journalist sardonically portrayed the nouveaux riches in the town. These are not the "Financiers" or the "Titans" whom Theodore Dreiser portrayed; these are bush-league robber barons:

> These men are mainly railroad men and manufacturers—not the heads of railways, but assistants and deputies and lieutenants. They have money in abundance without being vastly rich, and they come to Atlantic City because it so exactly suits their barbarous ideal of what is fine.
>
> They never think of anything outside the subject of iron or coal or pork or wheat or railway rates. They incarnate crass materialism in its most hopeless form.[15]

The *Daily Union* complained in 1892 that the resort was failing to attract "the patronage of millionaires" because it lacked a really posh hotel of the "first class Ponce de Leon" variety.[16] Indeed, by 1887 Atlantic City was already developing a suburb named Chelsea, to which its upper-middle-class natives were retreating.[17] The locals had begun to sniff at their customers.

Although the resort's nouveaux riches might be crass materialists, they were not always humorless. The *Inquirer*, observing that powerful Philadelphia politicians are often seen at the shore, mentions an anecdote of "George W. Ledlie, the generous and big-hearted Port Warden of the Thirty-second ward, and the gentleman who has 4300 men working for him on his electrical traction work in Philadelphia and other cities." The tale is not without relevance to Atlantic City's moneyed customers and to Gilded Age ethics:

> Mr. Ledlie tells a story, which is worth repeating, of an old firm of coal dealers who had as an employe an individual who was about as dumb and thick-headed as they come. This failing on the man's part became so apparent, finally, that the firm decided to discharge him. To bring this about, one of the members, with his visage full of foreboding portent, said: "Say, Bill, what do you know anyhow?"
>
> The employe said: "Well, not much, boss. But I know that 1800 pounds makes a ton." That the man was kept on the firm's payroll, it is needless to say.[18]

Quite apart from transient patrons, many of the resort's upper-middle-class users were resident throughout the summer in the city, renting the great number of cottages which the locals vacated for the season to pull in some extra money. Editor Hall estimated that there were over four thousand cottages on Absecon Island and that fully half of them were rented each summer.[19] Such seasonal residents were often professionals and executives who commuted from Philadelphia, apparently each day, leaving their families by the seaside. A Camden and Atlantic Railroad brochure of 1883 encouraged this trade,[20] while in

1893 the Reading Railroad sold twenty-trip commutation tickets for $17.50.[21] This portion of the resort's clientele was reliable and dull, the least colorful part of the visiting population. It was certainly welcome, yet the garish, intense pleasure industries of the Boardwalk were aimed at the more transient customers. The cottagers spent their money peacefully and left comparatively little historical record.[22]

At the other end of the social spectrum were the blacks, both resident and visiting. Evidence of their activities is hard to come by, for while the resort was highly dependent on black labor, it was anxious not to advertise the presence of blacks to potential white customers. Since most blacks were poor, they could hardly constitute a large tourist population. On the other hand, merely by working in Atlantic City they were able to avail themselves of some of the pleasures of the resort. The New Jersey state census of 1905 shows that, of 426 resident blacks, only 38 had been born in New Jersey. Of the vast majority not native to the state, 130 had been born in Virginia, 86 in Maryland, 43 in Washington, D.C., 34 in Pennsylvania, and 27 in North Carolina. A total of 47 were from fifteen other states, and individuals had come from Cuba, England, and Australia.[23] A great many no doubt lived in Philadelphia before seeking work in the resort. Nevertheless, directly or indirectly they found themselves in a very special community, some of whose pleasures could not be denied them.

It was a situation not entirely agreeable to the local establishment. In 1893 the *Inquirer* complained:

> What are we going to do with our colored people? That is the question. Atlantic City has never before seemed so overrun with the dark skinned race as this season, probably because the smaller proportion of visitors makes their number more prominent. At any rate, both the boardwalk and Atlantic avenue fairly swarm with them during bathing hours, like the fruit in a huckleberry pudding. This has gone so far that it is offending the sensitive feelings of many visitors, especially those from the South. . . . Of the hundreds of hotels and boarding houses which stud the island from one end to the other, it is probable that not a dozen could be found in which white help is employed. And when to the thousands of waiters and cooks and porters are added the nurse girls, the chambermaids, the barbers and bootblacks and hack drivers and other colored gentry in every walk and occupation of life, it will easily be realized what an evil it is that hangs over Atlantic City.[24]

Although this complaint is a good expression of the contradictory mentality of a white culture which employed blacks for every personal service and yet was distressed by the thought of mingling with them in the surf, it is nevertheless an admission that the city made no real attempt to exclude blacks from the beachfront. The article went on to say that in Asbury Park the problem had been solved by the founder and "original proprietor" of the resort, who restricted blacks to certain defined areas. But in Atlantic City, with owner-ship diffused in hundreds of hands, no such unified suppression was possible. The author conceded that only the collaboration of all the beachfront proprietors could keep the blacks in their place, a collab-oration which (one suspects) was unlikely.[25] Seven years later the *Washington Post* complained of the way local blacks by the hundreds were invading the bathing districts "heretofore patronized by the best visitors."[26] Conditions were similarly lax off the beach: "After the colored waiter serves his master's supper he can go out and elbow him on the Boardwalk, crowd him in the cars, or drink at the very next table to him in almost any cafe." But it would be wrong to imagine that blacks at the resort were always coldly viewed. In July 1900 the *Inquirer* good-naturedly (if condescendingly) mentioned "a beautiful young colored lady becomingly garbed in broad, longitudinal stripes of black and orange alternating and carrying an indescribable, unmentionable parasol into the surf with her to shield her complexion from tan and freckles while in water up to her neck."[27]

Of course, Atlantic City was not in fact completely integrated. Various kinds of informal segregation were practiced everywhere. The *Daily Union* records the criticism of a black Pennsylvania newspaper concerning the "color line" in the resort.[28] Although black servants could sit in the pavilions along the Boardwalk, wealthy black tourists were denied admission. Such inverted discrimination in favor of poor over wealthy blacks was perfectly logical, given the racial convictions of the whites. After all, the servants had to be in Atlantic City: the black tourists did not.[29]

The amount of black excursionism to Atlantic City is, as has been suggested, harder to determine than the use of facilities by local blacks. Nevertheless, it is clear that during the 1890s there was an annual outing to the resort for blacks from Philadelphia and the surrounding area. The *Daily Union* reported the visit of five thousand blacks to the Seaview Hotel and excursion district on September 3, 1891.[30] They used public conveyances, swam, and enjoyed themselves at the Seaview's dance hall and carrousel. The date, September 3, is interesting. At that time Labor Day had not yet been made a national holiday and September 1 marked the end of summer at the Shore, after which resort trade quickly dried up. It may be that the blacks who organized the excursion chose a date just after the close of the season to avoid offending the whites. Moreover, the money would be welcome as a post-season windfall.[31]

The *Inquirer* observed in September 1896 that "one of the harbingers of fall is . . . the annual excursion of colored citizens from Pennsylvania, Delaware and New Jersey to the seashore." The visitors that year remained in the lower Boardwalk area, and "the beach below Texas avenue was devoted exclusively to the dusky bathers." The newspaper approvingly commented on their orderliness, for there were very few arrests and "the race weapon, the 'razor,' was conspicuously absent." In September 1897 the annual black excursion drew eleven carloads over the Pennsylvania Railroad and twenty-five over the Reading. Some travelers reportedly came from as far away as Maryland for the event. The 1898 convocation prompted the *Inquirer* to remark that there was "no more disorder than there would be were the gathering composed of an equal number of whites."[32]

Whether Atlantic City's hospitality to blacks warmed as the decade advanced is not clear from the limited evidence, but in 1897 there was a holiday during the regular season in mid-August for "the belles and beaux of the colored quarter" of Philadelphia. They chartered two gaily decorated streetcars with musicians aboard for a round-trip party over the length of Absecon Island. Another August excursion took place the following year, and on August 22, 1899, the Baptist National Colored Congress met at Atlantic City, where "Miss G. H. Hoggers, of Philadelphia, caused a sensation when she said that God knew his business when he made the negro black, and that he should not seek to get white by using cosmetics." Black excursionism continued into the twentieth century, as evidenced by a postcard dated from Atlantic City in August 1909: "Never saw so many of the Colored race on any train. 11 cars of them. 27 whites *only.*"[33]

Thus it appears that while blacks suffered under the traditional exploitations and disadvantages of racial prejudice at the resort, they nevertheless enjoyed certain opportunities to outflank white society. Racial barriers more rigidly enforced elsewhere were hard to preserve at the seaside, and sometimes they were largely relaxed. Moreover, blacks were able to achieve some political power, as we shall see later. [Editor's note: This is discussed in a later section of Funnell's book.]

At the very bottom of the heap of the resort's users was a group which contributed neither money nor labor, and therefore was not welcome. Atlantic City wanted a smiling face, for important reasons shortly to be discussed, and the presence of tramps disturbed the smile. There was a good deal of pathos in their situation: "Ten tramps, like a flock of sheep, being chased down the railroad track by officer Piner was an amusing sight witnessed by many this morning. As the summer season progresses these undesirable visitors make their appearance, stealing rides in freight cars."[34] The city's policy was to hustle tramps as quickly as apprehended over the drawbridge back to the mainland. Bums who applied to the city jail, however, were given overnight lodging. Perhaps this service was granted on the condition of their leaving town, though this is only conjecture. At any rate, in 1897 a total of 471 persons were admitted as "Lodgers," "Tramps," and "Bums" to the city jail.[35] The authorities had a habit of categorizing them: 229 were classified as "Americans," 129 as Irish, 38 as black, 36 as German, 4 as Jews, and 2 as English. The *Daily Union* complimented the Jews on their "excellent showing," "considering the large numbers in this city and the fact that many are constantly traveling . . . in their effort to earn their livelihood."[36] The resort had particular trouble with tramps during the severe depression beginning in 1893 (the worst to hit America until the Great Depression of the 1930s); in that year a detachment of Coxey's Army passed through town, to the great amusement of the employed.[37] This was a novel incident, but hoboes were a recurrent problem. In 1908 it was observed: "There are no beggars around to bother [the visitor]; they and the tramps are run out of town as soon as discovered."[38] By 1912 the Salvation Army had an "industrial home" in the resort, and the Volunteers of America had a lodging house for transients of both sexes.[39] Such was seaside life for those who tarnished the Gilded Age.

Between the extremes of the rich and the déclassé stood the lower middle and lower classes. Certainly these two groups were distinct from each other, but together they comprised the great mass of visitors to the resort. Evidence points to the numerical preponderance of the lower middle class, with the lower class coming in its wake and enjoying whatever its modest means would allow. In terms of numbers, the greater part of the accommodation industry was directed toward the lower middle class, while the values expressed in the resort's entertainment were those of citizens vigorously striving for the good life which they believed they could attain and which they imagined the upper middle class and rich to enjoy. It seems likely that upper-middle-class observers tended to lump the lower middle and lower classes together. A laborer in clean shirt with wife and family would be as acceptable and as "respectable" as a petty clerk and his family. So long as the lower-class visitor had money to spend, he might "pass" as lower middle class. From the visitor's viewpoint, the clerk in an insurance office certainly would not consider himself on a par with the hod carrier. Nevertheless, both belonged to the less-moneyed group of tourists, instead of the blue-ribbon trade which some promoters fancied Atlantic City should attract. The local upper middle class who ran the large businesses, edited the newspapers, and cranked out the publicity for the town viewed this great mass of visitors with mixed feelings. Though the hosts wanted their money and recognized that the resort depended on their patronage, they often wished their guests were someone else.

It is necessary to consider how the hotel industry fit into the needs of the lower middle class. It is obvious that the great hotels were beyond their range. The Traymore charged $3.00 to $5.00 a day, as did the Brighton. The United States Hotel and the Dennis demanded $3.00 to $3.50, while Haddon Hall had accommodations from $3.00 to $4.00. No shopgirl from Wanamaker's or ticket agent for the Pennsylvania Railroad was going to pay that much unless he [or she] was on a mad spree. On the other hand, a study of 225 of the principal hotels in 1887 shows that most of them charged far less.[40] The most common daily charge (73 hotels) was only $1.50 to $2.00 for room and board. On a weekly basis, the cost was lower. A total of 91 hotels offered weekly room and board for $8.00 to $12.00, this being the most common price range of the many schedules available. In 1890 clerical workers in steam railroads and manufacturing averaged $848 a year; thus $8.00 for a week's lodging and food would represent about half a week's salary. It seems reasonable to suppose that such hotels would be well within their range. Annual real wages for other kinds of workers included: $1,096 for government employees in the executive branch, $878 for postal employees, $794 for ministers, $687 for workers in gas and electricity, $439 for workers in manufacturing (nonclerical), and $256 for teachers.[41] Here the economic blurring of the classes emerges, however different their aspirations and working conditions might be. Schoolteachers simply could not afford hotel rates; a trolley-car driver might. But in the main, the lower middle class could meet the prices of the majority of hotels in Atlantic City, assuming that their stay represented a holiday for which they had saved.[42] Qualifications are in order. The larger the hotel, the more expensive it tended to be: with one exception, the eleven largest were above the $1.50–$2.50 range. They comprised 5 percent of the total number of hotels, yet had 23 percent of the total number of rooms. The 91 hotels which offered room and board for $8.00–$12.00 weekly comprised 40 percent of the total number of hotels, yet had only 25 percent of the total number of rooms. In other words, only about one fourth of the hotel space could be had at the cheapest rates. Yet these smaller houses were probably more consistently full. A newspaper clipping in a scrapbook compiled in 1885 indicates that at peak season only the big hotels had room available, whereas second-rate hotels and boardinghouses were crammed full.[43] Moreover, when demand exceeded supply, hotel men practiced "doubling up" in the rooms, a maneuver which could hardly have been used in the most expensive and prestigious houses.[44] Thus the smaller, cheaper hotels, though lacking in space, utilized their space more fully.

The principal bailiwick of the lower middle class was the boardinghouse, not the hotel. Unfortunately, their rates are not recorded, though they must have ranged from the price of the cheapest hotels down to a good deal lower. In return for lower rates, the boardinghouse offered relatively humdrum accommodations and food. One fastidious reporter for the *New York Times* was reduced to desperation in his search for a hotel room on a summer evening in 1883:

> I passed a large boarding-house with a crowd on the front porch and somebody banging a piano in the parlor. I was almost far enough gone to seek for shelter in a boarding-house, but not quite. Even in my desolate condition I pitied the dwellers in an Atlantic City boarding-house and passed on.[45]

Still, boardinghouses, though lacking the glamour of even a small hotel, made available to the lower middle class a means of extended vacationing; without them they could have afforded only daily excursions. Estimating the number of boardinghouses is difficult, since there was no legal obligation for a proprietor to call his hostel by the name of "boardinghouse" or "hotel." In addition, the nebulous term "cottage" was often favored, no doubt for its implication of class as well as its lack of clarity. *Gopsill's Directory*, the standard Atlantic City guide in this period, lists the "hotels, cottages, and boardinghouses" for each year. A fair estimate would place boardinghouses, in name or in fact, at about three-fifths the annual total:[46]

1882–83	311	1896	610
1884	349	1897	582
1885	362	1898	590
1886	382	1899	621
1887	443	1900	649
1888	506	1901	715
1889	506	1902	739
1890	522	1903	665
1891	570	1904	689
1892	541	1905	696
1893	512	1906	683
1894	552	1907	682
1895	600	1908	716[47]

The table shows that, measured by the number of establishments, the accommodation industry developed steadily in the 1880s, wobbled but developed in the 1890s, and leveled off after 1902. Apparently the hard times of the 1890s did not drive many boardinghouses and hotels out of business.[48] Nevertheless, prosperity was not identical with being open for business. The impact of depression on a mass resort is apparent in an *Inquirer* article of 1893:

> Nearly every branch of business has felt the depression. The small hotel-keepers, who run their houses largely on speculation from season to season, have the most to fear, and several of them are tottering in the balance. A few weeks of good business would put them on their feet again, and this is what all are praying for. The big houses, like the Windsor, Brighton and Dennis, which draw their patronage almost exclusively from the fashionable and moneyed elements of society, are doing well, because these elements of society will always flock to seaside resorts as long as the resorts last.[49]

When the economic fortunes of average Americans faltered, those of Atlantic City faltered as well. Widespread hard times inevitably touched the majority of resort businessmen, and if the town's few most prestigious services had a clientele with a reserve to fall back on, it could only make the general drought more irksome.

Atlantic City could not have existed without the railroads, and the railroads could not have existed without the lower middle and lower classes. During summer weekdays, lower-middle-class families and young single people poured into town on their annual vacations, and their fares sustained the railroads, which waited for weekends to make the big killing. Just like the resort, the railroads needed successful weekends for a profitable season. On twelve or thirteen weekends hinged the prosperity of the entire year, and in fact Sundays were most critical of all. The six-day workweek was the general practice in the nineteenth century; thus employees not on vacation had one day a week into which to cram their summer pleasure. The excellent rail service between Atlantic City and Philadelphia made a round trip in one day feasible, and the railroads recognized that they must encourage this mass patronage with low rates. The narrow-gauge Philadelphia and Atlantic City Railway was built for this purpose in 1877, offering fares that Hall claims went as low as fifty cents for a round trip. Travel to the resort increased swiftly: "The crowds in the city were so large at times, especially over Sunday, as to nearly exhaust the supply of meat, milk, bread and provisions in stock."[50] Generally, round-trip excursions cost $1.00 or $1.50, and in 1880 the fare was increased to $1.75. A protest meeting was organized in the resort, probably as a response to the threat the raise posed to the excursion trade.[51] The West Jersey and Atlantic Railroad, controlled by the Pennsylvania, was organized in 1880 specifically to attract "the medium and poorer classes." The fare was "the astonishing sum of fifty cents each—less than hack-fare from Market street Philadelphia, to the Park."[52] The expense of travel could be reduced still further from prevailing excursion rates by organizing charters, a popular practice. In 1880 Hillman and Mackey advertised themselves as sole agents soliciting group excursions on the Camden and Atlantic Railroad, and invited churches, fraternal organizations, and other interested assemblies to make early reservations for choice summer dates.[53] On the mass patronage of the ordinary tourists the railroads were able to maintain service which provided for upper-middle-class and upper-class visitors as well.

There are many random indications of the essentially lower-middle-class appeal of the resort, in addition to the evidence of lodgings and transportation. Excursion houses had a long history at the seaside. Built at the terminals of railroads entering the city, they provided a reception point, an entertainment pavilion, a dining hall, and an amusement park for the weekend crowds. The Seaview Excursion House aimed at the popular market, with "its broad piazzas, its numberless facilities for amusement, and its enormous dining-hall, which can be changed on occasion into a Jardin Mabille, with flowers and fountains."[54] The West Jersey Excursion House featured solid excursion-oriented food, like "fish, chicken, roast meats, vegetables, pies, pudding, ice cream, tea and coffee." It provided free music and dancing in the ballroom, a bar, a bowling alley, and a pool room, and bathing suits and lockers could be rented for twenty-five cents.[55] The Seaview announced that "the large and spacious Ball Room will be used for Roller Skating every evening except Wednesday," while the Ocean House had a "Billiard Room Attached."[56] Later, in 1911, the Hygeia Hotel promised the "Free use of shower bath," whence, apparently, its name. Its price range went as low as fifty cents, because it was on the "European plan," which meant that the visitor of modest means could bring his own food. Most amusements admitted customers at five cents or ten cents apiece, aiming at high-turnover, low-cost entertainment. Applegate's Pier let in baby carriages for free, with an eye to thrifty mothers.[57] Heinz Pier, which charged nothing for admission, featured an "art exhibit" of fine rugs, ceramics, figurines, and paintings. But the company sought to develop a mass market for its "57 Varieties" through samples and demonstrations. A souvenir postcard introduced the housewife to the mysteries of canned goods. "Four Ways of Serving Heinz's Baked Beans

With Tomato Sauce" included "The Usual Way" ("Place the can in boiling water for ten to fifteen minutes, then open and serve. *Especially desirable for luncheons*") and a fearsome recipe for "Bean Salad" ("Place portions of the contents of a can of Heinz's Baked Beans in individual salad dishes. Pour over each portion a tablespoonful of Heinz's Mustard Salad Dressing").[58] Endless details reveal the mass orientation of Atlantic City.

If Atlantic City was primarily a lower-middle-class resort, then the next question concerns the basic function it performed for its clientele. In simplest terms, the answer is: it was there to dispense pleasure. The thousands of different people who flocked to the city shared an extraordinary community of feeling which could not exist under normal urban conditions, because, unlike the conventional city, Atlantic City had a single purpose. The Boardwalk was a stage, upon which there was a temporary suspension of disbelief; behavior that was exaggerated, even ridiculous, in everyday life was expected at the resort. The rigidities of Victorian life relaxed, permitting contact between strangers and the pursuit of fantasies. The imprimatur of the absurd was upon Atlantic City. In later years it would be the scene of fantastic stunts which came to be expected in the merrily bizarre atmosphere of the place—aviation feats, a gigantic operating typewriter, a colossal marathon dance derby, the gaudy and grotesque Miss America Pageant. Examples from the 1890s include a balloon ascension and parachute drop, Pain Pyrotechnic Company's Battle of Manila at Inlet Park (together with the explosion of the *Maine* and a mammoth portrait of Admiral Dewey in fireworks), a female baseball club, and a challenge supper of "oysters and sugar, pure soap, watermelon and molasses" undertaken by three visitors who wagered that "the one who first became ill after eating certain dishes agreed upon by the trio should 'set up' a wine supper for the less distressed members of the party."[59] The town was a gargantuan masquerade, as visitor deceived visitor, and entrepreneurs fooled them all. And people wanted to be deceived, to see life as other than it was, to pretend that they were more than they were. America was starved, as today, for festivals. The culture was groping toward common bonds in an industrial world, bonds that could humanize and integrate urban life without reimposing the restrictions of the old village form of society. Atlantic City provided a location of common understanding, together with a diminution of customary restrictions. The fluidity it offered was the countervailing force to a culture too rigid, with expectations in excess of possibility.

Pleasure at the resort meant not only fluidity but also the illusion of social mobility. Whether such an illusion is a good thing depends on the philosophical inclination of the observer, whose attitude will be affected by the degree to which the actual mobility of the society approximates the illusion. No attempt will be made here to improve upon Stephan Thernstrom's analysis in *Poverty and Progress*, which maintains that America did provide its citizens with real mobility, but not in the rags-to-riches manner of the Horatio Alger novel. For present purposes, let it be noted that the crowds at Atlantic City very much liked the fantasy world which surrounded them, and that it was skillfully and ingeniously presented by men who shared their hopes for the realization of the fantasy.

One form of fluidity found at Atlantic City was increased contact between the sexes. It is not possible here strictly to separate actuality from illusion, but only to make some observations. Common sense suggests that meetings between males and females of like class, socially and economically, were far easier in a resort than in the outside world. Young men with prospects, money to spend, and the desire to meet girls would take their annual vacations there. Single girls could visit the resort in the company of girl friends, or with relatives or parents who might well be understanding, or even alone.[60] The excursions seem to have been gay parties from beginning to end. With the anonymity provided by a great transient city went a kind of prior legitimation of contact. No one went to Atlantic City for solitude, at least not in summer. So anyone who went there could expect to meet strangers, and could feel relatively assured in seeking introductions. This process was similar to today's computer dating, in which selection of mutually compatible couples is not the point. Rather, the computer, with its prestige in a science-worshipping society, provides a technological and therefore social ratification of the meeting of strangers with like motivation. Single people who went to Atlantic City could expect that other single people would have motives similar to theirs. This was a great breaker of barriers, and was of real benefit to the people involved.

Of course, not all mingling at the resort was of the approved sort, nor did the easygoing informality of seaside life always yield wholesome fruit. In July 1896, a local constable invaded a Kentucky Avenue hotel at one in the morning to arrest a couple who had registered as "Mr. and Mrs. C. R. Duff." "Sensational developments are expected at the hearing," the *Inquirer* duly informed its readers, for the adulterous pair were allegedly well known in Philadelphia. A detective, hired by an outraged husband, had shadowed them to discover who was plumbing "Mrs. Duff." Sometimes the temptation to exceed social proprieties proved compelling, as in the case of a young man who "implanted four osculatory bits upon the ruby lips of a woman whose acquaintance he did not enjoy." The judge before whom this scapegrace appeared rejected his defense that he was unable to restrain himself, and "decided that there was not sufficient provocation, though he admitted that the victim of the kisser was fair to gaze upon." He nailed the culprit for five dollars a kiss, and "would not consent to a discount on a lot of four, but insisted that the trespasser upon the dignity of woman should pay $20." "Dan and Mary," a couple from Chicago, found Atlantic City a bit too casual for the prosperity of their relationship:

> She accused Dan of having boldly flirted with others of her sex, to which the lover mildly protested. With the cunning that is prover-bial in the feminine world, Mary pretended that she believed Dan, and matters went along smoothly again. But the storm broke in all its fury yesterday, when Daniel, after having enjoyed a surf bath, during which he cast sheep's eyes at a fair female bather, returned to his bath house. Mary had seen his doings, and she was mad clear through, so she decided that in order to prevent a reoccurrence of such scenes she would treat her derelict lover to another bath. Straightway she procured a box of lye, which she poured into a bucket of water. Then, as Daniel hove in sight she prepared for the act of her life. When within a few feet . . . Mary took good aim and fired.

Dan was obliged to seek a quick rinse before repairing to a magistrate to have his sweetheart arrested. But at length he gallantly declined to press charges, and was reunited with his fiery mistress. Incidents such as these doubtless were exceptions to the happier rule of pleasant boy-girl encounters.[61]

As an aid to the mixing of the sexes, Applegate's Pier had a "Lover's Pavilion."[62] The *Daily Union* snickered at a Baltimore ordinance forbid-ding public kissing, imagining what a riot such a law would cause if enacted at the seaside.[63] Guvernator's Mammoth Pavilion had an inner sanctum, curtained off, which sold liquor to young people and was accordingly a popular place among them.

> A noteworthy feature was that many of these young people who were entertaining each other did not seem to be very well acquainted. Their speech and actions did not indicate such, any how [*sic*]. As an example may be cited the determined efforts of a rosy-cheeked lad of not more than eighteen years, surely, to discover the "real name" of the maiden who accompanied him.[64]

Beyond this, increased sexual contact existed on the level of illu-sion. This in itself could have concrete results, because expectations encouraged fulfillment. It is undeniable that the public believed Atlantic City to be a great mingler of the sexes. A postcard from the turn of the century shows two ladies in a rolling chair who have just run down a well-dressed young man. Flat on his back, he gallantly salutes them. "Just ran across an old friend on the Boardwalk," says the caption, but behind the weak humor is substance, the fantasy of women assuming the role of sexual aggressors.[65] A flowery bit of prose in John F. Hall's history extols the romantic milieu of the resort: "It must be borne in mind that the Goddess of Love is the divinity that presides at the seashore and the matches that are made within sight of the sea, while not as numerous as the sands on the beach, are of frequent occurrence."[66] Such attitudes were congruent with the official sanction given the family, and in a city that prided itself on being the Family Resort, it is not surprising that faith in the availability of marriage is frequently proclaimed.[67] This did not deny the element of chance, which made the game more exciting and poignant. Heston's handbook for 1888 shows a male hand clasping a female hand, and the legend: "The Autumn Break-Up—They May Never Meet Again."[68] But at least they had met the first time, and getting contacts for the long winter was probably the strategic objective of many Philadelphians.

In spite of the make-believe atmosphere along the Boardwalk, however, it was necessary to bear in mind the prudent considerations of the real world which resumed after vacation's end. An 1873 article mentioned "whole rows of unmatched girls" who waited by the shore for partners "equal to them in social position."[69] There was much latitude for deception here, the making of alliances that would end in bitter disillusionment. But when the Cinderella romance did come true, and in an honorable way, it was cause for celebration, a vindication of the capitalistic faith that the individual could transcend class. A story from the *Inquirer* in 1893 is straight out of Horatio Alger:

> A wedding will take place quietly at this resort tomorrow, which if all the details were known, would disclose one of the most romantic stories of the season. The bride is a young Philadelphia girl who is well-known among the employes of Wanamaker's, where she has held a position as saleswoman for several years past. She came down last week to spend her vacation at the shore, and during the gay round of pleasure she encountered a young Western man.
>
> The pair were strangely attracted to one another, and the upshot of the acquaintanceship will be tomorrow's ceremony. The bride-groom comes from Colorado, and is reputed to be the sion [sic] of one of the wealthiest families of the Centennial State.[70]

But even without romance, the feeling of being part of a great crowd with a common purpose was intrinsically pleasurable. A promotional pamphlet exalted "the crowd itself," in which each participant figures as does another wave in the sea.[71] A visitor mentioned how he liked to "bathe in people" at the resort.[72] It was a huge party, with everyone putting on his best face as befitted the situation. The sores of industrial living and working were hidden from view, just as the resort took care to railroad its bums out of town.

Since there was a heightened awareness of forms of behavior appropriate to a pleasure city, fads arose which the masses seized upon. They conferred a feeling of belonging, a "society" of those outside society. Fads also testified to the loneliness that was a part of city living, for a fad is an artificial attempt, inherently frantic, to create or to heighten identity where insufficient identity is felt. Fads in Atlantic City took such diverse forms as the use of certain words, the wearing of particular objects and items of clothing, interest in what is *au courant*, and even the adoption of certain roles.

> Talking of love and pretty girls, we do not have any more flirtations, they are called "mashes"—"don't you forget it." This is the day of slang phrases; at cards you are told that "you can't sometimes most always generally tell how things will turn out"; as for the bathing "it is just too awfully nice for anything."[73]

The *Inquirer* warned its readers in July 1896 to avoid being judged "not in it" by laying in a supply of comic lapel buttons. Messages in use on the Boardwalk included: "If you love me, grin"; "I am somewhat of a liar myself, and there are others"; "I am mamma's darling, whose darling are you?"; and the succinct "Yes, darling." The young man could wear one proclaiming, "Give me your hand," to which the "summer girl" could respond with another which said, "I will be a sister to you."

In 1897, someone discovered that a burning incense taper carried in the coiffure would discourage Jersey's saber-toothed mosquitoes, and this practical innovation quickly became an item of fashion. As crowds of women strolled the Boardwalk by night, the effect was "quite startling, resembling somewhat the firefly." Vacationers also liked to have friends autograph their cigarettes as keepsakes, and white duck sailor hats were similarly used, the object being the hieroglyphic effect attained by great numbers of signatures. For a brief time, daring young men wore a single silk garter made of flashy ribbon with a silver buckle as they paraded the beach. Young women were fond of attracting attention by performing athletic exercises on the sand, such enthusiasts being generally of generous endowments and often of economical inclinations in the use of yard goods for bathing costumes.[74]

At the century's end, "Hello, My Baby" was so popular that this "mongrel ballad" could scarcely be escaped along the waterfront, while the "latest dude dress" was reported to be a white jersey shirt worn "Chinaman style outside of the pantaloons." Men were advised to turn up the cuffs of their white flannel trousers if they wished to be in style. Palmistry was in favor, especially among the ladies, who queued up to consult various "professors," "gypsy queens," and other savants "just arrived from Paris." The palmists had "all sorts of queer-sounding cognomens, some of which are regular jaw-breakers," and were attired in "some fantastic costume" to impress "the fair patron with the weight of their marvelous powers." Previously, phrenology had been the "summer girl's" pet interest, and her aspiring gallant might be cruelly diverted from "a conversation of particular personal interest" with "How's the development of your bump of amativeness?"[75]

Ladies' bathing suits became more abbreviated and more colorful as the end of the century approached. Part of the reason was the increasing number of women learning to swim (who appreciated not having to drag pounds of spare cloth through the water) and part the growing hedonism of American society. "Time was," said the *Inquirer*, "when women went into the water with long, baggy trousers down to their heels, while over these hideous garments hung flannel skirts. But that was in the old days before the world began moving at the pace it seems to be going at now." Women were eager to keep up with bathing-suit fashions, and the typical costume of 1898 "would scarcely fill the much talked of collar box." The more daring abandoned stockings and began to abbreviate their skirts. Bicycle clothing influenced bathing-suit design toward trimness, much to the delight of male "kodak fiends." A new female type emerged, "the bicycle girl, mayhap astride a man's wheel, scorching up and down the strand, with her golden hair hanging down her back and robed in a natty bathing suit, the colors of which outrival the noise of the bell, with her jaws going at a rapid pace because of the wad of tutti-frutti she has hidden within." Novelty was possible in street wear, too. For the Fourth of July 1896, one enterprising young lady "combined patriotism and style" by wearing a shirtwaist fashioned from a silken American flag, with a body of blue studded with stars and sleeves of red and white stripes.[76]

A more esoteric fad, the "widow craze," struck Atlantic City in 1893. The widow possessed a mystique of "experience" which the maiden never enjoyed, an earthly wisdom made respectable by the hand of God. The black clothing, drab in color but not necessarily in design, was an immediate attention getter, and widows were allegedly in demand. Their avowed bereavement recommended itself to the solicitations of gallant strangers. An attractive blond widow was to be seen every afternoon at a certain time on the merry-go-round, dressed in the "most exquisite style."[77]

The "summer girl" has joined the great auk in extinction, but she was once a prevalent shorebird. She deserves to be considered more as a role than a fad, perhaps, for she reappeared with each fin de siècle summer to bewitch male vacationists. "At a distance you would take this creature for an angel and no mistake, for she seems the personification of modesty and grace. Nudge up a little closer—if you can—and alas, you will observe that she has that naughty little twinkle in her eye." With her "coquettish commingling of sea shore freedom, natural feminine vanity and womanly longing for admiration," she was a sentimental favorite of journalists. But the efforts of young ladies to act the summer girl could make for amusement, too.

> A sensation . . . was furnished on Tuesday by three very pretty, stylish and modest young ladies who went into the water wearing, for the first time, suits that had been made especially for them, cut from thin white flannel. They didn't know, poor things, the terrible shrinking power of salt water, or they would not have gone in . . . They had not been in the water five minutes till a group of horrid men had assembled directly in front of where they were bathing. One of the girls, wonderingly, made a survey, and the result horrified her. The three of them were living pictures of "Venus Rising from the Sea." The white flannel was clinging with a tenacity worthy of a far better cause, and the black stockings showed through the material as though it was tissue paper, and indeed it was not much better. Being nice, modest girls they made a break at once for the bath house, but on their way thither ran a gauntlet far more awful than any ever encountered by Fenimore Cooper's Indian fighters.

Fashionable yet unspoiled, alluring yet virginal, surrounded by imploring suitors whom she coyly evaded, the summer girl was the archetype of female desirability. She was altogether too delicate a flower for the twentieth century.[78]

New York City might have its Four Hundred, but Atlantic City had its Forty Thousand. Anyone could join who had an aptitude for vogue and a fancy to belong to an "elite." In the confined area of the resort—and along its nerve track, the Boardwalk—fads could spread quickly. They occupied the evanescent middle range of repetitive behavior, halfway between the gesture too private to be stylish and the cliché too well known to be distinctive. In a normal city, fads applied to sections of the population, whereas Atlantic City was one great show on a city scale, and everyone was potentially in on the act.[79]

Imitation of the upper class was a primary component of the symbolic mobility which the resort afforded its lower-middle-class users. The many pseudo-sophisticated portraits of the city offered in promotional materials were designed to impart a patrician glamour to a plebeian spa, and far from substantiating the prestige of the place, they prove just the opposite. Atlantic City was low-flung, but it palmed itself off in high-toned terms. The promoters had a good ear for what appealed to their audience, and they were not wanting in boldness. Dr. Boardman Reed, a vigorous booster, composed a brochure for the Pennsylvania Railroad which touted the advantages of his home town as a health resort relative to Florida, the western states, and Europe, but these places were noncompetitive with Atlantic City for 95 percent of its customers.[80] The object could only have been to gild the Jersey coast with glamour rubbed off more remote utopias. Similarly, the imposingly titled "Academy of Music" presented lowbrow fare like comic opera and "Professor Bartholomew's Trained Horses."[81] Overstuffed names like these were usual throughout the town. Many called the fifth boardwalk, completed in 1896, the "Esplanade." But the events of 1898 generated a rumor that this elegant title had a Spanish origin, obliging the embarrassed Esplanadists to retreat hurriedly to the more humble "Boardwalk" to avoid "anything that savors of the Dons."[82]

Probably the most baroque and certainly the most long-lived ersatz phenomenon was the Boardwalk rolling chair.[83] It began as an aid for invalids, but one entrepreneur realized its wider potential. He started renting a fleet of them with attendants, and they rapidly caught on. They were floridly designed along the lines of Brown Decades' aesthetics, with swan-necked prows and heart-shaped dips in the backrests. Thickly padded with comfortable cushions and equipped with robes, they offered to the most proletarian customer willing to spend some change an American version of the sedan chair, the classic attribute of effete aristocracy. The chair pusher was probably the only servant most visitors ever had. Rolling chairs were popular subjects on postcards—just the thing to impress people back home. They were the epitome of nouveau bourgeois.

> Afterward, well wrapped up, a ride in a rolling chair is within the range of possibility, and when one has been wheeled for a stretch along the Boardwalk, dined at the celebrated tables for which our hotels are noted and afterward listened to a high-class concert, he or she is ready to smile a welcome to the sandman.[84]

One of the most important devices by which the lower-middle-class visitor created the illusion of having a higher-class status was clothing; for when nobody knew anybody else, clothes assumed an exaggerated importance in attributing status. Victorian styles allowed rather more yardage for creating effect than today's taste recommends.

The Piers at Atlantic City are the happy hunting grounds for those of the fair sex who love to see beautiful gowns or to display stunning ones in their own wardrobe. Saturday and Sunday nights the crowd is thickest . . .

[One] simple but vastly pretty gown [recently seen] was white organdy made over grape-colored silk. The yoke, which extended over the sleeve top, was of pleats and grape velvet ribbon . . . alternately arranged in groups, edged with a quilling of organdy, velvet bordered. The sleeves were mousquetaire, with a ruche at the wrist, and the waist itself repeated the perpendicular lines of the yoke, but at greater intervals.

The belt and stock were very deep violet satin ribbon and a big bow nestled at the left corner of the yoke. The skirt had a ruching laid in points, which was edged top and bottom with velvet, and above it following the same outline were three rows of the same ribbon. Ruche and ribbon rows were repeated at the foot of the circular flounce. Stunning little gown it was even if not specially original.[85]

Dress standards were high at Atlantic City, both in contemporary terms and even more so from the perspective of the melancholic informality of the present Age of Denim. Gowns, bonnets, and parasols for the ladies and suits, cravats, and skimmer hats for the men were in order for beach strolls. Victorian decorum prevailed right up to mean high-water mark.

While fancy clothing was usual throughout the season, on one particular occasion there was an immense resortwide competition to be the best-dressed. This was Atlantic City's Easter Parade, copied from the older event on New York's Fifth Avenue.[86] Like the Miss America Pageant at a later date, the Easter Parade was a ploy of local businessmen to pull in shekels outside the normal holiday season. The mild weather of springtime allowed promenading, even if the ocean was too brisk for swimming, and the event was highly popular. One weekend near the turn of the century, for example, allegedly drew nearly forty thousand passengers over the railroads.[87] The Boardwalk each year was jammed rail to rail by a crowd dressed in springtime finery. An army of the nouveaux bourgeois, like the fevered vision of a megalomaniac haberdasher, marched in review past equally well-dressed spectators. This was the white society which found cakewalks so amusing. Yet in its turn it performed a ceremony that to the unanthropological eye was every bit as ridiculous. It was a mass imitation of the upper class, an awkward assumption of the externals of elegance, and as such a parody of itself and its model.

Atlantic City was for sale. High society might be for sale too, in the long run, but it erected barriers against the too easy assault of wealth upon its ranks. A mellowing process was employed, to give time for the aura of the stockyard or the dime store or the roundhouse to dim a bit. New families seeking admission on the basis of wealth and power passed through a generational apprenticeship which allowed sons or grandsons into the ranks of the patriciate, but excluded the patriarch who had done the dirty work. Edward D. Baltzell in *Philadelphia Gentlemen* describes how this worked.[88] But Atlantic City sold its wares cash-on-delivery, and the pocketbook was its only coat of arms.[89] There was a limit to illusion, which the town never forgot: at the end of every fantasy was a hand poised over a cash register. An emphasis on buying and selling pervaded the resort and typified it throughout its history, producing an unabashedly vigorous commercial atmosphere. Every inch of the Boardwalk was engineered to tickle silver out of the jingling pockets of the throng. When the city of Chicago investigated the resort's water-recreation facilities in 1913 and compared them with its own, it was pleased to see that the difference was favorable to the boys in Cook County.[90] It was noted that maximum profit, not convenience and service to the public, was the overriding purpose of the Jersey resort. Searching for upper-class trappings, Atlantic City inaugurated an annual horse show in 1899, prompting editor Hall to express equal enthusiasm for the horseflesh and the profits of the display.[91] A visitor was disgusted when St. Nicholas' Church charged admission to its dedication, "in common with everything else" at the resort,[92] and an *Inquirer* article remarked how the city's businessmen "pile it on" in their systematic extortions.[93] That was a secret of Atlantic City. Though particular charges tended to be small, the methodical way in which everything had its fee led to cumulative effects unhappy for the visitor. The steady trickle of nickels and dimes was the making of fortunes and the undoing of personal budgets as well.

The principal shearing of sheep took place in the scores upon scores of small stores which abutted the Boardwalk on the land side. So long as the stroller was not looking at the ocean, he was looking at something for sale. These petty shops contrasted curiously with the pompous hotels, for they were lower in tone, a kind of lower-middle-class commercial foothills to the great structures behind them. They also moved huge quantities of goods to lower-middle-class customers who could not afford the swank hostelries. But, like the hotels, they encouraged a parallel impulse to consume, to revel in the first full flush of prosperity which urbanization and industrialization were bringing to the common people. The great hotels beyond the foothills would be conquered someday; today the masses could buy from the shops for a taste of high life. It was good stage setting. It encouraged the lower middle class to continue to struggle for utopia by way of materialism, in which it had unshakable faith. It peddled rhinestones by the curb, and held the diamonds a bit further off.

And the things that were sold! Racy postcards, "Genuine Japanese corylopsis talcum," tinsel brooches, agate ornaments, "lurid Naples landscapes on pearl shells," coral, Japanese fern seeds, "Indian" moccasins, Kewpie dolls, Swiss woodcarving, photographs bedizened with gold lacquer, and a heroic device to cut apples open in the shape of a water lily. The visitor could buy an improving tintype to grace his mantel back home ("A stalwart maiden . . . in a boat which stood on end, pulling through the surf with an oar, and dragging a drowning man . . . into the boat with her free hand. The legend was 'Saved'"). Or he could have a glass of "pure orange juice" from a big machine which consumed huge piles of ripe fruit before his eyes ("These machines in several instances are mere dummies, and the great stock of oranges that appear to be passing through the fake crusher is the same old pile that was doing business early in July"). Then there were deviled crabs, lemonade, soda pop, tutti-frutti, Gilt Edge Beer, Fralinger's Salt Water Taffy, Gage's Ice Cream, Zeno Chewing Gum, George Smith's Cream Java Coffee, and innumerable other syrups, jellies, doughs, liquids, and solids to lick, chew, munch, gulp, and swill.[94]

Confronted with so much wonderful junk so relentlessly proffered, visitors engaged happily in recreational buying, as dozens of desires not previously known to exist suddenly sprang into being and demanded fulfillment. All of life seemed to be for sale. Buying itself as a sort of pleasure was institutionalized for good and all in American culture. So far from being simply a convenience for the crowds, selling became a chief entertainment, engaging the passions more deeply and consistently than the ocean ever could. Recreational buying was a new phenomenon at the time. Whereas today it is an obvious element in the success of the suburban shopping center, through which it has become a principal locus of community, in Victorian America it was a novelty that the beneficiaries—the merchants—discovered slowly. The Boardwalk stores at first sold souvenirs and refreshments, and only later extended their wares as they discovered what the crowds wanted. But the entrepreneurs of the resort rose to the occasion handsomely, learning to speak a materialistic language the masses understood. Washington & Arlington's

New Unlimited Monster Shows shrewdly tacked on its bill of fare a note pointing out its "steam organ, costing [$]10,000." "Munkacsy's Christ Before Pilate" ("The young woman who recites a little piece and tells all about the picture, explains what is not on the bills, that the picture is 'after' Munkacsy") was touted as "the $100,000 painting." Roving Frank's Gypsies promised that the traditional service of palm reading would be done by "All New Gypsies," a message which belied the spirit of clairvoyance as completely as it fingered the pulse of the times.[95]

The merchants, promoters, and hotelkeepers themselves could only be impressed by the success which had descended on the town. Like their customers, they were a bit overwhelmed by the place, and, as though rubbing their eyes to make sure it was all real, they liked to reassure themselves with endless recounting of the growth in profits and numbers of visitors. They had many anxieties, for their welfare depended on factors that were either partially or totally out of their control: the press of Philadelphia, the laws of New Jersey, public taste, weather, the character of the resort, competition among themselves, and so forth. They had always predicted success for Atlantic City, and yet, now that it was here, was not a certain alchemy involved? Hence they searched for unique factors that would explain their city's fortune, that would imply permanence and eliminate the alchemy of success. The world of things for sale which so appealed to their customers appealed also to themselves. One could sell the goodness of life, and one could buy it—or so it seemed. And if this was true, then the goodness of life had descended upon both merchant and customer along the Boardwalk. Since happiness could be approached by measurable units, the businessmen of Atlantic City were measurers by nature. The Victorians were no Puritans. It was not for them to hasten through this vale of sorrow; they had made it a valley of opportunity. It was necessary now only to remind oneself that opportunity had no sorrows.

[Editor's note: The section of this chapter on entrepreneurs and vaudeville that appeared in the first edition of this Anthology has been deleted from this edition.]

◆ ◆ ◆ ◆ ◆ ◆

Atlantic City's role in presenting the illusion of social mobility must be seen in light of the class sensitivity evident in resort literature. The attention to class among resort commentators emphasizes the fundamentally lower-middle-class character of the town, and not only expresses satisfaction at the harmonizing potential of American society but also displays class antagonisms at variance with the supposed harmony. The history of the great plebeian resort demonstrates why it is possible to see turn-of-the-century America as either the Gilded Age or the Brown Decades, depending on the surface from which the light is reflected

Notes

1. *Atlantic City By the Sea* (Philadelphia, 1889), 7.

2. Thomas M. Dale speech at the Bourse, "Atlantic City in the Twentieth Century" (Philadelphia, 1897).

3. John F. Hall, *The Daily Union History of Atlantic City and County, New Jersey* (Atlantic City, 1900), 231.

4. John Steevens [sic], "The Charm of Eastertide at Atlantic City," *Harper's Weekly*, April 18, 1908, 20. Hereafter referred to as "Eastertide."

5. *Atlantic City Daily Union* (hereafter *ACDU*,) July 16, 21, 26, 28, 1890; December 1, 8, 15, 22, 29, 1890; February 22, 1892; June 3, July 24, 1893; July 2, 16, 23, 1894; December 3, 10, 17, 31, 1894; July 23, 1895; July 20, 23–25, 1900; August 6, 7, 1900. Hereafter referred to as *ACDU* Society Listings.

6. *Social Register, Philadelphia*, 1893, VII, 3 (New York: Social Register Association, November 1893); ibid., 1894, VIII, 2 (New York: Social Register Association, November 1893); *ibid.*, 1900, XIV, 3 (New York: Social Register Association, November 1899). The *Social Registers* for 1890–92 were not available to me, but the use of the 1893 volume (published in November 1892) probably makes little or no difference. It seems unlikely that the number of individuals listed in the *Social Register* in 1890, but not listed three years later, would be very large. Moreover, the *Social Register* had the habit of listing recently deceased members of society, so the loss of names by death would be further reduced.

7. "Society by the Seaside," *Philadelphia Inquirer* (hereafter *PI*), July 17, 1892, 12; "Society at the Seaside," *PI*, July 24, 1892, 12; "Society," *PI*, July 31, 1892, 12; "Summer Resorts," *PI*, July 22, 1894, 9; "Beside the Bounding Billows," *PI*, July 14, 1901, Summer Resort Section, 4; "Beach Costumes of Fair Bathers" and "The Social Whirl," *PI*, July 21, 1901, sec.2, 11.

8. *Social Register*, Philadelphia, 1893; *Social Register*, Philadelphia, 1894; *Social Register*, Philadelphia, 1901, XV (New York: Social Register Association, November 1900).

9. "Beside the Bounding Billows," *PI*, July 14, 1901, Summer Resort Section, 4.

10. *Social Register, Summer 1900*, XIV, 19 (New York: Social Register Association, 1900).

11. *ACDU* Society Listings.

12. Ibid.

13. Frank W. O'Malley, "The Board-Walkers: Ten Days with Bertha at Atlantic City," *Everybody's Magazine*, August 1908, 233.

14. "Atlantic City," *PI*, August 5, 1894, 9.

15. "The New Baedeker: Casual Notes of an Irresponsible Traveller," *The Bookman* 30 (September 1901): 46.

16. Editorial, *ACDU*, January 28, 1892, 4.

17. Alfred M. Heston, *Illustrated Hand-Book of Atlantic City, New Jersey* (Philadelphia, 1887), 73–74.

18. "Summer Resorts," *PI*, July 22, 1894, 9.

19. Hall, *Daily Union History*, 227–31.

20. *Summer Sketches of the City by the Sea: Atlantic City for Season* (Camden and Atlantic Railroad, 1883), 15–19. Hereafter *Summer Sketches.*.

21. "A Rush to the Seashore," *ACDU*, June 26, 1893, p. 1.

22. They did form a Cottagers' Association in 1889, primarily to protest the routing of train tracks through the city and to seek lower commutation rates to Philadelphia. The organization seems to have withered away after two years.

23. Trenton, New Jersey State Library, Archives and History Bureau, "New Jersey State Census, 1905. Atlantic City."

24. "Down by the Sea Shore—Atlantic City," *PI*, July 23, 1893, 10.

25. Ibid.

26. *ACDU*, July 23, 1900, 1.

27. "Some Curious Scenes Depicted on Beach at Gay Atlantic City," *PI*, July 28, 1900, 3.

28. *ACDU*, August 8, 1891, 1.

29. Little evidence has emerged of how such restrictions were enforced. It seems most probable that the white community had a fair consensus on how the blacks should be treated, and that a reproving word from a hostler, waiter, or passing citizen sufficed to enlighten black offenders of the code. Moreover, a black who sought his pleasures where he was not wanted had to calculate that appeal might be made to his employer by an angry white. Atlantic City must have had certain aspects of a "company town," since the single-purpose economy precluded most alternative kinds of employment. On the other hand, there were many employers, preventing the monopoly which made the disciplinary potential of the company town so oppressive.

30. *ACDU*, September 3, 1891, 1.

31. In one of Alfred Heston's scrapbooks is an undated clipping from a Bucks County (Pennsylvania) newspaper which, from internal evidence, must have appeared about 1904. It records: "Yesterday over 6,000 negroes were here to enjoy the annual colored excursion of the first Thursday in September." Heston, "Reminiscences of Absecon and Atlantic City" (1914), Local History Collection, Atlantic City Public Library.

32. "The City by the Sea, *PI*, September 6, 1896, 21; "Colored People Invade Atlantic," *PI*, September 2, 1897, 12; "Atlantic City," *PI*, September 4, 1898, 15.

33. "In the Merry Throng Down by the Sea," *PI*, August 18, 1897, 12; "Discussed Race Problem," *PI*, August 23, 1899, 5; New Brunswick, New Jersey, Rutgers University Library, New Jersey Collection, postcard file.

34. "Itinerant Visitors Warned," *ACDU*, June 21, 1893, 1.

35. "City Jail Records," *ACDU*, January 29, 1897, 1.

36. *ACDU*, June 23, 1893, 4.

37. "At the Seaside—Atlantic City," *PI*, August 12, 1894, 9.

38. O'Malley, "Board-Walkers," p. 238.

39. Margaret L. Brett, "Atlantic City: A Study in Black and White," *Survey* 27 (September 7, 1912): 725–726.

40. Heston, *Illustrated Hand-Book* (1887), 131–134.

41. Paul L. Douglas, *Real Wages in the United States, 1890–1926* (Boston: Houghton Mifflin, 1930), table following 392.

42. Comments one newspaper: "The grand hotels serve the wealthy, but the moderate ones give entertainment to thousands." Newspaper clipping from unidentified Bucks County (Pennsylvania) newspaper, ca. 1904, in Heston, "Reminiscences of Absecon."

43. *Summer Sketches*.

44. "Greatest and Best—Our Island City," *ACDU*, July 4, 1891, 1.

45. "A Sunday Sea-Side Resort," *New York Times*, August 14, 1883, 3.

46. In 1887, for example, Heston's handbook lists 212 "hotels," while *Gopsill's Directory* lists 443 "hotels, cottages, and boardinghouses." It is a safe bet that Heston did not omit anything worthy of the name "hotel." In fact he included many establishments with a dozen rooms or less. Thus, 47 percent (212/443) should certainly be reduced to obtain a rough estimate of the proportion of hotels to the total number of lodging places.

47. All figures in this table except that for 1884 were compiled from *Gopsill's Atlantic City Directory for 1882–1883* (Philadelphia, 1882) and *Gopsill's Atlantic City Directory* (Philadelphia, volumes for 1885–1908). The figure for 1884 was compiled from *Holdzkom and Company's Atlantic City Cottage and Business Directory for 1884* (Atlantic City, 1884).

48. It is possible that some might be induced to open a boardinghouse when depression struck. If, for example, an Atlantic Avenue merchant saw his trade dry up, his wife might decide to start a boardinghouse in their home, since even marginal profit was better than none.

49. "At the Summer Resorts—Atlantic City," *PI*, July 16, 1893, 10.

50. Hall, *Daily Union History*, 197.

51. Obviously, the excursion trade did not appeal equally to all business interests in the resort. Broadly speaking, there were two major economic camps in Atlantic City who were potential rivals. The first consisted of the proprietors of the large and prestigious hotels, other businessmen catering to upper-middle-class patronage, local professional and religious leaders, and citizens not directly dependent on a mass-resort economy. The second included small hotel and boardinghouse keepers, and amusement operators. On the fringes of the second group were businessmen of varying respectability and legality, such as Boardwalk hawkers, small-time entertainers like sand "sculptors," operators of unlicensed saloons and Sunday-closing violators, gamblers, brothel proprietors, and so forth. Conflict between the economic camps figures prominently in chapter 5, "Babylonian Days" [Funnell, *By the Beautiful Sea*], over the issue of Sunday liquor selling. Naturally,

the excursion crowd was of nil (or even negative) interest to the high-class resort businessmen, even if it was the lifeblood of the others.

52. A. L. English, *History of Atlantic City, New Jersey* (Philadelphia, 1884), 154.

53. *Summer Sketches.*

54. "A New Atlantis," *Lippincott's Magazine*, June 1873, 620.

55. *Summer Sketches.*

56. English, *History of Atlantic City*, 223.

57. Heston, *Illustrated Hand-Book* (1887), 15.

58. Postcard, author's collection; trade card, author's collection.

59. "Visitors of a Day at Atlantic City," *PI*, August 12, 1898, 2; "Atlantic City," *PI*, August 21, 1898, 15; "Rain Swept the Long Boardwalk," *PI*, August 24, 1897, 5; "With the Merry Throng at the Seaside Resorts," *PI*, August 10, 1899, 5.

60. Theodore Dreiser superbly describes the pleasures of newly found social opportunity in *Sister Carrie*, when Carrie meets Drouet on the train to Chicago.

61. "A Sunday Stroll at Atlantic," *PI*, July 13, 1896, 7; "Review of the Passing Show at Atlantic City and Cape May," *PI*, August 2, 1899, 6; "Atlantic City's Merry Throng of Seekers After Pleasure," *PI*, August 1, 1899, 14.

62. Heston, *Illustrated Hand-Book* (1887), 54.

63. *ACDU*, June 28, 1893, 4.

64. "At Atlantic City: The Evening Bulletin's' Exposure Bears Good Fruit," *Philadelphia Bulletin*, August 12, 1890, 1.

65. Atlantic City, Public Library, Local History Collection, scrapbook of postcards. Hereafter referred to as Atlantic City Postcards.

66. Hall, *Daily Union History*, 252.

67. Yet Atlantic City, by providing the opportunity for illicit sex, could be a threat to family values. The shopgirl's dream lover might turn out to be a rake, the shopgirl might discover a bit of the tart in her own soul, or the upstanding young man might avail himself of a lady of easy virtue. But it is possible that, on a higher level, illicit sex helped the family to survive.

68. Alfred M. Heston, *Illustrated Hand-Book of Atlantic City, New Jersey* (Atlatnic City, 1888), 68.

69. "A New Atlantis," 615.

70. "Atlantic City Romance," *PI*, August 23, 1893, 5.

71. *Cape May to Atlantic City: A Summer Note Book* (n.p.: Passenger Department, Pennsylvania Railroad Company, 1883), 39.

72. "The Spectator," *Outlook* 104 (July 26, 1913): 719.

73. *Summer Sketches*; "Atlantic City," *PI*, July 19, 1896, 18.

74. "Gay Atlantic," *PI*, August 8, 1897, 20; "The City by the Sea," *PI*, August 23, 1896, 18.

75. "Atlantic City," *PI*, August 6, 1899, sec. 3, 1; Atlantic City, Public Library, Local History

Collection, loose newspapers in folders, *Atlantic Journal*, July 30, 1890, 1; "Atlantic City," *PI*, July 22, 1900, sec. 2, 8; "Atlantic City," *PI*, July 12, 1896, 18.

76. "Atlantic City," *PI*, August 14, 1898, 15; "Atlantic City Sands," *PI*, August 15, 1897, 20; "The City by the Sea," *PI*, July 5, 1896, 18.

77. "At the Summer Resorts—Atlantic City," *PI*, July 2, 1893, 10.

78. "Belles of the Beach at Gay Atlantic," *PI*, July 22, 1900, Half-Tone Supplement, 1; "Atlantic City," *PI*, July 28, 1895, 14.

79. Fads not only are an attempt to create community, they are also (as a corollary) the expression of a felt lack of community. The feverish pleasures of Atlantic City bespeak not only what the culture could deliver—for a price—to its members, but also what it withheld from them.

80. Reprinted in English, *History of Atlantic City*, 183–194.

81. "Don't Be Slow: A Great Rush for the Academy's Opening Bill," *ACDU*, June 22, 1893, 1; William McMahon, *So Young...So Gay* (Atlantic City, 1870, 43–44).

82. "Atlantic City," *PI*, July 10, 1898, 13.

83. Somers Point, New Jersey, Atlantic County Historical Society, Silas R. Morse Scrapbook, 1840–1928.

84. Hall, *Daily Union History*, 237.

85. "Some Gowns Seen at Atlantic City," *PI*, September 3, 1899, Half-Tone Supplement, 7.

86. Steevens [*sic*], "Eastertide," 22.

87. Hall, *Daily Union History*, 247–249.

88. Edward D. Baltzell, *Philadelphia Gentlemen: The Making of a National Upper Class* (Glencoe, Ill.: Free Press, 1958).

89. In 1922, a visiting New Zealand woman exclaimed: "Dollars is the password here. You can have what you want if you are prepared to pay for it. Not so at Newport, where the amazing mansions of New York's Four Hundred are like a battlement along the cliff, warning off intruders." Nellie M. Scalon, "American Cities As Seen by a New Zealand Woman," *New York Times*, October 29, 1922, sec. 8, 2.

90. Special Park Commission, *Report of Investigation of Bathing Beaches* (n.p.: Chicago City Council, 1913).

91. Hall, *Daily Union History*, 243.

92. *Summer Sketches.*

93. "Down by the Sea Shore—Atlantic City," *PI*, July 30, 1893, 9.

94. "The Spectator," 718–719; Charles Dudley Warner, "Their Pilgrimage," *Harper's New Monthly Magazine* 72 (April 1886): 682; "Acid in the Juice," *PI*, September 2, 1899, 3.

95. Helen C. Bennett, "Come On In—The Water's Fine!" *American Magazine*, August 1926, 45, 144; *ACDU*, August 21, 1890, 4; "Atlantic City's Foul Blots," *PI*, August 4, 1895, Sunday Supplement, 21–22; *ACDU*, August 29, 1900, 4.

Raised and educated in New Jersey, Mahlon Pitney (1858–1924) served on the United States Supreme Court from 1912 to 1922. A champion of workmen's compensation laws but unfriendly to unions, he stood firmly in the mainstream of the Progressive movement. Photograph by Harris & Ewing, Collection of the Supreme Court of the United States.

11

Progressivism is a generic term American historians apply to the efforts of social reformers around the turn of the last century, but they differ on how precisely to define and use the word. Frustrated by the issue, Peter Filene concluded in 1970 that the term should be discarded. Progressives were a diverse group with different goals and values. Together, Filene observed, they displayed "a puzzling and irreducible incoherence." In contrast, Richard L. McCormick and Arthur S. Link in *Progressivism* (1983) willingly incorporated numerous reformers with varying philosophies and agendas under the term. In the article that follows, Michal Belknap argues that United States Supreme Court Justice Mahlon Pitney from New Jersey, whom previous authors had cast as a reactionary "capitalist tool," was in fact a Progressive.

Who were the Progressives? How did they differ from other reformers and from those whose practices they sought to reform? Was there a definable Progressive program or set of objectives? What did these reformers expect to accomplish, and how successful were they? What does Pitney's career show about Progressivism in the nation as a whole and in New Jersey specifically?

In *The Age of Reform* (1955), Richard Hofstadter argued that the Progressives were middle-class "victims of an upheaval in status" whose "deference and power" were challenged by the rise of big business and organized labor. Progressive reforms, he argued, in effect lashed out at opponents on both ends of the economic spectrum, at least in part to maintain the group's position in society. Numerous historians have attacked Hofstatder's premise. Based on profiles of Progressives and of their opponents, David Thelen concluded that there was no appreciable difference in class, occupation, or the tension each experienced from social change. Instead of being a movement restricted to urban middle-class professionals, historians have discovered rural, working-class, and immigrant support for Progressivism. As a middle-class lawyer from an old-stock New Jersey family, Pitney may have fit the old profile of a Progressive, but others with identical credentials were not reformers while some from very different backgrounds were.

Why did Pitney and others become Progressives? A number of developments at the end of the nineteenth century seem to have triggered their reaction. First, the social gospel theology of various religious groups heightened interest in social justice. This "new theology" included a concern for the general welfare and emphasized an active involvement in the community. Second, the depression that began in 1893 led many to conclude that new programs were necessary. Third, "muckraking" journalists had revealed widespread economic and political corruption. Progressives may have felt that preventive medicine was necessary; the way to avoid the spread of socialism and other radical movements was to temper the capitalist system. How did Pitney's support for Progressive measures emerge? What was there about New Jersey politics at the end of the nineteenth century that led men like him to conclude that reforms were necessary? What power did corporations and the trusts in the state possess?

Reflecting their diverse backgrounds, Progressive reformers had a wide variety of objectives. They advocated two methods for dealing with the trusts, either breaking them up or regulating them. They also proposed a series of political reforms, including the direct election of senators, the direct primary, the secret ballot, and laws to eradicate such corrupt practices as buying votes at the polls and in the legislature. Finally, they sought social measures such as minimum wages for women, restrictions on child labor, workmen's compensation, and pure food and drug laws. Which of these reforms did Pitney support and which did he oppose? Which succeeded and which did not? Based on his attitudes toward labor and corporations, including the railroads, was he a "conservative" or "liberal" Progressive? What, if anything, does Pitney's position suggest about the nature of the Progressive movement in New Jersey?

Belknap's essay on Pitney provokes two other questions about Progressives. The first considers their tolerance, or lack thereof, for differences and dissent. Some historians have described the Progressives as middle-class moralists who wanted to impose their standards on society as a whole and who, in the process, displayed a certain condescension toward the working classes, hostility toward immigrants, fear of radicals, and refusal to accept dissent, particularly during wartime. To what extent did Pitney exhibit these attitudes? What standards did Pitney and other judges in his time use to decide what was acceptable wartime dissent, and how do those standards compare to what prevailed in the Civil War years?

Second, how does one assess the historical role of such figures as Supreme Court judges? Legal historians ask whether or not a judge was "great"; political historians rank presidents. What standards are and should be used in this evaluative process? Should judges be compared only to others of their period or to those of later times? To compare historical figures to those who have succeeded them runs the risk of "presentism," evaluating the past by modern standards. Not to do so, on the other hand, may make their lives and history irrelevant to present-day readers.

Finally, Belknap, both a lawyer and a historian, wrote this chapter for a law review journal. Legal citation methods differ from those used by history journals (as well as those used by English professors, social scientists, and chemists). Compare the citations here with those in other chapters. Which style do you find easier to decipher?

Suggested Readings

Buenker, John D. "Urban, New-Stock Liberalism and Progressive Reform in New Jersey." *New Jersey History* 87 (1969): 79–104.

Chambers, John Whiteclay II. *The Tyranny of Change: America in the Progressive Era, 1890–1920.* 2d ed. New York: St. Martin's Press, 1992.

Filene, Peter. "Obituary for Progressivism." *American Quarterly* 22 (1970): 20–34.

Flanagan, Maureen A. *America Reformed: Progressives and Progressivems, 1890s–1920s.* New York: Oxford University Press, 2007.

Hofstadter, Richard. *The Age of Reform.* New York: Vintage Books, 1955.

Link, Arthur S. *Wilson: The Road to the White House.* Princeton, N.J.: Princeton University Press,1947.

McCormick, Richard L., and Arthur S. Link. *Progressivism.* Arlington Heights, Ill.: Harlan Davidson, 1983.

McGerr, Michael. *A Fierce Discontent: The Rise and Fall of the Progressive Movement in America.* New York: Oxford University Press, 2003.

Noble, Ransom E. *New Jersey Progressivism before Wilson.* Princeton, N.J.: Princeton University Press, 1946.

Paulsson, Martin. *Social Anxieties of Progressive Reform: Atlantic City: 1854–1920.* New York: New York University Press, 1994.

Thelen, David P. "Social Tensions and the Origins of Progressivism." *Journal of American History* 56 (1969): 323–341.

Tobin, Eugene M. "The Progressive as Humanitarian: Jersey City's Search for Social Justice, 1890–1917." *New Jersey History* 93 (1975): 77–98.

Wiebe, Robert H. *The Search for Order: 1877–1920.* New York: Greenwood Press, 1967.

◆ ◆ ◆ ◆ ◆ ◆

Mr. Justice Pitney and Progressivism

Michal R. Belknap

Introduction

In a book published in 1912, Marxist historian Gustavus Myers branded the United States Supreme Court a tool of the dominant capitalist class.[1] Part of the evidence he offered to support his characterization was the appointment that year of Associate Justice Mahlon Pitney, a native of what Myers called "that essentially plutocratic town," Morristown, New Jersey.[2] This was, he claimed, an event that gratified the great capitalist interests and "was inimical to the workers."[3] Summarizing Justice Pitney's career in 1969, historian Fred Israel also pictured him as a conservative bulwark against innovation,[4] notable mainly for his persistent hostility to labor.[5]

Such characterizations of Pitney are inaccurate. He did hand down a number of antiunion decisions, and he did interpret the income tax amendment in a manner arguably favorable to the wealthy, but this judge was no tool of the capitalists. Indeed, Pitney opposed monopoly in both the political and judicial arenas. Although hostile to trade unions, he wrote opinions that advanced the interests of unorganized workers, especially those victimized by industrial accidents. Far from being a die-hard reactionary, Mahlon Pitney was a judge whose career reflected the Progressivism that dominated American politics during the early years of the twentieth century. Some of Pitney's ideas seem illiberal today, but many of the reformers of his own time shared his views. Consequently, they gave him their political support. As a state judge, and later as a United States Supreme Court justice, he took positions on issues similar to those of contemporaries whom historians have labeled "Progressives." That appellation fits Pitney too, for his judicial opinions mirror concerns, values, and biases characteristic of Progressivism.

Seton Hall Law Review 16 (1986): 381–423. Reprinted by permission of the author and *Seton Hall Law Review.*

Progressivism

Pitney's judicial opinions link him to the "[c]onvulsive reform movements [that] swept across the American landscape from the 1890s to 1917."[6] These movements promoted a variety of economic, political, and social changes, which their proponents believed would "improve the conditions of life and labor" and stabilize American society.[7] Progressive reform crusades were extremely diverse. As several historians have pointed out, Progressivism was not a unified movement. Progressives pursued a variety of goals; indeed, they often disagreed among themselves, even about how to achieve commonly held objectives.[8]

On no issue were the disagreements among reformers sharper than on the question of what to do about the giant combinations of capital that Americans referred to inaccurately and pejoratively as "the trusts."[9] One group of Progressives, for whom Theodore Roosevelt was the most prominent spokesman, considered bigness in business inevitable and desirable. Rather than smashing the trusts, they argued, the federal government should subject them to continuous administrative supervision.[10] It should distinguish between those that behaved themselves and those that did not, and it should use intermittent law suits to discipline the miscreants.[11] Woodrow Wilson and his advisor in the 1912 presidential campaign, Louis Brandeis (later a colleague of Pitney on the Supreme Court), favored a vastly different approach. They idealized small economic units, and rather than regulating monopolies, they wanted to break them up by enacting legislation that would effectively outlaw giant combinations of capital.[12]

Progressives of this type held views deeply rooted in the American past, views that had been widely accepted since before the Civil War. Both Jacksonian Democrats and the leaders of the infant Republican Party of the late 1850s were deeply suspicious of corporations and economic concentration. They feared that these might restrict the options open to wage earners and small entrepreneurs and interfere with the efforts of these groups to attain economic independence and upward social mobility. The Democratic version of this antebellum ideology emphasized conflict between labor and capital, but most Republicans believed there was a harmony of interests between different social classes. For this reason, the Republicans opposed self-conscious, working-class actions such as strikes, which they saw as interfering with the rights of others. They believed that an individual might quit any job he chose, but that it was wrong for him to join with others to shut down his employer or to keep those who wanted to work from doing so.[13] Unions, like corporations, were aggregations of power that threatened the opportunities of enterprising members of the middle class.[14] Hostility toward combinations of both labor and capital was central to the thinking of the advocates of laissez-faire,[15] who gained intellectual preeminence in the United States during the decades after the Civil War.

Turn-of-the-century Supreme Court Justice John Marshall Harlan, known as a rigorous enforcer of the antitrust laws, also exhibited a distinct lack of sympathy for workers' organizations.[16] Even Brandeis, although a friend of the trade union movement, "was absolutely opposed to the closed shop as a form of labor despotism."[17] As late as 1909, Woodrow Wilson declared, "I am a fierce partizan [sic] of the Open Shop and of everything that makes for individual liberty."[18] To many small employers and middle-class professionals, unions seemed like just another type of monopoly—originated for the same reasons as the industrial monopoly and likely to produce similar results.[19] During the late 1890s and the early years of the twentieth century, the average middle-class citizen viewed himself as a member of an unorganized, and therefore helpless, consuming public, threatened from above by mushrooming trusts and from below by workers combining to protect themselves.[20]

Historian Richard Hofstadter once characterized Progressivism as "the complaint of the unorganized against the consequences of organization."[21] His thesis that it was caused by the status anxieties of the middle class[22] has by now been largely refuted by other scholars.[23] There were, however, other reasons for members of the unorganized middle class to feel threatened by the growing power of big business above and trade unions below. One was inflation. During the period from 1897 to 1913, the cost of living rose 35 percent. Although the increase was modest by today's standards, the country was then emerging from a period of deflation, and the public tended to blame rising prices on "the sudden development of a vigorous, if small, labor movement, and an extraordinary acceleration in the trustification of American industry."[24] The second important reason for the development of reform sentiments within the unorganized middle class was a sudden increase in public awareness of the extent to which big corporations were corrupting the political process in order to advance their own interests at the expense of other segments of American society.[25] The fears and resentments of the middle class were certainly not the only reasons for the development of Progressivism,[26] but they do explain the career of Mahlon Pitney and its relationship to that reform movement.[27]

The New Jersey Years

Background and Early Life

Progressives were mostly old-stock Americans with British ethnic backgrounds who came from economically secure middle-class families.[28] Religiously, they were most often Calvinists, affiliated with denominations such as the Congregationalists and the Presbyterians.[29] In a day when few Americans went to college, most Progressives were college graduates.[30] A majority of those active in politics were lawyers.[31]

In other words, the typical Progressive reformer was someone very much like Mahlon Pitney. Pitney's ancestors had come to New Jersey from England in the early 1700s, and the great-grandfather for whom he was named served in George Washington's army during the Revolutionary War.[32] The future justice was born the second son of attorney Henry C. Pitney on the family farm near Morristown on February 5, 1858.[33] He attended private schools in Morristown, and as befits a New Jersey Presbyterian, he enrolled at Princeton in 1875.[34]

Pitney studied hard at Princeton, and during his senior year, he played first base on and managed the baseball team.[35] Among his classmates were Robert McCarter, who would later serve as attorney general of New Jersey,[36] and Thomas Woodrow Wilson, who was destined to become president of the United States.[37] On November 30, 1915, the class of 1879 held a reunion at the White House hosted by President Wilson and attended by, among others, Justice Pitney.[38]

After graduating from Princeton, young Mahlon followed his father into what was rapidly becoming the family profession—law. H. C. Pitney, a country lawyer who had served as prosecutor of the pleas for Morris County in the 1860s, capped a successful career by becoming a vice chancellor in 1889, a position he held until 1907.[39] His sons, Henry C. Jr. and John O. H. (founding partner of Pitney, Hardin, Kipp & Szuch), also took up the practice of law.[40] "I could hardly have escaped it," Mahlon once remarked.[41] After discussing career options with his father, he decided that following graduation, he would read law in the elder Pitney's office.[42] That form of preparation for the bar proved to be less than thrilling. "I found the work very dull at first, and Blackstone very dry reading," the future Supreme Court Justice admitted later.[43] On the other hand, he learned an immense amount, "most of it from [his] father who was a walking encyclopedia of law."[44]

Law Practice

After a period of intense cramming with his close friend Francis J. Swayze (who would be his colleague on the New Jersey bench and rival for a seat on the United States Supreme Court),[45] Pitney took and passed the bar examinations. He was admitted as an attorney at law and solicitor in chancery in 1882, and three years later he became a counselor.[46] For the first seven years after his admission to the bar, Pitney practiced alone in Dover, New Jersey.[47] There he acted as counsel to the Cranbury Iron Company, which he also served as a director and an officer.[48] In addition, Pitney found time to manage a Dover department store.[49]

When his father was appointed vice chancellor in 1889, Mahlon returned to Morristown to take over H. C.'s firm, Pitney & Youngblood.[50] He achieved a reputation as both a skillful appellate advocate and a clever trial lawyer.[51] By 1894, Pitney was "justly regarded as one of the leading legal lights in New Jersey."[52]

Political Career

CONGRESS. In the fall of 1894, Pitney entered politics, running for the House seat from the Fourth Congressional District.[53] Like his father, Mahlon was a Republican, and the Fourth was normally a Democratic stronghold.[54] In 1894, the country was in the depths of a depression, however, and voters troubled by hard times were turning against the party of Democratic President Grover Cleveland.[55] Although a newspaper supporting his opponent, Johnston Cornish, stated that "no Democrat [could] be expected to vote for Mr. Pitney, because he represents in the most radical degree every principal [sic] of Republicanism that is distasteful to a Democrat,"[56] many obviously did. Pitney carried the district by 1,407 votes.[57]

During his first term in the House, Speaker Thomas B. Reed named him to both the Committee on Reform in the Civil Service and the powerful Appropriations Committee.[58] Although Pitney seldom opened his mouth on the floor,[59] the performance of the quiet freshman from New Jersey obviously pleased "Czar" Reed. When Pitney stood for reelection in 1896, the Speaker traveled to Morristown to give a major address and to endorse his candidacy.[60] Pitney again prevailed at the polls, defeating Democrat Augustus W. Cutler by 2,977 votes.[61]

During his second term in the House, he assumed a somewhat higher profile, frequently participating in debate.[62] Pitney spoke out against what he regarded as the excessively large appropriations proposed for various departments of the government.[63] He also served on the committee to which the Alaska boundary dispute was assigned.

All of its members were asked to prepare briefs on the controversy, and Pitney's was so "exhaustive that he was assigned to manage the passage of the . . . report" that the committee presented to the full House.[64]

STATE SENATE. Although successful, Pitney's second term ended prematurely. He resigned on January 5, 1899, to take a seat in the New Jersey senate.[65] Both he and his wife, the former Florence Shelton, "longed to return to Morristown and their friends" there.[66] In addition, Pitney wanted to be governor.[67] Early in 1898, he made the obligatory pilgrimage to the Camden railroad office that served as the headquarters of New Jersey's Republican boss, William J. Sewall, seeking Sewall's endorsement.[68] He did not get it. The boss, who favored another candidate, told Pitney that he had to broaden his base in state politics before seeking the governorship.[69] Assured by Sewall that if elected to the New Jersey senate he could have the minority leadership, Pitney ran for the Morris County seat in November of 1898,[70] winning by a plurality of 831 votes.[71]

When the Republicans gained control of the upper chamber in 1900, he became president of the senate.[72] During his three years in Trenton, Pitney won acclaim for a thorough "study of the proposed Morris Canal abandonment scheme," which he revealed was almost exclusively for the benefit of the lessee of the canal, the Lehigh Valley Railroad.[73] His efforts prevented consummation of this dubious project[74] and even won him praise from a newspaper otherwise highly critical of the state senate.[75]

Pitney's success in Trenton made him a leading contender for the Republican gubernatorial nomination and a likely winner of the state's highest office.[76] Before the 1901 election, however, the chief justice of the New Jersey Supreme Court, David A. Depew, resigned.[77] Governor Foster M. Voorhees elevated Associate Justice William S. Gummere to the chief justiceship, and on February 5, 1901, he nominated Pitney to fill the resulting vacancy.[78] On that day, Pitney also celebrated his forty-third birthday.[79] His fellow senators quickly confirmed their colleague from Morristown,[80] bringing an end to his career in elective politics.

PROGRESSIVE POLITICIAN. His career suggests that Pitney was part of the emergent Progressive movement that was just beginning to gather momentum around the country when he abandoned the political arena for the bench. To be sure, Pitney took traditional Republican positions on the issues in his two races for Congress.[81] As historian George Mowry has pointed out, however, most of those who would later be identified as Progressives were conservatives in the middle 1890s.[82] In the landmark presidential election of 1896, these nascent Progressives opposed

William Jennings Bryan, who, as the candidate of the Democratic and Populist parties, advocated the free and unlimited coinage of silver as a panacea for the economic woes of American farmers and workers.[83] Certainly, Pitney was part of this opposition. "What we need," he thundered, "is . . . not more money, but more confidence and more business."[84] Pitney's Princeton classmate Woodrow Wilson, now remembered as a Progressive governor and president, took a similar position. He denounced Bryan and cast his ballot for a breakaway faction of the Democratic Party that favored retention of the gold standard.[85]

What made reformers of men such as Wilson and Pitney were the economic and political abuses of the great corporations.[86] Such abuses were particularly serious in New Jersey, where during the 1880s and 1890s, the legislature adopted a series of laws designed to facilitate the formation of holding companies and monopolies.[87] Between 1896 and 1913, the state did a bargain-counter business in corporate charters, enriching its treasury with filing fees while giving a legal home to all of the largest holding companies in the Nation and a majority of the lesser trusts as well.[88] Their rush to incorporate in New Jersey earned her the nickname "the mother of trusts."[89] Particularly offensive to New Jerseyans themselves were the utility companies, which controlled gas, electric, trolley, and street railway service in the northern part of the state.[90] Backed by the major banks and insurance firms, these corporations enjoyed intimate relations with the leaders of both the Democratic and Republican parties, many of whom had financial interests in the companies.[91] It is hardly surprising that utilities benefited from extremely favorable franchise arrangements and quite low taxes.[92]

During the period from 1905 to 1912, these firms came under attack by reformers in both political parties. The first to take the offensive were the so-called New Idea Republicans, led by Jersey City Mayor Mark Fagan, his corporation's counsel, George Record, and Essex County Senator Everett Colby.[93] By 1906, the "New Idea" men had become such a potent force in the northern part of the state that the Republican majority in the legislature hastened to endorse their demands for increased taxation of railroad property and for legislation imposing limitations on the franchises that local governments routinely granted to utility corporations.[94] In 1911, Democratic Governor Woodrow Wilson joined the assault. His administration secured passage of legislation creating a board of public utility commissioners and investing it with the power to set rates and regulate service.[95]

Fourteen years before that measure became law, Mahlon Pitney had spoken out against abuse of the public by a utility corporation. In particular, he focused on the United States Electric Lighting Company, a firm that for years had enjoyed a monopoly franchise for lighting the streets of the nation's capital. In an 1897 debate on the floor of the House of Representatives, Pitney vigorously attacked the lighting company and endorsed the efforts of the District of Columbia commissioners to give some of its business to a competing firm.[96] No company "that has the full control in a matter of this sort can be trusted to care for the public interests," Pitney told his colleagues.[97] What would best serve the interests of consumers was competition.[98] The following year, in probably his most famous House speech, Pitney defended his home state against charges by Populist Congressman "Sockless" Jerry Simpson of Kansas that New Jersey was guilty of coddling the trusts. Although denouncing Simpson for preaching a doctrine that would "lead us directly to socialism," Pitney endorsed "reasonable measures of regulation for the government of corporations" and the use of the equity powers of the judiciary to prevent corporate abuses.[99] As he left the New Jersey senate for the bench in 1901, he denounced "bills . . . contrived for the purpose of establishing or bolstering up a partial or total monopoly."[100]

State Judge

Like his political rhetoric, Pitney's performance as a state judge reflected attitudes commonly associated with Progressivism. He served as an associate judge of the New Jersey Supreme Court from February 19, 1901, to January 22, 1908.[101] During this tenure, he wrote a total of 167 opinions, dealing with a wide variety of civil and criminal legal problems.[102] Only four times did the court of errors and appeals reverse one of his decisions.[103]

Pitney's performance earned him a promotion. When Chancellor William J. Magie retired in January of 1908, Governor J. Franklin Fort nominated him to a full seven-year term as Magie's successor.[104] The senate, not even bothering with the usual reference to committee, quickly confirmed the choice.[105] During Pitney's four years and two months as chancellor, he headed both the law and equity branches of the court of errors and appeals.[106] He handed down forty-seven decisions on the law side and approximately eleven on the equity side.[107] His responsibilities as chancellor also included coordinating the work of the vice chancellors, who presided over the various districts into which the state was then divided.[108] This made him briefly the superior of his father, who had already submitted his resignation before Mahlon's appointment, but remained on the job for a few months after his son took office.[109] As chancellor, Pitney inaugurated the practice of having all the vice chancellors meet two or three times a year to discuss any problems they were experiencing in their districts.[110] What attracted the attention of the press, however, was his "scoring [of] the Camden law firm of French & Richards for oppressive conduct in attempting to charge the Amparo Mining Company $75,000 for legal fees" by reducing the firm's fee to only $12,500.[111]

The Amparo Company had more reason to applaud Pitney's performance on the state bench than did most corporations. His decisions in cases challenging efforts to subject railroads to increased taxation revealed the continuing development of the incipient Progressivism that he had displayed as a politician. The constant in these rulings was the identity of the losing party; it was always the railroad. For example, Pitney spurned[112] the Bergen and Dundee Railroad's challenge to the constitutionality of the 1905 Duffield Act,[113] a measure subjecting all property of railroads and canals except their "main stem" to taxation by local governments. He also upheld the validity, under both the state constitution and the Fourteenth Amendment [of the federal Constitution],[114] of 1906 legislation that removed the main stem classification from property formerly so denominated[115] and equalized the tax rates on that part of railroad and canal property subject solely to state taxation with the rates on other New Jersey real property.[116]

Pitney again rebuffed railroads when they complained about the amount of their tax assessments[117] and when they objected to the inclusion of particular pieces of real estate in the "second class" category subject to local taxation.[118] He ruled in favor of the mayor and aldermen of Jersey City in a suit against both the State Board of Equalization and the Central Railroad Company of New Jersey.[119] The suit arose after the board, at the instigation of the railroad, ordered a reassessment of all real property in the community without giving notice to other taxpayers.[120]

Pitney also supported Jersey City's Progressive Republican administration in two disputes with local street railway companies. In 1905, he ruled that the municipality could collect a license fee from the North Jersey Street Railway Company.[121] Two years later, Pitney upheld as reasonable a municipal regulatory ordinance requiring North Jersey and another company to provide sufficient cars during rush hour so that all passengers could have a seat and no one would have to wait more than five minutes for a ride.[122]

This latter decision reflected Pitney's desire to see corporations regulated and controlled. Although he could wax eloquent about "the marvelous progress of the past half century in every line of human effort, carried on . . . more and more through the instrumentality of corporations,"[123] he deeply distrusted the increasing separation of ownership from control and the concentration of economic power into fewer and fewer hands,[124] two factors that distinguished corporate evolution at the turn of the century. His ideal corporation was a little democracy in which directors were elected annually for limited terms, real power rested with the shareholders, and minority rights were respected.[125] An equity judge, Pitney thought, should use his powers to preserve this ideal and at the same time to protect the public from corporate abuses such as restraint of trade.[126]

The nineteenth-century attitudes that permeated his corporation decisions also governed his approach to labor law. In the case of *Brennan v. United Hatters, Local 17*,[127] Pitney expressed his distaste for a union's claim that the value of belonging to it "consist[ed] in participation in a more or less complete monopoly of the labor market in the particular trade in question."[128] He subsequently cited *Brennan* as holding that the state constitution guaranteed a painter the "right to seek and gain employment in his lawful occupation,"[129] and added that, consequently, a union "had no right to interfere with him in his employment merely because he was not a member."[130] Finally, in *George Jonas Glass Co. v. Glass Bottle Blowers' Association*,[131] Chancellor Pitney upheld a sweeping injunction[132] issued by Vice Chancellor Bergen[133] against a labor organization that had attempted to pressure an employer into unionizing his factory. Besides instigating a strike and a boycott and picketing the plant, the union apparently had resorted to threats, intimidation, and even bribery to deprive Jonas Glass of a work force until the firm agreed to its demands.[134] Pitney characterized the union's actions as "a war of subjugation against the complainant corporation."[135] In issuing the injunction, Vice Chancellor Bergen was careful to emphasize that he was not disputing the right of workers to form a union or to state peacefully to others their position in a labor dispute.[136] Pitney, on the other hand, expressed distaste for a state statute that appeared to legalize both unions and strikes. He declared that if this law really permitted the use of peaceable measures to induce workmen to quit their jobs or refuse to enter someone's employment, it would have to be unconstitutional.[137]

Because Pitney's hostility toward unions was inspired by their tendency to monopolize in the labor market,[138] it did not extend to unorganized workers. In tort cases decided while he was on the New Jersey bench, he ruled in favor of injured workmen about as often as he ruled against them.[139] He did once make rather heartless use of the doctrine of contributory negligence, employing it to reverse a jury verdict in favor of a fourteen-year-old boy whose hand had been crushed in his employer's machine.[140] In another case, Pitney declined to adopt the so-called vice-principal exception to the fellow-servant rule, thus precluding a telephone lineman from recovering against his employer for injuries caused by the negligence of his foreman.[141] On the other hand, he consistently took the position that employers must furnish their employees with safe tools and a safe place in which to work, and he would not allow those who failed to do so to avoid liability by hiding behind the fellow-servant doctrine.[142] In viewing workers favorably while loathing their organizations, Pitney was not unique.[143] "[F]or many a progressive the rise of the labor union was as frightening as the rise of trusts."[144]

Pitney's hostility to unions placed him squarely within the mainstream of the Progressive movement, as did his support of governmental efforts to regulate saloons[145] and to combat other forms of vice.[146] In addition, Pitney impressed Progressives by prodding a Hudson County grand jury into indicting for election fraud some opponents of Jersey City's New Idea mayor, Mark Fagan, men who, according to the *Newark Evening News*, had concocted a "conspiracy to override the will of the people."[147] A charge to a Passaic County grand jury also attracted favorable attention. In it, Pitney lashed out at local officials for failing to enforce the liquor laws and called for action against election officers in Paterson, who were alleged to have submitted false returns.[148]

His judicial support for causes dear to their hearts made him politically appealing to Progressives.[149] In 1906, some Morris County friends launched a campaign to elect Pitney to the United States Senate.[150] Their bandwagon never really got rolling, however, and even his hometown backers finally abandoned it in the legislature. Nevertheless, Essex County's New Idea senator, Everett Colby, stuck with Pitney all the way by both nominating and voting for him.[151]

In the summer of 1907, President Theodore Roosevelt, then emerging as an outspoken champion of Progressivism,[152] encouraged New Jersey Republicans to nominate Pitney for governor.[153] That idea appealed to a Jersey City "Colbyite," who was impressed by the fact that the justice had made the railroads pay an additional $4,000,000 in taxes.[154] Pitney, however, did not get the gubernatorial nomination, despite being regarded as an acceptable candidate by a great majority of those who identified themselves with the New Idea movement.[155] He continued to be mentioned as a prospect for the governorship, though, and when Democrat Woodrow Wilson ran for that office in 1910, he thought his classmate might well be his opponent.[156]

Supreme Court Justice

Appointment

Pitney was headed not for the governor's office in Trenton, but for the Supreme Court in Washington. Although President William Howard Taft considered him for one of three open seats on the Court in 1910,[157] he ultimately gave those positions to other men.[158] Taft returned to Pitney after Associate Justice John Marshall Harlan died in October of 1911, but the chancellor was not his first choice for that appointment.[159] Scholars have never satisfactorily explained why the president finally chose Pitney for the Harlan seat.[160]

Perhaps the most important reason was his broad political appeal. During the early months of 1912, Taft was locked in a fight for control of the Republican Party with his predecessor, Theodore Roosevelt, who was seeking to deny him renomination and to capture the top spot on the GOP ticket for himself.[161] The president and his political strategists believed that New Jersey could become a crucial battleground in this contest.[162] Ultimately this belief proved decisive in Taft's choice of a replacement for Harlan.

The president first offered the appointment to his secretary of state, Frank Knox, who declined the honor.[163] For several months after that, the leading contenders appeared to be Secretary of Commerce and Labor Charles Nagel and Judge William C. Hook of the Court of Appeals for the Eighth Circuit. Nagel lost out because he was too old, lacked prior judicial experience,[164] and had made himself unpopular with labor by supporting immigration.[165] Some people objected to Hook because of his concurrence in a decision upholding an Oklahoma statute that allowed railroads to provide sleeping, dining, and chair cars for whites without making comparable facilities available to blacks.[166] Others disliked his issuance of an injunction prohibiting the city of Denver from constructing a new water plant and "requir[ing] it instead to buy [out] a private water company whose franchise had expired."[167] In addition, state railroad commissioners and Progressive governors from western states complained that Hook's approach to rate making was prorailroad.[168] That was not the sort of nominee Taft needed at a time when he was laboring to keep Progressives from deserting to the Roosevelt camp.[169]

Pitney was. Franklin Murphy, a former governor of New Jersey and then the state's Republican National Committeeman, pushed him for the job. Murphy was a strong Taft supporter,[170] and because he hoped to be selected as his running mate, he was anxious to ingratiate himself with the president. Taft was scheduled to give a speech in New York City in February of 1912. With the objective of promoting his political fortunes in New Jersey, Murphy arranged for Taft to stop over in Newark on the way there to attend a luncheon at the ex-governor's home and a Republican reception at the Essex County Country Club.[171] At Murphy's house, the president sat next to Chancellor Pitney.[172] They had a pleasant conversation,[173] and a week later, on February 19, Taft offered the chancellor a seat on the Supreme Court.[174]

Pitney was in many ways just what the president had been looking for. He was an experienced judge, but at fifty-four, he still had many years of judicial work before him.[175] In addition, he was from the Third Circuit, which had been unrepresented on the Supreme Court for a number of years.[176] A desire to correct that situation was one of the reasons Taft had approached Knox, and only reluctantly had he turned his attention to candidates from further west.[177] After dining with Pitney, the president, a former judge himself,[178] spent several hours reading a number of his opinions.[179] These apparently confirmed a favorable assessment of Pitney's abilities that Taft had received from New Jersey Vice Chancellor James E. Howell in 1910.[180] Finally, Pitney was from New Jersey. Taft had become convinced that he had to name someone from that state.[181]

Although the chancellor satisfied many of the president's other criteria, political considerations eventually earned him a seat on the Supreme Court. Taft considered at least three other New Jersey judges,[182] among them Pitney's friend Justice Swayze.[183] Swayze, who was Governor Murphy's initial choice for the job, had the support of United States Senator Frank O. Briggs[184] and even the chancellor himself.[185] Howell had advised the president, however, that Pitney was preferable because of his more extensive involvement in politics.[186] Eventually, Pitney became Murphy's choice.[187] The ex-governor was a conservative who considered the Progressive movement dangerous, but he recognized the value of appeasing those Republicans who were attracted to it because they needed their [Progressives'] vote.[188] Thus, he invited two or three Progressives, among them Senator Colby, to his luncheon, an event arranged to generate enthusiasm for the Taft movement.[189] The appointment of Pitney was almost certainly another move of the same kind, intended to curry favor with the New Idea men and thus help Taft retain control of the New Jersey Republican Party.[190]

Reaction to the nomination from within the state was extremely positive,[191] and Governor Wilson commended Taft's choice.[192] To the rest of the country, however, Pitney "was 'an unknown quantity.'"[193] The *New York Times* nevertheless predicted that the Senate would quickly and easily confirm him.[194]

The *Times* was wrong. First, the president of the Iowa Federation of Labor protested the Pitney appointment to senators from his state.[195] He failed to substantiate his objections, however, because his argument was based on *Frank & Dugan v. Herold*.[196] As the nominee swiftly pointed out, the Pitney who had granted a sweeping injunction against picketing and other union activity in that case was his father.[197] Mahlon Pitney claimed not to be an enemy of labor,[198] and the president of the New Jersey Federation of Labor, who was also a Hudson County assemblyman, supported him, claiming to be unable to recall any decision by the chancellor that had borne heavily against union interests.[199] He apparently had forgotten *Jonas Glass*. When the Senate took up the nomination on March 8, Charles A. Culberson, a Texas Democrat, raised objections to the *Jonas Glass* decision.[200] It aroused enough controversy that the Senate had the opinion printed.[201] For three days, senators read and debate raged.[202] At one point during the executive sessions on the nomination, Pitney's supporters reportedly lacked sufficient votes for confirmation.[203] Governor Wilson, Senator James E. Martine, and other leading New Jersey Democrats sprang to the defense of their state's native son,[204] and on March 13, the Senate approved Taft's choice by a vote of fifty to twenty-six.[205] The division was basically along partisan lines, although four insurgent Republicans did join twenty-two Democrats in voting no.[206]

Supreme Court Decisions

Five days later, Pitney took the oath of office,[207] beginning a tenure on the Supreme Court that would last for just under eleven years.[208] A durable justice, he was seldom absent from the Bench, participating in all but 19 of the 2,412 decisions that the Court rendered during his tenure.[209] Pitney authored a total of 268 opinions, speaking for the majority on 244 occasions, dissenting 19 times, and writing 5 concurrences.[210]

TAXATION. For lawyers practicing today, Pitney's most important opinion is *Eisner v. Macomber*.[211] In that case, he defined income for purposes of the Sixteenth Amendment, drawing the line between those additions to wealth that were subject to the federal income tax and those that were not.[212] The specific question in *Eisner* was whether stock dividends constituted taxable income.[213] Congress had passed a law in 1916 treating them as if they did,[214] but the financial community expected the Court to hold that measure unconstitutional. Early in his opinion, Pitney explained the intent of the disputed act.[215] Apparently, he mumbled as he did so.[216] An agent for Dow Jones misunderstood him as saying not that Congress had sought to tax stock dividends as income, but that the Court was holding it had the power to do this.[217] The Dow Jones man rushed out to wire the news to Wall Street.[218] The result was a brief plunge in stock prices.[219] When the false report was corrected, however, the market recovered what it had lost and more.[220]

The stock market's favorable reaction to Pitney's actual opinion probably did not surprise Justice Louis Brandeis. In a strong dissent, he charged, "If stock dividends representing profits are held exempt from taxation under the Sixteenth Amendment, the owners of the most successful businesses in America will . . . be able to escape taxation on a large part of what is actually their income."[221] Brandeis's populist rhetoric was nearly as unjustified a reaction to Pitney's opinion as the collapse of stock prices. Informed observers recognized that *Eisner* had not created much of an opportunity for the distribution of tax-free profits, and virtually all of the voluminous scholarly literature that the case generated supported Pitney's position.[222]

That is hardly surprising, for the justice from New Jersey had become something of a tax specialist. *Eisner* was only one of six majority opinions that he wrote explicating the concept of income as it related to the Sixteenth Amendment.[223] Pitney also spoke for the Court in cases involving federal taxation of corporations,[224] inheritances,[225] and imports.[226] In addition, he wrote a total of twenty majority opinions[227] and one dissent[228] dealing with various constitutional issues raised by state tax measures.

LABOR UNIONS. Although Pitney devoted more attention to taxation than to any other subject, as one of his biographers has pointed out, "It is in the area of labor decisions . . . that the Justice made his most significant contribution."[229] These were also the opinions that earned him his reactionary reputation.[230] As a member of the Supreme Court, Pitney continued to exhibit the hostility toward unions that he had displayed on the New Jersey bench.[231] In a 1915 case known as *Coppage v. Kansas*,[232] he held unconstitutional a state statute that made it unlawful for employers to require their workers, as a condition of employment, to agree not to join a labor organization.[233] Pitney insisted that he was not questioning "the legitimacy of such organizations," but added, "Conceding the full right of the individual to join [a] union, he has no inherent right to do this and still remain in the employ of one who is unwilling to employ a union man."[234] Pitney viewed the Kansas statute as one designed for "leveling inequalities of fortune" through "an interference with the normal exercise of personal liberty and property rights . . . and not an incident to the advancement of the general welfare."[235] Not even a national emergency, he argued in a later case, could justify legislative interference with management's freedom to negotiate with its workers for the employment terms it wanted.[236]

Pitney's antistatist attitudes did not cut both ways. Although hostile to governmental interference with employers' freedom of action, he generally gave enthusiastic support to governmental interference with the liberty of unions. Pitney remained a champion of the labor injunction. In *Paine Lumber Co. v. Neal*,[237] he argued unsuccessfully that open-shop sash and door manufacturers were entitled under the Sherman Antitrust Act[238] to have a federal court enjoin a boycott of their products by the Brotherhood of Carpenters and Joiners and certain unionized firms. Later, as a spokesman for the majority in *Hitchman Coal & Coke Co. v. Mitchell*,[239] Pitney held that a coal-mining company that had required its employees to agree to work on a nonunion basis might have a federal district court restrain the United Mine Workers from trying to organize its labor force.[240] In a revealing passage, he declared: "Defendants' acts cannot be justified by any analogy to competition in trade. They are not competitors of plaintiff; and if they were their conduct exceeds the bounds of fair trade."[241] Pitney believed that a union had no right to reduce an employer's freedom of choice through economic coercion, although he regarded it as perfectly acceptable for management to limit the independence of workers by making them agree not to join a union in order to obtain a desperately needed job.[242] *Hitchman Coal* and *Eagle Glass & Manufacturing Co. v. Rowe*,[243] which was decided the same day on *Hitchman Coal*'s authority, exhibit what one commentator has characterized as a "zeal bordering on vindictiveness in an effort to strike at labor."[244]

Despite his deep and long-standing hostility toward unions, Pitney wound up supporting their position in his last labor law decision. The New Jersey justice gave no preliminary indication that he would soon support a judicial inroad on the formidable restrictions on organized labor and union activity that he had helped to erect. Speaking for the Court in a January 1921 case called *Duplex Printing Press Co. v. Deering*,[245] he upheld the action of a federal district court, which had enjoined a secondary boycott organized by the International Association of Machinists in an effort to force a manufacturer to unionize.[246] Pitney ruled this way despite the fact that the district court had based its injunction on the antitrust laws.[247] He refused to acknowledge that by enacting section 20 of the Clayton Act[248] in 1914, Congress had made conduct of the type in which the machinists had engaged lawful and nonenjoinable under those statutes. Justice Brandeis responded with a powerful dissent in which he argued that rights were subordinate to the interests of the community and that how far "industrial combatants" might push their struggle was some thing for the community's representatives in the legislature to decide and "not for judges to determine."[249] Certainly that had never been Pitney's view, but he was not a man who clung to his own conclusions out of vanity, and he could be persuaded by study to change his mind.[250]

Twelve months later, in *Truax v. Corrigan*,[251] the New Jersey justice adopted Brandeis's position. Taft, who was then chief justice, assigned Pitney to write an opinion invalidating an Arizona statute that forbade the issuance of injunctions in labor disputes. Pitney soon received a memorandum from Brandeis opposing the decision, which he "read with interest."[252] The New Jersey justice then changed his vote, joining his critic in dissent.[253] Pitney's opinion suggested his sympathies still lay with businessmen seeking assistance from the courts rather than with unions,[254] and he declined to endorse "the wisdom, or policy, or propriety" of the Arizona law.[255] It now seemed clear to him that the labor injunction could be abolished "in the normal exercise of the legislative power of the State."[256]

INDUSTRIAL ACCIDENTS. Pitney's dissent in *Truax* "demonstrates that it would be an error to dismiss him simply as an antilabor judge."[257] Although too oriented toward the individualistic world of the nineteenth century to appreciate that unions might be necessary counterweights to rapidly expanding aggregates of capital (whose legitimacy he also could not accept), the justice from New Jersey did have some understanding of America's emergent industrial society. Like a number of his colleagues on the Supreme Court, he was willing, where union activity was not involved, to give a wide berth to state labor regulations.[258] Thus, for example, Pitney wrote opinions upholding the constitutionality of Missouri[259] and Oklahoma[260] statutes that required employers to give workers who either quit or were fired letters setting forth the nature and duration of their service and the reasons for its termination.

Like his *Truax* dissent, both of these decisions came near the end of his service on the Supreme Court. Much earlier, however, in cases arising under the Federal Employers' Liability Act (FELA) and state workers' compensation statutes, Pitney had displayed the sympathy for unorganized workers already apparent during his years as a New Jersey judge. Compensating laborers injured in the course of their employment, which was the purpose of these laws, was a long-standing Progressive objective, which he supported every bit as vigorously as did such outspoken champions of reform as Theodore Roosevelt.[261]

Four years before Pitney's appointment to the Supreme Court, Congress had enacted the FELA,[262] a statute that abolished the fellow-servant rule in cases where interstate railroad workers sued their employers for on-the-job injuries.[263] The FELA also greatly modified for purposes of such litigation two other common employers' defenses—

contributory negligence[264] and assumption of the risk.[265] During his tenure on the Court, Pitney decided a total of sixteen cases arising under the FELA. Twelve times he ruled in favor of the injured worker or his estate.[266] In two of the cases that the railroad won, the issue before the Court was not whether the railroad was liable, but only whether the damages that the plaintiff had recovered were excessive.[267] In a third case, Pitney disposed of all of the substantive issues in a manner favorable to the worker, but reversed a jury verdict in his favor because some local practice rules in the jurisdiction where the case arose had not been followed.[268] Similarly, in litigation arising under the common law of torts[269] and the Safety Appliance Act,[270] he ruled for railroad employees injured on the job.

It was in cases involving workers' compensation statutes, however, that Pitney aligned himself most dramatically with Progressivism. At the time of his appointment to the Supreme Court, states had begun to enact laws that made employers liable without fault for injuries that their workers suffered on the job; usually these statutes also limited the amount that the victim could recover.[271] New Jersey was a part of this national trend. In 1911, Woodrow Wilson secured enactment of a workers' compensation statute for the state.[272] By then, it had become apparent that traditional tort litigation served the interests of employers no better than it served those of employees; even the National Association of Manufacturers had concluded that compensation systems were inevitable and probably desirable.[273]

Nevertheless, in the 1911 case of *Ives v. South Buffalo Railway*,[274] the New York Court of Appeals unanimously struck down the first state law creating one, holding that it violated both the New York Constitution and the Fourteenth Amendment.[275] Constitutional law experts, led by Dean Roscoe Pound of Harvard, denounced the *Ives* decision in the press,[276] and Theodore Roosevelt expressed a desire to see every judge who had participated in the case removed from the bench.[277] In a February 1912 speech, Roosevelt, who was then mounting his challenge to Taft, urged giving the people the right to recall judicial decisions holding statutes unconstitutional.[278] Although denounced by the American Bar Association, Roosevelt's proposal and his concomitant attack on judicial power in general elicited a surprising amount of support, even within the legal community.[279]

If the judiciary were to avoid a successful assault on its authority, it had to adjust constitutional law to accommodate legislation ensuring compensation for the victims of industrial accidents. Mahlon Pitney did that. In the wake of the *Ives* decision, New York amended its constitution and then enacted a new workers' compensation law limited to employees in supposedly hazardous industries.[280] In 1916, that statute came before the Supreme Court in *New York Central Railroad v. White*.[281] The employer argued that this law struck "at the fundamentals of constitutional freedom of contract."[282] Speaking for the Court, Pitney disagreed, holding that it was "a reasonable exercise of the police power of the State."[283] Pitney reasoned that the pecuniary loss caused by an employee's death or injury had to fall somewhere and that these damages were, after all, the result of an operation out of which the employer expected to derive a profit.[284] Pitney concluded that it was not "arbitrary and unreasonable for the State to impose upon the employer the absolute duty of making a moderate and definite compensation in money to every disabled employee."[285]

In a companion case, in which the Court upheld an Iowa statute, Pitney declared "that the employer has no vested right to have these so-called common-law defenses perpetuated for his benefit, and that the Fourteenth Amendment does not prevent a State from establishing a system of workmen's compensation without the consent of the employer, incidentally abolishing [these] defenses."[286] The New Jersey justice also spoke for the Court in *Mountain Timber Co. v. Washington*.[287] The statute at issue in that case, unlike the New York law upheld in *White*, required employers in hazardous industries to contribute to a state fund for the compensation of injured workmen, whether or not any injuries had ever befallen their own employees.[288] Thus, a careful firm had to help pay for the harm caused by its negligent competitors. Nevertheless, stated Pitney, because "accidental injuries are inevitable," it could not "be deemed arbitrary or unreasonable for the State, instead of imposing upon the particular employer entire responsibility for losses occurring in his own plant or work, to impose the burden upon the industry."[289]

Four justices dissented in *Mountain Timber*.[290] This suggests that the Court had not been nearly as unified in support of the other two decisions as their reported unanimity indicates. Years later, Brandeis said of Pitney, "But for [him] we would have had no workmen's compensation laws."[291] Originally, the New Jersey justice "had been the other way," but "Pitney came around upon study,"[292] grasping the economic and sociological arguments for workers' compensation. He then voted to sustain those laws and wrote admirable opinions explicating the rationale for doing so.[293]

For the rest of his tenure on the Court, Pitney remained a champion of workers' compensation. He upheld as consistent with the Fourteenth Amendment the extension of New York's scheme to embrace all employers of four or more workers (even those in industries that were not hazardous)[294] and to provide payments for disfiguring injuries that did not deprive their victims of income-earning capacity.[295] Furthermore, when the Court held that a New York court's application of New York law to the case of a stevedore fatally injured while working upon the navigable waters of New York amounted to an impermissible invasion of the exclusive maritime jurisdiction of the federal judiciary, Pitney entered a vigorous dissent.[296] Although usually ruling in favor of the employee, he would go the other way when this was necessary to protect the integrity of a comprehensive workers' compensation system. This was also demonstrated in the case of an injured Texan who sought a higher recovery than his state's compensation act allowed by bringing a common law tort action against his employer.[297]

On the other hand, Pitney held that if a legislature gave laborers the option of either settling for the amounts authorized by a compensation statute or bringing tort actions against their employers (whose common law defenses it severely restricted), this violated neither the equal protection clause nor the due process clause.[298] The states, he wrote in the *Arizona Employers' Liability Cases*,[299] "are left with a wide range of legislative discretion, notwithstanding the provisions of the Fourteenth Amendment; and their conclusions respecting the wisdom of their legislative acts are not reviewable by the courts."[300] Novelty was not a constitutional objection.[301] The statute that the Arizona legislature had enacted imposed no new financial burden on hazardous industries; the very nature of these industries made damages from accidental injuries inevitable.[302] All this law did was require the party who organized and took the profits from an enterprise to treat these damages like other costs of doing business, such as paying wages.[303] He could consider them in setting prices and thus pass through the cost of accidents to the consumer, rather than leaving injured workers, their dependents, and public welfare agencies to bear the burden.[304] Acceptance of such modern notions about spreading the costs of accidents, so incompatible with the fundamental assumptions of turn-of-the-century tort law,[305] apparently did not come easily to Pitney.[306]

That it came at all is indicative of the extent to which one of the reform movements associated with Progressivism molded his thinking. Pitney did not always take a Progressive position in labor cases. For example, he voted against both a Federal child labor statute[307] and a state minimum-wage-for-women law.[308] Nevertheless, his positions in cases involving both unions and unorganized workers reflected the attitudes of Progressive reformers to a surprising extent.

Antitrust and Economic Regulation. The stands Pitney took in litigation arising under the antitrust laws and various state and federal regulatory statutes also mirrored the attitudes of Progressive reformers.

The lack of sympathy for railroads, which was such a notable feature of his career on the New Jersey bench, persisted after his appointment to the Supreme Court. In disputes between carriers and shippers, Pitney exhibited a consistent preference for the latter.[309] He rejected railroads' challenges to orders of the Interstate Commerce Commission,[310] and was almost equally unreceptive to their constitutional complaints about the rules and rates imposed upon them by state regulatory agencies.[311] Pitney also continued for the most part to support the efforts of municipal governments to regulate the corporations that provided their citizens with utility services.[312]

The antimonopoly bias that had animated him during his days as a New Jersey congressman and judge manifested itself in cases arising under the Sherman Antitrust Act. "As a rule, he joined with the majority where it upheld and gave vitality to the Act, and could be counted among the dissenters where the Court resorted to 'strained and unusual' interpretations of the facts to uphold the legality of challenged practices."[313] When a Supreme Court that was growing noticeably more conservative[314] ruled in 1917 that the exclusive leasing agreements that the United Shoe Machinery Company had used to dominate the entire shoe manufacturing business did not violate the Sherman Act, Pitney joined Justices Day[315] and Clarke[316] in protesting its decision. When the Court employed the "rule of reason" to justify rejecting the Government's efforts to dissolve the United States Steel Corporation, he again stood with these two colleagues in dissent.[317] Pitney was, according to one scholar, the Supreme Court's "most consistent supporter of congressional policy as detailed . . . in the antitrust law."[318]

CIVIL LIBERTIES. Although Theodore Roosevelt might not have applauded them, Pitney's votes in support of governmental efforts to control monopoly, like his rulings upholding federal attacks on liquor[319] and prostitution,[320] were very much in the Progressive tradition.[321] So too was Pitney's endorsement of the national government's attack upon dissent during World War I. For Progressives, among them President Wilson, American participation in "the war to end all wars" was a great crusade, in which the nation fought to eradicate militarism, to protect liberalism, and to spread democracy.[322] Believing shared convictions were the cement of society, the government resorted to publicity and appeals to conscience to unite the nation behind this greatest of all reform efforts.[323] The results were intolerance, vigilantism, and persecution.[324] Congress passed the repressive Espionage[325] and Sedition[326] Acts, and despite the apparent inconsistency between those measures and the first amendment, the Supreme Court affirmed their constitutionality and regularly sustained convictions obtained under them.[327] Even the great Justice Oliver Wendell Holmes Jr., before penning the first of his famous "clear and present danger" dissents, handed down three decisions in this vein.[328]

Pitney was in good Progressive company when, in *Pierce v. United States*,[329] he upheld the convictions of four Socialists under section 3 of the Espionage Act[330] based primarily on their distribution of a pamphlet called *The Price We Pay*.[331] This leaflet characterized the war as fought for the benefit of capitalists like J. P. Morgan, wailed about recruiting officers hauling young men away to awful deaths, predicted a rise in food prices, and accused the attorney general of being so busy jailing those who failed to stand for the playing of "The Star-Spangled Banner" that he had no time for prosecuting speculators.[332] "Common knowledge," Pitney believed, "would have sufficed to show at least that the statements as to the causes that led to the entry of the United States into the war against Germany were grossly false; and such common knowledge went to prove also that [the] defendants knew they were untrue."[333] In his opinion, a jury might have found that *The Price We Pay* could tend to cause insubordination in the armed forces and to obstruct recruiting.[334]

Brandeis, on the other hand, considered it inconceivable that the lurid exaggerations with which this pamphlet was filled could induce any serviceman of normal intelligence to risk the severe penalties prescribed for refusal of duty.[335] In dissent, he pointed out the harm that could be done to the democratic political process if arguments were treated as criminal incitements merely because they seemed unfair, mistaken, unsound, or intemperate "to those exercising judiciary power."[336] His was a message lost on Pitney, who joined the majority that upheld numerous other convictions under the Espionage and Sedition Acts and related state statutes.[337]

In voting to jail opponents of the war, Pitney reflected the temper of his times. His greatest weakness was an inability to question the accepted wisdom of his own day. Thus, he affirmed a district court decision that had denied a writ of habeas corpus to Leo Frank, who was convicted of murder in an Atlanta trial so dominated by a mob that the defendant had to be absent from the courtroom when the jury returned its verdict.[338] Because Frank had failed to raise the matter of his exclusion from the courtroom promptly and because the Georgia courts had considered and had rejected his contention that the jury had been influenced by the threatening atmosphere that surrounded the trial, Pitney ruled that the defendant had not been denied his Fourteenth Amendment right to due process of law.[339]

Such exaggerated deference to state authority and such callous insistence that violations of fundamental rights by state institutions lay beyond federal control were not peculiar to Pitney. They remained typical of the Court as a whole until well into the 1920s.[340] Furthermore, in refusing to impose national conceptions of due process on Georgia, Pitney was taking a position consistent with the one he adopted in other cases far less controversial than Leo Frank's.[341] Still, Holmes could see what Pitney could not: "Whatever disagreement there may be as to the scope of the phrase 'due process of law,' there can be no doubt that it embraces the fundamental conception of a fair trial. . . . Mob law [cannot be] due process."[342] Within less than a decade, the Court would inform the states, through a Holmes opinion, that the Fourteenth Amendment limited their discretion at least that much.[343]

Resignation and Death

By the time it did this, Mahlon Pitney was no longer on the bench. The justice who reflected so well the attitudes of the Progressive era departed from the Supreme Court soon after Progressivism came to an end in the sour aftermath of World War I.[344] In early 1922, while attending a rededication of the Philadelphia room where the Court had held its first session, Pitney suffered what doctors diagnosed as "a blood clot on the brain."[345] Chief Justice Taft urged him to take some time off,[346] and he did.[347] Upon his return to Washington, Pitney still could not resume a full workload. Taft regarded him as a "weak" member of the Court, and after his "breakdown," he assigned him no further cases.[348] Pitney wrote only three more opinions before the end of the term.[349]

Then, in August 1922, he suffered a massive stroke.[350] Pitney now recognized that he would have to leave the Court.[351] Unfortunately, if he did so, he would not be eligible for a pension; he had completed the required ten years of service, but was still six years short of the mandatory seventy years of age.[352] Congress enacted special legislation enabling Pitney to retire,[353] however, and he did so on December 31, 1922.[354] A little less than two years later, on December 9, 1924, New Jersey's third Supreme Court Justice died at his house in Washington.[355] Then, for the last time, he came home to Morristown.[356]

Conclusion

Neither contemporaries nor historians have ranked Pitney with the greats of the Supreme Court. Even among the four New Jersey justices, he tends to be the forgotten figure. [Editor's note: As of 2009, the total is six.] Nonetheless, Pitney deserves more credit than he has received. At the time he sat, a previously rural and agrarian America was struggling, often without really knowing quite how to go about it, to adjust to life as an urban and industrial society. That, at bottom, was what Progressivism was all about.[357] The country needed judges who would support, rather than use their judicial power to thwart, the sometimes unwise but mostly necessary initiatives of a great reform movement. The nation found one in Mahlon Pitney. Of all the justices who sat on the Supreme Court during his tenure, "Pitney was the most consistent supporter of national reform legislation."[358] His opinions are as murky as one critic has charged,[359] but he was not the reactionary some have made him out to be.[360] Thrust onto the national scene by New Jersey Progressivism, and a mirror of its values and biases, Justice Pitney was a contributor to whatever success the Progressive movement achieved, both in his native state and in the nation as a whole.

Notes

The author wishes to thank Ms. Loni Freeman for her invaluable help with the research for this article. [Editor's note, revised edition of the *New Jersey Anthology*: For the complete text of the footnotes see the original article or the first edition. Here citations have been retained, but not detailed comments, except where they provide valuable information about New Jersey history.]

1. *See* G. Myers, *History of the Supreme Court of the United States* 783–85 (1912, reprint 1925).

2. *Id.* at 783.

3. *Id.* at 784.

4. Israel, "Mahlon Pitney," in 3 *The Justices of the United States Supreme Court 1789–1978: Their Lives and Major Opinions* 2001 (L. Friedman & F. Israel eds. 1980).

5. *See id.* at 2005.

6. A. Link & R. McCormick, *Progressivism* 1 (1983).

7. *Id.* at 2.

8. *See id.*

9. Most of these big businesses were not true trusts. John D. Rockefeller did accomplish a horizontal combination of competing firms in the oil industry in 1882 by creating a trust. G. Porter, *The Rise of Big Business, 1860–1910*, at 56 (1973). After 1889, however, such a horizontal combination was normally achieved by creating a holding company incorporated under the laws of New Jersey. *See id.*

10. *See* J. Garraty, *A Short History of the American Nation* 368–69 (2d ed. 1974).

11. *See id.* at 369.

12. *See* T. McCraw, *Prophets of Regulation* 111 (1984).

13. *See generally* E. Foner, *Free Soil, Free Labor, Free Men: The Ideology of the Republican Party Before the Civil War* 16–17 (1970).

14. *See id.* at 20, 22, 25.

15. *See* Benedict, "Laissez-Faire and Liberty: A Re-evaluation of the Meaning and Origins of Laissez-Faire Constitutionalism," 3 *Law & Hist. Rev.* 293, 308 (1985).

16. *See* G. E. White, *The American Judicial Tradition: Profiles of Leading American Judges* 136–38 (1976); and his opinion in Adair v. United States, 208 U.S. 161 (1908).

17. P. Strum, *Louis D. Brandeis* 343 (1984).

18. A. Link, *Wilson: The Road to the White House* 127 (1947). During his 1910 campaign for governor, Wilson repudiated what he had said earlier about unions, claiming he had not really meant it. *Id.* at 159, 184.

19. G. Mowry, *The Era of Theodore Roosevelt: 1900–1912*, at 100 (1958).

20. R. Hofstadter, *The Age of Reform* 170 (1955).

21. *Id.* at 216. *Contra* R. Wiebe, *The Search for Order: 1877–1920 passim* (1967).

22. *See* R. Hofstadter, *supra* note 20, at 135.

23. *See* A. Link & R. McCormick, *supra* note 6, at 7.

24. R. Hofstadter, *supra* note 20, at 168–69.

25. *See id.* at 172–73.

26. A. Link & R. McCormick, *supra* note 6, at 7–8.

27. It may be that an interpretation of Progressivism that emphasizes the reaction of the middle class to what its members perceived as threats from above and below is more useful for explaining the development and nature of that phenomenon in the region from which Pitney hailed—the urban Northeast.

28. *See* G. Mowry, *supra* note 19, at 86.

29. *See id.* at 86–87.

30. *See id.* at 86.

31. *See id.; see also* Thelen, "Social Tensions and The Origins of Progressivism," 56 *J. Am. Hist.* 323, 330–34 (1969).

32. *See* Israel, *supra* note 4, at 2001.

33. *Id.*

34. *Id. See generally Obituaries*, 48 *N.J.L.J.* 29, 29 (1925) .

35. *Obituaries, supra* note 34, at 29.

36. *Id.; see also Princeton College, The Class Of 1879: Quindecennial Record 1879–1894*, at 85 (1894) [hereinafter cited as *Class of 1879*].

37. Israel, *supra* note 4, at 2001.

38. *Newark Evening News*, Dec. 1, 1915, in Mahlon Pitney Papers (in the personal possession of James C. Pitney, Morristown, New Jersey) [hereinafter cited as Pitney Papers]; *see* Letter from Woodrow Wilson to Mahlon Pitney (Nov. 22, 1915), in Pitney Papers, *supra*.

39. *See Bench and Bar of New Jersey* 209 (1942).

40. *See Obituaries, supra* note 34, at 29.

41. A. Breed, "Mahlon Pitney: His Life and Career—Political and Judicial" 8 (undated, unpublished thesis, Princeton University).

42. *See id.* at 8–9.

43. *Id.* at 9.

44. *Id.* at 10.

45. *See id.* at 9.

46. *See id.* at 9–10; Letter from Wilbur F. Sadler, Jr. to Mahlon Pitney (May 5, 1914), in Pitney Papers, *supra* note 38.

47. A. Breed, *supra* note 41, at 10.

48. *Id.*

49. *See id.*

50. *Id.*

51. *See id.* at 11.

52. *Class of 1879, supra* note 36, at 85; R. McCarter, *Memories of a Half Century at the New Jersey Bar* 88–89 (1937).

53. *See Obituaries, supra* note 34, at 29–30; A. Breed, *supra* note 41, at 12.

54. *See supra* note 53.

55. *See* Gould, "The Republican Search For a National Majority," in *The Gilded Age* 171, 183 (H. Morgan ed. 1970).

56. *True Democratic Banner*, Sept. 27, 1894, in Pitney Papers, *supra* note 38.

57. A. Breed, *supra* note 41, at 12.

58. *See id.*

59. It is interesting to note that the *New York Daily Tribune* later claimed, "Pitney surprised some of the old-timers by making a number of excellent speeches during his first term in Congress." *New York Daily Tribune*, May 10, 1897, in Pitney Papers, *supra* note 38. *The Congressional Record*, however, lends no support to this bit of Republican puffery.

60. *See Morris County Chronicle*, October 16, 1896, in Pitney Papers, *supra* note 38.

61. A. Breed, *supra* note 41, at 13.

62. *Id.*

63. *See id.*

64. *Obituaries, supra* note 34, at 30.

65. *See* A. Breed, *supra* note 41, at 14.

66. *Id.*

67. *See id.* at 16.

68. *Id.* at 15; Israel, *supra* note 4, at 2002.

69. *See* Israel, *supra* note 4, at 2002.

70. *Id.*

71. *Obituaries, supra* note 34, at 30.

72. *See id.*

73. *Id.*

74. *Id.*

75. *See* Letter from Mahlon Pitney to the Editor of the Sunday *Call* (March 28, 1901), in Pitney Papers, *supra* note 38.

76. Israel, *supra* note 4, at 2002; Obituaries, *supra* note 34, at 30; A. Breed, *supra* note 41, at 16.

77. A. Breed, *supra* note 41, at 17.

78. *Id.*

79. *Id.*

80. *Id.*

81. Besides defending the gold standard, Pitney also supported that traditional Republican bromide, the protective tariff. *See infra* notes 83–84 and accompanying text; *True Democratic Banner*, September 27, 1894, in Pitney Papers, *supra* note 38.

82. G. Mowry, *supra* note 19, at 87.

83. *See* Fite, "Election of 1896," in 2 *History of American Presidential Elections* 1787, 1822 (A. Schlesinger ed. 1971); J. Hicks, *The Populist Revolt* 315–16 (1931). As Pitney pointed out in a speech on the House floor on February 3, 1898, the free-silver issue caused New Jersey Democrats to desert their party by the thousands in 1896. *See* 31 *Cong. Rec.* 165 app., 167 app. (1898).

84. *Morris County Chronicle*, October 16, 1896, in Pitney Papers, *supra* note 38.

85. *See* A. Link, *supra* note 18, at 25.

86. *See id.* at 134–35.

87. *Id.* at 134; R. Noble Jr., *New Jersey Progressivism before Wilson* 4–6, 9–11 (1946); see McCurdy, "The Knight Sugar Decision of 1895 and the Modernization of American Corporation Law, 1869–1903," 53 *Bus. Hist. Rev.* 304, 322–23 (1979). Particularly useful to the great industrial combinations of the era were two Acts of the New Jersey Legislature. One authorized New Jersey corporations to do business outside the state and to issue their own stock in order to purchase stock in other corporations. *See* Act of May 9, 1889, ch. 265, §§ 1, 4, 1889 NJ. Laws 412, 412, 415. The other allowed corporations organized for any lawful purpose to carry on business anywhere, to hold securities in other concerns, and to issue their own stock in payment for property. *See* Act of Apr. 21, 1896, ch. 185, §§ 7, 49, 50, 1896 N.J. Laws 277, 280, 293–94, 294. The latter law also gave corporations organized under it wide power to alter their charters. *See id.* §28, 1896 N.J. Laws at 286.

88. *See* A. Link, *supra* note 18, at 134.

89. *Id.*

90. R. Noble, Jr., *supra* note 87, at 10–11.

91. *Id.* at 9–10.

92. *Id.* at 10–11.

93. *Id.* at 24, 51.

94. *Id.* at 65 n.3, 66–71.

95. A. Link, *supra* note 18, at 262–63; *see also* Act of April 21 1911, ch. 195, 1911 N.J. Laws 374 (creating the Board of Public Utility Commissioners).

96. *See* 29 *Cong. Rec.* 1448–55 (1897).

97. *Id.* at 1454.

98. *Id.* at 1455.

99. 31 *Cong. Rec.* 167 app. (1898).

100. Letter from Mahlon Pitney to the Editor of the Sunday *Call* (Mar. 28, 1901), in Pitney Papers, *supra* note 38.

101. Israel, *supra* note 4, at 2003; A. Breed, *supra* note 41, at 17–18.

102. Israel, *supra* note 4, at 2003.

103. *Id.*

104. *See* Obituaries, *supra* note 34, at 30.

105. *Id.* When his friend Francis Swayze expressed regret about his leaving the [state] supreme court, Pitney told him "that [he] would like to be *both* a Supreme Court Justice and Chancellor." Letter from Mahlon Pitney to John R. Hardin (January 25, 1908), in Pitney Papers, *supra* note 38.

106. Israel, *supra* note 4, at 2003, A. Breed, *supra* note 41, at 20.

107. A. Breed, *supra* note 41, at 20.

108. *See id.*

109. Family legend has it that Chancellor Pitney was once seen by a friend at a railroad station with a dour look on his face. Asked what was bothering him, he replied that he was on his way to reverse a decision of his father. Interview with James C. Pitney, grandson of Justice Pitney, in Morristown, New Jersey (Apr. 15, 1985). See also: "Jersey's Honor to Justice Pitney," 35 *N.J.L.J.* 139, 140 (1912) [hereinafter cited as "Jersey's Honor"].

110. A. Breed, *supra* note 41, at 20.

111. *Newark Evening News,* June 8, 1910, in Pitney Papers, *supra* note 38.

112. *See* Bergen & Dundee R.R. v. State Bd. of Assessors, 74 *N.J.L.* 742, 67 A. 668 (1907).

113. Ch. 91, 1905 N.J. Laws 189.

114. *See* Central R.R. v. State Bd. of Assessors, 75 *N.J.L.* 120, 67 A. 672 (Sup. Ct. 1907), aff'd, 75 *N.J.L.* 771, 69 A. 239 (1908).

115. *See* Average Rate Law, ch. 82, 1906 N.J. Laws 121.

116. *See* Perkins Act, ch. 280, 1906 N.J. Laws 571; *see also* Act of Apr. 18, 1906, ch. 122, 1906 N.J. Laws 220 (defining "main stem").

117. *See* Tuckerton R.R. v. State Bd. of Assessors, 75 *N.J.L.* 157, 67 A. 69 (Sup. Ct. 1907).

118. *See In re* New York Bay R.R., 75 *N.J.L.* 389, 67 A. 1049 (Sup. Ct. 1907); *In re* United N.J.R.R. & Canal, 75 *N.J.L.* 385, 67 A. 1075 (Sup. Ct. 1907), *rev'd*, 76 *N.J.L* 830, 71 A. 275 (1908).

119. *See* Mayor of Jersey City v. Board of Equalization of Taxes, 74 *N.J.L.* 753, 67 A. 38 (1907).

120. *See id.* at 754, 67 A. at 39.

121. *See* Mayor of Jersey City v. North Jersey St. Ry., 72 *N.J.L.* 383, 61 A. 95 (Sup. Ct. 1905). The Company, a successor in interest to the Jersey City & Bergen Railroad Company, claimed that a supplement to the charter of the Jersey City & Bergen, passed by the legislature in 1867, exempted it from license fees imposed by a local government. *Id.* at 387–88, 61 A. at 96. *But cf.* Fielders v. North Jersey St. Ry., 68 *N.J.L.* 343, 363, 53 A.404, 411 (1902) (stating that an ordinance requiring street railway companies to pave the portion of the street over which their tracks passed was an illegal tax not justifiable as an exercise of the police power).

122. *See* North Jersey St. Ry. v. Mayor of Jersey City, 75 *N.J.L.* 349, 67 A. 1072 (Sup. Ct. 1907). At the end of his opinion in the *North Jersey* case, Pitney announced that a like result had been reached previously in a similar case. *Id.* at 354, 67 A. at 1074; *see also* State v. Atlantic City & S. R.R., 77 *N.J.L.* 465, 72 A. 111 (1909) (sustaining effort of the attorney general to forbid a railroad from owning stocks and bonds of a street railway company).

123. *See* Warren v. Pirn, 66 NJ. Eq. 353, 399, 59 A. 773, 790 (1904) (Pitney, J., concurring). In this case, Pitney was part of a seven-to-six majority that affirmed a decision handed down by his father. *See id.* at 428, 59 A. at 802.

124. *See id.* at 364, 373, 378, 386–87, 59 A. at 777, 780, 782, 785 (Pitney, J., concurring).

125. *See id.* at 395–97, 59 A. at 789 (Pitney, J., concurring).

126. *See* 31 *Cong. Rec.* 167 app. (1898).

127. 73 *N.J.L.* 729, 65 A. 165 (1906).

128. *Id.* at 739, 65 A. at 169.

129. Levin v. Cosgrove, 75 *N.J.L.* 344, 347, 67 A. 1070, 1071 (Sup. Ct. 1907).

130. *Id.* at 347–48, 67 A. at 1071. It is not at all clear that this is really a holding of Brennan; the reasoning in the opinion is extremely murky. *See* Brennan, 73 *N.J.L.* at 742–43, 65 A. at 170–71.

131. 77 *N.J. Eq.* 219, 79 A. 262 (1908).

132. For the injunction restraining the defendants see: *Id.* At 221–22, 79 A. at 263.

133. *See* George Jonas Glass Co. v. Glass Bottle Blowers Assoc, 72 *N.J. Eq.* 653, 66 A. 953 (Ch. 1907), aff'd, 77 *N.J. Eq.* 219, 79 A. 262 (1908).

134. *See id.* at 655, 66 A. at 954.

135. *Jonas Glass*, 77 *N.J. Eq.* at 221, 79 A. at 263.

136. George Jonas Glass Co. v. Glass Bottle Blowers Assoc, 72 *N.J. Eq.* 653, 662, 66 A. 953, 957 (Ch. 1907), *aff'd*, 77 *N.J. Eq.* 219, 79 A. 262 (1908).

137. *See Jonas Glass,* 77 *N.J. Eq.* at 224, 79 A. at 264. For the statute see: Act of February 14, 1883, ch. 28, §1, 1883 N.J. Laws 36, 36. In a mildly critical editorial, the *Newark Evening News* argued that Pitney had not overlooked this statute, but had ignored the strikers'"constitutional rights of personal liberty and free speech." *Newark Evening News,* February 15, 1911, in Pitney Papers, *supra* note 38.

138. *See Jonas Glass,* 77 *N.J. Eq.* at 224, 79 A. at 264.

139. *See infra* notes 140–142 and accompanying text. He ruled for workers three times and against them four times. *See id.* If one discounts Delaney v. Public Serv. Ry., 82 *N.J.L.* 551, 552, 82 A. 852, 852 (1912), in which he affirmed a nonsuit because the plaintiff had presented no evidence of the defendant's negligence beyond the fact that its pneumatic jack had injured him, there is an even split.

140. *See* Diehl v. Standard Oil Co., 70 *N.J.L.* 424, 57 A. 131 (Sup. Ct. 1904). The decision in Gill v. National Storage Co., 70 *N.J.L.* 53, 56 A. 146 (Sup. Ct. 1903) seems also to be based on the doctrine of contributory negligence but it may rest on the principle of assumption of the risk; the opinion is extremely unclear.

141. *See* Knutter v. New York & N.J. Tel. Co., 67 *N.J.L.* 646, 52 A. 565 (1902).

142. *See* Burns v. Delaware & Atl. Tel. Co., 70 *N.J.L.* 745, 59 A. 220 (1904); Hopwood v. Benjamin Atha & Illingsworth Co., 68 *N.J.L.* 707, 54 A. 435 (1903); Smith v. Erie R.R., 67 *N.J.L.* 636, 52 A. 634 (1902).

143. *See generally* R. Hofstadter, *supra* note 20, at 238.

144. G. Mowry, *supra* note 19, at 99–100.

145. *See, e.g.,* Meehan v. Board of Excise Comm'rs, 75 *N.J.L.* 557, 70 A. 363 (1908); Croker v. Board of Excise Comm'rs, 73 *N.J.L.* 460, 63 A. 901 (Sup. Ct. 1906); Bachman v. Inhabitants of Phillipsburg, 68 *N.J.L.* 552, 53 A. 620 (Sup. Ct. 1902). The hostility of Progressives toward saloons arose from a belief that immigrants drank too much. *See* A. Link & R. McCormick, *supra* note 6, at 102–03.

146. *See, e.g.,* Ames v. Kirby, 71 *NJ.L* 442, 59 A. 558 (Sup. Ct. 1904). *See generally* A. Link & R. McCormick, *supra* note 6, at 68–69.

147. *Newark Evening News,* November 2, 1907, in Pitney Papers, *supra* note 38.

148. *See* clipping from unidentified newspaper, January 10,1907, in Pitney Papers, *supra* note 38.

149. Although his judicial rulings clearly served to enhance his political appeal, Pitney insisted in 1912 that he had never allowed politics to influence his decisions. " See: "Jersey's Honor," *supra* note 109, at 143.

150. *See* Letter from Frederick Gordon to the Editor of the *Newark Evening News* (Jan. 11, 1907), in Pitney Papers, *supra* note 38. The *Evening News* commented favorably on Pitney as a possible Senatorial candidate. *Newark Evening News,* September 4, 1906, in Pitney Papers, *supra* note 38.

151. R. Noble, Jr., *supra* note 87, at 83 n. 59; see *The Jerseyman,* January 25, 1907, in Pitney Papers, *supra* note 38.

152. *See* G. Mowry, *supra* note 19, at 210–12, 218–20.

153. *See Newark Public Ledger,* August10 (year unidentified), in Pitney Papers, *supra* note 38.

154. *See* Letter to the Editor of the *New York Times,* August 9, 1907, in Pitney Papers, *supra* note 38.

155. *See Newark Evening News,* July 27, 1907, in Pitney Papers, *supra* note 38.

156. *See* undated clipping from unidentified 1910 newspaper in Pitney Papers, *supra* note 38. In 1915, Morris County Republicans sought to promote the idea of a Pitney presidential candidacy. *See Newark Evening News,* November 24, 1915, in Pitney Papers, *supra* note 38. The Justice, however, then serving on the United States Supreme Court, released a letter to them saying he could not see his way clear to permit the use of his name as a candidate. *See Newark Evening News,* November 30, 1915, in Pitney Papers, *supra* note 38.

157. *See* Letter from William H. Taft to James E. Howell (September 15, 1910), in Pitney Papers, *supra* note 38.

158. Willis Van Devanter, Joseph R. Lamar, and Charles Evans Hughes. *See generally* 9 A. Bickel & B. Schmidt, Jr., *History of the Supreme Court of the United States: The Judiciary and Responsible Government 1910–21,* at 3–85 (1984).

159. *See infra* notes 163–169 and accompanying text.

160. Fred Israel attributes the appointment to the impression that Pitney made on Taft when they met at a dinner in Newark the week before the appointment was made. *See* Israel, *supra* note 4, at 2003. Henry J. Abraham attributes it to political strategy related to the struggle between Taft and Theodore Roosevelt for the 1912 Republican nomination, but he fails to explain the relationship between the two satisfactorily. *See* H. Abraham, *Justices and Presidents: A Political History of the Appointments to the Supreme Court* 162–63 (1974). After extensive research, the late Professor Alexander Bickel concluded, "The origins and the method of the Pitney selection are not discoverable." A. Bickel & B. Schmidt Jr., *supra* note 158, at 326.

161. *See* A. Link, *supra* note 18, at 468–69; W. Harbauch, *Life and Times of Theodore Roosevelt* 402 (rev. ed. 1963).

162. *See* H. Abraham, *supra* note 160, at 163.

163. A. Bickel & B. Schmidt Jr., *supra* note 158, at 318–19.

164. *Id.* at 326.

165. H. Abraham, *supra* note 160, at 163. Nagel's first wife was Louis Brandeis's sister. A. Bickel & B. Schmidt, Jr., *supra* note 158, at 326 n.26.

166. A. Bickel & B. Schmidt Jr., *supra* note 158, at 322–24. The case was McCabe v. Atchison, T. & S.F. Ry., 186 F. 966 (8th Cir. 1911), aff'd, 235 *U.S.* 151 (1914).

167. A. Bickel & B. Schmidt Jr., *supra* note 158, at 321. The case was City of Denver v. New York Trust Co., 187 F. 890 (8th Cir. 1911), rev'd, 229 *U.S.* 123 (1913).

168. A. Bickel & B. Schmidt, Jr., *supra* note 158, at 320–21. The decision to which the governors and railroad commissioners particularly objected was Missouri, Kan. & Tex. Ry. v. Love, 177 F. 493 (W.D. Okla. 1910), aff'd, 185 F. 321 (8th Cir. 1911).

169. *See generally* W. Harbaugh, *supra* note 161, at 401–06.

170. *See N.J.Journal*, February 21, 1912, in Pitney Papers, *supra* note 38.

171. *See N.J.Journal*, January 22, 1912, in Pitney Papers, *supra* note 38; *N.J.Journal*, February 12, 1912, in Pitney papers, *supra* note 38.

172. A. Breed, *supra* note 41, at 22.

173. *Id.* at 23. Pitney and Taft had met earlier, once having played golf together at Chevy Chase, Maryland. *Id.* at 22. The game of golf would continue to provide something of a bond between them after Pitney's appointment. *See* Letter from Mahlon Pitney to the President (June 18, 1912), in Pitney Papers, *supra* note 38.

174. *See* Letter from William H. Taft to Mahlon Pitney (February 19, 1912), in Pitney Papers, *supra* note 38;A Breed, *supra* note 41, at 23.

175. *See* H. Abraham, *supra* note 160, at 163; J. Semonche, *Charting the Future* 267 (1978).

176. *See* H. Abraham, *supra* note 160, at 163.

177. *See* A. Bickel & B. Schmidt Jr., *supra* note 158, at 318–19.

178. Taft had been a judge on the Ohio Superior Court from 1887 to 1890 and a judge on the United States Court of Appeals for the Sixth Circuit from 1892 to 1900. A. Mason, *William Howard Taft: Chief Justice* 12 (1964).

179. A. Breed, *supra* note 41, at 23.

180. *See* Letter from James E. Howell to William H. Taft (September 15, 1910), in Pitney Papers, *supra* note 38.

181. *See* "Jersey's Honor," *supra* note 109, at 143–44.

182. *See id.* at 140.

183. J. Semonche, *supra* note 175, at 266. Semonche claims that Swayze was the leading contender from New Jersey. *Id.* Certainly, that is what Pitney thought. *See* A. Breed, *supra* note 41, at 22.

184. *See* A. Breed, *supra* note 41, at 26–27.

185. *Id.* at 22. Briggs was also a Taft supporter. *See id.* at 26–27. According to Robert McCarter, Murphy at first urged Taft to appoint Swayze. Taft responded by offering to appoint Swayze to the United States Court of Appeals for the Third Circuit. R. McCarter, *supra* note 52, at 85.

186. Letter from James E. Howell to William H. Taft, *supra* note 180; *New York Times*, February 19, 1912, in Pitney Papers, *supra* note 38.

187. *See New York Times*, February 25, 1912, in Pitney Papers, *supra* note 38; *see also* A. Breed, *supra* note 41, at 22 (Murphy and Pitney were close friends).

188. R. Noble, Jr., *supra* note 87, at 23.

189. *See* A. Breed, *supra* note 41, at 22.

190. Bickel asserts that Taft "decided to nominate Pitney in the teeth of the progressives." A. Bickel & B. Schmidt Jr., *supra* note 158, at 328. Bickel is guilty of reading history backward, however, assuming that Taft knew at the time he made the appointment the sort of controversy that it would ignite. He also views the opposition to Pitney's confirmation as more Progressive than it was. *See infra* note 195–206 and accompanying text. Pitney was

a close friend of the conservative Franklin Murphy. A. Breed, *supra* note 41, at 22., *supra* notes 170–174 and accompanying text. In Washington, political observers commented that the Pitney appointment would have a sharp bearing on the political contest for control of New Jersey. *See N.Y. Times,* Feb. 19, 1912, in Pitney Papers, *supra* note 38.

191. *See* A. Breed, *supra* note 41, at 30–31.

192. *Id.* at 32.

193. A. Bickel & B. Schmidt Jr., *supra* note 158, at 329.

194. *New York Times,* February 19, 1912, in Pitney Papers, *supra* note 38.

195. A. Bickel & B. Schmidt, Jr., *supra* note 158, at 329.

196. 63 *N.J. Eq.* 443, 52 A. 152 (Ch. 1901).

197. A. Bickel & B. Schmidt Jr., *supra* note 158, at 330.

198. *Id.* at 330 n.41.

199. A. Breed, *supra* note 41, at 31–32.

200. A. Bickel & B. Schmidt Jr., *supra* note 158, at 331; *New York Times,* March 9, 1912, in Pitney Papers, *supra* note 38; *see also supra* notes 131–137 and accompanying text.

201. 48 *Cong. Rec.* 3011 (1912).

202. A. Bickel & B. Schmidt Jr., *supra* note 158, at 331.

203. *See Newark News,* March 13, 1912, in Pitney Papers, *supra* note 38.

204. *See id.;* A. Breed, *supra* note 41, at 33.

205. *Newark News,* March 13, 1912, in Pitney Papers, *supra* note 38.

206. A. Bickel & B. Schmidt Jr., *supra* note 158, at 329, 332. *See generally* A. Breed, *supra* note 41, at 33–36.

207. *See* A. Breed, *supra* note 41, at 36.

208. *See* Israel, *supra* note 4, at 2004. Pitney served for 10 years, 9 months, and 12 days. *Id.*

209. *Id.*

210. *Id.*

211. 252 *U.S.* 189 (1920).

212. *Id.* at 207.

213. *Id.* at 199.

214. *See* Revenue Act of 1916, ch. 463, §2(a), 39 Stat. 756, 757 (current version at 26 *U.S.C.* §61 (Supp. II 1984)).

215. *See* Eisner, 252 *U.S.* at 201–05.

216. *See* A. Bickel & B. Schmidt Jr., *supra* note 158, at 508.

217. *See id.*

218. *Id.*

219. *See id.*

220. *Id.* at 509.

221. Eisner, 252 *U.S.* at 237 (Brandeis, J., dissenting).

222. A. Bickel & B. Schmidt Jr., *supra* note 158, at 509. It is not surprising that Pitney defined income restrictively and thus limited what the national government could tax under the Sixteenth Amendment. New Jersey had refused to ratify that amendment. *See* A. Link, *supra* note 18, at 267–68.

223. *See, e.g.,* Miles v. Safe Deposit & Trust Co., 259 *U.S.* 247 (1922); Rockefeller v. United States, 257 *U.S.* 176 (1921); United States v. Phellis, 257 *U.S.* 156 (1921); Peabody v. Eisner, 247 *U.S.* 347 (1918); Lynch v. Hornby, 247 *U.S.* 339 (1918); Southern Pac. Co. v. Lowe, 247 *U.S.* 330 (1918).

224. *See, e.g.,* LaBelle Iron Works v. United States, 256 *U.S.* 377 (1921); United States v. Cleveland, C.C. & St. L. Ry., 247 *U.S.* 195 (1918); Hays v. Gauley Mountain Coal Co., 247 *U.S.* 189 (1918); Anderson v. Forty–Two Broadway Co., 239 *U.S.* 69 (1915); Stratton's Independence, Ltd. v. Howbert, 231 *U.S.* 399 (1913); McCoach v. Minehill & S.H.R.R., 228 *U.S.* 295 (1913).

225. *See, e.g.,* United States v. Field, 255 *U.S.* 257 (1921).

226. *See, e.g.,* St. Louis, J.M. & S. Ry. v. J.F Hasty & Sons, 255 *U.S.* 252 (1921).

227. *See, e.g.,* Texas Co. v. Brown, 258 *U.S.* 466 (1922); Citizens Nat'l Bank v. Durr, 257 *U.S.* 99 (1921); Bowman v. Continental Oil Co., 256 *U.S.* 642 (1921); F.S. Royster Guano Co. v. Virginia, 253 *U.S.* 412 (1920); Travis v. Yale & Towne Mfg. Co., 252 *U.S.* 60 (1920); Shaffer v. Carter, 252 *U.S.* 37 (1920); Wagner v. City of Covington, 251 *U.S.* 95 (1919); American Mfg. Co. v. St. Louis, 250 *U.S.* 459 (1919); Mackay Tel. & Cable Co. v. City of Little Rock, 250 *U.S.* 94 (1919); Leary v. Mayor of Jersey City, 248 *U.S.* 328 (1918); Postal Tel. Cable Co. v. City of Newport, 247 *U.S.* 464 (1918); United States Glue Co. v. Town of Oak Creek, 247 *U.S.* 321 (1918); Crew Levick Co. v. Pennsylvania, 245 *U.S.* 292 (1917); Illinois Cent. R.R. v. Greene, 244 *U.S.* 555 (1917); Louisville & N.R.R. v. Greene, 244 *U.S.* 22 (1917); Greene v. Louisville & Interurban R.R., 244 *U.S.* 499 (1917); St. Louis S.W. Ry. v. Arkansas, 235 *U.S.* 350 (1914); Singer Sewing Mach. Co. v. Brickell, 233 *U.S.* 304 (1914); Ohio Tax Cases, 232 *U.S.* 576 (1914); United States Fidelity Co. v. Kentucky, 231 *U.S.* 394 (1913).

228. *See* Union Tank Line v. Wright, 249 *U.S.* 275, 287 (1919) (Pitney, J., dissenting).

229. Israel, *supra* note 4, at 2004.

230. *See* J. Semonche, *supra* note 175, at 298.

231. *See* Levitan, "Mahlon Pitney—Labor Judge," 40 *VA. L. Rev.* 733, 748 (1954).

232. 236 *U.S.* 1 (1915).

233. *Id.* at 26. Such agreements were commonly referred to as "yellow-dog contracts." In striking down this statute, Pitney relied on an earlier case in which the Court had invalidated a federal statute outlawing yellow-dog contracts for railroad workers. *See id.* at 9–18 (citing Adair v. United States, 208 *U.S.* 161 (1908)). For a criticism of both Coppage and Adair, *see* Powell, "Collective Bargaining Before the Supreme Court," 33 *Pol. Sci. Q.* 396 (1918).

234. Coppage, 236 *U.S.* at 19.

235. *Id.* at 18.

236. *See* Wilson v. New, 243 U.S. 332, 377 (1917) (Pitney, J., dissenting). *See generally* Belknap, "The New Deal and the Emergency Powers Doctrine," 62 *Tex. L. Rev.* 67, 79–81 (1983) (discussing the Wilson case and the national emergency powers doctrine).

237. 244 *U.S.* 459, 472 (1917) (Pitney, J., dissenting).

238. Ch. 647, 26 Stat. 209 (1890) (codified as amended at 15 *U.S.C.* §§1–7 (1982)).

239. 245 *U.S.* 229 (1917).

240. *Id.* at 261–62.

241. *Id.* at 259.

242. *See* Powell, *supra* note 233, at 421–22.

243. 245 *U.S.* 275 (1917).

244. Levitan, *supra* note 231, at 744.

245. 254 *U.S.* 443 (1921).

246. *Id.* at 478–79.

247. *See id.* at 461.

248. Ch. 323, §20, 38 Stat. 730, 738 (1914) (current version at 29 *U.S.C.* §52 (1982)).

249. "Duplex Printing," 254 *U.S.* at 488 (Brandeis, J., dissenting).

250. *See* A. Bickel & B. Schmidt, Jr., *supra* note 158, at 585.

251. 257 *U.S.* 312 (1921).

252. Letter from Mahlon Pitney to Mr. Justice Brandeis (Nov. 3, 1920), in Louis D. Brandeis Papers, folder 14, manuscript box 114 (available at Harvard Law School Library) [hereinafter cited as Brandeis Papers]; Memorandum by Justice Pitney in No. 72, October Term 1920, in Brandeis Papers, *supra*, folder 9, manuscript box 7.

253. Conversations between L.D.B. and F.F., in Brandeis Papers, *supra* note 252 folder 14, manuscript box 114; see *Truax,* 257 *U.S.* at 344 (Pitney, J., dissenting).

254. *See Truax,* 257 *U.S.* at 346–47 (Pitney, J., dissenting).

255. *Id.* at 349 (Pitney, J., dissenting).

256. *Id.* at 348 (Pitney, J., dissenting). Somewhat earlier, Theodore Roosevelt had evolved from a defender to an opponent of the labor injunction. *See* J. Lurie, *Law and the Nation, 1865–1912,* at 59–63 (1983).

257. Levitan, *supra* note 231, at 748.

258. *See id.* at 752.

259. *See* Prudential Ins. Co. v. Cheek, 259 *U.S.* 530 (1922).

260. *See* Chicago, R.I. & Pac. Ry. v. Perry, 259 *U.S.* 548 (1922).

261. On the attitudes of Roosevelt, Congress, and the Progressive movement concerning compensation for the victims of industrial accidents, see A. Bickel & B. Schmidt Jr., *supra*

note 158, at 205–13. *See generally* Friedman & Ladinsky, "Social Change and the Law of Industrial Accidents," 67 *Colum. L. Rev.* 50 (1967).

262. Ch. 149, 35 Stat. 65 (1908) (codified as amended at 45 *U.S.C.* §§51–60 (1982)).

263. *Id.* §1, 35 Stat. at 65 (current version at 45 *U.S.C.* §51 (1982)).

264. *Id.* §3, 35 Stat. at 66 (current version at 45 *U.S.C.* §53 (1982)).

265. *Id.* §4, 35 Stat. at 66 (current version at 45 *U.S.C.* §54 (1982)).

266. *See, e.g.,* Philadelphia, B. & W.R.R. v. Smith, 250 *U.S.* 101 (1919); Southern Ry. v. Puckett, 244 *U.S.* 571 (1917); Erie R.R. v. Welsh, 242 *U.S.* 303 (1916); Spokane & I.E.R.R. v. Campbell, 241 *U.S.* 497 (1916); San Antonio & A.R Ry. v. Wagner, 241 *U.S.* 476 (1916); Chicago & N.W. Ry. v. Bower, 241 *U.S.* 470 (1916); Chesapeake & O. Ry. v. Proffitt, 241 *U.S.* 462 (1916); Great Northern Ry. v. Knapp, 240 *U.S.* 464 (1916); Seaboard Air Line Ry. v. Horton, 239 *U.S.* 595 (1916); Kanahwha & Mich. Ry. v. Kerse, 239 *U.S.* 576 (1916); North Carolina R.R. v. Zachary, 232 *U.S.* 248 (1914); Missouri, Kan. & Tex. Ry. v. Wulf, 226 *U.S.* 570 (1913).

267. *See* Chesapeake & O. Ry. v. Gainey, 241 *U.S.* 494 (1916); Chesapeake & O. Ry. v. Kelly, 241. *U.S.* 485 (1916).

268. *See* Chesapeake & O. Ry. v. De Atley, 241 *U.S.* 310 (1916).

269. *See* Gila Valley, G. & N. Ry. v. Hall, 232 *U.S.* 94 (1914).

270. *See* Texas & Pac. Ry. v. Rigsby, 241 *U.S.* 33 (1916); Southern Ry. v. Crockett, 234 *U.S.* 725 (1914).

271. *See* A. Bickel & B. Schmidt Jr., *supra* note 158, at 581; Friedman & Ladinsky, *supra* note 261, at 69–72.

272. A. Link, *supra* note 18, at 263. *See generally* Tynan, "Workmen's Compensation for Injuries," 34 *N.J.L.J.* 164 (1911).

273. *See* Friedman & Ladinsky, *supra* note 261, at 65–69; A. Bickel & B. Schmidt Jr., *supra* note 158, at 210; J. Weinstein, *The Corporate Ideal in the Liberal State: 1900–1918*, at 43 (1968).

274. 201 N.Y. 271, 94 N.E. 431 (1911).

275. *See id.* at 317, 94 N.E. at 448.

276. Friedman & Ladinsky, *supra* note 261, at 68.

277. J. Lurie, *supra* note 256, at 71; *see also* Friedman & Ladinsky, *supra* note 261, at 68 n.69.

278. Stagner, "The Recall of Judicial Decisions and the Due Process Debate," 24 *Am. J. of Legal Hist.* 257, 257–58 (1980).

279. *See id.* at 259–64.

280. *See* New York Cent. R.R. v. White, 243 *U.S.* 188, 192–97 (1917).

281. 243 *U.S.* 188 (1917).

282. *Id.* at 206.

283. *Id.*

284. *Id.* at 205.

285. *Id.*

286. Hawkins v. Bleakly, 243 *U.S.* 210, 213 (1917).

287. 243 *U.S.* 219 (1917).

288. *Id.* at 219–20.

289. *Id.* at 244.

290. *See id.* at 246.

291. A. Bickel & B. Schmidt Jr., *supra* note 158, at 585 (footnote omitted).

292. *Id.* (footnote omitted).

293. *See generally* Powell, "The Workmen's Compensation Cases," 32 *Pol. Sci. Q.* 542, 553–69 (1917). According to Bickel, "[W]hat Pitney came around to was a narrow and particular ground of decision." A. Bickel & B. Schmidt Jr., *supra* note 158, at 585. The Court accepted the reasonableness of the statute before it, but reserved the right to strike down others later if it did not like them. *Id.* Although offensive to proponents of judicial restraint such as Bickel, Pitney's reliance on this approach, rather than on deference to legislative judgments, serves to demonstrate his commitment to Progressive policies. See: Powell, *supra*, at 560, 569.

294. *See* Ward & Cow v. Krisky, 259 *U.S.* 503 (1922).

295. *See* New York Cent. R.R. v. Bianc, 250 *U.S.* 596 (1919).

296. *See* Southern Pac. Co. v. Jensen, 244 *U.S.* 205, 223 (1917) (Pitney, J., dissenting).

297. *See* Middleton v. Texas Power & Light Co., 249 *U.S.* 152 (1919).

298. *See* Arizona Employers' Liability Cases, 250 *U.S.* 400 (1919).

299. 250 *U.S.* 400 (1919).

300. *Id.* at 419.

301. *Id.*

302. *Id.* at 424.

303. *Id.*

304. *See id.* at 427.

305. *See generally* G. White, *Tort Law in America* 61–62 (1980).

306. Originally, the "Arizona Employers' Liability Cases" were assigned to Justice Holmes. *See* A. Bickel & B. Schmidt Jr., *supra* note 158, at 586, 586–88. He wrote an opinion that took the tack that all risk of damages should be imposed on the employer because he could pass them through to the public. Holmes's majority fell apart when the other members of it saw what he had written. The case was reassigned to Pitney. Yet, the opinion that he produced talked about the ability of employers to spread the cost of accidents and also stressed judicial restraint, the other theme Holmes had planned to emphasize.

307. *See, e.g.,* Hammer v. Dagenhart, 247 *U.S.* 251 (1918). *See generally* S. Wood, *Constitutional Politics in the Progressive Era: Child Labor and the Law* (1968). On this issue, Pitney was also out of line with New Jersey. *See* R. Noble, Jr., *supra* note 87, at 122–25.

308. *See, e.g.,* Stettler v. O'Hara, 243 *U.S.* 629 (1917) (per curiam); *But see* A. Bickel & B. Schmidt, Jr., *supra* note 158, at 593–603 (discussing Stettler). Although voting twice against a minimum-wage law for women, Pitney was part of the majority that upheld an Oregon statute setting maximum hours for both men and women and requiring time-and-one-half pay for overtime work. *See* Bunting v. Oregon, 243 *U.S.* 426 (1917). According to one scholar, the reason why he voted for this law, but against the one at issue in *Stettler,* was a strong hostility to wage setting. *See* J. Semonche, *supra* note 175, at 342 n.46.

309. J. Semonche, *supra* note 175, at 279; see, e.g., Spiller v. Atchison, T. & S.R Ry., 253 *U.S.* 117 (1920); Arkadelphia Milling Co. v. St. Louis S.W. Ry., 249 *U.S.* 134 (1919); Morrisdale Coal Co. v. Pennsylvania R.R., 230 *U.S.* 304, 315 (1913) (Pitney, J., dissenting); Mitchell Coal & Coke Co. v. Pennsylvania R.R., 230 *U.S.* 247, 267 (1913) (Pitney, J., dissenting); Pennsylvania R.R. v. International Coal Mining Co., 230 *U.S.* 184, 208 (1913) (Pitney, J., dissenting).

310. *See, e.g.,* O'Keefe v. United States, 240 *U.S.* 294 (1916); Kansas City S. Ry. v. United States, 231 *U.S.* 423 (1913).

311. *See, e.g.,* Darnell v. Edwards, 244 *U.S.* 564 (1917); Phoenix Ry. v. Ceary, 239 *US.* 277 (1915); Michigan Cent. R.R. v. Michigan R.R. Comm'n, 236 *U.S.* 615 (1915); Louisville & N.R.R. v. Finn, 235 *U.S.* 601 (1915).

312. *See, e.g.,* Lincoln Gas & Elec. Light Co. v. City of Lincoln, 250 *U.S.* 256 (1919); Puget Sound Traction, Light & Power Co. v. Reynolds, 244 *U.S.* 574 (1917). *But see* City of Denver v. Denver Union Water Co., 246 *U.S.* 178 (1918).

313. Levitan, *supra* note 231, at 761.

314. *See* A. Bickel & B. Schmidt Jr., *supra* note 158, at 415; J. Semonche, *supra* note 175, at 422–23.

315. *See* United States v. United Shoe Mach. Co., 247 *U.S.* 32, 75 (1918) (Day, J., dissenting).

316. *See id.* at 75 (Clarke, J., dissenting).

317. United States v. United States Steel Corp., 251 *U.S.* 417, 466 (1920) (Day, J., dissenting).

318. J. Semonche, *supra* note 175, at 423.

319. *See, e.g., Ex parte* Webb, 225 *U.S.* 663 (1912).

320. *See, e.g.,* Zakonaite v. Wolf, 226 *U.S.* 272 (1912).

321. On Progressive attitudes concerning the control of liquor and prostitution, see A. Link & R. McCormick, *supra* note 6, at 69, 79, 102–03.

322. *See* D. Kennedy, *Over Here: The First World War and American Society* 51 (1980).

323. *See id.* at 74–75.

324. *See id.* at 75–88.

325. Ch. 30, 40 Stat. 217 (1917).

326. Ch. 75, 40 Stat. 553 (1918).

327. *See generally* Levitan, *supra* note 231, at 763–67.

328. *See* Debs v. United States, 249 *U.S.* 211 (1919); Frohwerk v. United States, 249 *U.S.* 204 (1919); Schenck v. United States, 249 *U.S.* 47 (1919).

329. 252 *U.S.* 239 (1920).

330. Espionage Act, ch. 30, §3, 40 Stat. 217, 219 (1917).

331. *Pierce,* 252 *U.S.* at 253.

332. *See id.* at 245–47.

333. *Id.* at 251. Brandeis attributed Pitney's certitude that he knew the real causes of World War I to his Presbyterianism. Conversations between L.D.B. and F.F., in Brandeis Papers, *supra* note 252, folder 14, manuscript box 114.

334. *Pierce,* 252 *U.S.* at 249.

335. *Id.* at 272 (Brandeis, J., dissenting).

336. *Id.* at 273 (Brandeis, J., dissenting).

337. *See* Israel, *supra* note 4, at 2008.

338. *See* Frank v. Mangum, 237 *U.S.* 309 (1915). *See generally* L. Dinnerstein, *The Leo Frank Case* (1968).

339. Frank v. Mangum, 237 *U.S.* 309, 338–40 (1915); Conversations between L.D.B. and F.F., in Brandeis Papers, *supra* note 252, folder 14, manuscript box 114.

340. *See* P. Murphy, *The Constitution in Crisis Times: 1918–1969,* at 82–83 (1972).

341. *See, e.g.,* Collins v. Johnston, 237 *U.S.* 502 (1915); Lem Woon v. Oregon, 229 *U.S.* 586 (1913); Ensign v. Pennsylvania, 227 *U.S.* 592 (1913); cf. Prudential Ins. Co. v. Cheek, 259 *U.S.* 530 (1922) (applying federal due process principles to a state law).

342. Frank v. Mangum, 237 *U.S.* 309, 347 (1915) (Holmes, J., dissenting).

343. *See* Moore v. Dempsey, 261 *U.S.* 86 (1923).

344. *See generally* B. Noggle, *Into the Twenties* (1974).

345. A. Breed, *supra* note 41, at 164. Breed actually says Pitney suffered this illness in early 1921, but this appears to be a typographical error. *See* Israel, *supra* note 4, at 2009.

346. *See* Letter from Chief Justice Taft to Justice Pitney (January 20, 1922), in Pitney Papers, *supra* note 38.

347. Letter from Pitney to Chief Justice Taft (January 21, 1922), in Pitney Papers, *supra* note 38.

348. A. Mason, *supra* note 178, at 213.

349. A. Breed, *supra* note 41, at 164.

350. *Id.* at 165.

351. *Id.* According to certificates submitted to the Senate Judiciary Committee from four physicians, by November, Pitney was also suffering from hardening of the arteries and Bright's disease. S. 4025, 67th Cong., 3d Sess., 63 *Cong. Rec.* 272 (1922).

352. *See* A. Breed, *supra* note 41, at 165–66.

353. *Id.* at 166.

354. *Id.* at 165.

355. *Id.* at 167.

356. *See id.*

357. *See generally* S. Hays, *The Response to Industrialism: 1885–1914* (1957).

358. J. Semonche, *supra* note 175, at 308 n.7.

359. *See* H. Abraham, *supra* note 160, at 179.

360. *See id.* at 163–64; cf. Israel, *supra* note 4, at 2001 (Pitney adequately fulfilled the role of a Supreme Court justice).

This cartoon was a Democratic Party campaign advertisement in the Newark Evening News, *October 17, 1919. Supported by Republican Party bosses David Baird, Edward C. Stokes, and Edmund Wakelee, Newton A. K. Bugbee ran for governor in 1919 with equivocating positions on both Prohibition and the zone-based trolley fare increase proposed by the Republican controlled Public Service Railroad Corporation. State Democrats parodied Bugbee's fence-straddling, and in the end his argument that opposing Prohibition was tantamount to nullifying the Constitution fell on deaf ears in New Jersey. Photograph courtesy of the New Jersey Historical Society, Newark, New Jersey.*

12

Warren Stickle's article on the election of 1919 in New Jersey raises a broad spectrum of issues, the most obvious being how people vote, why they make their selections, and what the consequences have been. But the 1919 election also reveals much about attitudes toward law and liquor, the fear of dissent, and even the words people use to express dislike.

Government structure, issues, personalities, and culture influence voting trends, just as they help account for the origins and development of political parties. The decision to go to the polls in the first place can be affected by laws making it easy or difficult to exercise the franchise. Suffrage restrictions, the secret ballot, primary elections, and registration requirements have also affected turnout. Once in the polling booth, voters respond variably to issues and personalities based partly on cultural background—the ethnic, religious, and family ties that bind them to certain identities and associations.

In the election of 1919, as they often had before, New Jersey voters bucked the trend in the country at large, and in the Northeast in particular, by voting for the Democratic candidate for governor. To determine what lay behind their choice, political scientists and historians have analyzed voting returns by district, examined party platforms, and surveyed local newspapers and contemporary correspondence. Based on his research, Stickle determined that some factors were unimportant compared to the issues in the campaign, particularly trolley fares, Prohibition, and law and order. Prohibition, Stickle has argued, was the one question that clearly divided voters.

But what determined a voter's choice for or against Prohibition? In the country as a whole, advocates of Prohibition generally were rural, old-stock, evangelical Protestants. Prohibition's opponents tended to be urban, often Catholic immigrants. Does this cultural division define New Jersey's experience adequately?

New Jersey in 1919 is an interesting case study of the consequences when issues clash with culture-related political ties. The election was especially significant because it led to a political realignment. Many voters shifted their customary support from one party to another.

Historians have commonly identified 1928 or 1932 as the year when the "New Deal Coalition" was formed in the nation as a whole: immigrants, Catholics, laborers, and urban residents increasingly voted for Democratic candidates. The election of 1919 caused the shift to occur earlier in New Jersey than elsewhere and, Stickle has argued, opposition to Prohibition was behind it.

Unpopular and widely ignored, Prohibition not only changed the way people voted; it also affected their attitude toward law. What are the consequences for the legal system when government passes laws large numbers of citizens do not respect? What happened in New Jersey, and elsewhere, after the election of 1919? Can and should a government impose one standard of behavior on everyone?

The position of liquor in American society illustrates well how cultural attitudes change constantly. In the Jacksonian era many Americans saw liquor as the source of all social evils, the cause of poverty, insanity, and crime in weak individuals. By the early twentieth century Americans tended to blame society, or a person's environment, rather than individuals for such problems. Society's imperfections caused poverty, and poverty led to drinking; people drank to escape from the sorrow and inequity of the real world. Today many view such problems as a failure of both society and individuals working in tandem. And solutions also are perceived differently: Prohibition, once called the "noble experiment" and a governmental intervention of unprecedented scale, did not work after all.

Because Prohibition did not end drinking and led to widespread disrespect for the law, scholars have been critical of the movement. Like Progressive reformers, Prohibition advocates have been criticized for their intolerance of immigrants and workers, who tended to drink more than other members of society (or at least to do so in public places such as saloons). Yet during the health-conscious 1980s, a time of increased awareness of the connection between drinking, illness, and car accidents, Americans found it harder to dismiss the Anti-Saloon League as just an illiberal aberration in American history.

The rhetoric of the election of 1919 shows other prejudices as well. The Russian Revolution occurred in 1917, the Red Scare in the United States in 1919. The resultant wave of fear led to the deportation of radical immigrants. In New Jersey charges of Bolshevism, anarchism, treason, and sedition were leveled first against shipyard workers in Camden who rioted against trolley fare increases, and then against the "wet" candidate for governor. These allegations were as much a carryover from the wartime emphasis on 100 percent Americanism, patriotism, and conformity as they were a reflection of widespread interest in Prohibition. What do the terms politicians use to define and denigrate their opponents reveal about the prejudices and fears of their times?

Suggested Readings

Clark, Norman H. *Deliver Us from Evil: An Interpretation of American Prohibition.* New York: Norton, 1976.

Furnas, Joseph C. *The Life and Times of the Late Demon Rum.* New York: Capricorn Books, 1965.

Lender, Mark E., and James K. Martin. *Drinking in America: A History.* New York: Free Press, 1982.

Murray, Robert K. *The Red Scare: A Study in National Hysteria, 1919–1920.* Minneapolis: University of Minnesota Press, 1955.

Rorabaugh, W. J. *The Alcoholic Republic: An American Tradition.* New York: Oxford University Press, 1964.

Sinclair, Andrew. *The Era of Excess: A Social History of the Prohibition Movement.* New York: Harper & Row, 1964.

Timberlake, James H. *Prohibition and the Progressive Movement, 1900–1920.* Cambridge, Mass.: Harvard University Press, 1963.

◆ ◆ ◆ ◆ ◆ ◆

The Applejack Campaign of 1919: "As 'Wet' as the Atlantic Ocean"

Warren E. Stickle III

Prohibition had a pervasive social, religious, moral, economic, and political effect on New Jersey and the nation for more than a decade. Emerging as the dominant national issue of the 1920s, it changed American life in many ways—its social attitudes, its morals, its drinking habits, its religious fervor, its economic institutions, its concept of reform, its attempt at Americanization and its politics. Not least among its effects, Prohibition upset historic Republican roots and fostered the rejuvenation of the New Jersey Democracy. The ability of the Democratic Party to make its anti-Prohibition stance the central and winning issue of the gubernatorial campaign of 1919 constituted the beginning of a political realignment that would continue throughout the twenties, making the Democratic Party the party of urban America. This critical decade for New Jersey Democracy began with what one local newspaper appropriately labeled "The Applejack Campaign."[1]

After 1916 the Wilsonian coalition was in decline throughout New Jersey and the nation, marking a period of transition and defeat for the Democratic Party. In the Garden State, Republicans swept the presidential, gubernatorial, and senatorial campaigns of 1916, won both the long- and short-term senatorial posts in 1918, and controlled the congressional and legislative delegations throughout this period. With the armistice of 1918, a new era arrived—an era of adjustment and change, of conflict and tragedy for New Jersey and the nation. Racial disturbances rocked twenty-five municipalities throughout the nation. Labor unrest reached its peak with the Seattle general strike, the Boston police strike, and major strikes in the steel and coal industries. A series of bombings in the spring of 1919, creating fear of terrorism and Bolshevism, ignited the Red Scare. The League of Nations' crisis and the battle for ratification fragmented much of the national spirit

---

New Jersey History 89 (1971): 5–22. Reprinted by permission of the author and the New Jersey Historical Society.

and divided the nation. The continuation of wartime Prohibition and the implementation of the Volstead Act frustrated America's thirst, alienating thousands of immigrants and Newer Americans. A spiraling inflation gripped New Jersey and the nation as prices rose as much as 105 percent above 1914 levels.[2] "The mythical goose that lays golden eggs," quipped the *Paterson Evening News* on October 28, 1919, "has nothing on the hen which lays ordinary ones, at present prices." The events of 1919 led to a growing disenchantment with Wilsonian Democracy at home and abroad, and a national resurgence of Republicanism, a prelude to "normalcy." The Republican Party won almost all elections north of the Mason-Dixon line and west of the Mississippi, making a shambles of the Wilsonian coalition of 1916.[3] Only in the Garden State was the Democratic Party successful, and there only because the local party had put together a multifactional, urban, "wet" coalition of Newer Americans on the issue of opposition to prohibition.

As each political party, reflecting the unrest and turbulence of the times, struggled for self-definition, the party primaries took on added significance. The Republican Party witnessed a four-way battle for the gubernatorial nomination. William N. Runyon, president of the senate, became acting governor with the election of Governor Walter Edge to the United States Senate in 1918. A lawyer, municipal judge, and state senator from Union County, he was essentially a conservative, "dry" politician who had supported Taft in 1912. Tracing his ancestry back to the French Huguenot settlements in 1668, he represented Protestant old-stock America. His ultra-dry position garnered the support of the Anti-Saloon League in the primary of 1919.[4]

At the time of Runyon's elevation to the governorship, Newton A. K. Bugbee of Trenton was already campaigning for the nomination. A businessman, banker, and political moderate, Bugbee was well known to New Jersey Republicans because of his service as chairman of the powerful Republican State Committee from 1913 to 1919 and state comptroller from 1917 to 1919. He received the support of such local GOP bosses and organizations as David Baird of Camden County, the Edge machine of Atlantic County, and former Governor Edward C. Stokes, who had replaced Bugbee as GOP state chairman in 1919.[5] The support of the local party machinery was Bugbee's greatest asset in the primary battle.

The continuation of wartime Prohibition and the comparative "dryness" of Bugbee and Runyon brought a "wet" candidate into the primary struggle. A lawyer, district court judge, and prosecutor for the Pleas Court of Essex County, Thomas L. Raymond enjoyed much support in Newark and throughout Essex county because of his service as mayor and later city commissioner in charge of streets and public improvements in Newark. Although he was relatively unknown outside of northeastern New Jersey, his frank "wet" appeal attracted much support during the primary race.[6]

The fourth Republican candidate for governor, Warren C. King of Middlesex, was relatively unknown throughout the state and received no support from the state organization even in his own county. Although he had successfully organized the Manufacturers' Council of New Jersey, King's political appeal was severely limited. Despite large expenditures and a vigorous campaign, he polled less than 5 percent of the GOP primary vote and had no impact on its outcome.[7]

While Runyon, Bugbee, Raymond, and King fought for the Republican nomination, a struggle for the leadership of the Democratic Party was also taking place in the Garden State. A businessman, bank president, state comptroller from 1911 to 1917, and state senator from Hudson County, Edward I. Edwards received the support of Frank Hague's Hudson County machine, and of fourteen other county leaders. Although personally "dry," Edwards opposed Prohibition. One of his original supporters was Essex County's Democratic boss James Nugent. It appeared at first that Hague and Nugent had agreed upon the distribution of patronage if Edwards was victorious. But as Nugent's influence in the Edwards campaign declined, the Essex leader repudiated his former support of Edwards and declared his own candidacy, claiming that he was going to give the people a choice on Prohibition because Edwards was only "moist." The candidacy of James Nugent, an Irish-Catholic lawyer, who had served as chairman of the Democratic State Committee (1907–1912), and boss of Essex County, resulted in a confrontation with Frank Hague for control of the Democratic Party in the Garden State, a struggle that would determine party leadership for the next thirty years.

The third Democratic candidate for governor was a hardy perennial, Frank M. McDermit. An Irish-Catholic lawyer from Newark, he had lost an assembly race in 1886, a state senate race in 1908, and three campaigns for United States senator in 1910, 1912, and 1918. A supporter of Henry George's single tax and an advocate of federal ownership of public utilities, McDermit posed no threat to the Edwards-Nugent power struggle.[8]

Although Prohibition was the dominant issue in 1919, a conflict over trolley fares helped shape the campaign and set its tone. On August 1, 1919, the Republican-controlled Public Utility Board of Commissioners approved the nation's first trolley zoning fare system, which had been devised by the Public Service Railroad Corporation. Instead of paying a seven-cent flat fare and one cent for a transfer, riders under the new system would pay three cents for the first mile, two cents for each additional mile, and would have no transfer privileges. The purpose of zoning was to achieve a more equitable fare—the farther one traveled, the higher the cost.[9] However, the zoning fare plan quickly became a political football.

Before the new system went into effect on Sunday, September 14, the GOP gubernatorial candidates had voiced their disenchantment with Public Service and the new fares. Arguing for a "just fare," Bugbee suggested that the people "are not getting a square deal," but he offered no immediate solution. Raymond denounced the new system as "an unreasonable charge" and advocated postponement of its adoption. Governor Runyon, however, refused to act without a full investigation; consequently no action was taken before the zoning fare system was implemented.[10]

Edwards vigorously attacked the Utility Board for its "little regard for the interests of the people." Since Essex and Hudson counties, with one-half New Jersey's population, had no representation on the Board, he called for a Board elected according to districts. On the eve of the system's implementation, he vigorously attacked the Public Service Company and the zoning system, calling the latter "outrageous and nothing short of a gigantic swindle." In a full-page advertisement in sixty newspapers, Edwards asserted that the attitude of Public Service was: "The Public be Damned—We want the money." The President of Public Service labeled Edwards "mendacious, vicious, and debasing," a "vulgar demagogue," an "incendiary anarchist," and "Bolshevist agitator." Many began to respect Edwards for the enemies he was making.[11]

Of all the major candidates for governor, James Nugent contributed least to the zoning fare debate. The *Jersey Journal* noted on September 5, that Nugent was reluctant "to adopt the prevailing fashion and jump on the Public Utility Commission." As Nugent continued sidestepping the fare issue, Edwards's supporters pointed out that the Essex Democrat had previously acted as a counselor for Public Service and held shares of stock in the company. "I'll hang Jim Nugent with the Public Service before we get through this campaign," shouted Mayor Charles Gillen of Newark, an Edwards supporter.[12] Only on primary day did Nugent finally speak out against the zoning fare system.

The Garden State was rudely shocked by civil disorders that accompanied the implementation of the zoning fare system, especially in Camden. On the first working day of the new system, shipyard workers in Camden smashed doors and windows and refused to pay their fares. The next day, several trolleys were wrecked, and attempts were made to burn bridges and grease rails. Obstacles blocked the tracks and shots were fired at trolleys. When motormen and conductors refused to take their trolleys out, service was dispensed. The zoning fare system "has resolved itself into a question of law and order," declared Mayor Charles Ellis of Camden. "Anarchy in a mild form has raised its head in Camden and must be crushed . . . Bolshevism will not be tolerated." Finally, militia reserves were called to the scene on September 19 to preserve order and protect property. The shipyard workers responded with a trolley boycott, adopting a slogan of "Five cent fare or walk." And walk they did. The boycott was partially successful as trolleys carried few or no passengers, and daily receipts dropped from an average of $50 to $100 per car, to only $2 or $3.[13]

The Republican candidates reacted strongly to the uproar in this traditionally Republican bailiwick. Bugbee supported the demands of Mayor Ellis and other Camden citizens for a flat rate of five cents within Camden and one cent per mile beyond the city limits. Raymond charged that Adjutant-General Gilkyson, Bugbee's campaign manager, had "called out the militia to protect the Public Service in Camden." Governor Runyon ordered the Utility Board to show cause why it should not be removed from office for neglect of duty and misconduct of office. He claimed, furthermore, that the adjutant-general had dispatched the militia without requesting the governor's permission, and tried to link Bugbee with Public Service.

It is exceedingly difficult to draw any measurable conclusions as to who benefited from the zoning fare crisis. Although Bugbee polled 62.4 percent of the vote in Camden, the support of the Baird machine appears to have been more significant than the trolley issue. Since Edwards's margin of victory in Camden was less than 400 votes, the trolley issue seems not to have been decisive. The reaction to the zoning fare system was considerably less outside of Camden and elsewhere played only a relatively minor role in the election.[14] Clearly other issues such as Prohibition and control of local party machinery determined the outcome of both primaries.

Prohibition ultimately became the most significant issue in 1919. While all the Democratic candidates were "wet," the Republican Party found itself divided over Prohibition. Contending that "Prohibition is not a state issue," Governor Runyon declared that "the problem is one not of prohibition or non-prohibition, but rather respect for the fundamental law of the land." As the "dry" champion, he received the political and financial support of the Anti-Saloon League. Not only did the League support the Governor, but it threatened to run a separate candidate, Filmore Condit, should either Bugbee or Raymond win the primary.[15]

While Runyon sought to collect the "dry" vote, Raymond made a conscientious effort to cultivate the "wet" vote. Devoting his campaign to upholding "the personal liberty of the American people," he stressed New Jersey's equal and concurrent power with Congress and pledged himself to nullify a search law within the Garden State and to start proceedings to repeal the Eighteenth Amendment. Although he denounced "lawlessness in any form," the former Newark mayor was the only Republican candidate to oppose Prohibition.[16]

In contrast to the extremes of Raymond and Runyon, Bugbee tried to take a middle position. Since he was not known as a Prohibitionist and was believed to be personally "wet," his candidacy drew the support of known "wets" such as State Senator Charles O. Pilgrim of Essex and former Senator Emerson Richards of Atlantic County. By repudiating the platform of the State League of Republican Clubs which had called for a referendum on Prohibition, the Trentonian bypassed the fears of both "wet" and "dry" groups. Announcing that the "liquor question is already settled," he admonished the people to "stop chasing rainbows" and "get down to the realities of life" by cooperating "in the enforcement of the law." "I would as soon dishonor the flag or demolish the public school system," declared Bugbee, "as I would violate the Constitution of the United States." Accepting the enforcement of Prohibition as inevitable, Bugbee sought to neutralize it as a political issue. "Among Bugbee's supporters," declared the *Jersey Journal* on September 12, "are a lot of Republicans who prefer to pussy-foot on the liquor question." Bugbee's assumption of a middle position made him the candidate best able to unite the various factions of the Republican Party.[17]

"All of the Democratic candidates for the gubernatorial nomination are 'wet,'" declared the *Trenton Evening Times.* "Each is endeavoring to have it appear that he is the 'wettest' of the crowd." But James Nugent's vigorous, outspoken attack on Prohibition clearly identified him as the "wettest" candidate in either party: the raison d'etre of his candidacy was opposition to Prohibition. He carried this message to all sections of the state, bitterly attacking the Anti-Saloon League as "pseudo-reformers" who by "chicanery and deceit, by coercion and intimidation" wanted "to rule or ruin" America. "This election will decide," declared Nugent at a Sea Girt rally, "whether we shall lower the Stars and Stripes and replace 'Old Glory' with the banner of the arrogant Anti-Saloon League." Adopting a position similar to that of Raymond, Nugent claimed that the Eighteenth Amendment infringed on constitutional rights and denounced it as "a monstrosity of fanaticism and fundamental lawlessness." He promised to utilize "all the resources of our sovereign State to defeat Prohibition," and personally to take the Eighteenth Amendment to the Supreme Court and act as counselor for the people of New Jersey. "Prohibition will not come in this State," Nugent declared, "if we have the men in office to stand up against it." "The paramount issue of this campaign is the question of Prohibition," Nugent reminded the voters. "Everyone knows this. I made Prohibition the issue in this state." And, indeed, he had.[18]

Although every Nugent speech was devoted solely to his opposition to Prohibition, Edward I. Edwards was not to be outdone. He frequently reminded voters that he had cast one of the nine votes against ratification of the Eighteenth Amendment in the state senate. He stressed the concurrent powers of the sovereign state and promised to veto any legislation enforcing Prohibition within the Garden State. "If you do not believe that I will go farther than James R. Nugent in the matter of Prohibition," declared Edwards repeatedly, "and do it in an intelligent, legal way, do not vote for me—vote for Nugent." By the end of the primary campaign, Edwards' position had become so "wet" that the *Jersey Journal* suggested he was trying "to 'out-Nugent Nugent' in promises" on Prohibition.[19]

On primary day the voters clarified "the most puzzling race since the establishment of the primary system." The returns showed that Bugbee had won a narrow victory, polling 64,245 votes to 57,876 for Runyon, a slim margin of only 6,369. Raymond finished third with 39,373 votes and King received but 7,276 votes. In this four-way race, Bugbee polled only 38.07 percent of the GOP vote compared to 34.23 for Runyon, 23.39 for Raymond, and only 4.31 for King.[20]

Bugbee's moderate policies and his ability to straddle the Prohibition issue attracted many voters. He drew support from both "wets" and "drys" and ran especially well in his native South Jersey. Most significantly, he ran best where he had the support of the local organization, essentially in Camden, Atlantic, and Mercer counties. With the backing of Pierre P. Garven's organization, Bugbee was also able to carry Hudson County. In his native Trenton, he received a spectacular 71.8 percent of the vote and polled more than 62.0 percent in Camden. But in other areas of the Garden State, Bugbee fared poorly. He ran a poor third in Newark, and other cities like Elizabeth and Paterson revealed a disappointing vote. He polled less than 14 percent of the vote in populous Essex County. Clearly, the northeastern, urban, polyglot areas did not fall to the Trenton Republican.

Governor Runyon piled up a huge vote in his native Union County, especially in Elizabeth, and won ten of twenty-one counties. He ran well in the central and northwestern "dry" rural counties, where the endorsement of the Anti-Saloon League drew great support to his candidacy. A steady rain which fell throughout Election Day perhaps curtailed an even larger rural vote for Runyon, particularly in southern New Jersey.

Thomas Raymond swept his native city of Newark and polled 51 percent of the vote in Essex County. Significantly, his Essex County vote represented 40 percent of his statewide total, thus exhibiting the limited appeal of his candidacy in other areas of the state. However, he did carry the city of Passaic and ran well in Paterson; he also garnered scattered "wet" support in Camden, Trenton, and other cities.

No patterns emerged from the various sectors of the urban community. In the cities of 50,000 population or more, Newer Americans comprised at least 60 percent of the population in sixty-five wards.[21] Of these, Bugbee carried thirty-one, Runyon and Raymond seventeen each. Each candidate carried the Newer American wards where he was well known and where he had organizational support. The Republican primary returns thus revealed the importance of Prohibition and the local party machinery.

The fundamental problem confronting the Republican Party thus was the task of uniting all factions behind the Bugbee candidacy. How would the nominee run in the northeastern cities and the Newer American wards? Could the local organizations marshal the "wet" voters behind the "dry" candidate? Or would the Raymond vote defect to the Democrats? These questions confronted the Trenton Republican as he turned to face the Democratic primary victor in the general election.

The decisive factor in the Democratic primary was Edwards's ability to garner support from the local Democratic Party machinery throughout the Garden State. In early July most of New Jersey's twenty-one Democratic county chairmen pledged their support to the Hudson Democrat. But Edwards' greatest asset was Frank Hague's political machine in Hudson County. "We know how to get majorities," shouted Hague. "We've got the organization to do it."[22] On primary day, Hague made good his boast.

The primary returns revealed that Edwards had won a clear victory, polling 56,261 votes to 43,612 for Nugent, a margin of 12,649; McDermit gathered only 5,095 votes. Edwards's percentage of the vote reached 53.6, compared to 41.6 for Nugent and 4.8 for McDermit. Edwards piled up a huge majority in Hudson and carried fifteen counties. In Jersey City, the vote ran 9 to 1 for Edwards and individual districts showed spectacular results. The sixth district of Ward 2 (Hague's Horseshoe District) cast 300 votes for Edwards, 1 for Nugent; the seventh district was 178–0, the eighth ran 225–2, and the ninth was 190–1. Districts in wards one, three, four, five, ten, and eleven showed similar results. Hague's majority in Hudson neutralized Nugent's gains in Essex, Union, Passaic, and Mercer counties and carried Edwards to victory. Clearly, Hague emerged "from the Democratic primaries as the new Democratic State leader."[23] Proclaiming Hague "a genius in his field," the *Newark Evening News* on September 24, called him "a gentleman who promises to claim a larger share of public attention in the future than heretofore." Within six weeks, Hague provided new evidence to support these predictions.

Nugent's defeat has clouded the source and significance of his vote in the Democratic primary. Campaigning vigorously on the sole issue of Prohibition, the Essex boss ran well in the urban "wet" areas of the state, sweeping Newark, Trenton, Paterson, and Elizabeth, and consequently carrying Essex, Mercer, Passaic, and Union counties. He clobbered Edwards by a 6–1 margin in his native Newark and polled 79.9 percent of the vote in Essex County. But where in the cities did Nugent garner his support? He swept all eight Newer American wards in Trenton, all eleven in Newark, both in Irvington, seven of nine in Elizabeth, and nine of ten in Paterson. Only in Passaic did Edwards carry all three Newer American wards. He won only six of forty-three Newer American wards outside of Hudson. Obviously, Nugent had put together an urban coalition of Newer Americans outside of Hudson County on his anti-Prohibition issue. But the urban, "wet" Newer American coalition was not numerous enough to overcome the efficiency of the Hague machine. With Nugent's defeat, his supporters were left with no alternatives except to support Edwards or sit out the election. They chose the former because of his Nugent-like opposition to Prohibition.

After the primaries, each party held its state convention and drafted a platform amenable to the nominee.[24] On the utility problem, the Democratic Party denounced the "inequity and unfairness . . . [of the] miserable and botched zone system." It demanded the ousting of the existing Utility Board, the election of a new board, and the restoration of a five-cent flat rate. The Republicans proposed a fair, flat rate, based on an impartial valuation of the properties of the utility company, so that rates could be based on the actual money invested in such properties. Before the platform differences could have much impact on the campaign, however, the trolley crisis subsided. After two weeks of consultations between the Public Service Company and the Utility Board, a compromise solution was found. Instead of the original zone fare system of three cents for the first mile, two cents for each additional mile, and no transfer, the substitute plan called for five cents for the first two miles, one cent for each additional mile, and one cent for a transfer. Although the zoning plan was only modified and the Utility Board remained in office, the compromise diluted the issue; its impact on the campaign was negligible.

On the fundamental issue of Prohibition, the GOP platform declared that the Eighteenth Amendment had been ratified by more than the necessary two-thirds of the states and would become the law of the land on January 16, 1920. The party declared that "ratification can no longer be considered as necessary or as a political issue in this or any state," and pledged itself to uphold the Constitution and enforce the laws of the land. The Anti-Saloon League came out for Bugbee, and Filmore Condit of Essex Fells, as he withdrew from the race, announced that "We Anti-Saloon men can get more from the Republicans than we can from the Democrats." Quickly the Republican Party became associated with the "dry" issue and defense of law and order. Conversely, the Democratic Party proclaimed its decisive opposition to Prohibition. Announcing that "Prohibition has no proper place in the fundamental law of the nation," the party pledged itself "to oppose by all lawful means the ratification or enforcement" of Prohibition, and "to lead the movement which will eventually result in its repeal." Stressing "the concurrent powers granted to the states by that amendment," Democrats pledged that the "liberty of the individual citizen in New Jersey will be protected by legislation."[25] On the leading issues of the day, party lines had been drawn, and the five-week battle for "applejack" had begun.

While Edwards adopted a Nugent-like stand on Prohibition, Bugbee struggled to find a winning issue. Attacking "Frank Hague and his raiders from Hudson county," the Trentonian raised the issue of bossism, but Edwards's defeat of Boss Nugent and the conspicuous GOP bosses in southern New Jersey undermined Bugbee's charges.[26] Still groping for an issue, Bugbee desperately turned to national problems, contending that the election of Edwards would be viewed as an endorsement of Wilson's foreign and domestic policies. The attempt to stress national issues fell flat, as Prohibition dominated the campaign. "The last thing that the voters were thinking of," declared the *Newark Sunday Call* on November 9, "was the League of Nations or the effect of the election on next year's campaign."

As the deck of issues was shuffled and reshuffled, one card turned up continually—Prohibition. Although Bugbee contended that Prohibition was not an issue and pledged himself to support and defend the Constitution, he drank a glass of beer in Clifton to prove that he was personally "wet," although politically "dry."[27] Conversely, Edwards was personally "dry," but politically "wet." In mid-October he told one audience that "I am from Hudson County and I am as 'wet' as the Atlantic Ocean." On October 18, in Perth Amboy, Edwards allegedly stated that if he was elected governor, he would make New Jersey "as 'wet' as the Atlantic Ocean."[28] He defended states' rights and called for nullification of the Constitution.

Bugbee saw in this the issue he had sought; he quickly seized the banner of law and order and carried it throughout the remainder of the campaign. Edwards was not just "wet"; now he was a Bolshevik, an anarchist, guilty of treason and sedition. "The overshadowing, overwhelming question we Jerseymen are now called upon to decide," declared Bugbee in Camden on October 20, "is whether we are to be loyalists or nullificationists." Republican spokesmen compared Edwards to John C. Calhoun and "the South Carolina nullifiers of old." The next day the Trentonian suggested that "if it had not been for the fact that the Democrats have injected an issue into the campaign that has no place there, there would be no campaign."[29] While Bugbee attacked Edwards for "preaching treason and sedition" at a Singer plant rally in Elizabeth, one worker shouted: "To hell with him! He is the man who would take away our beer." Frequently, Bugbee and GOP speakers linked anarchy, treason, sedition, secession, nullification, and Bolshevism to Edwards's opposition to Prohibition.

The issue of Prohibition reached a climax when the Volstead Act was passed by a Republican-controlled Congress over Wilson's veto one week before Garden Staters went to the polls. New Jersey as well as the nation was officially "dry." Ballantine and Schlitz shifted their advertisements from beer to ginger ale. One saloon keeper who remained open observed: "It needed but a few flowers to make it a first class funeral."[30] The immediacy of Prohibition became acutely apparent to all.

In the last week of the campaign Edwards intensified his battle for "the preservation of personal liberty by all lawful means at our disposal." The Association Opposed to National Prohibition told Garden State voters: "Don't be fooled!! . . . New Jersey Need Not Concur." Bugbee, too, vigorously stepped up the tempo of his campaign. Discussing the "one overwhelming, overshadowing issue in this campaign," the Trentonian shouted that "the Democratic platform is a lie. The pledge of the Democratic candidate for governor is a lie." "Tomorrow New Jersey will vote on one question and one only. My opponent has raised only one issue in this campaign," declared Bugbee on election eve. "If he[Edwards] should be elected, . . . it will mean that the majority of the people of New Jersey desire the nullification of the Constitution." Later that same evening in Morristown, he concluded his campaign by declaring: "This is the issue: Loyalty as against nullification. Law and order against lawlessness. Patriotism as against sedition. You are at the crossroads tonight. Tomorrow you must take one of the two roads." The campaign had ended.[31] At the crossroads there was but one sign—"Applejack"—and without hesitation, Garden Staters took that path.

Seldom in the history of this or any state has a political campaign narrowed down to one issue. But in the "Applejack campaign," the issue had been clearly drawn by both parties and their spellbinders. As far as the man in the street was concerned, "liquor," declared the *Camden Post-Telegram* on November 4, "is the really big question." If ever a referendum was held on Prohibition (prior to 1932), it was the New Jersey gubernatorial campaign of 1919.

The "Applejack campaign" polarized Garden State politics as never before. Edwards swept the large cities, carrying Jersey City, Newark, Trenton, and Elizabeth. Republican Gibraltars were shocked as the "wet" vote went solidly to the Hudson Democrat. The Raymond vote in the primary shifted to Edwards, especially in Newark and Trenton. In Newark Bugbee ran behind the combined Republican primary vote in five wards largely dominated by Italians and German-Americans; in some wards, the drop off was nearly 30 percent. In Trenton, Bugbee ran behind the combined GOP primary vote in 39 of 71 districts, mostly Newer American areas. Without doubt a silent protest had occurred in 1919, and Newer Americans in the large urban centers began a shift to the Democratic Party.

The candidates and the press agreed that Prohibition had dealt the Republican Party a severe setback. "If the election of Edwards . . . means anything," declared the *Paterson Evening News*, "it indicates that the sentiment in this state is decidedly wet." In Newark, it was the same story. "The consensus of opinion is that Edwards' strong anti-Prohibition stand was unconquerable," noted the *Newark Star Eagle*. The voters had "but one purpose," declared the *Newark Sunday Call* on November 9, "to register their emphatic disapproval of Prohibition." The press throughout the state echoed the sentiment that the issue was the question of "wet" or "dry."[32]

The candidates agreed with the press. "I feel this election indicated that New Jersey is very 'wet,'" declared Newton A. K. Bugbee. "The ballots were not cast along the line of political partisanship. It was a matter of 'wet' and 'dry.'" "I construe my election," Edwards observed, "as an indication of the people of this state concerning national Prohibition."[33]

To the political parties, the candidates, the press, and the man in the street, the battle for "applejack" was real. Immediately after Edwards's victory, several hundred immigrants and Newer Americans started out on a tour of Paterson, looking for "applejack," but found that they could not buy a drink. Returning home, they charged that things would be different after Edwards was inaugurated.[34] It would be a long wait for a legal drink but in 1919, "New Jersey," declared a national magazine, "is decidedly wet."[35]

Notes

1. *Elizabeth Daily Journal*, November 4, 1919.

2. William E. Leuchtenburg, *The Perils of Prosperity, 1914–1982* (Chicago, 1958), 66–77; Frederick Lewis Allen, *Only Yesterday* (New York, 1981), 1–72; David A. Shannon, *Between the Wars: America 1919–1941* (Boston, 1965), 1–30; Robert K. Murray, *Red Scare: A Study of National Hysteria, 1919–1920* (New York, 1955); Andrew Sinclair, *Era of Excess: A Social History of the Prohibition Movement* (New York, 1962).

3. David Burner, *The Politics of Provincialism: The Democratic Party in Transition, 1918–1932* (New York, 1968), 28–74.

4. *Newark Star Eagle*, September 20, 1919.

5. *Newark Star Eagle*, September 18, 1919.

6. *Elizabeth Daily Journal*, September 20, 1919.

7. Ibid.

8. *Jersey Journal*, September 12–20, 1919; *Elizabeth Daily Journal*, September 12–20, 1919; *Newark Star Eagle*, September 12–20, 1919.

9. *Paterson Evening News*, August 1, 1919.

10. *Trenton Evening Times*, September 11, 1919; *Newark Star Eagle*, August 29, 1919.

11. *Trenton Evening Times*, July 25, 1919; *Jersey Journal*, September 13–20, 1919.

12. *Newark Star Eagle*, August 26, 1919.

13. *Camden Post-Telegram*, September 15–30, 1919.

14. *Camden Post-Telegram*, November 1–10, 1919.

15. *Newark Sunday Call*, August 10, 1919.

16. *Newark Star Eagle*, August 8, 1919.

17. *Trenton Evening Times*, July 7, 14, 17, 1919; *Newark Sunday Call*, August 17, 31, 1919.

18. *Trenton Evening Times*, July 7, 18, 28, August 15, 1919; *Newark Star Eagle*, September 13, 19, 1919; *Newark Sunday Call*, August 10, 1919.

19. *Jersey Journal*, September 19, 1919; *Elizabeth Daily Journal*, September 20, 1919.

20. All general election returns and final county primary returns were found in the *Legislative Manual of the State of New Jersey, 1920* (Trenton, 1920). City and ward returns for the primary were found in the local newspapers since no state records exist. The quotation is from the *Newark Star Eagle*, September 22, 1919.

21. Statistics are from the fourteenth and fifteenth censuses of the United States. The census defined Newer Americans as the foreign born and those of foreign-born or mixed parentage.

22. *Newark Star Eagle*, August 26, 1919.

23. *Jersey Journal*, September 24, 1919. "It was at bottom a factional fight [between Hague and Nugent] by which the public profited slightly." *Nation* 109 (October 4, 1919): 451. See also Dayton D. McKean, *The Boss: The Hague Machine in Action* (Boston, 1940), 46–51.

24. The platforms may be found in the *Legislative Manual of the State of New Jersey, 1920* (Trenton, 1920), 244–256.

25. *Trenton Evening Times*, September 30, October 1, 1919.

26. *Camden Post-Telegram*, October 16, 1919.

27. The *Newark Sunday Call* correctly suggested that "the voters are not interested in the private habit of candidates, but only in what may be expected of them if elected." October 19, 1919.

28. *Paterson Morning Call*, October 27, 1919. After the election Edwards confessed: "I did not say I would use legal means to make New Jersey as 'wet' as the Atlantic Ocean. I was misquoted. What I said was I would use legal power to prevent the enforcement of the Prohibition amendment. That I have always said." *Trenton Evening Times*, November 7, 1919. But during the last three weeks of the campaign Edwards made no effort to repudiate the statement. As far as the populace was concerned, Edwards was going to make the state "as 'wet' as the Atlantic Ocean."

29. *Newark Star Eagle*, October 21, 1919.

30. *Newark Evening News*, October 31, 1919.

31. The campaign dialogue can be found in all large city newspapers.

32. *Paterson Evening News*, November 5, 1919; *Newark Star Eagle*, November 5, 1919. Among other newspapers which saw Prohibition as the decisive factor were the *Trenton State Gazette*, November 5, 1919, the *Trenton Evening Times*, November 5, 1919, and the *Camden Post-Telegram*, November 13, 1919.

33. *Paterson Evening News*, November 5, 1919; *Literary Digest* 63 (November 22, 1919): 18.

34. *Paterson Evening News*, November 6, 1919.

35. *Review of Reviews* 60 (November 1919): 472.

WANTED

INFORMATION AS TO THE WHEREABOUTS OF

CHAS. A. LINDBERGH, Jr.

OF HOPEWELL, N. J.

SON OF COL. CHAS. A. LINDBERGH

World-Famous Aviator

This child was kidnaped from his home in Hopewell, N. J., between 8 and 10 p. m. on Tuesday, March 1, 1932.

DESCRIPTION:

Age, 20 months   Hair, blond, curly
Weight, 27 to 30 lbs.   Eyes, dark blue
Height, 29 inches   Complexion, light
Deep dimple in center of chin
Dressed in one-piece coverall night suit

ADDRESS ALL COMMUNICATIONS TO
COL. H. N. SCHWARZKOPF, TRENTON, N. J., or
COL. CHAS. A. LINDBERGH, HOPEWELL, N. J.

ALL COMMUNICATIONS WILL BE TREATED IN CONFIDENCE

March 11, 1932   COL. H. NORMAN SCHWARZKOPF
Supt. New Jersey State Police, Trenton, N. J.

As this ransom award poster indicated, Charles Lindbergh hoped to obtain the return of his kidnapped son by offering a reward. Unfortunately, he lost his son, despite paying the money. Poster from the New Jersey State Archives, Department of State.

13

On March 1, 1932, the son of Charles A. and Anne Morrow Lindbergh was kidnapped from the couple's new home in Hopewell, New Jersey. Although the couple paid $50,000 in ransom money, the baby was not returned. Ten weeks after the child was taken, his body was found in the woods about two miles from the Lindberghs' house. Two and a half years later, Bruno Richard Hauptmann was arrested in the Bronx. Charged with the crime, he was tried in Flemington in 1935 and executed in Trenton a year later. The kidnapping, trial, and execution all created a sensation in what was called "the crime of the century." In the years since, the case has produced a stream of books and articles, a play, and several made-for-television films, looking at the case from varied perspectives and arriving at widely different conclusions. In the selection that follows, Jim Fisher describes the last part of the trial, giving a clear sense of the drama in the courtroom. At the end of his book, he concludes that Hauptmann was guilty, while other possibilities suggested by other authors are noted below.

When you read this chapter, think about why some cases become famous, and what made this one important. At issue also is whether Hauptmann received a fair trial, his guilt or innocence (which is a separate matter), and if the death penalty was excessive. Today no one can be executed in New Jersey.

A series of twentieth-century cases have been called the "crime of the century": Leopold and Loeb (1924), Sacco and Vanzetti (1921), Scottsboro (1931), Hiss (1949), Rosenbergs (1951), and O. J. Simpson (1994), along with others. Alan Dershowitz has noted these are usually cases "about which only unreasonable zealots are absolutely certain." In all, the verdicts left at least some people unsatisfied as they raised issues about the use of evidence and the fairness of the American judicial system. In most, the accused denied guilt. The cases also reflected the issues and concerns of their times, including fear of radicalism, immigrants, blacks, or traitors in our midst. All drew international media interest, some because of the celebrity status of those involved. The Lindbergh case clearly shares some of these attributes. Historians have been interested in this, and other famous trials, for the insight they provide into America's past.

In the 1920s airplanes were still relatively new, small, and fragile devices flown by daredevil pilots. When Charles Lindbergh flew the *Spirit of St. Louis* solo to Paris, he became the first person to fly across the Atlantic nonstop; he immediately became an international hero. The media dogged his footsteps. Then he married Anne Morrow, daughter of a wealthy New York banker from Englewood who was minister to Mexico. Lindbergh taught her how to fly, and their joint escapades were newsworthy. It is not surprising that the kidnapping of their first child created a sensation. It occurred during the Great Depression when jobs and money were scarce, organized crime on the rise, and the number of kidnappings increasing. As a result the case played out in a circus atmosphere—from the numerous reporters who showed up the morning after the event and trampled the ground around the house, to the large crowds that descended on the small town where the trial was held. In addition, in what later proved to be hoaxes, several individuals proclaimed their willingness to help, sending Lindbergh and others off on several wild goose chases. For all who followed the case, it was a wild ride.

Bruno Richard Hauptmann served in the German army in World War I, had a difficult time during the economic turmoil that followed the war in Germany, and spent time in jail for burglary. He escaped, landed illegally in the United States where he went to work as a carpenter, married, and had a child. He was arrested after paying for gasoline using a $20 bill whose serial number was on the list of ransom money. The police later found more money, some $14,600, hidden in his garage. He claimed that it had been given to him by his friend Isidor Fisch, for safekeeping while Fisch returned to Germany. Fisch died soon afterward, and Hauptmann maintained he used the money in lieu of what he was owed for a joint business venture. He also insisted that for the past few years he had supported his family on earnings from successful stock investments.

In addition to the money, the evidence against Hauptmann included a ladder used in the kidnapping, handwriting analysis of the ransom notes, eyewitnesses who said they had seen him in Flemington earlier that day or when the ransom money had been delivered. This was all circumstantial evidence; there were no eyewitnesses to the crime. Experts at the trial, and authors ever since, questioned the evidence. The police were accused of manufacturing some of it, the handwriting analysis was disputed, and witnesses (including Charles Lindbergh) were seen as unreliable. There were questions about whether this crime could have been committed by a single person, or if it was the work of several individuals. Some authors have gone further, calling Hauptmann a scapegoat and suggesting that the real perpetrator was either a servant, an unknown criminal, Charles Lindbergh, his sister-in-law Elizabeth Morrow, or even a shadowy figure—Dwight Morrow Jr., an illegitimate, schizophrenic, and previously "hidden" half-brother of Anne Morrow Lindbergh. Other authors have argued that the body was a substitute and that the real Lindbergh child survived, pointing to a number of possible claimants. There are many other theories offered in numerous publications.

In addition to the question concerning Hauptmann's guilt or innocence, and if guilty whether he committed the crime alone or with others, there is the issue of whether he received a fair trial. The judge has been pictured as both fair-minded and biased, Hauptmann's legal team as shrewd or incompetent, David Wilentz (the main prosecutor) as brilliant or deceitful and vindictive. In his summation at the end of the trial, Wilentz, the state attorney general, deftly played on the prejudices of the times. With World War I a relatively recent memory and Hitler in power, he emphasized Hauptmann's German origins and noted that this was a crime "no American" would have committed. After a six-week trial, it took the jury eleven hours to return a guilty verdict. The case was later muddled when Governor Harold Hoffman visited the prisoner on death row, issued a stay of execution, and argued the case should be reopened. But all appeals, including two to the United States Supreme Court, were rejected, and Hauptmann was executed.

Jim Fisher, a former FBI agent who became a law school professor, argues that Hauptmann "murdered the baby in cold blood for the money." As you read his description of the trial and its enumeration of some of the evidence, evaluate what was presented to the jury. If you had been sitting there what would you have concluded? Was Hauptmann guilty or innocent? Did he receive (by the standards of the 1930s, not of today when the rules are not exactly the same) a fair trial? What about the imposition of the death penalty—was it justified in this particular case, when it was allowed? In your opinion, should it be used today? If so, under what circumstances? If you need more information before reaching a decision, look at some of the works cited below, but do not expect all the authors to agree. In the end you will have to reach your own conclusions.

Suggested Readings

Berg, A. Scott, *Lindbergh*. New York: Putnam, 1998.

Dershowitz, Alan, *America on Trial: Inside the Legal Battles That Transformed Our Nation*. New York: Warner Books, 2004.

Gardner, Lloyd. *The Case That Never Dies: The Lindberg Kidnapping*. New Brunswick, N.J.: Rutgers University Press, 2004.

Geis, Gilbert, and Leigh B. Bienen. *Crimes of the Century: From Leopold and Loeb to O. J. Simpson*. Boston: Northeastern University Press, 1998.

Hixon, Walter L. *Charles A. Lindbergh, Lone Eagle*. New York: Pearson Longman, 2007.

Kennedy, David. *Freedom from Fear: The American People in Depression and War, 1929–1945*. New York: Oxford University Press, 1999.

Lindbergh, Anne Morrow. *Hour of Gold, Hour of Lead: Dairies and Letters of Anne Morrow Lindbergh 1929–1932*. New York: Harcourt Brace Jovanovich, 1973.

Kennedy, Ludovic. *The Airman and the Carpenter: The Lindbergh Kidnapping and the Framing of Richard Hauptmann*. New York: Viking, 1985.

Milton, Joyce. *Loss of Eden: A Biography of Charles and Anne Morrow Lindbergh*. New York: HarperCollins, 1993.

Scaduto, Anthony. *Scapegoat: The Lonesome Death of Bruno Richard Hauptmann*. New York: Putnam, 1976.

◆ ◆ ◆ ◆ ◆ ◆

"Summing Up" and
"Wednesday the Thirteenth"

Jim Fisher

Summing Up

"Either this man is the filthiest and vilest snake that ever crawled through the grass, or he is entitled to an acquittal."

—David T. Wilentz

Before the jury had a chance to get used to the idea that the defense had rested, Wilentz put Joseph L. Farber, the State's first rebuttal witness, on the stand.

Farber, an insurance agent, said that at ten o'clock on the night of April 2, 1932, when alibi witness Benjamin Heier said that he had seen Isidor Fisch come out of St. Raymond's Cemetery, Farber's car and a vehicle driven by Heier collided in Manhattan on Sixth Avenue between Fifty-fourth and Fifty-fifth streets. The accident occurred nine miles from St. Raymond's Cemetery.

In his half-hearted cross-examination, Reilly questioned Farber without seriously challenging his testimony. Since Heier couldn't have been at two places at once, he obviously hadn't seen Isidor Fisch coming out of St. Raymond's Cemetery shortly after the ransom money was paid. If Benjamin Heier had intentionally lied, he had committed perjury.

Next, a middle-aged housepainter named Arthur Larson took the stand and swore that Elvert Carlstrom, another alibi witness, couldn't have been in Fredericksen's Bakery on March 1, 1932, because Carlstrom was with him that night in Dunellen, New Jersey. When Reilly couldn't

Jim Fisher, *The Lindbergh Case* (New Brunswick: Rutgers University Press, 1994), chapter 38, "Summing Up," and chapter 39, "Wednesday the Thirteenth," 359–373. Reprinted by permission of the author.

shake the witness on cross-examination, he released him. As Larson stepped from the stand, Hauptmann turned to the United States correspondent seated behind him and said, "I don't feel so good about this thing."[1]

Following the lunch recess, Cpl. George G. Wilton of the New Jersey State Police identified several photographs he had taken of rail 16 on March 8, 1932, which showed the four nail holes. Two of these photographs were marked exhibits 302 and 303 and admitted into evidence. Wilentz next called a U.S. Forest Service employee named Betts who said that he had examined the kidnap ladder on June 1, 1932, and found that it contained the four holes.

The next three rebuttal witnesses testified that Isidor Fisch, on the night of March 1, 1932, was at the home of Henry Jung, a resident of the Bronx. By showing that Fisch was not at the scene of the crime, Wilentz was disassociating him with the kidnapping, and in so doing, weakening Hauptmann's claim that Fisch had given him the ransom money.

Isidor Fisch's sister, Hannah, took the stand and through an interpreter testified that after Isidor had returned to Leipzig, Germany, he lived with her. She said that Isidor had come home with two suits, six shirts, a woolen shawl, two pairs of shoes, a few ties and 1,500 marks (about $500 in American currency). He entered the hospital on March 27, 1934, and two days later died of tuberculosis.

Wilentz next called John F. O'Ryan, New York City's police commissioner at the time of Hauptmann's arrest. Addressing this witness, Wilentz said, "It was testified here by this defendant that before certain moneys were found in his garage, that he told you where these moneys were; is that correct?"

"No, that is not correct."

"The moneys were discovered without any information from him?"

"Oh, yes. The money had been found before he told me about where the money could be found."

Mrs. Selma Kohl, Isidor Fisch's landlady from April 1932 until he left the country in December 1933, took the stand and said that Fisch could barely afford his $3.50-a-week room.

The final witness of the day was Princeton Police Officer William Konietsko who said that he had taken Lou Harding to the Lindbergh estate on the day after the kidnapping. Harding had testified that a man and a woman in a car with the kidnap ladder attached to it had asked him directions to the Lindbergh home. "At any time did he mention a ladder being in the automobile which he described to you?" Wilentz asked.

"Not at all."

"Did he mention seeing a woman in the car?"

"No, sir."

Reilly asked the officer a few token questions and the court was adjourned for the day.

That night, Reilly was upset when he heard that Judge Trenchard might invoke an old state law that would prohibit the jury from eating or sleeping until they reached a verdict. "I will protest vigorously against such attempt on the part of the prosecution to starve the jury into submission," he declared.[2]

Speaking to reporters, Lloyd Fisher said that Hauptmann was more impressed with his wood expert, Charles DeBisschop, than with Arthur Koehler. Fisher quoted the defendant as saying that "any man who works for thirty years in the wood business has got more brains in his head than a man from Washington."[3]

In order to speed things along, Judge Trenchard had authorized a special Saturday session. So, on the morning of February 9, Wilentz recalled Lt. Lewis J. Bornmann to the stand. Bornmann corroborated his previous testimony about finding the gap in Hauptmann's attic that corresponded to rail 16. Bornmann was followed to the stand by Arthur Koehler, who contradicted the testimony of Charles DeBisschop and the other lumber people put on by Reilly.

Following two inconsequential witnesses, Wilentz put four people on the stand who said that on the night of the crime, Violet Sharpe hadn't left the Morrow house in Englewood until eight o'clock. This discredited the testimony of Anna Bonesteel, who had said she had seen Violet in Yonkers that night at 7:30.

The final testimony of the day, and the State's last rebuttal witness, was Mrs. Elizabeth Morrow, Anne Lindbergh's mother. Mrs. Morrow, in the company of her daughter, had arrived at the courthouse that morning just before eleven. Although Lindbergh hadn't missed a day, Mrs. Lindbergh hadn't been back to court since the day she had testified.

Regarding Violet Sharpe's activities on the evening of the crime, Wilentz asked, "Now, Mrs. Morrow, will you tell us about what time you saw her that evening?"

"She served dinner at seven, then left the house at a quarter to eight."

"And you saw her again before twelve?"

"It was much earlier than that."

On cross-examination, Reilly, speaking softly and with obvious respect, asked a few questions then said, "I think that is all, Mrs. Morrow."

Wilentz stood up and said, "The State rests."

Since the defense had no sur-rebuttal, Reilly stated, "We rest."

It was almost over. After 29 court sessions, 162 witnesses, and 381 exhibits, all that remained were the summation speeches and the judge's instructions. Wilentz had lined up four new handwriting experts who, on rebuttal, would have testified that Hauptmann had written the ransom notes, but he didn't call them. Had the defense put on any kind of handwriting case, they would have been used, but as things turned out, they weren't needed.

Since it was too late in the day to begin the summations, Judge Trenchard adjourned until Monday morning.

That night, Anne Lindbergh put her impressions of the day into her diary: "We go through cameras the back way to the courtroom. I sat about in same place. I felt as if I'd been sitting there forever. The crowded rows, the slat chairs, the fat bored-looking woman opposite me in the jury, the high windows behind; outside the red bricks of an old building, lit by the sun."[4]

That evening, speaking to reporters in Englewood, Colonel Lindbergh stated that in his opinion the State had done all it could to obtain Hauptmann's conviction. He then said: "I am satisfied with their conduct of the case. As they conclude, I feel there's no possibility of a mistake in the outcome, I feel so, not only because of my own opinion that Hauptmann is guilty, but because, to my mind the defense has produced nothing of sufficient importance to outweigh the prosecution's evidence that he committed the crime."[5]

Saturday night, the turmoil and conflict within the Hauptmann camp broke out into the open when Lloyd Fisher announced that Hauptmann had asked him to deliver the closing speech before the jury. When Reilly came out of the jail after a short visit with Hauptmann, he was asked if Fisher was doing the honors. "I'm running this show and I'll do the talking," he snapped.

An hour or so later, Fisher emerged from the jail and quoted Hauptmann as follows:

"I think a New Jersey lawyer ought to take part in the summation. The best evidence on my side has been presented by the local lawyers. I have tried to get Mr. Reilly to agree with my wishes, and I will ask him again Monday morning."[6]

Fisher told reporters that he was on his way to Brooklyn to ask Reilly to consider letting him or one of the other local attorneys address the jury. Fisher said that Hauptmann had expressed a desire to speak to the jury himself, but that was out of the question.

On Monday morning, Judge Trenchard announced that Anthony

Hauck of the prosecution would be addressing the jury first. Edward Reilly would have his turn then Wilentz would be given the last word.

As the slender, easygoing Hunterdon County prosecutor addressed the jury in his matter-of-fact tone, Reilly looked surprised when Hauck announced that the prosecution had abandoned the felony-murder doctrine in favor of the theory that Hauptmann had murdered the Lindbergh child in cold blood. Hauck looked at the defendant then back at the jury, and said, "We have shown you that the infant child was forcibly taken from his crib. Miss Gow testified that the covers were pinned to the mattress. Further, we have the fact that it was a very short distance from the top of the blankets to the head of the crib which was proof that the baby must have been yanked from the crib. When Colonel Lindbergh went into the room after the baby was taken, the covers still bore the impression of that little body."

Hauck's speech, lasting only ten minutes, was well organized and clearly presented, but it lacked emotion. It was now Reilly's turn.

The flashy, red-faced defense attorney was Hauck's opposite. Hauck was cool and conservative, Reilly was emotional and unpredictable. Formally attired, with his hair slicked back and the diamond on his pinky finger sparkling, Reilly hurled himself at the jury. "I don't care about handwriting," he bellowed. "I don't care about the wood, nor do I care about the ransom money."

Undaunted in his belief that he could ram the inside-job theory down the jurors' throats, Reilly pointed the finger of guilt at the Lindbergh servants: "Colonel Lindbergh was stabbed in the back by the disloyalty of those who worked for him. A man can't come up to a strange house with a ladder and stack it against the wall and run up the ladder, push open a shutter, and walk into a room that he has never been in before. I say that ladder was a plant: that ladder was never up against the side of that house that night. Oh, it was so well planned by disloyal people, so well planned!"

This was Reilly at his best, while standing knee-deep in prosecution evidence, he was boldly serving up his own tray of suspects. The jurors looked on with reluctant fascination.

Reilly turned to another theme—bungling police: "They didn't even find fingerprints on the glass that Betty Gow had handled when she gave the child the physic." Going one step further, Reilly implied that the police had destroyed the evidence: "Now who rubbed those prints off the glass? Who rubbed them out?"

Reilly removed his glasses and wiped them clean with his silk handkerchief. "Now, they must prove the cause of death by direct evidence. So they call in the coroner's physician. You saw him—a big, swaggering, blustering individual who says he is a doctor. 'Are you connected to any hospital?' I asked. 'No,' he replied. Now, you and I know from our experience that every respectable, high-standing professional man is always connected with some hospital if he is a physician."

Referring to Inspector Walsh's handling of the corpse at the gravesite, Reilly said, "As a result of his picking up the head with the sharp stick, he punctured a hole in this little child's skull. The pressure of that stick on the little baby's skull was sufficient to crack it open. The cracks the doctor found in the skull are no indication that the baby in life received a blow."

Returning to his favorite theme, Reilly said, "The pressure of that stick by that police officer, careless and clumsy, more bungling, punctured the skull. That little child should have been treated with the greatest reverence in the world; it was easy to allow the little baby's body to stay there until some trained mortician came with a little basket, and who knew how to gather up the child, and then you wouldn't have this careless bungling of a great big copper with a stick, unfortunately puncturing the head and the skull of this child, and of course there was force enough for that undoubtedly to cause the little skull to crack, and that was the condition Doctor Mitchell found it in."

Although he had gone to great lengths to line up his own expert witnesses, Reilly reminded the jurors that experts were not to be taken seriously. "Expert evidence," he said, "is nothing more nor less than opinion evidence."

Dr. Condon was the next target. "Then we come to the picture of what General Wilentz describes as a 'patriotic gentlemen of the old school.' Well, General Wilentz, you are entitled to your opinion. Condon stands behind something in this case that is unholy. Now, I don't care anything about this man, but he stands out in this case, and Condon is always doing things alone, alone."

Violet Sharpe then came under attack. "Now, a girl who is as sophisticated and worldly enough as Violet Sharpe to go out on the road and flirt with a fellow—that may be harmless—doesn't commit suicide because she fears she might lose her job. Life is too sweet. But the net is closing in; the net is closing in. Sharpe has said something; Sharpe has given a clue. . . . Suddenly, suddenly detectives come back and they say, 'Bring Violet down here again.' And a poison which is never permitted in any house—cyanide of potassium I think it was—this girl drained when she knows Inspector Walsh and the police have checked up and found something. She didn't do it because she feared she would lose her job. She did it because a woman from Yonkers, Mrs. Bonesteel, told the truth. Violet was at a ferry with a blanket, with a child, and that child was the Colonel's. . . . I don't think Mrs. Morrow remembers correctly when she saw Violet Sharpe."

With that, Reilly was asking the jury to believe that in addition to Isidor Fisch, the kidnapping had been committed by John Condon, Betty Gow, the Whateleys, and Violet Sharpe. Reilly didn't bother to explain how these people had come together, who had done what, why Isidor Fisch had ended up with all the ransom money. The jury could put all of that together themselves. Reilly didn't bother with details—he painted with a big brush.

As for Arthur Koehler, the man who had connected the kidnap ladder to Hauptmann's attic, Reilly said, "Well, Mr. Koehler comes in, and we come back again to expert evidence against horse sense. I don't know why he got into the case. I assumed that the importance of the case compelled those in Washington at the time to send him up. He is nothing more or less than what we call a 'lumber cruiser.' He goes around the country spotting groves of trees to see what they are good for and reports down to Washington. . . . Now, he'd have you believe by his testimony—and I don't see how he can sleep at night after giving that testimony where a man's life is at stake—that this carpenter went out and got two or three different kinds of wood to make the ladder. Do you believe the defendant said to himself, 'My goodness, I am short a piece of lumber! What am I going to do?' There is a lumber yard around the corner. So he crawls up into his attic and tears up a board and saws it lengthwise and crosswise and every other wise to make this side of a ladder."

Referring to his own witnesses, Reilly said, "Well, we can't go out and pick these people out of colleges."

It was a little past twelve, so when Reilly paused long enough for the judge to get in a word, the court broke for lunch.

There were so many people in Flemington that day that several state troopers had to clear a path to the Union Hotel for the jury. The jurors walked single file to the hotel dining room through a crowd that was festive and a little loud, but nothing like the ugly mob the newspapers described.

A small restaurant on Main Street was advertising a "Special Trial Lunch," featuring Writer's Cramp Soup, Lindbergh Steak, Hauptmann Beans, Trenchard Roast, Jafsie Chops, and Gow Goulash. The dessert menu included such delights as Jury Pie and Reilly Pudding.

After lunch, Reilly was a different man: He looked haggard and his speech had lost its punch. He was repeating himself, relying on cliches, and at times rambling. Maybe he was tired, maybe it was the four drinks he had had over lunch, or maybe he had simply gotten tired of hearing himself talk.[7]

By 2:30, it was obvious that the jury had lost interest. Even Hauptmann was staring blankly at his shoes. With the sounds of the crowd outside filtering into the courtroom, those inside felt that all the excitement was out in the street.

Finally, at three o'clock, Reilly, on a maudlin note that embarrassed everyone in the room, concluded his summation this way: "May I say to Colonel Lindbergh, in passing, that he has my profound respect, and I feel sorry for him in his deep grief, and I am quite sure that all of you agree with me, his lovely son is now within the gates of heaven."

Reilly walked heavily to the defense table, and without looking at the defendant, sank onto his chair. None of the other defense attorneys greeted him. They were all busy doing other things or looking away. Nobody was smiling.

The next morning, Wilentz, wearing a dark blue double-breasted suit, a white starched shirt, and a blue striped tie, approached the jury. Talking to the jurors as though they were guests in his living room, he asked, "What type of man would murder the child of Charles A. Lindbergh and Anne Morrow?" Hitching his leg over the edge of the small, round table that sat in front of the jury box, Wilentz said, "He wouldn't be an American. No American gangster ever sank to the level of killing babies. Aah no! An American gangster who wanted to participate in a kidnapping wouldn't pick out Colonel Lindbergh. There are many wealthy people in the city of New York, much more wealthy than Colonel Lindbergh."

Wilentz pulled out the white linen handkerchief that had been folded into his breast pocket and dabbed his lips. Then he turned to Hauptmann with his finger pointed. "Oh no! It had to be a fellow that had ice water in his veins. It had to be a fellow who had a peculiar mental makeup, who thought he was bigger than Lindy. It had to be a fellow that was an egomaniac, who thought he was omnipotent. It had to be a secretive fellow. It had to be a fellow that wouldn't tell his wife about his money. It had to be a fellow that could undergo hardship; it had to be the kind of fellow that would stow away on a boat and travel three thousand miles to sneak into the country and when caught would go back and try again. It had to be the sort of man that, when he did break and enter a home, he would go through the window of the mayor's home in Germany, not the ordinary citizen; not because the mayor was a rich man, but because the mayor was a respected man. Yes, it would have to be the type of man that would hold up women at the point of a gun."

Hauptmann, having been told by Fisher to maintain a calm, detached manner, did his best to conceal his fury. But his flushed face and blinking eyes gave him away.

Gesturing before the jury like a bandleader before his musicians, Wilentz raised his voice in scorn, "And let me tell you, the state of New Jersey and the state of New York and the federal authorities have found that animal—an animal lower than the lowest form in the animal kingdom, Public Enemy Number 1 of this world—Bruno Richard Hauptmann; we have found him and he is here for your judgment!"

Wilentz took everyone by surprise when he swung around, and facing the courtroom, shouted, "Schwarzkopf, please stand up!"

Colonel Schwarzkopf, wearing a well-pressed business suit, got to his feet. "Jury," the prosecutor cried out, "look at Colonel Schwarzkopf. Take a look at his eyes. Does he look like a crook? A graduate of the United States Military Academy, a man who served his nation against his Fatherland on the fronts of Europe. Does he look like a crook? Don't you suppose he is sorry for a German? He has German blood running through his veins. Do you imagine Colonel Schwarzkopf is going to frame this fellow up?"

The colonel sat down, a little flushed from the attention. No sooner had he been seated when Wilentz said, "Inspector Bruckman, will you do me the honor to stand up, please!"

The big, dark-haired detective rose from his chair. "Jurors, look at Inspector Bruckman—one of the highest commanding officials in the New York Police Department. He became an inspector after twenty-seven years, risking his life many days and many nights, with an invalid wife at home. He has to listen over the radio that he is a crook. He is also a German—the man they say who wrote on the door trim, writing that the defendant had admitted was his."

Wilentz next reviewed the wood evidence then turned to the handwriting: "Did they tell you about their handwriting experts? I don't remember the names—they are in the record—Malone, Meyers, and others four or five more and only one man, all the way from East St. Louis, only one man would dare walk in this courtroom to say it wasn't Hauptmann."

Wilentz next pointed out numerous inconsistencies, contradictions, and implausibilities in the testimony of Reilly's alibi witnesses. Then he defended John Condon's character. At this point, Judge Trenchard interrupted Wilentz's summation to break for lunch.

The jurors had to make their way to lunch through the five thousand people who were in town for the verdict. As the jurors snaked their way behind the troopers, someone yelled, "Kill Hauptmann." But it was, on the whole, a good-natured crowd.

The hotel dining room was also noisier than usual and jammed with excited people. All of the noise and humanity was too much for Verna Snyder, the 265-pound juror from Centreville. She said she couldn't eat and asked one of the women jury guards to accompany her back to her room.

When the court got back into session at 1:30, Wilentz, still intense, crisp, and animated, immediately took command. Holding onto the railing with both hands and leaning into the jury box, he said, "But let me tell you this: This fellow took no chance on the child awakening. He crushed that child right in the room, into insensibility. He smothered and choked that child right in that room. That child never cried, never gave an outcry, certainly not. The little voice was stilled right in that room. He wasn't interested in the child. Life meant nothing to him. That's the type of man I told you about before—Public Enemy Number 1 of the World! That's what we are dealing with. You are not dealing with a fellow who does not know what he's doing."

Wilentz turned away from the jurors and pointed toward Hauptmann. "Take a look at him as he sits there. Look at him as he walks out of the room, pantherlike, gloating, feeling good!"

Wilentz stepped back from the jury box, took a deep breath, then launched into a sixty-minute interpretation of the testimony of several key witnesses. Next, he tore into the Fisch story, then came back to John Condon: "Now, what did Condon do? Condon risked his life, risked his life for Colonel Lindbergh, just as millions of people would. Colonel Lindbergh thinks Condon is all right. Colonel Breckenridge, a member of President Wilson's cabinet, thinks he is all right. He must have been all right."

Now facing Hauptmann, the prosecutor, his voice saturated with emotion, said, "Mr. Defendant here wanted to show you he didn't write 'Singnature' with the *n* in it. He said they dictated it to him that way-remember? I asked him, How do you spell 'Signature'? And he said, 'S-I-G-N-A-T-U-R-E. 'That was in court. You remember it. Did they tell you to spell it 'S-I-N-G-N-A-T-U-R-E?' I asked. They did, he said. But you can take the request writings. You can go through every one of those misspelled writings, and there isn't the word 'singnature' on one of them to show that we asked him to spell it, right or wrong. What do you think of that? And here he is in this courtroom. He knew the importance of that 'signature.'"

Several of the jurors cast furtive glances at Hauptmann, whose flushed face bore no expression. The prosecutor was now talking about Isidor Fisch: "We found no gold notes in his possession, either in this country or elsewhere, and during all this time there hasn't been one ransom bill that turned up in Germany, not one, not a single, solitary one—all in the Bronx."

Wilentz ridiculed the defense's lumber witnesses, talked about Hauptmann's bank accounts, reminded the jury that the word "boad" was written in one of Hauptmann's notebooks, then said, "Now, men and women, don't be weak. Don't be weak! If he got that sleeping garment from somebody else he had a chance to tell it to you. If he wrote those notes for somebody else he had the chance to tell it. He hasn't told his lawyer a thing. He hasn't told this court a thing. He didn't tell the judge a thing—he has got nothing to tell!"

Wilentz was approaching the end of his speech and was finishing strong. He wanted more than a guilty verdict; he wanted a first-degree murder conviction, and he wanted it without a recommendation of mercy that would automatically lead to a life sentence. Wilentz wanted death. "Now, men and women, as I told you before, there are some cases in which a recommendation of mercy might do, but not this one, not this one. Either this man is the filthiest and vilest snake that ever crawled through the grass, or he is entitled to an acquittal. If you bring in a recommendation of mercy, a wishy-washy decision, yes, it is your province, I will not say a word about it. I will not say another word. But it seems to me that you have the courage. If you are convinced, as all of us are—you must find him guilty of murder in the first degree."

The testimony and the speeches were over. Wilentz had held his audience spellbound for five hours. His summation had been scathing, emotional, purposeful, powerful—and effective. Wilentz took his seat, and Judge Trenchard was about to say something when one of the spectators cried out, "If it please Your Honor, I have a confession that was made to me by the man who committed the crime!" Before the man could say anything more, a detective clamped a hand over his mouth, then, with the help of two deputy sheriffs, hauled him out of the room. The speaker, dressed in a cleric's outfit, was the Reverend Vincent C. Burns of Palisades, New Jersey.[8]

Wilentz and Reilly rushed to the bench. "Did he say anything?" Wilentz asked.

"He shouted something," Reilly replied.

"If he did, it would be in your favor," Wilentz snapped.

"No, it wouldn't," Reilly growled.

"Did he say anything? I didn't hear anything." Wilentz said.

Judge Trenchard spoke. "I don't know whether he did or whether he didn't. I didn't hear anything myself except 'Your Honor.'"

"I think he ought to be committed to an insane asylum," Reilly said. "He came to me once and I threw him out. He was here the first day, dressed that way, and I had the troopers throw him out. They tell me he is the rector of a small church up on the banks of the Hudson here, more of a mission."

"I think he ought to be put in jail," Wilentz murmured.

"So do I," said Reilly.

Judge Trenchard turned to the jury and said, "Ladies and gentlemen of the jury, it is very unfortunate that this scene had to occur. I don't imagine that you heard anything that this man said, except his exclamations that he wanted to address the court; but if you did hear anything, my instruction to you is, at the request of counsel on both sides, that you utterly and entirely disregard anything that you heard and forget the scene."

Judge Trenchard looked at his watch and said, "Now, I had rather hoped to charge you this afternoon but the hour is now late. I think it is better for us to take an adjournment; it is better for you to get a good night's sleep and take the case in the morning with a fresh mind. The court is adjourned."

That night, Dr. Barclay S. Fuhrmann, the Hunterdon County Physician, examined Verna Snyder and reported that the crowd, the noise, the rigid confinement, and the pressure of the trial had given her a "case of the nerves." The doctor advised her not to eat so much and to go to bed early.

Wednesday the Thirteenth

"The trial is over. We must start our life again . . ."

—Anne Morrow Lindbergh[9]

February 13 was a Wednesday, the thirty-second and final day of the trial. That morning, at 9:55, Hauptmann entered the courtroom in his usual manner. With his head bowed and his eyes downcast, the defendant walked to his seat in the row of chairs just inside the rail that cut off the public part of the courtroom. The moment he sat down he raised his eyes and looked about the room. His face was very white, and his cheekbones appeared more prominent than ever. A reporter sitting behind him leaned over his shoulder and asked, "How do you feel, Bruno?"

"I feel fine," Hauptmann replied, not bothering to turn around.

"What do you think the verdict will be?"

"Your guess is as good as mine."

Reilly came into the room and took his place at the defense table without speaking to or looking at his client. Fisher and Pope came in and greeted the defendant warmly. Mrs. Hauptmann took a seat two chairs from her husband and spoke to him solemnly across the knees of a trooper and a deputy sheriff.

At ten o'clock, Judge Trenchard, his gray hair rumpled and his black robe flowing loosely from his shoulders, mounted the bench.

He was carrying a sheaf of papers and a yellow pencil. Despite the fact that streams of sunlight poured through the big side windows, all of the lights in the room were burning. The jurors were seated in the jury box beneath the huge American flag on the wall above and behind them.

The court was brought to order and Judge Trenchard, addressing the jury, said, "It now becomes your duty to render a verdict upon the question of the defendant's guilt or his innocence and upon the degree of his guilt." The judge next told the jury that they were the evaluators of the evidence, then explained that the State had the burden of proving the defendant guilty beyond a reasonable doubt. The judge covered the basic facts of the crime, then addressed the crucial subject of where the baby had been killed:

"The fact that the child's body was found in Mercer County raises a presumption that the death occurred there; but that, of course, is a rebuttable presumption, and may be overcome by circumstantial evidence. In the present case, the State contends that the uncontradicted evidence of Colonel Lindbergh and Dr. Mitchell, and other evidence, justifies the reasonable inference that the felonious stroke occurred in Hunterdon County, when the child was seized and carried out the nursery window and down the ladder by the defendant, and that death was instantaneous."

Judge Trenchard reviewed Dr. Condon's role in the case, then said, "If you find that the defendant was the man to whom the ransom money was delivered, as a result of the directions in the ransom notes, bearing symbols like those on the nursery note, the question is pertinent: Was not the defendant the man who left the ransom note on the windowsill of the nursery, and who took the child from its crib?" The judge next summarized Reilly's theory of the case: "It is argued by the defendant's counsel that the kidnapping and murder was done by a gang, and not by the defendant, and that the defendant was in nowise concerned therein. The argument was to the effect that it was done by a gang, with the help or connivance of one or more servants of the Lindbergh or Morrow households. Now do you believe that? Is there any evidence in this case whatsoever to support any such conclusion?"

Addressing the state's handwriting case, Trenchard said, "Numerous experts in handwriting have testified, after exhaustive examination of the ransom letters, and comparison with genuine writings of the defendant, that the defendant Hauptmann wrote every one of the ransom notes. On the other hand, the defendant denies that he wrote them, and a handwriting expert, called by him, so testified. And so the fact becomes one for your determination."

Following a discussion of the ransom money found in Hauptmann's garage, the Judge said, "The defendant says that these ransom bills were left with him by one Fisch, a man now dead. Do you believe that?"

Referring to Isidor Fisch's shoebox, the container Hauptmann said he had placed into his broom closet, Judge Trenchard said, "Mrs. Hauptmann, as I recall, said that she never saw it; and I do not recall that any witness excepting the defendant testified that they ever saw the shoebox there."

Except for Verna Snyder who at times had her eyes closed, the jury seemed attentive and interested in what the judge was saying. Trenchard next summarized the defendant's testimony and reminded the jurors that several alibi witnesses had testified that Hauptmann was in the Bronx on the night of the crime. Regarding these witnesses, the judge said, "You should consider the fact, where it is the fact, that several of the witnesses have been convicted of crimes, and to determine whether or not their credibility has been affected thereby; and where it appears that witnesses have made contradictory statements, you should consider the fact and determine the credibility."

The judge said that the State's case was completely circumstantial—no one had seen Hauptmann steal or murder the baby. "If the State has not satisfied you by evidence beyond a reasonable doubt that the death of the child was caused by the act of the defendant, he must be acquitted."

Regarding the felony-murder doctrine, Trenchard said, "Now, our statute declares: Murder, which shall be committed in perpetrating a burglary, shall be Murder in the First Degree. . . . If you find that the murder was committed in perpetrating a burglary, it is murder in the first degree, even though the killing was unintentional." He was nearing the end of his charge when he brought up the subject of New Jersey's death penalty. "If you find the defendant guilty of murder in the first degree, you may, if you see fit, recommend imprisonment at hard labor for life. If you should return a verdict of murder in the first degree *and nothing else, the punishment on that verdict would be death*."

It was 11:13 [A.M.] when Judge Trenchard finished instructing the jury. . . .

◆ ◆ ◆ ◆ ◆

. . . . At 10:28 [P.M.], Sheriff Curtiss ordered a deputy to mount the stairs to the cupola on the courthouse roof and ring the 125-year-old bell. This was the signal that a verdict had been reached. . . . . Charles Walton, the foreman, reading slowly from a slip of paper, said, "Guilty.

We find the defendant, Bruno Richard Hauptmann, guilty of murder in the first degree." Walton's hands were trembling so badly he almost tore the paper he was holding in two.

Notes

1. *New York Daily News*, February 8, 1935, 3.

2. Ibid., 1.

3. Ibid., 14.

4. Anne Morrow Lindbergh, *Locked Rooms and Open Doors: Diaries and Letters of Anne Morrow Lindbergh, 1933–1935* (New York: Harcourt Brace Jovanovich, 1974), 246–247.

5. Grace Robinson, "Lindbergh Sure of Bruno's Guilt," *New York Daily News*, February 9, 1935, 4.

6. *New York American*, February 9, 1935, 8.

7. Reilly's appearance and demeanor following the lunch break are noted in Russell B. Porter's reportage of the trial in the *New York Times*, February 12, 1935. Reilly's lunch-time drinking during the trial is noted in several accounts of the case. In his article, "Why the Lindbergh Case Was Never Solved," Alan Hynd writes: "He [Reilly] was never fully awake until after lunch, when he drank eight or ten orange blossoms out of a coffee cup in a hotel across the street" in Alan Hynd's *Murder, Mayhem and Mystery* (New York: A. S. Barnes, 1950), 37.

8. "Ejected Pastor Reticent on Story," *New York Times*, February 13, 1935, 15.

9. Lindbergh, *Locked Rooms and Open Doors*, 249.

Cartoon of "King Frank, The Last" 1929. Frank Hague (1875–1956) was mayor of Jersey City from 1917 to 1947. By the late 1920s he was being criticized for his strong-arm political methods, and violations of freedom of speech. Rather than his power diminishing with the New Deal, it actually increased, allowing him to remain in office. Bob Leach, The Frank Hague Picture Book, *Jersey City Public Library, 1998.*

14

The career of Jersey City mayor Frank Hague raises two questions with which American historians have wrestled for some time. The first is how to look at and evaluate the role of "bosses" in politics. The second is whether political machines controlled by bosses are a thing of the past or also of the present. If they are as extinct as the dinosaurs, when and why did they die out?

Historical opinion about bosses and their political role has changed over time. During the Progressive Era bosses were blamed for the corruption that was rampant in cities, criticized for their ties to the immigrant community, which seemed to trade its votes for favors, and faulted for their relationship to the business community, which paid bribes for preferential treatment. At the outbreak of World War II, party bosses were condemned for an excessive use of power compared at the time to that of the rising fascists in Europe. Historians and critics charged that boss control of government embraced an undemocratic and intolerable suppression of individual rights, as well as inefficiency and unwarranted expense.

In more recent years historians have been less inclined simply to condemn boss rule than to describe and explain how it operated and the services it provided. Machine politics reached significant proportions at the end of the nineteenth century when cities grew at a rapid pace and immigrants arrived in enormous numbers. The political boss bridged the gap between inadequate services and human needs. He provided job counseling when there were no unemployment offices, food baskets before food stamps and other welfare programs, assistance to businessmen before economic development bureaus, and a personal touch in an increasingly impersonal world.

Whether evaluating boss rule or trying to determine its balance of costs and services, historians have generally agreed that its days as a widespread American institution were numbered by the 1930s. The New Deal provided an assortment of social welfare services previously offered by the machine, such as social security, aid for families with dependent children, and subsidies for public works projects. The rise of big labor unions meant that they also took on some of the functions of the political machine, furnishing assistance in the event of arbitrary treatment, providing greater job security, and working for higher wages. At the same time, the end of large-scale immigration, a consequence of both the restrictive laws passed after World War I and of the Depression (which made the United States a less attractive destination), shrank the pool of traditional boss support. Bosses who survived the 1930s were an exception to the rule.

Hudson County's Frank Hague, like other bosses, has been roundly condemned for his dictatorial qualities. Dayton D. McKean in *The Boss* (1940) specifically charged that the Hague organization "systematically and successfully utilized the methods of terrorism . . . that have characterized the fascist régimes in Europe." The rights to freedom of speech and assembly were trampled in Jersey City. Government was inefficient and expensive; the school system was inadequate and plagued with cronyism. In contrast to this clear condemnation, Lyle Dorsett attempts a more detached appraisal. How does he evaluate Hague? What services did the Hague machine provide for residents, as well as for churches and businessmen, in return for their support? What, for example, did citizens receive in return for their investment in the large, expensive Jersey City Medical Center? Why did Jersey City voters keep Hague in office for so long?

Frank Hague first rose to power as a reform candidate in 1913. By 1932 criticism of his personal wealth and lifestyle, as well as his political methods and activities, was widespread. There were predictions that he could not remain in power much longer. But Hague outlasted even the New Deal, the reputed dragon slayer of boss rule. Dorsett has argued that the New Deal actually rescued Hague. Why did this happen? What did Hague have that Roosevelt needed, and what did Hague receive in return?

The relationship between the boss and the president was a pragmatic one, based on the needs of each. Roosevelt could be devious as well as practical. In 1940 he decided to try to oust Hague by quietly encouraging Charles Edison to act as a counterweight by running for governor of New Jersey. Although Edison was elected, the plan did not succeed, and Hague remained in office until 1947. Why did the reform effort fail? What does its failure suggest about the staying power not only of Hague but of political machines in general?

The Hague machine in Jersey City was replaced in 1949 by the Kenny machine, which lasted into the 1970s. Does machine politics still exist today? If it does, what functions does it perform, and where? To survive, boss-driven political machines need to provide something no one else offers in return for the votes and support they receive. Historians have come to agree that this process is reciprocal, not just the rule of bosses over voters.

Suggested Readings

Brownell, Blaine A., and Warren E. Stickle, eds. *Bosses and Reformers: Urban Politics in America, 1880–1920.* Boston: Houghton Mifflin, 1973.

Callow, Alexander B., Jr., ed. *The City Boss in America: An Interpretive Reader.* New York: Oxford University Press, 1976.

Colburn, David R., and George E. Pozzetta. "Bosses and Machines: Changing Interpretations in American History." *History Teacher* 9 (1976): 445–463.

Connors, Richard J. *The Cycle of Power: The Career of Jersey City Mayor Frank Hague.* Metuchen, N.J.: Scarecrow Press, 1971.

Fleming, Thomas J. *Mysteries of My Father.* Hoboken, N.J.: John Wiley & Sons, 2005.

Foster, Mark S. "Frank Hague of Jersey City: The Boss as Reformer." *New Jersey History* 86 (1968): 106–117.

Greene, Lee S., ed. "City Bosses and Political Machines." *Annals of the American Academy of Political and Social Science* 353 (1964): 15–121.

Lemmey, William. "Boss Kenny of Jersey City, 1949–1972." *New Jersey History* 98 (1980): 6–28.

———. "The Last Hurrah Reconsidered: The Kenny Era in Jersey City, 1949–1972." In *Cities of the Garden State: Essays in the Urban and Suburban History of New Jersey,* edited by Joel Schwartz and Daniel Prosser, 127–143. Dubuque, Iowa: Kendall/Hunt, 1977.

McKean, Dayton D. *The Boss: The Hague Machine in Action.* Boston: Houghton Mifflin, 1940.

Murray, Joseph M. "Bosses and Reformers: The Jersey City Liberty Movement of 1957." *New Jersey History* 103 (1985): 33–67.

O'Connor, Edwin. *The Last Hurrah.* Boston: Little Brown, 1956.

Rapport, George C. *The Statesman and the Boss: A Study of American Political Leadership Exemplified by Woodrow Wilson and Frank Hague.* New York: Vantage Press, 1961.

Stave, Bruce M., ed. *Urban Bosses, Machines, and Progressive Reformers.* Lexington, Mass.: Heath, 1972.

◆ ◆ ◆ ◆ ◆ ◆

Frank Hague, Franklin Roosevelt, and the Politics of the New Deal

Lyle W. Dorsett

William Dean Howells once said that "the kindlier view of any man is apt to be the truer view." This is probably true, but few journalists have applied it to Frank Hague. Aside from a 1937 feature article in the already disreputable *Literary Digest* (the *Digest's* days were numbered after it predicted Landon would defeat Roosevelt in 1936), most writers portrayed the boss of Jersey City as a "Dictator—American Style" or "King Hanky-Panky." Hague's city, it was argued, was an "occupied area" under the rule of New Jersey's "Hitler."[1]

There is some truth in the image journalists created of Hague. As with most images, though, the distance between reality and the impressions expressed by opponents is great. Hague was no angel, but he always had a large popular following. One of the reasons people in Jersey City liked Frank Hague was that they could identify with him and his humble beginnings. He was born in the Horseshoe in downtown Jersey City. The Horseshoe got its name in 1871 after the Republicans gerrymandered most of the city's Democrats into one assembly district, bordered by Hoboken in the north and the Hudson River on the east, and rounded off to the west and south in a horseshoe shape.

In 1876, the year Hague was born, Jersey City's population was approximately 120,000. About one-fifth of this number was foreign-born, and many of those came from Ireland. Most of the immigrants and native-born laborers were forced to raise their families in the Horseshoe, close to their places of employment, where rent was the lowest. It was down among the railroad yards, noisy wharves, and soot-blackened factories that Frank Hague was born. Although most of the neighbors lived in crowded tenements, Frank's Irish-born father managed to move his Irish bride and eight children into a dilapidated

New Jersey History 94 (1975–76): 21–35. Reprinted by permission of the author and the New Jersey Historical Society.

frame house when he graduated from a blacksmith's job to become a guard at a local bank.[2]

Frank nearly died as an infant, a fate which would not have been unusual in a late nineteenth century city, especially among slum children. But he had a strong constitution and grew into a tall, lean, strong boy with sandy-colored hair and striking blue eyes. A typical rowdy of the Horseshoe, Hague ran in a gang, swam in the river, and fought in the streets. His mother saw to it that he regularly attended Mass, but no one succeeded in getting him to school very often. Indeed, in the sixth grade at the age of fourteen, he was expelled for habitual truancy, thus ending his formal schooling. From P.S. 21 he went to work as a blacksmith's helper, and then took an unskilled job with the Erie Railroad. In his spare time he worked out in a gymnasium and became a rather good boxer. While fighting in the gym he met a professional lightweight named Joe Craig. Looking for an opportunity to get out of the railroad yards and into a suit and tie, Hague made a deal with Craig, became his manager, and was able to turn his back on work clothes, and common labor forever.[3]

During his years as Craig's manager, Hague became well-known in the Horseshoe. He spent many hours around the Cable Athletic Club and the Greenwood Social Club where he distinguished himself as the local fashion plate in impeccably clean shirts and four-buttoned, double-breasted plaid suits. Those who knew him believed his ambitions to be modest. He wanted to avoid the toil of manual labor, dress smartly, and eventually get a job on the police force. As a matter of fact, he demonstrated no particular interest in politics, and initially entered it unexpectedly on the initiative of others. Hague's political career began when a well-known saloonkeeper in the Horseshoe, Nat Kenny, decided to challenge the Democratic boss of the neighborhood, Denny McLaughlin. Kenny had no interest in holding public office himself, but he wanted to become the behind-the-scenes power in the Horseshoe Democracy. McLaughlin held no public office either, but he had many friends in the area and could deliver a large block of votes for candidates of his own choice at election time. Just prior to a special election in 1896 to elect constables and members of the Street and Water Board, Kenny was searching for some men who were popular in the Horseshoe. It was suggested that young Frank Hague, who was well-known in the clubs and as a fight manager, would be a good choice to run for constable. Hague was asked to run; he accepted, and went on to win.[4]

This victory was all Hague needed to realize that his calling was politics. The man of modest ambitions quickly developed a monumental appetite for power and prestige. He worked faithfully for the regular Democratic organization until Jersey City heard the nationwide clamor for reform. Then, in 1913, Hague became a reformer. He called for cleaning the "bosses" out of city hall and bringing honesty and efficiency to city government. The boy from the Horseshoe won the election and became a city commissioner and later mayor of Jersey City. And in the mayor's office he stayed until his voluntary retirement in 1947.[5]

During those early years in the mayor's office, Hague carefully tended to the business of building a political machine. His following was enlarged by keeping his promises of modernizing the city's fire and police departments. Eventually he had lieutenants in every ward of the city. Their job was to care for the needy and then get the vote out on Election Day. In middle-class neighborhoods the boss established social clubs where people could relax, play, and socialize. For the business community, both small and large, there were tax breaks and other favors. Hague also had the patent support of the Roman Catholic Church in Jersey City. The boss contributed large sums of money and some magnificent gifts to the church, and in return, he had its endorsement at election time. Furthermore, deliberate efforts were made to do favors for Jews and Protestants. Several well-known and influential rabbis and Protestant ministers were on the city payroll as "utility men" or "special inspectors."[6]

By the time Franklin Roosevelt launched the New Deal, Hague was a powerful and popular mayor with an efficient and loyal organization at his command. The seamier side of his character and the most ruthless tactics of his machine had not yet come to light. Consequently, Hague was the undisputed leader of the New Jersey Democratic Party by 1932, and he went to the national convention at Chicago militantly anti-Roosevelt. Hague's idol was Al Smith, and the New Jersey boss used every ounce of influence at his disposal to see him nominated. If Roosevelt had been inclined to hold a grudge against anyone in Al Smith's camp it would have been toward Hague. The arrogant, wisecracking boss of Jersey City was Smith's floor manager at the convention, and it was he who told reporters in Chicago that, if nominated, Roosevelt would not carry even one state east of the Mississippi.

This was a big crow to swallow, but Hague was an audacious man with enough appetite for the task. Immediately after the convention, Jim Farley went to Atlantic City to rest and recuperate from the strain and pressure of the battle for the nomination. He was not there long before he received a phone call from Hague. "He said," Farley remembered, "there was no soreness on his part over what had happened, that he was whipped in a fair fight, and that if Governor Roosevelt would come to New Jersey to open his campaign, he would provide the largest political rally ever held in the United States."[7]

Regardless of how much bitterness Roosevelt felt toward Hague, one thing was certain: he was not about to seek revenge. New Jersey, after all, was a populous state with a sizeable block of electoral votes, which traditionally went to the Republican candidate. For Roosevelt to refuse the aid of the state's most powerful Democrat would be suicidal. There was no hope of carrying New Jersey without Frank Hague's endorsement.

Always the realist, Roosevelt extended the olive branch, accepted Hague's invitation, and opened his presidential campaign with a speech delivered in front of Governor A. Harry Moore's home at Sea Girt. Jim Farley estimated that between 100,000 and 115,000 people were present to hear Roosevelt at what was probably the largest political rally ever to take place in the United States. Roosevelt was markedly impressed by the demonstration. If Hague could do this, he probably could put the state in the Democratic column in November. The boss of Jersey City was speaking the nominee's language, and it appeared that the hatchet was buried forever. Indeed, some months after the general election when Hague had delivered the vote for Roosevelt, he wrote a note to the president. "Your recognition of our State Organization had been substantially manifested and in return I feel we owe you this pledge of loyalty. Should the occasion ever arise when New Jersey need be counted, I am yours to command."[8]

This letter reveals the heart of the Roosevelt-Hague relationship. Hague delivered the vote as promised in 1932. In return, the president showered the New Jersey boss with favors. As long as the favors poured in, Hague would use his machine to support Roosevelt, and as long as Roosevelt needed Hague, the favors would be forthcoming.

The evidence shows that from the outset of the New Deal, Frank Hague was in complete control of all federal patronage in the state. Federal appointments were not filtered through the governor or New Jersey's senators. On the contrary, the mayor of Jersey City made all the decisions. Governor A. Harry Moore was inundated with appeals for help in finding various kinds of federal jobs. Almost invariably he answered the applicants in the way he wrote to a Newark, New Jersey, man in August, 1933. "I do not have the power," exclaimed the governor "to appoint to these Federal positions. They are made upon recommendation of the local organizations to Mayor Hague, who, in turn, sends them in . . . I would suggest that you also get in direct touch with the mayor."[9]

When Hague wrote to Roosevelt that "your recognition of our State Organization had been substantially manifested," he implied that everyone in the Roosevelt administration was being generous. No one wanted to offend Frank Hague and his organization. Jim Farley, the postmaster general, did his best to help if the cause was legitimate. He believed in party regularity. The Hague machine had put Roosevelt over in New Jersey, so it deserved New Jersey's share of the spoils. Typical of Farley's willingness to assist the Hague machine was an incident in 1934. Governor A. Harry Moore, a loyal Hague man, called upon Farley to use his influence to restore a friend to a post with the Civil Works Administration [CWA] as an aeronautical inspector. It seems that the man was competent, but that his services were already covered by others in the state. Farley took the case to the secretary of commerce, who controlled this particular level of appointment. Although the man did not get his old job back, he was given another post of equal caliber.[10]

It is true that Farley always worked well with the big-city bosses. He talked their language, believed in party organization, and held with the philosophy that the winners should take the spoils. It is also true that Farley hoped to become president some day, and he believed his friendship with bosses like Hague would enhance his chances. However, there were limits to which Farley would go to win political support, for he was a man of unimpeachable integrity. An issue surrounding Farley and Hague which sheds light on this point came in the late 1930s after Hague had faithfully delivered the delegates and the votes in two presidential contests. As postmaster general, Farley received evidence which proved that Frank Hague had one of his henchmen opening every piece of mail that went to or came from one of his political enemies. In a fit of anger, the usually jovial Farley stormed in to see the president for orders on how to proceed with arrest and prosecution. To Farley's disappointment, Roosevelt said: "Forget prosecution. You go tell Frank to knock it off. We can't have this kind of thing going on. But keep this quiet because we need Hague's support if we want New Jersey."[11]

Harry Hopkins was another who did his best to curry favor with Frank Hague. An ex-social worker, Hopkins learned the game of politics fairly well, and he too had ambitions that went beyond the cabinet and ministership of relief. Striving to please Jersey City's boss, Hopkins gave Hague charge of over 18,000 CWA jobs in 1934. Then Hopkins appointed Hague's man, William Ely, as the first director of the Works Progress Administration [WPA] in the state. During the 1930s New Jersey employed between 76,000 and 97,000 annually through WPA.[12]

That Hopkins lacked the courage or the will to clamp down on Boss Hague is abundantly clear. New Jersey was one of the worst states in the nation when it came to political abuses in FERA [Federal Emergency Relief Administration] and WPA. Hopkins was inundated with evidence from his own investigators and from injured citizens. Stacks of testimony and sworn affidavits testify to widespread political coercion. Men and women who held federal positions in New Jersey were forced to vote for the machine's candidates. Furthermore, it usually took connections to find employment in the first place. All jobholders were expected to "tithe" 3 percent of their salaries to the machine at election time. Politics became so flagrantly interwoven in WPA that one director always answered his office phone, "Democratic headquarters!" Even where it was argued that Republicans controlled relief programs it was well-known that Hague actually had his guiding hand in the system because he always rewarded a group of "machine Republicans" who worked faithfully for him by voting in Democratic primaries or becoming "Republicans for Hague."[13]

Hopkins not only ignored the overwhelming evidence of politics in relief programs, but he was up to his neck in it himself. New Jersey's state director of relief, William Ely, probably had some notion of ultimately building his own machine through the relief program. Consequently, he occasionally circumvented Hague's wishes on patronage if he thought he could do it and not get caught. Hopkins, however, used his personal influence to see that Hague's friends found jobs. In 1936, for example, Hopkins phoned Ely about a gentleman and said "Frank is very anxious to give him a job." Ely assured the federal minister of relief that "I think maybe we can work it out." Then on another occasion, after a plea from Hague, Harry Hopkins decided to stretch the letter of the law and take WPA funds which were earmarked for labor costs and use them to buy seats and plumbing for Jersey City's new baseball stadium. Hague knew he was asking Hopkins to violate the law but assured him it was for a good cause inasmuch as the facility was to be named Roosevelt Stadium and the president was going to be there for the grand opening. Once again Hopkins bowed to the throne in Jersey City and pressured Ely to look for a way to engineer the boondoggle for Hague.[14]

Besides these special favors from Hopkins, Frank Hague derived many other benefits from the New Deal. He estimated that his organization gave away approximately $500,000 a month through FERA to hungry families of the unemployed. WPA spent over $17,000,000 in Jersey City and Hudson County between 1933 and 1938, and by 1939, WPA had poured nearly $50,000,000 into the community. The machine took political advantage of every dollar and every job which the federal government provided.[15]

All of the federal support was helpful, but some of the projects could be used more advantageously than others. The monumental Jersey City Medical Center, for instance, was built largely with grants and loans from the Public Works Administration [PWA]. This gigantic complex was composed of seven buildings—the highest of which has twenty-three floors. All in all, the facility encompassed ninety-nine floors with 2,000 beds. At the time of construction it was the third largest hospital in the world. The Medical Center was Hague's pride and joy. To focus attention on his pet project, he got President Roosevelt to come and lay the cornerstone in October, 1936. The Hudson County boss humbly thanked Roosevelt for the federal funds which were making the project possible. Once the center was finished, though, Hague unabashedly took full credit for extending medical care to everyone who could not afford to pay. He likewise took great delight in attention-getting extravaganzas at the hospital. Without fail, Mayor Hague appeared at the children's ward each Christmas with a lieutenant who was dressed as Santa Claus and bearing gifts for all. With great resourcefulness Frank Hague squeezed every ounce of political advantage out of the Medical Center. When election time drew near, the boss saw to it that families who had received hospital services were sent bills with enclosed notes informing them that if they went to see their district leader they could get their bills reduced or completely written off.[16]

In the final analysis, the combined efforts of Roosevelt, Farley, Hopkins, and countless other administrators insured New Deal benefits for the Hague machine. As a careful student of Hague's career concluded, "the fact that the New Deal worked through, rather than in competition with, Frank Hague heightened the dependence of Jersey City families on his organization during the depression decade. The CWA, PWA, WPA, etc., provided resource strength for the Hague machine as it became a vast employment and relief agency."[17]

If it was not for the fact that Roosevelt needed the large majorities Hague turned out for him in Hudson County—indeed Roosevelt could not have carried New Jersey in 1932, 1936, 1940, and again in 1944 without those margins—it is difficult to imagine the president aligning himself with Frank Hague. Roosevelt probably would have allowed due process to take its course in 1938 when Farley exposed the mail-opening incident, except for reasons of political expediency. If Jersey City's mayor had not been a tried and true political asset, he would have gone the route of Kansas City's Tom Pendergast, upon whom Roosevelt unleashed the T-men in 1939. At least he would have met the fate of James Michael Curley [of Boston], who never received New Deal favors because Roosevelt considered him a liability. This is so because unlike Fiorello LaGuardia, Edward Kelly, and Edward Flynn—three urban bosses Roosevelt genuinely liked and enjoyed being with—Frank Hague disgusted him. A key to Roosevelt's personal feelings toward politicians was the frequency of their social visits to Hyde Park. While numerous people met the president at his birthplace for brief political meetings, only those Roosevelt thoroughly enjoyed picnicked there or socialized with their families overnight. It is significant that Hague attended only one luncheon at Hyde Park. The only time Mrs. Hague and the boss socialized with Roosevelt was on board a ship, *U.S.S. Indianapolis*, in 1934 to review the fleet. And this outing was a perfunctory political gathering which included a number of dignitaries and their wives from New Jersey and New York.[18]

Roosevelt, like many New Dealers, found Hague repulsive. A pushy, arrogant, domineering man, Hague once dictatorially boasted "I am the law" to a man who questioned the legality of one of his decisions. The New Jersey chieftain had the physique of an athlete, sharp features, and piercing ice blue eyes. He prided himself on his superb physical condition and enjoyed walking the feet and legs off his associates. His aggressive style complemented his obsessive personality. While he could be flexible when necessary for political advantage, he was a true believer when it came to several issues of the time.

Hague was militantly anti-Communist. Typical of many of the Americans he represented, he ignorantly equated Communism, socialism, and organized labor. In the name of preserving democracy, he pitched civil liberties to the wind. He said that civil liberties were bunk for anyone "working for the overthrow of the government," and he advocated the establishment of concentration camps in Alaska for American radicals.[19]

Intellectually Frank Hague never grew beyond the elementary grade education he received in Jersey City's Horseshoe district. The capitalistic system was good in his eyes, and 100 percent American. To the "Hudson County Hitler," as civil libertarians dubbed him, the Socialist Party and its leader, Norman Thomas, were subversive. Consequently, when Norman Thomas tried to speak in Jersey City, the Hague-controlled police force stood idly by while angry Hagueites pelted him with rocks and rotten vegetables. Thomas was detained by police without cause, and the mayor followed this up by banning the socialist from speaking in Jersey City.[20]

Inasmuch as the local industrialists whom he admired and from whom he received so much support were adamantly opposed to the CIO [Committee of Industrial Organizations], Hague did all in his power to oppose organized labor's entrenchment in New Jersey. However, this antilabor stand was not merely a facade to garner the continued support of the Chamber of Commerce and industrial magnates. That Hague, the true believer, really viewed it as a Communist conspiracy against the American system is evident in his dogged attempt to find evidence of Communist connections by scanning the mail of New Jersey's CIO organizers. While Hague viewed all organized labor as a threat, his most poisonous venom was saved for the CIO. Of cofounder John L. Lewis, the demagogue from Jersey City said he was merely "window dressing"—he was "a puppet of the Communist Party."[21]

By the late 1930s Hague unflinchingly resorted to police-state tactics of framing political opponents through the machine-controlled courts. Some apparently innocent persons were jailed for committing no crime other than challenging the "law" of Frank Hague. By 1937 and 1938, President Roosevelt drew increasing criticism from irate citizens, as well as from journalists who spoke for the liberal press. Given all of the adverse publicity and growing pressure, it is not at all surprising that Roosevelt allowed a situation to develop which could have worked to his advantage.[22]

It should be recalled that Roosevelt encouraged Joseph V. McKee to enter the mayoralty race in New York City in 1933 to insure Tammany's defeat—and hopefully to elect Fiorello LaGuardia. Regardless of who won, either McKee or LaGuardia, Roosevelt came out the winner. He had his hand in the contest but remained aloof enough to capitalize either way the race went. Then in 1938 in Missouri, Roosevelt played the game of subtly encouraging Lloyd Stark in his battle with Tom Pendergast. The president refused, however, to take sides openly until it was clear Stark had the Democratic Party fairly well in hand in Missouri. By 1940 a similar situation had developed in New Jersey. Hague was under constant attack for his fascist-style control of Hudson County, but to attack him openly as Farley suggested was dangerous. The danger lay in the fact that Hague did control the Democratic machinery and without his allegiance Roosevelt could not carry New Jersey.

Roosevelt's plan was to use his secretary of the navy, Charles Edison, son of Thomas A. Edison, to test the anti-Hague sentiment in New Jersey. If Edison could wrest control of the pro-Roosevelt forces in the state away from Hague, then Roosevelt could count New Jersey in the Democratic column in elections, yet be rid of the embarrassment of the notorious boss of Jersey City. Roosevelt's New Jersey scheme was delicate. The president had to encourage Edison to launch a reform crusade against the boss, but he had to appear above the battle himself. If Hague thought Roosevelt was in on the coup, then it could be "good-bye New Jersey" in 1940.

The plan seemed especially plausible in light of the Republican victories in Jersey's off-year elections in 1938. The word which reached the White House was that Republicans won for two reasons. First, citizens were embittered by Roosevelt's attempt to pack the Supreme Court. Secondly, laborers who ordinarily voted Democratic deserted the party because of Hague's bitter fight against the CIO. This was the first time Hague had not delivered for the New Deal. Was he losing his grip? The best way of finding out, given Roosevelt's way of thinking, was to send up a trial balloon and get a reading.[23]

Circumstances and events conspired to make Charles Edison the trial balloon. By 1940 Roosevelt knew war was imminent. In order to avoid making preparedness appear to be a Democratic Party monopoly, he wanted to appoint Republicans to key defense positions. How fortuitous it was that the secretary of [the] navy was from New Jersey. If Edison resigned and ran for governor of New Jersey, he could open a cabinet post for a Republican, and at the same time, test the wind for breaking Hague's hold on the state. Like McKee and LaGuardia, Charles Edison was taken in by Roosevelt's facade of sincerity. Like so many others, he went out to do battle for Roosevelt only to find that it was his own fight—the president's aid would never be forthcoming.

The plan was quickly implemented. Edison entered the Democratic primary and to the surprise of many received Hague's endorsement. He resigned from the cabinet and Republican Frank Knox was appointed. When Roosevelt accepted Edison's resignation he told him "I hope you will be elected—and I say this because you have a deep-seated feeling of responsibility to good government and efficient government, which I hope will be recognized by the people of your State." Edison was elected, and Roosevelt sent him a leather notebook as a gift of congratulations.[24] On the same day in 1940 that Edison was elected governor, Frank Hague delivered a whopping Hudson County vote for Franklin D. Roosevelt. Hague had worked hand-in-glove with Chicago's Edward Kelly at the national convention to railroad the president through for an unprecedented third term, and he followed up with a huge margin in Jersey City, which Roosevelt needed to carry the state.

Soon after Edison entered the governor's mansion, he launched an all-out crusade against the Jersey City boss. For the three years of his term he battled the boss, and frequently went to Washington to consult with the president. Although Roosevelt could lend behind-the-scenes encouragement to Edison, the trial balloon, he never publicly or openly declared his opposition to Hague and his tactics of repression and demagoguery.[25]

Charles Edison was in almost every way the antithesis of Hague. He was well educated and reflective, where Hague was ignorant and impetuous. Edison had warm eyes, a sincere smile, and calm and somewhat rounded, soft features, whereas Hague had dashing cold eyes, chiseled features, and the lean, hungry look of a hawk. Edison was a calm, reasonable, and articulate speaker, and Hague was hard, flamboyant, and impulsive. Edison was an idealist, and his rhetoric was reminiscent of early twentieth-century progressives. He had no organization and made no attempt to build one. Hague, on the other hand, was a calculating realist who understood that organization was essential to winning and keeping office, and that an organization was built on patronage and favors rather than party ideals.[26]

Edison also had the severe handicap of being unable to succeed himself as governor after one three-year term because of the state constitution. During his three years in office he managed to embarrass Hague, pushed forward the movement for a new state constitution, and gave the citizens some relief from the extraordinarily high taxes they were paying under the Hague-controlled, highly wasteful government. In the final analysis, though, the trial balloon showed Hague to be indestructible without more drastic action. A journalist with the *New Republic* summed up Edison's impact and Hague's reaction quite well. "After three years in office," wrote Willard Wiener, "Edison has retired to private life. He has materially weakened Hague's stronghold on the people of New Jersey and has provided a favorable opportunity to launch, with federal help, a campaign of liberation. But Hague is still strongly entrenched, with his chief support found in Washington and the Catholic Church, which he has played for all it is worth."[27]

As time passed, it was clear that Hague could be embarrassed but not destroyed. It would have taken action such as Farley suggested in the late 1930s but which Roosevelt would have no part of. In other words, Hague would have to be sent to prison if the Jersey City machine was to be toppled. But Frank Hague was destined to remain in power until he voluntarily retired from office in 1947 at the age of seventy-one. Roosevelt refused to destroy Hague—which he certainly could have done—because the man who ruled Jersey City politics for nearly half a century was more valuable to the President at the helm of New Jersey's Democracy than he was in prison.

Notes

The author thanks the American Philosophical Society for a grant which helped finance the research for this essay.

1. Marquis W. Childs, "Dictator—American Style," *Reader's Digest* 32(August 1938); Jack Alexander, "King Hanky-Panky of Jersey," *Saturday Evening Post* 213 (October 26, 1940); Willard Wiener, "Hague Is the Law," *New Republic* 110 (January 31, 1944); *Literary Digest* 123 (May 22, 1937).

2. Mark S. Foster, "The Early Career of Mayor Frank Hague" (M.A. thesis, University of Southern California, 1968), 5–7; Sutherland Denlinger, "Boss Hague," *Forum* 44 (March 1938).

3. Dayton D. McKean, *The Boss: The Hague Machine in Action* (Boston, 1940): 20–27; Denlinger, "Boss Hague,".

4. Foster, "Early Career," 7–8; McKean, *The Boss*, 26–29.

5. Mark S. Foster, "Frank Hague of Jersey City: The Boss as Reformer," *New Jersey History* 86 (Summer 1968): 106–117.

6. Richard J. Connors, "The Local Political Career of Mayor Frank Hague," (Ph. D. diss., Columbia University, 1966), ch. 3; Wiener, "Hague Is the Law," 110; McKean, *The Boss*, ch. 8 and 9; Foster, "Reformer," 107–108.

7. James A. Farley, *Behind the Ballots* (New York, 1938), 158.

8. Ibid., 158; Hague to Roosevelt, November 24, 1933, President's Personal File 1013, Roosevelt Mss., Roosevelt Library, Hyde Park, N.Y.

9. A. Harry Moore to Joseph Melici, August 12, 1933, A. Harry Moore Mss., State Library, Trenton, file "Federal 1932–1934."

10. Correspondence in A. Harry Moore Mss., Trenton, file "Federal, 1932–1934."

11. Interview with James A. Farley, December 18, 1966.

12. Connors, "Local Political Career," 130; Arthur Macmahon, John D. Millett, and Gladys Ogden, *Administration of Federal Work Relief* (Chicago, 1941), 199.

13. Political Coercion, New Jersey 610 WPF, National Archives; Lorena Hickok to Harry Hopkins, February 11, 1936, Box 89, Narrative Field Reports, FERA-WPA, Roosevelt Library, Hyde Park.

14. Hickok to Hopkins, February 11, 1936; transcripts of telephone conversations between Hopkins and Ely, January 6, 16, 1937, and between Hopkins and Hague, January 14, 1937, Harry Hopkins Mss., Box 93, Roosevelt Library.

15. McKean, *The Boss*, 103–104.

16. Ibid., ch. 10; Connors, "Local Political Career," 130.

17. Connors, "Local Political Career," 130.

18. President's Personal File 1013, Roosevelt Library; interview with James A. Farley, December 28, 1966.

19. Bruce Blivens Jr., "Will the Witness Step Down?" *New Republic* 95 (June 29, 1938).

20. "Liberty in Journal Square," *New Republic* 95 (May 18, 1938); "Mayor Hague's Long Shadow," *New Republic* 95 (June 15, 1938); McAlister Coleman, "Hague's Army Falls Back," *Nation*, 147 (November 26, 1938).

21. Heywood Broun, "Shoot the Works," *New Republic* 95 (January 19, 1938).

22. "Mayor Hague's Long Shadow"; "Baltimore C.I.O. Chief Jailed in Jersey City," *New York Times*, February 18, 1938, 12; McKean, *The Boss*, 144. See also materials in Official File 300, New Jersey 1938, and File 134, Roosevelt Library, for correspondence relating to Hague and civil liberties. Among the periodicals which put Hague under fire and sometimes Roosevelt for tolerating him, see especially the *Nation* and *New Republic* in 1937 and in 1938.

23. Edward Whalen to Roosevelt, December 29, 1933, Official File 300, Democratic National Committee, 1938, New Jersey, Roosevelt Library.

24. Charles Edison to Roosevelt, December 30, 1940, President's Personal File 3159, Roosevelt Library; press release, June 24, 1940, President's Personal File 3159, Roosevelt Library.

25. President's Personal File 3159, Roosevelt Library.

26. Edison's speeches and letters were in Charles Edison Mss., State Library, Trenton.

27. Wiener, "Hague Is the Law," 110; Jack Alexander, "Ungovernable Governor," *Saturday Evening Post* 215 (January 23, 1943).

Newark teachers who went out on strike in February 1971 picketed City Hall and also took turns picketing schools throughout the city. The strike was prolonged and very bitter. Staff photograph, (Newark) Evening News, *February 2, 1971. Courtesy of the Newark Public Library.*

15

Since 1945 there has been an important population shift in the United States from the cities to the suburbs, a change particularly dramatic in New Jersey. As the country and state also moved toward a postindustrial economy, manufacturing jobs were lost while new technology jobs located in suburban areas. The result was a dramatic loss in urban population and a related decline in the tax base (Camden, for example, had lost jobs and about half its population by 2000). The urban rioting of the 1960s compounded problems. Those who could afford to leave, most often whites, fled the cities in increased numbers. Camden, Paterson, Trenton, and other cities in the state, including small ones like Plainfield, all experienced problems, but Newark was particularly hard hit. Its population declined substantially, while the proportion of blacks increased from 11 percent in 1940 to 54 percent in 1970. These changes are important for understanding what happened in its schools in the 1970s.

An earlier chapter, on Sam Patch, showed Paterson mill workers participating in labor actions in the 1830s, but into the twentieth century workers in the United States faced legal obstacles to organizing unions. New Deal legislation in the 1930s legalized labor's right to organize, while providing for minimum wages and maximum hours. The result was a significant increase in union membership by industrial workers. Then labor's strength at the end of the 1940s contributed to a political backlash with restrictive legislation and, as manufacturing jobs began to decline, a reduction in membership. The exception was public sector unions, which grew dramatically in the 1960s, as government employees engaged in various types of work (including policemen, firemen, clerical workers, and teachers) joined. From the beginning they confronted two issues that were not faced by factory workers. First, particularly an issue for teachers, were they professionals and therefore different, or workers who needed to organize for their own protection? Second, could and should they strike? By the I960s the federal government and some states (New Jersey after a law passed in 1968) recognized their right to organize, but not to strike. Whether public employees could strike was an old issue going back at least to the Boston Police Strike of 1919, which dramatically illustrated the clash between frustrated workers and the safety needs of citizens. These two issues were central to the Newark teachers' strikes and are still worth thinking about today. What side would you take? Should teachers join unions? If public sector employees do strike, should they face heavy fines and jail sentences?

As public sector unions grew in the 1960s and 1970s, so did member militancy. From 1968 to 1981, there were 141 teacher strikes in New Jersey, including two in Newark (1970 and 1971). In the selection that follows, Steve Golin describes one of the Newark strikes. The teachers were angry about salaries, but also about the terrible conditions in the schools, and they resented the arbitrary actions of principals and central administrators who could involuntarily move them to different schools. They wanted a reduction of "nonprofessional duties" such as monitoring hallways and supervising lunch periods. The Newark Teachers Union, frustrated at its inability to win concessions, twice called for a strike. The first lasted three weeks. The second went on for eleven weeks, included violence against and by some of the teachers, and resulted in 347 suspensions and 178 teachers being sent to jail. Golin shows readers the bitterness of the strike. In writing his book he used published sources and oral interviews with 52 teachers who lived through the events. How do the oral interviews help him tell the story? What are the advantages, and pitfalls, of this form of historical research?

Golin also shows how complicated this story was. The teachers in Newark were divided by race, ethnicity, and religion. Many of the city's teachers were Jewish, but there were also large numbers of Italians and an increasing number of blacks. Three unions, the National Education Association (NEA), the Newark Teachers Union (NTU) affiliated with the American Federation of Teachers (AFT), and the Organization of Negro Educators (ONE), vied for members, but they had different perspectives on whether teachers were primarily professionals or primarily workers, and whether they should strike. In some schools many teachers went out on strike, in others just a few. Those who struck faced fines and the threat of jail, while those who crossed the picket lines were often torn by their agreement on the issues, confrontation with teacher-friends, and concern for their students. Even as the strikes took place, the city government changed. Ken Gibson became the first black mayor, a moderate in the midst of a growing black power movement. In a city with a majority black population, the issues of who controlled the schools (teachers, administrators, or the local community) and what was taught in them, were contested. Lyndon Johnson's Great Society programs emphasized community control, but by the 1970s much of the country was becoming more conservative, and moving away from such programs. If you had been teaching in Newark in 1971, what positions would you have supported: strike or not strike; for or against community control? Do you think your own ethnic, religious, or racial background influences your answer?

Legal remedies have been sought for some of the problems the Newark teachers faced in 1970 and 1971. On the heels of the Newark strike, Major Thomas J. Whelan of Jersey City, arguing that his city was too broke to pay for its schools, challenged how education was funded in New Jersey. A lawsuit called *Robinson v. Cahill* ultimately reached the state supreme court, which ruled the constitutional requirement for a "thorough and efficient education" could not be met by local property taxes alone. This led to the adoption in 1976 of the first state income tax. Continued inadequate funding resulted in the 1980s in another case, *Abbott v. Burke*, with which the courts are still wrestling. Creating poor and usually urban "Abbott districts" funded by the state raised the ire of middle-class and suburban residents. Some objected to higher taxes that would then be used for the education of "other people's children." In the debate that followed, one side pointed to urban school districts with lower teachers' salaries, inadequate tax bases, and disintegrating schools with insufficient supplies, while the other side complained of corruption, mismanagement, and wasted money. In response to some of these problems, the state took over schools in Paterson, Camden, Jersey City, and, in 1995, Newark. Still trying to deal with the problems, in 2008 New Jersey passed a School Funding Reform Act.

It has been nearly forty years since the Newark strikes of the 1970s took place, but some of the issues they raised are still with us. Urban decay and poverty continue to plague our cities. The state of the schools and the quality of the education they offer, especially in urban areas, are a matter of concern. The Bush administration promoted its "No Child Left Behind" program, which has increased the number of tests taken by New Jersey's K–12 students. Teach for America attracts high-achieving college graduates to serve as teachers in poor, usually urban, districts in the hope of increasing the ability and number of teachers. Some of these volunteers have been placed in New Jersey cities, including Newark. Have these programs helped? In your opinion, since the strikes, have the conditions in Newark and other cities become worse or better?

Suggested Reading

Braun, Robert J. *Teachers and Power: The Story of the American Federation of Teachers.* New York: Simon and Schuster, 1972.

Compton, Mary, and Lois Weiner, eds., *The Global Assault on Teaching, Teachers, and their Unions: Stories for Resistance.* New York: Palgrave Macmillan, 2008.

Cumbler, John. *A Social History of Economic Decline: Business, Politics and Work in Trenton.* New Brunswick, N.J.: Rutgers University Press, 1989.

Gillette, Howard, Jr. *Camden After the Fall: Decline and Renewal in a Post-Industrial City.* Philadelphia: University of Pennsylvania Press, 2005.

Gowaskie, Joseph. *Workers in New Jersey History.* Trenton: New Jersey Historical Commission, 1996.

McCartin, Joseph A. "Bringing the State's Workers In: Time to Rectify an Imbalanced Labor Historiography." *Labor History* 47 (2006): 73–94.

Mumford, Kevin. *Newark: A History of Race, Rights, and Riots in America.* New York: New York University Press, 2007.

Murphy, Marjorie. *Blackboard Unions: The AFT and the NEA, 1900–1980.* Ithaca, N.Y.: Cornell University Press, 1990.

Price, Clement A. "The Beleaguered City as Promised Land: Blacks in Newark, 1917–1947." In *Urban New Jersey since 1870*, edited by William C. Wright. Trenton: New Jersey Historical Commission, 1974.

Shaffer, Robert. "Where Are the Organized Public Employees? The Absence of Public Employee Unionism from U.S. History Textbooks, and Why It Matters." *Labor History* 43 (2002): 315–334.

Simon, Bryant. *Boardwalk of Dreams: Atlantic City and the Fate of Urban America.* New York: Oxford University Press, 2004.

Yaffe, Deborah. *Other People's Children: The Battle for Justice and Equality in New Jersey's Schools*, New Brunswick, N.J.: Rutgers University Press, 2007.

The 1971 Strike

Steve Golin

In form, the 1971 strike was similar to the 1970 strike: picketing, morning meeting, Sunday rally, occasional downtown demonstration. The feeling was different, however, frequently summed up in one word. "The second strike was vicious," says Phyllis Salowe. "That was vicious," says Martha Nolley. "The feeling that I got between the first strike and the second strike was totally different," says Beth Blackmon. "I mean this became vicious, incredibly vicious."[1]

Either/Or

There were not just two sides in 1971; there were also two ways of seeing. Striking teachers saw their struggle as one of working people against management. Their opponents saw Black parents and citizens against white teachers. There was tremendous pressure to choose between these competing views, rather than to seek what was true in each. Few people were able to look at the strike from both perspectives. Either the strike was seen through the lens of class, or it was seen through the lens of race.

E. Wyman Garrett looked through the lens of race. To Garrett, there was prehistory, when whites ruled Newark. And then there was Gibson's election and Jacob's appointment and his own push at South Eighth Street, when Blacks began to shape their own history, and teachers went on strike to reverse the progress of Blacks. In his view, the Board's power was never challenged, "but all of a sudden when it is controlled by black members, there is talk of taking that power away."[2] What Garrett didn't see was the 1970 strike. In 1970 the teachers fought for a share of power against a white-controlled Board. He was on that Board; he was there. But through the lens of race, the 1970 strike became invisible.

From Steve Golin, *The Newark Teacher Strikes: Hopes on the Line* (New Brunswick, N.J.: Rutgers University Press, 2002), 140–167. Reprinted by permission of the author.

And Carole Graves became a race traitor. In 1970, many Blacks saw her ascendancy as a sign of progress. Not in 1971. In reality she was more of a leader in 1971. But now she was seen as creating a major problem for the city's first Black mayor. Kenneth Travitt, the new head of ONE, denounced Graves and Clara Dasher as "colored lackeys." Travitt correctly interpreted some support for the strike as opposition to Mayor Gibson. He did not stop there; he believed the purpose of the strike itself was to hurt Gibson. "All of this rabble rousing is to discredit the Gibson administration."[3]

Either/or: workers against management, or whites against Blacks? Graves argued, defensively, "We are not a part of the establishment. We are workers." Seen through the lens of class, striking teachers were working people, underdogs against the establishment. "WHO ARE WE?" asked NTU, in a leaflet aimed at Newark citizens. "THE STRIKING TEACHERS ARE BLACK & WHITE *WORKERS*."[4]

Given the racial climate, NTU leaders worried that teachers would not want to strike. The Board of Education wouldn't negotiate a new contract, and the old one expired January 31, 1971. If teachers didn't strike, they would lose the gains they had won in 1970. If they did strike, they would strike against a nonwhite Board of Education, a Black mayor, and Black parent groups. "Gibson was the mayor," Jim Lerman recalls. "Baraka had been doing all this stuff about striking this time is a strike against the community. And the Black teachers for sure didn't want to go on strike. And the white teachers were afraid to go on strike."[5]

The decisive moment, Lerman says, occurred at a mass meeting at the end of January.

> Carole Graves walked into that hall and gave the performance of her life. She got pissed at everybody—the mayor, the commissioner of education, the superintendent of schools—and she was naming names, just like chapter and verse, and she was spitting mad. And for all these white people in that audience, to hear someone who was Black tell them that they had better go on strike, made that strike.[6]

Naming white as well as Black enemies of the teachers, the superintendent and commissioner as well as the mayor, Graves was saying that the dividing line between those who supported the teachers and those who opposed them was not the color line. The dividing line was the line between labor and management.

Before the strike, when a teacher had asked what would happen if they didn't strike, Graves had answered that going to work without a contract would subject teachers to the Board's power. To Graves, unions were in the forefront of the battle against bondage; the real Black freedom movement flowed with—not against—the movement of working people to organize. During the strike, she identified the "two great struggles in the history of the American people, the struggle of *my people* against slavery, culminating in the Thirteenth Amendment, which prohibited involuntary servitude, and the struggle of the labor movement for the right to create unions to obtain freedom *from the arbitrary power* of employers."[7]

Jim Brown, who began teaching in January, embraced the Union position. "We won, or else we went back to the master-or to the boss/employee type of thing, where the boss would tell you everything." He recalls an elegant formulation of the meaning of the strike. "I remember Bayard Rustin and to this day his saying: 'A boss is a boss is a boss.'" Brown remembers "everybody cheering, applauding."[8] Teachers were cheering because Rustin, as a Black, was saying that their strike was about class, not race.

NTU leaders always presented the struggle as labor versus management. When they distributed the Board's list of forty-eight demands to teachers, they put a star next to its rejection of binding arbitration. They did not star its rejection of the whole concept of nonprofessional chores; nonprofessional chores, as an issue, was already racialized. But they starred "There will be no time limit on any faculty meeting" and "Newark Board of Education will install in each school a time clock wherein all personnel are required to punch in and out, and pay will be based on the time clock."[9] In short, a boss is a boss is a boss.

The Board was boss. But was it the same boss, the same Board? Black activists like Garrett argued that Gibson's appointments made the Board new. They stressed the discontinuity in Board membership. Striking teachers stressed the continuity in Board function; they argued that despite appearances, the Board had not changed. "I've seen a lot of people come and go on the Board of Ed," says Beth Blackmon. "Somehow my perception of the Board of Ed remains constant through time," as if the Board has "a life of its own."[10]

Looking through the lens of class, Union leaders saw the conflict as union busters against Black and white workers. Young Black men attacked striking teachers on February 2, the second day of the 1971 strike, and sent several to the hospital. Graves insisted that the attack was not a racial incident but "strictly an anti-union incident."[11] The attackers did not discriminate. "What was heard was not 'Let's get the white b—' or 'Let's get the Black b—' but 'Let's get the union b—.'"[12]

NTU leaders believed that Gibson and Jacob wanted to bust their Union. They told other unions that "the City Administration and this Board of Education have set out to break any effective public employee union and trade union in the city and to turn back the clock for union members to pre-1930 days." This view of the strike was effective in reaching out to labor. "Help Stop Union Busting," urged a flyer signed by the local Teamsters, United Automobile Workers (UAW), and Building and Construction Trades, as well as by the New Jersey AFL-CIO and New Jersey Industrial Union Council.[13]

Local union leaders recognized that the Union was in danger and gave it crucial support. The UAW sent pickets. The Teamsters refused to cross the picket line to deliver food and heating oil. The New Jersey AFL-CIO, headed by Charles Marciante, lobbied local and state government, and gave between three hundred and six hundred dollars a day to support the strike, according to Ron Polonsky. "We couldn't do a thing without Marciante." Felix Martino adds: "The trade unions supported us to the extent that they could. They supplied speakers, they supplied moral support, they even supplied money and placards. Sometimes they even came on the picket line."[14]

There were limits to labor support, however. These limits derived from the limits of the trade union movement itself. Most trade unions, especially the old craft unions, were primarily white. Most were organized and controlled from the top down. And most had not been militant for years.

Local union leaders threatened to be militant in 1971. They called a one-day general strike in Newark to support the teachers. Newark business and political leaders pressed them to call it off. Two days before the general strike, claiming there had been progress in negotiations, Marciante cancelled it. Some teachers were bitter, saying labor leaders shouldn't threaten to strike if they didn't mean it.[15]

ONE focused on another limit of labor support when it charged that the unions backing the teachers strike were "predominantly lily-white." By the rules governing the discourse on race in 1971, only a Black could respond. Mae Massie, a civil rights director of the International Union of Electrical, Radio and Machine Workers, defended labor's effort to integrate Blacks, accused ONE of adding racial overtones to the strike, and asserted that the strike involved "pure and simple labor-management issues."[16]

The most serious limitation of the support provided by local trade unions was that it came from the top. Connie Woodruff, community affairs director of the International Ladies Garment Workers Union OLGWU), helped striking teachers present their side to the Black community, spoke at their rallies, raised money for them, lent them the ILGWU office for their strike headquarters, and let them use the phones and auditorium for free. But she couldn't get her own members in Newark to support the strike, or even keep their own children home.

Woodruff concluded, unhappily, that only union leaders backed the teachers; the Black community in Newark, including union members, did not support the teachers.[17]

Desperately seeking community support, striking teachers took it where they could get it, from the Italian communities of the North, East, and West Wards. And from Tony Imperiale, as Carole Graves acknowledged. "As far as welcoming support, I think when someone is drowning and going down for the third time, you don't look at where that hand is coming from, or what color it is."[18] In fact, the 1971 strike was never simply labor versus management. It was also Italian versus Black.

Imperiale had made his name in 1967 as the leader of Italian vigilantes, dedicated to saving Newark from the Black menace. His great strength as a leader, besides his readiness to use violence, was that he could not be shamed. After the 1970 mayoral election, he announced he was forming a conservative organization to fight Gibson and seeking help from supporters of George Wallace, the former Alabama governor and leading segregationist. Charges of racism bounced off Imperiale. "If racism means to be against communists, to be against those who are for insurrection, to be against those who advocate anarchy, then I'm proud to say I'm the head of a racist organization."[19]

Striking teachers accepted an alliance with Imperiale rather than let Jacob and Saunders strip away the gains made with such sacrifice in 1970, but because of his racism most accepted his help reluctantly. Carol Karman was troubled by the alliance with Imperiale; Graves clung to the pretense that his help was unsolicited. Polonsky took Imperiale's support but wouldn't let him speak at daily strike meetings.[20]

Tom Lawton was grateful to Imperiale for helping him when he was accused of attacking a Black strikebreaker, but Lawton's gratitude never translated into support for Imperiale. Growing up in Newark, Lawton made friends with the little girl next door. "I didn't know I wasn't supposed to like her, until my father told me I wasn't. And when I asked why, he says: 'She's Black.' . . . At that time, in the fifties, they didn't say Black. She was 'a nigger.'" Tom's father feared for his son's safety in the Black family's house. "His concept of a Black family was distorted." Lawton recognized that in many ways the 1971 strike "was becoming a Black and white situation," but he kept his distance from Imperiale, because he could not subscribe to Imperiale's distorted concepts about Blacks.[21]

Pete Petino embraced Imperiale. "Tony was a tremendous help," Petino says.

I did like him. I have a lot of respect for him. In fact if it wasn't for Tony Imperiale and his men, when we demonstrated with Bayard

Rustin at South Eighth, if it wasn't for Tony, I think we would have been in deep shit, quite frankly. Tony was there. He wasn't out on the line. He was there with his men, in cars and in trucks, making sure when the groups that came and converged on us that day— that even though the police were there, it didn't get out of hand. And we had known Tony was going to be there. In case.

Petino, Dominick Bizzarro, and Joe Del Grosso were the Italian connection, quietly assigned by NTU to coordinate activities with Imperiale. "We kind of were a liaison with him. We reached out," says Petino. The alliance with Imperiale heightened the danger of large-scale racial violence. It could not be publicized. "I think the correct term for that is 'covert.'"[22]

Italian Americans gave the strike the mass base in the community that it otherwise lacked. First Avenue School in the North Ward embodied Italian power, as South Eighth Street embodied Black power. Two women crossing the First Avenue picket line were hurt as they entered school, and hospitalized; the next day, Imperiale and a group of parents turned everyone away from the school, including the principal. One Black teacher still tried to go to work. Police escorted her through the line, using force to hold parents back, but she left after seeing no one else was in school. The Board assigned her and three other nonstriking Black teachers to another school. Imperiale, parents, and teachers kept First Avenue closed tight.[23]

Closing First Avenue was a communal effort. Almost everyone from the school was on the picket line, including the secretary, who lived in the neighborhood. Merchants opened their shops to pickets on cold mornings and gave free coffee. Parents brought doughnuts and coffee for pickets and sent their children to the alternative schools set up in basements and staffed by striking teachers. Closing the school helped the strike, because the Board only received state aid for schools that were open. A co-chair of the newly formed North Ward Community for Unity extended the logic of First Avenue to other schools. She said, "We should force the closing of the schools by any means—I mean any means."[24]

In Newark, Italian Americans appropriated the rhetorical style of Black Power. Across America, the heightened consciousness of white ethnics grew out of their encounter with Black pride and assertiveness; they reacted against, and borrowed from, Black nationalism. Deliberately quoting parents at South Eighth Street, First Avenue parents accused the Black teacher who went into school of "insensitivity to the community." Petino observed that when Blacks spoke at Board meetings and bargaining sessions, they claimed to speak "for the community," but only spoke for Blacks. Calling on North Ward residents to assert their power, he made the point that the idea of community was at least as meaningful to Italians as Blacks. "You're the community," thundered Petino.[25]

Italian Americans in Newark rose as a community in support of the strike. Their rallying cry was that they must stop Blacks in general, and Baraka in particular. Some already resented the preponderance of Jewish principals, especially in high schools. Were Blacks now going to take over the school system? During the strike, a group from the East Ward asked North Ward residents to join in defending the educational rights of "the white citizens of Newark."[26]

The strike was strong in the North Ward, where Imperiale was based, and even stronger in the East Ward, in the Ironbound district. The Ironbound was an industrial area with a strong blue-collar tradition and an Italian American core. A number of teachers crossed picket lines in the North Ward during the 1971 strike, but very few crossed in the Ironbound. Parents and teachers at Ann Street School were particularly aggressive, preventing anyone—teachers, aides, substitutes—from crossing the line. When nearly four hundred Ironbound residents met at Our Lady of Fatima Church to declare support for the strike, Louis Turco, the East Ward councilman and city council president, urged them to march on City Hall. Turco said, "Other people get together and make a lot of noise and they get the goodies."[27]

Turco had opposed the 1970 strike; a victory by teachers would cost the city too much money, he said. After Gibson's election, Turco became a leader of the opposition, and after Saunders framed the Board's stance as Black, he became a supporter of the teachers. He received a standing ovation when he unexpectedly showed up at a strike meeting in February. During the strike, he defended binding arbitration against "the radicals in Newark like Jesse Jacob, E. Wylnan Garrett and LeRoi Jones [Baraka]."[28]

Imperiale, Turco, and John Cervase gave leadership to the Italian community's support of the 1971 strike. Imperiale, with his paramilitary organization, led Italians in the street. Turco, as the most politically powerful Italian in Newark, led the council against the Board. Cervase became the voice of the Italian community on the Board.

Cervase was a wealthy lawyer, with a beautiful home in the Forest Hills section of the North Ward and a traditional management perspective, reinforced by social conservatism. Appointed to the Board of Education by Addonizio [the previous mayor], he became the first president of the Independent Board Members Association of New Jersey, founded in 1968 to combat subversive activity in the schools and prevent racial integration. Cervase condemned student demonstrations, sex education, forced busing, and the ban on school prayer; he blamed liberal teachers for fostering drug addiction and disrespect for lawful authority. He strongly opposed the 1970 strike, accusing the Union of wanting to share power with the Board. After the settlement, he helped block an effort to gain leniency for arrested teachers and shaped Board resistance to the new grievance procedure.[29]

But after Gibson's victory and Jacob's appointment, Cervase reversed his stand toward the teachers, their Union, and their contract. He saw the conflict in 1971 from the perspective of race, not class. Abandoning his management perspective, he now feared Black power more than teacher power. Above all, he was afraid of Baraka. Baraka wanted to teach Newark children to be African, not American; he "writes the word 'American' with a small letter, but uses a capital letter for the word 'Black.'"[30] Cervase embraced the Union in 1971 as a bastion of American civilization against Baraka and the militant hordes.

Cervase became the lone Board member to break publicly with Jacob, denouncing him as the captive of Baraka, Garrett, and Elayne Brodie. Jacob, who took direction from no one, called Cervase a liar. But Cervase lumped all angry Blacks together. Although he carefully made distinctions between Italians—criticizing Imperiale as too extreme, and dismissing a colleague on the Board as too working-class—he reduced all Blacks to followers or opponents of Baraka. The real battle in the strike, he said, was not between the Union and the Board but between the Union and Black militants.[31]

In 1971 the tendency to simplify was very powerful on both sides. People looked through the lens of class and saw conspiracy: Gibson wanted to break the Union and deprive teachers of their rights. Or they looked through the lens of race, and saw conspiracy: striking teachers were trying to undermine Gibson and prevent Blacks from coming into their own.

There was no middle ground. Early in the strike, Larry Hamm and the leaders of the Newark Student Federation claimed not to be on either side and to speak for white students as well as Black, but they too were affected by the spirit of 1971. Hamm, who was independent in 1970, identified with Baraka in 1971. He led the Student Federation to embrace a nationalist program of Black power in school curriculum and staffing. In April, the Federation urged the Board to reject a settlement with the teachers, even though not settling meant the strike would continue.[32]

Teachers, seen exclusively through the lens of race, were not working people, subject to the arbitrary decisions of bosses, but privileged persons. They were possessors of wealth and power greater than most Blacks, and they were the enemy. David Barrett, director of Newark's antipoverty program and an ally of Baraka, defended the violence against teachers on

February 2 as "the desperate actions of an abused, offended and aroused community." Barrett rejected the idea that teachers were working-class. "If they are members of the working class, then what class do the 25 percent unemployed, and the rest of us who are underemployed, then what class do they—do we—belong to?"[33]

The unemployed, the powerless, and those who spoke for them were good. The teachers were bad. An activist denounced the "so-called professional teachers" and their "so-called union." Elayne Brodie labeled NTU "a sick, barbaric teachers' union." The new Central Ward councilman, Dennis Westbrook, said teachers were "foreigners," meaning they didn't belong in the community. New Ark Community Coalition distributed a drawing of four white teachers. One wore a miniskirt; one had long sideburns. The four were holding hands and clutching money. The flyer proclaimed: "RUNT (Racist Union of Non Teachers) wants our community dollars for suburbs."[34]

The word "community" became reified, as if it was a thing, rather than a web of relationships. One activist said, "Too often the community is left out, and it is the community's children who are affected by the contract." The community's children: the community was not children. Nor was it parents. Most parents were not involved in the issues and did not attend PTA meetings, Don Saunders said; if he randomly stopped Blacks in Newark and asked them what they thought of nonprofessional chores, they probably wouldn't know what he was talking about. Saunders nevertheless claimed that the community wanted power over the schools. "The community didn't want to participate, they wanted control. . . . They wanted to control the school system."[35]

The idea of community was, finally, not about people. Community was the nationalist ideal: militant, Black, powerful. It was a weapon to use against teachers, the insensitive foreigners. The idea of community articulated by Garrett, Baraka, and Saunders tended to smother differences within the actual Black community. It pushed members of that community to simplify, or at least keep quiet.

Graves and Polonsky simplified too. They attacked the integrity of Black activists and blamed all racial conflict on them. "The issues have been intentionally muddled by unethical, irresponsible, and self-serving politicians and 'poverty pimps,'" asserted Graves. An NTU leaflet identified Baraka, Jacob, Saunders, Brodie, and others as "poverty pimps" and detailed the money they received from federal programs and city agencies. They were in a conspiracy with the powers-that-be. Polonsky asked whether "Dr. Garrett and LeRoi Jones might not be Agnew-type frontmen, saying the things ex officio that those in office would want to say." Graves told the teachers, "Once again it has become convenient to inject racism into a struggle which unites the working men and women of this country. The government and the courts, assisted by reactionary nationalists, have formed an amalgamation to destroy your dignity."[36]

There was a tendency to demonize opponents of the strike, especially Baraka. Many striking teachers regarded him as an evil genius and, without evidence, blamed him for the violent attack on February 2. In court, arguing against an injunction against the strike, the Union's lawyer asserted that the strike was necessary to block Baraka's attempt "to take over the schools and the board of education." Angela Paone, speaking at Fairleigh Dickinson University, was asked why Mayor Gibson wasn't doing more to settle the strike. She responded that the mayor was under Baraka's influence. A reporter telephoned Dasher, who verified that Paone was articulating the Union position.[37]

Just as opponents of the strike saw Graves and Dasher as puppets of whites, Union activists saw Jacob and Gibson as puppets of Baraka. They ridiculed Gibson, calling him "Mayor Jones." This view of Gibson cemented the Union's alliance with Italian Americans in the North and East Wards. "The union's charge that Jones is attempting to take over the school system and its references to 'Mayor Jones' have reinforced the belief of some persons that Gibson is in fact being directed by militant blacks," observed the *Newark News*. "In the North and East Wards . . . , those who had warned during the campaign that Gibson was the puppet of Jones and other black militants, are quick to say, 'I told you so.'"[38]

Each side in the 1971 strike attacked the motives and decency of the other. Neither saw the other merely as partisan, or even as wrong, but also as lacking integrity. Graves and Dasher were colored lackeys, Baraka and Brodie were poverty pimps. Those who insisted that class was central to the conflict were derided as "so-called professional teachers." Those who insisted that race was central were derided as "so-called leaders." It was hard for participants on either side to regard people on the other side as fully human. And the fact that, week after week, your side denied the humanity of my side was taken as proof that your side was humanly deficient.

Some participants managed to keep their balance. They knew the struggle was about both race and class. They took sides, but tried not to demonize their opponents. One NTU leaflet took a historical approach: many Black activists rejected unions because the labor movement had failed to integrate construction unions, to organize in the South, and to fight for jobs and housing for Blacks. These Black activists allied themselves with the establishment instead of allying with teachers and other working people. Written by someone who knew labor history and Black history, the leaflet granted Baraka's sincerity. "It would be wrong to dismiss Leroi Jones as an unrepresentative figure in Black America, or, as has been suggested, as an 'agent' of the city power structure."[39]

Not all Black groups joined in the condemnation of the strike. The Black Panthers picketed West Side High in support of the teachers and read a statement at a morning strike meeting. "We see the Board of Education as being one of the many oppressors located in our community," they said. "We view the present struggle of the Newark Teachers Union as one for progressive change for black and all oppressed people." The Nation of Islam also supported the strike. The Panthers, who always emphasized class as well as race, were a tiny group in Newark; the Nation of Islam, which was nationalistic, was larger. But what the two groups had in common was that their opposition to Baraka led to their support for the teachers. According to *Muhammad Speaks*, newspaper of the Nation of Islam, Baraka "tended to pit parents and students against teachers and place the Black community on the same side as the racist Board of Education."[40]

The teacher power movement and the Black Power movement both emerged during the 1960s. Each achieved its first major success in Newark in 1970: the teachers strike and the election of Gibson. In 1971, both movements were trying to protect what they had won. Neither felt secure or established. So they tore at each other. Hoping to gain legitimacy, each dismissed the other as illegitimate. In April, each side characterized the other as fascist.[41]

Either/or. The 1971 strike put terrible pressure on people to choose, not only between two sides, but also between two ways of viewing the struggle: Either solidarity with union brothers and sisters, or solidarity with Black brothers and sisters. Either Baraka was being used by the corporations, or Graves was being used by the white establishment. Either Gibson was trying to crush the Union, or the Union was trying to destroy Gibson.

Even before 1971, as Clara Dasher recognized, some Blacks tended to regard NTU as "a white racist union."[42] During the 1970 strike, teachers challenged this tendency, limiting its growth. But in 1971, they seemed to be striking against Black Power. As the strike continued, week after week, many intelligent and idealistic teachers felt increasing pressure to simplify. The chorus of Black voices portraying them as selfish, as striking in order to benefit their own kind at the expense of others less fortunate, challenged their understanding of themselves.

In 1971, Bob Lowenstein wrote to the *Newark News*, questioning the way that Black parents and community activists portrayed teachers. Lowenstein, who always advocated a teacher unionism that benefited students and the larger community, asked adults who had attended Newark schools whether their competent and devoted teachers "can have, almost overnight, become incompetent, negligent, and indifferent to the needs of their charges." His point was that teachers were not to blame for the failures of the school system. And then he too fell into blaming. Citing student absence, lateness, and lack of study, Lowenstein blamed the home and community.[43]

In 1970, Phyllis Salowe struck to help students. She didn't care about binding arbitration; she wanted more supplies. But 1971 was different. "There was more of a white/Black division in the second strike. And the parent groups, the community was making it that way." The hostility from parents bothered her. "The worst thing was being attacked as not caring about the children and only caring about ourselves. I guess that was the part that was most difficult for me to bear." Salowe's sense of innocence was shaken. "I couldn't understand why these people didn't think I was their ally. It was distressing, obviously. Distressing's the wrong word. I couldn't understand."[44]

For Salowe, 1971 had a terrible, clarifying effect. Feeling "torn," she observed, in herself and other young teachers, the narrowed choices, and the process of choosing. "There were a lot of people who were striking for very idealistic reasons the first time who didn't go out the second time. Or there were people who went out in the beginning and came back, because of . . . the effect that they thought it was going to have on the kids." But there was another group of young people who stayed out, who became less idealistic and "much more . . . militant, as a result." She was one of them. "The second strike was much more a strike of workers for better working conditions, and it was much clearer to me. . . . By the second strike, I wasn't striking for more pencils or different books."[45]

Dave Lieberfarb felt in 1970 that he was bringing "power to the people." By "people," he meant the teachers and parents. But in 1971, activist parents were saying that his struggle was opposed to their struggle, that he was the enemy. "We found much to our chagrin, especially in the second strike, that most local groups were against us." Lieberfarb stayed out again but was "probably a little less sure of myself that God was on our side." His uncertainty was heightened by the alliance with Imperiale. "Knowing that people like that were on our side was very disillusioning at times. [If you] judge people by who their friends are and who their enemies are, you have to wonder about your position sometimes, if you have more respect for some of your enemies than for some of your friends."[46]

Carol Karman had faith in the Union as one of the few places in the society where Blacks and whites could come together, and together struggle toward a better world. During the 1971 strike, she clung to that faith. Unlike Salowe or Lieberfarb, Karman was not shaken by charges that the strike was hurting the Black community. "I never felt guilty for one minute. I didn't buy that bullshit. I knew LeRoi Jones was being paid by Prudential Life Insurance, and that Gibson was out to break my Union, and was just using the race question to try to beat the Union. I was very convinced. I didn't waver at all."[47]

Most teachers who stayed out in 1971 or who crossed the picket line were hurt by the experience. The pressure was greatest on Black teachers. Torn between the conflicting solidarities of race and class, Black teachers faced painful decisions over and over again.

Phyllis Cuyler stayed out for a while. Afraid of violence, she didn't picket much. She was single, living alone, worried about her bills, paying off a loan from the 1970 strike, and confused because "there was so many viewpoints." Then she went back. She was pelted with eggs as she crossed the picket line. "I didn't feel good about it either way, because I didn't think I should be going in, but I didn't feel that anybody should throw eggs at me."[48] Cuyler's previous analysis, in which racial and class struggle converged, gave her little comfort in 1971. She was caught in the middle, between two solidarities.

Marion Bolden had stayed home in 1970. "I kind of followed the crowd, just being new." She didn't call in sick and didn't bond with other strikers; she supported the Union, but not in a passionate, transforming way. As the 1971 strike drew near, "I agonized more." She feared it would drag on and become "unfair to the kids." She decided to keep working. Inside Barringer, with a dozen Black teachers, Bolden experienced a camaraderie she had not felt in 1970. They took turns bringing food for lunch and became "a support group." She who had been shy found her voice in the group; it was the beginning of becoming a leader. But the decision to work did not end her choices. A striking Black teacher called her at home and asked her to stay out for just one day. She talked to others in the group, and they agreed: "Let's give our colleagues one day."[49]

To Avant Lowther, 1971 was "Black *versus* white." He decided to cross the picket line. "Here I am, a new young Black teacher . . . And here you have this Union with a Black president that's a figurehead, and you have Petino and all of these others, the Italian white males who were behind her." But inside West Kinney, the question of Black identity reemerged. Baraka was there, coaching volunteers. "It was always a constant conflict, because he was trying to push Black Black Black Black Black at the expense of everything else." Lowther's father didn't want Baraka and his volunteers in the school, because they taught Swahili, instead of skills the students needed to survive in America. Once Baraka "threatened my father, and one of the kids ran upstairs and got me." Lowther was so angry at Baraka that he could have killed him.[50]

Zenobia Capel was a veteran teacher. She told the Union rep at Peshine Avenue School that she would not strike. Although she thought the Union did more than the Association for teachers, she was not a joiner. And she had a baby, and bills to pay. Capel went to work during the 1971 strike, as she had in 1970. But she resisted the racial arguments used against the 1971 strikers. "When Jesse [Jacob] says that they're doing it to our kids, . . . I know that I don't sound really Black when I say it, but you can use that too often. After a while it doesn't mean anything. If everything is done to you because you're Black, then it gets to be a crutch for you, and also, no one pays attention to it."[51]

Janice Adams held on to her belief in the Union as a force for social progress. She knew many people saw the 1971 strike as "'those horrible teachers against the Black kids,' but that's not the way I felt about it. I felt that by forcing the issue, that an awful lot of substantive changes would take place"—such as new reading programs and counseling services, smaller classes, a better physical plant. She refused to believe there was no money for the schools. She told *Muhammad Speaks*: "Mayor Gibson is being manipulated by the corporate power structure. . . . He doesn't want big business to move out of Newark and so the corporations have had their property value reassessed downward. And then the cry is made that there is no money in the city." As a Black and a worker, Adams was a strike activist in 1971. "Nationalism was very strong, and I was a part of that also. I didn't see what I was doing as a contradiction."[52]

Harold Moore was active in the strike, picketing most days. One day he went to Seton Hall University to speak to a Black Studies class. "There were a lot of young militant Blacks in that program who had some opinions about the strike. . . . A lot of them felt that the fact that I was supporting the strike made me less Black." The charge annoyed him but didn't really get to him. "I never let anyone else define Blackness for me." Moore told the students how he felt about the strike. "I don't think I changed everybody's mind, but I think they saw that it wasn't just a black and white issue. I mean that in more ways than one. When young people become militant, it becomes very difficult for them to see any way but their way."[53]

Blessed with an inner calm and robust spirituality, Moore charted his own course through the ups and downs of the struggle. He was emotionally sustained by the camaraderie of strikers: "We were so close." Financially, he scraped by; Pat Piegari found him work on the docks. But the strike eventually hurt Moore. His wife, Alison, was worried about the violence. "We were getting warnings from people all over," she says. "I don't want anything bad to happen to him, because he's too good." Then came threats of suspensions and firings. Though

Alison put no pressure on him, Moore felt "what the strike was doing to her." He went to Piegari and Paone and, in tears, told them he was going back. The principal waited until school was over the next day before telling Moore he was suspended. Moore was furious at him for hiding the suspension all day. But he was also joyful. "He was so happy that he was suspended," Paone remembers. "He was thrilled because now the decision had been made, and that's it."[54]

The 1971 strike was brutal for everyone, especially for those who experienced conflicting claims of race and class. The longer it lasted, the more brutal it became; it seemed it would never end. Yet finally, in April, people torn by the conflicting claims would help end the strike.

Violence

The 1971 strike began on Monday, February 1. Half of the teachers—including most Black teachers—crossed the picket line on the first day of the 1971 strike.[55]

Few strikers picketed on Monday, February 1. They were afraid to picket because of the mood in the city, the free-floating anger. At most elementary schools, strikers were outnumbered by teachers who went to work, and they did not want to confront angry parents by themselves. Also, teachers arrested in 1970 had been warned by the Union's lawyer that their bail would be revoked if they were arrested again; they could go to jail for a long time. NTU leaders decided not to try to put pickets at every school, but rather to concentrate them at selected schools. Teachers willing to picket reported to the Union office on Clinton Avenue to get their picket assignment.[56]

It was still early on Tuesday, February 2, when fifteen teachers left the office with their assignments. Cars pulled up, surrounding them. "It was daylight," says Jim Brown. "So it was maybe seven-thirty or something, and we came walking out, with a lot of bravado, you know, high spirits. And that's when the incident happened." Young Black men, twenty or more of them, jumped out of the cars; the men were wearing fatigues and black army boots, running at the teachers, attacking males first. Stunned and terrified, teachers reacted individually. Brown, who had grown up in Newark, fought off one attacker. Then he ran.[57]

Brown had chosen to teach in Newark because he was from the city and knew he would be comfortable there. He was the son of a Newark fireman who had previously worked in a factory and always belonged to a union. Jim, the oldest of twelve children, grew up with the belief that "you wouldn't cross somebody's picket line." In college, he saw himself, with pride, as Nicky Newarker. He learned at a Union meeting in January that the Board refused to negotiate with the teachers. Like other young members of West Side High's math department, he knew what that meant. "We considered ourselves working-class teachers, rather than this high title of a professional. So there was no doubt in our mind that we were going to walk."[58]

In high school he had been on the track team. Now he ran. He ran to the corner of Clinton Avenue and turned left. Two men were after him, one carrying a broom handle, one a milk crate, but they could not keep up with him, "so I feel pretty safe." As he ran, a car pulled up. He imagined the police were on the way, and the car was there to help the two men escape. Instead, more men jumped out of the car, boxing him in. He yelled for someone to call the police. An older Black man came out of his door, and said, "I called the police." One young man threw the milk crate but missed. Brown looked for guns or knives and didn't see any. "I figured this is going to be a street fight." He blocked some punches and threw some but didn't connect. Blows from the broom knocked him to the ground. The men jumped in the car and left.[59]

He got up and walked the two blocks back to the Union office. After the attack, the office was locked tight. "I didn't realize how actually scared I really was until I walked back." He banged on the door, and someone let him in. "Carole Graves was there at the time, and Clara [Dasher] was there, and they look and they see that I'm all cut up, so they start washing my arms. Next thing you know I had to excuse myself, and I went in the bathroom and I threw up."[60]

Six teachers were taken to Beth Israel Hospital; two were kept overnight. Helen Cornish, who suffered a fractured skull, was released the next day. Terry Elman, who had fought back against the attackers, was kept longer. "I myself was hit in the back of the head with a whiffle bat that had nails coming out of it, causing 126 stitches," he explained. "I was hit in the face with a pipe that broke my nose, broke my elbow, and knocked me to the ground." One of the young men straddled him when he was on the ground and was going to hit him with a fire extinguisher. A striking teacher, a Black woman, ran over and pushed the attacker aside.[61]

Tuesday night, at a mass meeting, Brown told his story. One or two other victims also spoke. Television cameras were present (Only when he was watching the TV news did Brown notice a teacher in the front row weeping as she listened to him.) To further publicize the incident, the Union distributed a leaflet with a photo of a battered Terry Elman entering the hospital, and the words: "WE CARE! DO YOU?"[62]

Teachers cared. The attack shocked and angered them. Many were indignant that there were no arrests. On Wednesday, 227 more teachers stayed out to protest the violence; 20 more were out at Weequahic, 15 more at West Side. Nonstriking teachers at Sussex Avenue School decided to show sympathy with striking colleagues because of the assault; the Sussex Avenue PTA agreed to a one-day boycott, and on Thursday the school was closed. Pete Petino thinks the attack "gained us a lot of support, because those people that weren't out then decided to go out, because they were outraged that that would happen."[63]

But the increase in the percentage of striking teachers was only temporary. By the middle of the second week, the percentage was again hovering around 50, where it remained for a long time, before slipping even lower. The attack on February 2 scared some teachers away from picketing and hardened others. "That [assault] pretty much set the tone, that it was going to be a very hardball strike," says Jim Lowenstein. The violence against the teachers on the second day "cemented the strike" and "actually made the strike," according to Graves. Only 50 percent or fewer of the teachers were out, but after the attack, "they vowed to stay out forever."[64]

Petino says February 2 "triggered" a lot of violence. Tom Lawton says "everyone was fearing for their lives" after hearing what happened to Terry Elman. "We figured there would be roving bands of parents out there, beating teachers up. So everyone had something to protect themselves." Pickets began to carry screwdrivers, ice picks, knives. Carloads of strike opponents cruised around Newark in the mornings, intimidating pickets. "Teachers started retaliating," said Graves. "The picket lines were vicious scenes."[65]

Violence became characteristic of the 1971 strike. Cars were the preferred target for both sides. Someone poured soap powder down the carburetor of Carole Graves's 1970 Plymouth, then stuffed newspaper in the interior and set it on fire. The 1961 Cadillac of Elayne Brodie—a leading opponent of the Union, who helped Saunders with his community strategy—was burned at night. Someone broke the windows of Jesse Jacob's car, which made him even angrier at the Union.[66]

Attacks on the cars of strikebreakers became commonplace as the weeks went on and striking teachers became more desperate. At East Side High, on the first day of the strike, teachers who crossed the picket line found the tires of their cars punctured by an ice pick. After the assault on the Union teachers, there were reports from around the city of tires punctured, windows smashed, convertible tops slit, bodies scratched with keys or spray-painted. Violence against the cars of teachers who refused to strike was both an outlet for the anger of striking teachers and a picket line strategy. In 1970 there were enough pickets to intimidate teachers who wanted to work but wanted even more to avoid trouble. In 1971 violence made up for the lack of numbers.[67]

"Oh yeah, cars were expendable," says Petino, laughing. "Windows. Tires. You name it." Petino was one of a number of young activists who kept up their spirits by punishing teachers who crossed the picket line. Other strikers vicariously enjoyed the tales of revenge. The destruction was so widely accepted in the subculture of striking teachers that people who were not ordinarily violent became drawn into it. Elena Scambio called in sick in 1970, when she was not yet certified. In 1971, to retaliate against "people who were breaking the picket line," she gave flat tires. "I was a young teacher caught up in the activity of the moment. Because members of my family had always been strong union members, I wouldn't think of not participating."[68]

Tom Lawton, who drove a Rheingold beer truck during the strike to support himself, would stop in front of Garfield School to snarl traffic. To slow down teachers trying to get into school before the line formed, the band of young activists at Garfield would loop a chain (without a lock) around the gate and put bubble gum in the lock of the school door. They put objects in the tailpipes of cars belonging to teachers who were inside. "Not enough to ruin it, but just enough to foul them up for a while." The point was "to harass" strikebreakers without getting caught. "Little devious activities. We weren't really pugilists that would get out there and fight with people."[69]

Joe Del Grosso began teaching at Garfield late in 1970 and quickly became active in the Union. He used a BB gun. "When we could find teachers' cars that were scabbing, we would ventilate their windows." He shot out the windows of one car seven times, because the owner was a leader of those going in. "Finally after the seventh time, the teacher knew I did it, came to me, and said, 'That's it. I'm not going in any more. I surrender.'"[70]

Scambio, Lawton, and Del Grosso are unusual only in talking openly about what they did, when they were very young. Most activists felt the same way about people who were crossing the line. The feeling was: if we all stayed out, we would win quickly, and we could all go back. By going in, you prolong the strike. You collect a paycheck, while we go without. Yet you want it both ways. When we win, you'll benefit from the new contract as much as we will. If there's a raise, you'll take that too. But we are going to make you pay.[71]

Much of the violence was low-level vandalism. But it was intended to hurt. Pat Piegari and Angela Paone had a baby to feed, and they were not getting paid. "As the 1971 strike went on, I became more pissed and more militant," Piegari says. He threw pennies on the ground in front of teachers who were going in. "People hated that." He spray-painted the cars of teachers who were working and abused husbands who dropped off wives. Once he picked up a wooden police barricade and hurled it at the car of a teacher driving through a picket line.[72]

Many Americans treat cars almost as sacred objects: if you hurt my car, you hurt me. Charles Malone never supported the NTU or its strikes, going to work in 1965, in 1970, and in 1971. "But in the last one, I went in, and somebody banged my car. I'll never forget that." He was driving through the picket line at West Side High School when a picket struck the side of his car. Malone tried to shrug it off. Then the picket did it again. Malone got out of the car. "I'll tell you what," said Malone, who was a Tuskegee airman during World War II. "You touch the car again and your ass is mine." Although he protected his car, he still felt aggrieved. To him, the picket had gone too far. "We disagree, you call me scab. But don't touch my car."[73]

Ellen Cunniff was always critical of the Union and loyal to the Association. She and her mother drove to work at Abington Avenue during the strike. At night, she parked in her driveway in Belleville, just north of Newark. One night, someone took the trouble to find her house and puncture all four of her tires. She thought she knew who did it, a striker she knew and liked. As she saw it, it wasn't personal. It was because she and her mother were going to work.[74]

Unlike Cunniff and Malone, Phil Basile was a Union teacher. Basile struck in 1970 and was arrested. In 1971, he and his wife were trying to adopt a child; any further trouble with the law could ruin their chances. "I really felt bad. I certainly didn't want to cross—to this day, I won't cross a picket line." Painfully, he explained to friends at Barringer, and they said they understood. But that was before the strike began. After a few weeks, a friend took the distributor wire out of Basile's car. Basile confronted him. The friend was not apologetic. "What are you going to do about it?" asked the friend. "I didn't do anything," says Basile.[75]

Anyone on the "scab list" was fair game. At most schools, the building rep sent a list of strikebreakers to the Union office, where home addresses and telephone numbers were added. At night, strikers found and spray-painted the cars of some of the fifty-seven teachers and teacher aides on the Barringer list. During the day, Carmine Cicurillo, one of the oldest teachers, drove into the parking lot at Barringer. Pickets surrounded his car and wouldn't let him out. They rocked the car, terrifying him. Nick Cammesa had his tires shot out, apparently with an air pistol.[76]

Throughout the city, where activists gathered, conversation turned to violence. Violence didn't seem wrong to teachers who had grown up within the labor movement and knew that people who crossed picket lines were likely to suffer bodily harm. "A lot of us felt: uh-uh—we were just like the Teamsters—don't cross my picket line," says Jim Brown. "You cross my picket line, you're gonna get hurt" Others believed the situation required extraordinary measures. "It is very clearly a question of survival of the union—and when your survival is at stake, you don't play nice," said a striker from South Eighth Street.[77]

The violence of the 1971 strike developed during violent times in America. One nonviolent Newark teacher, arrested for striking in 1970, observed that people were setting off bombs nationally because they were frustrated by the seemingly endless Vietnam War and the plight of Blacks, particularly in central cities.[78] More bombs went off after the Cambodia bombing and the killing of students at Kent State and Jackson State in the spring of 1970. On the left, many young Americans romanticized violence. Violence against things, rather than against people, was particularly celebrated.

In practice, the line between violence against things and violence against people is hard to maintain. One woman, who asked me not to use her name, is still shocked that two male strikers conceived an idea involving explosives, directed against an older colleague who was crossing the line. "It was a terrible plan, really to immobilize this man's car." She emphasizes that they did not carry out the plan. Another discussion took place between NTU activists in a teacher's apartment. One said, "Something's got to blow." Asked to explain, he did: blow up a school building. Carol Karman loudly protested. Karman objected to violence on that scale, Carole Graves recalls, "because people who weren't a part of this were going to get hurt."[79]

Graves adds, "I don't think that the people who were fanning these flames understood the potential for real disaster that was in the making." She lived in the city, in the midst of the conflict, and so perhaps had a more realistic view of the danger. She feared an escalation of violence on both sides. "The rhetoric was heating, the physical attacks were heating up, our people were being roughed up by certain community people," threats were being made against families. "It had gone out of control very quickly." She tried to limit Union violence. But she was jailed for half the strike, which restricted her influence. And Graves too was affected by the overall atmosphere of the times, and the place. "Everybody suddenly seemed to be in a movie, playing some role in a movie, maybe myself included."[80]

The most violent thing done to cars in Newark was loosening the lugs on tires. A few male teachers who were crossing the line told Phyllis Cuyler that it had been done to them. According to Ellen Cunniff, the same thing was done to three nonstriking teachers at Garfield. One was Vicky Middleton. On the handwritten "scab list" from Garfield, Middleton was the one name underlined, because she was taking an active role against the strike. According to Cunniff, one of Middleton's tires came off on Route 22 as she drove home to Plainfield; she plunged into traffic, was so badly injured that she never returned to work, and later died as a result of her injuries.[81] Cunniff was ready to believe anything bad about the Union. But if she is right, and one teacher died as a result of violence in the strike, it would not be surprising. What would be surprising is that only one teacher died.

"It was an armed camp in Newark," said Graves. "Nobody talked about it. No one knows how close someone on either side came to being killed." She herself was a target. Her niece, the niece's husband, and their baby were visiting her on a Saturday evening in November, during the struggle at South Eighth Street. Someone shot out the windows at the back of the house, and the baby was cut on the foot by glass. Later, after the assault outside the NTU office and numerous bomb threats, its windows were sandbagged, and it became "a fortress." Newark assigned plainclothes detectives to Graves as her bodyguards. When a friend, a teacher activist, was attacked, two detectives guarding Graves broke it up.[82]

Newark was indeed an armed camp. Don Saunders had his own bodyguard. "I'm walking alone with a bodyguard who, when the pressure got so great, pulled a weapon on me. That's how jumpy people were." An anonymous caller to the house of Board member Tom Malanga complained that Malanga had once been "a good union man." Then a shot was fired through Malanga's living room window. A teacher's father was angry about how she had been treated; he was arrested with a gun before he hurt anyone. Another man was arrested with a gun at Franklin Street School, where he was interfering with pickets. Harold Moore knew several striking teachers who carried guns. He himself was not violent and carried no weapon. "But there was so much passion and so much anger, you could understand somebody being fearful enough to carry a gun."[83]

Bob Hirschfeld wanted a gun. He was an activist, arrested in 1970, a member of the Union's new executive board. He received anonymous phone calls threatening his family and asked the Livingston police to watch his children as they walked to school. But he still didn't feel they were safe. He himself just missed being in the group of teachers who were attacked on February 2; he arrived at the Union office late because he was arguing with his wife, who feared what would happen if he were arrested again. Now she put her foot down, saying he was not going to bring a gun into the house. As a compromise, he borrowed a dog, a German shepherd. "I kept the dog here for the next two weeks. . . . That was sort of my answer, or my wife's answer, to buying a gun."[84]

One reason the violence in 1971 wasn't worse is that guns were not as common then as they have become. Men and women carried less decisive weapons, and sometimes used them. For example, Cynthia

O'Neal was picketing at South Tenth Street, and Hattie Black wanted to go through. Black stabbed O'Neal in the arm with a small, sharp instrument. Janice Adams was there. "We were all shocked that an educator would do that."[85]

People on the picket line, and people crossing it, felt less vulnerable if they were armed with a weapon of some kind—a sharp or blunt instrument in their pocket, purse, or car. "Whether it was a pocket knife, or a set of brass knuckles, or a baseball bat, a lot of people were arming themselves for their protection," says Lawton."[86] In this way, violence created fear, and fear created the potential for more violence.

Jim Lowenstein picketed at South Eighth Street. "Talk about face-to-face confrontations with violence." About seventy teachers, and Bayard Rustin, faced community members. Jesse Jacob was personally serving injunctions. He served one on Rustin, who was hit with all kinds of insults—including signs saying "Fag go home"—but he maintained his dignity and composure. Garrett was threatening pickets: "Just stop one teacher or child, and even the police won't be able to help you." Lowenstein recognized some of the men on the other side. "They were the enforcers, the thugs," the Black equivalent of Imperiale's men, he says. No one was hurt. "But you could see—it could have been triggered off—someone could have thrown a punch."[87]

Lowenstein was afraid during the confrontation. After that day, he carried a weapon. "On a daily basis, it was either a screwdriver, [or] some kind of tool or implement with me, just in case. Nothing lethal, but something to give me a little more leverage, a little more of an edge. A screwdriver, possibly a little wrench, or something—just if I needed to buy a step or two between me and somebody else."[88]

Dave Lieberfarb hadn't been violent since the eighth grade, when he punched his friend Lowenstein, who was too shocked to hit back. But you didn't have to be particularly violent to pick up a weapon during the 1971 teachers strike. Lieberfarb was passing out leaflets at Weequahic, publicizing alternative schools run by strikers for students who weren't going to school. A man snatched away the leaflets; Lieberfarb went to get more from the other side of the building. "And I picked up an empty soda bottle . . . and stuck it in my pocket. And he came back—he came back at me again, and I pulled the empty soda bottle out, and he thought better of it, and he left."[89]

Zenobia Capel carried shears to protect herself. (To protect her car, she parked two blocks from school, in the alley of a friend of her mother's. "The car was never touched, because they didn't know where it was.") Once a woman picket angrily denounced Capel for being selfish. "But she never got too close," because the shears were sticking up out of Capel's bag. Capel, who taught physical education, thinks she would not have used the shears on a woman. "I'm too big, and I'm too strong." However, "I would have, on a man."[90]

It was hard for Avant Lowther to cross the line. "A lot of mornings I was actually physically sick for coming in." But he thought strikers would respect his decision. Instead, he and his wife received calls at home. "They were harassing my wife and it was making me angry." He was also angry because he heard rumors of pickets beating female teachers at other schools. He arrived at work one morning, already angry, and ran into a picket line. A white teacher from another school, a big man, blocked his way. He said to the teacher, "If you're not going to pay my bills, you're going to have to get out of my way." The teacher called him a scab and other names. Lowther told him to get out of the way, or he would go through him, and the teacher pulled a knife. In the ensuing scuffle, before others separated them, the teacher was wounded in the neck. "I cut him with his own knife, but he didn't die."[91]

A white teacher assaulted a young Black teacher trying to enter Ann Street School. A security guard was injured in a melee at Robert Treat School. Four striking teachers were attacked in their homes. Two reporters for the Liberation News Service were roughed up by teachers at a mass strike meeting. Pat Piegari confronted a Black substitute who was crossing the line. "We're trying to make things better for young Black kids," he said. "And you're in there for money, and I'm losing money." The substitute surprised him by punching him in the face, and a brawl began between the two men. Ellen Cunniff and her mother, driving to Abington, were blocked by pickets. Acting on impulse, her mother got out of the car, squared her shoulders, and advanced toward the line, where she was met by a young teacher. "All of sudden, my mother and this young girl are on the ground."[92]

Violence tended to drive away people, on either side, who were not prepared to get rough. Mary Abend, born in Spain, was in her first year of teaching in Newark, at Arts High, which was small and friendly. She was striking because she had grown up pro-union in Gary; her father, a steelworker, was in several strikes. NTU called for pickets at Arts High, and Abend went. A chair or table was hurled out of a third-floor school window, landing near the pickets. "I never in my wildest dreams expected that there would be danger." No one was hurt. But she never picketed again.[93]

Teachers felt safer when they were surrounded by people who seemed tough. Carol Karman, who picketed every day, picketed her own school once or twice. Clinton Avenue was a new elementary school in a Black neighborhood and no one else was striking. Parents harassed Karman when she picketed, but she wasn't afraid. Her closest girlfriends from other schools came to her picket line. Her brother, a per-diem sub in Newark, also picketed with her and yelled right back at the parents. "He was very tough and loud, so that made me feel good, having him there."[94]

Anna and Marty Blume crossed the picket line during the 1971 strike. They identified more with Black students and parents than with teachers; in a larger sense, they were more committed to the Black struggle than to the labor movement. They could park in the playground. But they first had to get their car through the line. "We had a lot of people in our face," says Anna. High school teachers and dockworkers pressed against the car. "They weren't messing around. You could get hurt over there, serious hurt. I'm not just talking about cars." But the Blumes were not alone. Most Bergen Street teachers were crossing the line. "We also had a lot of community people who were looking out for us," adds Marty. "We almost felt some kind of protection from them."[95]

Sometimes the protection was professional. When a young picket was assaulted, her brother, a powerful man in the labor movement in New Jersey, summoned Felix Martino. "This was the type of guy who when he said come now, you came." The man gave instructions. His sister would picket at Barringer, where Martino could look out for her. Just to be safe, the man would bring his own people, construction workers. "'And if they show up,'" said the man, referring to strike opponents, "'we're going to break heads.'"[96]

The strike went on and on, past the three and a half weeks of the 1970 strike, stretching into a second month, then into a third. The Board continued to take a hard line, insisting on gutting the contract. Striking teachers grew desperate. Their numbers were dwindling. The more fortunate found work at local breweries. Most ran out of money. Some used food stamps; some collected welfare; some cashed in life insurance. Jesse Jacob cancelled all the benefits of striking teachers, including health benefits: "I had stopped paying them and I had taken away their insurance. I was prepared to do what was necessary. If it meant that they had to stay out there in them streets until the next September, it had been all right with me."[97]

"First of all, we all went broke. I had five kids and I went broke," says Gene Liss. "Every single penny that I had in savings, which wasn't much, probably two thousand dollars, was gone. I borrowed money from my father." In the ninth week, he received a letter, suspending him. "We thought we were gonna lose our jobs." Jacob and the Board suspended 347 striking teachers and asked the New Jersey Commissioner of Education to determine whether they should be fired. Still Liss stayed out. After all, his father was a member of the Teamsters Union. But he worried: who would hire a teacher who was fired?[98]

The concern was real. During the summer of 1970, Superintendent Titus noted, without irony, "We haven't had any trouble recruiting teachers since we agreed on our new teacher salary guide." Nationally, there was a surplus of qualified teachers. Jacob told community groups that given the job market, it would be easy to replace striking teachers. Mayor Gibson, at the time of the suspensions, said it was "inevitable" the Board would fire strikers. "If the teachers who are supposed to do it won't, then we will get teachers who will."[99]

"Seventy-one was such a long strike," Angela Paone remembers, "and there were people who were breaking ranks at the end, and that was very painful. . . . People started folding very much at the end. We didn't know it was going to be the end, but we were folding toward the end." Ron Polonsky, the strike organizer, never gave the true figures of how many were still striking. Publicly, he continued to be optimistic. Costumed at the morning meeting in black leather jacket, sunglasses, and long hair, he would raise both arms, make a V with the fingers of each hand, and chant: "The strike is strong! The strike is strong!" His energy, enthusiasm, and humor helped some strikers keep going. But after so many weeks, Polonsky himself wondered when it would end, and how. Privately, he confessed to a national AFT organizer that he didn't know how much longer the strikers could go on; even the most dedicated were beginning to get demoralized.[100]

One day after the Board suspended teachers, the superior court of Essex County issued arrest orders for pickets. Sheriff's men invaded the morning meeting on April 1 to arrest two pickets, and Polonsky lost control. "The next time they'd better come with guns," he said in front of a TV camera. "No more teachers are going to be locked up. No more sacrificial lambs. If they want to come back, bring the National Guard."[101]

Under threat—financial, legal, physical—more and more teachers returned to work. The Board knew that its pressure was working. "I felt our position was good, because more teachers were going back," said Don Saunders. "Until we got to the hard core in the Union."[102]

Pete Petino observed the same shrinking numbers, and the same core.

As the weeks went on, more and more people went back. People started to go back. It got tougher and tougher economically for people. That's why I always used the figure—I don't know if it's right—when it came down to the settlement on April 19, we were like five hundred out there. We were just five hundred hard-core people in the whole district that no matter what happened that five hundred would never go back.[103]

Under pressure, the hard core became harder, angrier, more violent. "The first few weeks of the strike, for me, I was very calm, and not overly aggressive on the picket line," says Joe Del Grosso, who began teaching during the fall of 1970. "I was single, I was living home with my mother, I could survive. But I discussed with my colleagues who were trying to feed a family, who had to go drive a beer truck at night or take a second job to try and support the family." As time went by, "I have to say I succumbed, and became part of the violence myself."[104]

Del Grosso's initiation into violence began when he was a child in the North Ward. "I had to fight a lot of street battles myself, and if you ran home to Mommy you would have to fight a lot more battles, because then you would be a Mama's boy." On the first morning of the strike, he was driven to Garfield by Dominick Bizzarro, his building rep and mentor in unionism. "We got out of the automobile, and there is someone trying to get into the school. I saw Dominick tackle the person. . . . Then it really dawned on me that it was not a game." Once, leaving the Union office, Del Grosso and a few colleagues were threatened by young Black men. "We drove away, and they actually chased after us. And they caught me and they sideswiped my car, and . . . forced me into another car, and my car was pretty much banged up. It was an awakening. We learned that we had to be very, very careful, and not go anywhere alone, and be in groups, because it was getting very dangerous."[105]

At first, Del Grosso felt bad about what was happening to teachers. A Black teacher approached the picket line at Garfield, intending to cross, early in the strike. Imperiale had men at Garfield, "to make sure that we were protected." One of Imperiale's men began to shout at the teacher, which led to pushing and shoving, and eventually punching. "The police ironically arrested the teacher who was crossing the picket line, for assault, and they took him away. Because Mr. Imperiale's men were very close to the police." Del Grosso liked the teacher; before the strike they sometimes went to lunch together. As the teacher waited in the police car, Del Grosso went over to the window. "I just said to him, 'I'm sorry,' because he was still a teacher, and it was still tragic in the circumstances."[106]

Del Grosso's sense of tragedy diminished as the struggle went on. He knew he was headed for jail, because he was very militant and was photographed many times by the authorities. Giving himself to the battle of the picket line, he made it into a kind of game. "We had to become inventive. And we invented what we called the wild bus ride. The wild bus ride was where we rented a bus, and we got fifty of the craziest pickets we could find." A bus or a big truck would descend on a school. At Ridge Street School on March 24, for instance, pickets arrived suddenly in a bus and pelted the school with eggs. No one knew where the bus might show up, or what the teachers riding it might do.[107]

Del Grosso's inventiveness went further. He proposed a wild bus ride to his own school, to trap strikebreakers inside. Teachers parked in the Garfield playground during the strike. So when the wild bus, with fifty or sixty of the most militant teachers inside, swooped down and pulled into the parking lot, the cars were there. "I could see the teachers in the building, watching their cars being trampled." When the pickets finished with the cars—"like shooting fish in a barrel"—they formed a circle around the building. Several had attack dogs with them. Teachers could not leave the building. Some police arrived, but not enough; teachers were still afraid to come out. Husbands came to try to get their wives out, and pickets fought them. Teachers were captive in the building until four-thirty or five o'clock.[108]

As a guerrilla tactic, the bus ride worked. Only a handful of people returned to work at Garfield the next day. Tom Lawton agrees that guerrilla tactics at Garfield were successful in keeping many teachers home. "A lot of them were afraid that we were crazy and would cause them bodily harm, so they stayed out." The fear lasted. Two years after the strike, Ellen Cunniff was assigned to Garfield by the Board. She had heard how the wild bus riders came to Garfield "and sealed in the school" and had heard about other violent activities there. "They had so many bad things happen that when I was assigned there, I asked if there were any other openings. I was afraid to go there."[109]

Many parents kept their children home because of the violence. Though teacher attendance rose over time, pupil attendance remained low. "We wore 'em out," says Pete Petino.

> We disrupted the system. Even though we were small, we got into the trucks—you must have heard the stories about the trucks, the buses. And each day that passed, schools didn't know when they'd be hit. Either going in, in the morning, or in the afternoon. And it was a constant disruption. And then at the time, kids weren't going to school either, because there was a fear of violence.[110]

Petino coordinated the violence. Asked which side was more violent, he doesn't hesitate. "I think we were more violent." Hurting or harassing teachers as they went into school was difficult. "Of course there was a lot of that going on, but we had such heavy police presence, it became very difficult. So we did other things as it wore on, and that's where the nighttime rides and the nighttime visits and all that came in."[111]

Teachers were vulnerable at home. They received letters sarcastically urging them "to be in school on Monday to operate in my self-interest and not in the interest of my colleagues, the students, and the educational system." Then the anonymous calls began. Finally, for some teachers, there were nighttime visits, not only for their cars but for themselves. "Visits to their homes also," says Petino, laughing. "You paid people visits. It depends on how many people you had . . . who could make visits, who were into that."[112]

The nighttime visits were both secret and legendary—more legendary for being secret. Jerry Yablonsky heard stories about Union teachers shooting at houses at night. "I didn't know the details . . . and then didn't want to, once I found out what was going on." But Yablonsky felt sympathetic to the violence. His uncle led the Painters Union, and he grew up knowing that unions punish people who cross their picket line.[113]

Carol Karman liked the stories about the night visits.

> There were these brigades of guys who would go around at night and do mean things to scabs. Then we'd hear about them. It was almost mythological. There was no evidence and no proof, and no one knew exactly who they were talking about. . . . You'd hear about so-and-so got a punch in the nose, and so-and-so decked somebody else, and then they went to somebody's house, and they put his door on fire, and they put sugar in that guy's gas tank.[114]

Many of the myths of the strike are about violence. "You must have heard the stories," Petino said to me, referring to the wild bus rides. "To this day . . . people will have anecdotes about do you remember the '71 strike, when we did this, and we did that," says Jim Brown. "Talking about when we were all young, and maybe a little bit more brave." At the time, Graves disclaimed knowledge of violence toward cars or people; it was not NTU policy, she said. But it was policy. Three decades later, she acknowledges that teachers were armed; there were guns. "It was only a 50 percent strike, barely 50 percent," she explains. "Those that didn't get scared in just hunkered down, and said we're in this to the death."[115]

The 1971 Newark teachers strike was not incidentally but essentially violent. Both sides were violent, but the strikers used more violence. The Board had allies in the Black community who used violence, but the Board didn't need to rely on that kind of violence. It took away health insurance from all strikers, suspended most, and threatened to fire them. Everyone arrested in 1970 was threatened with a long sentence if arrested again; Graves and two NTU vice presidents were locked in jail during much of the strike. The Board had not only law but also time on its side. Unlike a private employer hit by a strike, it lost no money; only the striking teachers lost money— about three thousand dollars each, or 30 percent of a yearly salary. Jacob and the Board were in no hurry to settle. They could afford to turn up the pressure on teachers, one twist at a time. Their violence was institutionalized.

Teachers had no legal remedy. The 1968 law that created the Public Employment Relations Commission (PERC) gave it no power to force good-faith negotiations or determine unfair labor practices.[116] The violence by striking teachers effectively discouraged teachers from going to work and parents from sending children to school. Union leaders quietly embraced violence, even organized it, because the Board would not negotiate. They hoped the violence and disorder of 1971 would lead Mayor Gibson to intervene. Getting him to intervene, as Mayor Addonizio had intervened in 1970, was their last hope.

The Peace Movement

Mayor Gibson tried to make peace three times. He failed the first time, and Carole Graves was jailed. He failed the second time, and 347 teachers were suspended. But the third time, with the help of Clarence Coggins, he created a popular movement for peace. This time Graves was released from jail, the suspensions were rescinded, and the contract was signed.

Notes

1. Phyllis Salowe, interview with author, West Orange, N.J., August 10, 1995; Charles Nolley and Martha Nolley, interview with author, Montclair, N.J., September 14, 1995; Beth Blackmon, interview with author, South Orange, N.J., 1995.

2. Garrett quoted in *Newark Evening News* (hereafter *NN*), February 23,1971, 5; *NN*, April 15, 1971, 9.

3. Travitt quoted in *NN*, February 16, 1971, 8; Richard Wesley, interview with author, Montclair, N.J, July 21, 1993; *NN*, March 2, 1971, 6. See also Elayne Brodie, quoted in *Newark Star Ledger* (hereafter *SL*), February 26, 1971, 13.

4. Carole Graves, quoted in *Muhammad Speaks*, February 19,1971, NTU files; Newark Teachers Union, "WHO ARE WE?" leaflet, NTU files (emphasis in the original).

5. Jim Lerman, interview with author, Hoboken, N.J., October 29, 1993.

6. Lerman interview, October 29, 1993. As in 1970, a Black teacher was chosen to make the motion for the 1971 strike. *NN*, February 1, 1971, 1+.

7. "Statement by Carole Graves," press release, n.d., 2, in the possession of Carole Graves (emphasis in the original); *NN*, January 22, 1971, 5.

8. Jim Brown, interview with author, Belleville, N.J., August 17, 1995.

9. "Complete Text of Board Demands," NTU *Bulletin* (January 1971), 5.

10. Blackmon interview. A recent study agrees. In Newark, "There was no marked difference between the responses [to the pressure for school reform] of black- and white-dominated Boards of Education." Wilbur C. Rich, *Black Mayors and School Politics: The Failure of Reform in Detroit, Gary, and Newark* (New York: Garland, 1996), 97.

11. Graves, quoted in *SL*, February 3, 1971, 1+.

12. Carole Graves, quoted in *Muhammad Speaks*, February 19, 1971, NTU files.

13. Newark Teachers Union, "Report to Local Labor and Community Groups," n.d., 2, NTU files; "Rally," leaflet, NTU files; "What Does Union-Busting Mean To You?" leaflet, NTU files.

14. Polonsky quoted in *NN*, March 29, 1971, 21; Felix Martino, interview with author, Roseland, N.J., August 4, 1995; *NN*, February 3, 1971, 1+, and March 11, 1971, 23; *SL*, February 4, 1971, 1+, and February 7, 1971, 1+; Pete Petino, interview with author, Newark, November 5, 1995; Brown interview; Norman Eiger, "The Newark School Wars: A Socio-Historical Study of the 1970 and 1971 Newark School System Strikes" (Ed.D. diss., Rutgers University, 1976), 311; Frank Brown, letter to Ron Polonsky, March 11, 1971, NTU files.

15. Eiger, "Newark School Wars," 311–312; *NN*, March 17, 1971, 1; William M. Phillips, Jr. and Joseph M. Conforti, *Social Conflict: Teachers' Strikes in Newark, 1964–1971* (Trenton: New Jersey Department of Education, 1972), 49; Martino interview; *SL*, March 14, 1971, sec. 1, 1; "WORK STOPPAGE RALLY," leaflet, NTU files.

16. Kenneth Travitt, quoted in *NN*, February 19, 1971, 8. Travitt replaced Fred Means as president of ONE.

17. Connie Woodruff, interview with Norman Eiger, Newark, May 21, 1974; Connie Woodruff, "LIKE IT IS," leaflet, NTU files; *NN*, February 25, 1971, 1+.

18. Carole Graves, interview with Norman Eiger, Newark, May 21, 1974.

19. Imperiale quoted in *NN*, July 23, 1970, 8; Anthony Imperiale, letter to the editor, *SL*, February 6, 1971, 20; Peter D. Dickson, "The Sources of Italian Politics: The North Ward of Newark, New Jersey" (senior thesis, Princeton University, 1973), 102–103 and 106–107; Ron Porambo, *No Cause for Indictment: An Autopsy of Newark* (New York: Holt, Rinehart, and Winston, 1971), 339; Robert Curvin, "The Persistent Minority: The Black Political Experience in Newark" (Ph.D. diss., Princeton University, 1975), 102.

20. Carol Karman, interview with author, Bloomfield, N.J., March 17, 1994; Graves interview with Eiger; Robert J. Braun, *Teachers and Power: The Story of the American Federation of Teachers* (New York: Simon and Schuster, 1972), 272 and 273.

21. Tom Lawton, interview with author, Bloomfield, N.J., June 23, 1995.

22. Petino interview.

23. *NN*, February 8, 1971, 12; February 11, 1971, 1; February 16, 1971, 8; March 28, 1971, 1+; and April 21, 1971, 8; *SL*, February 9, 1971, 1, and February 18, 1971, 1+; *New York Times*, April 8, 1971, 50; "Scabs," list, NTU files.

24. Hilda Johnson, quoted in *NN*, March 29, 1971, 21; Elena Scambio, interview with author, Bloomfield, N.J., May 30, 1997. Scambio picketed First Avenue and taught in the basement schools.

25. Parents quoted in *NN*, February 25, 1971, 1+; Petino quoted in *NN*, March 2, 1971, 6; David Shipler, "The White Niggers of Newark," *Harper's Magazine* (August 1972), 77–83.

26. East Ward residents quoted in *NN*, April 6, 1971, 23; Tom Malanga, interview with Norman Eiger, Newark, December 10, 1974; Martino interview; Andy Thorburn, interview with author, Somerset, N.J., July 28, 1992; *NN*, April 1, 1971, 19.

27. Turco quoted in *NN*, February 11, 1971, 26; *New Jersey Afro-American*, March 13, 1971, 1; *NN*, February 4, 1971, 1+; February 24, 1971, 10; February 25, 1971, 1; and March 28, 1971, 1+; Karman interview, June 2, 1994. Italians also organized in support of the strike in the Vailsburg section of the West Ward. *NN*, March 19, 1971, 19.

28. Turco quoted in *NN*, April 6, 1971, 23; *SL*, February 2, 1970, 1+; Don Saunders, interview with Norman Eiger, East Orange, N.J., July 31, 1975; *NN*, March 1, 1971, 1; March 2, 1971, 6; April 1, 1971, 19; and April 8, 1971, 11; *SL*, March 1, 1971, 1+, and March 2, 1971.

29. *NN*, November 29, 1970, sec. 2, C8; Cervase interview with Eiger, Newark, December 24, 1979; *NN*, March 4, 1970, 4; September 11, 1970, 24; and October 28, 1970, 1+; Rich, *Black Mayors*, 95–96; Porambo, *No Cause*, 375.

30. John Cervase, letter to the editor, *NN*, March 3, 1971, 26; Cervase interview with Eiger; *SL*, June 20, 1971, sec. 1, 33. For a good analysis of why Cervase and Turco sacrificed labor-management issues in 1971 and backed the strikers, see Eiger, "Newark School Wars," 509.

31. Cervase interview with Eiger; *SL*, February 3, 1971, 21; *NN*, March 10, 1971, 8; *NN*, February 22, 1971, 5; February 26, 1971, 6; March 10, 1971, 1; and April 6, 1971, 23. Cervase offered to testify that Jacob forced the Union to violate the injunction. *NN*, September 4, 1970, 1; *SL*, February 25, 1971, 1+. Note that Jacob did not support the Black and Puerto Rican Convention candidate in the 1970 mayoral campaign; he supported John Caulfield. Porambo, *No Cause*, 370.

32. Eiger, "Newark School Wars," 314–318; Gus Henningberg, interview with Norman Eiger, Newark, November 26, 1974; Clara Dasher, interview with Norman Eiger, New Brunswick, N.J., June 21, 1974; *NN*, January 24, 1971, sec. 1, 4; January 29, 1971, 1+; February 8, 1971, 8; February 10, 1971, 42; and March 26, 1971, 28; *New Jersey Afro-American*, March 6, 1971, 1+; "Special Board Meeting," anonymous minutes, April 6, 1971, NTU files; K. Komozi Woodard, "The Making of the New Ark: Imamu *Amiri* Baraka (LeRoi Jones), the Congress of African People, and the Modern Black Convention Movement; A History of the Black Revolt and the New Nationalism, 1966–1976" (Ph.D. diss., University of Pennsylvania, 1991), 141–142. In June 1971, Mayor Gibson appointed Hamm, who had just graduated, to the Board of Education.

33. David H. Barrett, letter to the editor, *NN*, February 5, 1971, 26; Barrett, speaking at the Special Board Meeting, April 7, 1971, audio tape in possession of Norm Eiger.

34. Brodie quoted in Phillips and Conforti, *Social Conflict*, 38; Westbrook, quoted in *NN*, March 2, 1971, 6; Derek T. Winans, letter to the editor, *NN*, March 25, 1971, 26; New Ark Community Coalition, "RUNT," leaflet, NTU files; Eiger, "Newark School Wars," 489. Trying to refute the charge that teachers were suburbanites, NTU claimed that 40% lived in Newark. *New York Times*, April 8, 1971, 50; *American Teacher* (March 1971), 4; "Teachers residing in Newark," list, NTU files. Of the 187 teachers arrested in 1970, one third (63) lived in Newark. "Arrests Made by the Sheriff's Department during Newark School Teachers Strike," annotated list, NTU files.

35. Thomas Carmichael quoted in *NN*, March 17,1971, 1+; Saunders interview; Robert J. Braun, *Teachers and Power*, 272.

36. Carole A. Graves, letter to Brothers and Sisters, March 14, 1971, 2, NTU files; 'The Community's Choice? or Poverty's Pimps?" leaflet, NTU files"; Ron Polonsky, letter to Edward Chervin, March 10, 1971, 5, NTU files; *NN*, March 28, 1971, sec.1, 8, and April 11, 1971, 8; Graves interview with Eiger. Vice President Spiro Agnew was thought to say publicly the outrageous things President Nixon wanted to say but couldn't.

37. Seymour Cohen, quoted in *SL*, February 25, 1971, 1+; *New York Sunday News*, March 28, 1971, J12; Angela Paone, interview with author, Roseland, N.J., August 8, 1995; *NN*, April 20, 1971, 1; Marc Gaswirth, William M. Weinberg, and Barbara E. Kemmerer, *Teachers' Strikes in New Jersey: Studies in Industrial Relations and Human Resources, No.1* (Metuchen, N.J.: Scarecrow Press, 1982), 79. Many teachers told me Baraka was behind the February 2 attack, but they could offer no evidence.

38. Union activists quoted in *NN*, March 28, 1971, 8; *NN*, February 25, 1971, 1+; Graves interview with Eiger.

39. Newark Teachers Union, "Our Strike and the Two Sides of Black Nationalism," leaflet, NTU files.

40. "Black Panther Party," press release, February 21, 1971, NTU files; *Muhammad Speaks*, February 19, 1971, NTU files; Carol Karman, interview with author, Bloomfield, N.J., June 2, 1994; Petino interview; *SL*, February 23, 1971, 1+; Newark Teachers Union, "Our Strike and the Two Sides of Black Nationalism," leaflet, NTU files; Braun, *Teachers and Power*, 272; Eiger, "Newark School Wars," 510. The Black Panthers had backed the 1970 strike as well. *American Teacher/Special Issue* (February 16, 1970), 2.

41. *NN*, April 9, 1971, 1, and April 11, 1971, 1+; Eiger, "Newark School Wars," 380–381.

42. Dasher interview with Eiger.

43. Robert Lowenstein, letter to the editor, *NN*, February 9, 1971, 16.

44. Salowe interview.

45. Salowe interview.

46. Dave Lieberfarb, Jim Lowenstein, and Steve Shaffer, interview with author, Fair Lawn, N.J., November 19, 1995. Imperiale's support for the strike was one reason Marty Bierbaum decided to cross the picket line. Marty Bierbaum, interview with author, Berkeley Heights, N.J., September 16, 1995.

47. Karman interview, June 2, 1994; Carol Karman, phone conversation with author, May 29, 2000. Prudential contributed funds to the New Ark Coalition.

48. Phyllis Cuyler, interview with author, Woodbridge, N.J., July 21, 1994.

49. Marion Bolden, interview with author, Newark, October 2, 1995.

50. Avant Lowther Jr., interview with author, Newark, June 14, 1995.

51. Zenobia Capel, interview with author, East Orange, August 12, 1992. Jacob's posture of being the only one who cared about Black children alienated many people. Saunders interview with Eiger; Malanga interview with Eiger; Ron Haughton, interview with Norman Eiger, Princeton, N.J., November 19, 1974.

52. Janice Adams, interview with author, Newark, September 7, 1995; Adams quoted in *Muhammad Speaks*, April 1971, NTU files.

53. Harold Moore, interview with author, Montclair, N.J., August 21, 1995.

54. Harold and Alison Moore interview (Alison participated in parts of the interview); Paone interview.

55. Eiger, "Newark School Wars," 308; Dasher interview with Eiger; Lawton interview.

56. *SL*, February 2, 1971, 1+; *NN*, January 27, 1971, 19; Bob Clark, interview with author, Glen Ridge, N.J., October 17, 1995; Gene Liss, interview with author, Newark, August 29, 1995; Jim Lowenstein and Steve Shaffer, interview with author, Fair Lawn, N.J., July 26, 1994; Lieberfarb, Lowenstein, and Shaffer interview; Jerry Yablonsky, interview with author, Springfield, N.J., November 7, 1995; Dorothy Bergman, interview with author, New York City, October 11, 1995; Karman interview, March 17, 1994; Dasher interview with Eiger; Bob Hirschfeld, interview with author, Livingston, September 28,1995; Salowe interview; Cuyler interview; Petino interview.

57. Brown interview; *NN*, February 2, 1971, 1.

58. Brown interview.

59. Brown interview.

60. Brown interview.

61. Elman quoted in Newark Teachers Union, videotape, "Newark Teachers Union 50th Anniversary Celebration"; *NN*, February 2, 1971, 1+, and February 3 ,1971, 1+; *SL*, February 3, 1971, 1, and February 4, 1971, 1+; Hirschfeld interview; Carole Graves, discussion with author, Newark, June 14, 2000; *American Teacher* (March 1971), 4.

62. Newark Teachers Union, leaflet, NTU files; Brown interview.

63. Petino interview; *NN*, February 3, 1971, 1+, and February 4, 1971, 1+; Superior Court of New Jersey, Chancery Division-Essex County, "In the Matter of Newark Teachers Union Local 481, American Federation of Teachers, AFL-CIO, and unincorporated association, Defendant Charged with Contempt of Court," NTU files. Two months later, one man was indicted for beating Elman. *SL*, April 3, 1971, 4.

64. Lieberfarb, Lowenstein, and Shaffer interview; Graves interview with Eiger; Carole Graves, interview with author, Newark, May 24, 2000; Eiger, "Newark School Wars," 310; Fred Barbaro, "Mass Jailing of Teachers," *The Clearing House* (September 1973), 17; Nolley and Nolley interview.

65. Petino interview; Lawton interview; Graves interview with Eiger; Jim Lerman, "A Question of Survival," *American Teacher* (March 1971), 3.

66. *NN*, February 1, 1971, 1+, and February 12, 1971, 18; *New Jersey Afro-American*, February 20, 1971, 1, and March 13, 1971, 1+; Graves interview with Eiger; *SL*, March 3, 1971, 1+; Ben Epstein, interview with Norman Eiger, Newark, November 7, 1974.

67. *NN*, February 2, 1971, 1; February 4, 1971, 1+; February 16, 1971, 8; February 17, 1971, 1+; and March 13, 1971, 1+; *SL*, February 9, 1971, 1+; Phil Basile, interview with author, Verona, N.J., August 15, 1995; Bolden interview; Bierbaum interview; Capel interview; Hirschfeld interview.

68. Petino interview; Scambio interview, May 30, 1997.

69. Lawton interview. A teacher at another school, who does not want to be identified, put liquid lead on locks, to prevent teachers from going in before pickets got there.

70. Joe Del Grosso, interview with author, Newark, August 24, 1995.

71. Pat Piegari, interview with author, Caldwell, N.J., September 22, 1995; Blackmon interview; Lawton interview; Salowe interiew; Hirschfeld interview.

72. Piegari interview; Blackmon interview.

73. Charles Malone, interview with author, Orange, N.J., June 12, 1995.

74. Ellen Cunniff, interview with author, Bloomfield, N.J., August 14, 1995.

75. Basile interview.

76. Newark Teachers Union, "Scabs" list, NTU files; Basile interview; Blackmon interview.

77. Brown interview; South Eighth Street teacher, quoted in Lerman, "A Question of Survival," 3.

78. Asa Watkins, letter to the editor, *NN*, March 24, 1970, 16.

79. Graves interview with author. A school was firebombed in a New Orleans teachers strike in 1969. Braun, *Teachers and Power*, 15.

80. Graves interview with author.

81. Cuyler interview; Cunniff interview; "Scabs" list, NTU files. Tom Lawton confirms that Middleton died as a result of a crash and that some strike opponents suspected foul play. Lawton interview.

82. Graves interview with Eiger; Graves interview with author; *SL*, December 2, 1970, 31; Ron Polonsky, letter to Edward Chernin, March 10, 1971, NTU files; *NN*, January 25, 1971, 8, and February 8, 1971, 1+; Petino interview.

83. Saunders interview with Eiger; Malanga quoted in *NN*, March 2, 1971, 6; Moore interview; *SL*, March 3, 1971, 1+, and March 7, sec. 1, 16; Malanga interview with Eiger; Andy Thorburn, interview with author, Somerset, N.J., July 14, 1992.

84. Hirschfeld interview.

85. Adams interview; Janice Adams, telephone conversation with author, January 15, 2000; *NN*, March 19, 1971, 1+; *SL*, March 19, 1971, 1.

86. Lawton interview.

87. Lowenstein and Shaffer interview; Garrett quoted in *NN*, February 9, 1971, 1; Lerman interview, October 29, 1993; Phillips and Conforti, *Social Conflict*, 43; *SL*, February 10, 1971, 1+, and February 11, 1971, 1+; *NN*, February 25, 1971, 1+, and February 23, 1971, 5.

88. Lowenstein and Shaffer interview.

89. Lieberfarb, Lowenstein, and Shaffer interview.

90. Capel interview.

91. Lowther interview.

92. Piegari interview; Cunniff interview; *NN*, February 16, 1971 ,8, and February 24, 1971, 10; *SL*, March 1, 1971, 1+, and March 26, 1971, 10; Lerman, "A Question of Survival," 3.

93. Mary Abend, interview with author, Newark, June 14, 1995.

94. Carol Karman, interview with author, Bloomfield, N.J., March 17, 1994.

95. Anna Blume and Marty Blume, Berkeley Heights, N.J., October 1, 1995; Bierbaum interview.

96. Martino interview. Graves interview with author: "Some of the biggest names in labor racketeering . . . [were] on our side."

97. Jesse Jacob, interview with Norman Eiger, Newark, December 4, 1974; Arnold Hess, letter to instructional personnel, February 22, 1971, NTU files; *NN*, February 24, 1971, 10, and February 25, 1971, 1; *SL*, February 24, 1971, 7; March 29, 1971, 1+; and April 1, 1971, 1+; Paone interview; Shaffer interview, November 19, 1994; Lawton interview; Scambio interview, May 30, 1997; Hirschfeld interview; Blackmon interview; Dasher interview with Eiger. NTU made interest-free loans available.

98. Liss interview; *NN*, March 31, 1971, 1; *SL*, February 14, 1971, sec. 1, 4.

99. Gibson quoted in *NN*, April 1, 1971, 19; Titus, quoted in *NN*, August 9, 1970, sec. 1, 23; Dasher interview with Eiger. The school board in Minot, North Dakota, responded to a 1969 strike by firing all the striking teachers. *SL*, February 7, 1971, sec. 1, 36; Braun, *Teachers and Power*, 121–122.

100. Paone interview; Polonsky quoted in Jim Lerman, interview with author, Hoboken, N.J., December 10, 1993, and in Lowenstein and Shaffer interview; Clark interview; Karman interview, June 2, 1994; Eiger, "Newark School Wars," 349. Polonsky confided in Vinnie Russell, whom Eiger interviewed.

101. Polonsky, quoted in *SL*, April 2, 1971, 1+; *SL*, April 1, 1971, 1.

102. Saunders interview with Eiger.

103. Petino interview; Vic Cascella, Ralph Favilla, and Don Nicholas interview with author, Newark, December 1, 1995.

104. Del Grosso interview.

105. Del Grosso interview.

106. Del Grosso interview.

107. Del Grosso interview; *NN*, March 25, 1971, 1+, and March 27, 1971, 1+. At Broadway Elementary School, "roving busloads of teacher pickets show up two or three times a week." *NN*, March 28, 1971, 1+.

108. Del Grosso interview.

109. Lawton interview; Del Grosso interview; Cunniff interview.

110. Petino interview.

111. Petino interview. Carole Graves agrees that the strikers were more violent. Graves interview with author. Early on, there were only two policemen at most schools. As the mood became angrier, fifteen or more police were assigned to schools where violence was anticipated. *NN*, February 24, 1971, 10, and February 25,1971, 1.

112. Newark Teachers Union, letter to strikebreakers, NTU files; Petino interview; *SL*, February 7, 1971, sec. 1, 36; Cuyler interview.

113. Yablonsky interview. Gerald Meyer heard stories about the house visits from teachers in jail. Gerald Meyer, phone interview with author, February 5, 2000.

114. Karman interview, June 2, 1994.

115. Brown interview; Graves interview with author; *SL*, February 9, 1971, 1+.

116. Eiger, "Newark School Wars," 465–467. The law was changed in 1974 to give PERC more power.

This photograph shows an elegantly dressed Congresswoman Millicent Fenwick trying to make a point at a meeting. She was known for her constant attendance at House sessions, committee meetings, replies to constituent mail, and practice of speaking her mind. Millicent Fenwick Congressional Papers MC 834 Box 57 Folder 1, Prior to August 1979. Special Collections and University Archives, Rutgers University Libraries.

16

After the election of 2008, when Hillary Clinton came close to winning the Democratic nomination for president and Sarah Palin ran as the Republican vice presidential candidate, a brief look at the role of women in New Jersey politics seems appropriate. In some ways the New Jersey story in unusual, but in others it follows the pattern of women's experiences elsewhere. The same can be said for Millicent Fenwick, the subject of the following selection. A pipe-smoking grandmother with an independent streak when she was elected to Congress in 1974, she was unique, but her path to office and role once there are comparable to that of other women. Looking at New Jersey's record in hosting women in politics helps put her career in perspective. It also provides the opportunity to ask if gender is important in the role politicians play. Finally, this is a chapter from a biography, a specific form of history, which has its own advantages and problems. Questions at the end of this introduction note some of the issues.

Women in early New Jersey, as elsewhere in the American colonies, had limited economic and political rights. In most cases they were unable to possess property in their own names, to serve on juries, vote, or hold office. The exception, which did not occur elsewhere, was the ability of New Jersey widows owning £50 of property to vote under the terms of the hastily written 1776 state constitution. Then, in 1807, the legislature deliberately excluded women (and blacks) from voting in the future. Despite the efforts of state suffragists to "regain" the vote in the nineteenth century, it was not until passage of the Nineteenth Amendment to the U.S. Constitution in 1920 that this happened.

The period that followed saw women register to vote in large numbers, as well as run for office and win at rates not matched again for many years. What took place between 1920 and 1930 was that the expected "women's voting block" failed to materialize, as women divided in party allegiance and over issues. Consequently, male politicians then paid less attention and made fewer efforts to put women on the ballot. In addition, the Great Depression, which put men and their jobs first, and then the post–World War II emphasis on home life, discouraged women from pursuing careers (including careers in politics). With the civil rights movement of the 1960s and its emphasis on equality, an increasing number of women began to run for political office. Yet not until the 1980s, and most dramatically in the election of 2008, was significant change seen. Generally, New Jersey also followed this pattern, except that it started out stronger and ended up further behind. In 1927 the state ranked first in the number of women in its state legislature; in 1994 it was forty-first. Then in 2008 it rose in rank to fifteenth. Only five women have represented the state in Congress, all in the House. Although New Jersey elected its first female governor (Christine Todd Whitman) in 1993, overall it has lagged behind other states in the number of women holding political office. How can this be explained?

In the 1920s, when the state was preeminent in electing women to state office, it sent the first woman from an eastern state to Congress; she was also the first female Democrat elected to that body. Mary T. Norton, who came from Jersey City and had the backing of Frank Hague (the infamous political boss discussed in an earlier chapter of this volume), served from 1925 to 1951. Her staff was all female, and she supported a number of women's issues, including their right to serve on juries and be treated equally by immigration laws, but she was opposed to the Equal Rights Amendment (ERA), fearing it would erode necessary protections for women. On the other side of the aisle was Florence Dwyer, a Republican from Elizabeth who served from 1957 to 1973. Dwyer deemphasized her gender and denied she was a "feminist," but she supported the ERA, equal pay, consumer protection, and legislation that supported the welfare of children. As you read about Fenwick, think which of these two courses she took—to emphasize the fact she was a woman in political office or to deemphasize that fact?

Millicent Vernon Hammond Fenwick was descended from the prominent and wealthy Stevens family. Like Christine Todd Whitman, she was raised in the upper-class horse-riding, fox-hunting suburbs of New Jersey. Her mother was a prominent socialite who drowned when the *Lusitania* sank, and her father an insurance and real estate broker involved in local and state politics. Millicent briefly attended a boarding school in Virginia, then went off to Spain when her father was appointed ambassador. In 1932 she defied her family to marry Hugh Fenwick, who had been divorced. The marriage was of short duration. Left with two young children and his numerous debts, she found a job at *Vogue*, where she stayed for the next fourteen years. After retiring from the magazine, she became involved in local politics. In 1969 she ran for the state assembly, becoming one of two female members, and then served as the director of New Jersey's Division of Consumer Affairs. In 1974, when she was elected to Congress, there were eighteen women in the House, a record number. At that point Fenwick was sixty-four years old.

Like her father before her, Fenwick was a Republican. While conservative on fiscal issues, and generally opposed to government intervention, she was liberal on social matters. She supported the ERA, civil rights legislation, international human rights efforts, prison reform, child welfare, and was pro-choice. Independent minded in Congress, she did not always vote the party line. She traveled to Vietnam and China and locked horns with the House leadership. Fenwick could alternately be charming and feisty. Author Amy Shapiro's book subtitle, "Her Way," hints at these characteristics, and the approbation "Conscience of Congress" reflects the reputation she earned. In this and a number of other ways, she resembles Margaret Chase Smith of Maine, a Republican who served first in the House and then the Senate, where she stood up to Joseph McCarthy while male colleagues remained silent.

Fenwick was reelected to Congress three times, but in 1981, because of national population shifts, New Jersey lost a congressional seat. Her district disappeared when boundaries were redrawn. She then decided to run for the U.S. Senate, only to be defeated by Democrat Frank Lautenberg. She was later appointed ambassador to the United Nations Food and Agriculture Organization in Rome. In 1987 she retired for the second and last time. Looking over her political career, it is appropriate to ask, as have a number of political scientists and historians studying women who held or hold political office, whether her gender mattered. Did the fact that Fenwick was a woman make a difference in the positions she took and way she voted? Did her gender influence how she was perceived by the public and by other politicians?

History has many formats; this selection is part of a biography. In writing such works historians need to balance background information about the time period with details of the person's life, but they must also guard against their own prejudices either for or against the person studied. Another issue is how much to include, especially if it is of a sensitive nature. Does Shapiro present a balanced account? Is Fenwick glorified, or is she portrayed "warts and all"?

Suggested Readings

Burystyn, Joan, ed., and the Women's Project of New Jersey. *Past and Promise: Lives of New Jersey Women.* Metuchen, N.J.: Scarecrow Press, 1990.

Carroll, Susan J. *Women Candidates in American Politics.* 2nd ed. Bloomington: Indiana University Press, 1994.

Carroll, Susan J., and Richard Logan Fox, eds. *Gender and Elections: Shaping the Future of American Politics.* New York: Cambridge University Press, 2006.

Gertzog, Irwin. "Women's Changing Pathways to the U.S. House of Representatives: Widows, Elites, and Strategic Politicians." In *Women Transforming Congress,* edited by Cindy Simon Rosenthal, 95–118. Norman: University of Oklahoma Press, 2002.

Gordon, Felice D. *After Winning: The Legacy of the New Jersey Suffragists, 1920–1947.* New Brunswick, N.J.: Rutgers University Press, 1986.

Kartnoutsos, Carmela A. *New Jersey Women: A History of Their Status, Roles, and Images.* Trenton, N.J.: New Jersey Historical Society, 1997.

Lewis, Janet V., ed., *Women and Women's Issues in Congress 1832–2000.* Huntington, N.Y.: Nova Science Publishers, 2001.

McClure, Sandy. *Christie Whitman: A Political Biography for the People.* New York: Prometheus Books, 1996.

McCormick, Richard P., and Katheryne C. McCormick. *Equality Deferred: Women Candidates for the New Jersey Assembly, 1920–1993.* New Brunswick, N.J.: Center for American Women in Politics, Rutgers University, 1994.

Mitchell, Gary. "Women Standing for Women: The Early Political Career of Mary T. Norton." *New Jersey History* 96 (1979): 27–42.

Sherman, Janann. *No Place for a Women: A Life of Senator Margaret Chase Smith.* New Brunswick, N.J.: Rutgers University Press, 2000.

Tomlinson, Barbara. "Making Her Way: The Career of Congresswoman Florence P. Dwyer." *New Jersey History* 112 (1994): 41–77.

◆ ◆ ◆ ◆ ◆ ◆

The Conscience of Congress

Amy Shapiro

"The business of government is justice."
—President Woodrow Wilson

Millicent Fenwick arrived in Washington amid the fanfare of her victory as a sixty-four-year-old pipe-smoking grandmother. Resigned to the fact that she had been pigeonholed by the media, she pleaded to be referred to as the equally appropriate "hard-working congresswoman."

Fenwick wasted no time in making her mark in Washington. Her panache, pipe, age, gender, diction, candidness, and assertiveness soon set her apart from her male colleagues. Many members of Congress received their first introduction to Fenwick at the annual Washington Press Club dinner. She was one of six freshmen who received top billing from their unusually large class of 104 new members, representing a nearly 20 percent turnover; there were 92 new members of the House and 12 new members of the Senate.[1]

Dazzling the audience, Fenwick was touted as a new star. The next day the *Washington Star-News* reported, "A Republican—and a woman at that—was the funniest speaker at last night's Washington Press Club dinner honoring the returning Congress. The triumph of freshman Rep. Millicent Fenwick of New Jersey was the more noteworthy since women and Republicans both are somewhat endangered species in Congress. . . . Mrs. Fenwick confided she started off badly the first day by arriving 'in my best outfit, including a little fur hat,' only to be told that 'the hats are appropriate as a mark of respect in the house of God [and] are absolutely out of line in the House of Representatives.'"[2]

The thousand people in attendance at the dinner paled in comparison to the many thousands she had addressed decades earlier during her *Vogue* book tour. Over the decades she had honed her speaking skills and no longer worried about what to say or wear. Neatly tailored

From Amy Shapiro, *Millicent Fenwick: Her Way* (New Brunswick, N.J.: Rutgers University Press, 2003), 147–161. Reprinted by permission of the author.

designer suits, many acquired during her *Vogue* years, still lined her closet and fit her slender form. It was said that her suits endured because she did not dry clean them but instead aired them out of doors.[3]

A strand of pearls draped her narrow neck, sometimes wrapping around two, three, even four times. Large pearl earrings adorned her ears, and her left wrist was weighed down by her sister's gold chain-link bracelets. The small corncob pipe, while not always visible, was never far—usually on her desk or in her hand or purse if not in her mouth. Some quietly feared that one day ashes from her pipe would spark a fire in her bag. Also in her bag was a blend of Dutch amphora tobacco. While her pipe-smoking habit was well publicized she desperately tried to keep her pipe out of the camera's way. Being photographed with the pipe would only perpetuate her bad habit and set a poor example for others. Cognizant of being caught in the public eye she did not want children to see her pictured with a pipe or emulate her nicotine addiction.

When Fenwick moved into the tight quarters assigned to her in the Longworth House Office Building, she had assembled a young and relatively inexperienced staff. She sought bright people with an inner drive, ideally from her district. Among her two most esteemed employees were two Ivy Leaguers, Hollis McLoughlin and Larry Rosenshein, whom staffers referred to as Golden Boy #1 and Golden Boy #2, respectively.

Hollis, a Princeton University graduate, began working on the Fenwick campaign in the summer, after her primary victory. Initially, no one from the campaign was hired because Millicent was advised to hire people who knew the Hill and not the "kids" who had worked on her campaign. Within a few weeks she disregarded that advice and hired twenty-four-year-old Hollis because, as he said, "Of course, people on the Hill always think they know best, but after a few weeks I was hired because I knew where routes 24 and 287 were, and the issues of the campaign."[4] Hired as a file clerk for $8,000 a year, he quickly gained Millicent's confidence and was promoted on a trial basis to legislative assistant with the understanding that if it didn't work out because he was so young, he would return to his original position. That turned out not to be necessary.

Immediately following the election, Lou Vetter was Fenwick's administrative assistant, and when twenty-year-old Larry Rosenshein, a Dartmouth College student, came looking for an internship, Vetter offered him a full-time job. Larry, from Bound Brook in New Jersey's Fifth District, already had Hill experience. As a high school student at Exeter Academy he had participated in the school's Washington Internship Program and worked for Bronx Democrat Jack Bingham. Putting off plans to drive cross-country, Larry went to work for Millicent.

Larry hadn't worked on the campaign, and the fact that he was a college student had not gone unnoticed by the rest of the staff. A year and a half later, still working full-time, Larry received his degree from Dartmouth after taking evening classes at Georgetown University.

Three months into Fenwick's term, Vetter left and Hollis was running the show. He had Fenwick's complete trust. In an effort to staff the office, he hired John Schmidt, a twenty-two-year-old from the Princeton area who had volunteered on the campaign. Meanwhile, back in New Jersey, Roger Bodman, another campaign worker and recent college graduate, headed her district offices in Somerville and Morristown. Bodman's political career began as Fenwick's district office manager—representing her at meetings, accompanying her to events, and working with the Washington office—before he became a cabinet member in Governor Kean's administration. He later went on to be one of the top lobbyists in New Jersey.

❖ ❖ ❖ ❖ ❖ ❖

As a freshman member of Congress, Fenwick openly expressed discontent with her committee assignments and with the House leadership. She had naively thought that because she was elected to Representative Peter Frelinghuysen's seat she would replace him as a ranking minority member, on the House Foreign Affairs Committee. Instead, she found herself on the Banking, Currency and Housing Committee, often referred to as "Beirut" as an indication of its undesirability, and on the Small Business Committee. That was her first introduction to the power structure that dominated Capitol Hill. Fenwick disliked the Banking Committee and latched on to the Small Business Committee. At least, she thought, that committee would give her the opportunity to concentrate on the plight of individuals.

While Fenwick found issues of interest on the Small Business Committee, she had a more challenging time with the Banking Committee. In the evenings, she often read through regulations and other banking material so she could at least be informed, if not interested, about pressing matters. All the while she lobbied for an appointment to a committee where her true passion, human rights, resided. Meanwhile, fellow freshman Helen Meyner received a coveted slot from the Democratic majority to the International Relations Committee, which had been called the House Foreign Affairs Committee a year earlier when Frelinghuysen was the ranking Republican.

Meyner's election to Congress marked her first elected office, but not her introduction to politics, since she was a distant relative of Adlai Stevenson as well as the wife of Robert Meyner, New Jersey's governor from 1954 to 1962. When Helen first ran for Congress in 1972, she had little personal experience in politics and lost. Two years later her victory was aided by the Watergate scandal. She defeated Judiciary Committee member Joseph Maraziti of whom it was written in *The Almanac of American Politics*, "Maraziti might have remained, in fact would certainly have remained, an obscure backbencher were it not for the fact that he sat on the Judiciary Committee which decided to impeach Richard Nixon. Maraziti . . . was the oldish junior Republican [sixty-two years old], whose tongue-tied oratory always left him satisfied with the President's innocence. Named by *New Times* magazine as one of the ten dumbest members of Congress, Maraziti did precious little to dispel that reputation."[5]

Fortunately for New Jersey, and the country, another member of the state delegation, Democrat Peter Rodino Jr., served on the Judiciary Committee. A Newark native, Rodino was chairman of the House Judiciary Committee, and his handling of Nixon's impeachment hearings elevated his reputation. Although he staunchly believed Nixon should be removed from office, Rodino presided over the hearings in a fair and ethical manner that received praise from both sides of the aisle and respect from the nation.

◆ ◆ ◆ ◆ ◆ ◆

Because there were only eighteen women in the House of Representatives, the female legislators stood out. "Millicent came to Congress about the same time that we women felt we should have some type of organization whether it was informal or not," remembered Democrat Representative Lindy Boggs of Louisiana. "We would meet for lunch . . . and help with committee work, research, and so on. It was the beginning of the women's caucus which is now a lively sixty-nine members."[6] Notable Democratic colleagues included House Majority Leader Hale Boggs's widow, Lindy Boggs, who was well-versed on the Hill; the feisty New Yorker Bella Abzug, with whom the media begged to compare Millicent even before she was elected to Congress; two other New Yorkers, Shirley Chisholm and Elizabeth Holtzman; the energetic Patsy Mink; the politically astute Gladys Noon Spellman; the outspoken Pat Schroeder; the widows of George Collins and John Sullivan; Tennessean Marilyn Lloyd; Kansan Martha Keys; the eloquent and politically savvy Barbara Jordan; Yvonne Brathwaite Burke, the first member of Congress to give birth while in office; and Helen Meyner. Fenwick's three Republican peers were attorney Peggy Heckler, who later became ambassador to Ireland, and conservatives Marjorie Holt and Virginia Smith.

"By 1975, with more pressure coming to bear from outside women's groups, we finally were able to start the bipartisan Congressional Women's Caucus, under the chairmanship of Liz Holtzman and Peggy Heckler," said Pat Schroeder.[7] To help fund and staff the caucus, the women allocated a percentage of their staff funds and pooled it together. They also established the nonprofit Women's Research Institute to study issues of importance to the Congressional Women's Caucus. To raise money Millicent Fenwick and Lindy Boggs were sent to New York to tap into their philanthropic contacts. After that trip Boggs came away with a greater admiration for Fenwick's tenacity. "I was crazy about her," said Boggs. "Millicent had a very interesting life and she turned around every situation into a forward-looking situation—that was significant, that was interesting—and she didn't let adversity get her down."[8]

Although not a driving force of the Women's Caucus, Fenwick readily stepped up to the plate when it came to abortion issues and the Equal Rights Amendment, but she "didn't grasp equity issues," said Schroeder. When discussing pensions for widows, Schroeder felt Fenwick's perspective was a bit skewed. "Since her sister was married to a foreign service officer, and her sister wouldn't take the money, it was hard for her to understand the women who don't have money."[9]

Because of Fenwick's so-called equity gap and distaste for government intervention, women's organizations did not embrace her, nor did she embrace them. She argued that "if there's a need for them [women's organizations], then they really aren't women's issues at all but rather civil rights or citizenship issues."[10] Nor did Millicent adopt the political correct term "congressperson"; instead she preferred to be referred to as a Republican representative.

◆ ◆ ◆ ◆ ◆

Millicent lived two blocks from her office in the Longworth Building. She rented a narrow, two-story brownstone on South Capitol Street and often referred to it as her "shack," much to the dismay of her landlord, Pierre S. Du Pont, then the governor of Delaware. The decor of her Washington home was modest. A sofa, two overstuffed chairs, and a large stool created a simple living room setting. A small throw rug covered the hardwood floor. She often worked at a small table in the living room. Her literary favorites were housed in two nearby bookcases. Off the living room in the dining room stood a medium-size table that could seat six people, but rarely did. Millicent often ate alone. Her traditional dinner fare was a bowl of spaghetti with a little butter and a glass of wine. Her grandson, Joe Reckford, spent six weeks with his grandmother one summer while he interned for another member of Congress, and he remembered that she "would carry a box of store-bought spaghetti and a fresh loaf of bread from New Jersey to Washington. One box got her through the week."[11]

After a long day Millicent retired upstairs to her stark bedroom. It contained the basics—a bed, nightstand, straight-back chair, and small table. The only extra items were an overstuffed chair and a small television. A second bedroom was even barer. It had a bed, a small bookcase, a table, and a lamp—sufficient accommodation for a grandchild, Cousin Mary, or any other guest.

Millicent didn't spend much time in her bleak abode. Most of her waking moments were spent at her Longworth office or on the House floor. Often the first to arrive at the office, before seven in the morning, she picked up the bundles of mail piled outside the door and carried them in. Settling behind her desk, she carefully untied the twine and wound it into a ball—preventing unnecessary waste. Her drawers were filled with twine balls meant for recycling. Her staff didn't have the heart to tell her that there was no use for the small twine strands that she saved and they threw away.

Each day Fenwick plucked through the heaps of mail and separated the handwritten letters from the typed correspondence. Handwritten mail was a priority because, she believed, it was from real people. Fenwick opened, read, and responded to as many letters as she could. The sheer volume of mail she handled was quickly evident to an unsuspecting staff, who fielded calls flooding in from constituents who had received one of Millicent's handwritten responses. The staff, having no control over Fenwick or knowledge of the content of these letters, was helpless. They explained the problem to her and presented a solution—making carbon copies of her handwritten notes. These copies were affectionately referred to as pinky letters. The pinkies were then filed and available to staff as needed. Fenwick had always been an avid letter writer. Her handwriting crusade, which dated back to her campaign days with Senator Case and continued through her Consumer Affairs tenure, had evolved as part of her daily routine decades earlier when she faithfully wrote her children, friends, family, and Ghino, the husband of her late sister.

Fenwick carried a red satchel filled with constituent letters to the House floor, where she sat and composed her handwritten responses. She sometimes perched there for ten or twelve hours, listening to speeches and writing letters. She carefully reviewed each letter regardless of whether the person was from New Jersey or Idaho. Writing thousands of letters, Representative Fenwick became revered by the public for her personal touch, which she viewed as a gesture of thanks for voting her into office.

Personally prioritizing constituent mail, an atypical task for members of Congress, attracted widespread attention, as did the amount of time she spent on the House floor. The public loved Millicent's individual approach, but her congressional peers regarded it as another aspect of her eccentric nature. They didn't realize there was method to her idiosyncrasies.

Fenwick's letter writing kept her connected to her constituents, and her prolonged time on the floor was more calculated than her peers gave her credit for. In 1980, when Representative Marge Roukema joined the New Jersey congressional delegation, Millicent Fenwick dispensed this advice. "In those days," Roukema recalled, "we had significant debates on the floor. In recent years the debate forms have been more perfunctory, but in those days there were genuine debates and she advised me. 'Marge,' she said, 'you need to sit on the floor to get to know your colleagues. Get to know them, not only in committee, but on the floor when debates are going on. It is then you can learn to judge whose opinions you can trust, and whose opinions you must be skeptical of. Be able to evaluate them.'"

"That was wonderful advice," said Roukema. "The first year or so I spent a lot of time on the floor listening to the debates . . . and got a sense of things. Not only the issues but a sense of the evaluation of the people that were presenting things and who was being superficial and political and who was being substantive and incisive. It was excellent advice. Of course, she was always there. Third row on the aisle."[12]

Taking seriously her congressional duties and the voters' trust in her to represent them, Fenwick rarely missed a vote. If Congress was in session, she was there. "[Some] people in Congress felt she did not pay enough attention to a narrow agenda . . . and considered her time on the House floor to be a waste [because] she should have been working in committee and behind the scenes," said Hollis. "Now that is somewhat unfair because she never missed a committee meeting. I think if she could be faulted it was because she did not narrow her agenda . . . One of her strengths was that she was interested in all aspects of public policy and her effectiveness was her independence and willingness to speak out on a whole range of issues regardless of whether or not she had a say on that committee."[13]

As soon as Congress recessed for the week, Fenwick could be found on the next train to New Jersey, where she spent her time giving speeches, holding town hall sessions, and meeting with constituents. Often the local grocery store provided an ad hoc forum in which constituents took advantage of Fenwick's willingness to listen. Like clockwork, every Sunday, Fenwick boarded the 4:17 p.m. Metroliner from Trenton back to Washington to pursue the interests of her constituents.

To keep up with the demands of her job and the ever-present media, Fenwick's staff typed appointments on yellow unlined index cards to help keep their boss organized. By early May 1975, Fenwick generated enough attention to land on the cover of *Parade* magazine. The article, titled "Rep. Millicent Fenwick: A Star of the New Congress," characterized her as a "Republican version of Eleanor Roosevelt, though the taut elegance of her looks and assertiveness of her manner are more reminiscent of Katharine Hepburn."[14] As a former magazine writer, Fenwick gained "a respect for the press and an understanding of the needs of reporters," observed Bernardsville reporter Sandy Stuart.[15] Fenwick claimed to "never have been misquoted."[16] Her ease and candidness only added to her media appeal. "She's a strange combination," wrote Judy Bachrach in the *Washington Post*. "She reveals her wealth but won't mention, for instance, what kind of cancer she recovered from 15 years ago."[17]

◆ ◆ ◆ ◆ ◆ ◆

On Millicent's sixty-fifth birthday, she readied herself to board a military aircraft for her first congressional trip. President Ford was sending a congressional delegation to Vietnam and Cambodia to review his request to provide hundreds of millions of dollars more in supplemental military aid to Southeast Asia as part of a three-year phase-out plan. He hoped the trip would sway Congress to endorse his legislation.

Of the eight members on the trip, five Democrats and three Republicans, half were thought to support continued aid and the other half were believed to be opposed to it. Fenwick was one of the more open-minded members on the trip but was leaning against continued aid. Bella Abzug, the New York Democrat, was the only other congresswoman. For years the New Jersey media had compared Fenwick to Abzug. Both were characters in their own right. While Millicent was known for her pipe smoking, Bella was known for her ever-present hats. The pair was an odd couple—Millicent refined, Bella rough. Despite their contrasting styles their politics were not dissimilar. Both advocated abortion rights and the Equal Rights Amendment. Their records were fairly similar despite their different party allegiances. In Fenwick's first year in Congress she and Abzug voted together 61 percent of the time. The following year, 1976, that number increased to 77 percent while Fenwick voted with her party less than half the time—only 44 percent."[18]

Becoming better acquainted in Vietnam, each earned the respect of the other. Of Fenwick, Abzug said, "I always like style, and she has style. We both have a sense of ourselves. We're both women of the world. I have crossed many boundaries, and I am sure she has too."[19] Fenwick also admired Abzug for the same reason she admired Eleanor Roosevelt—she meant what she said. One *New York Times* writer characterized their relationship as an "odd couple who seek out each other's company, try to ease each other's paths and provide moral support, solace, humor and sympathy in what some feminists might call an expression of sisterhood."[20]

Upon arriving in Saigon the delegation met with the U.S. ambassador to the Republic of Vietnam, Graham Martin. From there the delegation was welcomed by South Vietnamese President Nguyen Van Thieu, who advocated the need for aid and candidly answered the delegation's questions. He also let them know they were free to travel and meet with anyone they pleased.

Splitting into groups, the delegation members pursued their own agendas. Fenwick, Abzug, and Democrat Don Fraser of Minnesota met with political prisoners, publishers, and opposition leaders, as well as with government officials regarding American soldiers still listed as missing in action. A visit to a political prisoner incensed Fenwick and incited a feud with Abzug. The Indochina Research Center, a United States–based organization, told them about a young medical student who was wrongly imprisoned and being tortured. Fenwick, Abzug, and Fraser made arrangements to make the tedious journey to investigate the allegations. What they found was a student, said Millicent, "who wouldn't admit he was a Communist so he was kept in lockup where he said himself he'd been perfectly well treated."[21] Upset about the wasted time and cost of the trip, Fenwick lashed out. She accused "the organization [Indochina Research Center] of being so pro-Communist that they simply had no sense or responsibility about telling the truth."[22] Those remarks sparked a screaming match between Fenwick and Abzug, who defended the Indochina Research Center. Fenwick shouted, "Listen here, Bella Abzug, I can scream just as loudly as you and I've got just as bad a temper." Once their heated exchange ended, Abzug tapped Fenwick on the elbow and said, "That was fun wasn't it?" thus, putting the whole episode behind them.[23]

In Cambodia, the delegation met with the U.S. ambassador there, John Dean, before spending time with Cambodian leader Lon Nol, who "offered to do anything that would result in a solution to the Cambodian war. Most people in attendance including myself understood this to mean that Lon Nol offered to resign if necessary," said Bob Wolthuis, special assistant to President Ford.[24]

At the conclusion of the trip President Thieu hosted a dinner for the delegation and delivered a speech in which he emphasized their freedom of movement to travel wherever they wished. He told the members of Congress, "I hope to destroy the myth carefully nurtured by the dissenters according to which the Republic of Viet-Nam is just another police state. Even though we are presently faced with aggression, you can see that there is much more freedom here than in many other countries living in peace and where national security is not at all threatened. Secondly, the evidence is here for all to see that, far from being the warmongers so often depicted in Communist literature, we are actually being attacked—and massively so—by North Vietnamese Communist Troops, in violation of every provision of the Paris Agreement of January 27, 1973. So it is evident to any impartial observer that the first thing to do in order to save the Paris Agreement is to stop the Communist aggression. Once the cease-fire is effectively implemented, all other provisions of the Agreement can be carried out. We are ready to do our part and we are disposed to resume the peace negotiations without any precondition," said Thieu.[25]

Upon the delegation's return Wolthuis wrote a memo to Max Friedersdorf, head of the White House Congressional Relations Office, in which he characterized Millicent as pensive. "I believe of all the people on the delegation she has wrestled harder with the problem than anyone else. She read everything she could get her hands on," wrote Wolthuis, "and while she spent a great deal of time with [Don] Fraser and [Bella] Abzug, she looked at both sides very carefully. I think a Presidential nudge may be helpful in her case based on the fact that she told one member of our party that when she was a little girl she learned that if a person made a commitment, that commitment should be kept."[26] Most likely Millicent contemplated the concluding remarks President Thieu made at the dinner in which he stated, "During the past two decades, the People of South Viet-Nam have been told time and again by five U.S. Presidents belonging to both parties of America— all of them supported by successive legislatures of the U.S—that the United States is determined to provide them with adequate assistance as long as they are willing to resist Communist aggression to preserve their freedom. That solemn commitment had been renewed at the time of the signing of the Paris Agreement. This issue boils down to one simple question: is the commitment made by the U.S. to be any value? Is the word of the U.S. to be trusted?"[27]

A few days after their return, the congressional delegation went to the White House to brief President Gerald Ford, Secretary of State Henry Kissinger, and National Security Adviser Brent Scowcroft. Aid to Vietnam and aid to Cambodia were viewed and discussed by the delegation as separate matters. The general consensus was that the Foreign

Affairs Committee would narrowly pass a limited aid package. The pros, cons, and limitations were candidly presented by members of the delegation. A majority seemed to view a phase-out aid package as feasible, but Abzug considered it unrealistic. Torn, Fenwick told the president, "If we can hold off until the rainy season, I would vote for ammunition. If we could get people out in the meantime—such as civil servants, teachers, refugees—I would vote for ammunition [to Cambodia]." As to Vietnam she was undecided and wary about Thieu's continued leadership and corruption problems. "If you asked who could replace Thieu, that is an unsettling question because there is no one. I find myself sharing [Rep. Paul] McCloskey and [Rep. Don] Fraser's view—that is we can't vote money without seeing a viable solution. We need a plan . . . I cannot go along with the idea of a phased-out aid program. I cannot see where it leads."

"If you have reservations about a phase-out would you stop [aid] period?" asked Ford.

"Not so," said Fenwick. "I will regret my vote no matter which way I vote."[28]

A couple of weeks after the White House meeting, she wrote an op-ed piece for the *New York Times*. It was entitled "Military Aid for Vietnam and Cambodia? No." After wrestling with the issue, she, like her constituents, felt the United States had given enough aid to the decades-long effort in Indochina. She thought continued aid would be misperceived as support for Marshal Lon Nol, the head of the Cambodian government, and on a more humanitarian note she was deeply affected by the dying children. "The children are so famished that they must be fed intravenously before their bodies can accept food. I have never seen or imagined such human suffering and the first thought that comes to mind is 'stop the killing.'" Where Vietnam was concerned she wrote, "I think we must face the fact that military aid sent from America will not succeed. It will only delay the development of the kind of stable situation—whatever form that takes—that will at least stop the horrible suffering of war."[29]

Public opinion mounted against providing further aid to Indochina, and the president's request of $300 million in aid to South Vietnam and $222 million for Cambodia floundered.

❖ ❖ ❖ ❖ ❖ ❖

One day, in the autumn of her first congressional term, Millicent was overcome by dizziness. She attributed it to the stifling Washington humidity, but when the House doctor examined her he noticed a slow heartbeat and recommended she go to the Bethesda Naval Hospital.

She did. After careful analysis, the doctors determined that Millicent needed a pacemaker to regulate her heartbeat.

Hollis was told to call two people—her daughter and Mary Baird—with very strict orders: her daughter was to call Hugo, then living in Italy, and neither of them was to come and see her. Not abiding by the patient's wishes, Mary Baird traveled with Archie Alexander to Washington. Knowing Millicent would be upset, they told her Archie had a meeting in Washington, which was true, although it was not until the following week. Hollis watched as Millicent chastised her two cousins for coming to see her. Quite a scene erupted as Mary and Millicent, two stubborn older women, yelled back and forth. Seeing that Millicent was back to her usual stubborn self, Archie took the next train back to New Jersey while Fenwick's staff tended to Mary Baird.

One day, while Millicent was supposed to be recuperating in the hospital, Hollis stopped by only to find her upright and busily answering each get-well card with a personal note. Scolding her, Hollis took the letters away. He explained that her staff would take care of it and ordered the Naval Hospital not to let Fenwick see any more mail. After that incident, he felt he had earned Mary Baird's complete trust."[30]

But even Hollis couldn't stop Millicent from returning to the House floor earlier than anticipated. The week after the surgery she was back. The heavy workload prompted her early return. She said she felt "just fine," despite "feeling as if I was hit by a small truck."[31]

She was candid about the procedure. Via her district newsletter, she informed constituents about the pacemaker operation and reassured them of her health. She had nothing to hide, made a swift recovery, and quickly returned to work and waged battles on behalf of her constituents.

Within a few months she went on her second congressional trip. The female members of Congress accepted an invitation from Chinese women officials to visit their country. As part of only the second congressional delegation to go to China since President Nixon's landmark visit, Millicent and several of her female colleagues were invited to bring a guest. Some, such as Helen Meyner, brought their spouses. Millicent, because of her pacemaker, brought a doctor.[32]

Helen's husband, Robert, the former governor of New Jersey, chatted with Fenwick and helped with her luggage. Thus, it came as a surprise to some members of the delegation to learn, upon their return, that Millicent had blasted Helen for bringing her husband on the trip at the expense of the taxpayer. Pat Schroeder, a member of the congressional delegation to China, said that incident "always said to me she is fascinating, go talk to her, but beware."[33]

Sixteen-year-old Joe Reckford also remembered his grandmother's trip to China. Aware that members of Congress could bring someone on the trip, Joe tried to convince his grandmother to take either him, his mother, or one of his siblings. "No," she sternly responded, "we are not invited to take somebody, we are invited to take spouses." "I knew she would say no," said Joe, "but the joke fell flat because she had no sense of humor . . . she felt it would have been an abuse of riding in a government plane." He conceded that she may have "protested if someone else took a friend or relative who was not a spouse. As she said, 'spouses were invited, not others.'"[34]

While the congressional delegation was in China, the country's premier, Chou En-lai, suffering from cancer, died at the age of seventy-eight. Chou En-lai, an adept politician, had ruled China since 1949 when the Communists assumed power. Flags were lowered to half-staff as radio stations continued to broadcast their regularly scheduled programming, something that would not have occurred a few years earlier. President Ford released a statement hailing "Premier Chou En-lai as a remarkable leader who has left his imprint not only on modern China but also in the world scene . . . We Americans will remember him especially for the role he played in building a new relationship between the People's Republic of China and the United States."[35]

As the congressional delegation—braving the bitter cold of January—traveled in Peking, Chengtu, Kewilin, and Shanghai, Millicent was struck by the warmth of the people. "I have never in all my travels, through India, Europe, and South America, I have never seen such friendly people," she said. "If you smiled at them, they would break into smiles, and the babies and teenagers would clap."[36] As congenial as the people were, Millicent still asked tough questions of her Chinese hosts. She prodded them about intellectual freedom, the criminal justice system, and their work ethic. "Maybe we were a little sharp sometimes, but you don't go 10,000 miles to show how charming you are."[37]

◆　◆　◆　◆　◆　◆

As the whirl of Watergate eased, Capitol Hill was rocked by another scandal in the spring of 1976. House leader Wayne Hays of Ohio, often referred to as the Mayor of Capitol Hill, took center stage in this scandal. Hays, a Democrat, was one of the most powerful and feared members of Congress. He chaired the Joint Committee on Printing; the Subcommittee on International Operations of the International Relations Committee; the House Administration Committee, which controlled payroll, telephones, and other vital necessities; and the Democratic National Congressional Committee (DNCC), which dispersed hundreds of thousands of dollars to congressional campaigns.

Many of Hays's peers dodged him. Opposing him often produced repercussions. Hays did not hesitate to threaten to stop payroll payments or disconnect phones, and he followed through on those threats. As chairman of the House Administration Committee he wielded the power to cut off vital resources. Despite his ominous reputation, Fenwick was not intimidated by him. When Hays proposed increasing congressional expense funds, something Fenwick deemed unnecessary, she called for a debate. In response, Hays reportedly bellowed, "If the Republicans think their expense allowance is too large, I can reduce it for them. I can strip them of their staffs." Fenwick, still a freshman with little political leverage, replied, "Mr. Chairman, I think we have heard something today for which we are all going to be sorry and ashamed."[38] With that, Fenwick scurried off the House floor to an anteroom where Bill Canis, one of her staffers, awaited. Flustered, she told Bill about her "critical exchange" with Hays. Bill listened in wonderment at his boss's willingness to take on the powerful Hays. "I don't care about offending such a powerful man," she said. "What he was advocating was wrong."[39] After cooling off Fenwick returned to the House floor and saw Hays emerge victorious. His provision passed, but he removed his remarks from the record. From that point forward Hays viewed Fenwick as a political adversary. "I've never heard any other man talk to another man as roughly as [Hays] did to me," Millicent recalled. "We got into some real fights."[40]

When the *Washington Post* revealed Hays's entanglement in a sex scandal, the mainstream media reported it in epic proportions. Within a week the story was plastered everywhere. It stemmed from allegations made by Elizabeth Ray, a committee secretary paid $14,000 a year (the median income at the time was $10,833),[41] to serve as Hays's mistress. Her famous quote, "I can't type. I can't file. I can't even answer the phone," did nothing to help Hays.[42] Ray's allegations triggered a Justice Department examination of criminal fraud based on her charges that she was on the public payroll for sexual, not secretarial, purposes. The investigations did not end there. *Newsweek* reported, "The House ethics committee voted unanimously to investigate Hays, one of the most powerful men in Congress. And Democrats on the Hill set out to topple him before he tarred his party and the House itself with a stain of guilt by association."[43]

A few weeks earlier the recently divorced sixty-four-year-old Hays had married the manager of his district office. She was half his age. It was in the aftermath of this second marriage that a scorned Ray revealed her two-year affair with Hays. He reluctantly admitted to the affair but insisted that Ray fulfilled her secretarial duties.

Many silently rejoiced at the compromising position in which the detested Hays found himself. Before the scandal erupted, few in Congress besides Fenwick were willing to oppose him. Now they were lining up. House Majority Leader Tip O'Neill urged Hays to relinquish his chairmanships, which he eventually did.

Fenwick's congressional peers gleefully watched as she passionately castigated Hays on the House floor for his behavior and breach of the public's trust and money. Unfortunately, her remarks have not survived because, according to *Congressional Record* rules "remarks or other materials that violate the rules of a house, such as derogatory statements about another member" can be expunged.[44] Age had given Fenwick a sense of security, and, unlike other members of Congress, she felt she had nothing to lose by doing what she did best, speaking her mind.

Curious why others were reluctant to challenge Hays, Fenwick asked a colleague, "Why does Hays command such influence? When he presents these terrible ideas, why does he always get 230 votes? Why?" The response was, "Well, he's got the goods on some of us, and goodies for the others." Millicent was horrified but understood. "He was the head of the House Admin. Committee. If he didn't sign your staff's checks, the staff wouldn't get paid," she said.[45]

Needless to say, not many members of Congress were upset that Hays's improprieties were made public. Capitalizing on the scandal, *Newsweek* showed a blonde bombshell resembling Ray on its cover. The leggy woman, scantily clad in a patriotic red, white, and blue bikini, was pictured leaping out of the Capitol dome as if it were a giant birthday cake. Despite the barrage of negative publicity in an election year, Hays won his primary. But two months before the general election, with a House ethics hearing pending, Hays finally resigned, bringing his nearly three-decade reign on the Hill to a woeful end.

The stain Hays's escapades left on Congress was mitigated to some extent by Fenwick's boldness in standing up to Hays, even before his political power was shattered. While some of her congressional colleagues viewed her as eccentric, they could not help but respect her adherence to her principles, which gave her the courage to challenge Hays.

In the scandal-ridden atmosphere of Washington, where Watergate, Vietnam, and sexual improprieties marred the public's faith in government, Fenwick's honesty and candor were not only refreshing but helped her do her job. Her work ethic, opposition to government waste, and advocacy for social justice prompted CBS news anchor Walter Cronkite to dub her the "Conscience of Congress" in the 1970s.[46]

Notes

1. *Congressional Quarterly Weekly Report*, 9 November 1975, 3060.

2. Isabelle Shelton, "Battle of Wits: Millicent Fenwick, a Republican, Puts Down the Men of Capitol Hill," *Washington Star-News*, 29 January 1975.

3. Catherine Rosenshein, interview by author, Montclair, N.J., 23 November 2001.

4. Hollis McLoughlin, interview by author, Washington, D.C., October 1993.

5. Michael Barone, Grant Ujifusa, and Douglas Matthews. *The Almanac of American Politics 1976* (New York: E. P. Dutton, 1976), 537.

6. Corinne (Lindy) Boggs, telephone interview by author, 16 November 2001.

7. Patricia Schroeder, *24 Years of House Work and the Place Is Still a Mess* (Kansas City, Mo.: Andrews McMeel, 1998), 30.

8. Boggs, interview, 16 November 2001.

9. Patricia Schroeder, interview by author, Washington, D.C., 19 December 2001, and Schroeder, *24 Years*, 28–29.

10. Peggy Lamson, *In the Vanguard: Six American Women in Public Life* (Boston: Houghton Mifflin, 1979), 33.

11. Joseph Reckford, telephone interview by author, 3 June 2002.

12. Marge Roukema, interview by author, Washington, D.C., 25 July 2001.

13. Hollis McLoughlin, interview by author, Washington, D.C., 19 March 1992.

14. Connecticut Walker, "Rep. Millicent Fenwick: A Star of the New Congress," *Parade*, 4 May 1975.

15. Sandy Stuart, "Millicent Fenwick—A Personal and Public Life Seem to Be One and the Same," *The Bernardsville News*, 20 May 1982.

16. Sandy Stuart, interview by author, Bernardsville, N.J., 10 January 1992.

17. Judy Bachrach, "Six from the Class of '75 . . . Millicent Fenwick," *Sunday Washington Post*, 23 February 1975.

18. Dennis Teti to J.B. [Jeff Bell], memo, "Fenwick and Abzug-Comparison of Voting Records," 3 May 1982, Box 128a, Millicent Fenwick Papers, Special Collections and University Archives, Rutgers University Libraries, New Brunswick, N.J.

19. Martin Tolchin, "An Odd Couple on Capitol Hill: Daughter of the Bronx and Well-Bred Jersey Lady," *New York Times*, 5 March 1976.

20. Ibid.

21. Lamson, *In the Vanguard*, 25.

22. Ibid.

23. Ibid., 26.

24. Bob Wolthuis to Max L. Friedersdorf, memo, "Viet Nam/Cambodia Congressional Trip," 3 March 1975, John Marsh Files, 1974–1977, box 43, folder Vietnam Congressional Trip 2/75–5175, Gerald R. Ford Library, Ann Arbor, Mich.

25. President Thieu's speech to the congressional delegation, 1 March 1975, Robert K. Wolthuis Files, box 5, folder Vietnam: Visit by Members of Congress Feb. 1975, Gerald R. Ford Library.

26. Wolthuis to Friedersdorf.

27. President Thieu's speech, 1 March 1975.

28. Memorandum of conversation, 5 March 1975, National Security Adviser, Memorandum of Conversations, 1973–1977, box 9, folder 5 March 1975, Ford, Kissinger, Congressional Vietnam Delegation, Gerald R. Ford Library.

29. Millicent Fenwick, "Military Aid for Vietnam and Cambodia? No," *New York Times*, 21 March 1975.

30. McLoughlin, interview, October 1993.

31. Robert W. Maitlin, "Fenwick Back in Action with Pacemaker Implant," *Newark Star-Ledger*, 1 October 1975.

32. Schroeder, interview, 19 December 2001.

33. Ibid.

34. Reckford, interview, 3 June 2002.

35. Gerald R. Ford, "Statement on the Death of Premier Chou En-lai of the People's Republic of China," 8 January 1976, *Public Papers of the Presidents* (Washington, D.C.: Government Printing Office, 1976), 24–25.

36. Mary Breasted, "China Tour: Warm Talk, Cold Hotels," *New York Times*, 18 January 1976.

37. Ibid.

38. Elisabeth Bumiller, "The Wit & Grit of Millicent Fenwick," *Washington Post*, 20 January 1982.

39. Bill Canis, interview by author, Washington, D.C., 18 May 2001.

40. Bumiller, "Wit & Grit."

41. Bureau of the Census, Statistical Abstract of the United States (Washington, D.C.: Government Printing Office, 1979), 425. The median income listed in the text is for 1975, when Elizabeth Ray was on the committee payroll.

42. Marion Clark and Rudy Maxa, "Closed Session Romance on the Hill," *Washington Post*, 23 May 1976.

43. Tom Mathews with Henry W. Hubbard, Anthony Marro, and Jon Lowell, "Capitol Capers," *Newsweek*, 14 June 1976, 18.

44. Walter Kravitz, *Congressional Quarterly's American Congressional Dictionary* (Washington, D.C.: Congressional Quarterly, 1993), 106.

45. Peter Jessup, "Interviews with Rep. Millicent Fenwick," Columbia University Oral History, 1980–1981, 15 April 1981, 444.

46. Marlene Adler, assistant to Walter Cronkite, confirmed on his behalf that he did call Millicent Fenwick the "Conscience of Congress," 7 September 2000.

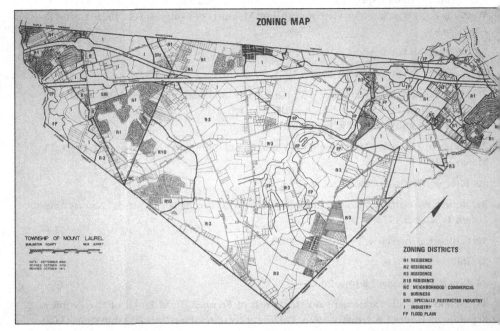

This 1971 zoning map for Mount Laurel was adopted even as the law case involving the town took shape. The size of building lots was set to discourage construction of multifamily housing and housing designed for low-income families. The lawsuit that contested this zoning led to a New Jersey Supreme Court ruling that "exclusionary zoning" was unconstitutional. Special Collections and University Archives, Rutgers University Libraries.

17

In 1970 a small group of African Americans in Mount Laurel, New Jersey, asked the all-white town council to approve a grant-funded proposal to build about one hundred units of low-income housing in the town. The units would replace inadequate residences, some of them literally converted chicken coops, enabling families to stay in a town some of their ancestors had inhabited for seven generations. They were refused and told that "if you people can't afford to live in our town, then you'll just have to leave." Five years later, with *Mount Laurel I*, in what would become a long string of cases, the New Jersey Supreme Court ruled that under the state's constitution municipalities had to consider the "general welfare," which meant providing housing for low- and moderate-income families, not just the wealthy. Mount Laurel, still in litigation at this writing, is a case with which towns and courts continue to wrestle. It raises a series of issues. Who makes decisions about the use of land, and who lives where? Who makes law: judges, the executive branch, or the legislature? What is fair housing, who provides it, where, and how? How do historians approach legal studies?

From the beginning, this case drew national interest because it raised issues about suburbs just as the United States became the first nation where more people lived in suburbs than cities or rural areas. In addition, New Jersey was and still is the most suburban state in the country. This was the culmination of a developing trend; owning a single-family home in a countrified setting long had been an American ideal. By the 1830s, wealthy Americans were moving out of urban areas, an exodus that increased in the late nineteenth century with the construction of trolley lines, picked up in the 1920s as automobiles became common, and then took off after World War II when a combination of mass-produced houses and federally supported highways opened ownership to many in the middle class. New Jersey not only participated in this ongoing transformation of settlement patterns, but at times led the way. In the 1850s, Llewellyn Park, a romantic enclave for the wealthy, was built in West Orange; in the 1920s, Radburn, a community designed with automobiles in mind, was constructed in Fairlawn; and in the 1950s, a Levitt project for veterans and others was developed in Willingboro (the company also built "Levittowns" in Pennsylvania and Long Island).

For many, the suburbs built in the 1950s and later were wonderful places to live and raise children. But they posed a number of problems. They drained cities of their wealthier citizens, and main streets of their stores, while also attracting offices and manufacturing plants. Left behind, as noted in chapter 15 about the Newark teachers strikes, were fewer jobs and poor, often minority residents who were unable to pay the taxes needed for schools and other facilities. Some suburban communities restricted who could live there. The Levitt Company, among others, did not sell to blacks. The cost of buying a home and the lack of apartments kept the poor out of other towns. By the 1970s, so did a practice called "exclusionary zoning." By setting the minimum lot for new houses at one-half, one, or two acres, specifying substantial home size, and prohibiting multifamily dwellings, towns made sure that only those with plentiful means could move in. Those who settled were then adamant about protecting the value of their property; for some this meant keeping out "others," the so-called riffraff. This also meant keeping out employees needed for lawn care and restaurants, as well as firemen and teachers.

What kind of place do you live in: rural, urban, or suburban? If it is suburban, what policies has the town followed? Who lives there in terms of race and economic status?

It was in this context of increased suburbanization, along with economic and racial segregation, that the New Jersey Supreme Court acted in the Mount Laurel case. New Jersey's 1947 constitution had substantially revised the state's court system, streamlining and centralizing it. As a result, both the power and the prestige of its judges increased. It also became an active judiciary, which in the 1970s took on difficult issues such as financing education, also noted in chapter 15, and zoning. In 1975 the court pointed to the state constitutional requirement that government needed to provide for the "general" welfare, not only for the well-to-do. When nothing changed, in 1983 in *Mount Laurel II* the court ordered towns to begin providing low- and moderate-income housing and appointed three judges to set specific proportions. While this encouraged those who had brought the lawsuit, it infuriated many residents of suburban towns, who contacted their legislators. In 1985 the state legislature, supported by Governor Thomas Kean, enacted a Fair Housing Act, which established a Council on Affordable Housing (COAH), to make decisions, taking them out of the hands of the courts. The state supreme court approved in *Mount Laurel III*, decided in 1986. Who makes or should make law—judges, the executive, or the legislature? What are the arguments for and against judicial activism?

Other aspects of this case help explain why it remains an unsettled matter for the state. Developers have used the requirement for low-income housing to force towns to approve projects, including additional units to ensure they make a profit. Coming at a time of concern about how suburban sprawl consumes more and more of remaining open land, the need for housing has collided with the need for preservation. Another issue is that while the original *Mount Laurel* decision pointed to a need for economic and racial desegregation, the Fair Housing Act included a provision for Regional Contribution Agreements (RCAs), enabling suburban towns to meet their obligations by paying urban areas to supply 50 percent of their required units. Thus Cranbury paid Perth Amboy to build housing for the poor. This provides more housing, but it does not end segregation.

In the nearly forty years since the Mount Laurel case was initiated, suburbs have changed. Some aging suburbs, often the "first ring" around a city, are now facing problems of decline similar to those experienced by cities. New, ever-farther out suburbs have been called "exurbs," "edge cities," "edgeless cities," and "technoburbs" as historians and other scholars try to describe a present that they see as different from the past. The landscape has become more complex than the single terms "rural," "urban," and "suburban" suggest. As new immigrants head straight for "suburbs" such as Edison, these locations have become even more racially and ethnically mixed, while age-restricted communities remain homogenous. Though small, New Jersey, with its 566 municipalities, now illustrates the increased diversity of place. Yet despite these changes, *Mount Laurel* continues to be of interest, the problems it raised still unresolved.

It is an example of a legal case that concerns scholars in different fields: political scientists, lawyers, and historians. That said, often their approach is not the same. Political scientists tend to start with the present and look backward, while historians usually begin in the past and work forward. Lawyers pick and choose from past cases to find examples they can use to win their arguments. Legal historians are concerned with context, what a particular case can teach about its time period. They try to understand all sides in a case: criminals and victims, winners and losers. What about the authors of the following selection: what field(s) do you think they are in and why?

Suggested Readings

Baxandall, Rosalyn, and Elizabeth Ewen. *Picture Windows: How the Suburbs Happened.* New York: Basic Books, 2000.

Birkner, Michael J. *A Country Place No More: The Transformation of Bergenfield, New Jersey, 1894–1994.* Rutherford, N.J.: Fairleigh Dickinson University Press, 1994.

Cammarota, Ann Marie T. *Pavements in the Garden: the Suburbanization of Southern New Jersey Adjacent to the City of Philadelphia, 1769 to the Present.* Madison, N.J.: Fairleigh Dickinson University Press, 2001.

Cohen, Lizabeth. *Consumer Republic: The Politics of Mass Consumption in Postwar America.* New York: Knopf, 2003.

Fishman, Robert. *Bourgeois Utopias: The Rise and Fall of Suburbs.* New York: Basic Books, 1987.

Haar, Charles M. *Suburbs Under Siege: Race, Space, and Audacious Judges,* Princeton, N.J.: Princeton University Press, 1996.

Jackson, Kenneth. *Crabgrass Frontier: The Suburbanization of the United States.* New York: Oxford University Press, 1985.

Lake, Robert W. *The New Suburbanites: Race and Housing in the Suburbs.* New Brunswick, N.J.: Center for Urban Policy Research, Rutgers University, 1981.

Marsh, Margaret S. *Suburban Lives.* New Brunswick, N.J.: Rutgers University Press, 1990.

Mattingly, Paul H. *Suburban Landscapes: Culture and Politics in a New York Metropolitan Community.* Baltimore: Johns Hopkins University Press, 2001.

Schwartz, Joel, and Daniel Prosser, eds. *Cities of the Garden State: Essays in the Urban and Suburban History of New Jersey.* Dubuque, Iowa: Kendal/Hunt Publishing, 1977.

Teaford, Jon C. *The American Suburb: The Basics.* New York: Routledge, 2008.

◆ ◆ ◆ ◆ ◆ ◆

Simple Justice

David L. Kirp, John P. Dwyer, Larry A. Rosenthal

In the annals of land use, the annals of poor people's justice too, the trilogy of *Mount Laurel* cases is renowned.[1] Because these were state-court rulings, they never unleashed the national passions of cases like *Brown v. Board of Education*, which outlawed racial segregation, or *Roe v. Wade*, which made abortion a constitutional right. Yet these are the most critical judicial decisions on zoning in this country since the U.S. Supreme Court first announced, nearly three-quarters of a century ago, that municipalities could tell landowners how their land could, and could not, be used.[2]

Like few other judicial decisions, *Mount Laurel* ignited powerful feelings. At church socials and backyard barbecues, at beach resorts and drinks at the nineteenth hole as well, even to say "Mount Laurel" was to start an argument. To some people it was shorthand for justice, while to others it stood for judicial busy bodying that threatened a hard-earned way of life.

These disturbances in the field were felt most powerfully in New Jersey, since that is where the cases were decided. But what the state judges said about the legal requirement of making available a "fair share" of land for the poor, and about the moral obligation to do the right thing, also appeared on the front page of the *New York Times* and on the nightly television news shows. Lawyers and planners who worked on the case found themselves in demand in courtrooms elsewhere. Planning schools and law schools taught their students new ways to think about housing and the general welfare. Legislators from across the country borrowed the themes of *Mount Laurel* in rewriting their states' rules about land use. And phrases like "fiscal zoning"—less euphemistically, snob zoning—became policy commonplaces. Because of *Mount Laurel*, the relationship changed between cities and their suburbs.

From David L. Kirp, John P. Dwyer, and Larry A. Rosenthal, *Our Town: Race, Housing, and the Soul of Suburbia* (New Brunswick, N.J.: Rutgers University Press, 1995), 61–82. Reprinted by permission of the authors.

Archaeologists in the Legal Trenches

None of these changes was remotely predictable to the lawyers from Camden Regional Legal Services who in 1970 were beavering away in the archives of Mount Laurel Township, pursuing what attorney Carl Bisgaier called an "archaeological dig." When they started out, these attorneys knew amazingly little about land-use law. "We didn't even know what zoning was," Bisgaier confesses—which was probably just as well, since it kept them from being discouraged by the utter lack of legal precedent for their arguments.

The press release accompanying the filing of their 1971 complaint called it "the first suit which asks a court to order a suburban community to develop an affirmative action plan for the construction of low and moderate income housing." That was a slight but pardonable exaggeration, for while similar cases were being brought elsewhere in New Jersey, the reform-minded attorneys did not discover one another until after they had filed the legal papers. These were truly legal innocents abroad in the land of reform. The task of researching the law was left to a Harvard law student named Ken Meiser, the house intellectual, who shuttled between Camden and Cambridge, and his inexperience showed. "It's all right here!" he exclaimed at one point, brandishing a New Jersey Supreme Court decision called *Vickers v. Gloucester Township*. Indeed, all the winning arguments *were* there, but in Meiser's excitement he failed to notice that he was reading not the majority opinion but the dissent.

While Meiser was guilty of wishful misreading, he was entirely right to focus on state, rather than federal, rulings. Because the issues in the Mount Laurel case potentially involved both federal and state constitutional law, the lawyers had to decide whether to take the dispute to a U.S. district court or to a New Jersey trial court. The former route was generally more familiar to reform-minded attorneys, and more glamorous too, since many attorneys think that federal court has more prestige and offers a more direct pathway to the U.S. Supreme Court. During the Warren Court era, federal judges had rewritten the law of equality, reconceiving the Constitution as an instrument to protect racial minorities and poor people against discrimination.

Yet even in its liberal heyday, the U.S. Supreme Court had been reluctant to say much about land use. Now, with Earl Warren replaced by conservative Warren Burger, there were unmistakable signs of retrenchment. In *James v. Valtierra*, decided in 1971, a closely divided Court upheld a California statute that required a public referendum before public housing could be built, rejecting the argument that this law effectively put a stop to such construction and so discriminated against the poor.[3] That retreat in Washington, coupled with the emergence of newly energized state tribunals, meant that the advocates needed to change their tactics, to emphasize state rather than federal constitutional law. Justice William Brennan, who himself had served on the New Jersey Supreme Court in the 1950s, had the *Mount Laurel* case specifically in mind when he reminded lawyers that "state decisions [based on state law] not only cannot be overturned by, they indeed are not even reviewable by, the Supreme Court of the United States."[4] In delivering this homily, Brennan was reminding reform-minded lawyers that the Warren Court was no more, and that they would do well to stay away from federal court.

For a generation, New Jersey's highest court had been as venturesome as any in the land. It was among the nation's most admired state tribunals, and judges in other states regularly followed its lead. While the court's opinions on land-use regulation had generally sided with the towns, recent dissents suggested that the New Jersey justices might be persuaded to change their minds. If that happened, there would be new law for the state and a model for the nation. That's why the activists began their legal campaign in the local trial court.

Jersey Justice

The New Jersey courts' fine reputation was of relatively recent vintage. In the 1940s, the august American Judicature Society pronounced those tribunals "the nation's worst."[5] Then, the state's sixteen-member high court, known as the Court of Errors and Appeals and partly comprised of lay jurists—its membership changing from case to case as judges shuffled on and off the bench, its precedents almost unintelligible—was derided by the *New York Times* as "too large to be a court and too small to be a mob."

Below the high court in unwieldy hierarchy sat no fewer than seventeen different kinds of specialized courts, law and equity tribunals rivaling one another, each court operating under its own distinct rules in a system as archaic as any that Dickens had described. As Denis Brogan, longtime British observer of American folkways, gleefully pointed out: "If you want to see the old common law in all its picturesque formality, with its fictions and fads, its delays and uncertainties, the place to look . . . is not London . . . but in New Jersey."[6]

New Jersey politics was boss run then, and the state courts were a valuable tool for the bosses. Frank Hague, Jersey City's mayor and for years the most powerful man in the state, deployed the judges to control elections and then to block legislative investigations of the fixes. In 1938, the governor appointed Frank Hague Jr., then just twenty-eight years old and a five-time loser on the bar exam, to the state's highest court—in order to "please his daddy," the governor admitted.[7]

It required immense effort, mainly on the part of a remarkable lawyer and politician named Arthur Vanderbilt, to rewrite the court rules.[8] Beginning in 1930 with his election to the state bar association's Judicial Council, Vanderbilt, the founder of the state's Clean Government Movement who became president of the American Bar Association and dean of New York University Law School, issued reports lambasting the court system, proposing to bring it up to date through consolidation and centralization. Boss Hague was, however, still running things from Jersey City—in a 1944 letter, Vanderbilt ruefully wrote that "the present chancellor [of the court of equity] has even outdone his predecessor in conforming to the readily ascertained wishes of the Hague machine"—and the politician kept the would-be reformer in check. In 1947, though, after several failed tries, a state constitutional convention finally pushed through Vanderbilt's proposals. The reformers showed that they had learned how to maneuver within smoke-filled rooms.[9] To win Hague's acquiescence, they agreed to delete a measure authorizing the legislature to investigate local officials and to revise tax proposals that assured higher taxation of railroad-owned property in Jersey City.

Arthur Vanderbilt became the first chief justice of the made-over New Jersey Supreme Court, and he quickly moved to assert the court's independence. Even as, during the early days of the Republic, Chief Justice John Marshall of the U.S. Supreme Court had separated court from politics with a piece of legal legerdemain known as *Marbury v. Madison*, Vanderbilt insisted that the New Jersey legislature had no power to veto court-made rules governing procedure and practice, even though the state constitution suggested otherwise.[10] More importantly, state politicians endorsed the ideal of judicial independence. In reaction to the political abuses of the Hague era, nonpartisanship became the norm for judicial appointments. Governors made it their practice to name an equal number of Republicans and Democrats to the bench; the senate confirmed those appointments and then, as the state constitution specified routinely reconfirmed them for life terms seven years later, unless they had broken the rules of "good behavior."

This admonition to "good behavior" didn't mean a judge was expected to be Caspar Milquetoast—far from it. Policy making was proper business of the state's judges, Vanderbilt believed, because the law "derives its life and growth from judicial decisions which . . . abandon an old rule and substitute . . . a new one in order to meet new conditions." Each of his successors as chief justice has maintained an equally broad vision of what judging means. The Supreme Court has "creative responsibility for making law," insisted Joseph Weintraub, who was appointed to succeed William Brennan on the state bench in 1956, when Brennan was tapped for the U.S. Supreme Court, and named to head the court a year later when Vanderbilt died.[11] As chief justice, Weintraub pushed the court to rewrite the law of torts to give consumers more rights against manufacturers, as well as to intervene in such sensitive policy areas as reapportionment and school finance. Richard Hughes, a former governor who succeeded Weintraub in 1974, carried the school-finance initiative forward; *Mount Laurel I* was also part of the Hughes court's judicial legacy.

"Judges have to mold the law into their concept of justice," one of Chief Justice Hughes's contemporaries on the bench told an interviewer. Another justice unselfconsciously marveled at how sensibly political the court could be—how "we can encourage the [state] legislature to pass laws or taxes without directing them to do that. This is the wonder of our system, and besides it works to accomplish our judicial objectives." While state judges, much more than federal judges, are expected to create public policy in their decisions, New Jersey's supreme court justices have been more openly political and politically strategic in their decrees than other states' judges.[12]

By no means were this court's opinions uniformly liberal. "The Constitution is not at all offended when a guilty man stubs his toe," Chief Justice Weintraub wrote in an opinion narrowly defining the scope of legal protection accorded defendants by the *Miranda* warning. "On the contrary, it is decent to hope that he will." But the state's high court was best known for its rulings that made it easier for injury victims to sue government agencies, gave union organizers access to farm workers, and guaranteed the public greater access to the state's beaches. Judicial innovation was the byword in New Jersey.[13]

All this was accomplished with little legislative direction or reaction. The great respect for the court and the politicians' desire to protect the judiciary's independence gave the justices maneuvering room. By the end of the 1960s, the New Jersey Supreme Court had grown accustom to its role—not as the "least dangerous branch of government," as the U.S. Supreme Court had been characterized in the *Federalist Papers*, but as a policy maker acting in parallel with the governor and the legislature.[14] Few indeed were the voices objecting that judicially led reform was antidemocratic.

"Suburban Blight" and the Court

The court's reformist bent did not, however, extend to zoning. On that subject, local autonomy became the dominant principle when, in its 1952 decision in *Lionshead Lake*, the state supreme court gave the suburbs carte blanche to write their own land-use rules.[15]

The Township of Wayne was once a bucolic place, rhapsodized as "a wondrously beautiful valley" by the first English settler who laid eyes on it. But by the mid-twentieth century Wayne was beset by fear that it would be spoiled by development, and to prevent that from happening it adopted a zoning ordinance setting a minimum size for new homes. When a landowner who wanted to build modest summer cottages on his property tested the new rule, the court backed the township. Wayne officials' only legal obligation, the justices ruled, was to advance the "community as a social, economic and political unit." Across the nation, state courts cited *Lionshead Lake* when blessing zoning ordinances that required mini-mansions built on multiacre estates. A decade later, Gloucester, Camden's neighbor—"the first white settlement on the Delaware River," according to a local historical-society report from the era, and "still virile and forward-looking"—banned all trailer parks. In the *Vickers* case, the state supreme court upheld this ordinance, and that decision was also widely mimicked.[16]

The New Jersey justices treated these disputes as pitting the rights of property owners to develop their land as they wished against the "general welfare" of the local community; and perceived that way, the correct result seemed obvious. A town should be able to "prevent suburban blight," said the court. There was reason to fear that, unless tough zoning measures were adopted, "the tide of suburban development" "would engulf the rustic character" of these bucolic places. Since zoning exists to create "community benefits," a town could exclude buildings—implicitly, people too—"repugnant to its planning scheme." But this formulation defines a "community" as consisting only of those already living there and financially able to stay put; anyone else is perceived as a stranger outside the gates.[17] To those outsiders—to *"you people,"* as Mount Laurel mayor Bill Haines said to the congregation at Jacob's Chapel—the community had absolutely no legal responsibility. In this way, parochialism became enshrined in state constitutional law.

The state supreme court was not, of course, entirely to blame for New Jersey's famed localism. This fragmented state has relied heavily on local property taxes to pay for government services. With no significant source of state tax revenues until the mid-1960s, and then only a pittance of a sales tax, state government was kept small and ineffectual. Real politics mostly transpired in the state's 567 municipalities. [Editor's note: There are now 566.] The court did not create this system, but its zoning decrees of the 1950s and 1960s reinforced it.

For the young Camden Legal Services attorneys researching the court's discouraging zoning precedents in preparation for the coming

Mount Laurel litigation, there were a few shards of hope amid the legal rubble. "If and when conditions change," the justices had declared in 1955, voicing Arthur Vanderbilt's activism, "alterations in zoning restrictions and pertinent legislative and judicial attitudes need not be long delayed."[18] In the 1962 *Vickers* case, a strong dissent written by Justice Frederick Hall (who early in his career had worked in Vanderbilt's Newark law firm) attacked "community-wide economic segregation" and "unquestioning deference to the views of local officials."

Later rulings also contained language helpful for the Mount Laurel cause. "Regional needs" matter, said the justices in 1966, approving a variance to a zoning ordinance that allowed a mental hospital to be built.[19] "General welfare . . . comprehends benefits not merely within municipal boundaries." A more critical ruling four years later involved the town of Englewood, which had donated ten acres of city-owned land to a nonprofit group.[20] The intention was to build multifamily housing, mainly for black families displaced by slum-clearance projects, in a neighborhood that was then all white. Irate white property owners took the town to court, only to be smartly swatted down. This wasn't the Mount Laurel situation, to be sure—Englewood was supporting, not opposing, low-income housing in this dispute—but the supreme court spoke plainly about the need to build housing for minorities and the poor.

The dominant voice in this and later rulings was Frederick Hall's. Writing for a unanimous court, he pointed out that "the critical Englewood housing situation cries out for the active and continuous exercise of the highest responsible citizenship by all segments of the population and all governmental bodies." A denial of the zoning variance "could not well be sustained"—language that fairly invited *Mount Laurel*-type litigation. (The people in Englewood "were really protesting because they didn't want black families living outside [the ghetto]," Hall subsequently said.) Two years later, the justice went to work once again, this time condemning "fiscal zoning"—zoning designed to boost tax revenues and limit expenditures for local services—as a "legally dubious stratagem."[21] In fact, fiscal zoning was Mount Laurel Township's best and only justification for its zoning ordinance, its "strategem."[22]

A bookshelf's worth of academic commentary on snob zoning sided with the *Mount Laurel* litigators.[23] Charles Haar, writing in the *Harvard Law Review* in 1953, the year after *Lionshead Lake*, condemned judicial endorsement of "localism" and "economic segregation." Many suburbs would emulate *Lionshead Lake*, Haar warned, and turn to protectionism to "avoid excessive immigration." At about the same time, Norman Williams, a rising authority on housing law, argued presciently that "local and exclusionist purposes" were the forces driving suburban zoning. Poor families were being condemned to substandard housing while the costs of social services were being "increasingly foisted on financially overburdened cities." A decade later, as the racial and economic divisions between city and suburb became deeper and clearer, the critics took off the gloves. "The resident of suburbia is concerned not with *what* but with *whom*," Richard Babcock wrote in *The Zoning Game*. "When they protest that a change in dwelling type will cause a decline in the value of their property, their economic conclusion is based upon a social judgment." Norman Williams, then a law professor at Rutgers and a good friend of Justice Hall's, was even more blunt: zoning "actually puts a premium on kicking the poor around." If state legislatures didn't limit local zoning authority, he wrote in 1969, the courts should declare exclusionary zoning unconstitutional.

When Ken Meiser, devising *Mount Laurel* legal strategy, came across this article, he and Carl Bisgaier made an appointment to meet with Williams at his Newark office. "We were in real deep water," Bisgaier acknowledges. "I was working with a kid who hadn't even finished law school." At the time, Williams was still writing his treatise on zoning, "and there were ten thousand note cards all over the place. He just brought us right in, said, 'How can I help you?'" Over the coming months, Williams gave the young lawyers a specialist's education. "He knew every land-use case written by every judge everywhere," said the awestruck advocate.

Activist lawyers and planners were already busily inventing litigation strategies to open up the suburbs. In the wake of Justice Hall's opinions and the spate of lawyerly critiques of localism, there followed what Norman Williams ruefully describes as the "great rush, in New Jersey and other states, to be the hero who slayed the dragon of exclusionary zoning, and all sorts of badly thought-out cases were brought by people necessarily in hurry."[24] The danger was that poorly designed cases would produce damaging precedents and so kill off the nascent reform movement.

Some of the first New Jersey lawsuits were brought by builders, prefiguring a later alliance between the developers and the dispossessed. After the population of suburban Madison Township leaped from seven thousand in 1950 to nearly fifty thousand in 1970, officials adopted a zoning ordinance meant to entice the kind of real estate—substantial homes, offices, and high-tech industries—that could be taxed to subsidize municipal services. The minimum lot size in some parts of town was two acres, and only a tiny amount of land was left for multi-unit housing. Three-bedroom apartments were banned entirely, on the theory that this would keep out poor families with children, who would increase the financial strains on the public schools. Oakwood-at-

Madison and the Beren Corporation, two builders whose developments had been blocked by the new ordinance promptly sued the township. At the same time, in Bedminster Township situated in rolling New Jersey countryside an hour's commute from Manhattan, Allan-Deane, a construction-industry subsidiary of Johns Manville, proposed to put up several hundred units of housing. The community drew together in outrage. This was a pastoral place where the population had grown by just 120 in more than a century, where the horses outnumbered the inhabitants and wealth was ubiquitous, if discreet; among the celebrities in hidden residence were Jacqueline Kennedy, Cyrus Vance, and Malcolm Forbes. Predictably, Bedminster said no, and in August 1971 Allan-Deane filed suit, claiming that the township's zoning ordinance was racially and economically discriminatory.

In Madison and Bedminster, the motivation for litigation was straightforward economics. Although poor people, would-be residents, were signed up as nominal plaintiffs, this was a merely tactical gesture. The developers' attorneys knew they had to demonstrate that their clients belonged in court—that, as lawyers say, they had standing to sue—and so they named people who could argue that, because of the zoning decision, they were denied a chance to live in the community. The real fight was between the developers and the old-guard townspeople.

In Mount Laurel, by contrast, the motivation for bringing the lawsuit was not to get rich but to do good, and the individual clients were entirely real. "Ethel Lawrence is a gentle and phenomenally wonderful person with integrity," Carl Bisgaier says of his client. "You could slice her up a hundred different ways, all you're going to find is integrity. She's a person of great personal strength, and the desire that things be right, and the willingness to take a stand. She did not fully comprehend what we [lawyers] were talking about, but she knew that this was wrong, what was happening to her people."

These three cases—concerning Madison, Bedminster, and Mount Laurel Townships—would simultaneously work their way up the judicial ladder. The Madison Township lawsuit was decided first at the trial-court level and at the time was the best known of the three; indeed, few of the legal high fliers could locate Mount Laurel on a map. But as things turned out, the events in Mount Laurel became the vehicle for ultimate judicial judgment.

"You Don't Have to Be a Weatherman"

With the community-action group's first attempts to build housing in Springville in the 1960s and all of the events that came afterward, Ethel

Lawrence found her true place in life. That observation does not detract from what she had already accomplished. As a teenager, she had gone with her mother to protest the practice of separating blacks and whites in a nearby movie theater. She had raised eight children and cared for her husband, Thomas, when illness made him quit work, and she would later spend many years nursing her ailing mother. She had been a Girl Scout troop leader, the first black troop leader in the region, had played the piano every Sunday at Jacob's Chapel, and had gotten out the vote for the local Democratic Party. When the Springville Action Council organized a preschool program, she earned the credential that she needed to teach there.

While those accomplishments would more than fill most people's biographies, Ethel Lawrence had not yet become a leader. When she was named to the community-action group, Reverend Stuart Wood remembers, she was quiet and deferential. The lawyers to whom Wood had introduced her, Peter O'Connor and Carl Bisgaier, were brash and smart, a couple of fast-talkers. She had never known anyone remotely like them. Because they respected her—not as the dutiful daughter, or the mother who baked the best rising bread around, or the wife who took good care of her husband, but as a wise woman who could describe the lives around her with richness and depth—they listened closely to what she had to say. And so she began speaking up, even as the attorneys started to construct a frame of legal rights around her story.

Plaintiffs in landmark cases are usually stand-ins, their identification a formality in what is really a dispute about principles, precedents, and policies. They are seldom fleshed-out human beings—a real black child barred from a segregated school, a real woman seeking an abortion—but instead someone named Brown or someone who gets assigned the fictitious name of Roe.

The *Mount Laurel* litigation wasn't like that at all. Ethel Lawrence was not a cutout on which the lawyers could paste their ideological agenda; she was a presence. Every single day that the case of *Southern Burlington County NAACP v. Township of Mount Laurel* was being argued in court—a matter of many months, stretched out over nearly a decade and a half—Ethel Lawrence and her mother, Mary Robinson, were there. Courtrooms were where she spent her vacations. While sometimes a handful of NAACP members were also present, mother and daughter were often the only spectators, sitting on hard wooden benches reminiscent of the pews in Jacob's Chapel. Whenever the judges looked up from the bench and saw these determined black women gazing back at them, it reminded them that lives as well as principles were at stake, that there were persons behind the tight-fitting masks of the law.[25]

The Legal Services attorneys handling the litigation—Peter

O'Connor, Carl Bisgaier, and Ken Meiser—represented a new generation of attorneys. They had gone to law school in the sixties, not with the intention of becoming partners in some stuffy Wall Street firm, but instead meaning to accomplish a quiet social revolution in the nation's courtrooms. These children of the Warren Court era regarded the law almost as a secular religion, and they had a faith in its power to undo injustice. The lawyers had already been successful in Camden, and more successes were to follow there, but now they were shooting higher. A triumph in *Mount Laurel* would be a frontal challenge to the ever widening divisions between blacks and whites, as well as between the poor and everyone else.

Peter O'Connor, who orchestrated the case and has made the cause of affordable housing central to his life ever since, excites the varied passions of others. "One of the most crazed and committed people to practice law," Bisgaier calls him admiringly, and his detractors say much the same thing, if with a less complimentary inflection. Characteristically, Ethel Lawrence, who has known him as well as anyone, describes a softer side. "If he had it within his power, there wouldn't be a hungry or a homeless person in the world."

As a boy growing up in suburban South Orange, though, there was little hint of a commitment to social justice. Throughout high school his passion was basketball, and he went to Holy Cross on an athletic scholarship. While he stood just six feet three inches, short by the standards of the game, he was a standout as guard, a natural leader who knew how to orchestrate his teammates on the floor, a player unafraid of elbowing his way past taller men when they tried to box him out of the flow of the game. Then and now, basketball has been a sport where black athletes excel, and for that reason many white players have found themselves enrolled in what amounts to Race Relations 101 on the court and in the locker room. "Basketball pricked my social conscience," O'Connor says, sounding like a better-known player from New Jersey named Bill Bradley. "Although things were fine among us as ballplayers, at the end of the game I went home to a very different place than the others did. Understanding just what that meant made the issues that the civil-rights movement was raising feel real to me, for the movement highlighted issues that I was living."

But civil rights was not yet his vocation. In the mid-1960s, during the time he was a student at Georgetown Law School, thousands of liberal northerners were putting their ordinary lives on hold, heading South to challenge Jim Crow laws by organizing voter-registration drives and freedom schools. Some, like Mickey Schwerner, James Cheney, and Andrew Goodman, murdered in Mississippi in the summer of 1964—Freedom Summer—became martyrs to the cause. Meanwhile,

O'Connor took out every student loan there was, spent his days in class and his nights holding down three jobs, including a stint as a Capitol policeman, in order to make it through Georgetown. He was called up for the draft after graduation, but because of an old basketball injury the army turned him down. While he thought about joining VISTA or the Peace Corps, instead he wound up, traveling in South America on a Rotary fellowship.

There were riots in the streets back home, and when the Latin Americans he met pressed him to explain why blacks were rioting, why there was so much poverty, he had no good answers for them, only new questions for himself. The racial conflagration that he witnessed firsthand in 1967 when he returned to Newark was the final push toward a lifelong commitment: he would be a lawyer who used his newly acquired tools to make things work better.

By the time he met Ethel Lawrence, O'Connor had packed a career's worth of legal hell-raising into a couple of years. As the senior in Camden Regional Legal Services' law-reform unit, had made so much noise that Vice President Spiro Agnew, on a fund-raising trip to nearby Cherry Hill, had lambasted Camden Regional Legal Services generally, and specifically the Camden urban-renewal litigation. That assault provoked a controversy in the chambers of the U.S. Senate, as Ted Kennedy criticized Agnew's heavy-handed attempt at intimidation. Back in Camden, the vice president's speech only boosted O'Connor's reputation.

Carl Bisgaier, who did much of the actual work on the *Mount Laurel* case, is a cooler customer. "I'm the cynic who was spurred on by Peter's perpetual enthusiasm," he says, and particularly at the outset of the case he was skeptical about the prospects for success. But Bisgaier too had what he calls his "personal epiphany," the moment when the rightness of what he was doing became transparently clear to him. During the fall of 1969, a year after beginning work with Camden Regional Legal Services, he took his family on a vacation to southern California. His experience in Camden had left him frustrated with cities, curious about the new towns that were then springing up in the West. But a visit to one of those invented places, Westlake Village, situated in the desert east of Los Angeles, "made me physically sick. 'My God,' I thought, 'there are no poor people here—the developers have created an environment that completely excludes the poor!' Then I realized that what this place had done overtly was why suburbs were what they were. It was all by design!" In the *Mount Laurel* case, Bisgaier would have his chance to expose that design.

The township's gentlemanly solicitor, Jack Gerry, defended Mount Laurel's zoning policies, not because he was personally committed to his client's cause, but because that was what he was hired to do—

privately, he believed that the town *was* giving poor and black families the bums' rush. The local politicians would win their case, he anticipated, because the law was so heavily on their side, but that didn't make their conduct admirable.

◆ ◆ ◆ ◆ ◆ ◆

The Legal Services attorneys charged that Mount Laurel's zoning ordinance unconstitutionally discriminated along race and class lines. But during the four-day trial in March 1972, town officials denied establishing "a pattern of economic and social segregation."[26] The market, they insisted, had done that. They rejected the claim that the township had any "legal duty to house the poor." There was nothing "arbitrary and capricious" about what Mount Laurel had done, Jack Gerry argued, citing the standard and, until that time, the successful defense in land-use disputes. The township permitted building on smaller lots than did nearby communities and in this respect really deserved plaudits, but beyond that Mount Laurel was unwilling to go.

The township admitted every important fact in the plaintiffs' complaint—the sorry condition of the housing in Springville and the doubling in the number of Mount Laurel's housing units during the 1960s, with not a single dwelling built for poor families. In effect, the township asked: *so what?* "We didn't even have to present all our testimony," says Carl Bisgaier, "because the defense was willing to accept statements from witnesses instead of testimony. They didn't care. It would be like me telling you I was going to prove you were green and your saying, 'Go ahead, prove I'm green, I know what color I am. Go ahead, do what you want to do, I don't give a damn.' Their response amounted to a declaration that, legally, we were out of our minds."

Trial court judge Edward Martino had sat on the Burlington County bench for nearly three decades. A Camden native, he was the most powerful jurist in the district, responsible for assigning all the cases, and a man with a reputation for being a martinet. Because he knew the controversial Mount Laurel dispute would make his judicial colleagues queasy, he decided to hear it himself. Political pressure often sways trial court judges, but Martino was regarded as an exception. Though he was a Republican loyalist on the bench he was neither particularly liberal nor especially conservative—just someone who let himself be guided by a sense of what seemed fair, within the boundaries of the law. Significantly, back in 1959, well before the heyday of activist judges in the field of civil rights, Martino found a Mount Holly restaurant guilty of race discrimination. In a statement that predates the national flap over racism in Denny's restaurants by more than thirty years, the judge declared, "Adequate service must be available to all citizens regardless of race, color, or creed, or national origin. The refusal of such equality of opportunity . . . is discrimination."

Martino had already been exposed to the Springville neighborhood's housing problems, since one of the plaintiffs in the lawsuit, Catherine Still, had earlier brought a case in his court that focused on conditions in the converted chicken coops. But the judge was nonetheless startled by the accounts of exploitation and ruined lives he heard during the Mount Laurel trial. "I took this never dreaming it was the type of case it turned out to be. I did not have any thought of taking care of the poor, but as I heard the testimony of the plaintiffs . . . and saw how the city fathers were treating a certain class of people, then I got a little agitated."

Judges are supposed to learn during cases, and profound judicial voyages of discovery do sometimes happen. At about the time Judge Martino was getting his lesson on misery in Mount Laurel, for instance, Stephen Roth, a federal trial court judge known to be unsympathetic to civil-rights claims, was learning to his amazement that the suburbs of Detroit practiced their own brand of apartheid—that they had contrived to keep black families out, forcing them to stay in the city and so had helped to make the public schools racially isolated. That revelation prompted the Detroit judge to arrive at the novel legal conclusion that the entire metropolitan area, not just the city, which by then had few white residents, should take responsibility for desegregation (a decision later overturned by a bare majority of the Burger Court).[27] In the Mount Laurel case, innovative legal arguments were less compelling to Judge Martino than the tangible plight of the people who came forward to tell their stories. "They were pushed around, and nobody came to their rescue. They were forced to leave their homes in a town where some of them had lived fifty years. Many of these people were born here, as were their parents and grandparents."

During his closing argument for the plaintiffs, Carl Bisgaier talked about how housing-design standards translated into tax dollars for the town's officials. "There was a money difference between a two-thousand-square-foot house and an eight-hundred-square-foot house, and that's the way they were thinking." He pointed to a map of the township that showed the approved planned unit developments. "It is just a matter of time before the whole town is closed off," he said, and then borrowed a refrain from the anthem of the day. "You don't have to be a weatherman to know which way the wind is blowing."

As the evidence piled up, abuse upon abuse, Judge Martino came to despise the politicians in Mount Laurel. "They were treating these people like cattle, even calling them scum of the earth and *telling them that if they can't afford to live in Mount Laurel they should leave"*—echoes of that fateful Sunday in 1970 when Mayor Bill Haines addressed the congregation in Jacob's Chapel. The case, as the judge saw it, boiled down to this: "The defendants . . . wanted to uplift the municipality, and these people were not going to help them, and they wanted to get rid of them." The speeches they made at township meetings said as much. "They wished to approve only those development plans which were to provide direct and substantial benefits to their taxpayers. This angered me."

State trial judges mostly handle mundane matters on which the law is well settled. In this instance, though, Martino reached out to invent law. While he dismissed several developers as defendants, concluding that they had no legal duty to build housing for the poor, and also rejected the argument that the region, not just the township, had an obligation to plan for affordable housing, he pushed far beyond the limits of precedent when it came to Mount Laurel itself.

The judge saw the case not as a challenge to an isolated zoning matter but as a test of deliberate and deeply imbedded policy. "This was no zoning case, this was development of a whole municipality," Martino says. "They didn't dream that I would enter into the ultimate conclusion that discrimination has no place in America . . . I had no hesitancy in determining that the attitude of the city fathers was contrary to the American way of life."

On May 1, 1972, six weeks after the trial and a year to the day after the lawsuit was filed, Judge Martino delivered his twenty-three-page opinion. It recites the damning facts lifted from the pages of the township council's minutes.

Early in 1968 the mayor, when a discussion arose as to low income housing, stated it was the intention of the township council to take care of the people of Mount Laurel Township but not to make any areas of Mount Laurel a home for the county. At a later meeting of the township committee in 1969 a variance to permit multi-family dwelling units was rejected because the committee did not see the need for such construction. At a meeting in 1970 a committeeman, during a discussion of homes being rundown and worthless, indicated that the policy was to wait until homes become vacant before the township took action, "because if these people are put out on the street they do not have another place to go" [and so, under the law, the township would have to take some responsibility for them]. At another meeting in September 1970

> a township committeeman [said] . . . "We must be as selective as
> possible . . . we can approve only those development plans which
> will provide direct and substantial benefits to our taxpayers."

At that time, the judge points out, two-thirds of the township still consisted of vacant land, and nearly a thousand acres of empty land was zoned for houses.

In concluding that Mount Laurel's zoning ordinance was unconstitutional "economic discrimination," Martino had no New Jersey precedent to back him up. Instead the judge cobbled together an opinion that relied on dissents, decisions from other states, and law review commentary. Justice Oliphant's 1952 dissent in *Lionshead Lake* could have been addressed by name to Ethel Lawrence and her family. "Certain well-behaved families will be barred from these communities simply because the income of the family will not permit them to build a house [there]. They will be relegated to the large cities . . . even though it may be against what they consider the welfare of their immediate families." Justice Hall's dissent in the 1962 *Vickers* case (the opinion that Ken Meiser had once believed was a majority ruling), also quoted in Martino's opinion, was even more scathing. "[L]egitimate use of the zoning power by . . . municipalities does not encompass the right to erect barricades on their boundaries . . . where the real purpose is to prevent feared disruption with a so-called chosen way of life. Nor does it encompass provisions designed to let in as new residents only certain kinds of people . . . or keep down tax bills of present property owners . . . [C]ourts must not be hesitant to strike down purely selfish and undemocratic actions . . . 'The Constitution nullifies sophisticated as well as simpleminded modes of discrimination.'"

Through an abuse of the power to plan for land use, Mount Laurel had cordoned off poor blacks—assigned them to a zone of disregard—and this, Judge Martino ruled, had to change. Without specifically telling the township what it must do, the judge set a planning process in motion, ordering local officials to work with the plaintiffs in identifying housing needs and crafting an "affirmative program" to meet those needs.

Martino's decision completed the transformation of the issue from a dispute over a minor zoning amendment to an argument about the much larger municipal obligation to the town's poor. The long-term implications of that decision remained unclear—the state supreme court could still reject the reformers' agenda—but the matter was bound for the high court. Given that court's hints that fiscal zoning was unconstitutional, as well as the justices' inclination to wade into political thickets, Martino's ruling promised to be the opening salvo in a long war over local authority to fence out the poor.

"Not an Inch"

As Edward Martino closed the record, Mary Robinson, Ethel's mother, broke down in tears of relief. But the judge's order depended for its success on the cooperation of local officials, and that was not forthcoming. Between the filing of the lawsuit and the announcement of the decision one year later, the Republicans had been swept out of office and the Democrats were again running the show. While this changeover had a direct impact on the pace of development—the planned unit development ordinance was repealed, although an exception was made for already approved projects—on the issue of affordable housing, the new political cast meant only that public debates would be even nastier.

"There was much reactionary sentiment" after the Democrats took over, the town planner recalls, though in fact it wasn't the sentiment that was new, just the rawness with which it was expressed. "There were some very noisy, obnoxious rednecks showing up [at township meetings]. They had heavy accents, and they were saying that they did not want blacks in our community, and there was talk about not creating a new ghetto."

The Democrats saw their position not as insensitive or racist but as morally compelled, says John Trimble, who took over for Jack Gerry as Mount Laurel's lawyer after the trial. "They didn't think it was right to subsidize those who wanted something for nothing. They envisioned somebody getting a free house next to their own house for which they had worked and slaved, to get out to their paradise, which was a one-hundred-foot by one-hundred-foot lot in Mount Laurel." This sentiment may explain why, despite Judge Martino's order, there was no interest—none whatsoever—in negotiating with the plaintiffs. Soon after the judge ruled, Carl Bisgaier came to a township council meeting with a simple proposition: pass a Resolution of Need, the first required step in obtaining federal funds for affordable housing, and we'll drop the lawsuit.

"Bullshit!" responded the Democratic mayor, Joe Massari, who had run for office to stop just such housing. "We're not giving an inch on this thing. We are going to fight it all the way."

When news of that exchange filtered back to Judge Martino, he was livid. He summoned Trimble to his chambers, the attorney recalls, and "he told me he knew that the town officials were sitting on their hands, and that if I didn't get my clients to pass a new zoning ordinance I should resign as an officer of the court because they were not fulfilling their moral obligation. 'I am going to put them in jail,' he said. I told the council what the judge had said. They said I should tell him to go to hell."

Negotiating is how political business is usually done, of course; and negotiation holds pride of place in the politics of mutual advantage that typically operates in small communities like Mount Laurel, where everyone knows everybody else and today's adversaries are likely to be tomorrow's allies. But in this single instance, the town-council members regarded bargaining as compromising a moral position—as giving away housing to people who hadn't sweated blood for it and so didn't deserve it. They also saw negotiating as an invitation to political disaster, and at that they balked. In the battle of Mount Laurel, the trial court's judgment marked only the end of the beginning.

"Fair Share"

On issue after issue, from equal education to consumers' rights, the New Jersey Supreme Court has been a reformer among state tribunals. But even this activist court caused a sensation in March 1975—three years after the trial court's ruling; seven years after Mount Laurel Township first rejected the proposal to amend its zoning ordinance and permit thirty-six apartments to be built—when Justice Frederick Hall delivered the court's unanimous judgment in the *Mount Laurel* case.[28] "I thought we had won the lottery," says plaintiffs' lawyer Carl Bisgaier.

The ruling was bolder in its rhetoric than the advocates ever hoped for. It demanded that developing towns across the state rewrite their zoning laws so that private developers, taking advantage of federal subsidies and market forces, could build homes for a "fair share" of the region's poor and moderate-income families. The decision drew national attention and quickly turned into a lightning rod; what *Brown v. Board of Education*, the school-desegregation case, had meant for southern whites, *Mount Laurel* became for suburbanites.

The case had been rushed to the state's highest court. When the township appealed Judge Martino's ruling, the supreme court, evidently eager to speak out on the issue, decided to hear the suit directly, skipping the intermediate appellate court. The justices had done the same thing in the *Madison* case, where the trial judge had sided with the developers and against the town, and both cases were scheduled to be heard by the high court, one after the other, on the same day in March 1973.

"Poor people simply can't afford to live in our township," Carl Bisgaier argued to the justices, speaking of Mount Laurel as "our town" as a way of emphasizing that his clients too had a stake in the community. "It's not because we've purposely kept them out, it's because the price of the land and the house is more than they can afford. . . . Mount Laurel is a typical town in New Jersey, and as long as the overriding factor [in the community's calculation] is the tax burden, the town has no obligation to provide for out-of-township residents. After all, we can't tax them."

Chief Justice Joseph Weintraub interrupted Bisgaier, to slice to the heart of the dispute. "What responsibilities does government have for low income housing," he asked, "and who has to pay for it?"

While still a law student at Cornell, Weintraub had acquired a reputation for precociousness when Supreme Court Justice Louis Brandeis wrote to praise a law review article he had written.[29] A former law clerk of Justice Weintraub's, Eugene Serpentelli, who as a trial court judge would manage some of the toughest *Mount Laurel*–type cases a decade later, remembers that Weintraub "needed law clerks only to fill chairs, to sit at his feet as the master. And of course he also had the impatience of a brilliant person."

"Have you got a model opinion we can use as guidance?" Weintraub had brusquely demanded of an attorney who, in the companion case, was challenging Madison Township's ordinance. "If not, don't ask the court to do something you cannot do yourself. You should draft a model judgment explaining the fair share concept and send it to us." Now he was turning his fire on Carl Bisgaier.

Questions about duties and cost were the very issues Bisgaier dreaded, yet when he tried to wriggle around them, the justice bore in relentlessly. The advocate had no good answers; he fled from the courtroom, for a "lost weekend," the moment the session ended. A few weeks later, when tapes of the oral argument became available, Bisgaier and his colleague Ken Meiser spent a dispiriting afternoon reliving his humiliation in the same Trenton courtroom where the proceedings had been held. "It was," he says, "like hearing yourself going to the toilet over and over."

Bisgaier hoped for an opportunity to redeem himself, and while the law seldom gives such second chances, this time he got it, when the New Jersey Supreme Court ordered the lawyers to argue *Mount Laurel* and *Madison* again. Evidently, the justices had struggled unsuccessfully to reach a decision before the end of the term, when three of them reached mandatory retirement age. Hence the summons to reargument. "Cases of this magnitude should be decided by [judges] who have to live with the decisions," said Chief Justice Weintraub, who was one of those leaving the bench. More retirements followed in the coming months, and so, of the six justices who had served with Joseph Weintraub, only Frederick Hall, the leading land-use jurist, remained when the case was heard a second time, in January 1974.

Rutgers law professor Norman Williams, who was by this time a nationally known expert on land use, represented the plaintiffs in *Madison*. Williams was supposed to lead off the argument, tackling the hardest questions, while the *Mount Laurel* attorneys, as Carl Bisgaier put it, would be "second sisters." But moments before the oral argument was scheduled to begin, lawyers for Madison informed the justices that the township had recently amended its zoning ordinance in an ostensible attempt to comply with the trial court's ruling. The astonished judges took one look at the redrawn maps and sent the case back to be tried a second time in light of the rewritten ordinance.

Suddenly, the klieg lights shifted to the *Mount Laurel* case and its novice litigators. "Many of those in the courtroom . . . did not even know where Mount Laurel was," says Williams. He was standing outside the courtroom preparing to leave, when Carl Bisgaier rushed over and asked him to participate in his case. The justices quickly granted the motion. "Slam dunk that they would grant it," says Bisgaier, "they wanted to hear him." Then, however, the burden of argument fell upon the Legal Services lawyer.

With the catastrophe of his earlier performance before the high court still vivid in his mind, the young advocate struck boldly and directly. Government was institutionalizing poverty, he contended, zoning out poor people by design and so deliberately creating racial and economic segregation. Only if towns were legally obliged to act differently, required to reverse that pattern, was there any hope that things would change. The justices had few questions for Bisgaier, but they bore down hard on John Trimble, the township's attorney. Trimble stuck to the familiar text: the zoning laws represented sound fiscal and legal planning. While this was the line the court had taken in earlier cases, it was evident from the barrage of questions that the justices no longer believed fiscal responsibility was a good enough reason for zoning out the poor.

When lawyer Trimble contended that "the Supreme Court has neither the authority nor the means to review local zoning decisions," one judge retorted that "one thing we *could* tell you is you can't prohibit multifamily dwellings." Allowing such housing would be "political suicide" for suburban politicians, Trimble said in exasperation. Justice Morris Pashman, who in his short time on the court had already acquired a reputation for painting justice in its broadest strokes, responded: "I don't know why they think the court won't assist them in political suicide. . . . We may even take them screaming and kicking." That exchange encapsulated one of the most troubling and enduring issues in the case: the limits of judicial activism in defining and enforcing newly created social rights and obligations.

Justice Hall's opinion in the *Mount Laurel* case was his valedictory to the bench, and he used the occasion like a latter-day Sinclair Lewis, scolding the suburbs for their Babbitry. After reciting chapter and verse concerning Mount Laurel's callous treatment of its own poor families, Hall went on:

> Through its zoning ordinance, Mount Laurel has exhibited economic discrimination in that the poor have been deprived of adequate housing and the opportunity to secure the construction of subsidized housing, and has used Federal, State, county and local finances solely for the benefit of middle and upper-income persons . . . There cannot be the slightest doubt that the reason for this course of conduct has been to keep down local taxes on property . . . and that the policy was carried out without regard for the non-fiscal considerations with respect to people.

Such behavior was not peculiar to Mount Laurel Township. "Almost every [municipality] acts solely in its own selfish and parochial interest and in effect builds a wall around itself to keep out those people or entities not adding favorably to the tax base."

A generation before, in the *Lionshead Lake* and *Vickers* decisions, the New Jersey judges had bowed to the wisdom of local governments, and courts elsewhere had followed their lead. But this was a tribunal that, since Arthur Vanderbilt's days, had made progressivism its credo. "Conditions have changed, and . . . judicial attitudes must be altered. . . . [T]he welfare of the state's citizens beyond the borders of the particular municipality . . . must be served." What the suburbs were doing, wrote Hall, was now legally unacceptable. It violated the command, inscribed in the state's zoning statute and implicit in its constitution as well, that government must serve "the *general* welfare," not just the interests of present residents or of the well off. The court's decision spoke to the ambitions of outsiders who wanted in—the general welfare, as Justice Hall constructed it, meant *regional* welfare.

The opinion was chock-full of the imperatives beloved by sermon writers and editorialists. "There cannot be the slightest doubt that shelter, along with food, are the most basic human needs"—but what about health, one might ask, or love, for that matter? "It is plain beyond dispute that proper provision for adequate housing of all categories of people is certainly an absolute essential in promotion of the general welfare required in all local land use regulation"—but if this were so plain, there would be no need for a *Mount Laurel* case.

Justice Hall did not even mention the federal constitutional rights of the poor, and there were good tactical reasons for this omission. The year before, in *Village of Belle Terre v. Boraas*, the U.S. Supreme Court had approved a zoning ordinance that permitted only families or unmarried couples, not groups, to reside in the community.[30] The ordinance was needed, said William O. Douglas, the most liberal justice on the bench, to preserve "a quiet place where yards are wide, people few," where "family values"—family values!—"youth values, and the blessings of quiet seclusion and clean air make the area a sanctuary for people." The single-family home, Douglas opined, was a place of "blessings," a "sanctuary," language that "connotes the sacred."[31] Zoning didn't affect any "fundamental rights" guaranteed by the U.S. Constitution, said the justices, and so, except where racial discrimination was deliberate, communities were left alone.

But the New Jersey constitution had sometimes been read as being "more demanding" than the federal Constitution, as Justice Hall pointed out, and he argued that it offered ample legal basis for striking down a local zoning law. Although there was no specific textual basis for the decision, just the capacious language of general welfare, the court established affirmative, constitutionally mandated municipal obligations. The state justices' strategy effectively insulated the *Mount Laurel* opinion from repeal by the legislators, who couldn't rewrite it by statute, as well as from review by the U.S. Supreme Court. This proved a prudent move when state politicians noisily if fecklessly complained; and just three months later the nation's high court held that neither poor city residents nor civil-rights-minded suburbanites could challenge a town's zoning ordinance.[32]

In New Jersey, all the burgeoning suburbs, from the snootiest enclaves in Bedminster's fox-hunting country to executive-class wannabe towns like Mount Laurel, were obliged to rewrite their zoning laws to assure that a "fair share" of the poor families in the region could live there. "'Developing municipalit[ies]," Justice Hall concluded, "must make *realistically possible* the opportunity for an appropriate variety and choice of housing for all categories of people who may desire to live there."

Despite this boldness, there was much that the court chose *not* to specify. There wasn't a word written about racial discrimination, even though such claims were part of the plaintiffs' case—instead, the new judicial doctrine focused entirely on the legally more novel territory of economic discrimination. Critical technical details went undiscussed: how a "region" was to be defined, what "fair share" meant. Nor, most critically, did the court say how it might enforce the judgment.

Left mainly to their own devices, the opinion suggested, the suburbs could be counted on to accept their "moral obligation," to do what was right. The court's proper role was to do good by doing little: the justices struck down, as too judicially intrusive, that portion of Judge Martino's order that required Mount Laurel to develop a plan under judicial supervision. It was improper for a judge to get so deeply involved in land-use particulars, Justice Hall maintained, warning trial judges against brokering settlements. "There is no reason," Hall opined, "why developing communities . . . may not become and remain attractive, viable communities providing good living and adequate services for all their residents in the kind of atmosphere which a democracy and free institutions demand."

Given the prevailing politics of hostility, Hall's vision was as fantastic as believing that raptors would nibble gently from the hand of Saint Francis. Yet there were practical reasons for this go-slow approach. Despite their attempt to anchor the ruling in the past, the justices had to know that their new doctrine was a radical reversal of their own precedents. The decision subverted engrained habits of local control; and with such thin legal support, the court's bold move risked political trouble. Better to give townships the opportunity to comply voluntarily, the justices may have concluded—if the towns did nothing, there would then be better reasons for the court to do more.

In a concurring opinion, Morris Pashman urged the court to move, even "farther and faster," to breathe "lifeblood" into "downright boring . . . culturally dead" suburbs. "Like animal species that over-specialize and breed out diversity and so perish in the course of evolution, communities, too, need racial, cultural, social and economic diversity to cope with our rapidly changing times." This Darwinesque passage was vintage Pashman. To his admirers, the justice's unabashed liberalism showed that he regarded "judicial activism" as something "not to be feared, but to be used to accomplish fairness," while to his critics, "[he did] not know what legislatures are for except to raise judicial salaries, and, since they do not do that fast enough, he would really like to take that function away from them too." His *Mount Laurel* concurrence gave ample ammunition to both camps. There is "an acute national housing shortage," the brunt of which is being borne by the poor, and "the growing movement of commerce and industry to the suburbs is imposing a heavy burden on employees who are unable to obtain housing in these suburban areas." That's why the court needed to "lay down broad guidelines for judicial review of municipal zoning decisions," including a declaration that, under certain circumstances, communities had "an affirmative duty to provide housing" for the poor.

In *Mount Laurel II*—eight years, several vacilating rulings, and much heartache later—the justices would embrace many of Pashman's ideas, setting up an elaborate structure of judicial management and laying out detailed rules to make the fair-share right a reality. Yet, as the judge reminded his brethren, "Even as we write [in 1975], development proceeds apace . . . There is a hazard that prolonged judicial inaction" will permanently lock out the poor.

This was prophecy. While the justices zigged and zagged in the next batch of zoning cases, state politicians plotted to undermine them and federal financial support for subsidized housing dried up. At the same time, the building market, responsive to the rhythms of the economy, was going through its own cycles of boom and bust. Whatever the courts might say about rights, the economics of housing would largely determine whether new construction was feasible—for poor families or anyone else.

Notes

1. *Southern Burlington County NAACP v. Township of Mount Laurel*, 67 N.J. 151, 336 A.2d 713, *appeal dismissed and cert. denied*, 423 U.S. 808 (1975) (*Mount Laurel I*); *Southern Burlington County NAACP v. Township of Mount Laurel*, 92 N.J. 158, 456 A.2d 390 (1983) (*Mount Laurel II*); and *Hills Dev. Co. v. Township of Bernards*, 103 N.J. 1, 510 A.2d 621 (1986) (*Mount Laurel III*).

2. *Village of Euclid v. Ambler Realty Co.*, 272 U.S. 365 (1926). See generally Richard Babcock and Fred Bosselman, *Exclusionary Zoning: Land Use Regulation and Housing in the 1970s* (New York: Praeger, 1973).

3. *James v. Valtierra*: 402 U.S. 137 (1971).

4. William Brennan, "State Constitutions and the Protection of Individual Rights," *Harvard Law Review* 90, no. 3 (January 1977): 489–504; see also Mary Cornelia Porter, "State Supreme Courts and the Legacy of the Warren Court: Some Old Inquiries for a New Situation," *Publius* 8, no. 4 (Fall 1978): 55–74.

5. "New Jersey Goes to the Head of the Class," *Journal of the American Judicature Society* 31 (1948): 131. See also G. Alan Tarr and Mary Cornelia Aldis Porter, *State Supreme Courts in State and Nation* (New Haven: Yale University Press, 1988).

6. D. W. Brogan, *The English People* (New York: Knopf, 1943), 11, 108.

7. See generally Dayton McKean, *The Boss: The Hague Machine in Action* (Boston: Houghton Mifflin, 1940); Richard Connors, A *Cycle of Power: The Career of Jersey City Mayor Frank Hague* (Metuchen, N.J.: Scarecrow, 1971).

8. See generally Eugene Gerhard, *Arthur T. Vanderbilt: The Complete Counselor* (Albany, N.Y.: Q. Corp., 1980); Arthur Vanderbilt II, *Changing Law: A Biography of Arthur T. Vanderbilt* (New Brunswick, N.J.: Rutgers University Press, 1976).

9. Henry Glick and Kenneth Vines, *State Court Systems* (Englewood Cliffs, N.J.: Prentice-Hall, 1973), 16.

10. *Twinberry v. Salisbury*, 5 N.J. 240, 74 A.2d 406, *cert. denied.*, 340 U.S. 877 (1950). Some

state legislators, angry at the justices, wanted to adopt a constitutional amendment restricting the court's rule-making powers, but they abandoned the idea when the bar and the press backed the court. Tarr and Porter (1988), 194.

11. Joseph Weintraub, "Justice Frederick W. Hall: A Tribute," *Rutgers Law Review* 29, no. 3 (Spring 1976): 499–501.

12. Glick and Vines (1953), 64. See also Henry Glick, *Supreme Courts in State Politics: An Investigation of the Judicial Role* (New York: Basic, 1971).

13. John Pittance, "The Courts," in *The Political State of New Jersey*, ed. Gerald Pamper (New Brunswick, N.J.: Rutgers University Press, 1986), 160–179. On the New Jersey Supreme Court's place in the context of high courts nationally, see generally Robert Kagan, Bliss Cartwright, Lawrence M. Friedman, and Stanton Wheeler, "The Evolution of State Supreme Courts," *Michigan Law Review* 76, no. 6 (May 1978): 961–1005; Lawrence Friedman, Robert Kagan, Bliss Cartwright, and Stanton Wheeler, "State Supreme Courts: A Century of Style and Citation," *Stanford Law Review* 33, no.5 (May 1981): 573–818; Dennis Coyle, *Property Rights and the Constitution: Shaping Society through Land Use Regulation* (Albany: SUNY Press, 1993), ch. 4 [comparison with Pennsylvania].

14. See Stanley Friedelbaum, "Constitutional Law and Judicial Policy Making," in *Politics in New Jersey*, ed. Richard Lehne and Alan Rosenthal, rev. ed. (New Brunswick, N.J.: Rutgers University 1979); Lawrence Baum and Bradley Canon, "State Supreme Courts as Activists: New Doctrines in the Law of Torts," in *State Supreme Courts: Policymakers in the Federal System*, ed. Mary Cornelia Porter and G. Alan Tarr (Westport, Conn.: Greenwood, 1982), 203–204.

15. *Lionshead Lake, Inc. v. Township of Wayne*, 10 N.J. 165 (1952), *appeal dismissed for want of a substantial federal question*, 344 U.S. 919 (1953).

16. *Vickers v. Township Committee of Gloucester Township*, 37 N.J. 232 (1962), cert. denied, 371 U.S. 233 (1963).

17. Babcock and Bosselman (1973).

18. *Pierro v. Baxendale*, 20 N.J. 17 (1955).

19. *Kunzler v. Hoffman* 48 N.J. 277 (1966); see also *Roman Catholic Diocese of Newark v. Ho-Ho-Kus Borough*, 47 N.J. 211 (1966).

20. *DeSimone v. Greater Englewood Housing Corp. No. 1*, 56 N.J. 428 (1970).

21. *Rutgers University v. Piluso*, 60 N.J. 142 (1972).

22. See generally Mary Mann, *The Right to Housing: Constitutional Issues and Remedies In Exclusionary Zoning* (New York: Praeger, 1976).

23. See, e.g., Norman Williams, "Zoning and Housing Policies," *Journal of Housing* 10, no. 3 (March 1955): 94–95; Charles Haar "Zoning for Minimum Standards: The Wayne Township Case," *Harvard Law Review* 66. no. 6 (April 1953): 1051–1063; Norman Williams, "Planning Law and Democratic Living," *Law and Contemporary Problems* 20, no. 2 (Spring 1953): 317–350; Richard Babcock, *The Zoning Game: Municipal Practices and Policies* (Madison: University of Wisconsin Press, 1966); Norman Williams and Edward Wacks, "Segregation of Residential Areas along Economic Lines: Lionshead Lake Revisited." *Wisconsin Law Review* 1969, no.3 (1969): 827–847; Lawrence Sager, "Tight Little Islands: Exclusionary

Zoning, Equal Protection, and the Indigent," *Stanford Law Review* 21, no. 4 (April 1969): 767–800.

24. Norman Williams, "The Background and Significance of *Mount Laurel II*," *Washington University Journal of Urban and Contemporary Law* 26 (1984): 3–23.

25. See generally John Noonan, *Person and Masks of the Law: Cardozo, Holmes, Jefferson, and Wythe as Makers of the Masks* (New York: Farrar, Straus, and Giroux, 1976).

26. Our account of the *Mount Laurel* relies on documents generated by the parties, interviews with many of the participants, and interviews quoted in Marianne Oross, "The Examination of the Social, Political, and Economic Conditions Associated with Exclusionary Practices in Mount Laurel, New Jersey" (Ed.D. diss., Rutgers University, 1989).

27. The Detroit schools case decided by the high court is *Milliken v. Bradley*, 418 U.S. 717 (1974).Two preceding trial court decisions are reported in *Bradley v. Milliken*, 338 F. Supp. 582 (E.D. Mich. 1971) and 345 F. Supp. 914 (E.D. Mich. 1972): the intermediate appellate decision is reported in *Bradley v. Milliken*, 484 F.2d 215 (6th Cir. 1973).

28. *Southern Burlington County NAACP v. Township of Mount Laurel*, 67 N.J. 151, 336, A.2d 713, *appeal dismissed and cert. denied*, 423 U.S. 808 (1975).

29. On Weintraub generally, see Milton D. Cornford, "Joseph Weintraub: Reminiscences," *New Jersey Law Journal* 96 (1973): 1205; John Francis, "Joseph Weintraub—A Judge for All Seasons," *Cornell Law Review* 59, no.2 (January 1974): 186–196; John Schupper, "Chief Justice Weintraub and the Role of the of the Judiciary," *Rutgers Camden Law Journal* 5, no. 3 (Spring 1974): 413–417; John Francis, "Chief Justice Joseph Weintraub: A Tribute." *Rutgers Law Review* 30, no. 3 (Spring 1977): 479–481.

30. *Village of Belle Terre v. Boraas*: 416 U.S. 1 (1974).

31. See Constance Perin, *Everything in Its Place: Social Order and Land Use in America* (Princeton, N.J.: Princeton University Press, 1977), 48.

32. *Warth v. Seldin*, 422 U.S. 490 (1975).

Index

geography, New Jersey's, politics and, 1

George, Henry, 326

George III, 87

George Jonas Glass Co. v. Glass Bottle Blowers' Assoc., 289, 293

German Americans, 34n71

Gerry, Jack, 452, 453, 457

gerrymandering, 2

Gethsemane Cemetery, 201

Gettysburg, Battle of, 222, 225, 234; burial of dead during, 235; Pickett-Pettigrew-Trimble charge, 234. *See also* Twenty-third New Jersey Volunteers

Gettysburg Campaign, of 23rd NJV, 237

Gibbons, Thomas, 10

Gibbons v. Ogden, 10–11

GI Bill of Rights, 22

Gibson, Mayor Kenneth A., 376, 380, 381, 383, 385, 386, 388, 389, 392, 403, 407

Gibson, Robin, 69

Gilded Age, 250, 271

Gillen, Mayor Charles, 327

Gillette, William, 223

Glenbervie, Lord. *See* Douglas, Sylvester

global warming, 25

Glorious Revolution, 43, 62

Gloucester, zoning ordinances in, 446

Gnadenhutten, murder of Delawares at, 117

Golin, Steve, 376

Goodman, Andrew, 451

Gorham, Nathaniel, 135

Gospill's Directory, 256

Gottfried, Bradley M., 225

government, financing of, 2

graft, "honest," 17

Grant, Pres. Ulysses S., 19

Graves, Carole, 380–381, 383, 387–389, 394, 395, 398, 399, 406, 407

Grayson, William, 135

Great Awakening, 6, 203

Great Depression, impact on women of, 415–416. *See also* depression: economic

Great Migration, 215

Great Society, 25

Greene, Larry, 188

Greene, Gen. Nathaniel, 93

Griffith, William, 14

Grimes, Quincy, 240n6

Grubb, Col., 228

gubernatorial campaign, of 1919, 332–335

Gummere, Justice William S., 285

Gutman, Herbert G., 160

Haar, Charles, 447

Hague, Mayor Frank, 2, 22, 23, 326, 331–332, 333, 358, 359, 366, 368, 416, 443, 444; antilabor stance of, 369; background of, 362–363; criticism of, 360; as mayor of Jersey City, 364; police-state tactics of, 370; political career of, 363–364; and Pres. Roosevelt, 365–366, 367, 368–369

Hague, Frank, Jr., 443–444

Hague machine, 360, 368

Haines, Alanson, 230

Haines, Mayor Bill, 446, 455

Haines, Gov. Daniel, 12

Haines, Rev. (NJV), 233, 236, 237

Hall, Justice Frederick, 447, 456, 458, 459, 461–463

Hall, John F., 247, 250, 262, 268

Halsey, Edmund (NJV), 229, 230, 236

Hamilton, Alexander, 38, 159, 164

Hamilton, Andrew, 43

Hamilton, Lt. Ellis (NJV), 235, 236–237

Hamm, Larry, 386

Hanoverian succession, 62

Harding, Silvester, 69, 70

Harlan, Justice John Marshall, 282, 291

Harper's Weekly, 247

Harrison, Charles (NJV), 229, 234

Hart, John, 7, 127

Hartz, Louis, 38

Hauck, Anthony, 346–347